D0396222

Trans-Siberian Railway

RU JUL 12

Simon Richmond

Marc Bennetts, Marc Di Duca, Michael Kohn,

Leonid Ragozin, Robert Reid, Mara Vorhees

ST PETERSBURG (p102)
Glide down canals past the glorious facades of palaces and mansions housing splendid museums in Russia's most elegant, bohemian city, birthplace of Russia's rail system

MOSCOW (p121)
From Red Square and Lenin's embalmed corpse to ultra-exclusive nightclubs and contemporary art, the nation's booming, never-say-die capital is the zenith of modern Russia

SUZDAL (p160)
Step back in time in the most photogenic and onion-dome-church-packed of the Golden Ring towns

TOBOLSK (p189)
Visit the historic town that both Dostoevsky and Nicholas II passed through during their detentions in Siberia

NIZHNY NOVGOROD (p163)
Cruise along the Volga River from Russia's 'third capital', an appealing city with an impressive kremlin and laid-back vibe

KAZAN (p168)
Learn about Tatar culture in its dynamic multicultural capital, an ideal base for a river trip to picturesque Sviyazhsk island

TOMSK (p199)
Siberia's most attractive city, this old university town boasts charming wooden mansions, grand century-old commercial buildings and a dynamic, contemporary outlook

0 ___ 1000 km
0 ___ 600 miles

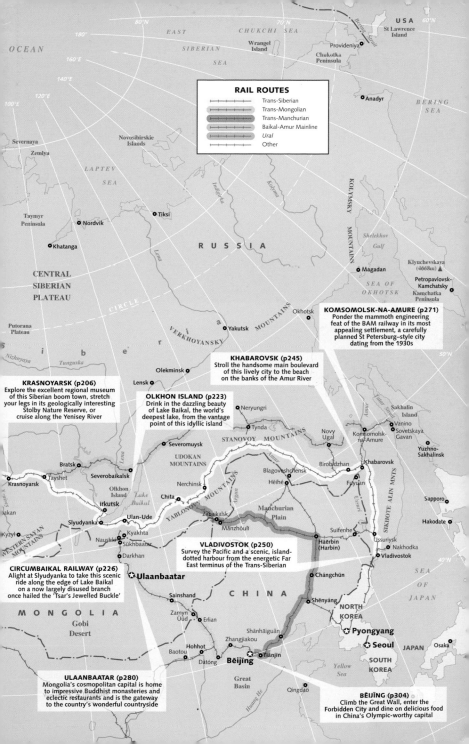

RAIL ROUTES

━━━━━━	Trans-Siberian
━━━━━━	Trans-Mongolian
━━━━━━	Trans-Manchurian
━━━━━━	Baikal-Amur Mainline
━━━━━━	*Ural*
━━━━━━	Other

KOMSOMOLSK-NA-AMURE (p271)
Ponder the mammoth engineering
feat of the BAM railway in its most
appealing settlement, a carefully
planned St Petersburg–style city
dating from the 1930s

KHABAROVSK (p245)
Stroll the handsome main boulevard
of this lively city to the beach
on the banks of the Amur River

KRASNOYARSK (p206)
Explore the excellent regional museum
of this Siberian boom town, stretch
your legs in its geologically interesting
Stolby Nature Reserve, or
cruise along the Yenisey River

OLKHON ISLAND (p223)
Drink in the dazzling beauty
of Lake Baikal, the world's
deepest lake, from the vantage
point of this idyllic island

VLADIVOSTOK (p250)
Survey the Pacific and a scenic, island-
dotted harbour from the energetic Far
East terminus of the Trans-Siberian

CIRCUMBAIKAL RAILWAY (p226)
Alight at Slyudyanka to take this scenic
ride along the edge of Lake Baikal
on a now largely disused branch
once hailed the 'Tsar's Jewelled Buckle'

ULAANBAATAR (p280)
Mongolia's cosmopolitan capital is home
to impressive Buddhist monasteries and
eclectic restaurants and is the gateway
to the country's wonderful countryside

BĚIJĪNG (p304)
Climb the Great Wall, enter the
Forbidden City and dine on delicious food
in China's Olympic-worthy capital

On the Road

SIMON RICHMOND
Coordinating Author
To not visit Moscow's Red Square (p130) at the start or finish of a Trans-Siberian journey is like skipping the view from the Empire State on a first visit to New York – unthinkable! This photo was taken on a chilly March day, hence the furry hat.

MARC BENNETTS This was taken near the end of my first trip to western Siberia after three weeks on the road. I was feeling tired and unshaven. The temperature in Novosibirsk that day was 22°C. Two days earlier, in Tomsk, it had been -9°C.

MARC DI DUCA Buryatiya (p235) is my favourite region of Siberia. Just behind me is the Tamchinsky Buddhist temple surrounded by the village of Gusinoe Ozero, just south of Ulan-Ude. When the Trans-Mongolian route was planned, in typical Soviet fashion a simple straight line was drawn from the village of Selenduma to Lake Gusinoe. When engineers were surveying the route, they discovered that the planned tracks cut the main temple building in half! The sharp swerve as you pass the village today is the result of a rare piece of Soviet consideration for a religious building.

LEONID RAGOZIN As a Lonely Planet author, you sometimes get excited about a certain destination, go to check it out, compare it to other places you've been to and then drop it for the lack of space in the book. Kozmodemyansk in the Mary-El republic is one such place. But at least I brought back this picture from a wooden architecture museum and a memory of sleeping in a terribly overpriced log house where the temperature never rose above 8°C. Still better than outside: -25°C.

MICHAEL KOHN I hopped off the train in Hǎilāěr (p295), between Hāěrbīn (Harbin) and the Russian border, and spent a relaxing day out on the grassy plains north of town. Most of the action was around a qer (yurt) camp where local Mongol herders rented out horses for the day and kept visitors entertained with traditional music. It was a dramatic place for a horse ride so I saddled up and galloped down to the river. My horse and I pose at the end of the ride.

ROBERT REID When pressed, I'll confess a dream: to create a Soviet bloc Car Museum in some place such as Newark or Tahlequah. Just buy the used ones no one wants over here, ship them back and set up. Then I found this: in the eastern neighbourhoods of Vladivostok, with a smokestack pumping black fumes nearby, a Soviet automobile museum (p253) with M&M-coloured beauts and propaganda posters touting Stalin's drive to beat the West. If you go, tell them to make T-shirts already.

MARA VORHEES Did you ever wonder what happened to Lenin, Stalin and all their comrades – the statues that used to stand on every square in Moscow? I found them congregated at Art Muzeon sculpture park (p135), now overshadowed by a behemoth bronze of Peter the Great. Ilych and I see eye-to-eye now that he's off his pedestal.

For full author biographies see p377.

Highlights

Trans-Siberian journeys are not short of wow moments. Only the most jaded of travellers will not get a kick out of marching across Moscow's Red Square or wandering around Běijīng's Forbidden City. The more adventurous will certainly want to explore and possibly plunge into icy Lake Baikal or ride with nomads across Mongolia's magnificent steppes. For many others the sharing of stories, vodka shots and slices of *kolbassa* (sausage) with fellow passengers on the train will provide the sweetest memories. A selection of our highlights and those of locals and Trans-Sib experts follow.

SIMON RICHMO

1 **SAVOUR THE EXPERIENCE**

We worked hard to make it [the movie] as real and authentic as my memories of it 20 years prior. We took a scouting trip on the train some months before we shot the film in 2006...the experience was exactly as I remember it all those years before – same trains, same food, same stern *provodnitsas* (female carriage attendants)! Nothing had changed...except for the fact that people were checking emails on their Blackberries as we rolled through the remote tundra!

Brad Anderson, Director & Cowriter, *Trans-Siberian*

BEAUTIFUL VITEBSK STATION

One of the great pleasures of taking a train from Eastern Europe and the Baltic States to St Petersburg (incidentally a great way to ease yourself into a Trans-Siberian journey) is that it arrives at Vitesbsky vokzal (p113), the most historic and gorgeously decorated of the city's train stations. Before leaving, take a peek at the amazing Style Moderne interior of the entrance hall and waiting room, beautifully restored in 2003 for St Petersburg's tricentenary.

Simon Richmond, Lonely Planet Author

A NIGHT AT THE MARIINSKY

I never pass up the opportunity to attend a performance at St Petersburg's majestic Mariinsky Theatre (p118). With maestro Valery Gergiev at the helm, a quality production is pretty much guaranteed, but nothing really can compare to the gilded beauty of the auditorium itself – it's like sitting inside the tsar's giant treasure box.

Simon Richmond, Lonely Planet Author

ГОСТИНИЦА ЛЕНИНГРАДСКАЯ

JONATHAN SMITH

④ KOMSOMOLSKAYA PLOSHCHAD

Trans-Siberian travellers can't go wrong if they begin or end their trip at the luxurious old Leningrad-skaya Hotel (p143). Occupying one of the iconic Stalinist skyscrapers known as the 'Seven Sisters', this new Hilton hotel overlooks Komsomolskaya pl in all its chaotic, commotion-filled glory. On one square, the three main train stations capture Moscow's architectural eclecticism, along with its diverse and dubious crowds.

Mara Vorhees, Lonely Planet Author

SIMON RICHMOND

⑤ ROSTOV-VELIKY

As you approach Rostov-Veliky (p151) by rail, an enigmatic apparition appears on the horizon: the tall towers and golden domes of the Monastery of St Jacob, sparkling in the sunlight. The monastery sits like Cinderella's castle, surrounded by the vast Russian countryside, evoking the magic and mystery of medieval Rus.

Mara Vorhees, Lonely Planet Author

SAMPLE *MEDOVUKHA* IN SUZDAL

No place evokes medieval Rus more than Suzdal (p160). The earthen ramparts of Suzdal's kremlin date to the 12th century, when this was the capital of the principality. A walk along the ramparts reveals magnificent views of three monasteries, two convents and some 30 smaller churches. A local speciality in Suzdal is *medovukha*, a mildly alcoholic honey drink. Visit the refectory, within the kremlin walls, to sample this preferred brew of medieval Russian princes.

Gerald Easter, Professor of Russian Politics & History, Boston College

MARTIN MOOS

WINTER'S JOURNEY TO NIZHNY

There is no more winter in Moscow. No snow, no frost, no red cheeks or hot donuts at the skating rink. Global warming, damn it! But travelling east to Nizhny Novgorod (p163), you'll see its effect weakening with every mile you pass. It gets sunnier, dryer and trees turn white instead of black. Four hours, and I am in the city full of things that were aplenty in the Moscow of my childhood, but not anymore – such as century-old gingerbread cottages. Quickly register the view from the kremlin, then dive into cafe Michelle for a glass of hot *glühwein* (mulled wine). Happiness.

Maria Makeeva, Silver Rain Radio Presenter

IMAGESTATE MEDIA PARTNERS LIMITED · IMPACT PHOTOS / ALAMY

TOBOLSK KREMLIN

The kremlin (p189) is the symbol of Tobolsk. It is intrinsically connected to the history of the town. The people across the entire area love it. It was recently voted the top sight for the region in an all-Russian poll. We don't get many tourists here right now, but the central government has been pumping money into the region of late to develop infrastructure, so all that should change soon!

Minsalim Timergazeev, Folk Artist, Tobolsk

SLACKER MONUMENT, OMSK

A very odd statue awaits visitors on Omsk's ul Lenina. Dating from the 1960s, this worker (p193) seems to be not so much dreaming of a socialist future but a pint and a pie after work.

Marc Bennetts, Lonely Planet Author

RICHARD I'ANSON

10 CIRCUMBAIKAL RAILWAY

Take an unhurried trundle along Lake Baikal's southern shore on the scenic Circumbaikal Railway (p226). The train dawdles along, giving you time to admire the tunnels and cuttings of this feat of early-20th-century engineering. The only slower way to make the journey is to hike – camping and bathing in the lake's cool waters as you go.

Marc Di Duca, Lonely Planet Author

PETER SOLNESS

11 A DIP IN LAKE BAIKAL

On a calm day, under a clear sky, Baikal's (p219) blueness is intense, peculiar, indescribable, heart-stopping... As one plunges into those blessed depths, all the famous statistics seem irrelevant.

Dervla Murphy, Travel Writer, *Through Siberia by Accident*

12 VLADIVOSTOK VIEW

On Vladivostok's grey streets, the Trans-Siberian's last stop looks a little cruddy at times close up – recently some locals even pulled out the flowers from a public display on its 'Arbat' (ul Fokhina) to plant vegetables! But it's as stunning as any cityscape seen from high above. Riding up the funicular (p251) to Eagle's Nest Hill gives a popular vantage point of the snaking, ship-lined Golden Horn Bay. Up there this time, an Azerbaijani couple shyly said 'hi' then wondered, 'In America, do you speak French or English?'

Robert Reid, Lonely Planet Author

13 BARGUZIN VALLEY

The incredibly remote and romantically timeless Barguzin Valley (p239), birthplace of Chinggis (Genghis) Khaan's mum, is one of the most attractive yet least-visited spots around Lake Baikal. Snow-dusted peaks and curious rock formations gaze down upon a landscape dotted with salt lakes and fairy-tale wooden villages – the perfect escape from civilisation.

Marc Di Duca, Lonely Planet Author

EASTERN SIBERIA'S TIMBER ARCHITECTURE

If there's one thing Siberia doesn't lack, it's wood! Siberians have been cobbling together dwellings and churches from larch and spruce since they arrived in the region almost 400 years ago, though not always as elaborately as this example at Taltsy Museum of Wooden Architecture (p219).

Marc Di Duca, Lonely Planet Author

14

MARC DI DUCA

HORSE SWEAT ANYONE?

Beyond the finish line at the Naadam horse-racing grounds (p289), the sweat collectors waited with baited breath. When the racers charged across the line the spectators were on them – reaching, scrambling and chasing the horses to scrape some of their sweat. Collecting sweat from racehorses is a time-honoured tradition in Mongolia. Having accrued a palm-full, the spectator will rub the perspiration on their own faces, thus earning themselves a year's worth of good luck. Attempting to protect the exhausted horses and jockeys, 100 policemen tried to fend off the crowds with tasers. I was content to stand back and photograph the ensuing mayhem.

Michael Kohn, Lonely Planet Author

BRADLEY MAYHE

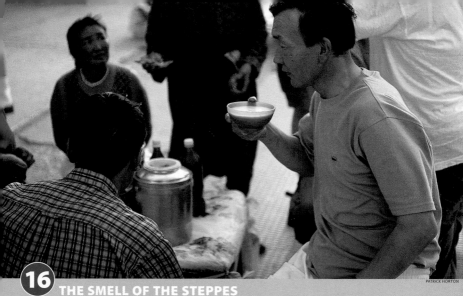

16 THE SMELL OF THE STEPPES

The best thing to do in the Mongolian countryside is drink *airag* (fermented mare's milk). I rarely drink it in the city but once I am out in the countryside I start to crave *airag*. I don't really know why but perhaps it's the smell of the grass that makes me think of the brew, or maybe just the endless steppes spreading out before me. I usually drink a good six or seven bowls in one sitting, but it never makes me drunk. The Mongolian body is basically immune to the alcoholic effects of *airag* – we can drink a lot of it but we'll never get drunk. For that we need vodka, but that is another story.

Onorjargal, Actor & Film Maker

17 BOWLFUL OF *BUUZ*

At first glance Hăilăĕr (p295) seemed like any mid-sized Chinese city. Yet after meeting a few locals I realised the city had quite a significant population of Buryats, an ethnic minority closely linked to the Mongols. It wasn't long before I was taken to a Buryat restaurant, which served Buryat *buuzy* (dumplings) and milk tea. Some of the patrons offered to take me out to the grasslands to meet a Buryat family who maintained a traditional lifestyle (except for the motorbike and DVD player in the ger (yurt). A bag of dried curds was thrust into my hands – it lasted all the way until Ulan-Ude!

Michael Kohn, Lonely Planet Author

PHIL WEYMO

⓲ BĚIJĪNG BY BIKE

At first Běijīng (p304) felt terribly difficult to navigate. It was big, spread out and exhausting to explore. I realised my mistake – I was travelling by foot. On day two I hired a bicycle and whizzed around the city at a wonderful pace. All those wide avenues, giant intersections and long distances were suddenly shrunk by two-thirds. I visited the highlights of the city, got some exercise and enjoyed the cool breeze in my face on an otherwise humid summer afternoon. Best of all, I felt like a local – pulling up to an intersection with thousands of Chinese on their bikes and taking off together as if we were in a massive bike rally.

Michael Kohn, Lonely Planet Author

Contents

Regional Map Contents

Central St Petersburg pp106-7

Central Moscow (Tverskoy) pp124-5

RUSSIA

Moscow to Yekaterinburg pp156-7

Yekaterinburg to Krasnoyarsk pp178-9

Tayshet to Sovetskaya Gavan by BAM pp262-3

Lake Baikal to Vladivostok pp230-1

CHINA

Krasnoyarsk to Lake Baikal p206

Chita to Běijīng pp296-7

MONGOLIA

Ulan-Ude to Běijīng p277

Central Běijīng p306

Trans-Siberian Railway

Once hailed as 'the fairest jewel in the crown of the Tsars', the Trans-Siberian Railway remains one of life's great travel experiences. Spanning seven time zones and some of Russia's most geographically challenging, yet resource rich and scenically splendid regions, the railroad represents a triumph of man over nature. But, together with its Trans-Mongolian and Trans-Manchurian tributaries into neighbouring China and Mongolia, travelling the Trans-Siberian is achievable by anyone with some time, a little money and a sense of adventure.

The classic journey links Moscow – Russia's awe-inspiring capital of the Kremlin and Red Square, Stalinist skyscrapers, and oil billionaires and their entourages – with the dynamic, physically stunning port of Vladivostok on the edge of the Pacific, 9288km away. The ever-popular Trans-Mongolian option joins up the dots between China's imperial capital of Běijīng, basking in its post-Olympic glory; Ulaanbaatar, the pulsating capital of Mongolia with access to exhilarating open spaces; and any number of fascinating destinations in Russia, including an essential pause at the sapphire dazzler that is Lake Baikal. Connoisseurs of the off-beat will gravitate towards the Baikal-Amur Mainline (Baikalo-Amurskaya Magistral, or BAM), an alternative Trans-Siberian route through some of the most remote and beautiful parts of Siberia.

With an average speed of around 60km/h, these Trans-Siberian services are not for travellers in a hurry. Nor, with a few exceptions, are these working trains particularly glamorous. Nonetheless, a Trans-Siberian trip is never dull, not least because of the chance you'll have to interact with your fellow passengers over several days of travel. Whether you experience the Trans-Siberian route nonstop, savouring the slowly evolving landscapes, or – as we'd strongly advise – hop off and on the train at the dozens of fascinating places en route, one thing is for sure: this will be a journey to remember.

Russia

In the past decade, Russia has evolved from an economically jittery, inefficient and disorganised basket case to a relatively slick petrodollar mover and shaker, and the world's No 1 luxury-goods market. Off the back of oil and gas, the world's biggest energy exporter has paid off its debts and stashed away reserves of R3.84 trillion (US$162.5 billion). With the economy growing at 7% per year, the Russian statistics agency reported that the average monthly salary rose by 27% in 2007 to R13,500 (US$550) and that unemployment was down to 6%. According to *Forbes* magazine, in 2007 19 of the 100 richest people in the world were Russians, while the country's tally of 87 US-dollar billionaires made it second only to the USA. Lenin is surely spinning in his mausoleum!

The global financial turmoil of late 2008 may have put a significant dent in their bank balances but it remains true that the *lyux* life enjoyed by the likes of aluminium mogul Oleg Deripaska or Chelsea-owner Roman Abramovich might as well be on an entirely different planet to that of the 20 million or so Russians who subsist on less than R4500 a month. Luxury is hardly common either among the growing Russian middle class, who nevertheless enjoy lives undreamt of by the vast majority of Soviet citizens less than two decades ago. Under such circumstances they have supported Putin and continue to support his successor Dmitry Medvedev, at the same time as gritting their teeth and tightening their purses to deal with steadily rising inflation, counted at 15% in the year to May 2008.

FAST FACTS

Russia

Population: 141.4 million

Surface area: 17 million sq km

Time zones: 11

National symbol: double-headed eagle

Extent of the Russian rail network: 87,000km

Gazprom profits in 2007: R658 billion (US$27.8 billion)

Rate of income tax: 13% flat

Number of deaths per year from alcoholic poisoning: 40,000

Number of languages spoken (other than Russian): more than 100

Number of Nobel Prize winners: 20

With no credible opponent, Medvedev's election to president in March 2008 was never in doubt, the only intangibles being how big his majority might be (71.3%) and how many Russians would bother to vote at all (73.7 million or 64% of potential voters). Non-Russian observers worried about how democratic this outcome really was, fretted even more in August of the same year when Russia came to blows with Georgia over the breakaway regions of Abkhazia and South Ossetia. While the controversy inevitably stirred up extreme reactions, more sober analysis would have that Russia – however heavy handed – is fumbling to find a way to deal with its sense of encirclement by newly NATO-leaning neighbours, such as Georgia, Ukraine and the Baltic States, who were once part of its 'sphere of influence' and whose borders continue to harbour many Russian nationals. While claiming to not want to defy the international community, Medvedev has said 'We are not afraid of anything, including the prospect of a new Cold War'.

Under such circumstances you may be wary about visiting Russia. We're not going to kid you that travel here is all plain sailing. On the contrary, for all the welcome that its people will show you once you're there, Russia's initial face can be frosty. Tolerating bureaucracy, an insidious level of petty corruption and some discomfort, particularly away from the booming urban centres, remains an integral part of the whole Russian travel experience. However, a small degree of perseverance will be amply rewarded. Russia remains its own unique, fascinating creation, that everyone should see for themselves.

China

A journey on the Trans-Mongolian or Trans-Manchurian routes will bring you to the nation currently on everyone's lips. The Asian and Western media are littered with images of China 'taking centre stage' and assuming its mantle as the 'powerhouse of the East'. Sitting on the world's largest foreign-exchange reserves, China grabbed the largest gold-medal tally at the 2008 Olympic Games, an achievement that could only assure the international respect China so craves.

When it runs out of superlatives, China simply generates a few more. The world's fastest intercity train started running in 2008 between Běijīng and Tiānjīn, but even that will be eclipsed in speed within a few years by the Běijīng–Shànghǎi high-speed rail link. China also recently overtook the USA as the world's largest broadband market. Lunar missions are a possibility as China's space program races through the gears.

China also finds itself at the heart of an apparent shift of world power from the West to the East. And despite downsizing, the country has the world's largest standing army (which could sponge up the world's largest number of permanent bachelors, a by-product of the country's one-child policy). The Olympics bequeathed Běijīng with a massively expanded metro system and extraordinary examples of modern architecture, making it a truly global city.

Impressive as these achievements are, any seasoned China traveller will tell you these success stories are not particularly useful yardsticks for quantifying this nation of 1.3 billion. You only have to wander a few kilometres from Běijīng for an immediate reminder that China remains a largely agricultural nation; its economy – measured by per capita wealth – is roughly in the same league as Morocco. As many as 500 million rural Chinese do not have access to clean drinking water. Even modest trips around the nation reveal China as a gigantic work in progress, caught somewhere between the 1950s and the early 21st century.

The fruits of the economic boom are tangible and easy to assess, but on other development indicators – take democracy, human rights, adequate education and healthcare, the rule of law, intellectual property rights and

FAST FACTS

China
Population: 1.3 billion

Surface area: 9.6 million sq km

Life expectancy male/female: 71/75 years

GDP growth: 10.8%

Extent of Chinese rail network: 78,000km

Literacy rate: 86%

Head of state: President Hu Jintao

Number of gold medals at 2008 Olympics: 51

Internet users: 134 million

Length of the Great Wall: 7200km

environmental degradation, to name a few – China is either making negligible or slow progress (or is indeed stationary or going backwards). See p71 for details on some of the indicators where China is making progress.

Despite the rebellious paroxysms of the 20th century, the Chinese are still a deeply pragmatic people. They are respectful and fearful of authority, so you won't see any antigovernment graffiti. You won't hear speakers standing on soap boxes to vent their political views (unless they chime with government opinion). Political debate is stifled and most Chinese keep their heads down and work hard for a living. This continues to create a country that is increasingly wealthy, for sure, but one that is intellectually muzzled.

Mongolia

Caught between two giants of the contemporary geopolitical landscape, Mongolia is a titan from the past, striving to make its mark in the present. Since the fall of communism nearly two decades ago, this remote, land-locked country has done just about everything in its power to open itself up to the world. While the old traditions of nomadic herding survive and its wild nature is still mostly intact, Mongolia has also reached out to Western countries for economic and cultural ties. It's not uncommon to meet Mongolians with degrees from universities in the USA, Europe or Australia. Everyone seems to have at least one relative working overseas.

Along with Japan and South Korea, Mongolia is one of the only legitimate democracies in the whole of Asia. A constant parade of street protests have forced policy change on everything from mining laws to bus fares. Elections have largely proven to be free and fair. However, the perceived irregularities in the June 2008 election sparked riots in the capital Ulaanbaatar leaving five dead and 300 injured. President Nambaryn Enkhbayar was forced to call a four-day state emergency.

This troubling development aside, democracy has given foreign investors enough confidence to stick with Mongolia during hard times. Attractive investment laws have lured some of the big boys of the mining world – the major target of Mongolia's economic reformers. The economy grows at a robust 7.5% per year – thanks mainly to China's insatiable appetite for Mongolia's raw materials. Even so, Mongolia still faces enormous economic and social challenges; it remains one of the poorest countries in Asia, with typical salaries at less than US$200 a month.

Tourism, along with mining and cashmere, has become a key feature of the economy. The limitations of poor infrastructure and a short travel season have kept receipts small, but Mongolia does have a growing network of ger (yurt) camps that cater to intrepid travellers seeking ecotourism adventures. Without fences or private property to restrict movement, Mongolia is a perfect destination for horse trekking, long-distance cycling or hiking. There is also plenty of scope for more leisurely activities such as fly-fishing, yak carting or just camping out under a sprawling mass of stars.

If this description perpetuates your belief in an untouched country of aimlessly wandering nomads, then you also need the scoop on the new Mongolia. Add to the above internet cafes in the middle of nowhere, herders chatting to one another on mobile phones and, in Ulaanbaatar, Manhattan-style cocktail bars and vegetarian cafes.

Most travellers come for Naadam, the two-day summer sports festival that brings Ulaanbaatar to a standstill. But Mongolia's unique charm will always lie in the countryside where, rather than being a spectator to the wrestling, you may find yourself making up the numbers! Outside the villages it's easy to meet nomad families whose relentless sense of hospitality can at times be nothing short of overwhelming.

FAST FACTS

Mongolia

Population: 3 million

GDP: US$3200 per capita

Leading 2008 exports: copper, wool, gold, cashmere, leather

Average life expectancy: 64 years

Literacy rate: 98%

Voter turnout: often over 75%

Horse-to-human ratio: 13 to 1

Annual economic aid received: about US$159 million

Telephone usage: 156,000 landlines; over 800,000 mobile phones

Proportion of people living below the poverty line: 33%

Head of livestock: 41 million

Getting Started

Given the number of options – which route to take, when to go, where to break the journey (if at all), whether to DIY or use the services of a tour operator, how to travel more responsibly – a Trans-Siberian trip requires some forethought. This chapter will help you sort your priorities, plan ahead and whet your appetite for the travelling pleasures to come.

See Climate Charts (p328) for more information.

WHEN TO GO

The main Trans-Siberian Railway tourist season runs from May to the end of September, with mid-July to early September being the busiest time for foreign visitors, as well as Russians taking their annual holidays. Tickets for all trains during this time should be booked well ahead, although note that Russian Railways sells tickets only up to 45 days in advance. The Moscow–Běijīng route is especially popular over the summer, with tickets for it selling very fast – you may find that to get the dates you want you'll be forced to deal with an agency or tour group.

Although July and August are the warmest months in Siberia (with temperatures rising as high as 40°C), they are often the dampest months in parts of European Russia, with as many as one rainy day in three. During these months the climate in Běijīng can also be murder with soaring humidity – the total opposite from Mongolia, where clear skies make the sunlight intense. Conditions are less extreme during May and June or September and the first half of October, when autumn brings stunning colours as the leaves turn, particularly in Russia's Far East.

Winter nights are long and freezing, but if you're prepared for it this time of year can also be fantastic. The theatres open, the furs and vodka come out, and the snow makes everything picturesque. In addition, Russian train tickets are sold at a discount in winter (particularly in November and most of December and January to April). The best winter month to visit Siberia is March, after the deep freeze of December to February, although note that March in St Petersburg and Moscow can be particularly grim.

Least liked everywhere are the first snows beginning in late October (but sometimes earlier) and the spring thaw (April), which turn everything to mud and slush.

Keep in mind major public holidays; for example manoeuvring around China with 1.3 billion others during Chinese New Year can be daunting. See p331 for details on the main festivals and events, and p333 for details on holidays.

WHAT KIND OF TRIP?
Independent Travel vs Group Tour

Independent travel in Russia, China and Mongolia can be a lot of fun, but don't expect it to be necessarily cheap or easy to organise. Away from the major cities your odds of meeting anyone who speaks English are slim; if you can speak and read some Russian and, on the Trans-Mongolian and Trans-Manchurian routes, Chinese and Mongolian, it will improve your trip no end. With limited language skills, everything you attempt will possibly be more costly and more difficult. However, it's far from impossible and if you really want to meet locals and have a flexible itinerary, this is the way to go.

To smooth the way somewhat, it's a good idea to consider using a specialist travel agency to arrange your visas, and make some of your train

HOW MUCH?

Russia

Midrange double room R1500-4000 (R3000-10,000 Moscow and St Petersburg)

1hr online R50-100

Meal and drink in a midrange restaurant R600-1000

Short taxi ride R200

1L of petrol R23-29

1L of bottled water R25

Bottle of local beer R70

Blin R50

Metro ticket R20

China

Midrange double room Y240

1hr online Y2-4

Meal and drink in a mid-range restaurant Y40

Short taxi ride Y10

1L of petrol Y6.2

1L of bottled water Y4

Bottle of local beer Y3

Souvenir T-shirt Y25

Large lamb kebab Y1

Metro ticket Y3

DON'T LEAVE HOME WITHOUT...

■ Getting your visas – for details, see p342.

■ Very warm clothes and a long, windproof coat, if you're visiting during winter.

■ Learning Cyrillic and packing a phrasebook or mini dictionary – having a handle on the Russian language will improve your visit immeasurably. Ditto knowing a few simple Chinese phrases and being able to recognise a handful of Chinese characters, if China is on your itinerary.

■ Slip-on footwear, such as thongs (flip-flops) or Chinese cloth sandals, and loose, comfortable clothes, such as a tracksuit for wearing on the train.

■ Thick-soled, waterproof and comfortable walking shoes.

■ Strong insect repellent for summer.

■ A plug for a bathroom basin.

■ Cards, books and photos of your family and home for breaking the ice with your cabin mates.

■ A stash of painkillers or other decent hangover cures.

■ A sense of humour.

and accommodation bookings. Most travel agencies will be happy to work on any itinerary. It's also possible to arrange guides and transfers through an agency, and the prices can sometimes be better than you'd be able to negotiate yourself with or without language skills. Note, though, that if you use an agency *just* to book train tickets, you will certainly pay more (sometimes far more) than what you'd pay for the same tickets if you buy them yourself once in Russia, China or Mongolia. For more on booking tickets, see p27.

On organised group tours everything is taken care of and all you need do is pay and turn up. Tours can cater to special interests and range from backpacker basics to full-on tsarist luxury, such as on the private Golden Eagle train (p360). You'll seldom be alone – which can be a curse as well as a blessing depending on the company. This will also cut down on your chances of interacting with locals: on some trips whole carriages of the train are filled with foreign tourists. Opportunities to head off the beaten track or alter the itinerary are also very limited, if not impossible. For a list of some overseas tour groups, see p352. Some local volunteer groups offer tours groups as well; see p31. Other local tour companies and travel agencies offering tours are mentioned in the destination chapters.

Staying on the Train vs Getting On & Off

Aficionados of going nonstop from Moscow to Vladivostok or Běijīng – both are journeys of seven days – often compare it to being on a sea voyage or having a beach holiday indoors. It's a chance to sleep and read, perhaps sharpen up your card-playing and chess skills with fellow passengers, while the landscape unreels in cinematic slow motion outside. Approached in this manner, the trip can be a relaxing, languorous experience, not to mention a chance to form some memorable relationships.

The aim, however, of this guide is to tempt you off the train and get you exploring the fascinating countries it passes through. At the very least we'd recommend breaking your journey once – the most obvious point being in Irkutsk (p211) to visit Lake Baikal. On the Trans-Mongolian route consider a stop in Ulaanbaatar (p280), while on the Trans-Manchurian route a pause in Hāěrbīn (Harbin; p299) is a possibility. See p24, p35 and the chapter highlights and route-planner boxes at the start of many destination

HOW MUCH?

Mongolia

Midrange double room T45,000-90,000

1hr online T700

Guanz (canteen) lunch T2000

Short taxi ride T3000

1L of petrol T820-1020

1L of bottled water T500

Can of Chinggis beer R1000

Local newspaper T500

Shashlyk T1800

Best seat at the Naadam opening T30,000

Outside of Russia's busy June to August travel period and over a few key holidays such as Easter, buying tickets yourself in the country shouldn't be too problematic.

TOP 10

Best Railway Stations

Many of the historic stations along the Trans-Siberian route are worth visiting in their own right. From St Petersburg, the following are ordered from west to east.

1 Vitebsk, St Petersburg (p113) Style Moderne delight and starting point of Russia's first public railway to Tsarskoe Selo.

2 Yaroslavl, Moscow (p148) A fitting start or finish to the Trans-Siberian is this 1902 stylised reproduction of a traditional Russian fort.

3 Novosibirsk (p196) Siberia's largest station is a temple to the Trans-Siberian.

4 Krasnoyarsk (p206) Big, grand and self-consciously spired, with a great mural of Lenin and comrades.

5 Irkutsk (p211) Admire the well-proportioned classicism of this station.

6 Severobaikalsk (p265) Le Corbusier–style station on the BAM line.

7 Slyudyanka 1 (p225) Built entirely of marble in 1904 to commemorate the construction of the technically challenging Circumbaikal line.

8 Tynda (p270) Futuristic Brezhnev meets *The Jetsons* structure, by far the city's most impressive architecture.

9 Birobidzhan (p244) The station's name is written in Hebrew; there's a star of David on the front of it, too, and a Jewish statue.

10 Vladivostok (p250) Restored old beauty, with detailed ceiling murals.

Our Favourite Festivals & Events

Many travellers schedule their journey to coincide with the events that take place during the year.

1 Ice Lantern Festival, Hāěrbīn (Harbin; 5 January to 15 February; p302)

2 Chinese New Year/Spring Festival, Běijīng and Hāěrbīn (January/February; p332)

3 Camel Polo Winter Festival, Ulaanbaatar (mid-March; p332)

4 Easter (Paskha), across Russia (March/April; p332)

5 Victory Day, across Russia (9 May; p332)

6 Sabantuy, Kazan (mid-June; p169)

7 White Nights Arts Festival, St Petersburg (mid-June; p115)

8 Naadam, Ulaanbaatar (11 and 12 July; p288)

9 Mid-Autumn/Moon Festival, across China (September/October; p332)

10 December Nights Festival, Moscow (December; p140)

Trans-Siberian Trivial Pursuit

These 'Did you knows' come courtesy of the Trans-Siberian Railway Web Encyclopaedia.

1 The real distance – Russian Railways calculates its Moscow–Vladivostok fare based on 9298km but the actual distance is 9288.2km.

2 The coldest place – between Mogocha (6906km) and Skovorodino (7306km), where temperatures can plummet to –62°C.

3 The highest point (1040m) – the Yablonovy Mountain pass (6110km) between Yablonovaya and Turgutui.

4 The lowest point – between Amursky Zaliv (9252km) and Ugol'naya (9253km) when the route skirts the Pacific Ocean.

5 The steepest descent – between Adrianovskaya and Slyudyanka-2 (5305km) when the railroad drops 400m.

6 The longest bridge – the 2616m Amur Bridge (8512km).

7 The longest tunnel – the 7km tunnel beneath the Amur built between 1937 and 1942 for strategic reasons and now used only by freight trains.

8 The longest tunnel used by passenger trains – Tarmanchukan tunnel (2km), built in 1915 and located between Arkhara (8080km) and Obluche (8190km).

9 The largest station – Novosibirsk built in 1939 to 1940.

10 Most expensive section – the 260km Circumbaikal line, which cost over R2 million per km.

chapters for other ideas of where to leave the train and how long to spend in each place.

Bear in mind that there's no such thing as a hop-on, hop-off Trans-Siberian ticket – every time you break your journey you'll have to buy a new onward ticket. Russian Railway's rules do allow passengers to break their journey once (for not more than 10 days) on any route, but the bureaucracy involved is off-putting, even to those who speak good Russian and have plenty of time on their hands.

Hence, if you are travelling from say from Moscow to Vladivostok, and plan on spending a night or two in Nizhny Novgorod and Irkutsk, you'll need three separate tickets: Moscow–Nizhny Novgorod, Nizhny Novgorod–Irkutsk, and Irkutsk-Vladivostok. The tickets will all be for a specific berth on a specific train on a specified day and can all be arranged in advance either online or via travel agencies or, once you're in Russia, at train station booking centres – see p27.

Also consider the direction in which you might travel. If you want to meet Russians, starting at Vladivostok and heading west is recommended, since far fewer foreign travellers take this route than the popular eastbound services from Moscow or westbound from Běijīng.

> Russian Prolife (www .russiaprofile.org) provides expert analysis of Russian politics, economics, society and culture that promises to unwrap 'the mystery inside the enigma'.

THE MAIN ROUTES

For full details of the routes covered here see the route descriptions at the start of many destination chapters. For the first four days' travel from Moscow, the main Trans-Siberian, Trans-Manchurian and Trans-Mongolian services all follow the same route through the Urals and into western Siberia, over the Yenisey River and on to Irkutsk in eastern Siberia.

On the fifth day, after rounding the southern tip of Lake Baikal, the Trans-Mongolian train branches off, heading south for the Mongolian border 250km away. The Trans-Manchurian stays with the main line for 12 hours past Lake Baikal, before it also peels off, heading southeast for Zabaikalsk on the Chinese border, some 368km away.

For information on the types of trains and carriages travelling these routes, see p357. For hints on reading a Russian train timetable, see p358.

Moscow to Vladivostok

The 1/2 *Rossiya* train is the top Moscow–Vladivostok service. If you're planning to stop off at Irkutsk, also consider using the 9/10 *Baikal*, reputed to be one of the best trains in Russia in terms of carriage standards and service.

Other good services that can be usefully included in a Moscow to Vladivostok itinerary include the 15/16 *Ural* between Moscow and Yekaterinburg; 25/26 *Sibiryak* between Moscow and Novosibirsk; 7/8 *Sibir* between Novosibirsk and Vladivostok; 55/56 *Yenisey* between Moscow and Krasnoyarsk; and 5/6 *Okean* between Khabarovsk and Vladivostok.

If you'd prefer to skip Moscow in favour of St Petersburg as the start or finish of a Trans-Siberian journey, the 71/72 *Demidovsky* between St Petersburg and Yekaterinburg is a recommended option.

If you're planning to frequently hop on and off trains and want to save some money along the way, it's a good idea to avoid the premium trains and go for the regular services, which offer *platskart* (*platskartny*; open carriage; see p359). Most of these services are perfectly acceptable and take pretty much the same travelling time point to point as the premium trains.

> *Black Earth: A Journey Through Russia after the Fall*, by Andrew Meier, is acutely observed and elegiac. In dispatches from Chechnya, Moscow, Norilsk, Sakhalin and St Petersburg, he paints a bleak picture of the country.

TRANS-SIBERIAN, THE MOVIE *Simon Richmond & Mara Vorhees*

The speeding carriages of a train, packed with intriguing strangers, are an ideal environment for generating suspense. This said, it's taken a while for movie-makers to get around to featuring one of the most famous trains of all – the Trans-Siberian – in a movie. Horror-movie fans can point to the 1973 cult classic *Horror Express*, directed by Eugenio Martin and starring Peter Cushing, Christopher Lee and Telly Savalas. However, this shlocky low-budget flick, which has an alien-inhabited prehistoric fossil turning Trans-Sib passengers into zombies, was actually filmed in Madrid and features only fake railway carriages and a model train that had previously served duty in the movie *Pancho Villa*.

Brad Anderson's far superior *Trans-Siberian*, released in 2008, used real Russian rolling stock but mostly had Lithuania stand in for Russia, and Vilnius Station was dressed up to resemble the one at Irkutsk. The entertaining and exciting thriller stars Woody Harrelson and Emily Mortimer as a likeable American couple, Roy and Jessie, travelling from Běijīng to Moscow by train. Along the way, they meet up with a charming but dangerous drug-running duo and a duplicitous narcotics detective (Ben Kingsley), thus entangling themselves in a very messy drug transaction.

The suspense-filled storyline unravels at the end. The *New York Times* review claims that 'it gets sidetracked' but we'll take it a step further and call the ending a train wreck – in more ways than one. In the movie's favour, the cinematography is spectacular, giving a wonderful sense of the vastness of the landscape and the emptiness of the countryside. It is also a pretty accurate depiction of life on the train – the close quarters in the cabins, the sometimes raucous atmosphere in the dining car, the less-than-tantalising toilet. If you've ever wondered what it's like to ride the Trans-Siberian railroad, this film will give you a good idea (minus the danger, death and destruction, most likely).

Actually, there is no guarantee that you won't be embroiled in some sort of intrigue. Part of the film takes place in the tiny Siberian town of Ilansky – the very same place where Simon Richmond – co-author of this guide – once was arrested for taking photos of the old locomotive and water tower at the station.

One recurring theme in the film is the unflinching nastiness of the *provodnitsa*, the train version of a flight attendant. In this film, the *provodnitsa* ignores the Americans' simple requests (no matter how loudly they are yelled at her in English); she pounds on doors and scowls at the camera; and she always, always yells. Relax. In all our years of riding trains in Russia, most of these ladies have been patient, pleasant and particularly attentive to foreigners on their carriage. Even the cranky ones are much more passive in their aggression.

The biggest thrill of this thriller? Not to toot our horn, but Roy and Jessie use Lonely Planet! A copy of the previous edition of this guide is prominently featured, lying enticingly on the bunk in the train cabin, while the action takes place in the background. Maybe we're not in the movies yet but our book is!

Moscow to Ulaanbaatar & Běijīng

The more popular of the two options running directly between Moscow and Běijīng is the 3/4 Trans-Mongolian service, a Chinese train that travels via Ulaanbaatar and the only one to offer deluxe carriages (see p358) with showers.

If you're planning to stop off in Irkutsk, there's also the less fancy daily 264/263 service to/from Ulaanbaatar.

The weekly 19/20 Trans-Manchurian service is a Russian train and takes half a day longer to reach Běijīng, but in doing so it avoids the need for a Mongolian visa.

TRAIN TICKET COSTS

In this book we typically quote *kupeyny* (*kupe*; compartmentalised carriage) fares. Expect SV (1st-class) fares to be double this amount and *platskartny* (*platskart*; open carriage) about 40% less. Children under five travel free if they share a berth with an adult, otherwise children under 10 pay half-fare for their own berth. On the Trans-Mongolian and Trans-Manchurian routes, kids under four travel free if they share a berth, while those under 12 pay around 75% of the full fare for their own berth.

Complicating matters is Russian Railways' policy of varying all fares according to seasons. In peak travelling seasons, for example early July to early August and around key holidays such as Easter and New Year, fares can be between 12% to 16% higher than the regular fare. During slack times of the year, such as early January to March, there are discounts on fares. On *skory poezd* (fast trains) and *firmennye poezdy* (premium trains) it's also possible to have two grades of *kupe* fare: with or without meals. We advise self-catering to putting your trust in what Russian Railways serves up.

Fares quoted in this book were collected between March and August 2008 and should be taken as a general guide only. The following table shows the cost for a *kupe* ticket:

As you chug towards Yekaterinburg from Moscow look out the window for the Europe-Asia obelisk at the 1777km marker.

SAMPLE KUPE TICKET PRICES

From	To Irkutsk	To Ulaanbaatar	To Běijīng	To Vladivostok
Moscow	R10,800	R12,600	R14,000	R16,000
Irkutsk	-	R4000	R10,100	R11,900
Ulaanbaatar	R4000	-	R6635	R10,400

For comparison, the following table shows the individual ticket costs and totals for those considering hopping on and off trains:

Itinerary 1: The Trans-Siberian route		Itinerary 2: Trans-Mongolian route	
Moscow-Vladimir	R240 *platskart*	Moscow–Nizhny Novgorod	R390
Vladimir–Nizhny Novgorod	R400 *platskart*	Nizhny Novgorod–Perm	R3570
Nizhny Novgorod–Yekaterinburg	R2827	Perm–Yekaterinburg	R1300
Yekaterinburg-Krasnoyarsk	R3491	Yekaterinburg-Tyumen	R1068
Krasnoyarsk-Irkutsk	R2040 *platskart*	Tyumen-Tobolsk	R710
Irkutsk–Ulan-Ude	R500 *platskart*	Tobolsk-Omsk	R2145
Ulan-Ude–Chita	R1470	Omsk-Tomsk	R1350
Chita-Khabarovsk	R6900	Tomsk-Krasnoyarsk	R1911
Khabarovsk-Vladivostok	R2700	Krasnoyarsk-Irkutsk	R2040
		Irkutsk-Ulaanbaatar	R4000
		Ulaanbaatar-Běijīng	R1382/6635 (for hard sleeper/*kupe*)
Total	**R20,568**	**Total**	**R19,866**

BOOKING TICKETS

Before setting off for your Trans-Sib journey you can buy tickets online (p28) and either have the ticket delivered to your home or hotel, or pick it up at an agency or from a courier at the train station.

Bookings cannot be made any earlier than 45 days before the date of departure – if you need to book for specific dates even further out than this your only option is to secure the services of an agency or tour company – the larger ones can almost always guarantee tickets for the dates you require for which you'll pay a premium.

You'd be wise to buy well in advance over the busy summer months and holiday periods such as New Year and early May, when securing berths at short notice on certain trains can be difficult. Tickets for key trains on the busy Moscow–St Petersburg route can also be difficult to come by, although those with flexible options should be able to find something.

Mongolian Matters (www.mongolianmatters .com) is a blog by an Ulaanbaatar expat, commenting on important news stories in Mongolia.

At most large Russian train stations you'll be confronted by several ticket windows. All will have different operating hours and generally un-helpful, non-English-speaking staff.

The sensible option, especially if there are horrendous queues, is to avail yourself of the *servis tsentr* (service centre) found at most major stations. At these air-conditioned centres – a godsend in summer – you'll generally encounter helpful, sometimes English-speaking staff who, for a small fee (typically around R200), can book your ticket. In big cit-ies and towns it's also usually possible to buy tickets at special offices and some travel agencies away from the station – individual chapters provide details.

> At Russian stations some ticket windows are reserved exclusively for use by the elderly or infirm, heroes of the Great Patriotic War or members of the armed forces. Check before queuing!

Even if you're told a particular service is sold out, it still may be possible to get on the train by speaking with the chief *provodnitsa* (female carriage attendant; see p361). Tell her your destination, offer the face ticket price first, and move slowly upwards from there. You can usually come to some sort of agreement.

Tickets for suburban trains are often sold at separate windows or from an *avtomat* (automatic ticket machine). A table beside the machine tells you which price zone your destination is in.

COSTS & MONEY
Russia

Avoid the major cities and use the *platskartny* ('hard' class, or 3rd class) carriages of overnight trains as an alternative to hotels and it's possible – just! – to get by on US$50 per day. However, if you visit the main cities, eat meals in restaurants and travel on *kupeyny* (2nd class) trains, US$150 to US$200 per day is a more realistic figure. Prices drop away from the metropolises, but not significantly, while in remote areas, such as the Russian Far East, everything can cost considerably more.

Dual pricing for sights and activities is also an issue (see the boxed text, p30). As a foreigner you'll sometimes be charged more at hotels, too, although not in Moscow or St Petersburg where hotel prices are the same for everyone. It's often fair game for taxi drivers and sometimes market sellers to try to charge foreigners more – check with locals for prices, but don't expect that knowledge to be much use unless you can bargain in Russian. You'll rarely be short-changed by staff in restaurants, cafes and bars, though.

BUYING TRAIN TICKETS ONLINE

There are several websites you can go to book train tickets online including that of **RZD** (www .rzd.ru, in Russian), which has plans to launch an English-language booking service. Other Russian-language websites include **UFS** (www.ufs-online.ru/rzhd/getInitParams.aspx) and **Tutu** (www.tutu.ru), which enables you to look up all train times, including those of *elektrichka* (local or suburban services) and to book airline tickets.

Sites in English, all with offices in Moscow, include the following:

- **Bilet.ru** (☎ 495-925 7571; www.bilet.ru/eng/) Partners with **Your Train** (www.poezda.net/en/), the CIS railway timetable search system.
- **Russian Rails** (☎ 916-202 6070; www.russianrails.com)
- **Trains Russia.com** (☎ in the USA 1888-263 0023, in Moscow 495-225 5012; www.trainsrussia.com/en /travels/) This is the authorised US agent for RZD. Tickets are issued in their Moscow office and can be picked up there or delivered to any address in Moscow for US$15, to any Moscow airport or train station for US$30 or sent via international DHL delivery to your home address.
- **VisitRussia.com** (☎ 1800-755 3080; www.visitrussia.com)

HOW TO BUY & READ YOUR TICKET

When buying a ticket in Russia, you can speed up the process immeasurably by arriving at the station or travel agent prepared. If you don't speak Russian, have someone who does write down on a piece of paper the following information in Cyrillic:

■ How many tickets you require

■ Where to

■ What class of ticket

■ The preferred date of travel and time of day for departure. Use ordinary (Arabic) numerals for the day of the month and Roman numerals for the month.

Also bring your passport as you'll be asked for it so that its number and your name can be printed on your ticket. The ticket and passport will be matched up by the *provodnitsa* (female carriage attendant) before you're allowed on the train – so make sure the ticket-seller gets these details correct.

Tickets are printed by computer and come with a duplicate. Shortly after you've boarded the train the *provodnitsa* will come around and collect the tickets: sometimes she will take both copies and give you one back just before your final destination; sometimes she will leave you with the copy. It will have been ripped slightly to show it's been used. It's a good idea to hang on to this ticket, especially if you're hopping on and off trains, since it provides evidence of how long you've been in a particular place if you are stopped by police.

Sometimes tickets are also sold with separate chits for insurance in the event of a fatal accident (this is a small payment, usually less than R30); for linen; and for some or all meals. The following is a guide for deciphering the rest of what your Russian train ticket is about.

1 Train number – the lower the number, the higher the standard and the price; the best trains are under 100. Odd-numbered trains head towards Moscow; even ones head east away from the capital.
2 Train type
3 Departure date – day and month
4 Departure time – always in Moscow time
5 Carriage number and class: Л = two-bed SV, M = four-bed SV, К = *kupe*, П = *platskartny*, О = *obshchiy*
6 Supplement for class of ticket above *platskartny*
7 Cost for *platskartny* ticket
8 Number of people travelling on ticket

9 Type of passenger: полный (*polny*, adult); детский (*detsky*, child); студенческий (*studenchesky*, student)
10 From/to
11 Bed number – if this is blank, the *provodnitsa* will allocate a bed on boarding
12 Passport number and name of passenger
13 Total cost of ticket
14 Tax and service fee
15 Arrival date
16 Arrival time – always Moscow time for long-distance trains

ABOUT MUSEUMS (AND OTHER TOURIST ATTRACTIONS)

Much may have changed in Russia since Soviet times, but one thing remains the same: foreigners typically being charged up to 10 times more than locals at museums and other tourist attractions. With the rouble strong, the economy booming and prices soaring, this practice is a Soviet hangover we'd prefer to see scrapped.

We understand that higher foreigner fees go towards preserving works of art and cultural treasures that might otherwise receive minimal state funding. The rub is that, Moscow and St Petersburg apart, non-Russian labels, guides or catalogues in museums are fairly uncommon. In our reviews we mention if there is good English labelling at a museum. Otherwise assume that you'll need a dictionary to work out the precise details of what you're seeing, or be prepared to pay even more for a guided tour – particularly if you wish that tour to be in a language you understand.

Some major Moscow attractions, such as the Kremlin, State History Museum and St Basil's have ditched foreigner prices. All adults pay whatever the foreigners' price used to be; all students, children and pensioners pay the low price. However, in St Petersburg foreigner prices rule, even at the Mariinsky Theatre, so awash with funds that it can afford to build not one but two brand new auditoria.

A few more working practices of Russian museums to keep in mind are as folllows:

■ Admittance typically stops one hour before the official closing time.

■ If you wish to take photos or film a video there will be a separate fee for this, typically an extra R100 for a still camera and R200 for video camera.

■ Once a month many places close for a 'sanitary day', in theory to allow the place to be thoroughly cleaned; if you specially want to see a museum, call ahead to check it's open.

China

The days are long gone when China was fantastically cheap; now costs can vary widely depending on the level of comfort expected. Living frugally by staying in dorms, travelling by bus, train or bicycle, eating from street stalls or small restaurants and refraining from buying anything means it is possible to live on less than US$20 (Y140) per day.

Food costs remain reasonable throughout China, and it's possible to eat for as little as US$5 to US$10 (Y35 to Y70) a day. Transport costs can be kept low by travelling hard seat on the train or by bus, but bus ticket prices have begun to rapidly increase in line with oil price hikes. Even travel by hard-seat sleeper is very good value and doubles as a good-value hotel.

Midrange hotel doubles start at around US$35 (Y240) and you can eat in midrange restaurants from around US$5 (Y35). Midrange comfort can be bought in China for around US$70 (Y480) a day.

Top-end travel in China? Five-star hotel double-room rack rates can reach US$300 (Y2000) a night in the big cities and you can expect to pay upwards of US$115 (Y800) for a meal at one of Běijīng's best restaurants.

In the Empire of Genghis Khan, by Stanley Stewart, is a mildly entertaining and brutally honest introduction to Mongolia by an Englishman who travelled 1000 miles on horseback across Central Asia and Mongolia.

Mongolia

Accommodation and food can cost as little as US$10 per day in Ulaanbaatar, but allow up to US$20 per day for better accommodation options, some tastier, Western-style meals, and trips to the theatre and museums.

Elsewhere within Mongolia, travellers on organised tours spend around US$100 per day (more for extra luxuries). Independent travellers can see the same sights and stay in midrange accommodation for around US$80 per day. If you share the cost of a private jeep or minivan and camp rather than stay in more expensive ger (yurt) camps, you can bring this down to about US$25 to US$40 per day. If you're hitching and using public transport around the countryside, allow about US$10 to US$15 per day.

TRAVELLING RESPONSIBLY

By using the train to get across the largest country in the world you're already doing your bit for the environment. In the Getting to the Railheads chapter (p39) we also provide some suggestions for reaching either Russia or China with minimal use of flights.

Once in the region you'll not fail to notice that as closely as some locals live with nature, they don't always respect it. Responsible travellers will be appalled by the mess left in parts of the countryside and at how readily rubbish is chucked out of train windows. Accept that you're not going to change how people live, but that you might be able to make a small impression by your own thoughtful behaviour.

It's obvious to not litter yourself, but also try to minimise waste by avoiding excess packaging. Rather than relying on bottled water, consider using purification tablets or iodine in tap water. Otherwise, use boiled water.

Also avoid buying items made from endangered species, such as exotic furs and caviar that isn't from legal sources. Poaching is a major problem in both Russia and China; there are laws against it – punishing both the poachers and the purchasers of their goods – so always check carefully the provenance of what you plan to buy and, if in doubt, don't.

WildChina (www .wildchina.com) organises far-flung treks around China, organised within China; it has a monthly email newsletter.

In China try to avoid simply tipping – the official line usually discourages this anyway. Instead, consider donating something that national park staff, or your tour guide or driver, would appreciate, especially if you feel they have a natural interest or talent. (For example, if you're about to leave the country you could leave behind your well-thumbed bird book.) Such gifts are way beyond the procurement power of most tour guides and will help further their interest in providing a sustainable tour experience.

Support local enterprises, environmental groups and charities that are trying to improve Russia, Mongolia and China's environmental and social scorecard. A good example is the Great Baikal Trail project helping to construct a hiking trail around Lake Baikal (see p224). Other possibilities include these:

Cross Cultural Solutions (www.crossculturalsolutions.org) Runs volunteer programs in a range of social services out of Yaroslavl.

Dersu Uzala Ecotours (www.ecotours.ru/english/) Works in conjunction with several major nature reserves across Russia on tours and projects.

EcoSiberia (www.ecosiberia.org) Has information on eco-attractions, projects and tours in Siberia.

Ger to Ger (☎ 011-313 336; www.gertoger.org) Mongolia's most innovative tourism concept combines hiking, sports, Mongolian language learning and visits with local families for cultural emersion.

International Youth Cultural Exchange (www.icye.org) Offers a variety of volunteer projects, mostly in Samara.

Language Link Russia (www.jobs.languagelink.ru/) Volunteer to work at language centres in Moscow, St Petersburg, Volgograd and Samara

Rinky Dink Travel Mongolia (☎ 9974 4162; www.rinkydinktravel.com) Small Ulaanbaatar-based tour company involved in social development programs in poor neighbourhoods and which invites tourists to volunteer for its projects.

World 4U (www.world4u.ru/english.html) Russian volunteer association promoting cultural, social and political awareness.

TRAVEL LITERATURE
Trans-Siberian

The Big Red Train Ride, by Eric Newby, is a classic, hilarious account of hopping on and off the *Rossiya* between Moscow and Nakhodka – it's as much a snapshot of the Soviet era as it is of life on a train.

Through Siberia by Accident and *Silverland,* by Dervla Murphy, are affectionate, opinionated discourses on the forgotten towns along Siberia's BAM rail route by one of the world's best travel writers.

Journey Into the Mind's Eye, by Lesley Blanch, is a semiautobiographical tale about the author's romantic obsession with Russia and the Trans-Siberian Railway.

Wall to Wall: From Beijing to Berlin by Rail, by Mary Morris, relates her personal experiences – which are not always positive – during a pre-Glasnost journey on the Trans-Mongolian route.

The Great Railway Bazaar, Riding the Iron Rooster and *Ghost Train to the Eastern Star,* all by Paul Theroux, include sections in which this erudite, opinionated traveller hauls his bags aboard the Trans-Siberian – each time he hardly seems to relish the experience.

Russia

Russia: A Journey to Heart of a Land and its People, by Jonathan Dimbleby – the hefty side product of a 16,000km journey the British journalist made for a BBC documentary across the country in 2007 – is a revealing snapshot of a multifaceted country and includes large sections on the Trans-Sib route.

Foreign Babes in Beijing, by Rachel DeWoskin, is an expat view of life in modern Běijīng in which the author dishes the dirt on her life in the capital during the 1990s when she became a soap-opera star.

Lost Cosmonaut and *Strange Telescopes,* by Daniel Kalder, are both blackly comic and serious explorations of some of Russia's quirkiest and least-visited locations. In the former the 'antitourist' author puts Kalmykia, Tatarstan, Mary-El and Udmurtia under the microscope. In the latter Kalder goes underground in Moscow, hangs out with an exorcist and extends his travels into Siberia to meet with the religious prophet Vissarion.

In Siberia, by Colin Thubron, is a fascinating, frequently sombre account of the author's journey from the Urals to Magadan during post-Soviet times; it's worth comparing with his *Among the Russians,* about a journey taken in 1981 from St Petersburg to the Caucasus.

China

China Road, by Rob Gifford, follows the National Public Radio correspondent as he travels Route 312 across the country from Shànghǎi to the border with Kazakhstan, expertly taking China's pulse as he goes.

River Town: Two Years on the Yangtze, by Peter Hessler, is full of poignant and telling episodes that occurred during the author's posting as an English teacher in the town of Fúlíng on the Yangzi River. Hessler perfectly captures the experience of being a foreigner in today's China in his observations of the local people.

Fried Eggs with Chopsticks, by Polly Evans, an occasionally hilarious account of travel around this huge country, is a good companion for those long, long train or bus journeys.

Mongolia

Dateline Mongolia: An American Journalist in Nomads Land, by Michael Kohn, is a memoir and travelogue written by a co-author of this guidebook. It recounts his memorable three years working as a reporter for the *Mongol Messenger.*

Lost Country: Mongolia Revealed, by Jasper Becker, describes the author's travels in Mongolia in the early 1990s and his attempts to uncover the secrets of the purge years that plagued Mongolia in the 1930s.

Wild East, by Jill Lawless, is a tightly written, very funny account of the author's experience in Mongolia, during which she spent two years editing the *UB Post.* This lightning-fast book serves as a good armchair read before visiting Mongolia.

INTERNET RESOURCES
Trans-Siberian Railway

Australian Broadcasting Corporation (www.abc.net.au/news/specials/transsiberia/default .htm) Slickly produced blog by the ABC's Russia correspondent Emma Griffiths about her 2005 Trans-Siberian journey.

Circumbaikal Railway (http://kbzd.irk.ru/Eng/index.htm) Best website for background on the historic Circumbaikal line.

Edrail.com (http://inbedwithjackanded.co.uk/edrail/table.html) Follow Ed Grieg's 2008 rail journey from Portugal to Vietnam in words, pictures and sound. Also see p40.

A Journey on the Trans-Siberian (www.trans-siberian-railway.co.uk) Clive Sampson's rail trip from the UK to China in 2006 with has plenty of inspiring photos and passion for the route.

Man in Seat 61 (www.seat61.com) Mark Smith's amazingly comprehensive website is one of the travel information wonders of the Web. It has great up-to-date sections on the Trans-Siberian routes, plus practically any other rail service that you might need.

Trans-Siberia.com (www.trans-siberia.com) John Pannell has some good personal accounts of the journey, photos of his Trans-Siberian trips and links to other useful sources of information.

Trans-Siberian Railway Web Encyclopaedia (www.transsib.ru) It's not been fully updated for several years, but this site still has tons of useful information and a huge photo library. (There's also a German-language version at www.trans-sib.de.)

Way to Russia (www.way torussia.net), written and maintained by Russian backpackers, is highly informative and on the ball. However, note that we've received complaints about buying train tickets through third parties associated with the site.

Russia

CIA World Factbook (www.cia.gov/library/publications/the-world-factbook/geos/rs.html) Read what the US spooks have on the Russkis.

English Russia (www.englishrussia.com) Daily entertainment blog that exists, as its strap line says, 'just because something cool happens daily on 1/6th of the world's surface'.

Moscow Times (www.moscowtimes.ru) All the latest breaking national news, plus links to the sister paper *St Petersburg Times* and a good travel-guide section.

Russia! (www.readrussia.com) There's more to Russia than ballet, Leo Tolstoy, or Maria Sharapova, as the website of this groovy quarterly magazine sets out to prove with its hip features on contemporary Russki culture.

Russian Beyond the Headlines (www.rbth.ru) Wide-ranging online magazine, with interesting features, sponsored by the daily paper *Rossiyskaya Gazeta.*

China

China Culture Center (www.chinaculturecenter.org) Bĕijīng-based outfit with tours around the capital and China plus China-related lectures and background info.

China Daily (www.chinadaily.com.cn) Get with the party line at the online mouthpiece of the Chinese Communist Party (CCP).

China National Tourist Office (www.cnto.org/aboutchina.asp) US site for the country's official tourism body.

China.org.cn (www.china.org.cn) Sanitised info on all aspects of China and up-to-the-minute news in 10 languages, including Esperanto.

CIA World Factbook (http://www.cia.gov/library/publications/the-world-factbook/geos/ch.html) What the US intelligence service publicly knows about China.

Human Rights in China (www.hrichina.org) Organisation set up in 1989 to promote human rights in China, with useful links.

Learn Chinese with the BBC (www.bbc.co.uk/languages/chinese/) A very useful introduction to learning Mandarin Chinese, with video.

Zhongwen: Chinese Characters and Culture (www.zhongwen.com) Includes a Pinyin chat room and an online dictionary of Chinese characters.

Mongolia

UN in Mongolia (www.un-mongolia.mn) gives development news and has links to UN agencies.

Living in Mongolia (www.living-in-mongolia.com) News and information site geared towards expats living in Mongolia.

Mongolia Expat (www.mongoliaexpat.com) Up-to-date website with sights and activities in contemporary Mongolia.

Mongolia National Tourism Centre (www.mongoliatourism.gov.mn) Includes lists of hotels, ger camps and travel agencies.

The Mongol Society (www.mongoliasociety.org) An excellent resource on news and events, with lots of links.

Mongolia Today (www.mongoliatoday.com) A colourful online magazine covering all aspects of Mongolian culture.

Mongoluls.net (www.mongoluls.net) Cultural articles, links and handy language tutorial.

Shaggy Yak (www.shaggyyak.com) A great starting point, with handy tips on visas, planning and logistics for a trip to Mongolia.

Itineraries
CLASSIC ROUTES

THE TRANS-SIBERIAN ROUTE One to Four Weeks / Vladivostok to Moscow
Although this route can be done in either direction, we suggest going
against the general flow by starting in **Vladivostok** (p250), at the far eastern
end of Russia, so you can finish up with a grand party in either **Moscow**
(p121) or, better yet, **St Petersburg** (p102).

Vladivostok, situated on a stunning natural harbour, merits a couple of
days, and it's also worth taking a break at **Khabarovsk** (p245), a lively city
on the banks of the Amur River that's an overnight hop to the west. Save
a couple of days for **Ulan-Ude** (p234), a fascinating city where Russian and
Buryat cultures mingle, and from where you can venture into the steppes
to visit Russia's principal Buddhist monastery, **Ivolginsky Datsan** (p238). Just
west of Ulan-Ude the railway hugs the southern shores of magnificent
Lake Baikal (p219). Allow at least four days to see the lake, visit the equally
lovely **Olkhon Island** (p223) and spend time in **Irkutsk** (p211), one of the
Trans-Siberian's most important rail junctions.

Krasnoyarsk (p206), on the Yenisey River, affords the opportunity for
scenic cruises along one of Siberia's most pleasant waterways. Crossing
the Urals into European Russia, schedule a stop in **Yekaterinburg** (p179),
a bustling historic city stocked with interesting museums and sites connected to the murder of the last tsar and his family. Finally, pause in the
tranquil Golden Ring towns of **Vladimir** (p158) and/or **Suzdal** (p160), both
packed with onion-domed churches, and a million miles away from the
pace of the megacities to come.

This 9288km jour-
ney can be done
nonstop in a week,
but we recom-
mend hopping on
and off the train
and making more
of an adventure
of it. Spend time
seeing the sights
in St Petersburg,
Moscow and along
the route, and you
could stretch this
trip to a month.

THE TRANS-MONGOLIAN ROUTE   One Week / Moscow to Běijīng

This highly popular journey between **Moscow** (p121) and **Běijīng** (p304) goes via the Mongolian capital of **Ulaanbaatar** (p280), allowing you to compare and contrast the three countries' cultures and people.

Get creative by breaking away from the regular Trans-Mongolian route. Take a boat from **Nizhny Novgorod** (p163) along the mighty Volga River to the charming artists' town of **Gorodets** (p168). From Nizhny Novgorod, there's a choice of ways to go: either the regular route to the industrial hub of **Perm** (p172) from where it's possible to take a trip to see the remains of a Gulag camp or an ice cave; or the southern route via the Tatarstan capital of **Kazan** (p168), with its World Heritage–listed kremlin.

Branch off from pleasant **Tyumen** (p186) in favour of the atmospheric old Siberian town of **Tobolsk** (p189), then return to the Trans-Sib route at the appealing city of **Omsk** (p192). A direct train from here will allow you to bypass Novosibirsk and head straight to **Tomsk** (p199), a Siberian gem packed with gorgeous wooden architecture. **Krasnoyarsk** (p206) with river cruises and fine theatres is the next logical overnight stop, from where you can push on to Irkutsk and Lake Baikal. Stop in either the southern lakeside town of **Port Baikal** (p223) or **Slyudyanka** (p225), both of which offer a trip along the **Circumbaikal Railway** (p226).

Crossing into Mongolia will seem to take forever. Reward yourself by alighting at Ulaanbaatar and taking time to explore the beautiful surrounding countryside, perhaps staying at a ger (yurt) camp in the **Gorkhi-Terelj National Park** (p292). Two more nights on the train and you'll finally reach China's fascinating capital.

Trains linking Moscow and Běijīng run just once a week, taking just under seven days for the total 7865km journey. By hopping on and off other trains you can make up your own itinerary, and so fully explore the three countries this route passes through.

ROUTES LESS TRAVELLED

OFF THE BEATEN SIBERIAN TRACK One Week

The 3400km Baikal-Amur Mainline (Baikalo-Amurskaya Magistral, or BAM) travels through some of the most rugged and unforgiving Siberian landscapes. The line officially starts in the drab town of **Tayshet** (p260), but the closest big city, **Krasnoyarsk** (p206), has an airport if you wish to skip all points further west.

At **Bratsk** (p261) the train crosses a 1km-long dam. The town also has an excellent open-air ethnographic museum where you can see many of the traditional Siberian buildings rescued when the dam was built. Pleasant **Ust-Kut** (p264) can be used as a base for hydrofoil trips up and down the Lena River. If you're short on time, push on to **Severobaikalsk** (p265), on the northern tip of Lake Baikal. This is the best base for exploring this relatively unvisited end of the lake and it also has a small BAM museum.

The most technically difficult section of the BAM to construct comes en route to **Tynda** (p270), where the line climbs over and burrows through mountains, the longest tunnel being 15.34km at **Severomuysk** (p260). Home of the BAM construction company's headquarters, Tynda is a must-stop for its BAM museum and good *banya* (hot bath). Having cleaned up, continue working your way east to the St Petersburg–styled **Komsomolsk-na-Amure** (p271), the largest and most pleasant city on the line and a great place to ponder the sacrifices and achievements made by hardy Soviet pioneers. Some 500km further east the BAM terminates at the naval base of **Sovetskaya Gavan** (p273), from where you can pick up a train that doubles back along the line to bring you to **Vladivostok** (p250).

Rail enthusiasts and adventurous travellers will not want to miss this alternative Trans-Siberian journey which, from Krasnoyarsk to Vladivostok, covers 5500km and takes at least six days without overnight stops. Begin in Moscow and you'll add on an extra 4098km and four days on the train.

THE BĚIJĪNG LOOP
One to Four Weeks / Běijīng to Běijīng

You will want to schedule plenty of time in historic, dynamic **Běijīng** (p304) either at the start or end of the trip. A day each is needed to tick off the Forbidden City and Tiananmen Square, the Great Wall and the Summer Palace.

An excellent overnight service connects the capital with **Hāěrbīn** (Harbin; p299), famous for its ice sculptures during its midwinter Ice Lantern Festival. Russians came here at the end of the 19th century to build the railway and handsome architectural evidence of their stay lies at the city's heart close to the Songhua River. Take a couple of days to enjoy Hāěrbīn's cosmopolitan atmosphere and visit the nearby **Siberian Tiger Park** (p300).

The Chinese–Russian border lies an overnight train ride away at **Mǎnzhōulǐ** (p297); if you're not on one of the weekly Trans-Manchurian services through to Moscow, it's a simple process of hopping on a bus across to **Zabaikalsk** (p295) on the Russian side where you can reconnect with trains through to **Chita** (p239). That pleasant city is a great base for exploring a relatively unvisited area of Siberia where you'll discover a couple of beautiful Buddhist monasteries and a holy mountain at **Alkhanay** (p243). From **Ulan-Ude** (p234) you could immediately branch down towards Mongolia, but since you've come this far it would be a great shame not to first venture further west to see **Lake Baikal** (p219). Apart from Ulan-Ude, possible bases for exploring the lake include **Slyudyanka** (p225), **Irkutsk** (p211), **Listvyanka** (p220) and **Olkhon Island** (p223).

Ulaanbaatar (p280) is certainly worth at least a couple of days. Its highlight is the lively and colourful Gandan Khiid monastery. From Ulaanbaatar, it's a two-night journey back to Běijīng through the Gobi Desert.

> Arrange your Russian visa at home before starting out and also get a double-entry visa for China. The 6148km journey can be done in a week, but you'll want to schedule up to a month to get the most out of the trip.

Getting to the Railheads

Green was the last word on anyone's lips when, a century and a half ago, dreams of building a railroad across Siberia began to coalesce into reality. And yet today, the Trans-Siberian Railway and its various tributaries are an integral option for travellers seeking to reduce the environmental impact of a journey between Europe and Asia or vice versa. As well as enjoy one of travel's most fascinating experiences.

Rather than flying to Moscow or Běijīng to start your journey, pause to consider the benefits of overland travel to the railheads. Sure, it takes more time and costs more money, but it does give you the chance to check out many interesting places en route and interact with locals – all up, far more fun than being squashed up for hours on a cheapo flight. International trains and buses (see p350) are plentiful, and as the carbon emissions comparison table shows (see below) it's possible in some cases to make more than a 50% cut in your environmental footprint by using them.

The following suggested routes can all be combined with a Trans-Siberian, Trans-Mongolian or Trans-Manchurian rail journey. It's time to get off the plane and get on the train!

Read up on Marc and Patricia's *Around The World Overland Adventure*, including a Trans-Siberian leg, at their blog on www.travelpod.com/travel-blog/marc-patty/marc_patty/tpod.html.

THE UK & CONTINENTAL EUROPE

There are no direct trains from the UK to Russia. The most straightforward route you can take is on the **Eurostar** (www.eurostar.com) to Brussels, and then a two-night direct train to Moscow via Berlin, Warsaw and Minsk (Belarus). The total cost can be as low as UK£150 one way.

There are many possible routes through Central Europe and Northern Europe, including Scandinavia. For example, from Moscow and St Petersburg there are regular services to Amsterdam, Berlin, Budapest, Helsinki, Paris, Prague, Vienna, Vilnius and Warsaw; see p148 for Moscow, and p120 for St Petersburg details.

Crossing the Poland-Belarus border at Brest takes several tedious hours while the wheels are changed for the broader Russian track. All foreigners visiting Belarus need a visa, including those transiting by train – sort this out before arriving in Belarus. To avoid this hassle consider taking the train to St Petersburg from Vilnius in Lithuania, which runs several times a week via Latvia. There are daily connections between Warsaw and Vilnius.

CARBON EMISSIONS COMPARISON TABLE

Journey	Transport	Carbon emissions (tonnes)	Travel time
London–St Petersburg (2315km)	Train	0.139	2 days
	Flight	0.3	3½hr
London-Moscow (3097km)	Train	0.186	2 days
	Flight	0.359	3½hr
London-Irkutsk (8282km)	Train	0.499	5½ days
	Flight	0.75	8½hr
London-Vladivostok (12,386km)	Train	0.773	8½ days
	Flight	0.983	10½hr

Calculations made on www.carbonfootprint.com.

AN UNEXPECTED JOURNEY ON THE LOVE TRAIN *Ed Greig*

In 2004 somewhere between Běijīng and Moscow, a small paragraph in my Lonely Planet caught my eye. It revealed that while the Trans-Mongolian, my temporary home, was undoubtedly a long train journey, the longest of them all stretched from Portugal to Vietnam, covering a total of 17,852km. The idea of adding 10,000km either side of my current odyssey seemed ridiculous, and I laughed heartily at the thought that there would be anyone out there foolish enough to attempt it.

Four years later I was standing on the platform of a small station in the town of Villa Real de Santa Antonio, in southern Portugal. My goal, after crossing 13 countries, was Ho Chi Minh City in Vietnam, which I explained to the station master, using expansive gestures and my phrasebook Portuguese. He let out a familiar hearty laugh. To add to the complications of three months of train travel, I planned to interview as many of my fellow passengers as possible, to chart my journey from some other perspectives. On the first train, which I was certain would be empty, I was lucky enough to find Elders Nelson and Croshaw, Mormon missionaries spreading the word of the Prophet to the Algarve. With one interview safely on tape I continued up through Europe, spending one or two nights in each city until I reached Warsaw.

From Poland I took a detour to St Petersburg, through Vilnius, avoiding Belarus. Up to this point I had recorded my journey in a professional and objective manner, but then the love train pulled, unscheduled, into life's station, in the form of the lovely Natasha. She came with me as far as Moscow but we vowed to stay in touch. On through Russia, stopping this time at all those places that I'd only glimpsed on the previous trip, finally getting to take a dip in the icy waters of Baikal. Then wild horses, a Bird's Nest, an Oriental Pearl, a Dragon's Bay and the stories of many passengers carried me finally to the platform at Ho Chi Minh City Station.

As I hadn't taken the most direct route, my total distance covered was 21,477km) over a period of three months on 42 different trains for around UK£500 in train tickets, half of which was for a 22-day Eurail pass. Such a journey might not be for everyone and requires a fair amount of planning. However, if you are tempted to follow in my tracks, my best advice is don't rush from sight to sight: leave room for the unexpected because, as I found in St Petersburg, this might well be the best bit.

For European rail timetables check www.railfaneurope.net, which provides a central link to all of Europe's national railways. Also see www.seat61.com/Russia.htm, an excellent resource for planning a Europe to Russia train journey, as well as **Way To Russia** (www.waytorussia.net/Transport /International/Bus.html), which includes ideas on using the inter-Europe bus routes of **Eurolines** (www.eurolines.com).

ASIA

Ferries from Japan and Korea to Vladivostok (see p250) make an overland journey from the Russian Far East to Europe a sinch (albeit a lengthy sinch). Likewise there are several regular ferry connections between Japan or Korea with various ports in China, including Shànghǎi and Tiānjīn, from where you can make the fastest intercity rail journey in the world to Běijīng, the start or terminus of the Trans-Manchurian and Trans-Mongolian routes.

Běijīng is connected with Hong Kong every second day and with Hanoi, Vietnam by two weekly trains. From Hanoi there are many trains onwards to Ho Chi Minh City (Saigon). A rail journey from London to Saigon will take you around two weeks; again, for details, of how to do it, consult the **Man in Seat 61** (www.seat61.com/Vietnam.htm).

Alternative overland approaches to and from Russia and China through Asia are numerous since the continent is threaded with rail networks. Where these peter out, there's almost always bus connections – the route

The emissions that would be generated by taking a (nonexistent) bus from London to Vladivostok (1.104 tonnes) are actually more polluting than a flight – take note, Trans-Siberian drivers!

you take is pretty much only limited by your time, budget and occasional security concerns.

THE USA & AUSTRALIA

If travelling from the USA, unless you find a berth on a yacht (cruise ships can be as polluting as aircraft) you'll need to fly to Europe or Asia and travel overland from there. To minimise your environmental impact, consider taking a train to the east or west coast before flying out.

As for Australia, Tony and Maureen Wheeler hitched a ride on a yacht between Timor and Darwin in 1972, thus capping off their London to Australia overland journey. Sadly, due to unrest in East Timor, this trans-continental hop is currently pretty much dead in the water.

Consider overlanding to Darwin from where it's possible to make a 1¼-hour flight on **Air North** (www.airnorth.com.au) to Dili, East Timor. From there, hopping by boat and bus through Indonesia to the Asian mainland is a tried-and-true route.

For more options from Australia, see www.seat61.com/Australia-over land.htm.

For a story of travelling overland from London to Thailand, using the Trans-Mongolian route, see www.guardian.co.uk /travel/2006/oct/25/travel news.travelsenvironment alimpact.environment

History of the Railway

Simon Richmond & Mara Vorhees

In the second half of the 19th century, the more advanced industrial states engaged in a worldwide contest for strategic advantage, economic fortune and imperial expansion. The competition took the form of continental conquest. Across Africa, Asia and the Americas, expeditions set off to explore hidden interiors, exploit material riches and tame 'uncivilised' natives. As industrial empires arose, railways became a means to, as well as a symbol of, great power and status. The number of kilometres of laid track and the production of more-powerful locomotives became indicators of industrial might, while the exquisite designs of railway stations and great halls became expressions of imperial pomp.

Russia's ambitions turned eastward towards the immense Siberian hinterland and distant Pacific coastline. Russia sought to consolidate existing holdings and to extend her influence in the region. At stake was Russia's claim over the still undeveloped and even undiscovered natural wealth of Inner Eurasia. But these ambitions were checked by the Russian state's limited reach across these far-flung eastern territories. Until this time, the distance between St Petersburg and the Pacific was measured in an arduous overland trek or a hazardous sea voyage. The solution was found in the construction of the world's longest railroad, the great Siberian railway.

For general histories of Russia, China and Mongolia flick through the following: Nicholas Riasanovsky's A History of Russia, *Stephen Haw's* A Traveller's History of China *and Charles Bawden's* The Modern History of Mongolia.

THE BIRTH OF RUSSIAN RAILWAYS

Russia was a latecomer to the industrial revolution. Russian society had long been dominated by a bloated autocratic state with close ties to an obsolete, landowning aristocracy. With industrial entrepreneurs in short supply, the state was compelled to take the initiative in economic innovation – often by granting special concessions to foreign developers.

By the mid-19th century, Russia was slipping from the ranks of Europe's great powers. In 1857, Tsar Alexander II issued a railway decree, through which the state determined to reinvigorate the economy's preindustrial infrastructure with modern railway routes. Between 1860 and 1890, Russia constructed more kilometres of track than any other country except the USA.

The new railroads connected the central industrial region to the raw materials of the Urals and the agricultural products of the Black Earth region. Moscow became the hub of the national rail system, as the terminus of nine different lines. This spurt of construction was mostly confined to European Russia, but fear of British encroachment from the Indian subcontinent prompted the construction of a trans-Caspian line, which penetrated deep into Central Asia in the 1880s. Siberia, however, continued to remain a distant and undeveloped land.

Well worth tracking down is the out-of-print To the Great Ocean *by Harmon Tupper, a heavily researched and lively take on the construction of the Trans-Siberian Railway.*

TIMELINE

1580	1628–39	1649–51
Yermak Timofeevich and his band of Cossack brigands capture Tyumen from the Turkic khanate Sibir, and two years later the Sibir capital Isker, initiating Russia's expansion into Siberia.	Russian pioneers reach the Lena River in 1628, found the fort of Yakutsk in 1637 and, two years later, sail out of the Ulya River into the Sea of Okhotsk.	Siberian explorer Yerofei Khabarov leads 150 men from Yakutsk, down the Olekma River towards the Amur River, which he reaches in the winter of 1650. He ruthlessly subdues the local Daur tribe, encroaching on Chinese territory.

THE CONQUEST OF SIBERIA

Long before Russia claimed Siberia and the Far East for its empire, other nations tried – as much as they could – to control this vast and largely inhospitable territory. First came the Mongols, then the Tatars, followed by the Turkic empire of Timur (Tamerlane), based in Samarkand. The name Siberia comes from Sibir, a Turkic khanate that ruled the region from the late 14th century.

From 1563, Sibir started raiding what were then Russia's easternmost flanks. A Volga brigand called Yermak Timofeevich was sent to counter-attack. Though he had only 840 Cossack fighters, the prospect of battle seemed better than the tsar's death sentence, which hung over him from past misdemeanours. With the advantage of firearms, the tiny Cossack force managed to conquer Tyumen in 1580, turning Yermak into a Russian hero. Two years later, Yermak occupied Sibir's capital Isker (near today's Tobolsk), continuing Russia's extraordinary eastward expansion. By 1639 Cossacks had reached the Sea of Okhotsk in the Far East.

Initially, small Cossack units set up an *ostrog* (fortress) at key river junctions such as Krasnoyarsk (1628), Irkutsk (1651) and Ulan-Ude (1666, originally Verkhneudinsk). The wealthy fur-trader Yerofei Khabarov (after whom Khabarovsk is named) set out from Yakutsk to exploit the Amur region of the Far East, treating the indigenous peoples barbarously by some accounts. Hailed as an empire builder by the tsar, Khabarov was handsomely rewarded for his efforts.

In the wake of the Cossack pioneers came traders from European Russia, who pressed natives into supplying sable and other fur pelts at bargain prices. Russian peasants followed in large numbers, and the original defensive forts grew into ramshackle timber towns. Banished prisoners were the next group to make the treacherous journey from the west, and Old Believers (outcasts from the reformed Russian Orthodox Church) followed after the religious rift of 1653. Other banished troublemakers included the influential Decembrists, who'd failed to pull off an 1825 coup against Nicholas I, and political prisoners from the uprisings in Russian-occupied Poland.

Siberia's fur-based economy rapidly diversified, and the discovery of gold further encouraged colonisation. Following the treaties of Nerchinsk (1689) and Kyakhta (1728) trade with China brought considerable wealth. Until they were put out of business by the Trans-Siberian Railway, lucrative tea caravans continued trudging the Siberian post road.

Suddenly, the fortune of a city relied on whether or not it was on the railway line. Kyakhta, on the Mongolian border, was once one of the richest towns in Russia, but plunged into provincial obscurity when the tea trade dried up and it was bypassed by the railway.

RAILWAY VISIONARIES

In the 1840s, a geological expedition had discovered that the Chinese had left the Amur River region unsettled and unfortified. Shortly thereafter, the tsar appointed the ambitious and able Nikolai Muravyov as the governor-general of eastern Siberia. But unlike his predecessors, Muravyov was not content merely to reap the harvest that came with the office. He believed it was Russia's destiny to develop the Siberian Far East. With the tsar's approval, he collected some Cossacks and cruised the Amur, establishing towns for Russia and provoking fights with China. Preoccupied with foreign encroachment

1689	1833–35	1837
Russia and China sign the Treaty of Nerchinsk, defining the Sino-Siberian frontier and halting Russia's expansion further east of the Amur. Russia gains right of passage to Běijīng for its traders.	Father and son mechanics EA and ME Cherepanov construct Russia's first steam locomotives, following ME's research visit to England to learn about this new technology. One of the engines is sent to St Petersburg.	On 30 October, Russia's first passenger railway, the 24km Tsarskoe Selo line connecting St Petersburg with Pavlovsk, is opened. Its purpose is to prove the value of railways to the country.

RUSSIA'S EARLIEST RAILS

In 1833, inspired by newfangled steam technology from overseas, EA Cherepanov and his son ME Cherepanov invented Russia's first steam railway locomotive at Nizhny Tagil in the Urals (there's a model of it in Yekaterinburg, opposite the railway station). The locomotive and first Russian rail line, just 2km long, were built to support the Urals' mining industry, although the Cherepanovs also sent one of their engines to Tsar Nicholas I in St Petersburg.

It was here in St Petersburg that Russia's first public railway opened, in 1836. Built by Austrian engineer Franz Anton von Gerstner and operating with British-built locomotives, it was a 24km line connecting the imperial capital to the tsar's summer residence, Tsarskoe Selo. Nicholas I was so impressed with this new form of transport that plans were quickly made to roll out a rail network across European Russia.

Legend has it that in 1850, when the tsar commanded that a 650km rail line be built between Moscow and St Petersburg, he accidentally drew around his own finger on the ruler as he traced out a straight line between the cities. Engineers, too afraid to point out the error, duly incorporated the kink into the plans, which became a 17km bend near the town of Novgorod.

The truth is somewhat more prosaic. The curve was actually built to circumvent a steep gradient that Russian steam locomotives of the time were not powerful enough to climb. In October 2001, the line was closed for 24 hours so that workers could finally straighten it out.

along the eastern seaboard, China was in no mood for hassles over Siberian forests. Thus, without bloodshed, Muravyov was able to redraw the border with China along the Amur River in the north and the Ussuri River in the east in exchange for some cash and a promise of mutual security. At the tsar's request, Muravyov henceforth attached the sobriquet 'Amursky' to his name.

Muravyov-Amursky continued to pursue his vision of Siberian colonisation, becoming a leading advocate of a railway that would connect European Russia to the Far East. He attracted a long line of suitors from Russia, England and the USA, offering their own proposals for a railroad to the Pacific, including Howard Duff, a British gent who came up with the somewhat bizarre idea of using wild Siberian horses to pull trains across Siberia until steam engines could be afforded.

Konstantin Chevkin, Russia's minister of ways of communication, was unimpressed with the schemes presented to him. With neither political support nor financial backing, the various petitions went unheeded by the tsar Alexander, whose approval was crucial. In the last quarter of the 19th century, however, events prompted a change in attitude in St Petersburg.

First, Russia's state economy came under stress in the 1880s. Population growth and bad weather caused widespread famine and led to peasant unrest in the countryside. As a solution to the overcrowded villages and bread shortages, the government considered a policy of migration to the uncultivated lands of Western and Southern Siberia. As reports of pummelled foremen

In *Road to Power: the Trans-Siberian Railroad and the Colonization of Asian Russia*, Steven Marks argues political concerns over competition with China and Korea contributed as much to the success of the railway as economic interests in developing Siberia.

1847	1851	1854–56
Nicholas I appoints the ambitious lieutenant-general Nikolai Muravyov governor-general of eastern Siberia. As part of a vision of Siberian colonisation, Muravyov becomes the chief advocate for a railway connecting the region to European Russia.	On 1 November the first passenger train on the 649.7km St Petersburg–Moscow railway, Russia's second such transport line, leaves the imperial capital at 11.15pm. It takes 21 hours and 45 minutes to reach Moscow.	During the Crimean War, Muravyov bolsters Russian settlements and military posts along the Amur River against possible attack by British and French forces, securing more of the Far East for Russia.

and torched manor houses became more frequent, the landowning nobility were persuaded of the policy's merits.

Second, in the late 19th century a regional intelligentsia began to write resentfully about Siberia's colonial status, and admiringly about the American west. Regional elites tried to define a distinct Siberian cultural identity, which was rooted in the region's multiethnic frontier society. Their words fuelled fears that Siberia might go the same way as the Americas and seek political independence. In response, a consensus formed in Russia's ruling circles that Siberia's radicals and renegades needed to be reined in.

Third, the decline of the Chinese empire spurred the avaricious appetites of the great powers in the Far East. Russia's vulnerability in the Pacific was made very clear as early as the 1850s, when British and French warships launched assaults on the coastal town of Petropavlovsk-Kamchatsky on the Kamchatka peninsula during the Crimean War. The opening of the Suez Canal and the completion of the Canadian-Pacific Railway provided the British with easy access to the region. As a result, the 'great game', in which Russia and Great Britain vied for strategic leverage along the mountain passes of Central Asia, now spread to the coast of the Far East.

Finally, the most important event was a leadership change. In 1881 Tsar Alexander II was assassinated and succeeded by his son. Alexander II had earned a reputation as the 'tsar reformer', instituting sweeping internal changes meant to modernise and liberalise Russian society. Among his most notable reforms were the abolishment of serfdom and the introduction of local representative assemblies. By contrast, Alexander III was a political reactionary. He embraced the old regime's ideological pillars: autocracy, orthodoxy, empire. He aspired to rule through a strong centralised state. Much more so than his father, Alexander III embodied the nationalist spirit that infused the Age of Industrial Empire. He was anxious to join the competition for territorial possessions.

In 1886 Alexander III responded to a petition for support sent from the governor-general of Irkutsk: 'How many reports from Siberian governors have I not read already, and I have to admit with shame and grief that until now the government has done nothing to satisfy the requirements of this rich but neglected region. It is time, high time.' In March 1891 the tsar officially proclaimed the undertaking of a Trans-Siberian Railway, from the Urals to the Pacific, and dispatched his son and heir apparent, Nicholas, to lay the first stone at Vladivostok.

A STATE WITHIN A STATE

The task of building the Trans-Siberian Railway fell to one of imperial Russia's most industrious and talented statesmen, Sergei Witte. His rise to the highest levels of state service, given his modest pedigree, was testimony to his skills and shrewdness.

Victor Mote's *Siberia: Worlds Apart*, packed with pictures, graphs, maps and personal anecdotes, briefly covers the area's prehistory and then moves into the 20th century.

A Voyage Down the Amoor by Perry McDonough Collins, first published in 1860, can be read online at http://books.google .com.au.

1857	1858	1860
Tsar Alexander II issues a railway decree to build a Russian rail network, the same year in which American Perry McDonough Collins proposes the Amur Railroad be built between Chita and Irkutsk.	Khabarovsk, the city named after Yerofei Khabarov, is founded by Muravyov, Siberia's governor-general, at the confluence of the Amur and Ussuri Rivers.	The Treaty of Peking sees China cede all territory east of the Ussuri and as far south as the Korean border to Japan, including the newly established port of Vladivostok (meaning 'lord of the east').

Witte was entrusted by the tsar with overseeing the pedestrian details underlying the imperial vision. The Siberian Railway Committee, a special panel with enhanced powers, was created to override the inevitable bureaucratic obstacles. At Witte's urging, the tsar appointed his son Nicholas to head the Committee. In so doing, Witte was able to exert influence on, and curry favour with, the 23-year-old *tsarevitch*.

As work progressed, the committee's scope expanded. It assumed responsibility for peasant resettlement to Siberia, diplomatic relations in the Far East and security forces along the route. Feeling left out of the process, the minister of foreign affairs remarked that Witte had built his own 'state within a state'.

For decades, proposals for a transcontinental railway had been quashed by frugal finance ministers. But that situation changed once the post was occupied by Witte, a devout Keynesian (even before Keynes!). Making Witte's task difficult, Alexander III was swayed by the argument of economic nationalists, who warned against foreign participation in a project of such great strategic value. So Witte was forced to raise money from a lean domestic economy.

Witte implemented a host of financial policies and manoeuvring to raise the necessary funds, including issuing bonds, raising taxes and taking out foreign loans. Finally, he set off a wave of inflation by printing extra roubles to cover the soaring construction costs. 'Better to lose money than prestige', he explained to the concurring tsar.

The Trans-Siberian Railway also provided Witte with the opportunity to play diplomat, when he proposed to build a 560km short cut across Manchuria, rather than follow the northern bend in the Amur to Vladivostok. Already besieged with foreigners, the Chinese emperor rejected the proposal.

A determined Witte changed tactics. He bought the influence of senior Chinese statesmen, offered a generous loan to the close-to-bankrupt Chinese government and repackaged his proposal to look like a Chinese-Russian joint venture. The result was an 80-year lease agreement over a corridor of territory for the railway. The Manchurian diversion led to the formation of the East Chinese Railway Company and the Russo-Chinese Bank, which were both in fact fronts for the Russian Ministry of Finance.

In 1898 Witte negotiated further territorial concessions, allowing Russia to build a Southern Manchurian line to a warm-water outlet at Port Arthur (Dàliàn), located on the southern tip of the Liaodong Peninsula. The minister of finance, in effect, became the tsar's chief envoy to the Far East.

Before the Trans-Siberian Railway was built, it was quicker to travel from St Petersburg to Vladivostok by crossing the Atlantic, North America and the Pacific than by going overland.

WORKING ON THE RAILROAD

Construction on the railway got under way almost immediately after the tsar's decree was issued in 1891. Beginning at Chelyabinsk, in the southern Urals, it was decided the line would run parallel to the old post road as far as Irkutsk.

1876	1886–89	1890
China's first railroad, the Woosung Railway, connects Shànghǎi with Woosung (now Baoshan District). However, the private project, constructed without government approval, is demolished the following year.	Following Tsar Alexander III's approval of the idea of a Trans-Siberian Railway, topographical surveys are taken along part of the proposed route between Tomsk and Sretensk, and around Vladivostok.	Russian playwright Anton Chekhov and American journalist George Kennan travel along the Trakt, the rough road across Siberia and the Far East, inspecting the penal colonies of the region on their way.

FROM TICKET SELLER TO EMPIRE BUILDER

The son of a colonial bureaucrat in the Caucasus and a graduate in mathematics, Sergei Witte (1849–1915) took a job selling train tickets in Odesa for the Southwest Railway Company just as Russia's railway boom got under way. He quickly mastered the logistics and finances of rail transport and was promoted to stationmaster, and then company director.

Witte's rare ability to turn a profit from the line and his efficient dispatch of troops during the first Balkans war earned him a post in the central railway administration in St Petersburg. His ascent continued with appointments as minister of transport and minister of finance, the latter probably the most powerful portfolio in the government.

Elite society considered Witte an outsider; his forceful personality and sudden appearance inside the tsar's court was much resented. But in Alexander III he had a most admiring patron. Moreover, Witte genuinely shared the tsar's vision of a Trans-Siberian Railway, describing it as 'one of the largest and most important undertakings of the 19th century, not only for the Motherland, but for all the world'. Truly a character of historic magnitude, Witte saw himself as Russia's Cecil Rhodes, and the Trans-Siberian Railway gave him the opportunity to become an empire builder.

Then it would blaze an iron trail eastward through the untamed Baikal, Amur and Ussuri regions to Vladivostok, the eastern terminus on the Pacific.

This route was selected out of consideration for the south's warmer weather conditions and more arable lands, which would hopefully encourage new agricultural settlements. But it didn't please local industrialists and merchants, since it bypassed many larger mining colonies and river towns in the north. The line was later altered to accommodate these influential economic lobbies by including Perm, Yekaterinburg and Tyumen.

Building the railroad across a formidable landscape posed ongoing challenges of engineering, supply and labour. The railroad cut through thick forests, crossed countless rivers, scaled rocky mountains and traversed soggy quagmires. Work brigades were poorly outfitted. The heavy work was carried out using shovels and picks, while horses and humans did the hauling.

No ready labour supply existed for this immense project. Workers were recruited, or conscripted, from all over the empire as well as from abroad. They toiled from dawn to dusk in the sweltering heat and freezing cold, and were preyed on by deadly diseases, forest bandits and hungry tigers.

Despite the many obstacles, construction moved apace. For state leaders, time was of the essence, so the work brigades pressed on. The construction work was divided into seven territorial segments, starting simultaneously from the eastern and western terminus points.

In A Ribbon of Iron, *Annette Meakin, the first Englishwoman to circumnavigate the globe by rail in 1900, recounts her generally favourable impressions of the early Trans-Siberian train services.*

Western Siberian: 1892–96

From Chelyabinsk in the west (which is no longer part of the official Trans-Siberian route), the railway ran through Omsk and on to the Ob

1891	1892–96	1893–99
Following a grand tour of Greece, Egypt, India, Indo-China and Japan (where he narrowly escaped assassination), Nicholas, Alexander III's son and heir, arrives in Vladivostok to lay the first stone of the Ussuri line to Khabarovsk.	With the Trans-Siberian route divided into the six geographical sectors of Russia, construction of the western Siberian line from the tea-trading city of Chelyabinsk in the Southern Urals to the Ob River (present-day Novosibirsk) commences.	Mountains and steep river valleys, including that of the Yenisey River, prove the chief challenges for the construction of the central Siberian line from the Ob River to Lake Baikal, via the city of Krasnoyarsk.

It's estimated that by the time the Trans-Siberian Railway was completed in 1916 it had cost around R1400 million, over four times its original estimated cost of R300 million.

River, the site of present-day Novosibirsk. The Western Siberian section was 1440km long and the easiest to build. For the engineers, the main challenge was spanning the many rivers that fed the Ob Basin. The crossings for the Irtysh and Ob Rivers both required the building of bridges that were almost 1km long. The region did not suffer from a shortage of materials or labour – the free peasants of Western Siberia willingly enlisted in the work brigades, although many disappeared during the harvest season.

Central Siberian: 1893–98

The central Siberian section covered a distance of 1920km from the Ob through Krasnoyarsk and on to Irkutsk, west of Lake Baikal. The work of the engineers became more complicated on this leg, because of the mountainous terrain and the steep river valleys. The Yenisey River required a steel bridge nearly 1km in length. The earth – frozen until July and then swampy after the thaw – was less than ideal for digging. Water from the drained bogs collected in stagnant pools, which bred swarms of bloodthirsty mosquitoes around work sites.

Starting in 1888, George Kennan produced 25 articles for The *Century* (later collected in *Siberia and the Exile System*) in which he attacked the tsarist government's policy of using Siberia as a prison camp.

Supply and labour now became chronic. Unlike on the plains, the line ran through forests with few settlements to tap for workers (particularly those skilled with stone) or provisions. The builders advertised throughout the empire, offering higher wages and bonuses to entice fresh forces. In August 1898, the first train rolled into the station at Irkutsk.

Ussuri: 1891–97

Meanwhile, construction was under way in the east on the Ussuri section of the railway. Beginning in Vladivostok, the line ran northward through the Ussuri River Valley to Khabarovsk, a distance of about 800km. The forest

---

TRAVELLING THE TRAKT

When the playwright Anton Chekhov set off in 1890 to investigate the notorious penal colony on the Russian Far East island of Sakhalin, he travelled along the Great Siberian Trakt (post road). It was much more a rough track than an actual road; travellers could arrange transport at the posting stations spaced at about 40km intervals from each other. The mode of transport depended on the season, with a sledge being used in winter and either a *kibitka* (covered cart) or a slightly more comfortable *tarantass* (carriage) available at other times. These were pulled by a *troika,* a group of three horses, driven by a *yamshchik* (driver) who was typically inebriated. Despite the undoubted discomfort and great length of the journey (it took Chekhov 2½ months to cross Siberia at what was considered a fast clip!) the American journalist George Kennan called transport along the route 'the most perfectly organised horse express service in the world'. Read Chekhov's impressions in *Journey to Sakhalin*.

1896	1895	1898
China grants Russia a concession to build the Chinese Eastern Railway (the Manchurian line) from Chita to Vladivostok via Hāěrbīn in Manchuria, drastically reducing the distance along the original main route, which stayed within Russia's borders.	Construction starts on the Trans-Baikal line from Lake Baikal to Sretensk. Two years later a torrential flood washes away over 300km of the track and 15 bridges, wrecking a further two irreparably.	To gain access to the deep-water port at Lüshun (also known as Port Arthur, the present-day Dàliàn) near the tip of the Liaodong Peninsula, Russia starts to build the 550km South Manchurian Railway as a branch from Hāěrbīn.

terrain was more difficult for the engineers. Moreover, after the first tracks had been laid, it was discovered that the Amur rose as much as 10m during the spring, which meant redrawing the route and starting again. The builders faced severe labour shortages in this remote corner of the Far East. Despite initial misgivings, the construction brigades recruited over 8000 workers from the local Korean population and migrant Chinese labourers, over one-half of the total workforce for this section. They received lower wages than the Russian workers because, the foremen said, their work was inferior (though it may have been because they did not run tabs in the company canteen).

The builders of the Ussuri line introduced convict labour to the railroad, when 600 prisoners destined for incarceration on Sakhalin Island were instead ordered to start digging. Some prisoners escaped from their inexperienced handlers and went on to a local crime spree. The project as a whole eventually employed nearly 15,000 convicts and exiles, with far better results. Many brigade foremen praised their contribution. Convicts, in turn, could work time off their sentences, and the living conditions were a small improvement on the tsar's prisons.

> In 1911 Siberia recorded about nine million inhabitants; by 1959, the number had increased to nearly 23 million.

Trans-Baikal: 1895–1900

The Trans-Baikal section ran from the eastern shore of Lake Baikal past Ulan-Ude and Chita, then on to Sretensk on the Shilka River. For the engineers, this section of 1072km of dense forest was nearly as daunting as the Circumbaikal section was a few years later, and would prove more frustrating. The railroad had to scale the Yablonovy Mountains, rising 5630m above sea level. The rivers were not so wide, but they ran in torrents and cut steep valley walls. The tracks were laid on narrow beds along high mountain ledges. Harsh weather, including summer droughts and heavy rains, exacerbated the difficulties. The great flood of 1897 washed away over 300km of laid track and 15 completed bridges.

> The price of a 1st-class ticket from Moscow to Vladivostok on the initial Trans-Siberian trains was R114.

Circumbaikal: 1901–04

Heading east from Irkutsk, the builders encountered their most formidable obstacle; Lake Baikal. No previous experience prepared the engineers for the frigid lake's steep rocky cliffs, which dominated the shoreline.

Engineers initially decided that construction of a railroad line around the lake would be impossibly expensive. Instead, the steamship *Baikal*, strong enough to smash through ice and big enough to carry train carriages, was commissioned from Britain. From April 1900, it transported trains and passengers between Port Baikal and Mysovaya (now Babushkin), while more passengers followed on the *Angara* – now moored in Irkutsk. However, the ships proved less than efficient, being prey to severe storms and sometimes impassable ice. This hindrance became a national security threat in 1904 – when Russia needed

> An exquisite miniature version of a Trans-Siberian train, complete with luxury carriages and church car, was created in 1900 to go inside one of the famous jewelled eggs made by Fabergé for the tsar; it can be viewed today at the Armoury of Moscow's Kremlin.

1900	1901	1904
The first Trans-Siberian services go into operation, utilising the train-ferry *Baikal* to transport passengers across Lake Baikal. This ice-breaking ship is later supplemented by the smaller *Angara* ferry, transporting passengers and freight only.	The ferries having proved a less than successful solution to crossing Baikal, the decision is made to start the technically difficult construction of the Circumbaikal line along the southwestern shore of the lake.	Port Arthur comes under attack from the Japanese, provoking the Russo-Japanese War. The Trans-Siberian Railway buckles under the strain of transporting troop reinforcements to the Far East, and the outcome looks bleak for Russia.

to transport troops and supplies to the front during the Russo-Japanese War, temporary tracks were actually laid across the ice in an attempt to expedite the military movement. Tragically, the ice cracked under the first train to attempt this crossing, and it sank into Baikal's icy waters.

Despite earlier hesitation, the decision was made in 1901 to begin construction of a railway line that would skirt the southern edge of the lake, connecting Port Baikal and Mysovaya. The project was overseen by VA Savrimovich, a highly regarded engineer and surveyor. The cliffs around the lake made this the most challenging section of all to build. Tsar Alexander III brought in Armenian and Italian masons to design the elaborate portals and arched bridges. The pride of Mother Russia at the time, this section was nicknamed 'the Tsar's Jewelled Buckle'.

In the 1950s the Angara River was dammed, raising Lake Baikal by about 6m and submerging the railway line between Irkutsk and Port Baikal. A short cut bypassing this flooded section was built between Irkutsk and Slyudyanka – today's Trans-Siberian mainline. The remaining 94km of the Circumbaikal became a neglected branch line, along which a few weekly minitrains still chug, much to the delight of train buffs; see p226 for details.

> The Circumbaikal consumed four times as much stone as the entire Trans-Baikal section. Workers chiselled 39 tunnels into the lake's craggy capes and erected over 100 bridges and viaducts.

Amur: 1907–16

The 2080km-long Amur section presented similar engineering, supply and labour challenges. The Amur required some of the longest and most complicated bridges, including a span of almost 2km across the Amur. The builders relied heavily on convict labour, supplemented by army units and Chinese migrants. Building materials, including iron rails, had to be imported from British and North American suppliers.

The Amur was the last section of the Trans-Siberian Railway to be built, going into operation in 1916. The railway's first travellers transferred into boats at Sretensk for a long river voyage down the Amur to Khabarovsk, where they could reboard the train. The completion of the East Chinese Railway in 1898 bypassed the Amur, diverting passengers through northern China.

> In the 1907 Peking–Paris car rally, contestants followed what would become the Trans-Mongolian rail route. The winners were Italians Prince Borghese and journalist Luigi Barzini.

East Chinese: 1897–1901

In 1894 Russia secured the agreement from the weak Chinese empire that allowed for a Manchurian section of the Trans-Siberian Railway. From Chita, the 1440km-long East Chinese Railway turned southeast, crossing the Argun River and rolling through Hāěrbīn (Harbin) to Vladivostok. It sliced over 600km off the journey and, after a one-sided negotiation, the Russian wide gauge was used. The terrain of flat steppe lands, wide mountain passes and fertile river valleys elated the exhausted builders.

However, other problems soon arose. In 1899 Chinese nationalism mobilised into a rancorous antiforeigner movement, the self-proclaimed 'Fists of Higher Justice'. Better known as the Boxer Rebellion, the movement quickly

1905	1906	1907
The Russian fleet is annihilated in the Tsushima Straits in May and Russia sues for peace. The Treaty of Portsmouth turns Southern Manchuria over to Japan, allowing Russia to keep control of the East Chinese Railway.	Japan founds the South Manchurian Railway Company within Japanese-controlled southern Manchuria. The railway runs from the southern tip of the Liaodong Peninsula to Hāěrbīn where it connects to the Chinese Eastern Railway.	To protect Russian access to the Pacific Coast and her territory in the Far East, the decision is made to construct the Amur line from Sretensk to Khabarovsk, the final portion of the Trans-Siberian Railway.

spread to Manchuria and the Russian-controlled railway. Stations and depots were set ablaze, 480km of track were torn up and besieged railroad workers took flight. The line was only able to return to service after the Russian military intervened.

A LUXURIOUS PROMISE

At the dawn of the 20th century, Russia was ready to launch its engineering achievement to the world. Prince Mikhail Khilkov, the communication minister, made arrangements with a Belgian company to create 'an ambulant palace of luxury' and had promotional brochures printed up in four languages proclaiming how it would now only 'take 10 days to cover the 5500 miles between Moscow and Vladivostok, or Port Arthur'.

Bernardo Bertolucci's *The Last Emperor* (1988) is a lavish, epic-scale story of Puyi, China's last imperial ruler.

To further press home the Trans-Siberian Railway's advantages a 'Palace of Russian Asia' pavilion was constructed at the Exposition Universelle in Paris in 1900. Inside the pavilion, visitors were treated to images of Siberia's pristine rugged landscape and exotic native cultures – including, incongruously, stuffed polar bears clinging to papier-mâché icebergs. Much more impressive were the luxuriously decorated mock wagons. The 1st-class sleepers offered comfortable and commodious compartments decorated with French Empire and Chinese-style furnishings.

The imitation dining car served caviar, sturgeon and other Russian delicacies, while allowing visitors to admire moving Siberian scenery through the window, as recreated by a complex, multilayered painted panorama (see p52). The exhibit also featured a handsome smoking car, a music salon with piano, a well-stocked library, a fully equipped gymnasium and a marble and brass bath. Here on display was elegance and efficiency, provided in high Russian style.

TRANS-SIBERIAN REALITY

The personal accounts of early Trans-Siberian Railway travellers suggest that the actual journey did not live up to its advance billing. Although 1st-class accommodation was comfortable enough, most of the other promised indulgences were underwhelming, to say the least. East of Baikal, the train routinely ran out of food and had to stop once a day at small stations en route. 'Today we did not eat until 3pm, and then it was vile', wrote one cranky American traveller in 1902. 'There was one wretched little eating room filled with Russians. You may stand around and starve for all they care.'

Trains buffs can flick through evocative historic and more contemporary images of past Trans-Siberian locos and carriages at Trains-World Expresses (http://trains-worldexpresses.com).

In addition, the Trans-Siberian did not succeed in providing a more expeditious route to the Far East. The hastiness that went into construction was exposed in operation. Travellers experienced frequent delays, sometimes lasting days. The Trans-Siberian had the highest accident rate of any line in the empire. Ties splintered, bridges buckled and rails warped. The locomotives chugged along at no more than 25km/h because of the risk of derailment

1908	1915	1916
Two-year-old Puyi ascends the throne as China's last emperor. As new railways are financed and built in Chinese territory by foreigners, the anti–Qing dynasty Railway Protection Movement is born and gathers support.	Having declared its independence from the dying Manchu empire in 1911, Mongolia signs the Treaty of Kyakhta with China and Russia, and is granted limited autonomy.	The completion of the Khabarovsk bridge (at 2.6km the longest on the Trans-Siberian route) over the Amur River allows the opening of the 1920km Amur line, establishing the Trans-Siberian route as it exists today.

THE TRANS-SIBERIAN RAILWAY PANORAMA

The sensation of the 1900 Paris Exhibition was not so much the mock Trans-Siberian Railway carriages but rather the painted panorama that unreeled behind them creating a simulated journey lasting one hour. Created by Pavel Pyasetsky, the panorama entitled *The Great Siberian Route: the Main Trans-Siberian Railway* was based on sketches the artist had made across Siberia starting in 1897 and included images of Moscow, Omsk, Irkutsk, the Great Wall of China and Běijīng. Consisting of rolls of watercolours glued to canvas, the work was not fully completed until 1903 but even so it gained a gold medal in Paris, and the Legion of Honor medal for Pyasetsky.

The panorama, last seen at the 1904 St Louis World's Fair, is part of the Hermitage's collection in St Petersburg. In 2004, the museum announced plans in conjunction with Russian Railways to restore the work and exhibit it, possibly in Vitebsk Station, St Petersburg, as well as make copies that could be displayed elsewhere in Russia.

---

at higher speed. One Běijīng-bound passenger scribbled in resignation: 'A traveller in these far eastern lands gradually loses his impatience and finally ceases to care whether his train goes fast or slowly, or does not go at all. Certainly we have been two hours at this station for no apparent reason.' (This sentiment may ring true even for travellers today.)

A principal goal of the railway was to facilitate the resettlement of European Russia's rural inhabitants, in the hopes of easing social tensions and offering economic opportunities for the country. In the 1800s the tsar had officially lifted restrictions on internal migration and opened up Siberia for colonisation. Between 1860 and 1890 fewer than 500,000 people moved to Siberia. But once the train came on line, the population's eastward drift turned into a raging torrent.

Between 1891 and 1914, over five million new immigrants settled in Siberia. Station halls were packed with hundreds of waiting peasants sleeping on the floor. Third-class fares were kept low so that ordinary subjects could ride the rails. One could travel for more than 3200km on the Trans-Siberian for less than R20. These wagons dispensed with any pretension of style or comfort. A 1st-class rider observed: 'The 3rd-class passengers are packed like sardines. Their cars hold nothing save wooden bunks, two tiers thereof, and each has four and sometimes six. One's health would certainly be jeopardised by a passage through them. I notice that our car is constantly guarded. I am not surprised, and do not object in the least.'

Published in 1897, *Roughing it in Siberia* by Robert Louis Jefferson is an amusing account of the eccentric English adventurer's journey on the Trans-Siberian as far as Krasnoyarsk and then by road to Minusinsk.

WAR & REVOLUTION

Alexander III saw the Trans-Siberian Railway as the means by which the Russian empire would act as a great power in the Far East. Under his less able successor, Nicholas II, the construction of the railway instead provoked confrontations that exposed the manifold weaknesses of imperial

1917	**1918**	**1918–20**
The February Revolution forces the abdication of Nicholas II, and is followed by the Lenin-led Bolshevik coup in October. The moderate Socialist party win the November election, a result ignored by the increasingly authoritarian Bolsheviks.	Lenin pulls Russia out of WWI and moves the capital to Moscow. As Nicholas II, his immediate family and servants are executed in Yekaterinburg, civil war ensues throughout the country.	The Czechoslovak Legion, a volunteer army who fought with Britain, France and Russia in WWI, seizes control of the western half of the Trans-Siberian Railway. A deal with the Red Army allows their evacuation from Vladivostok.

Russia. The railway and railroad workers played prominent supporting roles in the tumultuous political events that subsequently toppled the tsarist autocracy and brought radical socialism to power in the early 20th century.

The Russo-Japanese War

The East Chinese Railway involved Russia in the multilateral dismemberment of the Chinese empire. In the subsequent grab for territorial and commercial concessions in Manchuria, Russia came into direct conflict with imperial Japan. Witte was always inclined towards diplomacy in Russia's Far Eastern policy, but Nicholas fell under the sway of more adventurous advisors. 'What Russia really needs,' the minister of interior opined, 'is a small victorious war'.

The tsar's aggressive stance in the Far East provoked Japan to attack Port Arthur in February 1904. The overconfident Nicholas was dazed by the rapid string of defeats that subsequently took place in the field. Japanese forces quickly seized the advantage over Russia's outnumbered troops, while the reinforcements remained stalled at Lake Baikal. The single-track, light-rail Trans-Siberian was simply overwhelmed by the demands of war. The tsar dispatched his prized Baltic fleet. In May 1905 the war concluded when – upon reaching the Tsushima Straits – the fleet was annihilated in just one afternoon.

Nicholas summoned Witte to salvage Russia's dignity in the peace negotiations. Under the Treaty of Portsmouth, Russia agreed to vacate southern Manchuria, but managed to hold on to the East Chinese Railway. The Japanese went on to extend this line as the South Manchurian Railway from Hăĕrbin southeast to the Liaodong Peninsula.

At turns anecdotal and specific, *A People's Tragedy: The Russian Revolution 1891–1924*, by erudite scholar Orlando Figes, paints a vivid picture of this tumultuous period in Russian history.

The 1905 Revolution

Russia's woeful performance in war unleashed a wave of anti-tsarist protest at home. The reactionary impulses of the regime were fully displayed in January 1905 when peaceful demonstrators, led by an Orthodox priest, were

---

RELIGION ON THE RAILS

The original pre-1917 Trans-Siberian trains included a Russian Orthodox church car, complete with icons, bells and a travelling priest. At stations along the route where a church had yet to be built the church car was used to hold services for the locals, railway workers and any interested passengers.

Jump forward a century to April 2005 and the Russian Orthodox Church signed an agreement with Russian Railways to cooperate on, among other things, restoring chapels and mobile carriage chapels to the railway transport system.

1920	1922	1924
Admiral Alexander Kolchak, leading the counter-revolutionary White Army, suffers a decisive defeat by the Red Army at Omsk. He retreats to Irkutsk where he's captured and shot. The civil war is over two years later.	Josef Stalin, born Josef Dzhugashvili in Georgia, is appointed Communist Party general secretary. The USSR is established with Russia, Ukraine, Belarus and Transcaucasia (the republics of Georgia, Armenia and Azerbaijan).	At the age of 53, Lenin dies without designating a successor. In his honour St Petersburg, which had become Petrograd prior to WWI, changes its name to Leningrad.

shot down in front of St Petersburg's Winter Palace. The 'Bloody Sunday' massacre did not quell the unrest, but instead incited more people to take to the streets. Among the most radical participants in the 1905 Revolution were the railroad workers.

It's believed that Russia adopted the wider 5ft gauge track for its railways, as opposed to the 4ft 8.5in track favoured by the rest of Europe and American railways, to stop foreign invaders being able to use standard-width rolling stock.

Like most Russian workers, railroad employees laboured under harsh conditions, received scant wages and suffered tyrannical bosses. Unlike other sectors, however, the railroad workers could paralyse the economy by going on strike. To tackle this hazard, the government maintained a special railway police force, 8000 strong, which spent its time intimidating labour organisers.

Railroad workers were quick to join the protest movement, as 27 different lines experienced strikes in the first two months of 1905. In April, they co-ordinated their efforts by forming an All-Russia Union of Railroad Workers. At first, they demanded economic concessions, such as higher wages and shorter hours, but soon their demands became more political, such as the rights to organise and strike.

The government attempted to impose martial law over the railway system. The railway union responded by calling for a total shutdown of service. The strike started in Moscow, spread to every major railway line and sparked a nationwide general strike. The movement only subsided after the tsar issued the October Manifesto, which promised to reform the autocracy into a constitutional monarchy.

The Bolshevik Revolution

Radical railroad workers also played a crucial role in the Bolshevik Revolution of 1917. Exhausted by its involvement in WWI, the tsarist regime lost its ability to rule and fell to street demonstrators in February 1917. Nicholas' abdication created a power vacuum in the capital. The liberal provisional government hesitated to make decisions and work out how to deal with the war, which swung public sentiment towards the more radical political parties.

Robert Service is the author of both a biography of Vladimir Ilych Lenin and the *History of Twentieth Century Russia*, both excellent introductions to the dawn and progress of the Soviet era.

In an attempt to restore order, General Kornilov ordered his troops at the front to march on St Petersburg, with the intention of declaring martial law. Radicals and liberals alike took cover. But Kornilov's men never made it. Railroad workers went on strike, refusing to transport them, and the putsch petered out. Within weeks, Vladimir Ilych Lenin and the Bolsheviks staged a palace coup, deposed the provisional government and declared themselves rulers of Russia.

The Russian Civil War

The Bolsheviks' claim on power was soon challenged. In the spring of 1918, as the war in Europe continued without Russia, a legion of Czech POWs tried to return home to rejoin the fighting. Unable to cross the front line in

1926	1929	1930s
Chicago Daily News correspondent Junius B Wood reports that the post-revolution Trans-Sib Railway is in poor condition and seldom on time. In the dining car he's served 'pre-cooked cauliflower warmed with a sauce of unknown texture'.'	As part of the first of Stalin's Five-Year Plans – a program of centralised economic measures, including major investment in heavy industry, designed to turn the USSR into a superpower – the electrification of the Trans-Siberian line begins.	Slave labour from Siberia's infamous Gulag system is used to start construction of the Baikal-Amur Mainline (BAM), an ambitious project to provide a backup Trans-Siberian Railway, should the main line become incapacitated.

the west, they headed east. Along the way, they provoked a confrontation with the Bolsheviks. When the White Army, hostile to the Bolsheviks, came to support the Czechs, the Russian Civil War began.

The Czech legion seized control of the western half of the Trans-Siberian Railway; in the meantime, the Japanese, who had landed in Vladivostok, took control of the railway east of Baikal. A separatist Siberian Republic was formed in Omsk, that is, until tsarist naval officer Admiral Kolchak overthrew the Omsk government and declared himself supreme ruler of Siberia. Another former tsarist general reigned over the East Chinese Railway in Manchuria. Cossacks menaced the Trans-Baikal and Amur regions. Siberia had returned to the era of warlords.

It took the Bolsheviks more than three years to secure complete control over the Trans-Siberian Railway and to establish Soviet power across Siberia. Kolchak was arrested, tried and shot.

DEVELOPMENT OF SIBERIA

The construction of the Trans-Siberian Railway was intended to foster industrial development in Siberia. As such, an engineering and technical school was founded in the late 19th century in the city of Tomsk, to become Siberia's first university. Scores of factories, mills and mines sprung up along the route to feed the railroad's huge appetite for iron, bricks and lumber. However, Siberia's fledgling industries could not keep pace with the growing demand.

The project served as an economic stimulus for other regions too. The mining and metal works in the Urals became the chief supplier of iron and steel. The sprawling manufacturing works around St Petersburg and Moscow were contracted to supply the rolling stock. By 1905 over 1500 locomotives and 30,000 wagons had rolled out of Russian factories. At the same time, the railway system as a whole employed over 750,000 workers involved with engines and rolling stock, traffic management, track maintenance and administration. Higher wages, as much as 50% above the norm, attracted railway employees to the Trans-Siberian line.

After coming to power, Russia's new Soviet rulers were committed to rapid industrial development. To meet this goal, they needed to gain wider access to Siberia's plentiful raw materials. Thus, they invested heavily in upgrading the Trans-Siberian Railway. A second track was built alongside the original single line. The light rails were replaced with heavier, more durable rails. Wooden bridges and supports were replaced with iron and steel. Working conditions on the railway did not improve much under the new socialist regime, but railway workers were now extolled for being in the vanguard of the industrial proletariat.

In the 1930s the Soviet regime launched a state-managed campaign of industrialisation, in which large-scale projects in Siberia figured prominently.

Seventeen Moments in Soviet History (www .soviethistory.org) is a well-designed and highly informative site that covers all the major events that occurred during the life of the USSR.

The Pulitzer Prize–winning *Gulag: A History* by Anne Applebaum is the definitive account of the forced labour camps of Russia's most desolate regions.

1931	1934	1935
A turn-of-the-century proposal to connect the Trans-Siberian Railway with the tsarist-built Trans-Caspian Railway is realised with the opening of the Turkestan-Siberian line from Novosibirsk to Luguvoi, in Kazakhstan.	The Asia Express starts running on the South Manchurian Railway between Dàliàn and Hsinking, capital of Japanese-controlled Manchuria. Reaching a speed of 134km/h, it is the fastest scheduled train in the world at the time.	Russia sells the East Chinese Railway in Manchuria to Japan for ¥170 million (around US$48.3 million), the same year that Mao Zedong is recognised as the head of the Chinese Communist Party.

THE RAILROAD OF DEATH

It's impossible to tally the human toll of building railways across Siberia's notoriously inhospitable terrain, but one section of track in the far north of the region was so perilous that it was known as the Railroad of Death. The 1297km railway between Salekhard and Igarka was planned under Stalin's rule for three reasons: to aid the export of nickel from Norilsk; to connect the ports of Salekhard and Igarka with Russia's railway network; and as work for the thousands of prisoners herded into the Gulag system of forced-labour camps.

Construction started in 1949 but was immediately hampered by terrible weather and perma-frost. Poorly treated workers died in droves. Only Stalin's death in 1953 put a halt to the railway's construction, by which time 699km of track had been laid, at a cost of nearly R42 billion. After construction ceased, the elements quickly finished off what was left of the railway. All that remains today is the ghostly presence of abandoned villages, rusting rails and machinery and rotting sleepers amid dense forests. For images see www.englishrussia.com/?p=1305.

The Kuznets Basin became a prodigious supplier of coal, coke, iron and steel.

At the same time, the paranoid and vengeful Soviet dictator, Josef Stalin, was engaged in a purge against his own citizens and comrades. The victims of Stalin's terror who were not shot were sent to forced labour camps known as the Gulag (standing for *Glavnoe Upravlenie Lagerey* – Main Administration for Camps). Siberia's industrial revolution was built on the backs of millions of real and imaginary 'enemies of the people'.

WWII & Beyond

In WWII, Nazi Germany's blitzkrieg invasion was an unintended impetus for further development of Siberia, when the industrial stock of European Russia was hastily evacuated to safer interior locations. During the German occupation, the Trans-Siberian Railway served as a lifeline for Soviet survival. It furnished the front with the reinforcements and equipment that eventually wore down the formidable Nazis.

In the 1950s and 1960s Siberian development was energised by the dis-covery of oil and gas. While these deposits were in the north, they promoted development in the cities along the railway, such as the oil refinery in Omsk and the chemical plant in Irkutsk.

Stalin's reform-minded successor, Nikita Khrushchev, denounced his former boss and liberated millions of labour-camp inmates. Meanwhile, incentive-laden offers lured new workers to the region, and the Siberian population became highly skilled. A uniquely planned academic community was created near Novosibirsk. Military industry flourished in secret cities, sheltering well-tended scientists and technicians. By 1970, 13 Siberian cities had populations of 250,000 or more.

1937	1939	1941
Under the leadership of Stalin's henchman Lazar Kaganovich, Russia's railways, including the Trans-Siberian, are revived. The largest plant east of the Urals for building and repairing loco-motives and rolling stock goes into operation in Ulan-Ude.	Japan invades Mongolia from Manchuria in May. With help from the Soviet Union, and after heavy fighting, the Mon-gols defeat Japan by Septem-ber – just as WWII is kicking off in Europe.	In June, Hitler invades the Soviet Union in Operation Bar-barossa, beginning what is re-ferred to in Russia as the Great Patriotic War. The Red Army is unprepared and German forces advance rapidly across Russian territory.

During this time, Siberia's indigenous populations were increasingly assimilated into the lifestyle and culture of Soviet Russian society. In 1900 native peoples accounted for more than 15% of Siberia's total population but, by 1970, this number was less than 4%. Simultaneously, Siberia's development was having detrimental effects on the environment (see p98).

BRANCHING OUT

The Soviet regime intended to further develop overland access to the Eurasian continent so that travellers could reach ever more remote corners of the Far East. The construction and operation of branch lines throughout the Far East were entangled in the politics of the region for most of the 20th century.

The Trans-Manchurian

The Trans-Manchurian line connects Běijīng to the Trans-Siberian at Chita, via the Russian-built East Chinese Railway and also the South Manchurian Railway. The South Manchurian, however, fell to Japan as spoils of war in 1905. At this time, American railroad baron EH Harriman made several generous bids to buy these routes from their respective operators. He saw a rare opportunity to realise his ambition of building a railroad line that circumnavigated the globe. Harriman's offers, however, were rebuffed.

In 1922 China persuaded Soviet Russia – which was weakened by war and revolution – to renegotiate the status of the East Chinese Railway between Vladivostok and Port Arthur. The Soviet government renounced its special economic privileges in Manchuria and agreed to joint custody of the railway. As Manchuria was the scene of an ongoing power struggle, the Russians had to continuously defend their (partial) claim to the railway line. During the 1920s the Russian managers were arrested by a Manchurian warlord and again by Chiang Kaishek (leader of the Kuomintang, the Chinese Nationalist Party), both of whom seized control of the railroad. In each case the aggressors were forced to relinquish their prizes and prisoners. In 1932 the Japanese took control of Manchuria, renaming it Manchukuo and installing the last Manchu emperor, Puyi, as a puppet ruler. Under pressure, Russia sold her interest in the East Chinese Railway to the new rulers in 1935.

This was not the end of the line, however. According to the secret protocols negotiated at Yalta, Winston Churchill and Franklin D Roosevelt conceded back to Stalin the East Chinese and South Manchurian rail lines, as part of the price of Soviet entry into the Pacific War. Russia's return to Manchuria was brief; the lines were given back to China in 1952 as a goodwill gesture to its new communist regime.

Ironically, geopolitics proved stronger than ideology. By the mid-1960s relations between China and Russia soured and the border was closed, thus stopping the Trans-Manchurian service. The low point was in 1969 when

For a very personal history of China through the 20th century read *Wild Swans* by Jung Chang. She followed this epic tale in 2005 with her collaborative warts-and-all portrait of Mao Zedong, *Mao: The Unknown Story*, cowritten with Jon Halliday.

1945	1947–49	1950–52
The USSR declares war against Japan. Soviet troops occupy Manchuria. When Japan surrenders, Moscow signs a 30-year treaty with Chiang Kaishek's Nationalist government, placing the Manchurian railway under Sino-Russian administration.	Construction of the Trans-Mongolian line begins in 1947, with an extension from Ulan-Ude stretching south towards the border town of Naushki. In 1949 the line reaches Mongolia's capital of Ulaanbaatar.	On 14 February 1950 the USSR signs a treaty with the People's Republic of China, shifting its support from Chiang Kaishek's Nationalists to Mao's Communists. Two years later China assumes control of Manchuria's East Chinese Railway.

armed clashes occurred over Damansky Island in the Ussuri River, part of the border between the two communist neighbours. The so-called Sino-Soviet Split lasted until the early 1980s, and since this time Russian–Chinese relations have warmed considerably, allowing the Trans-Siberian to be reconnected to the Trans-Manchurian.

In 2005 China and Russia settled a post-WWII dispute over 2% of their 4300km common border. For the first time, the whole border was legally defined.

The Trans-Mongolian

The 2080km Trans-Mongolian line was built along the route travelled by the ancient tea caravans, from Běijīng through Mongolia to Ulan-Ude. The line was built piecemeal, a direct result of fluctuations in the relationship between Russia and China.

During the late 19th century, Mongolia was formally part of the Chinese Manchu empire. After centuries of neglect, China's officials became more interested in the region, much to the irritation of the Mongols. Plans were made to construct a railroad from Běijīng to Örgöö (Ulaanbaatar). Instead, the Chinese empire collapsed in 1911.

Mongolia was very eager to be rid of its Chinese overlord but was too weak to fend for itself. Russia emerged conveniently as a protective patron of Mongolian independence. The Soviet Union consolidated its influence in 'independent' Mongolia through the signing of agreements on economic and military cooperation. In 1936 the announcement came of construction of a short rail route linking Mongolia and Soviet Buryatiya, whose peoples shared close ethnic ties. This new line between Ulan-Ude and Naushki was completed in 1940, and in 1949, it was extended to the capital, Ulaanbaatar.

In the early 1950s, relations between the Soviet Union and communist China relaxed a bit, allowing the Chinese to finally begin work on the long-planned railroad connecting Běijīng with Ulaanbaatar. Although train service began on this line in 1956, the Sino-Soviet Split in the 1960s closed the border. Like the Trans-Manchurian, the Trans-Mongolian line was reopened in the 1980s.

The Turkestan-Siberian

The Turkestan-Siberian (Turk-Sib) connects the Trans-Siberian to Central Asia. From Novosibirsk, the 1680km line heads south over the Altai Mountains and across the Kazakh steppe to Almaty. The line was first planned in the last years of the tsarist empire, when the initial segment of track was laid between Barnaul and Semipalatinsk. It was not completed, however, until the Soviet period, after Stalin made the Turk-Sib one of the more prominent construction projects of the first five-year plan.

Learn more about the Turk-Sib line at Mysterious Turksib (www.turksib.com)

The route was opened in 1931. The railway was built to facilitate the exchange of Central Asian cotton for western Siberian grain. This trade

1956	1961	1961–63
The Gobi Desert is spanned; the Trans-Mongolian Railway connecting Moscow with Běijīng via Ulaanbaatar is completed. Chinese and Russian trains operate on different gauges, requiring a long delay to change wheels at the China–Mongolia border.	Mongolia is admitted to the UN as an independent country, but the Soviet Union continues to occupy Mongolia with troops and run it as a satellite state.	The Trans-Siberian Railway is used to transport cosmonaut hardware to Baikonur (in present-day Kazakhstan). The first man in space, Yury Gagarin, blasts off in 1961, followed by the first woman, Valentina Tereshkova, in 1963.

FUTURE PLANS FOR RUSSIAN RAILWAYS

The Trans-Siberian has always travelled at a slow speed – an average of 60km/h. But this may change, as Russian Railways (RZD) plans to upgrade sections of the track in order to slash journey times, particularly for the transport of freight, which is where the railway makes its money. We interviewed RZD spokesman Pavel Moskov about this and other developments along Russia's rails:

How far along is RZD with its development of high-speed train lines? RZD is implementing a program for the development of high-speed and super high-speed services until 2020. Eighteen routes, covering 2500km, with a steady passenger flow, have been picked as being suitable for the introduction of such services. The most relevant routes for travellers are Moscow–St Petersburg, Moscow–Nizhny Novgorod and Omsk–Novosibirsk.

What kind of trains will operate on these routes? Eight super high-speed Velaro RUS trains will run on the Moscow–St Petersburg and Moscow–Nizhny Novgorod lines. The first will arrive in Russia in December 2009. Trains on the Moscow–St Petersburg line will reach 250km/h on some sections and cover the distance in 3¾ hours. In the future, the speed can be increased further. Trains travelling at 160km/h will appear on the Moscow–Nizhny Novgorod line in 2010. We are also acquiring Pendolino Sm6 trains (which can reach 200km/h) to serve on the St Petersburg–Helsinki line.

We understand RZD plans to form a new company to take care of passenger services. The RZD board has approved the plan to create the Federal Passenger Service Company by 2010. This new joint-stock company, 100% owned by RZD, will control the entire fleet of passenger carriages, maintenance depots, administrative buildings and sales terminals currently owned by RZD. The plan envisages a number of initiatives to improve the service quality and increase the competitiveness of passenger services. Private business will be involved in projects to improve ticket sales and new products, as well as for outsourcing.

How concerned are you about increased competition from airlines? If you compare SV (1st class) prices with prices for business-class air tickets, the railway prices will be cheaper. For example, an SV ticket to Vladivostok costs €650, while a business-class air ticket costs €1800. RZD is hoping that with the introduction of high-speed services between Moscow, St Petersburg and Nizhny Novgorod, most passengers will prefer travelling by train. We are also competing with airlines in the luxury sector. For example, we launched the Express XXI night train between Moscow and St Petersburg in 2007 which has four- and two-berth compartments and VIP carriages. All compartments have individually controlled air-conditioning, DVD players and showers. In the future, VIP carriages will have internet access. The luxury-car ticket is only slightly more expensive than an air ticket.

As told to Simon Richmond

would keep the looms busy in the textile factories of the north, while the import of cheap food would free up more land for cotton cultivation in the south. The construction of the Turk-Sib was also meant to stimulate industrial development in the region, hence its nickname, 'the Forge of the Kazakh Proletariat'.

1965	1969	1974
Oil begins to flow in Siberia as Prime Minister Alexey Kosygin tries to shift the Soviet economy over to light industry and producing consumer goods. His reforms are stymied by Brezhnev, resulting in economic stagnation.	Political relations between China and Russia deteriorate and armed clashes erupt along the Ussuri River. The Trans-Mongolian and Trans-Manchurian routes into China are suspended.	As work resumes on the long-abandoned BAM, Leonid Brezhnev, General Secretary of the Communist Party, announces the railroad will become a huge Komsomol (Communist youth league) project with its completion scheduled for 1982.

In 1996 newly independent Kazakhstan took over its section of the line. From the southern terminus at Lugovaya, the line extends to Chimknet in western Kazakhstan and to Bishkek in Kyrgyzstan. In 1992 a long-planned third connection through to China from Kazakhstan was opened, enabling direct services between Almaty and Ürümqi.

The 1929 silent documentary *Turksib* about the Turk-Sib railway is a classic example of socialist-realist cinema by Soviet film director Viktor Turin.

The Baikal-Amur Mainline

The 4234km Baikalo-Amurskaya Magistral (Baikal-Amur Mainline, or BAM) begins west of Irkutsk and passes north of Lake Baikal on its way east to the Pacific coast; see p259. The route was first considered as an option for the Trans-Siberian line in the 1880s, but it would not be until the 1930s that work actually started on its construction, beginning at Tayshet.

Although parts of the far-eastern end of the line were built from 1944 (partly using Japanese and German POWs as labour), the project was put on indefinite hold in 1953 after the death of Stalin. Its resumption, amid much fanfare, came in 1974, when Leonid Brezhnev hailed it the 'Hero Project of the Century'. The call went out to the youth of the Soviet Union to rally to the challenge of constructing the BAM. The response is evident from the names of towns along the line: Estbam, Latbam and Litbam, so called for the young workers from the Baltic states who built them.

Go to www.eng.rzd.ru to read Russian Railway's PR version of the history of the BAM line.

The BAM was badly mismanaged. Instead of a construction chief, 16 different industrial ministries organised their own separate work teams with minimal coordination. By 1980, 50% of the managers had been replaced because of 'unsatisfactory work'. The project employed 100,000 workers, including 20,000 communist youth league 'volunteers'. Lacking housing and electricity, few workers reenlisted and others simply deserted.

The BAM epitomised the best and worst of Soviet industrialisation. It blazed a trail through inhospitable climate and terrain, providing access to the region's mineral-rich basins. The BAM towns expanded with the new railway, which was being forced through virgin wilderness. Overcoming Siberia's swamps, its seven mountain ranges, its seemingly infinite number of rivers and, in particular, its vast swath of permafrost, pushed the cost of the project to a staggering US$25 billion (the original Trans-Siberian is estimated to have cost the equivalent of US$500 million).

The Russian railway system, covering 85,500km of track, is the second-largest in the world after the USA's 228,464km of track.

The BAM was officially opened in 1991, when it became possible to travel the whole length from Tayshet to Sovetskaya Gavan on the Pacific coast. However, the line's 15.34km Severomuysk tunnel, the longest in Russia, was only completed in 2003. Work continues very slowly on the Amuro-Yakutskaya Magistral (Amur-Yakutsk Mainline or AYaM), a branch line that already extends south from Tynda on the BAM to Bamovskaya on the Trans-Siberian line, and will eventually terminate in the north at Yakutsk, capital of the Republic of Sakha. At the time of research passenger trains stopped at the coal mining town of Neryungri on the AYaM.

1980s	1984	1990
Following a thaw in international relations between Russia and China, the Trans-Mongolian and Trans-Manchurian lines reopen for business.	On 24 September a golden spike is used to connect the eastern and western ends of the BAM at Balbukhta. Only a third of the BAM's 3115km of track and only one of its tunnels is fully operational.	Democracy demonstrations break out in Ulaanbaatar. Soviet troops begin withdrawal in March and in June the first free, multiparty elections are held, with the Mongolian People's Revolutionary Party winning 85% of the vote.

A CHAT WITH THE BIG BOSS OF A TRANS-SIBERIAN TRAIN *Marc Bennetts*

Every train in Russia has its own *nachalnik* or *nachalnitsa*, the person responsible for seeing that everything flows smoothly on the journey, as well as managing the *provodniki* (carriage attendants). One snowy night in April 2008, we spoke to Ludmila Kalugina, the *provodnitsa* (female carriage attendant) in charge of train 038A, serving the Omsk–Tomsk route. With 15 years on the trains, Ludmila was clearly a woman who knew a lot about the Trans-Siberian express, and she was happy to reveal the secrets of the trade to us.

Have things changed much in the one-and-a-half decades that you've been in the job? Of course. In the past conditions were awful. The carriages were terrible; there was snow everywhere…

In the train? [laughing] Yes, in the train. But now they've changed the actual carriages, and things are a lot more comfortable.

What about your staff, the provodniki? There have been changes there as well. In the past, they were less qualified, and most of them just saw the job as temporary employment. But now, as wages have begun to rise, people have generally been sticking with us. And if they stay on the trains, naturally they want promotion, so they begin to study.

What does it mean exactly to be the boss of a train? Well, I'm completely responsible for the comfort and safety of the passengers. Sometimes it's hard, but, you know, I wouldn't do the job if I didn't like it.

What's the hardest thing about the job? Being away from home so much. It makes family life tough when you are always travelling.

And the best thing? The feeling I get when I sense that my team and me have done something pleasant for people, when I can see the fruits of our labour.

What's your favourite city along the route? [again laughing] What? Do you think we see anything of the cities we go to? We see train stations, and that's all! Even if we have to wait for 10 hours at a station, the girls have to clean the train, we have to check everything…there's a lot to be done. Of course, summer is the best time to travel. Even if it's hot, almost all the trains have modern air-conditioning now so that's not much of a problem. In winter, things can go wrong, parts of the train can freeze over…it's a lot more stressful.

Before we left, we asked Ludmila if we could take a photo of her. 'Not now,' she said. 'I'll have to put my make-up on first. ' We assured her that she looked fine, but she was adamant. 'Come back in an hour, ' she insisted.

At the appointed time she wasn't ready, and hadn't even made a start on her make-up. 'The Inspectors are here. My bosses,' she whispered. 'I'll have to give it a miss.' We understood. Life as the boss of a Trans-Siberian train is hard, with little time for photo shoots.

The Trans-Korean

Re-creating the early-20th-century Kyongwan Railway, the proposed Trans-Korean line, from Seoul in the south to Wonsan in the north, is slowly edging closer to reality, though a breakdown in relations between

1991	**1992**	**2002**
The BAM's official opening is overshadowed by an attempted coup against USSR president Mikhail Gorbachev, and the demise of the Soviet Union. Boris Yeltsin becomes the first popularly elected president of the Russian Federation.	A third route into China from Russia is established when the Chinese extend their railway from Ürümqi to the border of Kazakhstan, to connect with a line completed in 1960 to Aktogai, between Almaty and Semey.	The electrification of the Trans-Siberian line, started in 1929, is finally completed, allowing a doubling of train weights to 6000 tonnes.

North and South in late 2008 threatens to delay further progress. The line will connect with the Trans-Siberian near Vladivostok.

A small but significant step forward was taken in 2000, when North and South Korean leaders agreed to restore a short train service across the world's most heavily fortified border. To promote the project, North Korean leader Kim Jong Il made a much publicised trip on the Trans-Siberian in 2001.

For the first time since the border was closed during the Korean War of 1950–53, a train crossed from South to North Korea in May 2007. The following year Russia and North Korea agreed to reconnect their countries via the Khasan-Tumangan border crossing, with Russia helping to construct the line on the Korean side of the border onwards to the port of Rajin.

Geoffrey Elliot's From Siberia with Love, a family history of the author's Russian-exile grandfather, is fleshed out with almost manic attention to detail, with much of the action occurring in Chita and Irkutsk.

SIBERIA IN TRANSITION

After decades of overbearing central control, the demise of the Soviet Union in 1991 ignited a spontaneous diffusion of power across Russia's regions. This process was accelerated by Russia's President Boris Yeltsin, who urged regional leaders to 'take as much sovereignty as you can swallow'.

In Siberia, these dramatic events rekindled the separatist spirit. Siberian Accord, a confederation of regional political actors, was founded in Novosibirsk in 1991. Resentful of Moscow's grabbing hand, they were determined to wrest control of Siberia's natural resources.

During this early post-Soviet period Siberia came to resemble the 'Wild Wild East' of olden days. The privatisation of state property gave rise to a new breed of economic adventurer. Those who succeeded in gaining control over Siberia's prized natural resources reaped great fortunes. Siberia's regional governors openly defied the Kremlin's edicts and pillaged the local economy for private gain.

In 1999 a 2612m combined road and rail bridge over the Amur River replaced the original 18 span, 2568m-long construction – the longest such bridge on the Trans-Siberian Railway.

President Yeltsin, a former regional governor himself, defused the conflict through a negotiated compromise, by which Siberia's regions were granted greater political autonomy and a larger share of the region's wealth. His successor, Putin, however, pursued a policy of gradual recentralisation.

Along the Trans-Siberian route it's impossible not to notice how much life has improved in those big cities where Russia's economic resurgence, built on the back of Siberian natural resources, is having the most impact. Yekaterinburg, Novosibirsk and Krasnoyarsk – all firmly off limits to foreign visitors during the Soviet period – are booming at the same time as outlying towns and villages are being abandoned for lack of work and food.

In foreign affairs, the improvement in Russian–Chinese relations has reopened the border in the Far East and boosted cross-border trade and smuggling. Some things, however, never change. For reasons of national security and public service, the Trans-Siberian remains a state-managed monopoly. It continues to be one of the busiest train lines in the world. Most importantly, the Trans-Siberian endures as the vital lifeline for the people of Siberia.

2003	2004	2008
Russian Railways is turned into a joint-stock company, with the federal government the sole owner of shares estimated at R1545.2 billion (more than US$50 billion) in value.	BAM trains start running through the 15.34km-long Severomuysk tunnel, avoiding a lengthy detour around a mountain, and allowing the transportation of 6 million tonnes of freight a year to be shifted from the Trans-Siberian line.	Representatives of 100 Japanese firms, and Japanese government ministers, meet in St Petersburg to thrash out the details of assisting Russia in a ¥69 trillion (US$638 billion) upgrade of the Trans-Siberian Railway by 2030.

The Cultures

Scratch a Russian, a local saying goes, and you'll find a Tatar – meaning that under that European veneer beats an Asian heart. With a history shaped by imperial expansion, forced movements and migration over many thousands of years, it's not surprising that Russian society has multicultural traits. Similarly, Mongolians call themselves Asian by ethnicity but Western by culture – not such a strange abstraction once you visit this freedom-loving country, where the modern world has found a place alongside the traditional. By contrast, the commercially dynamic and creatively energetic Chinese are very certain and proud of their Asian heritage. The following chapter covers the basics of each nation's culture to help you start making some sense of the three distinct countries that you'll encounter on a Trans-Siberian, Trans-Mongolian or Trans-Manchurian journey.

RUSSIA
The National Psyche
Compared with the Chinese and Mongolians, Russians can initially come across as rather unfriendly. Although surly uncommunicative Russians are still found in certain 'service' industries (things are, however, rapidly improving), the overarching Russian character trait is one of genuine humanity and hospitality. But once you've broken the ice with Russians on the train and in the towns you pass through, you'll typically find yourself being regaled with stories, drowned in vodka and stuffed full of food. This can be especially true outside the big cities, where you'll meet locals determined to share everything they have with you, however meagre their resources.

Unsmiling gloom and fatalistic melancholy remain archetypically Russian characteristics, but these are often used as foils to a deadpan, dry sense of humour. You'll soon learn how deeply most Russians love their country. They will sing the praises of Mother Russia's great contributions to the arts and sciences, its long history and its abundant physical attributes, then just as loudly point out its many failures. The dark side of patriotism is the tendency of some to display an unpleasant streak of racism. Don't be put off, and take heart in the knowledge that as much as foreigners may be perplexed about the true nature of the Russian soul, the locals themselves still don't have it figured out either! As the poet Fyodor Tyutchev said, 'You can't understand Russia with reason…you can only believe in her'.

Although a little out of date, *Teach Yourself World Cultures: Russia* by Stephen and Tatyana Webber is a decent decoding of all aspects of Russian culture for the layperson.

Lifestyle
Travel into the more remote areas of Russia, and you'll see people living very different lives from those of their compatriots residing in the prosperous urban centres of Moscow and St Petersburg. Sometimes, a trip to the countryside can feel like a trip back in time to the USSR – as demonstrated by any of the preserved-in-Soviet-formaldehyde towns along the Baikal-Amur Mainline (or Baikalo-Amurskaya Magistral; BAM).

That said, there are common features to life across Russia. For the vast majority of urban Russians, home is within a drab, ugly housing complex of Soviet vintage. Although quite cosy and prettily decorated on the inside, these apartments are typically cramped and come with no attached garden. Instead, a large percentage of Russian families have a *dacha* (a small country house). Often little more than a bare-bones hut (but sometimes quite luxurious) these retreats offer Russians refuge from city life and figure prominently in the national psyche. As half-warm weekends approach, big cities begin to

THE RULES OF RUSSIAN HOSPITALITY & BEHAVIOUR

Blame it on the days of Soviet rules and regulations – many Russians are sticklers for formality. They're also rather superstitious. Follow these tips and you should fit right in:

- When you're in any setting with other people, even with strangers in a train compartment, it's polite to share anything you have to eat, drink or smoke.
- Refusing offered food or drink can cause grave offence (see p79 for what to say to avoid offence).
- Vodka is for toasting, not for casual sipping; wait for the cue.
- If you're invited to a Russian home, always bring a gift, such as wine or a cake.
- Shaking hands across the threshold is considered unlucky; wait until you're fully inside.
- If you give anyone flowers, make sure there's an odd number of flowers, as even numbers are for funerals.
- Remove your shoes and coat on entering a house; also be sure to deposit your coat in cloakrooms at restaurants, bars and the theatre.
- Be sure to dress up, rather than down, for fancy restaurants, the theatre and other formal occasions.
- Traditional gentlemanly behaviour is not just appreciated but expected – as you'll notice when you see women standing in front of closed doors waiting for something to happen.

The Country Studies website (www.country-studies.com/russia/) includes a comprehensive series of essays on many aspects of Russian life.

empty out early on Friday as people head to the country. Around Siberian cities such as Irkutsk and Chita, the small wooden dwellings you see close to the train tracks will be *dachi* too.

One of the most important aspects of *dacha* life is gardening. Families grow all manner of vegetables and fruit to eat over the winter. Flowers also play an important part in creating the proper *dacha* ambience, and even among people who have no need to grow food, the contact with the soil provides an important balm for the Russian soul. It's also quite likely that a *dacha* will have a traditional *banya* (bathhouse; see p67) attached to it.

Cohabitation remains less common than in Western countries, so when young couples get together they usually get married (which also partly explains why a very high proportion of marriages end in divorce).

As the economy has improved, so has the average Russian's lifestyle, with more people than ever before taking holidays abroad (something impossible for all but the favoured few during Soviet times), and owning a car, a computer and a mobile phone. The lives of today's Russian teenagers couldn't be more different from those of their parents, who just a generation ago had to endure shortages of all kinds of goods, on top of the bankrupt ideology of Soviet communism. It's not uncommon to meet young adults who have only the vaguest, or no, idea who Lenin and Stalin are.

Read the results of studies carried out by the UN Development Programme in Russia on issues such as poverty reduction, HIV/AIDS and democratic governance at www.undp.ru/?iso=RU.

On the other hand there's the older generation, who remember the former Soviet leaders only too well and are now suffering as the social safety-net that the State once provided for them has been largely withdrawn. It's hard not to be moved by the plight of the elderly trying to get by on pensions of a few hundred roubles, after a lifetime of struggle.

Population

Close on three-quarters of Russia's 142 million people live in cities and towns. Rural communities are withering: in the 2002 census, of Russia's 155,000 villages, 13,000 had been deserted and 35,000 had populations of fewer than 10 people.

Russia is also facing a decline in its population – around 0.5% per year – that is a concern to authorities. The population has plummeted by some six million people in the last decade alone. The average life expectancy for a Russian man is 61.5 years, for a woman 74. Much of this is the result of poor health, often caused by a diet high in alcohol and fat. Accidental deaths due to drunkenness are also frequent. The birth rate has dropped significantly and there are more deaths than births in a year, despite government attempts to reverse this statistic (see p68).

About 80% of Russia's people are ethnic Russians. The next largest ethnic groups are Tatars with 3.8%, followed by Ukrainians (2%), Bashkirs (1.15%), Chuvash (1.13%), Chechens (0.94%) and Armenians (0.8%). The balance belongs to dozens of smaller ethnic groups, all with their own languages and cultural traditions (in varying degrees of usage), and varied religions.

Over 30 original indigenous Siberian and Russian Far East peoples now make up less than 5% of the nation's total population. Along the trans-Siberian routes, the main ethnic groups you'll encounter are Mongol Buryats in and around Ulan-Ude (see p235) and Lake Baikal; and the Nanai in the lower Amur River basin near Khabarovsk.

Go to www.unpo.org and www.eki.ee/books/red book for profiles of over 80 ethnic groups in lands currently or once ruled by Russia.

Media

Russia is a TV country, with radio and newspapers sidelined to a greater extent than elsewhere in Europe or the USA. The internet has exploded in recent years with all manner of blogs on *LiveJournal,* the main platform for free political and cultural debate in Russia, with both the opposition and pro-government forces broadly represented. Social-networking sites such as **Odnoklassniki** (http://odnoklassniki.ru) and **Vkontakte** (http://vkontakte.ru), similar to Facebook, number members in the millions. So far censorship, which is prominent in the old media (mainly in the form of self-censorship to avoid any potential clashes with the authorities), hasn't significantly affected the web, but there are fears that this freedom-of-speech loophole may also be removed.

The best newspapers offer editorial opinions largely independent of their owners' or the government's views. That said, both the most popular paper (and one of the most respected) *Kommersant* (http://kommersant.com), and its main rival *Izvestia* (http://izvestia.com, in Russian) have financial ties with Gazprom, the state-owned gas monopoly, leading some groups to claim that both publications are muted in their criticism of the government.

The most famous antiestablishment newspaper is the tabloid *Novaya Gazeta* (http://en.novayagazeta.ru), for which the crusading journalist Anna Politkovskaya wrote before her murder in 2006. Other tabloid (but not necessarily tabloid in format) papers, *Komsomolskaya Pravda* (www.kp.ru,

---

RUSSIA'S RAILWAY GAZETTE

Although those in charge at the old Soviet mouthpiece *Izvestia* may challenge it, *Gudok* claims to be the oldest continuously published daily newspaper in Russia. *Gudok*, which means signal and also denotes the whistle sound of trains, has been in business since December 1917. The importance of a newspaper for the railway workers was instantly recognised by Lenin and the Bolsheviks, who knew that the way they could gain a grip on such a huge country would be to control the railways.

Still partly owned by Russian Railways and the trade union of railway workers, the broadsheet had writers of the calibre of Mikhail Bulgakov (author of *The Master and Margarita*) working for it in the 1920s and 1930s. In today's competitive media market, *Gudok* takes a populist approach to news coverage. Published daily Monday to Friday, you should be able to find it – only available in Cyrillic – on sale at stations across the country or online at www.gudok.ru, in Russian.

CHURCHGOING DOS & DON'TS

As a rule, Russian working churches are open to one and all, but as a visitor take care not to disturb any devotions or offend sensibilities. On entering a church men bare their heads, while women usually cover their heads. Female visitors can often get away without covering their heads, but miniskirts are unwelcome and even trousers on women sometimes attract disapproval. Hands in pockets, or crossed arms or legs, may attract frowns. Photography at services is generally not welcome; if in doubt, you should ask permission first.

---

in Russian), and the weekly *Argumenty i Fakty* (www.aif.ru, in Russian), are viewed by most people as being pro-government publications.

With a population habituated to receiving the party line through the tube, conventional wisdom has it that in Russia, he who controls the TV, rules the country. Ex-president Putin grasped this fact and through a variety of take-overs and legal challenges succeeded in putting practically all TV channels under the Kremlin's direct or indirect control. News and analysis on Russian TV is generally uncontroversial.

Russian TV provides a wide choice of programs, some modelled on Western formats, some unique – although the channels are sometimes dominated by crime series in which shaven-headed veterans of the war in Chechnya pin down conspiring oligarchs and politicians. There's also a boom of sitcoms and comedy shows, which is perhaps a sign of the times. The national channel Kultura, dedicated entirely to arts and culture, is always worth a look. For news, **RenTV** (www.ren-tv.com, in Russian) has coverage that tends to be more objective than the norm. Don't expect to hear English spoken on the TV, though. See also p323.

Religion

One of the most noticeable phenomena in Russia since the end of the atheist Soviet Union has been the resurrection of religion. Since 1997 the Russian Orthodox Church has been legally recognised as the leading faith, and takes an increasingly prolific role in public life, just as it did in tsarist days. The Russian constitution enshrines religious freedom – in theory protecting the rights of Muslims (Islam is Russia's second-largest religion with up to 20 million practitioners), Jews, Buddhists and members of the nation's myriad animist religions.

Along the Trans-Siberian route you'll have chances to encounter many of these religions in buildings ranging from St Petersburg's **Grand Choral Synagogue** (☎ 713 8186; Lermontovsky pr 2; ☷ 11am-3pm Mon-Wed, 11am-2pm Thu & Fri, services 10am Sat; Ⓜ Sadovaya or Sennaya Ploshchad) to Kazan's Kul Sharif Mosque (p169) and the Buddhist *datsans* (temples) near Ulan-Ude (p238) and Chita (p242) in Siberia. Most often, though, it will be the Russian Orthodox churches, many with soaring onion-dome cupolas, that will leave the most vivid impression.

Russian Orthodoxy is highly traditional, and the atmosphere inside a church is formal and solemn. Churches have melodic chanting, no seats and many icons (see p69), before which people will often be seen praying, lighting candles and even kissing the ground. The Virgin Mary (*Bogomater;* translates as Mother of God) is greatly honoured. The language of the liturgy is 'Church Slavonic', the Southern Slavic dialect into which the Bible was first translated for Slavs. Paskha (Easter) is the focus of the church year, with festive midnight services launching Easter Day.

In most churches, Bozhestvennaya Liturgia (Divine Liturgy), lasting about two hours, is held at 8am, 9am or 10am Monday to Saturday, and usually at

---

Anna Reid's The Shaman's Coat is both a fascinating history of the major native peoples of Siberia and the Russian Far East and a lively travelogue of her journeys through the region.

In 2005, in an effort to present Russia's viewpoint to the outside world, the state set up the digital channel Russia Today (www.russiatoday .ru), a CNN/BBC news and current affairs station that even broadcasts in Arabic to cover the Al Jazeera audience.

7am and 10am on Sunday and festival days. Most churches also hold services at 5pm or 6pm daily.

Arts

Much of Russia's enormous contribution to world culture has been since the 19th century.

CLASSICAL MUSIC, BALLET & OPERA

Many visitors will want to see a Russian ballet or opera performance at either Moscow's famous Bolshoi Theatre (p145), or St Petersburg's Mariinsky (p118), home of the Kirov Ballet. Ballet and opera are generally performed at the same venues, which are often impressive buildings in themselves such as Novosibirsk's gigantic Opera & Ballet Theatre (p184).

The roots of Russian music lie in folk song and dance and Orthodox Church chants. Mikhail Glinka (1804–57), in operas like *A Life for the Tsar* and *Ruslan and Lyudmila,* was the first to merge these with Western forms. Modest Mussorgsky (1839–81), Nikolai Rimsky-Korsakov (1844–1908) and Alexander Borodin (1833–87) continued to explore and develop Slav roots.

Pyotr Tchaikovsky (1840–93) also used folk motifs but was closer to the Western tradition. His *1812 Overture,* his ballets *Swan Lake* and *The Nutcracker,* and his opera *Eugene Onegin* are still among the world's most popular works. Sergei Rachmaninov (1873–1943), Igor Stravinsky (1882–1971) and Dmitry Shostakovich (1906–75) are other influential composers of the 20th century.

Russian opera has produced many stars, from Fyodor Chaliapin in the early years of the 20th century to the current diva, soprano Anna Netrebko, who started as a cleaner at the Mariinsky and now commands the stages of top opera houses around the world.

ROCK & POP

Russian music is not all about classical composers. Ever since the Beatles broke through the Iron Curtain of the 1960s, Russians both young and old have been keen to sign up for the pop revolution. By the 1970s and '80s, punk and heavy metal were influencing local groups such as Akvarium,

In its Freedom of Conscience report for 2007 the SOVA Center (www .sova-center.ru) found that 'nontraditional' religious organisations faced 'serious difficulties' in relation to the construction of buildings or leasing of facilities.

THE TRADITIONS OF THE BANYA

For centuries, travellers to Russia have commented on the particular (in many people's eyes, peculiar) traditions of the *banya* (bathhouse). To this day, Russians make it an important part of their week and you can't say you've really been to Russia unless you've visited a *banya*.

The main element of the *banya* is the *parilka* (steam room). Here, rocks are heated by a furnace, with water poured onto them using a long-handled ladle. A few drops of eucalyptus or pine oils (sometimes even beer) are often added to the water, creating a scent in the burst of scalding steam that's released into the room. You'll note that even though people are naked in the *banya*, some wear a *chapka* (felt cap) to protect their hair from the effects of the heat.

As they sweat it out, some bathers grab hold of a *venik* (a tied bundle of birch branches) and beat themselves or each other with it. Though it can be painful, the effect can also be pleasant and cleansing: the birch leaves (sometimes oak or, agonisingly, juniper branches) and their secretions are supposed to help rid the skin of toxins. After the birch-branch thrashing, bathers run outside and, depending on their nerve, plunge into the *basseyn* (ice-cold pool) or take a cooling shower. The whole process is then repeated several times for anything up to two hours.

Many city *banya* are rundown and unappealing (a classy exception is Moscow's splendid Sanduny Baths, p138). Grab any chance to try a traditional countryside *banya*: nearly all the guesthouses on Olkhon Island (p223) in Lake Baikal have them.

HAVE A BABY FOR RUSSIA

In 2008, designated the Year of the Family by ex-president Putin, there were signs that government policies aimed at reversing Russia's decrease in population were starting to take effect. Cash payouts of R250,000 (US$10,300) for women who have more than two children, and stunts such as awarding prizes of fridges, TVs and cars to those who give birth on Russia's national day have helped slow the rate of population decrease, delivering roughly 20,000 more babies in 2007 than in 2006.

However, more Russians are dying than are being born, the number of deaths exceeding the number of births at a rate of 1.3. Similarly, there are far more abortions than births. There are many reasons why some 1.6 million women a year chose to abort, but one of the most commonly cited is that they can barely afford to have one baby, let alone two or more. A feature deflating 2008's baby boom in online magazine *Slate* (www.slate.com/id/2195133/) illustrated how desperate some Russian women were to give birth to win prizes that they were putting their health, and that of their babies, at risk.

DDT and Nautilus Pompilius. The god of Russian rock, though, was Viktor Tsoy, lead singer of the group Kino. His premature death in a 1990 car crash ensured his legendary status; his grave, at the Bogoslovskogo Cemetery in St Petersburg, has been turned into a shrine, much like Jim Morrison's in Paris. There's also the 'Tsoy Wall' on ul Arbat in Moscow, covered with Tsoy-related graffiti.

The likes of techno-pop girl duo tATu and pretty-boy singer Dima Bilan, winner of the 2008 Eurovision Song Contest, are the tame international faces of Russia's contemporary music scene. The ageing diva Alla Pugacheva, a survivor from the 1960s, is also still around. Among the more interesting artists to listen out for are **Leningrad** (www.myspace.com/leningradru), an entertaining group of rockers from St Petersburg; the female rock/jazz singer **Zemfira** (www.zemfira.ru, in Russian); and **Markscheider Kunst** (www.mkunst.ru, in Russian), with their Afro-beat-infused sounds.

LITERATURE

Natasha's Dance: A Cultural History of Russia, by Orlando Figes, is a fascinating book that offers plenty of colourful anecdotes about great Russian writers, artists, composers and architects.

Russia's Shakespeare equivalent is Alexander Pushkin (1799–1837); he's revered as the father of Russian literature and you'll find many Russians who can recite some of his work, usually from his most famous work, *Yevgeny Onegin*. Mikhail Lermontov (1814–41) is another major figure, who like Pushkin died young in a duel.

Nikolai Gogol (1809–52) was a master of romantic realism; his classics include the mordantly satiric *Dead Souls* and *The Inspector General*. Fyodor Dostoevsky (1821–81) is best known for the St Petersburg–based *Crime and Punishment, The Idiot* and *The Brothers Karamazov*. His four years of hard labour in a camp near Omsk formed the basis of *The House of the Dead*. Other giants of literature include Leo Tolstoy (1828–1910; *War and Peace* and *Anna Karenina*) and the playwright Anton Chekhov (1860–1904). Boris Pasternak (1890–1960) wrote *Doctor Zhivago,* which was filmed on an epic scale by David Lean, and possibly did more than any other work to influence Western perceptions of Siberia. It's a richly philosophical, epic novel offering personal insights into the revolution and Russian Civil War. Pasternak had to smuggle it out of Russia to get it published (simultaneously in Italian and Russian) in 1957.

Preceding *glasnost* was native Siberian writer Valentin Rasputin, who is best known for his stories decrying the destruction of the land, spirit and traditions of the Russian people. His 1979 novel *Farewell to Matyora* is about a Siberian village that is flooded when a hydroelectric dam is built.

Russian publishing is currently booming, with the traditional Russian love of books as strong as ever. One of the most popular novelists is Boris Akunin, whose series of historical detective novels feature the foppish Russian Sherlock Holmes, Erast Fandorin. Titles include *The Winter Queen* and *Turkish Gambit,* recently made into a Russian hit movie.

Poet, journalist, media talent and prose writer Dmitry Bykov is one of the biggest names currently in Russian literary circles. In 2007 he published a well-regarded biography of Boris Pasternak, and his latest novel *ZhD* is a satirical, anti-utopian, conspiracy theory–laden tale of civil war set in near-future Russia. Also of note is Perm-based Alexey Ivanov, whose historical novels, such as *Heart of Parma,* focus on the Russian colonisation of the Urals.

> For a review of some interesting contemporary Russian artists go to www.waytorussia.net /WhatIsRussia/Art.html.

The award-winning novels of Andrei Makine, born in the Russian Far East but long based in France, where he has won the country's top two literary awards, are also worth discovering, especially *A Hero's Daughter,* which charts the impact of the Soviet Union on a family from WWII to the 1990s. His *Once Upon the River of Love* is about life in a small village near the Trans-Siberian Railway.

VISUAL ARTS

Up until the 17th century, religious icons were Russia's key art form, though clearly they were conceived as religious artefacts and only in the 20th century did they really come to be seen as works of art.

In the 18th century, Peter the Great encouraged Western trends in Russian art, which led to the Peredvizhniki (Wanderers) movement in the following century. The movement gained its name from the touring exhibitions with which it widened its audience, and its leading figures included Vasily Surikov, infamous for painting vivid Russian historical scenes; Nikolai Ghe, who depicted biblical and historical scenes; and Ilya Repin, perhaps the best loved of all Russian artists. The best places to view works by these artists are St Petersburg's Russian Museum (p109) and Moscow's Tretyakov Gallery (p134).

At the start of the 20th century, Russian artists dabbled in Impressionism, art nouveau and symbolism as well as a home-grown avant-garde futurist movement, which in turn helped Western art go head over heels. Notable artists of this period include Natalia Goncharova, Vasily Kandinsky and Kasimir Malevich. Socialist realism was the driving force during the early and mid-Soviet periods when art had to serve the state's political purposes.

> An excellent website devoted to Russian architecture is http://archi .ru/english/, which has an index of the country's key buildings.

Artists are now freer than they ever were in the past to depict all aspects of Russian life with even the government pitching in to fund prestigious events such as the **Moscow Biennale of Contemporary Art** (http://3rd.moscowbiennale.ru/en/).

CINEMA

From Sergei Eisenstein's *Battleship Potemkin* (1925) right through to Alexey German's *My Friend Ivan Lapshin* (1982), Soviet cinema excelled in producing classic movies. Eisenstein's *Alexander Nevsky* (1938) contains one of cinema's great battle scenes. Mikhail Kalatozov's tragic WWII drama *The Cranes are Flying* (1957) was awarded the Palme d'Or at Cannes in 1958. Of later Soviet directors, the dominant figure was Andrei Tarkovsky, whose films include *Andrei Rublyov* (1966) and *Solaris* (1972), the Russian answer to *2001: A Space Odyssey.*

The romantic comedy *Irony of Fate* (Eldar Ryazanov, 1975) has a special place in all Russian hearts, while the most popular film in the Ostern genre (the Eastern European take on Western movies) is *White Sun of the Desert* (Vladimir Motyl, 1969), a rollicking adventure set in Turkmenistan during the civil war of the 1920s. The cult classic, still one of the top-selling DVDs in Russia, is traditionally watched by cosmonauts before blast-off.

PHOTOGRAPHING RUSSIA

The Trans-Siberian Railway and its branches were instrumental in enabling two photographers in two different centuries to fulfil commissions to document Russia in all its glory. In 1909 Sergei Prokudin-Gorsky, an early proponent of colour photography, set out to shoot all of the 'lands and people living on Russian land' using his own photographic technique.

To assist this ambitious project Prokudin-Gorsky was presented with documents from Tsar Nicholas II that allowed him to travel anywhere in the empire, and papers from the minister of railways requesting that all officials should assist 'in any place, at any time'. He was also provided with a special Pullman wagon with hot water, an icebox for food and a photo studio so he could develop his film on the road.

The revolution of 1917 put a stop to Prokudin-Gorsky's work, but a year later the photographer managed to escape to Norway, taking his amazing collection of thousands of unique images with him. Four years after his death in Paris in 1944, Prokudin-Gorsky's heirs sold his photographic collection to the US Library of Congress where they remain. Parts of the collection can be viewed at http://lcweb2.loc.gov/pp/prokhtml/prokabt.html and www.prokudin-gorsky.ru/collection.htm.

Building on the historical roots of Prokudin-Gorsky's original project, a new exhibition 'Russia Through a Train Window' opened in Moscow in April 2008. This joint venture, by the Russian photographer Anton Lange and Russian Railways, presents over 200 images shot across the country between November 2006 and April 2008. There are plans to show the photographs at the 20 largest railway stations in 17 cities across Russia, as well as mount international exhibitions in 2009. It's all part of the cultural project **1/9 Objective Reality** (www.fotorussia.su/en), which aims to present the Russia of the 21st century to the world.

Nikita Mikhalkov's *Burnt by the Sun* won the Oscar for Best Foreign Film in 1994 but, at that time, Russian film production was suffering as state funding dried up and audiences stayed away from cinemas. By the end of the decade the local industry was back on track with hits such as Alexey Balabanov's gangster drama *Brother* (1997) and Alexander Sokurov's *Molokh* (1999). Among recent Russian cinema to look out for is the ambitious art film *Russian Ark* (2002) filmed in one 96-minute take inside the Hermitage; Andrei Zvyaginstev's moody thriller *The Return* (2003); and Timur Bekmambetov's Moscow-based vampire thrillers *Night Watch* (2004) and its sequel *Day Watch* (2006).

CHINA
The National Psyche

Despite having experienced tremendous social upheaval over the past century, the Chinese are an energetic and optimistic people, excited about the rapid modernisation taking place in their country. Běijīng's hosting of the 2008 Olympics was painted as China's coming-out party, a chance to introduce their long-standing cultural traditions to the world and be accepted as a modern, progressive nation.

The Chinese proudly extol their country's inventions of gunpowder, printing and paper currency, while simultaneously embracing Western business ideas and spending hours at late-night English classes. Some sections of the community worry that Western values may destroy the heart of traditional Chinese culture, but there's also a strong drive to transform the insularity that has defined China for hundreds of years.

Modernisation has brought its share of headaches – overcrowding of cities, rising crime, pollution and unemployment, to name a few. The government has incentives in place to deal with these issues, but progress is very slow. Above all, traditional values persist. Many beliefs derive largely from the pervasive influence of Confucian philosophy, which forms the very core of

Chinese identity. The Chinese value the family, the cultivation of morality and self-restraint, and the emphasis on hard work and achievement.

Lifestyle

Chinese culture is traditionally centred on the family. In the past, the family provided long-term support for every member. Extended family remains exceedingly important in Chinese society, with grandparents commonly acting as caretakers for grandchildren and with adult children working and financially supporting their ageing parents.

The website http://chin eseculture.about.com is a good resource on culture and society in China with links to a variety of topics including food, holidays and martial arts.

The end of cradle-to-grave welfare (the 'iron rice bowl') has brought increasing pressure on families who struggle to meet the rising costs of health care and education. Economic pressures have had an impact on many young Chinese who are putting off marriage or having children until they've acquired enough money to ensure their financial security.

The rapid development of the 1990s has raised the standard of living for many Chinese, who now face a dazzling array of consumer choice and live a very different lifestyle from that of earlier generations. Unfortunately, recent educational and economic opportunities are only available to a small segment of the population. The majority of Chinese live in the countryside, shut off from the benefits of China's economic reforms.

The growing gap between China's rich and poor is one of the worst in the world. The rural communities in inland China are the most poverty stricken, but those on the investment-laden east coast fare better. Farmers who can least afford it are expected to pay for their own health care and the education of their children. Many rural families have been forced to move to the cities, where they often find low-paying jobs in unsafe conditions. The government has promised to address these devastating trends, but few incentives have been put in place.

Disillusionment with Communist Party policies has resulted in more people speaking out and demanding changes. Private action groups are springing up all over the country, seeking to address social needs that are ignored or neglected by the government, including care of the disabled, equal rights for gays and lesbians, AIDS prevention, environmental protection, help for battered women and workers' conditions. Artists and writers are starting to free themselves from earlier political restraints, contributing to a burgeoning literary and art scene that has been stifled for many years. Censorship is still common, though what defines something as 'taboo' or 'off limits' can be arbitrary.

Red Azalea, by Anchee Min, is a moving story of a young woman caught up in the horrors of the Cultural Revolution.

ARCHITECTURE IN SIBERIA

Although you'll find traditional Russian wooden architecture across European Russia, Siberia has the best examples. Many villages, relatively accessible around Lake Baikal and in the Barguzin Valley, retain whole streets of *izba* (log houses) whose main decorative features are carved, brightly painted window frames. This construction style was taken further in Siberian city town houses, where the carvings of eaves and window frames became so intricate that they're now known as 'wooden lace'. The classic place to see this is Tomsk (p200), although some great individual examples have survived in Krasnoyarsk, Irkutsk (p211), Tobolsk (p190) and Tyumen (p187).

Before the Russians colonised Siberia, native Siberians were mostly nomadic. Their traditional dwellings fall into three main types: tepee-style cones of poles covered with skins or strips of bark (the Evenki *chum*); hexagonal or cylindrical frameworks of poles covered with brush and earth (the Altai *ail,* or similar western Buryatian equivalents); and round, felt-covered tent houses (the yurts of nomadic Tuvan and Kazakh herders). Examples of all these dwellings can be found in open-air museums, including near Bratsk (p261), Taltsy near Listvyanka (p219) and Ulan-Ude (p235).

CHINESE ETIQUETTE DOS & DON'TS

- When beckoning to someone, wave them over to you with your palm down, motioning to yourself.
- If someone gives a gift, put it aside to open later to avoid appearing greedy.
- Always take off your shoes when entering a Chinese home.
- When meeting a Chinese family, greet the eldest person first, as a sign of respect.
- Always present things to people with both hands, showing that what you are offering is the fullest extent of yourself.
- Be aware of the concept of 'face'. If you lose your temper in public, not only will the person targeted lose face, so will you for being seen as weak and unable to control your emotions.

Population

China is home to 56 ethnic groups, with Han Chinese making up 92% of the population. China's other ethnic groups are usually referred to as *shaoshu minzu* (minority nationals). One of the largest minority groups is Mongolian, found in the Inner Mongolia region in the north of the country, bordering Mongolia proper.

China faces enormous population pressures, despite comprehensive programs to curb its growth. Over 40% of China's population live in urban centres, putting great pressure on land and water resources. It's estimated that China's population will continue to grow at a rate of eight to 10 million each year, even with population programs such as the one-child policy. The unbalanced gender ratio (in some parts of the country 119 boys to every 100 girls) and a rapidly ageing population represent serious national problems.

For in-depth articles and reviews on contemporary Chinese arts and artists, head to www.newchinese art.com, a website run by the Shanghai-based gallery Art Scene China.

Media

All media is strictly controlled and censored. China's largest-circulation Chinese-language daily is the *People's Daily*. It has an online English-language edition at http://english.peopledaily.com.cn.

Chinese Central TV (CCTV) has an English-language channel, CCTV9. CCTV4 also has some English programs. Your hotel may have ESPN, Star Sports, CNN or BBC News 24. See also p323.

Religion

Religion in China has been influenced by three streams of thought: Taoism, Confucianism and Buddhism. All three have been inextricably entwined in popular Chinese religion along with ancient animist beliefs. The founders of these traditions have been deified; the Chinese worship them and their disciples as fervently as they worship their own ancestors and a pantheon of gods and spirits.

The Chinese communist government professes atheism. It considers religion to be base superstition, a remnant of old China used by the ruling classes to keep power. Nevertheless, in an effort to improve relations with the Muslim, Buddhist and Lamaist minorities, in 1982 the Chinese government amended its constitution to allow freedom of religion. However, only atheists are permitted to be members of the Chinese Communist Party (CCP). Since almost all of China's 55 minority groups adhere to one religion or another, this rule precludes most of them from becoming party members.

Muslims and Christians are believed to be the largest identifiable religious group still active in China today, both numbering perhaps 3% to 5% of the nation's population. The government has not published official figures of the number of Buddhists – hardly surprising given the ideological battle it has been waging with Tibetan Buddhists, who have been fighting for decades to preserve their culture and their nation. It's impossible to determine the number of Taoists, but the number of Taoist priests is very small.

Traditional Chinese religious beliefs took a battering during the Cultural Revolution when monasteries were disbanded, temples were destroyed and the monks were sometimes killed or sent to the fields to labour. Since Mao's death, the Chinese government has allowed many temples (sometimes with their own contingent of monks and novices) to reopen as active places of worship. All religious activity is firmly under state control and many of the monks are caretakers within renovated shells of monasteries, which serve principally as tourist attractions and are pale shadows of their former selves.

Arts

With its long, unbroken history and culture, China has made one of the greatest artistic contributions to humankind. Sadly, many of China's ancient art treasures have been destroyed in times of civil war or dispersed by invasion or natural calamity. Many of China's remaining great paintings, ceramics, jade and other works of art were rescued by exile beyond the mainland – in Taiwan, Singapore, Hong Kong and elsewhere. Fortunately, a great deal of work has been done since the early 1970s to restore what was destroyed in the Cultural Revolution.

Today China has a flourishing contemporary art scene, with private galleries competing with government-run museums and exhibition halls. Chinese artists are increasingly catching the attention of the international art world and joint exhibitions with European or American artists are now common. Over 700 artists from 81 countries took part in the third Beijing International Art Biennale held in August 2008. In the capital you'll also have the chance to see the traditional performance art of Chinese opera (see below).

Along the Trans-Manchurian route the architecture stands out from the rest of China, primarily as a result of foreign influences in the region. At the turn of the 20th century, much of Manchuria was occupied – either economically or militarily – by Russia, Japan and various European powers, all of whom left their mark on the cities in this region. The best example is Tiānjīn, which contains quarters once dominated by Austro-Hungarians, Belgians, Germans, Italians and Japanese. In Dàolǐqū (p299),

---

CHINESE OPERA

Chinese opera has been in existence formally since the northern Song dynasty (AD 960), developing out of China's long balladic tradition. Performances were put on by travelling entertainers, often families, in teahouses frequented by China's working classes. Performances were drawn from popular legends and folklore. Over 300 different types of opera developed throughout the country, with Běijīng opera being officially recognised in 1790, when performances were staged for the imperial family.

Chinese opera is fascinating for its use of make-up, acrobatics and elaborate costumes. Face-painting derives from the early use of masks worn by players and each colour suggests the personality and attributes that define a character. Chinese audiences can tell instantly the personality of characters by their painted faces. In addition, the status of a character is suggested by the size of headdress worn – the more elaborate, the more significant the character. The four major roles in Chinese opera are the female role, the male role, the 'painted-face' role (for gods and warriors) and the clown.

the oldest part of Hāěrbin (Harbin), onion domes and ornamental facades reveal the city's Russian roots.

MONGOLIA
The National Psyche
The nomadic life of the people, the timelessness of the land and the delicate relationship with the earth and its resources have all had a profound effect on the Mongolian character. These factors have made Mongolians humble, adaptable, unfettered by stringent protocol, good-humoured and uncannily stoic. You may well wonder if these are the same people who for centuries were vilified in the West as the 'scourge of God'. Indeed, compared with Russians and Chinese you're likely to find Mongolians the most easily approachable in terms of attitudes.

The great emptiness of their landscape has seemingly kindled a strong curiosity about outsiders. But, more significantly, it has also made hospitality a matter of sheer necessity rather than a chore or social obligation. Hospitality is something that is, quite simply, crucial to survival. In effect, every home on the steppes serves as a hotel, restaurant, pub, repair shop and information centre. This hospitality extends readily to strangers and it is usually given without fanfare or excitement.

The Mongolian ger (or yurt, a traditional, circular felt tent) plays a vital role in shaping both the Mongolian character and family life. Its small confines compel families to interact with one another, to share everything and to work together, tightening relationships between relatives. It promotes patience, makes inhibitions fade away and prevents privacy. It also hardens the sensibilities: ger dwellers must fetch their own water and fuel, difficult tasks especially in the dead of winter.

Lifestyle
Half the population of Mongolia lives permanently in urban areas, while the other half are either truly nomadic, or seminomadic, living in villages in the winter and grazing their animals on the steppes during the rest of the year. Urban Mongolians typically live in Russian-style apartment blocks while the nomads live in the one-room, felt ger.

Ovoo (large piles of rocks on Mongolian mountain passes) are repositories of offerings for local spirits. Walk around an *ovoo* clockwise three times, toss an offering onto the pile (another rock should suffice) and make a wish.

Usually equipped with traditional furnishings that are painted bright orange with fanciful designs, most gers are set out in a like manner with three beds around the perimeter, a chest covered with Buddhist relics at the back wall and a low table for dining. Everything revolves around a central hearth, with the women's side to the right and the men's to the left. The head of the household sits at the northern end of the ger with the most honoured guest to the right. The area near the door is the place of lowest rank and the domain of children.

Although one-third of Mongolians live well below the poverty line (less than US$30 per month), and unemployment hovers at 30% to 40%, this does not necessarily mean that people are going hungry. The reason is the strong family network. One family member with a decent job has the responsibility to support their family and distribute their wealth among siblings. Approximately 100,000 Mongolians live and work abroad, about 8% of the workforce, and many send money home to their families. In Ulaanbaatar, government salaries are less than US$100 per month while those in the private sector can be two or three times higher (sometimes much more).

Since the late 1990s there has been a major shift to urban areas, especially Ulaanbaatar, whose population hit the one million mark in 2007. With the exception of a handful of places benefiting from either mining or tourism, rural areas languish in neglect.

Population

The great majority (about 86%) of Mongolians are Khalkh Mongolians (*khalkh* means 'shield'). The other sizable ethnic group, the Kazakhs, make up about 6% (110,000) of the population and live in western Mongolia. The remaining 8% of the population are ethnic minority groups, including some 47,500 ethnic Buryats who live along the border with Russia. Population growth is at an all-time low, having fallen from 2.4% to 1.4% over the 15 years to 2005. The government offers economic benefits for newly weds and newborns.

Media

Mongolia's media is pretty free to express antigovernment opinions compared with that in Russia and certainly China. Major daily newspapers in Mongolia include *Ardiin Erkh* (People's Right), *Zunny Medee* (Century News), *Odriin Sonin* (Daily News) and *Önöödör* (Today).

All the TV stations have political allies; Channel 25 favours the Democrats, Channel 9 prefers the Mongolian People's Revolutionary Party (MPRP) and the others go with whomever is in power. Local TV stations don't start broadcasting until the afternoon and switch off around 11pm. See also p323.

Religion

Freedom of religion has opened up again only since the fall of communism in 1990 and there is growing competition between Buddhism and Christianity in both urban and rural areas. Most Mongolians practise some form of Buddhism, typically following the Mahayana school of Tibet. With the past two generations having essentially been raised atheist, most people no longer understand the Buddhist rituals or their meanings but a few still make the effort to visit the monasteries during prayer sessions. Numbers swell when well-known Buddhist monks from Tibet or India (or even Western countries) visit Mongolia.

Minority religions include Islam, followed mainly by ethnic Kazakhs living in the west of the country, and Christianity, Mongolia's fastest-growing religion. In Ulaanbaatar there are now more than 50 non-Buddhist places of worship with Mormons and Catholics represented in the largest numbers. Shamanism, the dominant belief system of Chinggis Khaan and the Mongol hordes, has been pushed to the cultural fringes.

A Mongol is a member of the Mongol ethnic group; a Mongolian is a citizen of Mongolia. More Mongols live outside Mongolia than in it – around 3.5 million ethnic Mongols are Chinese citizens and nearly a million are Russian citizens.

MONGOLIAN ETIQUETTE DOS & DON'TS

When meeting Mongolians or visiting a ger, note the following customs and habits:

- Avoid walking in front of an older person, or turning your back to the altar or religious objects (except when leaving).
- If someone offers you their snuff bottle, accept it with your right hand. If you don't take the snuff, at least sniff the top part of the bottle.
- Try to keep ger visits to less than two hours to avoid interrupting the family's work.
- Don't point a knife in any way at anyone; when passing a knife to someone ensure that the handle is facing the recipient; and use the knife to cut towards you, not away.
- Don't point your feet at the hearth, at the altar or at another person. Sleep with your feet pointing towards the door.
- If you have stepped on anyone, or kicked their feet, immediately shake their hand.
- Don't stand on, or lean over, the threshold, or lean against a support column.
- Don't touch another person's hat.

THE GREAT MONGOLIAN HERO

In the West, Chinggis (Genghis) Khaan (c AD 1167–1227) is reviled as a bloodthirsty barbarian, and with good reason; he left a trail of blood and destruction as he engaged in his relentless conquests. However, Chinggis is regarded a national hero in Mongolia. His legacy is very much a modern-day rallying point for Mongolians who are proud of what their fearless ancestor achieved. Chinggis' face adorns money, stamps, even vodka, and an Ulaanbaatar hotel, rock band and brewery are named after him.

Having been voted 'Man of the Millennium' by both the *Washington Post* and *Time* magazine, the tide of opinion on the great Khaan is changing somewhat. Adding weight to the argument that he was as much a skilful diplomat as brutal warrior are books such as *Genghis Khan and the Making of the Modern World,* by Jack Weatherford. Chinggis Khaan is credited by many as having introduced the first written system of Mongol law as well as traditional Mongolian script. He promoted his empire as a meritocracy and was tolerant of differing religious beliefs. Trans-Mongolian travellers might also want to ponder how he practically pioneered travel from China to the eastern edge of Europe way back in the 13th century.

Arts

The Story of the Weeping Camel (2003), directed by Byambasuren Davaa with Luigi Falomi, is a moving documentary about a camel that rejects its offspring, and how the family that owns it attempts to reconcile their differences.

From prehistoric oral epics to the latest movie from MongolKino film studios in Ulaanbaatar, the many arts of Mongolia convey the flavour of nomadic life and the spirit of the land. Traditional Mongolian music, which can be heard at concerts in Ulaanbaatar, is usually played on a *morin khuur* (horsehead fiddle), a two-stringed vertical violin and a lute. These instruments are also used by some of Mongolia's popular rock bands, including Hurd and Legend.

There are also several unique traditional singing styles. The enigmatic *khöömii* – throat singing – has the remarkable effect of producing two notes simultaneously – one low growl and the other an ethereal whistling. Translated as 'long songs', *urtyn-duu* use long trills to relate traditional stories about love and the countryside.

Mongolia's best-known modern poet and playwright is Dashdorjiin Natsagdorj (1906–37), regarded as the founder of Mongolian literature. His dramatic nationalist poems and plays are still performed in Mongolian theatres today. There's also been a recent revival in Mongolian cinema with the brightest star being director Byambasuren Davaa, whose 2005 movie *Cave of the Yellow Dog* describes the life of a nomad family and the changing life on the steppes.

Developed by the Arts Council of Mongolia, the website www.mongolart.mn has extensive information on dance, music, film, theatre and art.

Much of Mongolia's visual arts is religious in nature. Religious scroll paintings, depicting deities and their enlightened qualities, can be found on family altars in many homes. Another traditional style of painting is *zurag* – landscape storytelling. These landscapes include intricate sketches depicting every aspect of Mongolian life. Balduugiyn Sharav (1869–1939) is Mongolia's best-known painter in this style. The sculptor Zanabazar (1635–1723) is one of Mongolia's most revered artists, as well as religious and political leaders. He is known primarily for his bronze cast statues, which are now on display in monasteries and museums around Ulaanbaatar. For an interview with an artist working to resurrect Buddhist-inspired art in Mongolia, see p285.

There is also a vibrant modern-art scene in Ulaanbaatar, where you can see contemporary pieces by the likes of M Erdenebayar and his wife S Munkhjin at the Mongolian Artists' Exhibition Hall.

Food & Drink

Travellers on the Trans-Siberian route will have ample opportunities to sample the very best (and sometimes the worst) of Russia's kitchens. Those heading into or out of China will have a mind-boggling array of regional delicacies to explore, while those travelling the Trans-Mongolian route can add in hearty nomadic-inspired Mongolian dishes. One thing's for sure: you won't go hungry!

STAPLES & SPECIALITIES
Russia

Russia has a great culinary heritage enriched by influences from the Baltic to the Far East. Its waterways yield a unique range of fish and, as with any cold-climate country, there's a great love of fat-loaded dishes – Russia is no place to go on a diet!

Typical *zavtrak* (breakfast) dishes include bliny (pancakes) with savoury or sweet fillings, various types of *kasha* (porridge) made from buckwheat or other grains, and *syrniki* (cottage-cheese fritters), delicious with jam, sugar and the universal Russian condiment, *smetana* (sour cream). *Khleb* (bread) is freshly baked and comes in a multitude of delicious varieties.

Whether as the preamble to lunch or dinner, or something to nibble on between shots of vodka, *zakuski* (appetisers) are a big feature of Russian cuisine. Including lots of different salads, *zakuski* are usually a good choice for vegetarians. Soups, such as borsch or borscht, made with beetroot, *lapsha* (chicken noodle) and *solyanka* (a thick broth with meat, fish and a host of vegetables) can be a meal in themselves, served with piles of bread and a thick dollop of sour cream. Main dishes often come with a salad garnish, but you'll usually have to order rice or potatoes as side dishes.

During summer outdoor pizza and shashlyk (kebab) stalls pop up all over the place. Another standard snack you'll find are *pirozhki* (pies) with a range of fillings. Useful for nibbling on long journeys is *kolbasa*, a salami-like sausage, which is made in a wide variety of styles and can go down pretty well with bread, tomato and raw onion.

Sweet-toothed Russians adore *morozhenoe* (ice cream) and gooey *torty* (cream cakes), often decorated in lurid colours. *Pecheniye* (pastries) are eaten at tea time in the traditional English style and are available at any *bulochnaya* (bakery). Locally made chocolate and *konfetki* (sweets) are also excellent and, with their colourful wrappings, make great presents.

China

In northern Chinese cuisine, the *fàn* (grain) in the meal is usually wheat or millet, rather than rice. Its most common incarnations are as *jiǎozi* (steamed dumplings) or *chūnjuǎn* (spring rolls). The most famous northern dish, Peking duck (or Beijing duck as it is called today), is also served with typical ingredients: wheat pancakes, spring onions and fermented bean paste. The range of *cài* (vegetable or other accompanying dishes) is limited in the north. The cuisine relies heavily on freshwater fish, chicken and, most of all, cabbage.

The influence of the Mongols is evident in northern Chinese cuisine. Mongolian hotpot and Mongolian barbecue are adaptations from Mongol field kitchens. Animals that were hunted on horseback could be cooked in primitive barbecues made from soldiers' iron shields on top of hot coals. Alternatively, a soldier could use his helmet as a pot, filling it with water, meat and condiments. Mutton is now the main ingredient in Mongolian hotpot.

In most Russian cities it's common to find restaurants serving set three-course *biznes* lunches from noon to 4pm, Monday to Friday; these cost as little as R200 (up to R400 in Moscow and St Petersburg).

In *A Year of Russian Feasts*, Catherine Cheremeteff-Jones recounts how Russia's finest dishes have been preserved and passed down through the feast days of the Russian Orthodox Church.

TRAVEL YOUR TASTEBUDS

The following are among the variety of regional food specialities you'll find along the rail routes:

- *Omul* (a cousin of salmon and trout) – endemic to Lake Baikal and considered a great delicacy.

- *Oblyoma* (dried, salty fish found in the Volga) – most often eaten as a snack food with beer.

- *Kasylyk* (dried horsemeat sausages) and *zur balish* (meat pies) – both from Tatarstan, where *chek chek* (honey-drenched, macaroni-shaped pieces of fried dough) are also an essential part of celebrations.

- *Manti* (steamed, palm-sized dumplings) – known as *pozy, buuz* or *buuzy* in Buryatiya and *pyan-se* (a peppery version) in the Russian Far East.

- *Húntun* (wontons) – filled with leeks and minced pork, served in northern China.

- Noodles topped with *lǘròu huáng miàn* (sliced donkey meat) or hearty *kǎo yángròu* (roasted mutton) – also popular in northeastern China.

- *Öröm* (sometimes called *üürag;* a rich, sweet-tasting Mongolian cream) – made by warming fresh cow's milk in a pot and then letting it sit under a cover for one day.

The most common method of cooking in Běijīng is 'explode-frying', or deep-frying in peanut oil. Although northern Chinese cuisine has a reputation for being bland and unsophisticated, it has the advantage of being filling and therefore well suited to the cold climate.

In Běijīng, of course, every region of China and most regions of the world are represented in the splendid restaurant scene. The options range from the street stalls at Donghuamen Night Market to chic (and pricey) fusion restaurants where East meets West.

The following websites will teach you more about Russian, Chinese and Mongolian cuisine, respectively: www .ruscuisine.com, www .eatingchina.com and www.mongolfood.info.

Mongolia

The culinary masters of Mongolia's barren steppes have always put more stock in survival than taste. Mongolian food is therefore a hearty, if somewhat bland, array of meat and dairy products. Out in the countryside, potatoes are often considered exotic, leavened bread a treat and spices a cause for concern.

The streamlined diet reflects Mongolia's nomadic lifestyle. Nomads cannot reasonably transport an oven, and so are prevented from producing baked goods. Nor can nomads plant, tend to or harvest fruits, vegetables, spices or grains. Nomads can, however, eat the food that their livestock produces.

Many of the recipes in Imperial Mongolian Cooking: Recipes from the Kingdoms of Genghis Khan, by Marc Cramer, are from the author's grandfather, who worked as a chef in Siberia.

Dairy products – known as 'white foods' – are the staple for herdsmen in the summer. Camel's milk, thick cream, dried milk curds and fermented cheese are just a few of the delicacies you may sample (most of which taste like sour, plain yogurt). During winter the vast majority of Mongolians survive on boiled mutton and flour. A summer treat is Mongolian blueberry jam.

DRINKS
Russia

There are hundreds of different brands of vodka for sale, including ones that you'll certainly have heard of such as Stolichnaya and Smirnoff. Also look out for Moskovskaya, Flagman and Gzhelka.

Beer, however, is Russia's most popular alcoholic beverage, not least because it's cheap and very palatable. The local market leader is Baltika, making a range of 10 different brews; No 3, the most common, is a very quaffable lager.

Russian vineyards produce mainly saccharine *polusladkoe* (semisweet) or *sladkoe* (sweet) dessert wines. *Bryut* (very dry and only for sparkling wine), *sukhoe* (dry) and *polusukhoe* (semidry) reds can be found, though getting a palatable Russian dry white can be pretty tough. The cheapness of locally produced sparkling wine, known as *shampanskoye* (around R300 a bottle), accounts for its popularity rather than its taste.

The best Russian *konyak* (brandy) comes from the Caucasus and is generally a very pleasant surprise. *Kvas* is fermented rye-bread water, and is often dispensed on the street from big, wheeled tanks. It tastes not unlike ginger beer, and is a wonderfully cool and refreshing drink in summer.

Dodgy tap water has caused sales of bottled water to proliferate to the point where almost half the water drunk in Russia comes from a bottle. For those concerned about the environment as well as their health, boiling water and using a decent filter are sufficient if you want to drink what comes out of the tap (see p365 for more information).

Russians are world-class tea drinkers: the traditional brewing method is to make an extremely strong pot, pour small shots of it into glasses and fill the glasses with hot water from the kettle. Putting jam, instead of sugar, in tea is quite common.

Coffee comes in small cups, and unless you buy it at kiosks or stand-up eateries, it's usually quite good. There's been an explosion of Starbucks-style cafes all across Russia's bigger cities – cappuccino, espresso, latte and mocha are now as much a part of the average Russian lexicon as elsewhere.

Other drinks, apart from the ubiquitous canned soft drinks, include *sok* (juice) and *kefir* (yogurtlike sour milk).

> The question '*Nǐ chī fànle ma?*' (Have you eaten yet?) is a common greeting among Chinese people and is taken to show the significance of food in Chinese culture.

China

Legend has it that tea was first cultivated in China about 4000 years ago in the modern-day province of Sichuan. Today tea is a fundamental element of Chinese life, with green tea the most popular beverage throughout the country. Other local beverages include sugary soft drinks and fresh, sweet yogurt, available from street stalls and shops across the country. The latter is typically sold in small milk bottles and consumed through a straw.

Beer is also very popular, the best-known Chinese brew being Tsingtao, produced in the formerly German town of Qīngdǎo (the Chinese inherited

---

DRINKING ETIQUETTE IN RUSSIA & MONGOLIA

At bars, restaurants and on trains, it's odds-on if you get talking with Russians they'll press you to drink with them. Even people from distant tables, spotting foreigners, may be seized with hospitable urges.

If it's vodka being drunk, they'll want a man to down the shot in one, neat, of course; women are usually excused. This can be fun as you toast international friendship and so on, but vodka has a knack of creeping up on you from behind and the consequences can be appalling. It's traditional (and good sense) to eat a little something after each shot.

Refusing a drink can be very difficult, and Russians will probably continue to insist until they win you over. If you can't stand firm, drink in small gulps with copious thanks, while saying how you'd love to indulge but you have to be up early in the morning (or something similar). If you're really not in the mood, one sure-fire method of warding off all offers (as well as making people feel quite awful) is to say '*Ya alkogolik*' (*Ya alkogolichka* for women): 'I'm an alcoholic'.

Mongolians are not quite so pushy when it comes to drinking alcohol, but it's worth noting at least one local vodka drinking tradition. Before the first sip, honour the sky gods and the four directions by dipping your left ring finger into the glass and flicking drops into the air four times as well as touching the finger to your forehead.

the brewery). A notable Běijīng brand is Yanjing. Note that Chinese 'wines' are actually spirits, many used primarily for cooking or medicinal purposes. Chinese red and white wines tend to unanimously get the thumbs down from Westerners.

Imported beverages, such as soda, beer and coffee, are available at many shops and restaurants. And yes, Starbucks has made it to Běijīng, inspiring many local cafes in the process.

Mongolia

Mongolians commence every meal with a cup of weak tea to aid digestion. In the countryside, many people drink *süütei tsai* (salty tea), which is a taste that is hard to acquire.

The most famous Mongolian alcoholic drink is *airag* (sometimes called *koumiss*), fermented mare's milk. Herders make it at home with an alcohol content of about 3%. If further distilled, it becomes the more potent *shimiin arkhi*, a clear spirit with 12% alcohol content. The Mongolians taste for vodka has been inherited from their former Russian patrons; they used to export vodka to Russia, but now consume much of it themselves. Several pubs in Ulaanbaatar brew their own light and dark beers (see p288 for ideas).

> Mongolians consider eating wolf meat and lungs good for respiratory ailments, while consuming the intestines can aid digestion. Powdered wolf rectum is used for haemorrhoids and hanging a wolf's tongue around one's neck is said to cure gland and thyroid ailments.

SCENES FROM FOUR DINING CARS

Ratings are from 1 (very poor) to 5 (excellent).

May 2008: Train 71, Westbound between Yekaterinburg & St Petersburg *Simon Richmond*
Ambience: 5
Cleanliness: 4
Quality of food: 5
Quality of service: 4
Range & availability of items on the menu: 4

The *Demidovsky* is the premier train linking Yekaterinburg and St Petersburg. As I approached its dining car for lunch, I had a view into the cramped kitchen occupied by a middle-aged woman in a tall white chef's hat who looked as if she'd been cooking all her life. The dining car was impressively opulent with art-nouveau decorative flourishes, plush moss-green upholstery on the chairs and pale gold trimmings. The menu listed tempting salads, a classic range of soups and main dishes such as grilled trout and escalope of pork. There were even children's options, including the charming *nyam nyam* (yum yum) rice pudding. My fish soup, delivered with a smile by the waiter, had a delicious peppery broth and was generously laced with chunks of salmon, trout and potato.

June 2008: Train 270, Eastbound between Ulan-Ude & Chita *Marc Di Duca*
Ambience: 1
Cleanliness: 5 (completely uncontaminated by food)
Quality of food: never got to find out
Quality of service: 1
Range & availability of items on the menu: 5 for range, 0 for availability

Having boarded at 4am in Ulan-Ude, I woke up five hours later fancying breakfast. The *provodnitsa* (carriage attendant) informed me there was no boiling water for tea, so I decided to head for the dining car. Twenty heavy doors and six scary gaps between the carriages later, I found myself in a suspiciously empty restaurant. Though presented with a menu, a Monty Python-esque scene unfolded as my enquiries regarding the availability of meals met with a *nyet* every time. In the end I gave up. 'What do you have?' I asked. 'Wafer biscuits and juice', the waiter replied. 'What about a cup of coffee?' 'No boiling water', she said, almost apologetically.

WHERE TO EAT & DRINK
On the Trains

A trip on the Trans-Siberian Railway can often seem like an endless picnic, with all manner of foods being enjoyed in the compartments. Although it's possible to buy limited provisions on board (such as drinks and snack foods) and at stations along the way, it's a good idea to stock up on anything special or more substantial before you start the journey – that way you'll be able to join in the ritual sharing with your fellow passengers. To make the best impression, bring some unique foods from your home country.

Dining cars on all Russian trains are private operations, hence the food served in them can vary enormously in quality. They are best favoured as a place to meet fellow travellers and have a drink rather than for any gastronomic qualities (see the boxed text, opposite). The dining cars are changed at each country's border, so en route to Běijīng you will get Russian, Chinese and possibly Mongolian menus (although it's unlikely there'll be a car attached between the Russian border and Ulaanbaatar). A meal with accompanying drink will typically cost US$20 to US$30, paid in local currency. Dining cars are open from approximately 9am to 9pm

> Scientists claim that drinking a few cups of *airag* (fermented mare's milk) on a constant basis can improve health, clear the skin and sharpen the eyesight.

July 2008: Train 24, Southbound between Ulaanbaatar & Běijīng *Michael Kohn*
Ambience: 4
Cleanliness: 3
Quality of food: 2.5
Quality of service: 3
Range & availability of items on the menu: 2.5

Chinggis (Genghis) Khaan would definitely be proud of this dining car! It was decked out in traditional Mongolian wood panels, with beautifully carved animal motifs and nature-inspired designs. Bows, arrows and old guns hung on the walls, as well as Mongolian landscape paintings. Menu items were not unlike those found in basic Mongolian cafes: globs of mashed potatoes, lukewarm pieces of meat and tightly packed mounds of rice with a dollop of ketchup. I tried the decidedly average potato and meat soup. A passenger near me was tucking into a cheese omelette, which seemed like a better call. Mongolian milk tea and black tea were available and little snacks, such as Vietnamese candies, were also for sale. Food quality was not extraordinary but the service was friendly enough, the atmosphere was great and the locals seemed to be enjoying themselves. Most tables were filled by large Mongolian men huddled around bottles of vodka.

August 2008: Train T11, Northbound between Běijīng & Shěnyáng *Michael Kohn*
Ambience: 2
Cleanliness: 2.5
Quality of food: 3
Quality of service: 3
Range & availability of items on the menu: 3

The dining car on Chinese train T11 was built with one purpose in mind: serve the people. It was decidedly unelaborate, with red vinyl chairs, white tablecloths and brown walls. Waiters scuttled about the car, doling out platters of food and wiping tables as endless rounds of passengers rolled through. The staccato chatter of the patrons rose into the air, along with the clicks and taps of chopsticks. I was shunted onto one of the tables and set about ordering. Rather than try to decipher the menu I put in a personal request: chicken and cashews, plus fried vegetables. I have never been in a Chinese restaurant where the chef could not fulfil my exact request and the same was true of train T11. Tea was continuously replenished and the food came hot and fast. I ate slowly, read, wrote in my notebook and simply watched as the fast and furious pace of a Chinese meal unfolded before my eyes.

local time, although this is by no means certain, and with the time-zone differences knowing when to turn up can be a constant guessing game.

During the peak summer season on the more popular Trans-Siberian services, such as the *Rossiya* and *Baikal,* the dining car can be booked out at certain times by tour groups. On both these trains and a few others it's possible to buy a ticket that includes all meals – probably not the best of ideas given the variable nature of what's on offer, and only worth considering if you have a total aversion to shopping en route. On some overnight trains, an airline-style breakfast tray of provisions is provided to SV and *kupe* (1st- and 2nd-class compartmentalised carriage) passengers.

In the dining car you will often find a table of pot noodles, chocolate, alcohol, juice and the like being peddled by the staff. They sometimes make the rounds of the carriages, too, with a trolley filled with various snacks and drinks. The *provodnitsas* (female carriage attendants) also offer their own drinks and nibbles. Prices are cheap but not as cheap as what you would pay at the kiosks or to the babushkas at the station halts.

Off the Trains

Shopping for supplies at Russian stations is part of the fun of a journey on the Trans-Siberian Railway (note that this is not the case, though, in Mongolia and China, where you will find very little food available on the platforms). It's a good idea to have plenty of small change on hand, but you'll rarely have to worry about being overcharged.

'Shopping for supplies at Russian stations is part of the fun of a journey'

The choice of items can be excellent, with fresh milk, ice cream, grilled chicken, boiled potatoes, home cooking such as *pelmeni* (dumplings) or *pirozhki* (savoury pies), buckets of forest berries and smoked fish all on offer. Through Siberia you'll always find sellers of fresh pine or cedar nuts. There can also be surprises: 'What looked like candy…turned out to be sap twisted into chewing gum, with a Blu-Tak-like consistency', said one Lonely Planet correspondent.

In all the main cities along each of the train routes there are plenty of choices when it comes to places to eat. Meals in the best new restaurants (where you'd typically pay between R500 and R1000 for a meal) can be fine renditions of Russian classics made with fresh and tasty ingredients. In contrast, a *stolovaya* is a cafeteria-style place often found outside train stations, and in office blocks and government institutions, where a meal rarely tops R200.

Ulaanbaatar has a fine range of restaurants, but if you leave the capital be prepared for gastronomic purgatory. In cheap restaurants throughout Mongolia, mutton is the special of the day, every day: mutton with rice, mutton in goulash etc. A *guanz* is a canteen that often offers little but mutton and noodles. In the countryside, the *guanz* is often housed in a ger (yurt) and may be a traveller's only eating option apart from self-catering.

Fortunately, many places in Ulaanbaatar – as well as ger camps that cater to foreigners – have expanded their menus. A few restaurants serve Mongolian hotpot and Mongolian barbecue, but these are really Chinese adaptations of ancient Mongolian cooking techniques. You are more likely to sustain yourself on *buuzy* (steamed dumplings) and *khuushuur* (fried pancakes with mutton).

It's hard to go hungry in China as just about everywhere you go there will be myriad food options to suit most budgets. The word *fàngdiàn* usually refers to a large-scale restaurant that may or may not offer lodging. A *cānguǎn* is generally a smaller restaurant that specialises in one particular type of food. The most informal type of restaurant is the *cāntīng*, which has low-end prices, though the quality of the food can be quite high.

VEGETARIANS & VEGANS

Russia is pretty tough on vegetarians, although some restaurants have thankfully caught on, particularly in Moscow, St Petersburg and the other large cities. Note that vegetable and fish soups are usually made using meat stock. If you're a vegetarian, say so, early and often. You'll see a lot of cucumber and tomato salads, and – if so inclined – you will develop an eagle eye for *baklazhan* (eggplant). *Zakuski* include quite a lot of meatless ingredients, such as eggs and mushrooms. If you're travelling during Lent, you'll find that many restaurants have special nonmeat menus.

Despite vegetarianism having a 1000-year history in China, eating meat is a status symbol, symbolic of health and wealth. Many Chinese remember all too well the famines of the 1950s and 1960s, when having anything to eat at all was a luxury. Even vegetables are often fried in animal-based oils, and soups are most commonly made with chicken or beef stock. In Běijīng, vegetarianism is slowly catching on, and there are new chic vegetarian eateries appearing in fashionable restaurant districts. These are often pricey establishments and you pay for ambience as well as the food.

A traditional Chinese vegetarian menu will often consist of a variety of 'mock meat' dishes made from tofu, wheat gluten and assorted vegetables. Some of the dishes in China are quite fantastic to look at, with vegetarian ingredients expertly sculpted to look like spare ribs or fried chicken. Sometimes the chefs will even go to great lengths to create 'bones' from carrots and lotus roots. Some of the more famous vegetarian dishes include vegetarian 'ham', braised vegetarian 'shrimp' and sweet and sour 'fish'.

Mongolia is a difficult, but not impossible, place for vegetarians. If you don't eat meat, you can get by in Ulaanbaatar, but in the countryside you will need to take your own supplements and preferably a petrol stove. Vegetables other than potatoes, carrots and onions are rare, relatively expensive and usually pickled in jars. The best way for vegetarians to get protein is from the wide range of dairy products. Vegans will either have to be completely self-sufficient, or be prepared to modify their lifestyle for a while.

'If you're a vegetarian, say so, early and often'

EAT YOUR WORDS

This glossary is a brief guide to some basics. The italics in the transliterations indicate where the stress in the word falls; see p368 for further tips on pronunciation.

Useful Phrases
RUSSIA
Do you have a table ...?

	Есть свободный столик ...?	u vas yest' sva·*bod*·nih *sto*·lik ....
for two	на двоих	na dva·*ikh*
for three	на троих	na tra·*ikh*

Do you have an English menu?

	Английское меню можно?	an·*gli*·ska·ye mi·*nyu mozh*·na

Can we see the menu?

Дайте, пожалуйста меню. *dai*·tye, pa·*zhal*·sta, mi·*nyu*

Please bring a ...

Принесите, пожалуйста … pri·ni·*si*·tye pa·*zhal*·sta ...

fork	вилку	*vil*·ku
knife	нож	nosh
plate	тарелку	ta·*ryel*·ku
glass of water	стакан воды	sta·*kan* va·*dih*
with/without ice	со льдом/без льда	so l'·*dom*/byez l'·*da*

I'm a vegetarian.

Я вегетарианец/Я вегетарианка. ya vi·gi·ta·ri·*a*·nits/ya vi·gi·ta·ri·*an*·ka (m/f)

I don't eat meat.

Я не ем мясного. ya nye yem myas·*no*·va

I can't eat dairy products.

Я не ем молочного. ya nye yem ma·*loch*·na·va

Do you have any vegetarian dishes?

У вас есть вегетарианские блюда? u vas yest' vi·gi·ta·ri·*an*·ski·ye *blyu*·da

Does this dish have meat?

Это блюдо мясное? *e*·ta *blyu*·da myas·*no*·ye

Does it contain eggs?

В этом блюде есть яйца? v *e*·tam *blyu*·dye yest' *yai*·tsa

I'm allergic to nuts.

У меня аллергия на (орехи). u min·*ya* a·lir·*gi*·ya na (a·*rye*·khi)

Please bring the bill.

Принесите, пожалуйста счёт. pri·ni·*si*·tye pa·*zhal*·sta shchot

CHINA

I don't want MSG.	我不要味精	*Wŏ bú yào wèijīng.*
I'm vegetarian.	我吃素	*Wŏ chī sù.*
not too spicy	不要太辣	*bù yào tài là*
menu	菜单	*càidān*
bill (cheque)	买单/结帐	*măidān/jiézhàng*
set meal (no menu)	套餐	*tàocān*
let's eat	吃饭	*chī fàn*
cheers!	干杯	*gānbēi*
chopsticks	筷子	*kuàizi*
knife	刀子	*dàozi*
fork	叉子	*chāzi*
spoon	调羹/汤匙	*tiáogēng/tāngchí*
hot	热的	*rède*
ice cold	冰的	*bīngde*

MONGOLIA

I can't eat meat.

Би мах идэж чадахгүй. bi makh i·dej cha·dakh·gui

Can I have a menu please?

Би хоолны цэс авч болох уу? bi khool·nii tses avch bo·lokh uu

How much is it?

Энэ ямар үнэтэй вэ? e·ne ya·mar ü·ne·tei ve

What food do you have today?

Өнөөдөр ямар хоолтой вэ? ö·nöö·dör ya·mar khool·toi ve

When will the food be ready?

Хоол хэзээ бэлэн болох вэ? khool khe·zee be·len bo·lokh ve

Food Glossary
RUSSIA
Breakfast

am-*lyet*	омлет	omelette
blin-chi-ki	блинчики	bliny rolled around meat or cheese and browned
bli-*nih*	блины	leavened buckwheat pancakes; also eaten as an appetiser or dessert
ka-sha	каша	Russian-style buckwheat porridge
ki-fir	кефир	buttermilk, served as a drink
tva-*rok*	творог	cottage cheese
ya-*ich*-ni-tsa	яичница	fried egg
yiy-*tso*	яйцо	egg

Lunch & Dinner

di-*syer*-tih	десерты	sweet courses or desserts
gar-*ya*-chi-ye *blyu*-da	горячие блюда	hot courses or 'main' dishes
pyer-vi-ye *blyu*-da	первые блюда	first courses (usually soups)
vto-*ri*-ye *blyu*-da	вторые блюда	second courses or 'main' dishes
za-*ku*-ski	закуски	hors d'oeuvres

Methods of Preparation

at-var-*noy*	отварной	poached or boiled
fri	фри	fried
pi-*chyo*-nih	печёный	baked
va-*ryo*-nih	вареный	boiled
zhar-nih	жареный	roasted or fried

Appetisers

gri-*bih* f smi-*ta*-nye	грибы в сметане	mushrooms baked in sour cream
ik-*ra*	икра	black (sturgeon) caviar
ik-*ra kras*-na-ya	икра красная	red (salmon) caviar
sa-*lat* iz pa-mi-*do*-raf	салат из из помидорав	tomato salad
sa-*lat* sta-*lich*-nih	салат столичный	salad of vegetable, beef, potato and egg in sour cream and mayonnaise
zhul'-*yen* iz gri-*bof*	жульен из грибов	another name for mushrooms baked in sour cream

Soup

ak-*rosh*-ka	окрошка	cold or hot soup made from cucumbers, sour cream, potatoes, eggs, meat and *kvas*
borsch	борщ	beetroot soup with vegetables and sometimes meat
khar-*cho*	харчо	traditional Georgian soup of lamb, rice and spices
lap-*sha*	лапша	noodle soup
sal-*yan*-ka	солянка	thick meat or fish soup
shchi	щи	cabbage or sauerkraut soup
u-*kha*	уха	fish soup with potatoes and vegetables

Fish

a-sit-*ri*-na	осетрина	sturgeon
fa-*ryel'*	форель	trout
rih-ba	рыба	fish
su-*dak*	судак	pike, perch
syom-ga	сёмга	salmon

Poultry & Meat Dishes

an·tri·*kot*	антрекот	entrecôte – boned sirloin steak
ba·*ra*·ni·na	баранина	lamb or mutton
bif·*shteks*	бифштекс	'steak', usually a glorified hamburger
bif·stra·ga·*nof*	бифстроганов	beef stroganov – beef slices in a rich cream sauce
ga·lub·*tsih*	голубцы	cabbage rolls stuffed with meat
gav·*ya*·di·na	говядина	beef
kal·ba·*sa*	колбаса	a type of sausage
kat·*lye*·ta	котлета	usually a croquette of ground meat
kat·*lye*·ta pa *ki*·if·ski	котлета по-киевски	chicken Kiev; fried chicken breast stuffed with garlic butter
kat·*lye*·ta pa·*zhar*·ski	котлета по-жарски	croquette of minced chicken
mya·sa	мясо	meat
mya·sa pa ma·nas·*tir*·ski	мясо по-монастирски	meat topped with cheese and sour cream
pil'·*mye*·ni	пельмени	small meat dumplings
plof	плов	pilaf – fried rice with lamb and carrots
po·zi	пози	large meat dumplings
pti·tsa	птица	chicken or poultry
shash·*lihk*	шашлык	skewered and grilled mutton or other meat
svi·*ni*·na	свинина	pork
tef·ti·li	тефтели	meat-and-rice balls
zhar·ka·ye pa da·*mash*·ni·mu	жаркое по-домашнему	meat stewed in a clay pot 'home-style', with mushrooms, potatoes and vegetables

Vegetables

a·gur·*yets*	огурец	cucumber
bak·la·*zhan*	баклажан	eggplant/aubergine
chis·*nok*	чеснок	garlic
gar·*ni*·rih	гарниры	any vegetable garnish
ga·*rokh*	горох	peas
gri·*bih*	грибы	mushrooms
ka·*pus*·ta	капуста	cabbage
kar·*tosh*·ka/kar·*to*·fil'	картошка/картофель	potato
mar·*kof'*	морковь	carrots
o·va·shchi	овощи	vegetables
pa·mi·*dor*	помидор	tomato
zye·lin'	зелень	greens

Fruit

ab·ri·*kos*	абрикос	apricot
a·pil'·*sin*	апельсин	orange
ba·*nan*	банан	banana
fruk·tih	фрукты	fruit
gru·sha	груша	pear
vi·na·*grat*	виноград	grapes
vish·nya	вишня	cherry
ya·bla·ka	яблоко	apple

Other Foods

khlyep	хлеб	bread
mas·la	масло	butter
pye·rits	перец	pepper
ris	рис	rice
sa·khar	сахар	sugar

| sihr | сыр | cheese |
| sol' | соль | salt |

Desserts

kam·*pot*	компот	fruit in syrup
ki·*syel'*	кисель	fruit jelly/jello
ma·*ro*·zhih·na·ye	мороженое	ice cream
pi·*rozh*·na·ye	пирожное	pastries

CHINA
Methods of Preparation

chǎo	炒	fry
hóngshāo	红烧	red-cooked (stewed in soy sauce)
kǎo	烤	roast
yóujiān	油煎	deep-fry
zhēng	蒸	steam
zhǔ	煮	boil

Rice Dishes

jīchǎofàn	鸡炒饭	fried rice with chicken
jīdàn chǎofàn	鸡蛋炒饭	fried rice with egg
mǐfàn	米饭	steamed white rice
shūcài chǎofàn	蔬菜炒饭	fried rice with vegetables
xīfàn; zhōu	稀饭; 粥	watery rice porridge (congee)

Noodle Dishes

húntun miàn	馄饨面	wontons and noodles
jīsī chǎomiàn	鸡丝炒面	fried noodles with chicken
jīsī tāngmiàn	鸡丝汤面	soupy noodles with chicken
májiàng miàn	麻酱面	sesame paste noodles
niúròu chǎomiàn	牛肉炒面	fried noodles with beef
niúròu miàn	牛肉汤面	soupy beef noodles
ròusī chǎomiàn	肉丝炒面	fried noodles with pork
shūcài chǎomiàn	蔬菜炒面	fried noodles with vegetables
tāngmiàn	汤面	noodles in soup
xiārén chǎomiàn	虾仁炒面	fried noodles with shrimp
zhájiàng miàn	炸酱面	bean and meat noodles

Bread, Buns & Dumplings

cōngyóu bǐng	葱油饼	spring onion pancakes
guōtiē	锅贴	pot stickers/pan-grilled dumplings
mántóu	馒头	steamed buns
ròu bāozi	肉包子	steamed meat buns
shāo bǐng	烧饼	clay-oven rolls
shuǐjiān bāo	水煎包	pan-grilled buns
shuǐjiǎo	水饺	boiled dumplings
sùcài bāozi	素菜包子	steamed vegetable buns

Soup

húntun tāng	馄饨汤	wonton soup
sān xiān tāng	三鲜汤	three kinds of seafood soup
suānlà tāng	酸辣汤	hot and sour soup

Beef Dishes

| gānbiǎn niúròu sī | 干煸牛肉丝 | stir-fried beef and chilli |
| háoyóu niúròu | 蚝油牛肉 | beef with oyster sauce |

hóngshāo niúròu	红烧牛肉	beef braised in soy sauce
niúròu fàn	牛肉饭	beef with rice
tiěbǎn niúròu	铁板牛肉	sizzling beef platter

Chicken & Duck Dishes

háoyóu jīkuài	蚝油鸡块	diced chicken in oyster sauce
hóngshāo jīkuài	红烧鸡块	chicken braised in soy sauce
jītuǐ fàn	鸡腿饭	chicken leg with rice
níngméng jī	柠檬鸡	lemon chicken
tángcù jīdīng	糖醋鸡丁	sweet and sour chicken
yāoguǒ jīdīng	腰果鸡丁	chicken and cashews
yāròu fàn	鸭肉饭	duck with rice

Pork Dishes

biǎndòu ròusī	扁豆肉丝	shredded pork and green beans
gūlǔ ròu	咕噜肉	sweet and sour pork
guōbā ròupiàn	锅巴肉片	pork and sizzling rice crust
háoyóu ròusī	耗油肉丝	pork with oyster sauce
jiàngbào ròudīng	醬爆肉丁	diced pork with soy sauce
jīngjiàng ròusī	京酱肉丝	pork cooked with soy sauce
mùěr ròu	木耳肉	wood-ear mushrooms and pork
páigǔ fàn	排骨饭	pork chop with rice
qīngjiāo ròupiàn	青椒肉片	pork and green peppers
yángcōng chǎo ròupiàn	洋葱炒肉片	pork and fried onions

Seafood Dishes

gélí	蛤蜊	clams
gōngbào xiārén	宫爆虾仁	diced shrimp with peanuts
háo	蚝	oysters
hóngshāo yú	红烧鱼	fish braised in soy sauce
lóngxiā	龙虾	lobster
pángxiè	螃蟹	crab
yóuyú	鱿鱼	squid
zhāngyú	章鱼	octopus

Vegetable & Bean Curd Dishes

báicài xiān shuānggū	白菜鲜双菇	bok choy and mushrooms
cuìpí dòufu	脆皮豆腐	crispy-skin bean curd
hēimùěr mèn dòufu	黑木耳焖豆腐	bean curd with wood-ear mushrooms
hóngshāo qiézi	红烧茄子	red-cooked aubergine
jiācháng dòufu	家常豆腐	'home-style' tofu
jiāngzhī qīngdòu	姜汁青豆	string beans with ginger
lúshuǐ dòufu	卤水豆腐	smoked bean curd
shāguō dòufu	砂锅豆腐	clay pot bean curd
sùchǎo biǎndòu	素炒扁豆	garlic beans
sùchǎo sùcài	素炒素菜	fried vegetables
tángcù ǒubǐng	糖醋藕饼	sweet and sour lotus root cakes
yúxiāng qiézi	鱼香茄子	'fish-resembling' aubergine

Fruit

bālè	芭乐	guava
bōluó	菠萝	pineapple
gānzhè	甘蔗	sugar cane
lí	梨	pear
lìzhī	荔枝	lychee

lóngyǎn	龙眼	longan/'dragon eyes'
mángguǒ	芒果	mango
píngguǒ	苹果	apple
pútáo	葡萄	grape
xiāngjiāo	香蕉	banana
xīguā	西瓜	watermelon

MONGOLIA

ban·shtai shöl	банштай шөл	dumpling soup
goi·mon·tai shöl	гоймонтой шөл	noodle soup
gu·ril·tai shöl	гурилтай шөл	handmade noodle soup
shöl	шөл	soup
bai·tsaan zuush	байцаан зууш	cabbage salad
bif·shteks	бифштекс	patty
bu·daa·tai	будаатай	rice
buuz	бууз	steamed mutton dumplings
kho·ni·ny makh	хонины мах	mutton
khor·khog	хорхог	meat roasted from the inside with hot stones
khuu·rag	хуурга	fried food
khuu·shuur	хуушуур	fried meat pancake
khuur·ga	хуурга	fried meat and flour in sauce
luu·van·giin zuush	луувангийн зууш	carrot salad
makh	мах	meat
niis·lel zuush	нийслэл зууш	potato salad
no·goo·toi	ногоотой	vegetables
no·goon zuush	ногоон зууш	vegetable salad
shar·san ön·dög	шарсан өндөг	fried egg
shar·san ta·khia	шарсан тахиа	fried chicken
shni·tsel	шницель	schnitzel
talkh	талх	bread
tom·stei	төмстэй	potato
tsö·tsgii	цөцгий	sour cream
tsui·van	цуйван	fried slices of dough with meat
za·gas	загас	fish
zai·das/so·sisk	зайдас/сосиск	sausage

DRINKS
Russia

va·da	вода	water
mi·ni·ral'·na·ya va·da	минеральная вода	mineral water
ko·fe	кофе	coffee
chai	чай	tea
ma·la·ko	молоко	milk
sok	сок	juice
biz·al·ka·gol'·nih na·pi·tak	безалкогольный напиток	soft drink
vot·ka	водка	vodka
ig·ris·ta·ye vi·no/sham·pan·ska·ye	игристое вино/шампанское	sparkling wine/champagne
kras·na·ye vi·no	красное вино	red wine
bye·la·ye vi·no	белое вино	white wine
kan·yak	коньяк	brandy
pi·va	пиво	beer
kvas	квас	fermented bread drink

China

bái pútáo jiǔ	白葡萄酒	white wine
báijiǔ	白酒	Chinese spirits
chá	茶	tea
dòujiāng	豆浆	soya bean milk
hóng pútáo jiǔ	红葡萄酒	red wine
kāfēi	咖啡	coffee
kāi shuǐ	开水	water (boiled)
kěkǒu kělè	可口可乐	Coca-Cola
kuàngquán shuǐ	矿泉水	mineral water
mǐjiǔ	米酒	rice wine
nǎijīng	奶精	coffee creamer
niúnǎi	牛奶	milk
píjiǔ	啤酒	beer
qìshuǐ	汽水	soft drink (soda)
suānnǎi	酸奶	yogurt
yézi zhī	椰子汁	coconut juice

Mongolia

tsai	цай	tea
ban·shtai tsai	банштай цай	dumplings in tea
süü·tei tsai	сүүтэй цай	Mongolian milk tea
ra·shaan us	рашаан ус	mineral water
shar ai·rag	шар айраг	beer
air·ag	айраг	fermented mare's milk

Environment

Part of the Trans-Siberian Railway's attraction for travellers is the variety of terrain along the route and the abundance of wildlife it holds. Much of the region's wildlife is naturally shy, hidden from view or too distant to be observed well. Nevertheless, it's still possible to see interesting wildlife and vegetation from the train compartment, sometimes very close to the track. There are also frequent opportunities to get off and explore the countryside at leisure and in more detail, the most popular stop being World Heritage–listed Lake Baikal.

THE LAND

Russia, China and Mongolia – the three nations linked by the Trans-Siberian routes – cover over a quarter of the globe in total, with Russia being the world's largest country, China the fourth biggest and Mongolia the eighteenth biggest. The bulk of the railway traverses the geographical entity known as Inner Eurasia, an immense territory bounded by Europe in the west, the Middle East and India in the south, and China in the east. Its physical environment has shaped its social evolution from prehistoric times to the present day. Most notably, the region remained only sparsely populated for centuries (and it's hardly overpopulated these days!).

Inner Eurasia's remote interior location, far away from the oceans and moisture-bearing winds, fosters a climate of harsh extremes. When global warming forced back the great ice sheets that covered the continent more than 10,000 years ago, it resulted in four distinct ecological zones in Inner Eurasia: tundra, taiga, steppe and desert. The tundra includes the upper reaches of Siberia, extending to the Arctic coast. Under snow for nearly two-thirds of the year, the ground remains in a frozen condition of permafrost, even in summer. The tundra supports little vegetation and fauna, though the wintry northern coast is home to sea mammals.

South of the tundra, the taiga comprises a dense forest belt that runs from Scandinavia across Siberia to the Pacific coast. The taiga's soil is poor for farming, but its woods and rivers were rich in fauna until relatively recently. Below the taiga lies the steppe, which spans the continent from the plains north of the Black Sea across Central Asia through Mongolia to the western edge of China. This gently rolling, semiarid grassland is unsuitable for cultivation, but it provides sufficient vegetation to support large herds of grazing animals. To the south, the steppe becomes arid and gives way to the deserts of central and eastern Asia. The Gobi Desert in Mongolia and China retains a thin grass cover that sustains some of the hardier herbivores.

RIVERS & LAKES

Six of the world's 20 longest rivers are in Russia. Forming the China-Russia border, the east-flowing Amur (4416km) is nominally the longest, along with the Lena (4400km), Yenisey (4090km), Irtysh (4245km) and Ob (3680km), all of which flow north across Siberia ending up in the Arctic Ocean. In fact, if one was to take the longest stretch, including tributaries (as is frequently done with the Mississippi–Missouri River System in North America), the Ob–Irtysh would clock up 5410km and the Angara–Yenisey a phenomenal 5550km. The latter might, in fact, be the world's longest river if you were to include Lake Baikal and the Selenga River (992km), which directly feed into it.

The Wild Russia website (www.wild-russia.org) belongs to the US-based Center for Russian Nature Conservation, which assists and promotes nature conservation across Russia.

The Russian taiga is a major carbon sink, re-moving an estimated 500 million tonnes of carbon from the atmosphere each year.

Beautiful Lake Baikal itself is the world's deepest lake, holding nearly one-fifth of all the globe's unfrozen fresh water. Formed by rifting tectonic plates, Baikal is also the world's oldest lake, dating back 25 million years. It was enshrined as a Unesco World Heritage Site in 1996. The rift, which widens by about 2cm per year, is thought to be 9km deep, of which 7km of depth is covered by sediment.

Europe's longest river, the Volga (3690km), rises northwest of Moscow and flows via Kazan and Astrakhan into the Caspian Sea, the world's largest lake (371,800 sq km). Lake Onega (9600 sq km) and Lake Ladoga (18,390 sq km), both northeast of St Petersburg, are the biggest lakes in Europe.

WILDLIFE

The extent and variety of habitat in Russia, China and Mongolia support a huge range of species; so many, in fact, that we can only sketch an outline of the rich fauna and flora here.

Animals

The wild animals living in the area bordering the railway are amazingly varied, recalling what Western Europe was like before civilisation took its toll. What follows is a selection of the most characteristic (if not always the most easily observable) species.

Lesley Chamberlain's *Volga Volga* recounts the author's voyage back and forth along the great river in 1993 as she digs into its history, environmental decline and place in Russian culture.

BIRDS

Birds are numerous and seen more often than other animal species on the journey. However, many birds are shy and secretive, have restricted habitat preferences or are absent in winter.

Geese you can spot include the greylag goose *(Anser anser)*, the largest of the 'grey' geese and familiar as the ancestor of the domestic farmyard goose; and the bean goose *(A. fabalis)*, smaller and darker than the greylag. Breeds of duck include the common mallard *(Anas platyrhynchos)*, the less common Baikal teal *(A. Formosa)* and the falcated teal *(A. falcate)*.

Coots *(Fulica atra)* prefer the more open areas of lakes, so are easily visible. The common or mew gull *(Larus canus)* is widespread throughout the region, particularly on the larger lakes and rivers, as is the black-headed gull *(L. ridibundus)*. The little gull *(L. minutus)*, the world's smallest at only 26cm long, is usually seen gliding and dipping over lakes, picking mosquitoes off the surface in summer.

The common tern *(Sterna hirundo)* may be seen hovering over lakes and wide rivers before plunging in to catch fish. Not as common, despite its name, is the common crane *(Grus grus)*. In autumn, large flocks set off on migration with loud bugling calls, returning the following spring to breed.

USSURILAND

At the far-eastern end of the Trans-Siberian route, in Primorsky Kray, is Ussuriland, an environmentally unique area largely covered by a monsoon forest filled with an exotic array of plants and animals found nowhere else in Russia. The mix of flora and fauna, from tree frogs to tigers, originates from the taiga to the north and also from neighbouring China, Korea and the Himalayas. The topography is dominated by the Sikhote-Alin Range, which runs, spinelike, for more than 1000km parallel to the coast. Unlike the sparsely vegetated woodland floor of the taiga, the forests of Ussuriland have a lush undergrowth, with lianas and vines twined around trunks and draped from branches. But it's the animal life that arouses the most interest – not so much the wolves, sables or Asian black bears (tree-climbing, herbivorous cousins to the more common brown bears, also found here), as Russia's own tiger, the Siberian, or Amur, tiger (see p95).

THE ECOLOGY OF LAKE BAIKAL

Lake Baikal's wildlife is unique. Thanks to warm water entering from vents in the bottom of the lake, and the filtering action of countless millions of minute crustaceans called epishura, the water is exceptionally clear and pure – although unfortunately less so now than formerly (see p99).

Over 1700 species of plants and animals live in the lake (nearly all endemic), including over 200 of shrimp and 80 of flatworm; one of the latter is the world's largest and eats fish! Uniquely for a deep lake, life exists right down to the bottom.

The many kinds of fish include the endemic *omul,* Baikal's main commercial fish. A remarkable species, the *omul* (a white fish of the salmon family) is reputed to emit a shrill cry when caught. It spawns in the Selenga River, but its main food source is the endemic Baikal alga, *melosira,* which has declined drastically because of pollution.

The *golomyanka* – a pink, translucent oilfish with large pectoral fins – is endemic to Baikal. It's unusual in having no scales and being viviparous – giving birth to live young, about 2000 at a time. It is the lake's most common fish, although its numbers have been depleted by pollution. By day it lives in the deep, dark depths, rising at night to near the surface.

Golomyanka is the preferred food of the *nerpa* (Baikal seal, *Phoca siberica*), the world's only freshwater seal, with no relatives nearer than the ringed seal of the Arctic. The *nerpa* is an attractive, gentle creature with unusually large eyes set in a round, flat face, enabling it to hunt down to at least 1500m below the surface – even at night. Despite their size (less than 1.5m, making them the world's smallest seal), they have particularly strong claws for forcing their way through winter ice and keeping their breathing holes open. Pups are born in late winter. At the top of the food chain, Baikal seals have been greatly affected by pollution and are still harvested by local people. According to research by Greenpeace, the seal population hovers around the 60,000 mark – not sufficient for the animal to be endangered but meaning it could be in the future as its under threat from excessive hunting.

There is plenty of other wildlife around the lake. The huge delta, nearly 40km wide, formed by the sediment brought down to the lake by the Selenga River, is a great attraction to wild fowl and wading birds. In summer such beautiful and rare species as the Asiatic dowitcher and white-winged black tern nest there, while in autumn vast numbers of waterfowl from the north use the mudflats and marshes to rest and feed on their migration south – a sort of international bird airport – while many overwinter there, too.

Vast numbers of caddis flies and other insects hatch and swarm on the lake in summer, providing a rich and vital food source for all kinds of wildlife from fish to birds. Despite their lack of visual impact for the Trans-Siberian traveller, these tiny insects, along with the microscopic plant and animal organisms, form the base of the pyramid of wildlife that graces this unique area.

The grey heron *(Ardea cinerea)* is the only waterbird likely to be seen near the train line. Tall and grey, with a long shaggy crest, it will be seen wading cautiously through shallow water or standing hunched on the shores of lakes and rivers. The lapwing *(Vanellus vanellus)* is a widespread, attractive wading bird, easily identified by its wispy crest and, in flight, very rounded wings. The little ringed plover *(Charadrius dubius),* a member of the same wader family, is much smaller, sandy brown above, and white below with a black collar. The dainty yellow wagtail *(Motacilla flava)* is a summer visitor to marshes, water meadows and lake edges throughout the region. The male is mainly yellowish, the female more buff-coloured.

The magnificent white-tailed eagle *(Haliaeetus albicilla)* is easily identified by its huge size, broad wings and short wedge-shaped tail. The equally impressive golden eagle *(Aquila chrysaetos)* is slightly smaller, with a longer tail and, in the adults, a golden-brown head and hind neck.

The common buzzard *(Buteo buteo)* is one of the most numerous and often-seen raptors. Its general shape is not dissimilar to an eagle, but a buzzard is considerably smaller, with a less protruding head. With more angled

Heavy on photographs, *Baikal, Sacred Sea of Siberia* is a pictorial tribute to the great lake with text by travel writer and novelist Peter Matthiessen.

and longer wings than a buzzard, the black kite *(Milvus migrans)* is another soaring raptor. Its most distinctive feature is its long, shallowly forked tail.

The peregrine *(Falco peregrinus)* rises above its intended victim – perhaps a flying duck or pigeon– and with lightning speed (over 150km/h) strikes a deadly blow with its outstretched talons. Like all falcons, the peregrine has rather pointed wings in comparison with those of eagles, buzzards and hawks.

The goshawk *(Accipiter gentiles)* is the largest of the hawks. Capable of catching prey up to the size of a goose (hence its name), surprise is the key to its hunting success; it glides low to the ground, swerving in and out of the trees, hoping to catch its victim unawares. A smaller and more common version of the goshawk is the sparrowhawk *(A. nisus)*.

CANINE FAMILY

Although largely hunted to extinction in Europe, wolves *(Canis lupus)* remain a significant and important part of the ecosystem in Siberia and Mongolia. You're much more likely to hear their unmistakable distant howling than see them, though. (The howl, incidentally, is a contact call to assemble or keep the pack together.) Resembling an Alsatian dog, the wolf is typically greyer with a broader head, smaller ears and pale yellow eyes.

In wolf society there is a strong sense of responsibility, obedience, co-operation and sharing. The species also performs a useful function in keeping populations of other animals under control and should only be destroyed when its activities are in direct conflict with raising domestic animals.

A member of the same family as the wolf, the fox *(Vulpes vulpes)* is much more familiar and easily observed. Apart from being a useful scavenger, an efficient predator of rats and mice, and an aesthetically attractive animal in its own right, the fox is also faithful to the same mate for life.

CERVINE FAMILY

Among the largest and most easily spotted of animals along the route are deer. The roe deer *(Capreolus capreolus)* is the one you'll most likely see out at the edge of the forest and in the fields. Its small size and antlers also enable it to move quickly through dense undergrowth or conceal itself.

The impressive moose, or elk *(Alces alces)*, the largest of the deer family, is common, particularly in the wetter and more open parts of the forest. The males sport antlers up to 2m wide and can stand over 2m high at the shoulders. It's unlikely that you'll see the timid red, or maral deer *(Cervus elaphus)*. The sturdy stag carries impressive antlers, shed annually in early spring. In late summer he sheds the velvety skin that covers the new antlers.

Even rarer is the musk deer *(Moschus moschiferus)*, long hunted for the pungent secretion produced in its abdominal glands and widely used in expensive perfumes. The males don't grow antlers; instead, both sexes have tusks (actually extended upper canines) protruding about 6cm in males, less in females. These are used with deadly effect in the rutting season in December and January.

FELINE FAMILY

The lynx *(Felis lynx)* is rarely seen, but easily identified by its tufted ears and short black-ringed tail. This solitary, nocturnal animal's much-prized coat of fur is reddish or greyish in background colour, more or less covered with indistinct dark spots.

The Siberian tiger *(Panthera tigris altaica)*, also known as the Amur or Manchurian tiger, used to occur throughout the vast forests of Ussuriland and Manchuria, but its valuable fur and taste for domestic animals and humans

SPECIES UNDER THREAT

The largest of all wild cats, the Siberian tiger can measure up to 3.5m in length. In 2005 there were estimated to be between 430 and 530 tigers in Russia's Ussuriland, which is incredible considering it was designated a protected species in 1948, with somewhere between 20 and 30 animals. In 2007 the 81,000-hectare Zov Tigra (Roar of the Tiger) National Park was established in the region, partly to help monitor and safeguard the cats. The following year Vladimir Putin posed in the park with a drowsy tiger that he'd shot with a tranquilliser dart – as good a publicity moment for the prime minister as it was for Russia's conservation success.

Across the border in China the situation is not so rosy – there is thought to be no more than a dozen or so Siberian tigers living there freely. Though protected by Chinese law and recognised as one of the world's most endangered species, the animal's survival hangs by a thread due to urban encroachment on its territory and a lucrative poaching industry. Tiger bones are prized in traditional Chinese medicine, while tiger skins also fetch a hefty price on the black market. One Siberian tiger can earn up to 10 years' income for a Chinese poacher.

In response to the tigers' plight, the Chinese government set up a number of breeding centres, including the Siberian Tiger Park (p300) outside Hāěrbin (Harbin). The centres aim to restore the natural tiger population by breeding and reintroducing them into the wild. However, conservationists stress the need for the tigers to have minimal human contact, and for the centres to emulate as much as possible the life that the tigers will face once released. China's centres, which see busloads of tourists snapping photos of big cats munching on cows and chickens, may instead produce tigers with a taste for livestock, and who will associate humans with feeding time.

has led to its demise over virtually all of its former territory. See the boxed text, above, for more details on these magnificent animals and how you can get an up-close look at them in Hāěrbin's Siberian Tiger Park.

Ussuriland is also home to the Amur leopard, a big cat significantly rarer than the Siberian tiger, though less impressive and consequently less often mentioned. Around 30 of these leopards roam the lands bordering China and North Korea. Sadly, the leopard is also under threat from constant poaching by both Chinese and Russian hunters. For more about this beautiful animal see **ALTA Amur Leopard Conservation** (www.amur-leopard.org).

MUSTELID FAMILY

Mustelids include otters (*Lutra lutra*), stoats and weasels, all of which occur widely in the Trans-Siberian region. Otters, being nocturnal hunters, are best spotted in early morning or dusk on land, where they always eat their fish (or other prey). Well adapted to the bitterly cold conditions of the Siberian winter, otters have no need to hibernate or migrate, so are active and visible year-round.

The largest of the mustelids, the wolverine (*Gulo gulo*) somewhat resembles a long brown badger in shape, but its fur is brown, with lighter patches on its head and flanks. Immensely strong, it can rip the head off its prey. Heads from decapitated animals as large as reindeer have been found high up in conifer trees! Like all fur-bearing animals it has suffered at the hands of trappers. However, this species has got its own back to some extent, as it is well known (and unpopular) for robbing traps.

The sable (*Martes zibellina*) is almost exclusively a Siberian animal. It is confined to the vast stretches of forest east of the Yenisey River and notably in the forests around Lake Baikal. The sable's luxurious dark brown fur almost brought it to the brink of extinction as a result of relentless trapping. Now there are perhaps several thousand in the wild, counting those inside and outside national park areas around Baikal. Though sometimes

In *The River Runs Black*, Elizabeth Economy gives a fascinating account of China's environmental crisis. Her perspective is neither melodramatic nor dull, and very readable.

The website www.wwf china.org has details of the World Wide Fund for Nature (WWF)'s projects for endangered and protected animals in China.

still obtained by trapping and shooting wild animals, most sable furs now come from farmed animals.

RODENT FAMILY

The beaver *(Castor fiber)* is the largest rodent in the northern hemisphere, growing up to a grand 1.3m in length and weighing up to 40kg. Exclusively vegetarian, its favourite food is the bark and branches of waterside trees. It stores branches and other vegetation for the winter in underwater chambers inside its lodge, where the young are also born. These lodges are wonderful feats of engineering, with an elaborate system of interconnected chambers and tunnels for different purposes, with ventilation shafts incorporated.

Though beavers are not frequently seen by the casual observer (nowadays they are rarer because they are being hunted for fur), conspicuous dams and lodges along stretches of river are clear evidence of their presence. They're most common in the taiga areas of Russia between Karelia (north of St Petersburg) and the Ural Mountains.

Other rodents, including muskrats, squirrels, chipmunks, rats, voles and mice, form an integral part of the ecosystem. On a massive scale, they replenish the soil through their regular burrowing and eating routines, and provide an indispensable food source for creatures higher up the food chain.

URSINE FAMILY

In Russian the brown bear *(Ursus arctos)* is called *medved,* reflecting the animal's love of *med* (honey). Unfortunately, bears are not usually held in high esteem by Russian hunters, who kill them even in winter, when specially trained dogs are used to scent out the lairs in which they hibernate. Despite this, and also the high mortality of the cubs who are dependent on their mothers for two or three years, brown bears still occur widely, if sparsely, in Siberia, with several distinguishable subgroups. It is easily the heaviest animal of the area, with males weighing up to 350kg and females up to 250kg. If you see one in the wild, you should stay well clear as they are highly dangerous.

Plants

The taiga is the habitat through which much of the railway passes in Siberia. In some places it is dominated by conifers, particularly Siberian pine *(Pinus sibirica),* in others by mixed conifer and deciduous trees, and in yet other places it's all deciduous. Silver firs, spruce, larch and birch often mingle with maple and aspen, while by the innumerable lakes, ponds and rivers willows and poplars dominate – in June and July the poplars' white fluffy seeds float everywhere like snow.

A particularly beautiful species of birch *(Betula dahurica)* with an unusual dark bark grows near Lake Baikal, while at the far eastern end of the journey, in Ussuriland, you will see the impressively tall white-barked elms *(Ulmus propingua)* and Manchurian firs *(Abies holophylla)* – the latter with pink, purple or orange-buff bark – as well as the more familiar cork, walnut and acacia trees. The almost subtropical climate here is quite different from the harsher conditions further west in Siberia, allowing a lush profusion of exotic flowers.

The leaf litter at the base of trees swarms with invertebrate life, which not only transforms dead vegetation into fertile humus, but also provides food for animals and birds. On the forest floor mosses, lichens, ferns and fungi thrive, including the colourful but deadly fly agaric *(Amanita muscaria).* The dense leaf canopy above inhibits the growth of flowering plants and shrubs, but in more open areas and clearings it is a different picture; in such places flamboyant rhododendrons, azaleas, ryabina, spiraea, asters, daisies, gentians and vetches delight the eye in summer.

Among Lake Baikal's unique species of sponge is one that has been traditionally used to polish silverware.

China is one of the Earth's main centres of origin for plants. It claims more than 17,300 species of endemic seed plants.

Though still extensive, much of the forest has been cleared for agricultural purposes or to sell for timber, so large tracts of cultivated fields and eroded scrubland where trees once stood are a common sight. There are also extensive but natural open, treeless steppes. Of the many kinds of grass that grow wild here the most attractive are the aptly named feather grasses, which rise and ripple in the wind like the surface of the sea.

NATIONAL PARKS & NATURE RESERVES
Russia
Russia has around 100 official nature reserves *(zapovedniki)* and 35 national parks *(natsionalniye parki)*. Along or close by the Trans-Siberian route you'll find several, including Russia's oldest protected reserve, the Barguzin Nature Reserve (p239) within the 269-sq-km Zabaikalsky National Park. These are areas set aside to protect fauna and flora, often endangered or unique species. Some reserves are open to visitors and, unlike in the old days when your ramblings were strictly controlled, today you can sometimes hire the staff to show you around.

Apart from the parks around Lake Baikal, also see p258 for details of the Sikhote-Alin Nature Reserve near Vladivostok and p207 for information on Krasnoyarsk's Stolby Nature Reserve. Also see p224 for details of the Great Baikal Trail project passing through the three national parks and four nature reserves surrounding Lake Baikal.

China
China has an incredibly diverse range of natural escapes scattered across the country. Since the first nature reserve was established in 1956, around 2000 more parks have joined the ranks, protecting about 14% of China's land area, and offering the traveller a wonderful variety of landscapes and diversity of wildlife. Many of the parks are intended for the preservation of endangered animals, while others protect sacred mountains.

Before you pack your hiking gear and binoculars, be prepared to share many of the popular reserves with expanding commercial development. This means pricey hotels, more roads, gondolas, hawkers and busloads of tourists. With a little effort, you can often find a less-beaten path, but don't expect utter tranquillity.

Along the Trans-Manchurian route birdwatchers should consider a visit to the Zhalong Nature Reserve (p303).

Mongolia
The 60 protected areas in Mongolia constitute a very impressive 13.8% of the country (21.52 million hectares). The Ministry of Nature and Environment (MNE) in Mongolia classifies protected areas into four distinct categories. In order of importance:

Strictly Protected Areas Very fragile areas of great importance; hunting, logging and development are strictly prohibited, and there is no established human influence.

National Parks Places of historical and educational interest; fishing and grazing by nomadic people is allowed and parts of the park are developed for ecotourism.

Natural and Historical Monuments Important places of historical and cultural interest; development is allowed within guidelines.

Natural Reserves Less important regions protecting rare species of flora and fauna, and archaeological sites; some development is allowed within certain guidelines.

The strictly protected areas of Bogdkhan Uul, Great Gobi and Uvs Nuur Basin are biosphere reserves included in Unesco's **Man and Biosphere Programme** (www.unesco.org/mab).

The Moscow-based Biodiversity Conservation Center (BCC; www.biodiversity.ru/eng/) is a nonprofit, nongovernmental organisation working for the restoration and protection of pristine nature all over northern Eurasia.

To visit these parks – especially the strictly protected areas, national parks and some natural and historic monuments – you will need a permit. These are provided by the local Special Protected Areas Administration (SPAA) office, or from rangers at the entrances to the parks. The permits are little more than an entrance fee, but they are an important source of revenue for the maintenance of the parks. Entrance fees are set at T3000 per foreigner and T300 per Mongolian (although guides and drivers are often excluded).

Close to Ulaanbaatar, you'll find the Gorkhi-Terelj National Park (p292) and the Bogdkhan Uul Strictly Protected Area containing the temple Mandshir Khiid and the holy mountain Tsetseegün Uul (p290).

The WWF website (www .wwf.mn) has relevant news on Mongolia's environment and includes statistics, data and information on conservation threats.

ENVIRONMENTAL ISSUES
Russia

Obsessed with fulfilling production plans, Siberian managers during the Soviet years showed little regard for the harmful practices of their factories. As a result, the major industrial areas in the Kuznets Basin, Irkutsk and Krasnoyarsk have since been declared environmental catastrophes, with irreparably damaged soil and water. Lake Baikal served as a receptacle for raw waste discharged from a paper mill and towns along its shore.

The USSR's demise was an unexpected boon to Russia's environment, as many of the centrally planned – and massively polluting – industries collapsed. However, as the economy has recovered, concerns have resurfaced about environmental damage, particularly in relation to the country's extraction of oil and gas. Higher standards of living have put many more cars on the road- and solid-waste generation has substantially increased.

Russia has the world's largest natural-gas reserves, the second-largest coal reserves and the eighth-largest oil reserves – just as well, since it's the world's third-largest energy consumer.

At the same time, environmental awareness is growing in Russia. In June 2008 President Dmitry Medvedev signed a decree ordering the government to develop legislation that encourages efficiency in electricity, construction, housing and transportation. Tax cuts for environmentally conscious companies are being considered, environmental education at schools is being introduced, and on 5 June 2008 Russia observed its first Day of the Environmentalist. The Natural Resources and Environment Ministry is working on legislation that would toughen up rules on pollution emissions and increase fines for environmental offenders. Enforcing these and existing laws is another thing entirely.

Pressure groups such as Greenpeace Russia have managed to mount successful campaigns and there are several ways, as a visitor, that you can get involved in helping clean up and preserve Mother Russia (see p31).

AIR POLLUTION

The Oslo-based Bellona Foundation (www.bellona .org) is a respected environmental organisation tackling nuclear waste and other pollution problems in Russia.

According to a 2007 report by Russia's Natural Resources and Environment Ministry, air pollution is either 'high' or 'extremely high' in 69% of Russian cities, affecting over half the population.

One positive step came in 2004 when Russia ratified the Kyoto Protocol. Its greenhouse-gas-emission targets were set based on levels measured in 1990 during the polluting Soviet times, and since then the actual emissions have fallen by around one third. Should the quotas market ever start functioning, Russia is currently in the position of being able to earn itself billions of dollars by selling carbon credits.

WATER POLLUTION

Russia's network of antique pipes and lax safety standards result in tap water that is, at best, tainted with rust and large doses of chlorine, and at worst, positively harmful. As a result many locals have turned to bottled water, creating a litter problem.

BAIKAL'S ENVIRONMENTAL ISSUES

Home to an estimated 60,000 *nerpa* seals, Lake Baikal is beautiful, pristine, and drinkably pure in most areas. As it holds an astonishing 80% of Russia's fresh water, environmentalists are keen to keep things that way. In the 1960s, despite the pressures of the Soviet system, it was the construction of Baikal's first (and only) lakeside industrial plant that galvanised Russia's first major green movement. That plant, the Baikalsk paper-pulp factory, is still monitored today while the owners argue over a costly, World Bank–assisted clean-up plan.

These days some two-thirds of Baikal's shoreline falls within parks or reserves, so similar factories would not be allowed. But the ecosystem extends beyond the lake itself. Another challenge includes polluted inflows from the Selenga River, which carries much of Mongolia's untreated waste into the lake. The most contentious of recent worries is the US$16 billion Eastern Siberia oil pipeline from Tayshet to the Pacific coast. The route deliberately loops north, avoiding the lakeshore itself. Nonetheless, when finished, some 80 million tonnes of oil a year will flow across the lake's northern water-catchment area, an area highly prone to seismic activity. Environmentalists fear that a quake-cracked pipeline could spill vast amounts of oil into the Baikal feedwaters.

A more recent, and potentially ominous, development was the July 2008 exploration of the bottom of Lake Baikal by a team of Russian submarine explorers (the same group that rather comically planted a Russian flag on the bottom of the Arctic Ocean in 2007). Some claim the team was secretly looking for oil reserves, prompting local environmentalists to fear the worst.

For more information see the websites of regional ecogroups **Baikal Wave** (www.baikalwave .eu.org/eng.html) and **Baikal Watch** (www.earthisland.org/baikal/) and the wonderful **Baikal Web World** (www.bww.irk.ru), which has lots about the wildlife, history and legends of the lake.

The Volga River in particular is severely polluted by industrial waste, sewage, pesticides and fertilisers. In 2008, the *Chicago Tribune* described the river as possibly Russia's 'most abused waterway'. A chain of hydroelectric dams along the river blocks the spawning routes of and slows the current, which encourages fish parasites.

The most documented instance of water pollution has centred on Lake Baikal (above).

RADIOACTIVITY & NUCLEAR WASTE

Maintenance, and security against terrorist attacks, have improved in recent years at Russia's 10 nuclear power plants, all managed by the federal agency Rosenergoatom. Still, many of the reactors at these plants are similar to the flawed ones that operated at the Chornobyl nuclear power plant in Ukraine, and accidents and incidents continue to occur across Russia.

Post-*glasnost* (the free-expression aspect of the Gorbachev reforms) disclosures have revealed that the Russian navy secretly dumped nuclear waste, including used reactors from submarines, in the Sea of Japan (off Vladivostok) and in the Arctic Ocean.

Go to Greenpeace Russia (www.greenpeace.org /russia/en) for more details on the environmental problems being faced by Russia.

LOGGING & FOREST FIRES

Logging companies from China, Japan, South Korea and the USA, in partnership with Russia, are queuing up to clearfell the Siberian forests. According to the Federal Agency for Forestry, illegal logging in the Zabaikalsky region (between Lake Baikal and the Russian Far East) accounts for more than 2 million cu metres a year. The agency warned that the region could be stripped of wood reserves in five years if nothing is done to stop the criminal trade.

In recent years, huge fires have swept uncontrollably through Russia's forests too, causing much damage. Because these forests act as a major carbon sink, removing an estimated 500 million tonnes of carbon from the atmosphere each year, their destruction is cause for global concern.

OIL & NATURAL GAS ISSUES

The oil and gas industry, through greed, inattention and a failing infrastructure, has been perhaps Russia's greatest environmental desecrator. The Ob River, which flows across Russia's major oil fields on the Western Siberian Plain, has been subject to oil spills and pollution for decades.

The delicate tundra ecosystem has been destabilised by the construction of buildings, roads and railways and the extraction of underground resources. At the mouth of the Ob, parts of the low-lying Yamal Peninsula, which contain some of the world's biggest gas reserves, have been crumbling into the sea as the permafrost melts near gas installations. The traditional hunting and reindeer-herding way of life of Siberian native peoples has been further impeded by gas pipelines blocking migration routes.

Green Cross International (www.gci.ch), based on an idea of ex-president Mikhail Gorbachev, aims to find solutions to ecological and environmental issues and problems that span national boundaries.

China

As a developing country experiencing rapid industrialisation, it's not surprising that China has some hefty environmental issues to contend with. Unfortunately, China's huge population makes its environmental plight infinitely bigger than that of other nations. Air pollution, deforestation, endangered species, and rural and industrial waste are all taking their toll.

The World Bank has reported that 16 of the 20 most polluted cities in the world are Chinese. The biggest source of this pollution is coal. It provides some 70% of China's energy needs and around 900 million tonnes of coal go up in smoke each year. The result is immense damage to air and water quality, agriculture and human health, with acid rain falling on about 30% of the country.

See http://china.org.cn, a Chinese government site, for a link to a page covering environmental issues.

Across the north of China, rampaging natural fires in coal fields are believed to consume more than 200 million tonnes of coal each year, further exacerbating China's contribution to global warming.

The build-up to the 2008 Olympics and China's entry into the World Trade Organization have seen the country change its policy of 'industrial catch-up first, environmental clean-up later' to one of tidying up its environmental act now. Nevertheless, some analysts continue to point to an impending

---

THE GREEN WALL OF CHINA

If you visit Běijīng in spring and experience the sandstorms that send residents rushing around with plastic bags over their heads, you may not be surprised to hear that the city may one day be swallowed up by the Gobi Desert. The desert is only 150km away, and the winds are blowing the sands towards the capital at a rate of 2km a year, with 30m dunes closing in. These massive dust storms have left entire towns abandoned and environmental refugees numbering in the millions. They've also brought about bizarre weather effects, such as 'black winds' and 'mud rains'. Experts blame the problem on overgrazing and deforestation; every month 200 sq km of arable land in China becomes a desert.

In an attempt to fend off the desert, China's government has pledged US$6.8 billion to build a green wall between Běijīng and the sands; at 5700km long, it will be longer than the Great Wall of China. Under the scheme, the government pays farmers to plant trees and is claiming a partial victory despite ongoing problems, such as trees dying, over-irrigation, erosion and corruption. According to **Global Access China** (www.gac-china.com) the area of desertification, which is 2.62 million sq km or about 27% of China's land territory, far exceeds the nation's total farmland. Although the rate of desertification has been curbed in some areas, it still is expanding at a rate of more than 3000 sq km every year. But while the frequency of sand storms has apparently decreased since the 1990s, their intensity has increased: one storm in 2006 dumped an estimated 330,000 tonnes of dust on the capital. In 2006 China agreed to work with neighbouring countries to combat desertification in Northeast Asia.

environmental catastrophe, fearing that the efforts could well be too little, too late. Like Russia, the impact of China's environmental problems unfortunately doesn't stop at its borders (see opposite).

Mongolia

The natural environment of Mongolia remains in good condition compared with that of many Western countries. The country's small population and nomadic subsistence economy have been its environmental salvation.

However, it does have its share of problems. Communist-era production quotas put pressure on grasslands to yield more crops and support more livestock than was sustainable. The rise in the number of herders and livestock through the 1990s has wreaked havoc on the grasslands; some 70% of pasture is degraded and around 80% of plant species near village centres have disappeared.

Forest fires, nearly all of which are caused by careless human activity, are common during the windy spring season. Other threats to the land include mining (there are over 300 mines), which has polluted 28 river basins. The huge Oyu Tolgoi mine in Ömnögov will require the use of 360L of water *per second,* which environmentalists say might not be sustainable. Neighbouring China's insatiable appetite for minerals and gas is prompting Mongolia to open up new mines, but the bigger threat is China's hunt for the furs, meat and body parts of endangered animals. Chinese demand has resulted in a 75% decline in the number of marmots and an 85% drop in the number of saiga antelope.

Urban sprawl, along with a demand for wood to build homes and to use as heating and cooking fuel, is slowly reducing the forests. This destruction of the forests has also lowered river levels, especially the Tuul Gol near Ulaanbaatar. In recent years the Tuul Gol has actually gone dry in the spring months due to land mismanagement and improper water use.

Large-scale infrastructure projects are further cause for concern. Conservationists are worried about the new 'Millennium Road', which is being built before the finalisation of environmental-impact studies. Its completion is likely to increase mining and commerce inside fragile ecosystems. The eastern grasslands, one of the last great open spaces in Asia, will come under particular threat.

Air pollution is becoming a serious problem, especially in Ulaanbaatar. At the top of the Zaisan Memorial in the capital, a depressing layer of dust and smoke from the city's three thermal power stations can be seen hovering over the city. This layer is often appalling in winter, when all homes are continuously burning fuel and the power stations are working overtime. Ulaanbaatar has also suffered from acid rain, and pollution is killing fish in the nearby Tuul Gol in central Mongolia.

Mongolia's Wild Heritage by Christopher Finch, written in collaboration with the Mongolian Ministry of Nature and Environment, is an outstanding book on Mongolia's fragile ecology, along with excellent photos.

St Petersburg
Санкт Петербург

It may not officially be part of the Trans-Siberian route, but there's every reason to consider starting or finishing your journey in St Petersburg. Beautiful, complex and imperious, with a hedonistic, creative temperament, the city that Peter the Great ordered built on an uninhabited swamp has matured into the ultimate Russian diva. Constantly in need of repair and, with her devil-may-care party attitude, a prime candidate for rehab, Piter, as she's affectionately known by locals, retains the power to seduce all who gaze upon her grand palaces, glittering spires and gilded domes.

Visual arias come naturally to Europe's fourth-largest city. The Neva River and surrounding canals reflect unbroken facades of handsome 18th- and 19th-century buildings, housing a spellbinding collection of cultural storehouses, culminating in the incomparable Hermitage. It's easy to imagine how such an environment, warts and all, was the inspiration for many of Russia's greatest artists including the writers Pushkin, Gogol and Dostoevsky, and musical maestros such as Rachmaninoff, Tchaikovsky and Shostakovich.

'St Petersburg is Russia, but it is not Russian.' The opinion of Nicholas II, the empire's last tsar, on his one-time capital still resonates. St Petersburg remains a 'window on the West', a fascinating hybrid where one moment you can be clapping along to fun Russian folk music in a baroque hall, the next grooving on the dance floor of an underground club. The long summer days of the White Nights season are particularly special; this is when the fountains flow, parks and gardens burst into colour and Piter's citizens hit the streets to party. However, the ice-cold winter has its own magic and is the perfect time for warming body and soul in all those museums and palaces.

HIGHLIGHTS

- Lose yourself amid the artistic treasures and imperial interiors of the **Hermitage** (p105)
- Cruise the **canals** (p114) for a different perspective on the city's architecture and pretty bridges
- Enjoy a world-class opera or ballet performance at the beautiful **Mariinsky Theatre** (p117)
- Admire the Grand Cascade's symphony of fountains at **Petrodvorets** (p114)
- Learn about Russia's train history at one of the city's two **railway museums** (p112) and marvel at the old-world glamour of elegant **Vitebsky vokzal** (see the boxed text, p113)

Hermitage
Canals ★ ★ Vitebsky Vokzal
Mariinsky ★ ★ Railway Museums
Theatre
ST PETERSBURG
★
Petrodvorets

- TELEPHONE CODE: 812 | - POPULATION: 4.6 MILLION

HISTORY

Starting with the Peter & Paul Fortress, founded on the marshy estuary of the Neva River in 1703, Peter the Great and his successors commissioned a city built to grand design by mainly European architects. By the early 19th century St Petersburg had firmly established itself as Russia's cultural heart. But at the same time as writers, artists and musicians, such as Pushkin, Turgenev and, later, Tchaikovsky and Dostoevsky, lived in and were inspired by the city, political and social problems were on the rise.

Industrialisation brought a flood of poor workers and associated urban squalor to St Petersburg. Revolution against the monarchy was first attempted in the short-lived coup of 14 December 1825. The leaders (who included members of the aristocracy and who became known as the Decembrists) were banished to the outer edges of the empire (see p217).

The next revolution was in 1905, sparked by the 'Bloody Sunday' of 9 January when more than a hundred people were killed and hundreds more were injured after troops fired on a crowd petitioning the tsar outside the Winter Palace. The tsar's government limped on, until Vladimir Lenin and his Bolshevik followers took advantage of Russia's disastrous involvement in WWI to instigate the third successful revolution in 1917. Again, St Petersburg (renamed a more Russian-sounding Petrograd in 1914) was at the forefront of the action.

To break with the tsarist past, the seat of government was moved back to Moscow, and St Petersburg was renamed Leningrad after the first communist leader's death in 1924. The city – by virtue of its location, three-million-plus population and industry – remained one of Russia's most important, thus putting it on the frontline during WWII. For 872 days Leningrad was besieged by the Germans, and one million perished in horrendous conditions.

During the 1960s and 1970s Leningrad's bohemian spirit burned bright, fostering the likes of dissident poet Joseph Brodsky and underground rock groups such as Kino and Akvarium with its lead singer Boris Grebenshchikov. As the Soviet Union came tumbling down, the city renamed itself St Petersburg in 1991. Millions of roubles were spent on restoration for the city's tricentenary celebrations and St Petersburg looks better now than probably at any other time in its history, which is a source of great pride to two local boys made good: President Dmitry Medvedev and former president and current prime minister Vladimir Putin.

ORIENTATION

St Petersburg sprawls across and around the delta of the Neva River, which divides into many branches creating several large islands as it nears the Gulf of Finland.

If you arrive by train from Moscow, your entry point will be Moskovsky vokzal (Moscow Station) at the eastern end of Nevsky pr, St Petersburg's main thoroughfare, which heads west for about 3km through the heart of the city towards the south bank of the Neva and the Winter Palace. All trains from the Baltic countries and Eastern Europe arrive at Vitebsky vokzal (Vitebsk Station), 2km southwest of Moscow Station. Trains from Helsinki end up either at Finlyandsky vokzal (Finland Station) or at Ladozhsky vokzal (Ladoga Station), both across the Neva in an area known as the Vyborg Side.

Other main areas north of the Neva are Vasilevsky Island, on the westernmost side of the city – at its eastern end is the Strelka (Tongue of Land), where many of the city's early buildings stand – and the Petrograd Side, a cluster of delta islands marked by the Peter & Paul Fortress.

MAPS

Dom Knigi (below) has the best map selection, including maps of transport routes and several street directories.

INFORMATION
Bookshops

Anglia (Map p110; ☎ 579 8284; nab reki Fontanki 30; ◷ 10am-7pm; Ⓜ Gostiny Dvor) English-language bookshop.

Dom Knigi (Map p110; ☎ 448 2355; www.spbdk.ru, in Russian; Nevsky pr 28; ◷ 9am-midnight; Ⓜ Nevsky Prospekt)

Emergency

All of the following numbers have Russian-speaking operators. If you need to make a police report and don't speak Russian, first contact the Tourist Information Centre (p105).

Ambulance ☎ 03
Fire ☎ 01
Gas Leak ☎ 04
Police ☎ 02

Internet Access

Internet cafes and wi-fi access are common across the city. For wi-fi, many places use either the **Peterstar** (www.peterstar.com, in Russian), **Quantum** (www.wifizone.ru) or **Yandex** (http://wifi .yandex.ru, in Russian) networks; the last is free. Internet access cards can be bought at computer shops and kiosks.

Café Max (Map p110; ☎ 273 6655; Nevsky pr 90/92; per hr R40; ☺ 24hr; Ⓜ Mayakovskaya) Wi-fi available here. Also has a branch in the Hermitage.

FM Club (Map p110; ☎ 764 3674; ul Dostoevskogo 6A; per hr R35; ☺ 10am-8pm; Ⓜ Vladimirskaya)

Quo Vadis? (Map p110; ☎ 333 0708; Nevsky pr 66; per hr R100; ☺ 24hr; Ⓜ Mayakovskaya) Enter from Liteyny pr.

Internet Resources

www.encspb.ru The St Petersburg Encyclopaedia is encyclopaedic in its coverage of art, architecture, geography, society, economy and more.

www.saint-petersburg.com One of the best places to start. There's information on sights, current events and listings, a virtual city tour, online hotel booking, and a great, up-to-date travellers' message board.

www.visit-petersburg.com The city's tourist information bureau's site is best used for its downloadable walking tours. Sadly, other information can be inaccurate, out-of-date or too brief to be of much use.

www.yell.ru/spbeng Yellow Pages for St Petersburg.

Laundry

Stirka (Map p110; ☎ 314 5371; Kazanskaya ul 26; ☺ 11am-11pm; Ⓜ Sadovaya/Sennaya Ploshchad) Cafebar and laundrette – what a good idea! A 5kg wash costs R140. The dryer is R90.

Media

The following English-language publications are available free at many hotels, hostels, restaurants and bars across the city.

In Your Pocket (www.inyourpocket.com/city/st_peters burg.html) Monthly listings booklet with useful up-to-date information and short features.

Pulse (www.pulse.ru) Slick colour monthly with fun features and reviews.

St Petersburg Times (www.sptimes.ru) Published every Tuesday and Friday (when it has an indispensable listings and arts review section), this plucky little newspaper has been fearlessly telling it like it really is for over 15 years.

Medical Services

The clinics listed here are open 24 hours and have English-speaking staff.

American Medical Clinic (Map pp106-7; ☎ 740 2090; www.amclinic.ru; nab reki Moyki 78; Ⓜ Sadovaya)

Medem (Map p110; ☎ 336 3333; www.medem.ru; 6 Marata ul; Ⓜ Mayakovskaya)

PHARMACIES

Look for the sign *apteka*, or the usual green cross to find a pharmacy.

36.6 Pharmacy (http://spb.366.ru, in Russian) Gorokhovaya ul 16 (Ⓜ Sadovaya); Liteyny pr 41 (Ⓜ Mayakovskaya); Zagorodny pr 6/8 (Ⓜ Vladimirskaya) A chain of 24-hour pharmacies around the city.

Apteka Petrofarm (Map p110; ☎ 314 5401; Nevsky pr 22; ☺ 24hr; Ⓜ Nevsky Prospekt)

ST PETERSBURG IN...

One Day

Take a tour of the **Hermitage** (opposite). Move on to the polychromatic **Church of the Saviour on Spilled Blood** (p108) after lunch, combining a visit here with a stroll down **Nevsky Prospekt** (see Walking Tour, p113). Hop on a boat for an early evening **cruise** (p114). If you're quick, you could also squeeze in a visit to **St Isaac's Cathedral** (p109), climbing its colonnade for a bird's-eye view of the city. Cap off the day with dinner at **Teplo** (p116).

Two Days

Cross the Neva River to explore the **Peter & Paul Fortress** (p113). Continue around to the **Strelka** (p112) to see the museums there, or just to enjoy the view. In the afternoon, take a masterclass in Russian art at the splendid **Russian Museum** (p109) or, if contemporary art is more your bag, drop by **Pushkinskaya 10** or **Loft Project Floors** (p112).

Four Days

Following on from the previous two days, spend a day each exploring the imperial parks and palaces at **Petrodvorets** and **Tsarskoe Selo** (p114). Cap off your trip with a performance at the **Mariinsky Theatre** (p117), combined with dinner at **Sadko** (p116).

Money

ATMs are ubiquitous and there are currency-exchange offices all the way along and around Nevsky pr.

Post

Post office branches are scattered throughout the city. All the major air-courier services are available in St Petersburg.

Central post office (Map pp106-7; ☎ 312 8302; Pochtamtskaya ul 9; ⏰ 24hr; Ⓜ Sadovaya/Sennaya Ploshchad) Worth visiting just to admire its recently renovated, elegant Style Moderne interior. The express mail service EMS Garantpost is available here.

Telephone

Local *telefonnaya karta* (phonecards) are available from shops, kiosks and metro stations and can be used to make local, national and international calls from any phone. Using a call centre (see p339) is better value for international calls – look for the Mezhdunarodny Telefon sign.

You can buy a local SIM card at any mobile-phone shop, such as **Dixis** (www.dixis.ru, in Russian) or **Euroset** (www.spb.euroset.ru), both chains with several branches across the city, from as little as R150, including R100 credit. See p338 for information on the main mobile providers.

Tourist Information

From May to September the city sponsors 'angels' (ie guides) who roam Nevsky pr, Palace Sq and the like, ready to assist tourists.

City Tourist Information Centre (www.visit-petersburg .com) airport booths (⏰ 10am-7pm Mon-Fri); Hermitage booth (Map p110, Dvortsovaya pl 12, ⏰ 10am-7pm, Ⓜ Nevsky Prospekt); Sadovaya ul (Map p110; ☎ 310 8267; Sadovaya ul 14/52; ⏰ 10am-7pm Mon-Sat; Ⓜ Gostiny Dvor) Sadovaya ul is home to the main centre. The English-speaking staff are vague about most things but will do their best to help.

Travel Agencies

All the following agencies have English-speaking staff.

Budget Travel (www.budget-travel.spb.ru) Apart from visa support, transfers and buying transport tickets, this small agency also offers inexpensive guides and, hopefully, will have found new premises for its budget hostel by the time of publication.

City Realty (Map p110; ☎ 570 6342; www.cityrealty.ru; Muchnoy per 2; ⏰ 10am-6pm; Ⓜ Nevsky Prospekt) Can arrange all types of visas (tourist visas from US$25) including business ones, as well as accommodation and transport tickets. Very reliable.

Ost-West Kontaktservice (Map p110; ☎ 327 3416; www.ostwest.com; Nevsky pr 105; ⏰ 10am-6pm Mon-Fri; Ⓜ Ploshchad Vosstaniya) The multilingual staff here can find you an apartment to rent, and organise tours and tickets.

Parallel Sixty (☎ 928 0739; www.parallel60.ru; Room 415, ul Avtogennaya 6; ⏰ 10am-6pm; Ⓜ Elizarovskaya) Friendly and efficient agency that can arrange visas, accommodation and tours. It also runs VB Excursions (p115).

Sindbad Travel (Map p110; ☎ 332 2020; www.sindbad .ru, in Russian; 2-ya Sovetskaya ul 12; ⏰ 9am-10pm Mon-Fri, 10am-6pm Sat & Sun; Ⓜ Ploshchad Vosstaniya) A genuine Western-style, discount air-ticket office, staffed by friendly knowledgeable people. It also sells train tickets and ISIC/ITIC/IYTC cards and can book youth hostel accommodation through the IBN system.

DANGERS & ANNOYANCES

Watch out for pickpockets, particularly along Nevsky pr around Griboedova Canal and in crowded places such as theatres and cinemas. Non-Caucasians should be aware that St Petersburg is notorious for race-related violent attacks. Avoid wandering around alone late at night or venturing out to the suburbs solo at any time.

Every year in early spring and during winter thaws, several people die when hit by giant icicles falling from rooftops and balconies; take care to make sure one of these monsters is not dangling above your head. From May to September mosquitoes are another nightmare.

Never drink unboiled tap water in St Petersburg as it could contain harmful bacteria, such as *Giardia Lamblia*, a parasite that plays havoc with your stomach and bowels.

SIGHTS

The following are the major sights; for more information, see Lonely Planet's *Russia & Belarus* or *St Petersburg City Guide*.

The Hermitage & Dvortsovaya Ploshchad

Mainly set in the magnificent Winter Palace, the **State Hermitage** (Map p110; ☎ 571 3465; www .hermitagemuseum.org; Dvortsovaya pl 2; adult R350, ISIC cardholders & under 17yr free; ⏰ 10.30am-6pm Tue-Sat, to 5pm Sun; Ⓜ Nevsky Prospekt) fully lives up to its sterling reputation. You can be absorbed by its treasures for days and still come out wishing for more. The following are the must sees:

The Jordan Staircase Directly ahead when you pass through the main entrance inside the Winter Palace

CENTRAL ST PETERSBURG

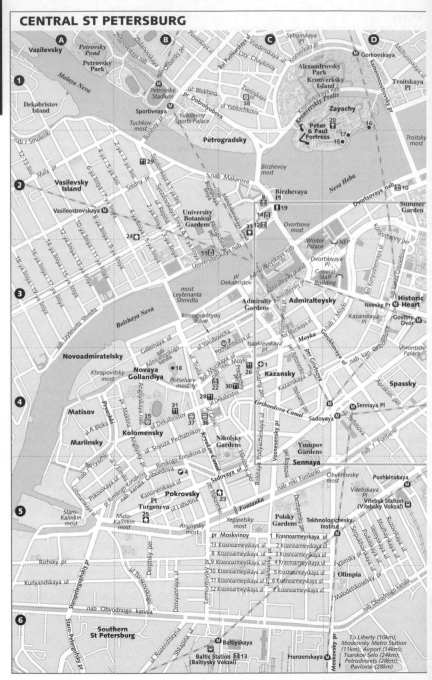

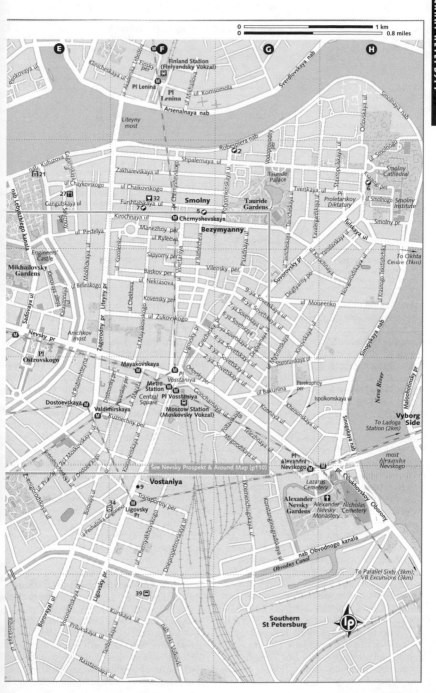

INFORMATION
American Medical Clinic
Американская Медицинская
Клиника.................................. **1** C4
Belarusian Consulate
Консульство Беларусии **2** G2
Central Post Office Почтамт...........**3** C3
Chinese Consulate
Консульство Китая **4** B5
German Consulate
Консульство Германии **5** F2
UK Consulate
Консульство Великобритании ...**6** H2
US Consulate Консульство США.. **7** F2

SIGHTS & ACTIVITIES
Central Naval Museum
Центральный военно-морской
музей **8** C2
Loft Project Floors **9** F5
Marble Palace
Мраморный дворец **10** D2
Menshikov Palace
Дворец Меншикова **11** B3
Museum of Anthropology &
Ethnography Музей
антропологии и этнографии..... **12** C2

Museum of Railway Technology
Музей Железнодорожной
Технологии **13** C6
Museum of Zoology
Музей зоологии **14** C2
Naryshkin Bastion
Нарышкинский бастион **15** D2
Nevskaya Panorama
Невская панорама **16** D1
Nevsky Gate
Невские ворота........................... **17** D2
New Holland
Новая Голландия **18** B4
Rostral Columns
Ростральные колонны **19** C2
SS Peter and Paul Cathedral
Собор св Петра и Павла **20** D1
Summer Palace
Летний дворец **21** E2
Yusupov Palace
Юсуповский дворец.................... **22** B4

SLEEPING 🛏
Alexander House
Дом Александра..........................**23** C5
Art Hotel Terezinni...........................**24** B2
Seven Bridges Hostel **25** B5

EATING 🍴
Café Idiot **26** C4
Olyushka & Russkye Bliny
Олюшка и Русские Блины **27** E2
Sadko Садко **28** B4
Stolle Штолле **29** B2
Stolle Штолле **30** C4
Stolle Штолле **31** B4

DRINKING 🍷
City Bar Сити Бар...........................**32** F2
Die Kneipe Град Петров **33** C2

ENTERTAINMENT 🎭
Griboedov Грибоедов.................... **34** F5
Mariinsky Concert Hall
Мариинский Концертный зал..**35** B4
Mariinsky Theatre
Мариинский театр **36** B4
New Mariinsky Theatre
Новый Мариинский театр **37** B4
Underground Club
Тунель...**38** C1

TRANSPORT
Avtovokzal No 2 (Main Bus Station)
Автовокзал Но 2............................**39** F6

Rooms 178–98 Imperial stateroom and apartments including the Malachite Hall, Nicholas Hall, Armorial Hall and Hall of St George
Room 204 The Pavilion Hall
Rooms 207–238 Italian art, 13th to 18th centuries
Room 229 Raphael and his disciples
Rooms 239–40 Spanish art, 16th to 18th centuries
Rooms 244–47 Flemish art, 17th century
Rooms 249–52 & 254 Dutch art, 17th century
Room 271 The Imperial family's cathedral

Concentrate the rest of your time on rooms 333–50 for late-19th-century and early-20th-century European art, including works by Matisse and Picasso.

The museum's main entrance is on Dvortsovaya pl (Palace Sq), one of the city's most impressive and historic spaces. Stand back to admire the palace and the central 47.5m **Alexander Column**, named after Alexander I and commemorating the 1812 victory over Napoleon. Enclosing the square's south side is the **General Staff Building** (Map p110; ☎ 314 8260; www.hermitagemuseum.org/html_En/03/hm3_11.html; Dvortsovaya pl 6-8; adult/student R200/free; ⏰ 10am-6pm Tue-Sun; Ⓜ Nevsky Prospekt), which has a branch of the Hermitage in its east wing.

Queues for tickets, particularly from May to September, can be horrendous. The museum can also be very busy on the first Thursday of the month when admission is free for everyone. Apart from getting in line an hour or

so before the museum opens or going late in the day when the lines are likely to be shorter, there are a few strategies you can use. The best is to book your ticket online through the Hermitage's website: US$17.95 gets you admission to the main Hermitage buildings, plus use of a camera or camcorder, and US$25.95 is for the two-day ticket to all the Hermitage's collections in the city (except the storage facility). You'll be issued with a voucher that allows you to jump the queue and go straight to the ticket booth.

Joining a tour is another way to avoid queuing. These whiz round the main sections in about 1½ hours but at least provide an introduction to the place in English. It's easy to 'lose' the group and stay on until closing time. To book a tour call the museum's **excursions office** (☎ 571 8446; ⏰ 11am-1pm & 2-4pm); staff there will tell you when they are running tours in English, German or French and when to turn up.

Church of the Saviour on Spilled Blood

This multidomed dazzler of a **church** (Spas na Krovi; Map p110; ☎ 315 1636; http://eng.cathedral.ru/saviour; Konyushennaya pl; adult/student R300/150; ⏰ 11am-7pm Thu-Tue Oct-Apr, 10am-8pm Thu-Tue May-Sep; Ⓜ Nevsky Prospekt), partly modelled on St Basil's in Moscow, was built between 1883 and 1907 on the spot where Alexander II was assassinated in 1881 (hence its gruesome name).

The interior's 7000 sq metres of mosaics fully justify the entrance fee.

Russian Museum

Facing onto the elegant pl Iskusstv (Art's Sq) is the former Mikhailovsky Palace, now the **Russian Museum** (Russy Muzey; Map p110; ☎ 595 4248; www.rusmuseum.ru; Inzhenernaya ul 4; adult/student R350/150; ☼ 10am-5pm Mon, to 6pm Wed-Sun; Ⓜ Gostiny Dvor), housing one of the country's finest collections of Russian art. After the Hermitage you may feel you have had your fill of art, but try your utmost to make some time for this gem of a museum.

The museum owns three other city palaces (see www.rusmuseum.ru), all worth visiting if you have time, where permanent and temporary exhibitions are held: the **Marble Palace** (Mramorny Dvorets; Map pp106–7; ☎ 312 9196; Millionnaya ul 5; adult/student R350/150; ☼ 10am-5pm Wed-Mon; Ⓜ Nevsky Prospekt); the **Mikhailovsky Castle** (Mikhaylovsky Zamok; Map p110; ☎ 595 4248; Sadovaya ul 2; adult/student R350/150; ☼ 10am-5pm Mon, to 6pm Wed-Sun; Ⓜ Gostiny Dvor), also known as the Engineer's Castle; and the **Stroganov Palace** (Map p110; ☎ 312 9054; Nevsky pr 17; adult/student R350/150; ☼ 10am-5pm Tue-Sun; Ⓜ Nevsky Prospekt). A ticket for R600, available at each palace, covers entrance to them all within a 24-hour period.

St Isaac's Cathedral

The golden dome of this **cathedral** (Isaakievsky Sobor; Map p110; ☎ 315 9732; http://eng.cathedral.ru; Isaakievskaya pl; adult/student R300/150; ☼ 10am-8pm Thu-Mon, closed last Mon of the month; Ⓜ Sadovaya/Sennaya Ploshchad) dominates the city skyline. Its lavish interior is open as a museum, but many visitors just buy the separate ticket to climb the 262 steps up to the **colonnade** (adult/student R150/100; ☼ 10am-7pm Thu-Mon, closed last Mon of the month) around the dome's drum to take in the panoramic views.

Summer Garden

St Petersburg's loveliest park, the **Summer Garden** (Letny Sad; Map pp106–7; admission free; ☼ 10am-10pm May-Sep, to 8pm Oct–mid-Apr; Ⓜ Gostiny Dvor) is a great place to relax. In its northeast corner is the modest, two-storey **Summer Palace** (Muzey Letny Dvorets Petra 1; ☎ 314 0374; adult/student R300/150; ☼ 10am-5pm Wed-Mon early May–early Nov), built for Peter from 1710 to 1714. Inside it's stocked with early-18th-century furnishings of limited appeal.

Sheremetyev Palace

Facing the Fontanka Canal, the splendid Sheremetyev Palace (1750–55) houses two lovely museums. The **Museum of Music** (Map p110; ☎ 272 3898; www.theatremuseum.ru/eng/index_eng.html;

NEVSKY PROSPEKT & AROUND

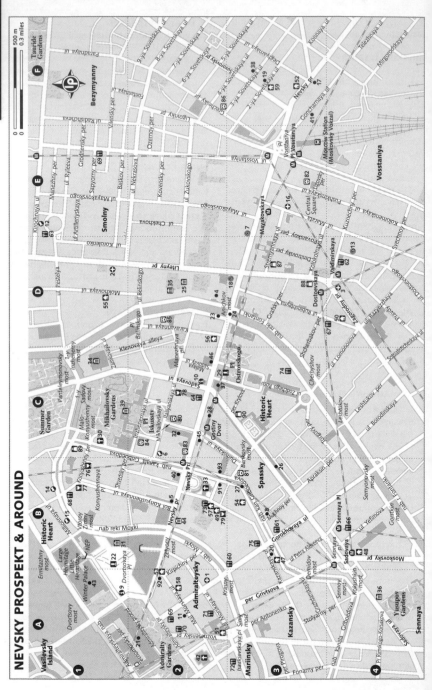

nab reki Fontanki 34; adult/student R180/90; noon-6pm Wed-Sun; M Gostiny Dvor) contains a lovely collection of beautifully decorated instruments. Upstairs the palace rooms have been wonderfully restored; you get a great sense of how cultured life must have been here.

In a separate wing of the palace, reached from Liteyny pr, is the charming **Anna**

Akhmatova Museum at the Fountain House (Map p110; ☎ 579 7239; www.akhmatova.spb.ru; Liteyny pr 53; adult/student R120/80; 10.30am-6.30pm Tue & Thu-Sun, 1-9pm Wed, closed last Wed of month; M Mayakovskaya), filled with mementoes of the poet and her family, all persecuted during Soviet times. Admission also includes the Joseph Brodsky 'American Study'. The poet did not live here, but his connection with Akhmatova was strong. His office has been recreated, complete with furniture and other 'artefacts' from his adopted home in Massachusetts.

Yusupov Palace

In a city of glittering palaces, the sumptuous interiors of the **Yusupov Palace** (Map pp106–7; ☎ 314 9883; www.yusupov-palace.ru; nab reki Moyki 94; adult/student R500/280; ⏰ 11am–5pm; Ⓜ Sadovaya/Sennaya Ploshchad) more than hold their own. Best known as the place where Rasputin met his untimely end, the palace sports a series of sumptuously decorated rooms culminating in a gilded jewel box of a theatre, where performances are still held. Admission includes an audio tour in English or several other languages. Places are limited to 20 daily for each of the two English-language 'Murder of Rasputin' tours (adult/student R300/150).

Railway Museums

Every child's and railway enthusiast's dream will be realised at the **Museum of Railway Transport** (Map p110; ☎ 315 1476; http://railroad.ru/cmrt, in Russian; Sadovaya ul 50; adult/student R100/50; ⏰ 11am–5pm Wed–Sun, closed last Thu of month; Ⓜ Sadovaya/Sennaya Ploshchad), which holds a fascinating collection of scale locomotives and model railway bridges, often made by the engineers who built the real ones. As the oldest such collection in the world (the museum was established in 1809, 28 years before Russia had its first working train!), it includes models of Krasnoyarsk's *Yenisey Bridge*, the ship that once carried passengers and trains across Lake Baikal. It also has a sumptuous 1903 Trans-Siberian wagon complete with a piano salon and a bathtub.

Train spotters should also hasten to view the impressive collection of full-sized locomotives at the **Museum of Railway Technology** (Tsentralny Muzey Oktyabrskoy Zheleznoy Dorogi; Map pp106–7; ☎ 768 2063; nab Obvodnogo Kanala 118; adult/student R150/80; ⏰ 11am–5pm; Ⓜ Baltiyskaya), behind the old Warsaw Station. Around 75 nicely painted and buffed engines and carriages are on display, some dating back to the late 19th century.

Contemporary Art Galleries

St Petersburg has a thriving contemporary art scene and the best places to see examples are at the several galleries occupying **Pushkinskaya 10** (Map p110; ☎ 764 5371; www.p10.nonmuseum.ru; Ligovsky pr 53; admission free; ⏰ 3–7pm Wed–Sun; Ⓜ Ploshchad Vosstaniya) and **Loft Project Floors** (Loft Proekt Etazhi; Map pp106–7; Ligovsky pr 74; admission free; ⏰ 2–10pm Tue–Sat; Ⓜ Ligovsky Prospekt). The former dates back to an artists' squat established in 1988. Now a fully legit nonprofit organisation, this legendary locale also houses the cool music clubs **Fish Fabrique** (p118) and **Experimental Sound Gallery** (p118). While the art centre commonly goes by the name 'Pushkinskaya 10', note that the entrance is through the archway at Ligovsky pr 53.

Hidden away off the main road in the former Smolensky Bread Bakery, Floors consists of four large and industrial-looking gallery spaces, the main one being **Globe Gallery** (www.globegallery.ru). At the time of research there were plans to create a summer cafe and viewing space on the roof and to install a wine bar at the rear of the gallery.

Vasilevsky Island

Some of the best views of St Petersburg can be had from Vasilevsky Island's eastern 'nose' known as the **Strelka**. The two **Rostral Columns** (Map p106–7) on the point, studded with ships' prows, were oil-fired navigation beacons in the 1800s; on some holidays, such as Victory Day, gas torches are still lit on them. From May to October a massive **floating musical fountain**, shooting jets up to 60m into the air, is anchored in the Neva just opposite here.

The best of many museums gathered on Vasilevsky Island is the riverside **Menshikov Palace** (Menshikovsky Dvorets; Map pp106–7; ☎ 323 1112; www.hermitagemuseum.org; Universitetskaya nab 15; adult/student R200/100; ⏰ 10.30am–6pm Tue–Sat, to 5pm Sun; Ⓜ Vasileostrovskaya), built in 1707 for Peter the Great's confidant Alexander Menshikov. Now a branch of the Hermitage (p105), the palace's impressively restored interiors are filled with period art and furniture.

The **Museum of Anthropology & Ethnography** (Kunstkamera; Map pp106–7; ☎ 328 1412; www.kunstkamera.ru; entrance on Tamozhenny per; adult/student R200/100; ⏰ 11am–6pm Tue–Sat, to 5pm Sun; Ⓜ Vasileostrovskaya) was established in 1714 by Peter the Great, who used it to display his ghoulish collection of monstrosities, notably preserved freaks, two-headed mutant foetuses and odd body parts: they still draw the crowds today.

Housed in what was once the Stock Exchange, the **Central Naval Museum** (Tsentralny Voenno-Morskoi Muzey; Map pp106–7; ☎ 328 2502; www.museum.navy.ru, in Russian; Birzhevoy proezd 4; adult/student

---

HISTORIC RAILWAY STATIONS

St Petersburg's oldest and most elegant station is **Vitebsky vokzal** (Vitebsk Station; Map pp106-7; Ⓜ Pushkinskaya), originally built in 1837 to serve the line to Tsarskoe Selo. The current building dates from 1904 and is partly graced with gorgeous Style Moderne (Russian art nouveau) interior decoration.

While at **Moskovsky vokzal** (Moscow Station; Map p110; Ⓜ Ploshchad Vosstaniya) look up at the expansive ceiling mural in the main entrance hall. There's a striking giant bust of Peter the Great in the hall leading to the platforms.

Finlyandsky vokzal (Finland Station; Map pp106-7; Ⓜ Ploshchad Lenina), rebuilt after WWII, is famous as the place where, in April 1917, Lenin arrived from exile and gave his legendary speech atop an armoured car. Lenin's statue, pointing across the Neva towards the old KGB headquarters, stands outside the station.

For more historic train stations along the Trans-Siberian route, see p24.

R320/110; ◔ 11am-6pm Wed-Sun, closed last Thu of the month; Ⓜ Vasileostrovskaya), is a must for naval enthusiasts. Next door, the **Museum of Zoology** (Zoologichesky Muzey; Map pp106-7; ☎ 328 0112; www.zin .ru/mus_e.htm, Universitetskaya nab 1; adult/child R150/50, free Thu; ◔ 11am-6pm Sat-Thu; Ⓜ Vasileostrovskaya) has some amazing exhibits, including a complete woolly mammoth, thawed out of the Siberian ice in 1902, and a live insect zoo!

Peter & Paul Fortress

There's plenty to see and do at this **fortress** (Petropavlovskaya krepost; Map pp106-7; ☎ 238 4550; www .spbmuseum.ru/peterpaul; ◔ grounds 6am-10pm, exhibitions 11am-6pm Thu-Mon, 11am-5pm Tue; Ⓜ Gorkovskaya), dating from 1703. The oldest building in St Petersburg, planned by Peter the Great as a defence against the Swedes, never saw action, and its main use up to 1917 was as a political prison. To get a sense of its scale, and for river views, walk the **Nevskaya Panorama** (adult/student R100/60) along part of the battlements, then enter the **SS Peter & Paul Cathedral** (adult/student R170/80), whose 122m-tall, needle-thin gilded spire is one of the city's defining landmarks. Its magnificent baroque interior is the last resting place of all Russia's prerevolutionary rulers from Peter the Great onward, except Peter II and Ivan VI.

At noon every day a cannon is fired from **Naryshkin Bastion**. In the south wall is **Nevsky Gate**, where prisoners were loaded onto boats for execution. Notice the plaques showing water levels of famous floods.

Individual tickets are needed for each of the fortress's attractions so the best deal is the combined entry ticket (adult/student R250/130), which allows access to all the exhibitions on the island (except the bell tower) and is valid for 10 days.

WALKING TOUR

Walking **Nevsky Prospekt** – Russia's most famous street – is an essential St Petersburg experience. All the sights listed can be found on the map, p110.

Starting at Dvortsovaya pl, notice the gilded spire of the **Admiralty** to your right as you head southeast down Nevsky towards the Moyka River. Across the Moyka, Rastrelli's baroque **Stroganov Palace** (p109) houses a branch of the Russian Museum, as well as a couple of restaurants and a chocolate shop masquerading as a 'museum'.

A block beyond the Moyka, on the southern side of Nevsky pr, see the great arms of the **Kazan Cathedral** (Kazansky Sobor; ☎ 571 4826; Kazanskaya pl 2; admission free; ◔ 10am-7pm, services 10am & 6pm; Ⓜ Nevsky Prospekt) reach out towards the avenue. It's a working cathedral, so please show some respect for the local customs if you enter.

Opposite the cathedral is the **Singer Building**, a Style Moderne beauty restored to its original splendour when it was the headquarters of the sewing machine company. Inside is the bookshop **Dom Knigi** (p103) and a branch of the coffee shop **Shokoladnitsa**, with a great view over the street.

A short walk south of the cathedral, along Griboedova Canal, sits one of St Petersburg's loveliest bridges, the **Bankovsky most**. The cables of this 25.2m-long bridge are supported by four cast-iron griffins with golden wings.

View the lavish **Grand Hotel Europe** (Mikhaylovskaya ul 1/7), built between 1873 and

DETOUR: PETRODVORETS & TSARSKOE SELO ПЕТРОДВОРЕЦ & ЦАРСКОЕ СЕЛО

Among the several palace estates that the tsars built around St Petersburg as country retreats, the ones not to miss are **Petrodvorets** (☎ 427 0073; www.peterhof.ru, in Russian; ul Razvodnaya 2), 29km west of St Petersburg, and **Tsarskoe Selo** (Tsar's Village; ☎ 465 2281; http://tzar.ru/en; Sadovaya ul 7), 25km south of the city in the town of Pushkin.

If time is limited, Petrodvorets, also known as Peterhof, with its breezy Gulf of Finland location is the one to opt for, mainly because of its **Grand Cascade & Water Avenue**, a symphony of over 140 fountains and canals. To see them you are required to pay to enter the **Lower Park** (Nizhny Park; adult/student R300/150; ⏰ 9am-8pm Mon-Fri, to 9pm Sat & Sun). They only work from mid-May to early October (from 11am to 5pm Monday to Friday, to 6pm Saturday and Sunday), but the gilded ensemble still looks marvellous at any time of the year.

Tsarskoe Selo's big draw is the baroque **Catherine Palace** (Yekaterininsky dvorets; adult/student R500/250; ⏰ 10am-6pm Wed-Mon, closed last Mon of the month), built between 1752 and 1756, but almost destroyed in WWII. The exterior and 20-odd rooms have been expertly restored; the Great Hall and the Amber Room are particularly dazzling.

Getting There & Away

Buses and *marshrutky* (fixed-route minibuses) to Petrodvorets (R45, 30 minutes) run frequently from outside the Avtovo (424), Leninsky Prospekt (103) and Prospekt Veteranov (N639B or K343) metro stations. There's also the K404 bus from outside the Baltisky vokzal (R50, 40 minutes). All stop near the main entrance to the Upper Garden, on Sankt Peterburgsky pr.

From May to September, the *Meteor* hydrofoil (one-way/return R400/700, 30 minutes) goes every 20 to 30 minutes from 9.30am to at least 7pm from the jetty in front of St Petersburg's Hermitage.

Marshrutky regularly shuttle to Pushkin (R30, 30 minutes) from outside metro Moskovskaya. Infrequent suburban trains run from St Petersburg's Vitebsky vokzal. For Tsarskoe Selo (R36) get off at Detskoe Selo station, from where *marshrutky* (R15) frequently run to the estate.

1875, redone in Style Moderne in the 1910s and completely renovated in the early 1990s. Across Nevsky pr, the historic department store **Bolshoy Gostiny Dvor** (Big Merchant Yard; www.bgd.ru, in Russian; Nevsky pr 35; Ⓜ Gostiny Dvor) is another Rastrelli creation dating from 1757–85. Beside it stands the clock tower of the former **Town Duma**, seat of the prerevolutionary city government.

At 48 Nevsky pr, the **Passazh** (⏰ 10am-10pm; Ⓜ Gostiny Dvor) department store has a beautiful arcade (notice the glass ceilings), while on the corner of Malaya Sadovay ul is the Style Moderne classic **Yeliseyevsky**, once the city's most sumptuous grocery store. At the time of research the building was closed but its grand exterior is well worth a look.

An enormous statue of **Catherine the Great** stands at the centre of **Ploshchad Ostrovskogo**, commonly referred to as the Catherine Gardens. The square's western side is taken up by the lavish **National Library of Russia**, St Petersburg's biggest with some 31 million items; at the southern end is **Aleksandrinksy Theatre**, where Chekhov's *The Seagull* premiered in 1896.

Nevsky pr crosses the Fontanka Canal on the **Anichkov most**, with its famous 1840s statues (sculpted by the German Pyotr Klodt) of rearing horses at its four corners.

TOURS

The following operations can arrange city tours on foot and Anglo Tourismo can also organise tours by boat. For something more private than Anglo Tourismo's cruises, there are many small boats that can be hired as private water taxis. You'll have to haggle over rates: expect to pay around R2000 an hour for a group of up to six people.

Anglo Tourismo (Map p110; ☎ 8-921 989 4722; anglotourismo@yahoo.com; nab reki Fontanki 21; Ⓜ Gostiny Dvor) From May to September it runs one-hour cruises with English commentary at 11am, 1pm, 5pm and 8pm from near Anichkov most. It also offers walking tours (adult/student R500/400) from early April to October, departing daily at 10am from Café Rico, just off Nevsky pr at Pushkinskaya ul.

Peter's Walking Tours (☎ 943 1229; www.peterswalk.com) In business for over 12 years, Peter Kozyrev and his brilliant band of guides can give you an insight into the city like no one else. The standard walking tour (R500) departs from the HI St Petersburg Hostel (Map p110; 3-ya Sovetskaya ul 28; **M** Ploshchad Vosstaniya) at 10.30am daily.

Skatprokat (Map p110; ☎ 717 6836; www.skatprokat .ru; Goncharnaya ul 7; rental per day R500; ⏱ 24hr; **M** Ploshchad Vosstaniya) Arranges cycling tours in conjunction with Peter's Walking Tours.

VB Excursions (☎ 8-911 999 5678; www.vb-excursions .com; Room 415, ul Avtogennaya 6; **M** Elizarovskaya) Offers excellent walking tours with clued-up students on themes including Dostoevsky and revolutionary St Petersburg. Its 'Back in the USSR' tour (R925 per person) includes a visit to a typical Soviet apartment for tea and bliny (pancakes).

FESTIVALS & EVENTS

The city's biggest event is the **White Nights Arts Festival**, which includes numerous events ranging from folk to ballet. The official festival dates are the last 10 days of June, but all kinds of arts events and performances take place across the city throughout June and often into July, with the Mariinsky Theatre taking the lead.

SLEEPING

Unless otherwise noted, the accommodation rates in St Petersburg are for the high season and include breakfast.

In addition to City Realty (p105), Ost-West Kontaktservice (p105) and Zimmer Nice (right), the following can arrange apartment rentals and homestays.

Andrey & Sasha's Homestay (Map p110; ☎ 315 3330; asamatuga@mail.ru; nab kanala Griboedova 49; **M** Sadovaya/Sennaya Ploshchad) Photographer Andrey and doctor Sasha have a couple of apartments they rent rooms out in, including this one, which is also their delightfully decorated home. Rates are around €60 for a double room, all but one with shared facilities.

Host Families Association (HOFA; Map pp106-7; ☎ 8-901 305 8874; www.hofa.ru) The most established and reliable agency for homestays and rental of private flats, with rates for a single/double/apartment without breakfast starting at €29/44/118.

Budget

Seven Bridges Hostel (Map pp106-7; ☎ 572 5415; http: //7bridges.night.lt; Apt 34, ul Labutina 36; dm/s/d US$18/ 23.50/26; ⏷ ; **M** Sadovaya/Sennaya Ploshchad) Run by an English Trans-Siberian tour guide and his Russian girlfriend, this convivial place is named after the seven bridges that tether Pokrovsky ostrov – the hostel's location – to the rest of St Petersburg. The two dorm rooms have four beds each and there's a very comfy lounge well stocked with books and videos.

our pick **Cuba Hostel** (Map p110; ☎ 921 7115, 315 1558; www.cubahostel.ru; Kazanskaya ul 5; dm R550; ⏷ ; **M** Nevsky Prospekt) This funky hang-out presses all the right buttons in terms of atmosphere, friendliness, price and location. Each of the dorms – holding from four to 10 beds – is painted a different colour and arty design is used throughout.

Hostel Pilau (Map p110; ☎ 572 2711; www.hostelpilau .ru; Apt 12, ul Rubinshteyna 38; dm from R550, s & d from R2100; ⏷ ; **M** Vladimirskaya/Dostoevskaya) Occupying a renovated 19th-century flat, the 10-bed dorm here is in the best-appointed room with beautiful plaster mouldings on the walls and ceiling. Smaller dorm rooms are simpler in design but all have newly polished parquet flooring, high ceilings and big windows.

Crazy Duck (Map p110; ☎ 310 1304; www.crazyduck .ru; Apt 4, Moskovsky pr 4; dm from R750; ⏷ ; **M** Sadovaya/ Sennaya Ploshchad) This cheery newcomer to the city's hostel scene offers plenty of home comforts to supplement its eight-, six- and four-bed dorms, including a fab lounge, kitchen with top-notch facilities, and a Jacuzzi.

Zimmer Nice (Map p110; ☎ 973 3757; www.zimmer .ru; Apt 7, Malaya Morskaya ul 8; dm/s/d from R750/1300/2000; ⏷ ; **M** Nevsky Prospekt) If this one is full, there's another at 2-ya Sovetskaya ul 19 (apartment 86; Map p110), as well as several centrally located apartments for rent.

Midrange

our pick **Art Hotel Terezinni** (Map pp106-7; ☎ 332 1035; www.trezzini-hotel.com; Bolshoy pr 8; s/d from R2500/3360; ⏷ ⏷ ; **M** Vasileostrovskaya) All the rooms are very appealing at this arty hotel, even the compact economy singles. Stand-outs are rooms 201 and 214, which have little balconies and overlook the neighbouring St Andrew's Cathedral.

Nevsky Prospekt B&B (Map p110; ☎ 325 9398; www.bnbrussia.com; Apt 8, Nevsky pr 11; s/d €80/100; ⏷ ; **M** Nevsky Prospekt) This delightfully decorated B&B has just five rooms sporting antique furnishings and the oldest functioning radio and TV you're likely to see anywhere. The only downside is the shared bathroom facilities. Airport transfers are included in the price.

Hotel Repin (Map p110; ☎ 717 9976; www.repin-hotel .ru, in Russian; Nevsky pr 136; s/d R2800/3700; ⏷ ; **M** Ploshchad Vosstaniya) The Repin's jolly, flower-bright colours make it one of the city's more pleasant minihotels, with bigger than usual rooms, preserved original features, including antique ceramic wall stoves, and a spacious lounge area where reproductions of Ilya Repin's most famous works hang.

Polikoff Hotel (Map p110; ☎ 314 7925; www.polikoff
.ru; Nevsky pr 64/11; r from R3000; ✂ 🖳 ; 🅜 Gostiny Dvor)
Tricky to find (the entrance is through the
brown door on Karavannaya ul, where you'll
need to punch in 26 for reception), the Polikoff
is worth hunting out for its rooms brimming
with contemporary cool decor, quiet but central location and pleasant service.

Pio on Mokhovaya (Map p110; ☎ 273 3585; www
.hotelpio.ru; Apt 10 & 12, Mokhovaya ul 39; s/d/tr/q €100/
120/150/170; 🖳 ; 🅜 Chernyshevskaya) Split across
two apartments, the rooms at this appealing
guest house are named after Italian towns.
They're simply but elegantly furnished, with
modern fixtures and dusky, pastel-coloured
walls. There's a sister property at **Pio on Griboedov** (Map p110; Apartment 5, nab kanala Griboedova
35), with canal views and a few cheaper rooms
sharing bathrooms.

Rachmaninov Antique-Hotel (Map p110; ☎ 327
7466; www.hotelrachmaninov.com; 3rd fl, Kazanskaya ul 5;
s/d/ste R4400/4550/12,680; ✂ 🖳 ; 🅜 Nevsky Prospekt)
Super-stylish minihotel, where minimalist
decor is offset by antiques.

Top End

ourpick **Alexander House** (Map pp106-7; ☎ 575 3877;
www.a-house.ru; nab Krukova kanala 27; s/d from R7140/7820,
apt s/d R12,920/13,600; ✂ 🖳 ; 🅜 Sadovaya/Sennaya
Ploshchad) The 19 spacious rooms at this lovely
boutique hotel are each named and tastefully
styled after the world's top cities. It also offers
a comfortable lounge area with an attached
kitchen for guests' use, a library, *banya* (bathhouse), restaurant and lush garden.

Hotel Astoria (Map p110; ☎ 494 5757; www.rocco
fortecollection.com; Bolshaya Morskaya ul 39; s/d/ste from
R17,150/19,250/24,500; ✂ 🖳 ; 🅜 Nevsky Prospekt) The
very essence of old-world class, the pricier
rooms and suites here are decorated with
original period antique furniture.

EATING
Restaurants

Schaste (Happiness; Map p110; ☎ 572 2675; www.schaste
-est.com, in Russian; ul Rubinshteyna 15/17; mains R250-
400; ☯ 9am-midnight Mon-Thu, 9am-7am Fri, 10am-7am
Sat, 10am-midnight Sun; 🅜 Dostoevskaya/Vladimirskaya)
Romantic cherubs are the motif at this charming cafe-bar, even on the dot-to-dot puzzles
that are printed on the place mats. The vaguely
Russian food is tasty and its three-course
lunch for R250 is a steal.

Teplo (Map p110; ☎ 570 1974; Bolshaya Morskaya ul 45;
mains R260-500; 🅜 Sadovaya/Sennaya Ploshchad) You'll

instantly warm to Teplo's cosy living-room
atmosphere; cuddly soft toys are liberally scattered around for the kids. The food – roast
chicken, salmon in Savoy cabbage, sweet and
savoury pies, and pastries baked daily – is
equally comforting.

ourpick **Sadko** (Map pp106-7; ☎ 920 8228; www.probka
.org; ul Glinki 2; mains R260-650; 🅜 Sadovaya/Sennaya
Ploshchad) This impressive restaurant's decor
applies traditional floral designs to a slick
contemporary style. It has a great children's
room and is ideal as a pre– or post–Mariinsky
Theatre dining option. Serving all the Russian
favourites, it makes its own *pirozhki* (pies)
and cranberry *mors* (fruit drink). The waiters,
many music students at the local conservatory, give impromptu vocal performances.

Terrassa (Map p110; ☎ 337 6837; www.terrassa.ru;
Kazanskaya ul 3; mains R300-700; 🅜 Nevsky Prospekt) Atop
the Vanity shopping centre, this cool bistro
boasts unbelievable views towards Kazan
Cathedral. In the open kitchen, chefs busily
prepare fusion cuisine, exhibiting influences
from Italy, Asia and beyond.

Makarov (Map p110; ☎ 327 0053; Manezhny per 2;
mains R400-500; ☯ noon-11pm Sun & Mon, 8am-11pm Tue-
Fri, 11am-midnight Sat; 🅜 Chernyshevskaya) Charming
place, overlooking the Cathedral of the
Transfiguration of our Saviour; serves traditional Russian with a twist in a relaxed setting.
Child friendly.

Yerevan (Map p110; ☎ 703 3820; www.en.erivan.ru; nab
reki Fontanki 51; mains R500-1000; 🅜 Gostiny Dvor) This
top-class Armenian restaurant with an elegant
ethnic design serves delicious traditional food
made with ingredients the chefs promise are
from 'ecologically pure' regions of Armenia.

Also recommended:

Kharbin (Map p110; ☎ 311 1732; nab reki Moyki 48;
mains R300-400; 🅜 Nevsky Prospekt) Inexpensive, reliable
Chinese restaurant.

Kilikia (Map p110; ☎ 327 2208; Gorokhovaya ul 26/40;
mains R200-300; ☯ noon-3am; 🅜 Nevsky Prospekt)
Excellent value, tasty Armenian food.

Tandoori Nights (Map p110; ☎ 312 8772; Voznesensky
pr 4; mains R300-400; 🅜 Nevsky Prospekt) Stylish Indian
restaurant.

Taverna Oliva (Map p110; ☎ 314 6563; Bolshaya
Morskaya ul 31; mains R200-400; 🅜 Nevsky Prospekt) A
little piece of Greece in St Petersburg.

Cafes & Quick Eats

Herzen Institute Canteen (Map p110; Herzen Institute
courtyard, nab reki Moyki 48; mains R50-100; ☯ noon-6pm
Mon-Sat; 🅜 Nevsky Prospekt) This no-frills Chinese

outlet, which uses the same kitchen as Kharbin (opposite), caters to the students of the Herzen Institute who come here in droves at lunch.

our pick Stolle (www.stolle.ru; pies R60-100; 🕑 8am-10pm) Konyushennaya per 1/6 (Map p110; **M** Nevsky Prospekt); ul Vosstaniya 32 (Map p110; **M** Chernyshevskaya); ul Dekabristov 33 (Map pp106-7; **M** Sadovaya/Sennaya Ploshchad); ul Dekabristov 19 (Map pp106-7; **M** Sadovaya/Sennaya Ploshchad); Vasilevsky Island (Map pp106-7; Syezdovskaya & 1-ya linii 50; **M** Vasileostrovskaya) We can't get enough of the traditional Russian savoury and sweet pies at this expanding chain of cafes, and we guarantee you'll also be back for more. It's easy to make a meal of it with soups and other dishes that can be ordered at the counter.

Olyushka & Russkye Bliny (Map pp106-7; Gagarinskaya ul 13; mains R/0-100; 🕑 11am-6pm Mon-Fri; **M** Chernyshevskaya) The students at the nearby university quite rightly swear by these authentic canteens that hark back to the simplicity of Soviet times. Olyushka serves only *pelmeni* (dumplings), all handmade, while Russkye Bliny does a fine line in melt-in-the-mouth pancakes.

Zoom Café (Map p110; www.cafezoom.ru, in Russian; Gorokhovaya ul 22; mains R200-400; **M** Nevsky Prospekt) Popular boho/student hang-out with regularly changing art exhibitions on its walls. Serves unfussy tasty European and Russian food, has wi-fi access, a very relaxed ambience and a no-smoking zone.

Pelmeny Bar (Map p110; Gorokhovaya ul 3; meals R200-540; **M** Nevsky Prospekt) Dine with witches and a very dapper wolf at this whimsical *dacha*-style (country cottage) cafe specialising in *pelmeni*. It's a favourite with the naval recruits from the Admiralty across the road.

Café Idiot (Map pp106-7; ☎ 315 1675; nab reki Moyki 82; meals R400; 🕑 11am-1am; **M** Sennaya Ploshchad) This long-running vegetarian cafe charms with its prerevolutionary atmosphere. It's an ideal place to visit for a nightcap or late supper. It also has free wi-fi.

Self-Catering

Kuznechny Market (Map p110; Kuznechny per; 🕑 8am-8pm; **M** Vladimirskaya) The best fresh-produce market in town.

Recommended supermarkets:

Lend (Map p110; Vladimirsky Passazh, Vladimirsky pr 19; 🕑 24hr; **M** Dostoevskaya)

Passazh (Map p110; Nevsky pr 48; 🕑 10am-10pm; **M** Gostiny Dvor)

Perekrestok (Map p110; PIK, Sennaya pl 2; 🕑 24hr; **M** Sennaya Ploshchad)

DRINKING

our pick Achtung Baby (Map p110; Konyushennaya pl 2; cover after 10pm Fri & Sat R300; 🕑 6pm-6am; **M** Nevsky Prospekt) The best of several bars and clubs that have taken over the old tsarist-era stables makes great use of the vast, high ceiling space. We love the furry globes that hang over the bar.

Sochi (Map p110; Kazanskaya ul 7; 🕑 6pm-6am; **M** Nevsky Prospekt) Occupying half of the same building as the microbrewery Tinkoff is this new venture by the woman who launched St Petersburg's DJ-bar scene. Prop yourself at the long bar or groove along with the hipsters to bands and eclectic DJ selections.

Other Side (Map p110; www.theotherside.ru; Bolshaya Konyushennaya ul 1; 🕑 noon–last customer, concerts 8pm Sun-Thu, 10pm or 11pm Fri & Sat; **M** Nevsky Prospekt) There's live music most nights at this fun and funky bar as well as decent food (mains R200 to R500), but most people turn up to enjoy its seven beers on tap and other alcoholic libations.

City Bar (Map pp106-7; Furshtatskaya ul 20; 🕑 11am-2am; **M** Chernyshevskaya) Always busy with expats and travellers, and locals who enjoy their company. Offers free wi-fi access, fine food and live entertainment. Music, poetry readings and stand-up comedy are all on the agenda, depending on the day.

Die Kneipe (Grad Petrov; Map pp106-7; ☎ 326 0137; www.die-kneipe.ru; Universitetskaya nab 5; 🕑 noon–last customer; **M** Vasileostrovskaya) The refreshing ales are reason enough to stop by this fine microbrewery with a view across the Neva from its outdoor tables. Its German style sausage meals are also the business.

SevenSkyBar (Map p110; www.sevenskybar.ru; Italiyanskaya 15; 🕑 noon-2am Sun-Thu, to 6am Fri & Sat; **M** Nevsky Prospekt) This hyper-fashionable DJ bar atop the Grand Palace mall acts like a magnate for the city's body-beautiful crowd on weekends (when there's a R400 cover charge after 10pm).

ENTERTAINMENT

Check Friday's *St Petersburg Times* for up-to-date listings.

Classical Music, Ballet & Opera

The main season is September to the end of June. In summer many companies are away on tour, but plenty of performances are still staged.

Mariinsky Theatre (Map pp106-7; ☎ 326 4141; www
.mariinsky.ru; Teatralnaya pl 1; ❤ box office 11am-7pm;
Ⓜ Sadovaya/Sennaya Ploshchad) Home to the world-
famous Kirov Ballet and Opera company. A
visit here is a must, if only to wallow in the
sparkling glory of the interior. Use the website
to book and pay for tickets in advance, for
both here and its acoustically splendid new
concert hall nearby (ul Pisareva 20).

Mikhaylovsky Opera & Ballet Theatre (Map p110;
☎ 585 4305; www.mikhailovsky.ru; pl Iskusstv 1; Ⓜ Nevsky
Prospekt) Challenging the Mariinsky in terms
of the standards and range of its performances is this equally historic and beautifully
restored theatre.

Bolshoy Zal (Big Hall; Map p110; ☎ 710 4257; www
.philharmonia.spb.ru; Mikhailovskaya ul 2; Ⓜ Gostiny Dvor)
The St Petersburg Philharmonic's symphony
orchestra is particularly renowned, and this
grand venue is one of its two concert halls;
the other being the **Maly Zal imeni Glinki** (Small
Philharmonia; Map p110; ☎ 571 8333; Nevsky pr 30;
Ⓜ Nevsky Prospekt).

Live Music

Check the Russian-language websites of
the following venues for details on current
gigs. Bands also play at the Other Side and
Sochi (p117).

Fish Fabrique (Map p110; ☎ 164 4857; www.fishfab
rique.spb.ru; Ligovsky pr 53; cover R100-150; ❤ 3pm-late;
Ⓜ Ploshchad Vosstaniya) This legendary bar is
set in the building that's the focus of the
avant-garde art scene, thus it attracts an interesting crowd who give the cramped space
its edge.

Mod Club (Map p110; ☎ 881 8371; http://modclub.spb
.ru; Konyushennaya pl 2; cover Fri & Sat R200; ❤ 6pm-6am;
Ⓜ Nevsky Prospekt) There's a groovy mix of live
and spun music at this fun, invariably packed
place, with two bars and little balconies for a
prime view of the stage.

Zoccolo (Map p110; ☎ 274 9467; www.zoccolo.ru;
3-ya Sovetskaya ul 2/3; cover R200-300; ❤ 7pm-midnight
Sun-Thu, to 6am Fri & Sat, concerts 8pm; Ⓜ Ploshchad
Vosstaniya) Urgently orange and green underground space with a positive vibe and a
great line-up of sounds, including indie rock,
Latin-hip-hop-reggae and even 'if Radiohead
played punk'.

Experimental Sound Gallery (GEZ-21; Map p110;
☎ 764 5258; www.tac.spb.ru; 3rd fl, Ligovsky pr 53; cover
R100-150; ❤ concerts from 9pm; Ⓜ Ploshchad Vosstaniya)
You know that a place called 'experimen-
tal' is going to be out there. Also catch film
screenings, readings and other expressions
of creativity. The attached cafe is a very
groovy hang-out.

Nightclubs

Griboedov (Map pp106-7; ☎ 764 4355; www.griboedov
club.ru, in Russian; Voronezhskaya ul 2A; cover after 8pm R100-
400; ❤ 5pm-6am; Ⓜ Ligovsky Prospekt) This eternally
hip club in an artfully converted bomb shelter
is a fun place most nights. It's recently extended above ground with the groovy cafe-
bar Griboedov Hill, which hosts live music
performances in the evenings.

Underground Club (Map pp106-7; ☎ 572 1551; www.un
dergroundclub.ru, in Russian; cnr Lyubansky per & Zverinskaya
ul; cover R250-350; ❤ midnight-6am Fri & Sat; Ⓜ Gorkovskaya) Quite literally underground since this
club's four dance floors occupy a sprawling
bomb shelter. DJs spin hard-core electronic
dance music.

Central Station (Map p110; ☎ 312 3600; www.central
station.ru, in Russian; ul Lomonosova 1/28; cover after midnight
R100-300; ❤ 6pm-6am; Ⓜ Gostiny Dvor) Glamtastic
gay club featuring two dance floors, several
bars, a cafe and souvenir shop (in case you
have such a good time that you just have to
have a pair of Central Station boxer shorts).
Open-minded straights will feel very comfortable here as most people just come here
to dance.

Purga (Map p110; ☎ 570 5123; www.purga-club.ru,
in Russian; nab reki Fontanki 11; cover R100-300; ❤ 4pm-
6am; Ⓜ Gostiny Dvor) You can celebrate New Year
Russian-style every night in one room of this
intimate, fun-packed club, while in the other
a traditional wedding celebration is likely to
be in full flow.

SHOPPING

Souvenir Market (Map p110; Konyushennaya pl; ❤ 10am-
dusk; Ⓜ Nevsky Prospekt) This very well-stocked
souvenir market is diagonally across the
canal from the Church of the Saviour on
Spilled Blood.

Tovar dlya Voennikh (Map p110; Sadovaya ul 26;
❤ 10am-7pm Mon-Sat; Ⓜ Gostiny Dvor) The best
place to buy cool Russian military clothes
and memorabilia. Look out for the circular green-and-gold sign with Military Shop
written in English; the entrance is inside
the courtyard.

La Russe (Map p110; ☎ 572 2043; www.larusse.ru;
Stremyannaya ul 3; ❤ 11am-8pm; Ⓜ Mayakovskaya) Lots
of rustic old what nots and genuine antiques
are for sale at this quirky, arty store.

GETTING THERE & AWAY
Air
Pulkovo-1 (☎ 704 3822; www.pulkovoairport.ru/eng) and **Pulkovo-2** (☎ 704 3444; www.pulkovoairport.ru/eng) are, respectively, the domestic and international terminals that serve St Petersburg. There are direct air links with most major European capitals and cities across Russia.

Tickets for all airlines can be purchased from travel agencies and from the **Central Airline Ticket Office** (Map p110; ☎ 315 0072; Nevsky pr 7; 8am-8pm Mon-Fri, to 6pm Sat & Sun; M Nevsky Prospekt), which also has counters for train and international bus tickets.

Boat
From June to August, **DFDS Lisco** (☎ 4012-660 404; www.dfdslisco.ru) runs a weekly ferry service on the *George Ots,* travelling between Baltiysk in Russia's Kaliningrad region and St Petersburg. **Trans-Exlin** (☎ 4012-660 408; www.transexlin.ru) also runs weekly car ferries between Baltiysk and Ust-Luga, 150k west of St Petersburg. Prices and schedules vary, so book through a travel agency such as **Baltic Tours** (Map p110; ☎ 320 6663; www.baltictours.ru; Sergei Tyulenina per 4-13; M Nevsky Pr).

It's also possible to take a boat to/from Moscow; see p146 for details.

Bus
St Petersburg's main bus station, **Avtovokzal No 2** (Map pp106-7; ☎ 766 5777; www.avokzal.ru, in Russian; nab Obvodnogo kanala 36; M Ligovsky Prospekt) – there isn't a No 1 – has both international and European Russia services.

Tickets can be purchased here and at the Central Airline Ticket Office (above).

BUSES FROM ST PETERSBURG

Destination	Buses per day	Duration	One-way fare
Helsinki	2	8hr	R1700
Moscow	1	12hr	R1000
Riga	2	11hr	R700-1050
Tallinn	7	7½hr	R900

Train
The four major long-distance train stations are: **Finlyandsky vokzal** (Finland Station; Map pp106-7; ☎ 768 7687; pl Lenina 6; M Ploshchad Lenina), for services to/from Helsinki; **Ladozhsky vokzal** (Ladoga Station; off Map pp106-7; ☎ 768 5304; Zhanevsky pr 73; M Ladozhskaya), for services to/from Helsinki, the far north of Russia and

towards the Urals; **Moskovsky vokzal** (Moscow Station; Map p110; ☎ 768 4597; pl Vosstaniya; M Ploshchad Vosstaniya), for Moscow and Siberia; and **Vitebsky vokzal** (Vitebsk Station; Map pp106-7; ☎ 768 5807; Zagorodny pr 52; M Pushkinskaya), for the Baltic states, Eastern Europe, Ukraine and Belarus. Suburban services also run from these stations, as they do from **Baltisky vokzal** (Baltic Station; Map pp106-7; ☎ 768 2859; Obvedny Kanal 120; M Baltiyskaya).

Tickets can be purchased at the train stations, the **Central Train Ticket Office** (Map p110; ☎ 762 3344; nab kanala Griboedova 24; 8am-8pm Mon-Sat, to 4pm Sun; M Nevsky Prospekt), the Central Airline Ticket Office (left) and many travel agencies around town.

DOMESTIC SERVICES
There are 12 to 14 daily trains to Moscow, all departing from Moscow Station; see the table (p120) for the best services. If you want to save money, four services (19, 27, 29 and 55) have *platskartny* (3rd-class open-carriages) with tickets for R940.

INTERNATIONAL SERVICES
There are two daily direct trains between St Petersburg and Helsinki: the *Repin,* which is Russian-operated, and the *Sibelius,* run by **Finnish Railways** (www.vr.fi). The *Leo Tolstoy* service between Moscow and Helsinki also transits via Ladozhsky vokzal. For details on services going to Helsinki, see the table, p120; check online or at the stations for current departure times.

Services to Berlin, Budapest, Kaliningrad, Kyiv, Prague and Warsaw pass through Belarus; for these journeys you must hold a transit visa. Note that border guards have been known to force people off trains and back to where they came from if they don't have a visa.

GETTING AROUND
St Petersburg's excellent public transport system makes getting around the city simple and inexpensive. Pack walking shoes, because the city centre is best seen on foot.

To/From the Airport
Pulkovo Airport, 17km south of the centre, is easily and (very) cheaply accessed by metro and bus. From Moskovskaya metro, 6km north of the airport, bus 39 runs to Pulkovo-1, the domestic terminal, and bus 13 runs to

RAIL ROUTES FROM ST PETERSBURG

From St Petersburg to Moscow

Train name & no	Departure time	Duration	Fare
Avrora (159)	4pm	5½hr	R2700
Ekspress (3)	11.59pm	8hr	R2180
Grand Express (53)	11.40pm	9hr	R5310-13,000
Krasnya Strela (1)	11.55pm	8hr	R2060
Nevsky Ekspress (165)	6.30pm*	4½hr	R2060
Nikolaevsk Ekspress (5)	11.30pm	8hr	R2500
Yunost (23)	1.05pm	7½hr	R2060

Notes: *Sun-Fri

From St Petersburg to Other Russian Cities

Destination & train no	Departure time & station	Duration	Fare
Kaliningrad (079)	6.16pm, Vitebsky	27½hr	R3000
Kazan (103)	6.29pm, Moskovsky*	26hr	R4300
Nizhny Novgorod (Gorky; 59)	5.32pm, Moskovsky	15½hr	R3800
Yekaterinburg (072E)	5.04pm, Ladozhsky	35hr	R6000

Notes: *odd days

International Trains from St Petersburg

Destination	Train name & no	Departure time & station	Duration	Fare
Brest	49	3pm, Vitebsky	18½hr	R2325
The Brest train 49 has carriages that are detached there and go on to Budapest and Prague.				
Budapest	49	3.01pm, Vitebsky	45hr	R6300
Prague	49	3.01pm, Vitebsky †	40½hr	R4700
Helsinki	*Repin* (034)	7.27am, Finlyandsky	6hr	R2100
Helsinki	*Sibelius* (036)	4.44pm, Finlyandsky	6hr	R2100
Helsinki	*Tolstoy* (032)	6.09am, Ladozhsky	6hr	R2100
Kyiv	053	9.20pm, Vitebsky	24hr	R1790/2025*
Minsk	051	7.08pm, Vitebsky	15hr	R3000
Odessa	19	11.40pm, Vitebsky	35½hr	R2100
The Odessa train has carriages that are detached along the way and go on to Berlin and Warsaw.				
Berlin	19	11.40pm, Vitebsky §	31hr	R6000
Warsaw	19	11.40pm, Vitebsky §	29hr	R3000
Riga	037	10.08pm, Vitebsky	13hr	R3280
Tallinn	649	9.50pm, Vitebsky	9½hr	R1485
Vilnius	391	8.28pm, Vitebsky||	15¼hr	R2230/2735#

Notes: *Russian/Ukrainian train   † Mon, Wed, Thu, Sun   § Tue, Wed Thu, Sat ||odd days   #Russian/Lithuanian train

Pulkovo-2, the international terminal. There are also plenty of *marshrutky* (fixed-route minibuses). The trip takes about 15 minutes and costs just R16 to R22. Alternatively, take the buses and *marshrutka* K3 all the way from the airport to Sennaya pl in the city centre or K39 to pl Vosstaniya (R35). Buses stop directly outside each of the terminals.

By taxi you should be looking at around R600 to get to the city (R400 is the price from the city to the airport). Most taxi drivers will request more from foreigners so be prepared to haggle or take the bus.

Public Transport

The **metro** (🕐 5.30am-midnight) is usually the quickest way around the city and you'll rarely wait more than three minutes for a train. *Zhetony* (tokens; R17) can be bought from booths in the stations. If you are staying more than a day or two, however, it's worth buying a 'smart card' (a plastic card that the machine reads when you touch the circular light), which is good for multiple journeys over a fixed time period. There's around a R30 deposit for the card, on top of which you'll pay a minimum of R140 (10 trips/seven days).

Moscow Москва

Moscow is the start or the end point for your train journey across Mother Russia. If you are travelling east to west, you will be relieved – after days (or weeks) on the train – to reach the cultured, cosmopolitan capital, brimming with opportunities to immerse in history; to indulge in world-class music and art; to feast on fabulous food, both exotic and familiar; and to sample the nightlife in a city that never sleeps. If you are travelling west to east, you may be relieved to depart – to escape the overwhelming urbanity – the bumper-to-bumper traffic; the nonstop noise; the panic-inducing prices. Either way, Moscow is an exhilarating and confounding contrast to the rest of Russia.

These days, the capital city is experiencing a burst of creative energy, undoubtedly fuelled by economics but evident in all aspects of contemporary culture. Former factories and warehouses are converted into edgy art galleries. Foodies flock to wine bars, coffee bars, sushi bars and even beer bars. Nightlifers enjoy a dynamic and diverse scene out on the town – at exclusive clubs, bohemian art cafes, underground blues bars, get-down discos and drink-up dives. Tchaikovsky and Chekhov are well-represented at the theatres, but you can also see world premiers by up-and-coming composers and choreographers.

The ancient city has always been a haven for history buffs. The red-brick towers and sturdy stone walls of the Kremlin occupy the founding site of Moscow; the remains of the Soviet state are scattered around the city. Now history is being examined in innovative ways, as institutions such as the Gulag History Museum broach subjects long brushed under the carpet.

Soak it up. Examine the art and move to the music; splurge on a ritzy restaurant; stay out til sunrise; get lost in the crowds. Once you get on that train, you may not get to do it again.

HIGHLIGHTS

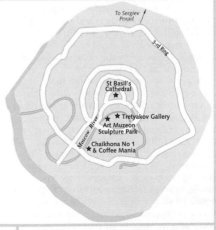

- Marvelling at the magnificent multi-coloured, multidomed **St Basil's Cathedral** (p131).

- Admiring the world's largest collection of Russian art at the **State Tretyakov Gallery** (p134)

- Seeing eye to eye with the fallen heroes at the **Art Muzeon sculpture park** (p135)

- Doing the cafe scene at sweet summer spots such as **Chaikhona No 1** (p145) or **Coffee Mania** (p144).

- Lighting a candle to St Sergius at **Sergiev Posad** (p149).

- TELEPHONE CODE: 495, 499

- POPULATION: 10.4 MILLION

MOSCOW МОСКВА

HISTORY

Moscow's recorded history dates to the mid-12th century, when Yury Dolgoruky constructed the first Kremlin on a strategic spot atop the Borovitsky Hill. Moscow soon blossomed into an economic centre.

In the 13th century, the Mongols burned the city to the ground. The Golden Horde was interested in tribute, and Moscow was conveniently situated to monitor the river trade and road traffic. Moscow's Prince Ivan acted as tax collector, earning himself the moniker 'Moneybags' (Kalita), and Moscow developed into a regional capital.

Towards the end of the 15th century, the once diminutive duchy emerged as an expanding state under the reign of Grand Prince Ivan III (the Great). To celebrate his successes, he imported a team of Italian artisans for a complete renovation of the Kremlin. The city developed in concentric rings outward from this centre. Under Ivan IV (the Terrible), the then capital city earned the nickname of 'Gold-Domed Moscow' because of its multitude of monastery fortresses and magnificent churches.

In 1712 Peter the Great startled the country by announcing the relocation of the capital to St Petersburg. In the early 1800s, Moscow suffered further at the hands of Napoleon Bonaparte. But after the Napoleonic Wars, Moscow was feverishly rebuilt and industry prospered.

When the Bolsheviks gained control of Russia in 1917, the capital returned to Moscow. Stalin devised an urban plan for the city: historic cathedrals and monuments were demolished; in their place appeared the marble-bedecked metro and neo-Gothic skyscrapers. In the following decades, Moscow expanded at an exponential rate.

Moscow was the scene of the most dramatic events of the early 1990s' political transition. Boris Yeltsin led crowds protesting the attempted coup in 1991; and two years later, he ordered the army to blast the parliament into submission. Within the Moscow city government, the election of Mayor Yury Luzhkov in 1992 set the stage for the creation of a big-city boss: his interests range from the media to manufacturing and from five-star hotels to shopping malls. While the rest of Russia struggled to survive the collapse of communism, Moscow emerged as an enclave of affluence.

Early in the new millennium, Moscow was a target for terrorist attacks linked to the ongoing crisis in Chechnya. Over the course of several years, hundreds of people in Moscow were wounded or killed when suicide bombers attacked a theatre, a rock concert, metro stations and airplanes.

In 2007 Mayor Luzhkov was reappointed for his fifth term in office. Under his oversight, the city continues to undergo a massive physical transformation, with skyscrapers shooting up along the Moscow River. The population continues to climb. And Moscow – political capital, economic powerhouse and cultural innovator – continues to lead the way as the most fast-dealing, free-wheeling city in Russia.

ORIENTATION

The Kremlin is at Moscow's heart in every way. Red Square lies along its eastern side while the Moscow River flows to the south. From this centre, radial roads spoke out across the city in all directions, the most important being the northbound Tverskaya ul.

Four ring roads spread out from the centre, although the outermost rings are only of interest to drivers. The Boulevard Ring (Bulvarnoe Koltso) is about 1km from the Kremlin, while the Garden Ring (Sadovoe Koltso) is about 2km out. Most of the sights are concentrated within the Garden Ring.

About 2.8km northeast of the Kremlin is Komsomolskaya pl, Moscow's transport hub. Three bustling train stations dominate this square, including Yaroslavsky vokzal (Yaroslavl Station), the most important station for Trans-Siberian travellers. Next door is Leningradsky vokzal (Leningrad Station), for services to and from St Petersburg, while across the road is Kazansky vokzal (Kazan Station), the terminus for some trains from the Urals including the main service from Yekaterinburg.

If you're arriving in Moscow on trains from Western and Eastern Europe, your likely entry points will be Belorussky vokzal (Belarus Station), 2.8km northwest of the Kremlin, or Kievsky vokzal (Kyiv Station), 2.4km to the southwest.

Maps

An excellent, up-to-date map in English is the *Moscow Today City Map*, published in 2007 by **Atlas Print Co** (☎ 495-984 5604; www.atlas-print.ru).

MOSCOW IN...

Two Days

Spend one day seeing what makes Moscow famous: **St Basil's Cathedral** (p131), nearby **Lenin's Mausoleum** (p130) and the **Kremlin** (p127). Allow a few hours in the afternoon to gawk at the gold and gems in the **Armoury** (p130). In the evening, attend an opera at the **Bolshoi Theatre** (p145) or dine like the tsars at **Café Pushkin** (p144).

Art lovers can spend the next day at the **Pushkin Fine Arts Museum** (p133) or **Tretyakov Gallery** (p134), both housing world-class collections. In the late afternoon, head to whimsical **Art Muzeon** (p135) and fun-filled **Gorky Park** (p135), stopping for a drink at **Chaikhona No 1** (p145).

Four Days

Take in all of the activities suggested in the two-day itinerary. On day three, visit **Novodevichy Convent & Cemetery** (p134), where so many political and cultural figures are laid to rest. Have lunch at **Stolle** (p144) or work out the blues at **Roadhouse** (p146). Reserve one day for a trip out of the city to **Sergiev Posad** (p149) or **Rostov-Veliky** (p151).

INFORMATION
Bookshops

Atlas (Map pp124-5; ☎ 495-928 6109; Kuznetsky most 9/10; ☉ 9am-8pm Mon-Fri, 10am-6pm Sat, 11am-5pm Sun; Ⓜ Kuznetsky Most) A map shop with city and regional maps covering the whole country.

Dom Inostrannoy Knigi (Map pp124-5; ☎ 495-628 2021; Kuznetsky most 18/7; ☉ 9am-9pm Mon-Fri, 10am-9pm Sat, 10am-8pm Sun; Ⓜ Kuznetsky Most) The 'House of Foreign Books' is a small place with the widest selection of literature in foreign languages.

Respublika (Map pp124-5; ☎ 495-251 6527; Tverskaya-Yamskaya ul 10; ☉ 24hr; Ⓜ Mayakovskaya) If you take your browsing seriously, Respublika is the place for you, with comfy couches, cosy cafe and stay-all-day atmosphere. Also sells music, posters and souvenirs.

Emergency

Ambulance ☎ 03, in Russian
Emergency assistance ☎ 495-937 9911
Fire ☎ 01
Police ☎ 02

Internet Access

Cafemax Zamoskvorechie (Map pp136–7; ☎ 495-950 6050; Pyatnitskaya ul 25; per hr R50-90; ☉ 24hr; Ⓜ Novokuznetskaya); Tverskoy (Map pp124–5; ☎ 495-741 7571; Novoslobodskaya ul 3; per hr R120; ☉ 24hr; Ⓜ Novoslobodskaya) Discounts available for late-night and early-morning hours.

NetLand (Map pp124-5; ☎ 495-781 0923; Teatralny proezd 5; per hr R80-100; ☉ 24hr; Ⓜ Kuznetsky Most/Lubyanka) A loud, dark club that fills up with kids playing games. Enter from ul Rozhdestvenka.

Pronto Internet Cafe (Map pp124-5; ☎ 495-692 5181; Tverskaya ul 10; per hr R130-160; ☉ 9am-10pm;

Ⓜ Pushkinskaya) Computers and coffee on the 2nd floor of the Tsentralnaya Hotel

Time Online Okhotny Ryad (Map p128; ⌂ 495-988 8428; Manezhnaya ul; per hr R70-100; ☉ 24hr; Ⓜ Okhotny Ryad); Komsomolskaya (Map p132; ☎ 495-266 8351; Komsomolskaya pl 3; per hr R70-100; ☉ 24hr; Ⓜ Komsomolskaya) Offers copy and photo services, as well as over 100 zippy computers or free wi-fi access.

Internet Resources

www.expat.ru Run by and for English-speaking expats. Provides useful information about real estate, restaurants, children in Moscow, social groups and more.

www.maps-moscow.com An energetic group of international journalists raising awareness of architectural preservation issues in Moscow.

www.moscowmaximum.blogspot.com An anonymous blog providing in-depth club reviews and insiders' info on Moscow nightlife.

www.moscow-taxi.com Viktor the virtual taxi driver provides extensive descriptions of sites inside and outside of Moscow, as well as info on hotel bookings and other tourist services.

www.redtape.ru Like expat.ru but better. Forums offer inside information on any question you might ask.

Media

element (www.elementmoscow.ru) This oversized newsprint magazine comes out weekly with restaurant reviews, concert listings and art exhibits.

Moscow News (www.mnweekly.ru) This long-standing news weekly focuses on domestic and international politics and business.

Moscow Times (www.themoscowtimes.com) This first-rate daily is the undisputed king of the hill in locally published English-language news. The Friday edition is a great source for what's happening at the weekend.

CENTRAL MOSCOW (TVERSKOY)

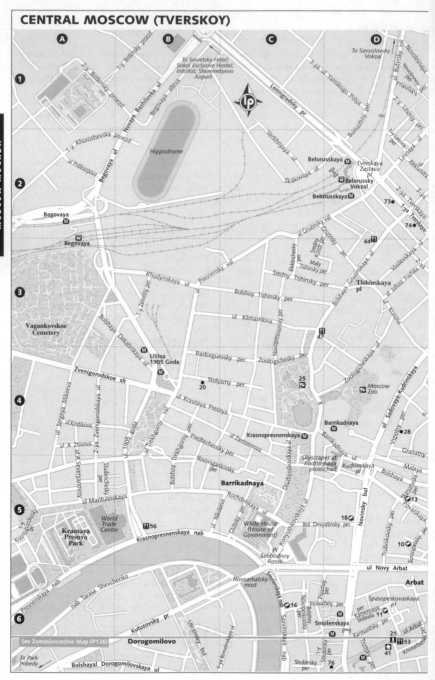

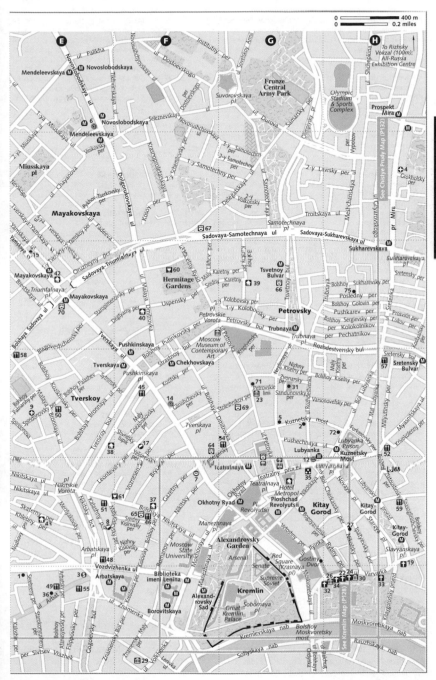

Passport Magazine (www.passportmagazine.ru) An excellent monthly lifestyle magazine.

Medical Services

36.6 Chistye Prudy (Map p132; ☎ 495-923 2258; ul Pokrovka 1/13; Ⓜ Kitay-Gorod/Lukyanka); Tverskoy (Map pp124-5; ☎ 495-623 4718; Kuznetsky most 18/7; Ⓜ Kuznetsky Most); Arbat (Map pp124-5; ☎ 495-203 0207; ul Novy Arbat 15; Ⓜ Arbatskaya) A chain of 24-hour pharmacies with outlets all over the city.
American Medical Centre (Map pp124-5; ☎ 495-933 7700; www.amcenter.ru; Grokholsky per 1; Ⓜ Prospekt Mira) Offers 24-hour emergency service, consultations and a full range of medical specialists, including paediatricians

and dentists. Also has an on-site pharmacy with English-speaking staff.
European Medical Centre (Map pp124-5; ☎ 495-933 6645; www.emcmos.ru; Spiridonevsky per 5; Ⓜ Mayakovskaya) Includes medical and dental facilities, which are open around the clock for emergencies. The staff speak 10 different languages.

Money

Banks, exchange counters and ATMs are ubiquitous in Moscow. Credit cards, especially Visa and MasterCard, are widely accepted in upscale hotels, restaurants and shops.

Alfa Bank (8.30am-8pm Mon-Sat) Kitay Gorod (Map p128; ul Varvarka 3; Kitay-Gorod); Tverskoy (Map pp124-5; Kuznetsky most 9/10; Kuznetsky Most); Arbat (Map pp124-5; ul Arbat 4; Arbatskaya); Zamoskvorechie (Map pp136-7; ul Bolshaya Ordynka 21; Tretyakov-skaya) ATMs at the branches listed dispense roubles, euros and US dollars.

American Express (Map p128; 495-543 9400; Vetoshny per 17; 10am-9.30pm; Teatralnaya) The most reliable place to cash American Express travellers cheques. It also offers an ATM, mail holding and travel services for AmEx cardholders.

Post, Telephone & Fax

Moscow payphones operate with cards that are available in shops, kiosks and metro stations.

Central telegraph (Map pp124-5; Tverskaya ul 7; post 8am-10pm, telephone 24hr; Okhotny Ryad) This convenient office offers phone, fax and internet.

Main post office (Map p132; Myasnitskaya ul 26; 8am-8pm Mon-Fri, 9am-7pm Sat & Sun; Chistye Prudy) It's on the corner of Chistoprudny bul.

Tourist Information

Moscow City Tourist Information Centre (Map p128; 495-232 5657; www.moscow-city.ru; ul Ilynka 4; 9am-6pm Mon-Fri; Kitay-Gorod/Ploshchad Revolyutsii) Located in Gostiny Dvor, the capital's official tourist office does not answer the phone, nor is it open on weekends.

Travel Agencies

Glavagentstvo-Service (Map pp124-5; 495-745 6548; 1-ya Tverskaya-Yamskaya ul 15; Belorusskaya) Sells plane and train tickets with many outlets around town.

Maria Travel Agency (Map p132; 495-725 5746; ul Maroseyka 13; Kitay-Gorod) Offers visa support, apartment rental and some local tours, including the Golden Ring.

Unifest Travel (Map pp136-7; 495-234 6555; www.unifest.ru; Komsomolsky pr 13; Park Kultury) Formerly Infinity Travel, this on-the-ball travel company offers rail and air tickets (recommended), visa support, and Trans-Siberian and Central Asian packages.

DANGERS & ANNOYANCES

Unfortunately, street crime targeting tourists has increased in recent years, although Moscow is not as dangerous as paranoid locals may have you think. As in any big city, be on your guard against pickpockets and muggers. Be particularly careful at or around metro stations at Kursky vokzal (station) and Partizanskaya, where readers have reported specific incidents.

> **WI-FI MOSCOW**
>
> Wireless access is becoming very common around Moscow. It's not always free, but it is ubiquitous. Take advantage of wi-fi access at many hotels and hostels, as well as at Time Online and Cafemax (see p123). Look also for the internet icon in the listings for restaurants (p143), bars and cafes (p145). A more-complete listing of clubs and cafes with wi-fi access is available in Russian at http://wifi.yandex.ru.

Some policemen can be bothersome, especially to dark-skinned or otherwise foreign-looking people. Other members of the police force target tourists. Reports of tourists being hassled about their documents and registration have declined. However, it's still wise to carry a photocopy of your passport, visa and registration stamp. If stopped by the police, do not hand over your passport! It is perfectly acceptable to show a photocopy of the relevant pages instead.

SIGHTS
Kremlin

The apex of Russian political power and once the centre of the Orthodox Church, the **Kremlin** (Map p128; 495-202 3776; www.kremlin.museum.ru; adult/student R300/50, audio guide R200; 9.30am-4pm Fri-Wed; Aleksandrovsky Sad) is not only the kernel of Moscow but of the whole country. It's from here that autocratic tsars, communist dictators and democratic presidents have done their best – and worst – for Russia.

Occupying a roughly triangular plot of land covering Borovitsky Hill on the north bank of the Moscow River, the Kremlin is enclosed by high walls 2.25km long with Red Square outside the east wall. The best views of the complex are from Sofiyskaya nab across the river.

Before entering the Kremlin, deposit bags at the **left luggage office** (Map p128; per bag R60; 9am-6.30pm Fri-Wed), beneath the Kutafya Tower near the main ticket office. The main ticket office is in the Alexandrovsky Garden, just off Manezhnaya pl. The ticket to the 'Architectural Ensemble of Cathedral Square' covers entry to all five church-museums, as well as Patriarch's Palace and exhibits in the Ivan the Great Bell Tower. It does not include the Armoury or the Diamond Fund

MOSCOW МОСКВА

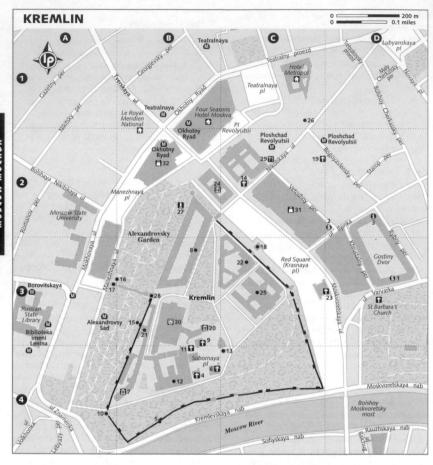

KREMLIN

0 — 200 m
0 — 0.1 miles

Exhibition. In any case, you can and should buy tickets for the Armoury here.

Photography is not permitted inside the Armoury or any of the buildings on Sobornaya pl (Cathedral Sq). Visitors wearing shorts will be refused entry.

TOURS

Make advanced arrangements for the tour 'One Day at the Kremlin' at the **Kremlin Excursion Office** (Map p128; ☎ 495-290 3094; Ⓜ Alexandrovsky Sad) in Alexandrovsky Garden. Capital Tours (p140) offers standard daily tours of the Kremlin and Armoury, while Patriarshy Dom Tours (p140) offers more in-depth tours. Numerous freelance guides also tout their services near the Kutafya Tower.

GOVERNMENT BUILDINGS

The **Kutafya Tower** (Map p128), which forms the main visitors' entrance today, stands away from the Kremlin's west wall, at the end of a ramp over the Aleksandrovsky Garden leading up to the **Trinity Gate Tower** (Map p128). On the way to central Sobornaya pl you'll pass a series of buildings that are closed to visitors. On the right is the 17th-century **Poteshny Palace** (Map p128), where Stalin lived, and the bombastic marble, glass and concrete **State Kremlin Palace** (Map p128), built from 1960 to 1961 for Communist Party congresses and now used by the Kremlin Ballet Theatre (see p145). On the left is the **Arsenal** (Map p128), home to the Kremlin guard and ringed by 800 captured Napoleonic cannons; and the yellow, triangular former **Senate** (Map p128) building, now the ultimate seat of power in the modern Kremlin, the offices of the president of Russia. Next to the Senate is the 1930s **Supreme Soviet** (Map p128) building.

PATRIARCH'S PALACE

The palace contains an exhibit of 17th-century household items, including jewellery, hunting equipment and furniture. From here you can access the five-domed **Church of the Twelve Apostles** (Map p128), which has a gilded, wooden iconostasis and a collection of icons by leading 17th-century icon painters.

The Patriarch's Palace often holds **special exhibits** (adult/student R150/70), which can be visited individually, without access to the other buildings on Sobornaya pl.

ASSUMPTION CATHEDRAL

On the northern side of Sobornaya pl, with five golden helmet domes and four semicircular gables facing the square, is this **cathedral** (Map p128), built between 1475 and 1479. As the focal church of prerevolutionary Russia, it's the burial place of most heads of the Russian Orthodox Church from the 1320s to 1700. The iconostasis dates from 1652 but its lowest level contains some older icons, including the *Virgin of Vladimir* (Vladimirskaya Bogomater), an early-15th-century Rublyov-school copy of Russia's most revered image,

the *Vladimir Icon of the Mother of God* (Ikona Vladimirskoy Bogomateri).

The delicate little single-domed church beside the west door of the Assumption Cathedral is the **Church of the Deposition of the Robe** (Map p128), built between 1484 and 1486 by masons from Pskov.

IVAN THE GREAT BELL TOWER

With its two golden domes rising above the eastern side of Sobornaya pl, the 16th-century **bell tower** (Map p128; adult/student R100/50) is the Kremlin's tallest structure, visible from 30km away. Exhibitions from the Kremlin collections are shown on the ground level.

Beside the bell tower (not inside it) stands the **Tsar Bell**, which is the world's biggest bell. Sadly, this 202-tonne monster never rang. North of the bell tower is the **Tsar Cannon**, cast in 1586 for Fyodor I, whose portrait is on the barrel. Shot has never sullied its 89cm bore – and certainly not the cannonballs beside it, which are too big even for this elephantine firearm.

ARCHANGEL CATHEDRAL

Back on Sobornaya pl, this 1508 **cathedral** (Map p128) at the square's southeastern corner was for centuries the coronation, wedding and burial church of tsars. The tombs of all of Moscow's rulers from the 1320s to the 1690s (except Boris Godunov, who is buried at

Sergiev Posad – see p149) are here. Tsarevich Dmitry (Ivan the Terrible's son, who died mysteriously in 1591) lies beneath a painted stone canopy.

ANNUNCIATION CATHEDRAL

At the southwest corner of Sobornaya pl, this **cathedral** (Map p128), built by Pskov masters in 1489, was the royal family's private chapel. Ivan the Terrible's first marriage disqualified him under Orthodox law from entering the church proper, so he had the southern arm of the gallery converted into the **Archangel Gabriel Chapel**, from which he could view services through a grille.

The cathedral contains the celebrated icons of master painter Theophanes the Greek (at the right-hand end of the diesis row, the biggest of the six tiers of the iconostasis). *Archangel Michael* (the third icon from the left on the largest of the six tiers of the iconostasis) is ascribed to Andrei Rublyov.

ARMOURY

The 700-room State Kremlin Palace is used for official visits and receptions, but isn't open to the public. In the Kremlin's southwestern corner is the **Armoury** (Map p128; adult/student R350/70, audio guide R200; ☺ 10am, noon, 2.30pm, 4.30pm), a numbingly opulent collection of treasures accumulated over time by the Russian State and Church. Tickets specify entry times. Look for royal regalia such as the joint coronation throne of boy tsars Peter (the Great) and his half-brother Ivan V (with a secret compartment from which Regent Sofia would prompt them); the 800-diamond throne of Tsar Alexey Mikhailovich; and the coronation dresses of 18th-century empresses.

If the Armoury doesn't sate your diamond lust, there are more in the separate **Diamond**

STAND ON CEREMONY

Every Saturday at noon on Sobornaya pl, the Presidential Regiment shows up in all their finery for a ceremonial procession, featuring some very official-looking prancing and dancing, both on foot and on horseback. The price of admission to the Kremlin allows access to the demonstration. Otherwise, on the last Saturday of the month, the demonstration is repeated at 2pm for the masses on Red Square.

Fund Exhibition (Map p128; ☎ 495-629 2036; admission R500; ☺ 10am-1pm, 2-5pm Fri-Wed), which is in the same building as the Armoury. The lavish collection shows off the precious stones and jewellery garnered by tsars and empresses over the centuries, including the largest sapphire in the world.

ALEKSANDROVSKY GARDEN

A good place to relax is the pleasant **garden** (Map p128) along the Kremlin's western wall. At the garden's northern end is the **Tomb of the Unknown Soldier**, containing the remains of a soldier who died in December 1941 at Km41 of Leningradskoe sh – the nearest the Nazis came to Moscow. The changing of the guard happens every hour from 10am to 7pm in summer, and to 3pm during winter. Opposite the gardens is Manezhnaya pl and the underground Okhotny Ryad shopping mall.

Red Square & Kitay Gorod

Immediately outside the Kremlin's northeastern wall is the renowned **Red Square** (Krasnaya ploshchad; Map p128). It was once a market square adjoining the merchants' area in Kitay Gorod. Red Square has always been a place where occupants of the Kremlin chose to congregate, celebrate and castigate for all the people to see.

Incidentally, the name 'Krasnaya ploshchad' has nothing to do with communism or the blood that flowed here: *krasny* in old Russian meant 'beautiful' and only in the 20th century did it come to mean 'red', too.

LENIN'S MAUSOLEUM

Visit this granite **tomb** (Map p128; ☎ 495-623 5527; admission free; ☺ 10am-1pm Tue-Thu, Sat & Sun; Ⓜ Ploshchad Revolyutsii) while you can, since the former leader may eventually end up beside his mum in St Petersburg. For now, the embalmed leader remains as he has been since 1924 (apart from a retreat to Siberia during WWII).

Before joining the queue at the northwestern corner of Red Square, drop your camera at the left-luggage office in the State History Museum (see opposite), as you will not be allowed to take it with you. After trooping past the embalmed, oddly waxy figure, emerge from his red and black stone tomb and inspect where Josef Stalin, Leonid Brezhnev and many of communism's other heavy hitters are buried along the Kremlin wall.

MOSCOW MOCKBA

LENIN UNDER GLASS

Red Square is home to the world's most famous mummy, that of Vladimir Lenin. When he died of a massive stroke (on 22 January 1924, aged 53), a long line of mourners gathered patiently in winter's harshness for weeks to glimpse the body as it lay in state. Inspired by the spectacle, Stalin proposed that the father of Soviet communism should continue to serve the cause as a sacred relic. So the decision was made to preserve Lenin's corpse for perpetuity, against the vehement protests of his widow, as well as his own expressed desire to be buried next to his mother in St Petersburg.

Boris Zbarsky, a biochemist, and Vladimir Vorobyov, an anatomist, were issued a political order to put a stop to the natural decomposition of the body. The pair worked frantically in a secret laboratory in search of a long-term chemical solution. In the meantime, the body's dark spots were bleached, and the lips and eyes sewn tight. The brain was removed and taken to another secret laboratory, to be sliced and diced by scientists for the next 40 years in the hope of uncovering its hidden genius.

In July 1924 the scientists hit upon a formula to successfully arrest the decaying process, a closely guarded state secret. This necrotic craft was passed on to Zbarsky's son, who ran the Kremlin's covert embalming lab for decades. After the fall of communism, Zbarsky came clean: the body is wiped down every few days, and then, every 10 months, thoroughly examined and submerged in a tub of chemicals, including paraffin wax. The institute has now gone commercial, offering its services and secrets to wannabe immortals for a mere US$1 million dollars.

Every so often, politicians express intentions to heed Lenin's request and bury him in St Petersburg, but it usually sets off a furore from the political left as well as more muted objections from Moscow tour operators. It seems that the mausoleum, the most sacred shrine of Soviet communism, and the mummy, the literal embodiment of the Russian Revolution, will remain in place for at least several more years.

ST BASIL'S CATHEDRAL

No picture can prepare you for the crazy confusion of colours and shapes that is **St Basil's Cathedral** (Map p128; ☎ 495-698 3304; adult/student R100/50; ☼ 11am-5pm Wed-Mon; Ⓜ Ploshchad Revolyutsii), technically the Intercession Cathedral. This ultimate symbol of Russia was created between 1555 and 1561 (replacing an existing church on the site) to celebrate the capture of Kazan by Ivan the Terrible.

The misnomer 'St Basil's' actually refers only to the northeastern chapel, which was added later. It was built over the grave of the barefoot holy fool Vasily (Basil) the Blessed, who predicted Ivan's damnation.

STATE HISTORY MUSEUM

At the northern end of the square, the **State History Museum** (Map p128; ☎ 495-692 3731; www.shm.ru; adult/student R150/60, audio guide R110; ☼ 10am-5pm Wed-Sat & Mon, 11am-7pm Sun; Ⓜ Ploshchad Revolyutsii) has an enormous collection covering the whole Russian empire from the Stone Age on. The building, dating from the late 19th century, is itself an attraction – each room is in the style of a different period or region. A joint ticket (adult/student R230/115) allowing access to the State History Museum

and St Basil's Cathedral is available at either spot.

Tiny **Kazan Cathedral** (Map p128; Nikolskaya ul 3; admission free; ☼ 8am-7pm; Ⓜ Ploshchad Revolyutsii) is opposite the museum entrance. It's a replica of the original, which was founded in 1636 and demolished on Stalin's orders in 1936, allegedly because it impeded the flow of parades through Red Square.

KITAY GOROD

The narrow old streets east of Red Square are known as Kitay Gorod. It translates as 'Chinatown', but the name derives from *kita*, meaning 'wattle', and refers to the palisades that reinforced the earthen ramp erected around this early Kremlin suburb. Kitay Gorod is one of the oldest parts of Moscow, settled in the 13th century as a trade and financial centre.

The busiest street of Kitay Gorod is Nikolskaya ul, once the main road to Vladimir, while the greatest concentration of interesting buildings is along ul Varvarka. See p138 for a walking tour of Kitay Gorod.

Tverskoy District

The streets around Tverskaya ul comprise the vibrant Tverskoy District, characterised

MOSCOW МОСКВА

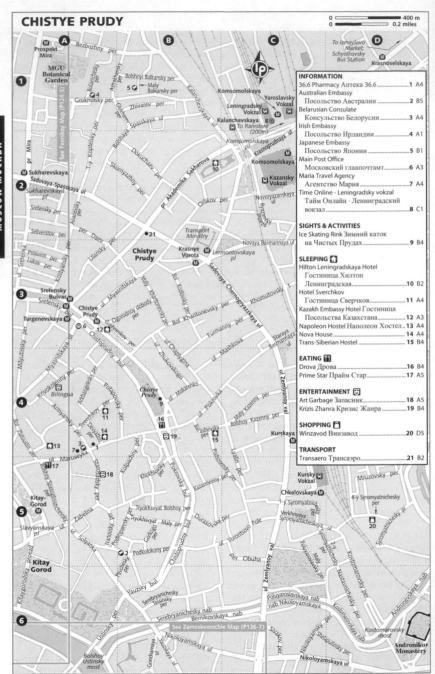

CHISTYE PRUDY

0 ————————— 400 m
0 ————————— 0.2 miles

INFORMATION
36.6 Pharmacy Аптека 36.6 ....1 A4
Australian Embassy
 Посольство Австралии 2 B5
Belarusian Consulate
 Консульство Белорусии 3 A4
Irish Embassy
 Посольство Ирландии 4 A1
Japanese Embassy
 Посольство Японии 5 B1
Main Post Office
 Московский главпочтамт.................6 A3
Maria Travel Agency
 Агентство Мария 7 A4
Time Online - Leningradsky vokzal
 Тайм Онлайн - Ленинградский
 вокзал 8 C1

SIGHTS & ACTIVITIES
Ice Skating Rink Зимний каток
 на Чистых Прудах............................9 B4

SLEEPING 🏠
Hilton Leningradskaya Hotel
 Гостиница Хилтон
 Ленинградская................................10 B2
Hotel Sverchkov
 Гостиница Сверчков.........................11 A4
Kazakh Embassy Hotel Гостиница
 Посольства Казахстана...................12 A3
Napoleon Hostel Наполеон Хостел..13 A4
Nova House 14 A4
Trans-Siberian Hostel 15 B4

EATING 🍴
Drova Дрова.....................................16 B4
Prime Star Прайм Стар 17 A5

ENTERTAINMENT 🎭
Art Garbage Запасник......................18 A5
Krizis Zhanra Кризис Жанра 19 B4

SHOPPING 🛍
Winzavod Винзавод..........................20 D5

TRANSPORT
Transaero Трансаэро........................21 B2

by old architecture and new commerce. Small lanes such as **Kamergersky per** and **Stoleshnikov per** are among Moscow's trendiest places to sip a coffee or a beer and watch the big-city bustle.

In the midst of the swanky shops on ul Petrovka, an archway leads to a courtyard strung with barbed wire and where hang portraits of political prisoners. This is the entrance to the **Gulag History Museum** (Map pp124–5; ☎ 495-621 7346; www.museum-gulag.narod.ru in Russian; ul Petrovka 16; ☷ 11am-4pm Tue-Sat; Ⓜ Chekhovskaya). Guides dressed like camp guards describe the vast network of labour camps that existed in the former Soviet Union and recount the horrors of camp life. The museum also serves as a memorial to the millions of victims of the system.

Nearby, the **Moscow Museum of Modern Art** (ММОМА; Map pp124–5; ☎ 495-694 2890; www.mmoma .ru; ul Petrovka 25; adult/student R200/100; ☷ noon 7pm; Ⓜ Chekhovskaya) is housed in a classical 18th-century merchant's home. It contains 20th-century paintings, sculptures and graphics, including some works by Marc Chagall, Natalia Goncharova, Vasily Kandinsky and Kasimir Malevich. Don't bypass the whimsical sculpture garden in the courtyard.

Arbat District

Bound by the Moscow River in the southeast, this district includes the area south of ul Novy Arbat (or Vozdvizhenka ul), including ul Arbat, the 1.25km pedestrian mall stretching from Arbatskaya pl on the Boulevard Ring to Smolenskaya pl on the Garden Ring.

Moscow's most famous street, **The Arbat** is something of an art market, complete with instant-portrait painters, soapbox poets, jugglers and buskers (and some pickpockets). It makes an interesting walk, dotted with old pastel-coloured merchant houses and tourist-oriented shops and cafes. Near ul Arbat's eastern end, the **Wall of Peace** (Map pp124–5) is composed of hundreds of individually painted tiles on a theme of international friendship. The statue at the corner of Plotnikov per is of **Bulat Okudzhava** (Map pp124–5), the 1960s cult poet, singer and songwriter who lived at No 43 (see p134).

Khamovniki

The Moscow River surrounds this district on three sides, as it dips down south and loops back up to the north.

PUSHKIN MUSEUM OF FINE ARTS

Moscow's premier foreign-art museum is the **Pushkin Museum of Fine Arts** (Map pp136–7; ☎ 495-203 7998; www.museum.ru/gmii; ul Volkhonka 12; adult/student R300/150, audio tour R200; ☷ 10am-6pm Tue-Sun; Ⓜ Kropotkinskaya), which shows off a broad selection of European works, mostly appropriated from private collections after the revolution. The highlight is perhaps the Dutch and Flemish masterpieces from the 17th century, including several Rembrandt portraits, and the Ancient Civilisation exhibits, which include the impressive Treasures of Troy.

The Pushkin has moved its amazing collection of Impressionist and post-Impressionist paintings next door to the new **Gallery of European & American Art of the 19th & 20th Centuries** (Map pp136–7; ☎ 495-203 1546; ul Volkhonka 14; adult/student R300/150; ☷ 10am-6pm Tue-Sun, 10am-8pm Thu; Ⓜ Kropotkinskaya). The new gallery contains the famed assemblage of French Impressionist works, including Degas, Manet, Renoir and Pisarro, with an entire room dedicated to Monet. Post-Impressionist masterpieces include those by Matisse, Picasso, Rousseau and Van Gogh, as well as an incredible collection of Gauguins.

There is a cluster of other, smaller art museums in the vicinity:

Glazunov Gallery (Map pp136–7 ; ☎ 495-291 6949; www.glazunov.ru; ul Volkhonka 13; adult/student R160/80; ☷ 11am-6pm Tue-Sun; Ⓜ Kropotkinskaya) Ilya Gazunov's work depicting scenes from Russian history.

Museum of Private Collections (Map pp136–7; ☎ 495-203 1546; ul Volkhonka 14; adult/student R300/150; ☷ 10am-6pm Wed-Sun; Ⓜ Kropotkinskaya)

Rerikh Museum (Map pp136–7; ☎ 495-203 6419; Maly Znamensky per 3/5; adult/student R220/110; ☷ 11am-5pm Wed-Sun; Ⓜ Kropotkinskaya) The artwork, archaeology and spirituality of Nikolai Rerikh.

Russian Academy of Art (Map pp136–7; ☎ 495-637 2569; www.rah.ru; ul Prechistenka 21; admission R80; ☷ 11am-8pm Tue-Sun; Ⓜ Kropotkinskaya) Has rotating exhibitions.

Tsereteli Gallery (Map pp136–7; ☎ 495-637 4150; ul Prechistenka 19; admission R200; ☷ noon-7pm Tue-Sat; Ⓜ Kropotkinskaya) Countless works by Zurab Tsereteli.

CATHEDRAL OF CHRIST THE SAVIOUR

Dominating the skyline along the Moscow River, the gargantuan **Cathedral of Christ the Saviour** (Map pp136–7; ☎ 495-202 4734; www.xxc.ru; admission free; ☷ 10am-5pm; Ⓜ Kropotkinskaya) sits on the site of an earlier and similar church of the

---

ARBAT, MY ARBAT

Arbat, my Arbat, you are my calling
You are my happiness and my misfortune.

Bulat Okudzhava

For Moscow's beloved bard Bulat Okudzhava, the Arbat was not only his home, it was his inspiration. Although he spent his university years in Georgia dabbling in harmless verse, it was only upon his return to Moscow – and to his cherished Arbat – that his poetry adopted the free-thinking character for which it is known.

He gradually made the transition from poet to songwriter, stating that, 'Once I had the desire to accompany one of my satirical verses with music. I only knew three chords; now, 27 years later, I know seven chords'. While Bulat and his friends enjoyed his songs, other composers, singers and guitarists did not. The ill feeling subsided when a well-known poet announced that '…these are not songs. This is just another way of presenting poetry'.

And so a new form of art was born. The 1960s were heady times – in Moscow as elsewhere – and Okudzhava inspired a whole movement of liberal-thinking poets to take their ideas to the streets. Vladimir Vysotsky and others – some political, some not – followed in Okudzhava's footsteps, their iconoclastic lyrics and simple melodies drawing enthusiastic crowds all around Moscow.

The Arbat today – crowded with tacky souvenir stands and overpriced cafes – bears little resemblance to the hallowed haunt of Okudzhava's youth. But its memory lives on in the bards and buskers, painters and poets who still perform for strolling crowds on summer evenings.

---

same name, built from 1839 to 1883 to commemorate Russia's victory over Napoleon. The original was destroyed during Stalin's orgy of explosive secularism. Stalin planned to replace the church with a 315m-high 'Palace of Soviets' (including a 100m statue of Lenin) but the project never got off the ground – literally. Instead, for 50 years the site served an important purpose as the world's largest swimming pool.

NOVODEVICHY CONVENT & CEMETERY

A cluster of sparkling domes behind turreted walls on the Moscow River, **Novodevichy Convent** (Map pp136-7; ☎ 499-246 8526; adult/student R150/60; ☺ grounds 8am-8pm daily, museums 10am-5pm Wed-Mon; Ⓜ Sportivnaya) was founded in 1524 to celebrate the taking of Smolensk from Lithuania. The convent is notorious as the place where Peter the Great imprisoned his half-sister Sofia for her part in the Streltsy rebellion. The oldest and most dominant building in the grounds is the white **Smolensk Cathedral**, its sumptuous interior covered in 16th-century frescoes.

Adjacent to the convent, **Novodevichy Cemetery** (Map pp136-7; admission free; ☺ 9am-5pm; Ⓜ Sportivnaya) is among Moscow's most prestigious resting places – a veritable 'who's who' of Russian politics and culture. You will find the tombs of Chekhov, Gogol,

Mayakovsky, Stanislavsky, Prokofiev, Eisenstein and many other Russian and Soviet notables. The most recent notable addition is former president Boris Yeltsin, who died in 2007.

Zamoskvorechie

Zamoskvorechie (meaning 'Beyond Moscow River') stretches south from opposite the Kremlin, inside a big river loop.

STATE TRETYAKOV GALLERY

Nothing short of spectacular, the **State Tretyakov Gallery** (Map pp136-7; ☎ 495-951 1362; www .tretyakovgallery.ru; Lavrushinsky per 10; adult/student R250/150, audio tour R300; ☺ 10am-5.30pm Tue-Sun; Ⓜ Tretyakovskaya) holds the world's best collection of Russian icons and an outstanding collection of other prerevolutionary Russian art, particularly the 19th-century Peredvizhniki (see p69). It is wheelchair friendly.

NEW TRETYAKOV

The premier venue for 20th-century Russian art is the new building of the State Tretyakov Gallery on Krymsky val, better known as the **New Tretyakov** (Map pp136-7; ☎ 499-238 1378; adult/student R225/150; ☺ 10am-6.30pm Tue-Sun; Ⓜ Park Kultury). Besides the plethora of socialist realism, the exhibits showcase avant-garde artists such as

Kasimir Malevich, Vasily Kandinsky, Marc Chagall, Natalia Goncharova and Lyubov Popova.

In the same building as the New Tretyakov, the **Tsentralny Dom Khudozhnikov** (Central House of Artists; Map pp136-7; ☎ 499-238 9843; admission R100, special exhibits R200; ☼ 11am-7pm Tue-Sun; Ⓜ Park Kultury) is a huge exhibit space used for contemporary art shows.

Behind the complex is the wonderful, moody **Art Muzeon sculpture park** (Map pp136-7; ☎ 499-238 3396; ul Krymsky val 10; admission R100; ☼ 9am-9pm; Ⓜ Park Kultury). Formerly called the Park of the Fallen Heroes, this open-air park started as a collection of Soviet statues put out to pasture when they were ripped from their pedestals in the post-1991 wave of anti-Soviet feeling. These discredited icons have now been joined by fascinating and diverse contemporary work. A monumental but controversial **statue of Peter the Great** by sculptor Zurab Tsereteli stands on the riverbank, overlooking the park.

GORKY PARK
Part ornamental park, part funfair, Gorky Park is one of Moscow's most festive places to escape the hubbub of the city. Officially the **Park Kultury** (Map pp136-7; ☎ 495-237 1266; ul Krymsky val; adult/child R80/20; ☼ 10am-10pm; Ⓜ Park Kultury), it's named after Maxim Gorky, and stretches almost 3km along the river upstream of Krymsky most. You can't miss the showy entrance, marked by colourful flags waving in the wind and the happy sounds of an old-fashioned carousel. Inside, Gorky Park has a small Western amusement park with two roller coasters and a dozen other terror-inducing attractions.

Outer Moscow
ALL-RUSSIA EXHIBITION CENTRE
No other place sums up the rise and fall of the Soviet dream quite as well as the **All-Russia Exhibition Centre** (Vserossisky Vystavochny Tsentr, VVTs; ☎ 495-544 3400; www.vvcentre.ru, in Russian; ☼ pavilions 10am-7pm, grounds 8am-10pm; Ⓜ VDNKh), north of the centre. The old initials tell the story – VDNKh stands for Vystavka Dostizheny Narodnogo Khozyaystva SSSR (USSR Economic Achievements Exhibition).

VDNKh was originally created in the 1930s to impress upon one and all the success of the Soviet economic system. Two kilometres long and 1km wide, it is composed of wide pedestrian avenues and grandiose pavilions, glorifying every aspect of socialist construction from education and health to agriculture, technology and science. The pavilions represent a huge variety of architectural styles, symbolic of the contributions from diverse ethnic and artistic movements to the common goal. Here you will find the kitschiest socialist realism, the most inspiring of socialist optimism and, now, the tackiest of capitalist consumerism.

The grounds of VVTs are huge, so you may wish to catch a ride on the **tourist train** (R30) that leaves from the front gate. Otherwise, you can **rent bicycles and in-line skates** (R100/300 per hour/day) just outside.

The soaring 100m titanium obelisk is a monument to Soviet space flight. In its base is the **Memorial Museum of Cosmonauts** (☎ 495-683 8197; Ⓜ VDNKh), a high-concept series of displays from the glory days of the Soviet space program. The museum was closed for renovations at the time of research.

PARK POBEDY
This huge memorial complex, west of the centre, celebrates the Great Patriotic War. The park includes endless fountains and monuments, as well as the memorial **Church of St George**. The centrepiece **Museum of the Great Patriotic War** (☎ 495-142 4185; ul Bratiev Fonchenko 10; adult/child R100/40; ☼ 10am-5pm Tue-Sun Nov-Mar, till 7pm Apr-Oct; Ⓜ Park Pobedy) has a diorama of every major WWII battle. Exhibits highlight the many heroes of the Soviet Union, plus weapons, photographs, films, letters and other wartime memorabilia. Make

MOURNING TRAIN
Paveletskaya pl is the wide square on the Garden Ring, dominated by Paveletsky vokzal (Pavelets Station). The finest loco in the neighbourhood, however, stands idle in an air-conditioned pavilion east of the station. It is the 'mourning train' (Map pp136-7) that brought Lenin's body to Moscow from Gorki Leninskie, where he died, in January 1924. The old steam engine is in beautiful condition, but does not attract many visitors these days. In fact, it is technically closed to the public but the security guard might let you in for a small fee, especially if you show up after hours. From Kozhevnichenskaya ul, cut behind the row of kiosks and through the overgrown park to the pavilion in the back.

MOSCOW МОСКВА

ZAMOSKVORECHIE

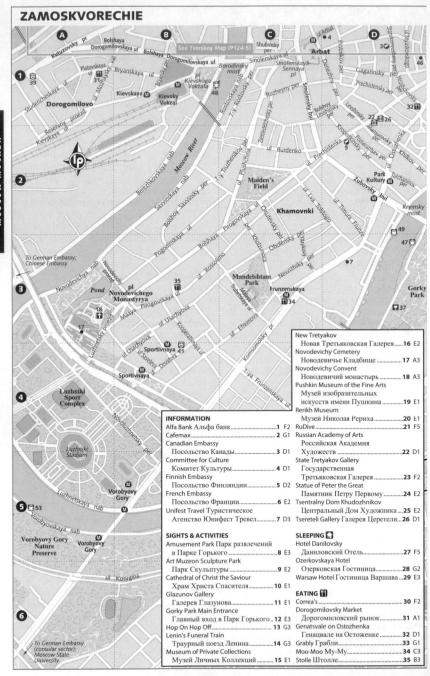

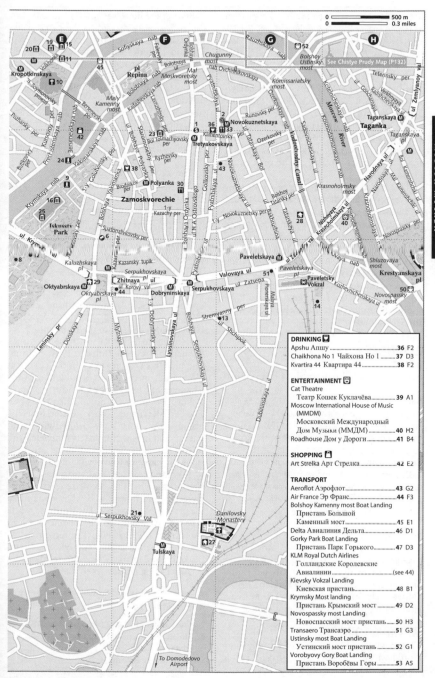

MOSCOW МОСКВА

arrangements in advance to visit the **Museum of Jewish Legacy History & Holocaust** (☎ 495-148 1907; Minskaya ul; admission free; ☒ 10am-6pm Tue-Thu, noon-7pm Sun; Ⓜ Park Pobedy).

VOROBYOVY GORY

The best view over Moscow is from **Universitetskaya pl** on Vorobyovy Gory (Sparrow Hills). Behind the square is the 36-storey spire of **Moscow State University** (Moskovsky Gosudarstvenny Universitet; Ⓜ Vorobyovy Gory), one of Stalin's 'Seven Sisters' that is visible from most places in the city thanks to its elevated site.

This is also a convenient access point for the **Vorobyovy Gory Nature Preserve** (☎ 499-739 2708; www.vorobyovy-gory.ru, in Russian; admission free; Ⓜ Vorobyovy Gory). Following the south shore of the Moscow River, the narrow strip of land contains a network of wooded trails and a sandy beach. An **eco-train** runs along the bank of the river; otherwise you can rent bicycles or in-line skates at the southeastern entrance. From the riverbank, the walking trails lead up to Universitetskaya pl, as does the **ski lift** (R100).

ACTIVITIES
BANYA

See p67 for a full description of the *banya* experience.

Banya on Presnya (Map pp124-5; ☎ 495-253 8690; Stolyarny per 7; general admission R700-800; ☒ 8am-8pm Wed-Mon, noon-8pm Tue; Ⓜ Ulitsa 1905 Goda) This pleasant, efficient place has an excellent, segregated *banya* as well as spa services and an on-site cafe.

Sanduny Baths (Map pp124-5; ☎ private 495-628 4633, general 495-625 4631; www.sanduny.ru; Neglinnaya ul 14; private room per hr from R1300, general admission per 2hr R600-800; ☒ 8am-10pm; Ⓜ Chekhovskaya) The oldest and most luxurious *banya* in the city.

WINTER SPORTS

There's no shortage of winter in Moscow, so take advantage of it. You can rent ice skates and see where all those great Russian figure skaters come from at **Gorky Park** (p135) or **Chistye Prudy** (Map p132; Chistoprudny bul; Ⓜ Chistye Prudy). Bring your passport to rent skates.

WALKING TOUR

This walking tour winds its way through Kitay Gorod, which – settled in the 13th century – is one of the oldest parts of Moscow.

Start at the **Hotel Metropol (1)** and walk east down Teatralny proezd to the gated walkway. This historical complex is **Starye Polya (2)**, and includes excavations of the 16th-century fortified wall that used to surround Kitay Gorod and the foundations of the 1493 Trinity Church, as well as the memorial statue of Ivan Fyodorov, the 16th-century printer responsible for Russia's first book.

Walk down Tretyakovsky proezd to busy Nikolskaya ul. Turn right to head southwest on Nikolskaya ul, which used to be the main road to Vladimir.

The green and white building, with the lion and unicorn above its entrance at No 15, is the **Synod Printing House (3)**, where Ivan Fyodorov reputedly produced Russia's first printed book in 1563. Up until the early 19th century, Kitay Gorod was a printing centre, home to 26 out of Moscow's then 31 bookshops. The **Zaikonospassky Monastery (4)** at No 7 refers to the busy icon trade that also took place here.

Turn left on Bogoyavlensky per and head south, looking for the Moscow Baroque Epiphany Cathedral on the right-hand side. The church was built in the 1690s, but the **Monastery of the Epiphany (5)** dates to the 13th century.

Continue to ul Ilyinka, which was Moscow's financial heart in the 18th and 19th centuries. The old **Stock Exchange (6)** is on the corner at No 6. Built in the 1870s, it now houses the Chamber of Commerce and Industry.

Turn left and walk down Khrustalny per. The Old Merchants' Court – **Gostiny Dvor (7)** – occupies the block between uls Ilyinka and Varvarka. It is now completely renovated and filled with shops, including some excellent stops for souvenir hunters.

Take another left and head east on ul Varvarka, which is crowded with tiny churches, old homes and what remains of the giant Hotel Rossiya. The pink and white **St Barbara's Church (8)**, now government offices, dates from 1795 to 1804. The reconstructed 16th-century **Old English Court (9)**, white with peaked wooden roofs, was the residence of England's first emissaries to Russia.

WALK FACTS

Start Hotel Metropol (Ⓜ Teatralnaya)
Finish Staraya pl (Ⓜ Kitay-Gorod)
Distance 1.5km
Duration Two hours

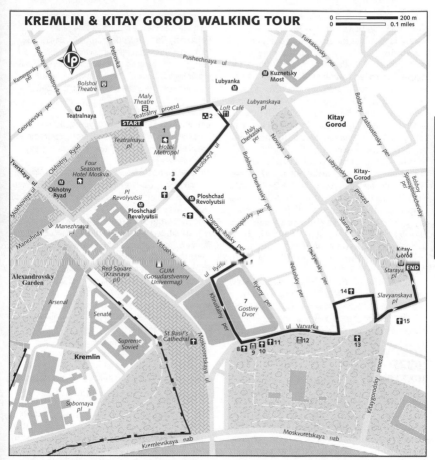

KREMLIN & KITAY GOROD WALKING TOUR

Built in 1698, the **Church of St Maxim the Blessed (10)** at No 4 is now a folk-art exhibition hall. Next along is the pointed bell tower of the 17th-century **Monastery of the Sign (11)**, incorporating the monks' building and a golden-domed cathedral.

Tucked in between the street and the former Hotel Rossiya is the small but interesting **Romanov Chambers in Zaryadie Museum (12**; Map pp124-5; ☎ 495-692 1256; ul Varvarka 10; admission R100; ♥ 10am-5pm Thu-Mon, 11am-6pm Wed), which is devoted to the lives of these high-ranking nobles. The colourful **St George's Church (13)** at No 12 dates from 1658.

Cross ul Varvarka and walk up Ipatyevsky per. The enchanting 1630s **Church of the Trinity in Nikitniki (14)** is an exquisite example of Russian

baroque hidden amid the overbearing facades of the surrounding buildings.

Head east on Ipatyevsky per out to Slavyanskaya pl. At the southern end of Slavyanskaya pl **All Saints Cathedral on the Kulishka (15)** was built in 1687. In 1380, Dmitry Donskoy built the original wooden church on this site to commemorate those who died in the battle of Kulikovo. Some remains of the old city wall can be seen in the underground passage at the corner of ul Varvarka and Staraya pl.

MOSCOW FOR CHILDREN

Kids may not appreciate an age-old icon or a Soviet hero but Moscow has plenty to offer the little ones. For starters, the city is filled with parks, such as **Gorky Park** (p135) and the **All-Russia Exhibition Centre** (p135).

Russia excels at the circus, and crazy clowns and daring acrobatics are all the rage at the atmospheric **Nikulin Circus** (p145). **Obraztsov Puppet Theatre and Museum** (Map pp124-5; ☎ 495-699 7972; www.puppet.ru; Sadovaya-Samotechnaya ul 3; adult R300-1000, child R200-600; ☻ box office 11am-2.30pm & 3.30-7pm; Ⓜ Tsvetnoy Bulvar) runs colourful Russian folk tales and adapted classical plays; kids can get up close and personal with the incredible puppets at the museum.

What better fun for kiddies than performing kitties? At the **Cat Theatre** (Map pp136-7; ☎ 499-249 2907; Kutuzovsky pr 25; tickets R200-700; Ⓜ Kievskaya), Yuri Kuklachev's acrobatic cats do all kinds of stunts to the audience's delight. Kuklachev says, 'We do not use the word *train* here because it implies forcing an animal to do something; and you cannot force cats to do anything they don't want to. We *play* with the cats.'

Bigger cats are the highlight of the **Moscow Zoo** (Map pp124-5; ☎ 499-255 5375; www.moscowzoo.ru; cnr Barrikadnaya & Bolshaya Gruzinskaya uls; adult/child R150/free; ☻ 10am-7pm Tue-Sun May-Sep, 10am-5pm Tue-Sun Oct-Apr; Ⓜ Barrikadnaya), an obvious destination for children.

TOURS

BOAT TOURS

For a leisurely cruise or good old-fashioned transport, a boat ride (adult/child R400/150, 1½ hours, every 20 minutes) on the Moscow River is one of the city's highlights. The main route runs between Kievsky vokzal (Map pp136-7) and the Novospassky most near Novospassky Monastery, with stops at Vorobyovy Gory, Gorky Park and Ustinsky most near the Kremlin. The boats are operated by the **Capital Shipping Company** (☎ 495-225 6070; www.cck-ship.ru) from May to September.

For boats that go further afield, see p148.

OTHER TOURS

Capital Tours (Map p128; ☎ 495-232 2442; www.capital tours.ru; Gostiny Dvor, ul Ilinka 4; Ⓜ Kitay-Gorod) This spin-off of Patriarshy Dom offers a twice-daily Kremlin tour (adult/child R1400/700, ☻ 11am & 2pm Fri-Wed) and Moscow city bus tour (adult/child R750/360, ☻ 10.30am & 2.30pm). Tours depart from Gostiny Dvor.

Hop On Hop Off (Map pp136-7; ☎ 495-787 7335; www .hoponhopoff.ru; ul Shchipok 1; adult/child R750/400; ☻ 10am-5pm; Ⓜ Serpukhovskaya) This colourful bus circulates around the city centre, stopping at designated points. As the name implies, you can hop on and off as many times as you like within a 24-hour period.

Patriarshy Dom Tours (Map pp124-5; ☎ 495-795 0927; http://russiatravel-pdtours.netfirms.com; Vspolny per 6, Moscow school No 1239; Ⓜ Barrikadnaya) Provides unique English-language tours on many specialised subjects; some provide access to otherwise closed museums.

FESTIVALS & EVENTS

Golden Mask Festival (www.goldenmask.ru) Two weeks of shows by Russia's premier drama, opera, dance and musical performers. Brightens up otherwise dreary March and April.

Moscow Biennale (www.moscowbiennale.ru) Aimed at making Moscow a centre for contemporary art, this month-long program hosts exhibits at venues around the city. Odd years only, usually in autumn.

Moscow Forum (www.ccmm.ru) A contemporary music festival held every year in April at the Moscow Conservatory.

Moscow International Film Festival (www.moscow filmfestival.ru) Russia's premier film festival in June attracts film-makers from around the world, although the highlight is the retrospective on the great Soviet artists.

City Day (Den Goroda) Celebrates the city's birthday every year on the first weekend in September. The day kicks off with a festive parade, followed by live music and plenty of food, fireworks and fun.

December Nights Festival (www.museum.ru/gmii) Perhaps Moscow's most prestigious music event, this annual festival involves a month of performances by high-profile musicians and an art exhibit for accompaniment.

SLEEPING

Staying within the Garden Ring guarantees easy access to major sights and plenty of dining and entertainment options. The Tverskoy and Arbat Districts are particularly lively. If you do find yourself far from the centre (which may be the case if you are on a tight budget), look for easy access to the metro.

Budget

For the purposes of this chapter, budget accommodation is less than R3000. Budget accommodation is usually dorm-style, although there are some private rooms available in this range. Prices include coffee and tea, but no breakfast.

CHISTYE PRUDY

Trans-Siberian Hostel (Map p132; ☎ 495-916 2030; www .transsiberianhostel.com; Barashevsky per 12; dm R630-700, d R1750; Ⓜ Kitay-Gorod; ✕ ▣) If you can snag one of the two double rooms in this tiny hostel, you're getting one of the capital's best bargains: you won't find a private room at this price anywhere else in central Moscow. A train-themed decor brightens the place up.

Nova House (Map p132; ☎ 495-623 4659; novahostel@nm.ru; Devyatkin per 4, apt 6; dm R680, d R2600-2800; Ⓜ Kitay-Gorod; ✗ ▣) It's hard to say who at Nova House is friendlier: Oleg, the owner, or Vasya, the loveable resident cat. Both ensure a homey atmosphere, enhanced by the funky contemporary decor, mural-painted ceilings and walls, and a beautiful upright piano in the common living room. Bonus: bikes!

Napoleon Hostel (Map p132; ☎ 495-628 6695; www.napoleonhostel.com; Maly Zlatoustinsky per 2, 4th fl; dm R800-1000; Ⓜ Kitay-Gorod; ✗ ▣) Ignore the decrepit entryway and climb to the 4th floor, where you'll find a fully renovated hostel: the light-filled rooms have six to 10 wooden bunks, for a total of 47 beds (but only two toilets and two showers – do the math!), plus a clean kitchen and a comfy common room that is well stocked with board games and a plasma TV.

TVERSKOY & ARBAT

our pick Home from Home Hostel (Map pp124-5; ☎ 495-229 8018; www.home-fromhome.com; ul Arbat 49, apt 9; dm R700-800, d R2000; Ⓜ Smolenskaya; ✗ ▣) In an attempt to make this your 'home away from home' the owners have spruced up the entryway, putting comfy couches and potted plants on the landing and creating a pleasant first impression – rare indeed in Moscow! Once inside, original art and mural-painted walls create a bohemian atmosphere. Enter the courtyard from Plotnikov per and look for entrance No 2. If this place is full, the owners can recommend a few other hostels in the neighbourhood.

Godzillas Hostel (Map pp124-5; ☎ 495-699 4223; www.godzillashostel.com; Bolshoy Karetny per 6; dm/d/tr R725/1740/2175; Ⓜ Tsvetnoy Bulvar; ✗ ▣) Godzillas is the biggest and most professionally run hostel in Moscow, with 90 beds spread out over four floors. The rooms come in various sizes, but they are all spacious and light-filled and painted in different colours. There are bathroom facilities on each floor, three kitchens and a big living room with satellite TV.

our pick Sokol Exclusive (☎ 8-916 572 3664; www.moscowhostel.org; Leningradsky pr 71, apt 109; dm/r R900/2700; Ⓜ Sokol; ✗ ▣) This newish place is trying to cash in on the capital's obsession with exclusivity. But as hostels go, Sokol Exclusive really is a step up. The two spacious light-filled rooms have only three beds, wood floors and attractive minimalist Tudor-style

decor. It's northwest of the centre, well outside the Garden Ring, but only a few steps from the metro.

Midrange

Midrange accommodation in Moscow falls between R3000 and R10,000 per night. This wide-ranging category includes a variety of Soviet-era properties that have not come completely into the 21st century, though many are very atmospheric (as reflected in the price). Prices include breakfast unless otherwise noted.

CHISTYE PRUDY

Hotel Sverchkov (Map p132; ☎ 495-625 4978; per Sverchkov 8; sverchkov8@mail.ru; s/d from R3800/4400; Ⓜ Chistye Prudy) On a quiet residential lane, this is a tiny 11-room hotel in a graceful 18th-century building. The hallways are lined with green-leafed plants, and paintings by local artists adorn the walls. Though rooms have old-style bathrooms and faded furniture, this place is a rarity for its intimacy and hominess.

Kazakh Embassy Hotel (Map p132; ☎ 495-608 0994; hotel@kazembassy.ru; Chistoprudny bul 3; s/d R5500/7400; Ⓜ Chistye Prudy; ▣) Caters – as you might guess – to guests and workers of the nearby Kazakh embassy. But anyone can stay in this grand, modern building that fronts the prestigious Boulevard Ring. The recent revamp has brought rooms into line with a generic international style. Convenient to the train stations at Komsomolskaya pl.

TVERSKOY & ARBAT

Kita Inn (Map pp124-5; ☎ 8-926 664 4118, 8-919 772 4002; www.kitainn.com; 2-ya Tverskaya-Yamskaya 6/7, apt 9-10; r R3325; Ⓜ Mayakovskaya; ✗ ▣) Finally, somebody has opened a proper pension in Moscow. It's a modest place, offering private rooms that are simple and sweet – Ikea beds, posters on the wall and windows overlooking a shady courtyard. Three rooms share access to a small, remodelled kitchen and a brand new bathroom. The owner has a few flats in the neighbourhood all offering similar facilities – see also **Flamingo B&B** (www.flamingobed.com).

Melodiya Hotel (Map pp124-5; ☎ 495-723 5246; www.melody-hotel.ru, in Russian; Skatertny per 13; s/d R5500/6900; Ⓜ Arbatskaya) Unique for its small size, Melodiya has only 46 small but comfortable rooms. Fantastic location on a residential street just off the Arbat.

FIND A FLAT

Hotels in Moscow can break your bank. In response to the shortage of affordable accommodation, some entrepreneurial Muscovites now rent out flats on a short-term basis. Flats are equipped with kitchens, and sometimes with other useful amenities such as internet access. Often, a good-sized flat is available for the price of a hotel room, or less. It is an ideal solution for travellers in a group, who can split the cost. Apartments are around R2800 to R3500 per night; expect to pay more for fully renovated, Western-style apartments.

■ **www.cheap-moscow.com** Heed the disclaimers, but this site has loads of listings for apartments to rent direct from the owner.

■ **www.enjoymoscow.com** Rick's apartments are off the Garden Ring between Sukharevskaya and Tsvetnoy Bulvar metro stations. Studios start at US$135, or pay about US$215 for one with two-bedrooms.

■ **www.evans.ru** Caters mainly to long-term renters, but also offers some apartments for US$150 to US$250 per night.

■ **www.flatmates.ru/eng** A site for travellers looking for somebody to share short- or long-term accommodation.

■ **www.hofa.ru** Apartments from €62 per night and a variety of homestay programs.

■ **www.moscowapartments.net** Not-too-fancy but fully-furnished apartments for €85 to €100.

■ **www.moscow4rent.com** Most flats are centrally located, with internet access, satellite TV and unlimited international phone calls. Prices start at US$150 per night.

---

ourpick Assambleya Nikitskaya Hotel (Map pp124-5; ☎ 495-933 5001; www.assambleya-hotels.ru, in Russian; Bolshaya Nikitskaya ul 12; s R7110-7900, d R9450-10,500; Ⓜ Okhotny Ryad; ⊠ ✖ ☐) Nikitskaya offers a rare combination: superb location, reasonable prices and Russian charm. While the building and rooms are freshly renovated, it preserves an anachronistic atmosphere, with heavy floral drapes and linens. But it's all very cosy and comfortable.

Sovietsky Hotel (☎ 495-960 2000; www.sovietsky.ru; Leningradsky pr 32/2; r from R7200; Ⓜ Dinamo; ⊠ ✖ ☐ ⍾) Built in 1952, this historic hotel north of the centre shows Stalin's tastes in all of its architectural details, starting from the gilded hammer and sickle and the enormous Corinthian columns flanking the front door. Even the simplest rooms have ceiling medallions and other ornamentation. The legendary restaurant Yar – complete with old-fashioned dancing girls – is truly over the top. The location is not super convenient, but this throwback is still fun for a Soviet-style splurge.

East-West Hotel (Map pp124-5; ☎ 495-232 2857; www.eastwesthotel.ru; Tverskoy bul 14/4; s/d R9000/10,000; ⊠ ✖ ☐ ; Ⓜ Pushkinskaya) Located on the loveliest stretch of the Boulevard Ring, this small hotel evokes the atmosphere of the 19th-century mansion it once was. It is a kitschy but charming place with 24 individually decorated rooms and a lovely fountain-filled courtyard. The price comes down significantly on weekends; it goes up if you do not pay in advance.

ZAMOSKVORECHIE

Hotel Varshava (Map pp136-7; ☎ 495-238 7701; warsaw@sovintel.ru; Leninsky pr 2/1; s R3600-4100, d R4750-5000; Ⓜ Oktyabrskaya; ⊠ ✖ ☐) The location is the main drawcard here: the Warsaw Hotel offers lots of restaurants, easy access to the metro and a short walk into the heart of Zamoskvorechie. The hotel itself does not exactly add to the aesthetics of the surrounding square; however, the interior has recently undergone extensive renovations and offers good value.

ourpick Ozerkovskaya Hotel (Map pp136-7; ☎ 495-951 7644; www.cct.ru; Ozerkovskaya nab 50; s/d from R5400/6300; Ⓜ Paveletskaya; ⊠ ☐) This comfy, cosy hotel has only 25 rooms, including three that are tucked up under the mansard roof. The rooms are simply decorated, but parquet floors and comfortable queen-sized beds rank it above the standard post-Soviet fare. Add in attentive service and a central location (convenient for the express train to Domodedovo airport), and you've got an excellent option.

Hotel Danilovsky (☎ 495-954 0503; www.danilovsky.ru; bul Starodanilovsky per; s/d/ste R5500/6000/9000; Ⓜ Tulskaya; ⊠ ✖ ☐) Moscow's holiest hotel is on the grounds of the 12th-century Danilovsky monastery – where the exquisite setting comes complete with 18th-century churches and well-maintained gardens. The modern five-storey hotel was built so that nearly all the rooms have a view of the grounds. The recently renovated rooms are simple but clean, and breakfast is modest: no greed, gluttony or sloth to be found here.

Top End

Top end accommodation starts at R10,000 and goes all the way up. Prices include breakfast.

Hotel Akvarel (Map pp124-5; ☎ 495-502 9430; www .hotelakvarel.ru; Stoleshnikov per 12; s/d R10,500/12,250; Ⓜ Chekhovskaya; ☒ ☒ ☐) Set amid all the grandeur of Stoleshnikov per is this intimate business-class hotel, offering 23 simple but sophisticated rooms, adorned with watercolour paintings. The friendly Akvarel is tucked in behind Simachyov Bar & Boutique (p146). It has reduced rates on weekends.

Golden Apple (Map pp124-5; ☎ 495-980 7000; www.goldenapple.ru; ul Malaya Dmitrovka 11; s/d from R12,000/12,500; Ⓜ Pushkinskaya; ☒ ☒ ☐) A classical edifice fronts the street, but the interior is sleek and sophisticated. The rooms are decorated in a minimalist, modern style – subdued whites and greys punctuated by contrasting coloured drapes and funky light fixtures. Comfort is also paramount, with no skimping on luxuries.

Hilton Leningradskaya (Map p132; ☎ 495-627 5550; www.hilton.com; Kalanchevskaya ul 21/40; d from R19,000; Ⓜ Komsomolskaya; ☒ ☒ ☐ ☒) If you want to indulge in high-thread-count sheets and feather pillows before you get on the train, here is your chance. Occupying one of the iconic Stalinist skyscrapers, the old Leningradskaya Hotel has a new life, thanks to Hilton and its multiyear upgrade (finally completed in 2008). Right on Komsomolskaya pl, this is the most convenient option for Trans-Siberian travellers. It is wheelchair friendly.

EATING

Many restaurants, especially top-end eateries, accept credit cards, and almost all restaurants have English-language menus.

Restaurants

BUDGET

Grably (Map pp136-7; ☎ 495-545 0830; Pyatnitskaya ul 27; meals R200-300; Ⓨ 10am-11pm; Ⓜ Novokuznetskaya) The big buffet features an amazing array of fish, poultry and meat, plus salads, soups and desserts. After you run the gauntlet and pay the bill, take a seat in the elaborate winter-garden seating area.

Moo-Moo (meals R200-300; Ⓨ 9am-11pm) Arbat (Map pp124-5; ☎ 495-241 1364; ul Arbat 45/24; Ⓜ Smolenskaya); Kitay Gorod (Map pp124-5; ☎ 495-623 4503; Myasnitskaya ul 14; Ⓜ Lubyanka); Khamovniki (Map pp136-7; ☎ 495-245 7820; Komsomolsky pr 26; Ⓜ Frunzenskaya) You will recognise Moo-Moo by its black-and-white Holstein-print decor. A cafeteria-style service offers an easy approach to Russian favourites.

Drova (meals R200-400, all-you-can-eat buffet R350; Ⓨ 24hr) Arbat (Map pp124-5; ☎ 495-202 7570; Nikitsky bul 8a; Ⓜ Arbatskaya); Kitay Gorod (Map p128; ☎ 8-901 532 8252; Nikolskaya ul 5; Ⓜ Ploshchad Revolyutsii); Chistye Prudy (Map p132; ☎ 495-916 0445; ul Pokrovka 17; Ⓜ Chistye Prudy) The self-serve buffet features offerings ranging from *solyanka* (a salty vegetable and meat soup) to sushi to sweet-and-sour pork. It's not the best place to sample any of these items, but the price is right.

MIDRANGE

Vostochny Kvartal (Map pp124-5; ☎ 499-241 3803; ul Arbat 45/24; meals R400-600; Ⓜ Smolenskaya; Ⓥ) Vostochny Kvartal used to live up to its name, acting as the 'Eastern Quarter' of the Arbat. Uzbek cooks and Uzbek patrons assured that this was the real-deal place to get your *plov* (pilaf rice with diced mutton and vegetables). The place has since gone the way of the Arbat itself, drawing in more English-speakers than anything else. Nonetheless, it still serves some of the best food on the block.

Skromnoe Obayanie Burzhuazi (Modest Charms of the Bourgeoisie; Map pp124-5; ☎ 495-623 0848; ul Bolshaya Lubyanka 24; meals R400-600; Ⓨ 24hr; Ⓜ Lubyanka; Ⓥ) The main draw of the 'Bourgeoisie' is the cool, casual setting. The menu is reasonably priced and wide-ranging, from pizza to sushi to sandwiches, but don't expect gourmet fare.

Correa's (Map pp124-5; ☎ 495-605 9100; Bolshaya Gruzinskaya ul 32; brunch R400-600, sandwiches R200-300, meals R600-1000; Ⓨ 8am-midnight; Ⓜ Belorusskaya/ Barrikadnaya; Ⓥ) It's hard to characterise a place that's so simple. It is a tiny space – only seven tables. The menu – sandwiches, pizzas and grills – features nothing too fancy, but everything is prepared with the freshest ingredients and the utmost care. The **outlet** (Map pp136-7; ☎ 495-725 6035; ul Bolshaya Ordinka 40/2; Ⓜ Tretyakovskaya) in Zamoskvorechie is roomier, but reservations are still recommended for Sunday brunch. Enter from the courtyard.

Botanika (Map pp124-5; ☎ 495-254 0064; Bolshaya Gruzinskaya ul 61; meals R500-700; ⏱ 11am-10pm; Ⓜ Belorusskaya; Ⓥ) Rare is the restaurant in Moscow that is both fashionable and affordable. Somehow Botanika manages to be both, offering light, modern fare, with plenty of soups, salads and grills.

Mayak (Map pp124-5; ☎ 495-291 7503; Bolshaya Nikitskaya ul 19; meals R600-800; Ⓜ Arbatskaya) Named for the Mayakovsky Theatre downstairs, this is a remake of a much beloved club that operated in this spot throughout the 1990s. More cafe than club, it still attracts actors, artists and writers, who come to see friendly faces and to eat filling European fare.

Genatsvale on Arbat (Map pp124-5; ☎ 495-203 9453; ul Novy Arbat 11; meals R600-800; Ⓜ Arbatskaya; Ⓥ) Moscow's favourite Georgian restaurant has a new outlet on the Arbat. But what better setting to feast on favourites such as *khachipuri* (cheesy bread) and lamb dishes. If you prefer a more intimate atmosphere, head to the original location, **Genatsvale on Ostozhenka** (Map pp136-7; ☎ 495-202 0445; ul Ostozhenka 12/1; Ⓜ Kropotkinskaya), in Khamovniki.

TOP END

Café Pushkin (Map pp124-5; ☎ 495-739 0033; Tverskoy bul 26a; business lunch R750, meals R1500-2000; ⏱ 24hr; Ⓜ Pushkinskaya) The queen mother of *haute-russe* dining, with an exquisite blend of Russian and French cuisines, where service and food are done to perfection. The lovely 19th-century building has a different atmosphere on each floor, including a richly decorated library and a pleasant rooftop cafe. Next door, a marble-trimmed, chandelier-bedecked **ice-cream parlour** (⏱ 11am-midnight) is an enticing destination for coffee or dessert.

Mari Vanna (Map pp124-5; ☎ 495-650 6500; Spiridonovsky per 10; meals R1000-1500; ⏱ 9am-11pm; Ⓜ Pushkinskaya) Remember when the best Russian food was served in somebody's crowded living room, on tiny mismatched plates, on a table cluttered with dried flowers in vases and framed photographs? Mari Vanna invites you to recall these days – don't look for the sign (there's none), just ring the doorbell at No 10. You will be ushered into these homey environs and served delicious Russian home cooking.

Shinook (Map pp124-5; ☎ 495-255 0204; ul 1905 goda 2; meals R1000-1500; Ⓜ Ulitsa 1905 Goda; Ⓥ) In case you didn't think that Moscow's theme dining was really over the top, Shinook has re-created an indoor Ukrainian peasant farm in the city centre. As you dine, you can look out the window at a cheerful babushka tending the farmyard animals (who are very well taken care of, we are assured).

Cafes & Quick Eats

Prime Star (meals R200-300; ⏱ 7am-11pm) Arbat (Map pp124-5; ☎ 495-290 4481; ul Arbat 9; Ⓜ Arbatskaya) Tverskoy (Map pp124-5; ☎ 495-692 1276; Kamergersky per; Ⓜ Teatralnaya); Chistye Prudy (Map p132; ☎ 495-781 8080; ul Maroseyka 6/8; Ⓜ Kitay-Gorod) Here's a novel concept: a sandwich shop. And not only that, a *healthy* sandwich shop, also serving soups, salads, sushi and other 'natural food'. Everything is pre-prepared and neatly packaged, so you can eat in or carry out.

Volkonsky Keyser (Map pp124-5; ☎ 495-699 4620; Bolshaya Sadovaya ul 2/46; meals R200-400; Ⓜ Mayakovskaya) The queue often runs out the door, as loyal patrons wait their turn for the city's best fresh-baked breads, pastries and pies. It's worth the wait, especially if you decide on a fruit-filled croissant or to-die-for olive bread. In Chistye Prudy there is another **outlet** (Map p132; ☎ 495-741 1442; ul Maroseyka 4/2; Ⓜ Kitay-Gorod).

Stolle (Map pp136-7; ☎ 499-246 0589; Malaya Pirogovskaya ul 16; meals R200-500; ⏱ 9am-9pm; Ⓜ Sportivnaya; ✗) A 'stolle' is a traditional Saxon Christmas cake: the selection of sweets and savouries sits on the counter, fresh from the oven. It is difficult to decide (mushroom or meat; apricot or apple?) but you can't go wrong.

Coffee Mania (Map pp124-5; ☎ 495-775 4310; Bolshaya Nikitskaya ul 13, Moscow Conservatory; meals R600-800; ⏱ 24hr; Ⓜ Alexandrovsky Sad; ✗ 🖥) With all of Moscow's opportunities for high stepping, fine dining and big spending, where is the most popular place for the rich and famous to congregate? Can you believe it's a place called Coffee Mania? The friendly, informal cafe is beloved for its home-made soups, fresh-squeezed juices and steaming cappuccino, not to mention its summer terrace overlooking the leafy courtyard of the conservatory.

Self-Catering

Ramstore (Map p132; ☎ 495-207 0241; Komsomolskaya pl 6, Moskovsky Univermag; ⏱ 24hr; Ⓜ Komsomolskaya) The Turkish-owned supermarket – just opposite Yaroslavsky vokzal – is an ultraconvenient place to stock up for your Trans-Siberian journey.

Dorogomilovsky market (Map pp136-7; Mozhaysky val 10; ⏱ 10am-8pm; Ⓜ Kievskaya) Even if you are not buying, it's fun to see what's for sale at the *rynok* (market): tables piled high with fresh produce; golden honey in jars that are as big as basketballs; vibrantly coloured spices pouring out of plastic bags; and also silver-coloured fish posing on beds of ice. Convenient to Kievsky vokzal.

DRINKING

Kvartira 44 (Map pp124-5; ☎ 495-291 7503; Bolshaya Nikitskaya ul 22/2; ☺ noon-2am Sun-Thu, noon-6am Fri & Sat; Ⓜ Okhotny Ryad) Somebody had a great idea to convert an old Moscow apartment into a crowded, cosy bar, with tables and chairs tucked into every nook and cranny. There is another **location** (Map pp136-7; ☎ 495-238 8234; ul Malaya Yakimanka 24/8; Ⓜ Polyanka) in Zamoskvorechie.

Apshu (Map pp136-7; ☎ 495-953 9944; Klimentovsky per 10; ☺ 24hr; Ⓜ Tretyakovskaya; 🖳) It was a little fishing village on the Baltic coast that inspired this trendy place. Once discovered by worldly Muscovites, the village was transformed into a bohemian beacon – a magnet for artists and other creative-types. This so-called club-cafe tries to do the same in Moscow, offering inexpensive food and drinks, board games, art exhibitions, concerts…basically something for everyone.

Chaikhona No 1 Hermitage Garden (Map pp124-5; ☎ 495-971 6842; ☺ 2pm–last guest; Ⓜ Chekhovskaya); Gorky Park (Map pp136-7; ☎ 495-778 1756; Ⓜ Frunzenskaya) Housed in an inviting, exotic tent, laid with Oriental rugs and plush pillows, this cool Uzbek lounge and cafe is one of the best chill-out spots in the city. If you are hungry, there is *plov* and shashlyk on the menu.

ENTERTAINMENT

To find out what's on see the weekly magazine *element* (www.elementmoscow.ru) and the weekly entertainment section in Friday's *Moscow Times* (www.themoscowtimes.com).

Classical Music, Opera & Ballet

Bolshoi Theatre (Map pp124-5; ☎ 495-250 7317, hotline 8-800 333 1333; www.bolshoi.ru; Teatralnaya pl 1; tickets R200-2000; Ⓜ Teatralnaya) An evening at the Bolshoi is still one of Moscow's most romantic options, with an electric atmosphere in the glittering six-tier auditorium. Both the ballet and opera companies perform a range of Russian and foreign works. At the time of research, the Bolshoi was preparing to re-open its main stage after a multiyear renovation. In the meantime, the smaller New Stage (Novaya Stsena) has been hosting performances.

Kremlin Ballet Theatre (Map p128; ☎ 495-620 7729; www.kremlin-gkd.ru; ul Vozdvizhenka 1; Ⓜ Alexandrovsky Sad) The Bolshoi does not have a monopoly on ballet and opera in Moscow. Leading dancers also appear with the Kremlin Ballet, which performs in the State Kremlin Theatre (inside the Kremlin).

Moscow International House of Music (Map pp136-7; ☎ 495-730 1011; www.mmdm.ru; Kosmodamianskaya nab 52/8; tickets R200-2000; Ⓜ Paveletskaya) A graceful, modern, glass building, the venue for the Russian Philharmonic towers over the Moscow River. It has three halls, including Svetlanov Hall, which has the largest organ in Russia. So the organ concerts are impressive.

Tchaikovsky Concert Hall (Map pp124-5; ☎ 495-232 5353, box office 495-699 0658; www.classicalmusic.ru; Triumfalnaya pl 4/31; tickets R100-1000; Ⓜ Mayakovskaya) Home to the famous State Symphony Orchestra, which specialises in the music of its namesake composer and other Russian maestros.

Theatre & Circus

Moscow Art Theatre (MKhAT; Map pp124-5; ☎ 495-629 8760; http://art.theatre.ru; Kamergersky per 3; Ⓜ Teatralnaya) Also known as the Chekhov Moscow Art Theatre, this is where method acting was founded more than 100 years ago. Watch for English-language versions of Russian classics performed by the American Studio.

Maly Theatre (Map pp124-5; ☎ 495-623 2621; Teatralnaya pl 1/6; Ⓜ Teatralnaya) A lovely theatre founded in 1824, which hosts performances of mainly 19th-century works.

Nikulin Circus on Tsvetnoy Bulvar (Map pp124-5; ☎ 495-625-8970; www.circusnikulin.ru; Tsvetnoy bul 13; tickets R250-2000; ☺ shows 7pm Thu-Mon, 2.30pm Sat; Ⓜ Tsvetnoy Bulvar) Named after the beloved actor, director and clown Yury Nikulin, this building has housed the circus since 1880 (though it has been thoroughly modernised). Its thematic shows are also acclaimed.

Nightclubs

Propaganda (Map pp124-5; ☎ 495-624 5732; www.propagandamoscow.com; Bolshoy Zlatoustinsky per 7; meals R500-700; ☺ noon-6am; Ⓜ Kitay-Gorod) This long-time favourite looks to be straight from the warehouse district, with exposed brick walls and pipe ceilings. It's a cafe by day, but at night they clear the dance floor and let the DJ do his stuff. This is a gay-friendly place, especially on Sunday nights.

Krizis Zhanra (Map p132; ☎ 495-623 2594; www.kriziszhanra.ru; ul Pokrovka 16/16; ☺ concerts 9pm daily, 11pm Fri

& Sat; M Chistye Prudy) Everybody has something good to say about Krizis: expats and locals, old-timers and new-comers, young and old. What's not to love? Good cheap food, copious drinks and rockin' music every night, all of which inspires the gathered to get their groove on.

Simachyov Bar & Boutique (Map pp124-5; ☎ 495-629 8085; www.denissimachev.com; Stoleshnikov per 12/2; ☾ 11am–last guest; M Chekhovskaya) By day, it's a boutique and cafe, owned and operated by the famed fashion designer of the same name. By night, the place becomes a hip-hop happening nightclub that combines glamour and humour. You have to look sharp to get in here, but at least you can be bohemian about it.

Live Music

Art Garbage (Map p132; ☎ 495-628 8745; www.art-garbage.ru; Starosadsky per 5; ☾ noon-6am; M Kitay-Gorod) Enter this funky club-cafe through the courtyard that is littered with sculpture. Inside, the walls are crammed with paintings of all genres, and there are DJs spinning or live music every night. The restaurant is relatively minimalist in terms of decor, but the menu is creative. Is it art or is it garbage? We'll let you decide.

Roadhouse (Map pp136-7; ☎ 499-245 5543; www.road house.ru; ul Dovatora 8; ☾ noon-midnight, concerts 9pm; M Sportivnaya) If your dog got run over by a pick-up truck, you can find some comfort at the Roadhouse Blues Bar, with down-and-out live music nightly, plus cold beer and a whole menu of salty cured meats.

SHOPPING

Artists set up their stalls on ul Krymsky val, opposite the entrance to Gorky Park (p135), and in the underground walkway. There are also galleries within the Tsentralny Dom Khudozhnikov (p135) in the New Tretyakov.

Izmaylovo market (admission R15; ☾ 9am-6pm Sat & Sun; M Partizanskaya) This sprawling area, northeast of the centre, is packed with art, handmade crafts, antiques, Soviet paraphernalia and almost anything you need for a souvenir.

GUM (Map p128; ☎ 495-788 4343; www.gum.ru; Krasnaya pl 3; ☾ 10am-10pm; M Ploshchad Revolyutsii) On the east side of Red Square, this 19th-century building is a sight in itself. It houses a huge collection of pricey shops.

Winzavod (Map p132; ☎ 495-917 4646, www.winza vod.ru; 4-Siromyatnichesky per 1; ☾ noon-8pm Tue-Sun; M Chkalovskaya) This former wine-bottling factory was converted into exhibit space and is now home to five of Moscow's most prestigious art galleries.

Art Strelka (Map p136-7; ☎ 8-916 112 7180; Bersenevskaya nab 14/5; ☾ 4-8pm; M Novokuznetskaya/Polyanka) The garages at the old Red October candy factory now serve as studio and gallery space. The place is perhaps less polished than Winzavod, but that may be the appeal.

GETTING THERE & AWAY

Air

Of Moscow's five airports, two of them service most international flights and most flights to destinations along the Trans-Siberian Railway. Moscow's main international airport is **Sheremetyevo-2** (☎ 495-232 6565; www.sheremetyevo -airport.ru), 30km northwest of the city centre. Across the runways (and accessible by shuttle bus), Sheremetyevo-1 services many domestic flights, especially to/from St Petersburg and northern European Russia.

Domodedovo (☎ 495-933 6666; www.domodedovo.ru), 48km south of the city centre, has undergone extensive upgrades in recent years in order to service more international flights. Most notably, British Airways and American Airlines flights now fly in and out of Domodedovo.

You can buy airline tickets at most travel agencies (see p127). Airline offices in Moscow:

Aeroflot (www.aeroflot.ru; ☾ 9am-8pm Mon-Sat, to 4pm Sun) Tverskoy (Map pp124-5; ☎ 495-223 5555; ul Petrovka 20/1; M Chekhovskaya); Kuznetsky Most (Map pp124-5; ☎ 495-924 8054; ul Kuznetsky Most 3; M Kuznetsky Most); Zamoskvorechie (Map pp136-7; ☎ 495-223 5555; Pyatnitskaya ul 37/19; M Tretyakovskaya)

Air France (Map pp136–7; ☎ 495-937 3839; www .airfrance.com; ul Korovy val 7; M Oktyabrskaya)

British Airways (Map pp124–5; ☎ 495-363 2525; www.britishairways.com; Business Centre Parus, 1-ya Tverskaya Yamskaya ul 23; M Belorusskaya)

Delta Air Lines (Map pp136–7; ☎ 495-937 9090; www .delta.com; Gogolevsky bul 11; M Kropotkinskaya)

KLM Royal Dutch Airlines (Map pp136–7; ☎ 495-258 3600; www.klm.com; ul Korovy val 7; M Oktyabrskaya)

Lufthansa (Map pp124–5; ☎ 495-980 9999; www .lufthansa.com; Posledny per 17; M Tsvetnoy Bulvar)

Transaero (☎ 495-788 8080; www.transaero.com; ☾ 9am-6pm Mon-Sat) Krasnoselsky (Map p132; Sadovaya-Spasskaya ul 18/1; M Krasnye Vorota); Zamoskvorechie (Map pp136-7; Paveletskaya pl 2/3; M Paveletskaya)

Boat

There are many cruise boats plying the routes between Moscow and St Petersburg,

DOMESTIC FLIGHTS FROM MOSCOW

Destination	Flights per day	Duration	One-way fare
St Petersburg	20	1hr 20min	R2200
Nizhny Novgorod	2	1hr	R2300-3300
Kazan	2	1½hr	R2200-3200
Perm	5	2hr	R2700-3200
Yekaterinburg	16	2½hr	R4600
Tyumen	7	3hr	R3800-5200
Omsk	4	3½hr	R6400
Novosibirsk	16	4hr	R11,200
Tomsk	3	4½hr	R9500
Krasnoyarsk	2	4½hr	R12,400
Irkutsk	9	5½hr	R14,000
Ulan-Ude	1	6hr	R12,000
Chita	1	6hr	R12,800
Khabarovsk	3	8hr	R13,000-15,000
Vladivostok	4	8½hr	R18,200

many stopping at some of the Golden Ring towns on the way. Longer cruises south along the Volga also originate in Moscow. Some cruises are specifically aimed at foreign tourists. Generally, for lower prices, you can also sail on a boat aimed at Russian holidaymakers. Boat operators and agencies include the following:

Infoflot (Map pp124–5; ☎ 495-684 9188; www.infoflot .com; ul Shchepkina 28; Ⓜ Prospekt Mira) The market leader.

Mosturflot (☎ 495-221 7222; www.mosturflot.ru, in Russian)

Orthodox Cruise Company (☎ 499-943 8560; www .cruise.ru; ul Alabyana 5; Ⓜ Sokol) Also has an office in Rostov-on-Don.

Rechflot (☎ 495-363 9628; www.rechflot.ru, in Russian)

Rechturflot (☎ 495-638 6611; www.rtflot.ru, in Russian)

Vodohod (☎ 495 223 96 11; www.vodohod.com/eng)

Bus

Buses run to a number of towns and cities within 700km of Moscow. Bus fares are similar to *kupe* (*kupeyny*; compartmentalised carriage) train fares. Buses tend to be crowded, but they are usually faster than the *prigorodny* (suburban) trains. To book a seat go to the long-distance bus terminal, the **Shchyolkovsky bus station** (Ⓜ Shchyolkovskaya), 8km east of the city centre.

Buses also depart from outside the various train stations, offering alternative transport to the destinations served by the train. These buses do not run according to a particular schedule, but rather leave when full. Likewise, they cannot be booked in advance.

Train

Moscow has nine main stations. Multiple stations may service the same destination, so confirm the arrival/departure station.

Belorussky vokzal (Belarus Station; Map pp124-5; Tverskaya Zastava pl; Ⓜ Belorusskaya) Serves trains to/from Smolensk, Kaliningrad, Minsk, Warsaw, Vilnius, Berlin; some trains to/from the Czech Republic; and suburban trains to/from the west.

Kazansky vokzal (Kazan Station; Map p132; Komsomolskaya pl; Ⓜ Komsomolskaya) For trains to/from Kazan, Izhevsk, Ufa, Ryazan, Ulyanovsk, Samara, Novorossiysk, Central Asia; some to/from Vladimir, Nizhny Novgorod, the Ural Mountains, Siberia; the Volga; and suburban trains to/from the southeast, including Bykovo airport.

Kursky vokzal (Kursk Station; Map p132; pl Kurskogo vokzala; Ⓜ Kurskaya) Serves trains heading south and east, including to the Caucasus, eastern Ukraine, Crimea, Georgia, Azerbaijan. It also has some trains to/from Vladimir, Nizhny Novgorod and Perm.

Kievsky vokzal (Kyiv Station; Map pp136-7; Kievskaya pl; Ⓜ Kievskaya) Serves Kyiv and Prague, as well as suburban trains to/from the southwest.

Leningradsky vokzal (Leningrad Station; Map p132; Komsomolskaya pl; Ⓜ Komsomolskaya) Serves Tver, Novgorod, Pskov, St Petersburg, Vyborg, Murmansk, Tallinn, Helsinki.

Paveletsky vokzal (Pavelets Station; Map pp136-7; Paveletskaya pl; Ⓜ Paveletskaya) For trains heading south, including the express train to Domodedovo airport.

Rizhsky vokzal (Riga Station; Rizhskaya pl; Ⓜ Rizhskaya) Serves Latvia, as well as suburban trains to/from the northwest.

Savyolovsky vokzal (Savyolov Station; pl Savyolovskogo vokzala; Ⓜ Savyolovskaya) For suburban trains to/from the north, including the express train to Sheremetyevo airport.

TRAINS DEPARTING MOSCOW

From Moscow (Leningradsky Station) to St Petersburg

The trains below are the best trains to the listed destinations. There are also other services to many of these destinations. The costs are for *kupe,* unless otherwise stated.

Train no & name	Departure time	Duration	Fare
2 *Krasnaya Strela*	11.55pm	8hr	R2600-3000
4 *Ekspress*	11.59pm	8hr	R2380
6 *Nikolaevsky Ekspress*	11.30pm	8hr	R2750
54 *Grand Express*	11.40pm	9hr	R5000-6200 *(lyux)*
160 *Avrora*	4.30pm	5½hr	R2450 *(platskart)*
166 *ER200* (platskart)	6.30pm	4½hr	R3300-3650

International Trains from Moscow

Destination & train no	Departure time & station	Duration	Fare
Almaty 007	10.40pm (odd days), Paveletsky	3 days, 6hr	R6260
Beijing 020 *Vostok*	11.55pm Fri, Yaroslavsky	6 days	R14,000
Kyiv 001	11.23pm, Kievsky	9½hr	R2000-2400
Minsk 001	10.25pm, Belorussky	10hr	R2850
Riga 001	7.10pm, Rizhsky	16hr	R4020
Tallinn 034	6.05pm, Leningradsky	15½hr	R3300
Ulaanbaatar 006 *Trans-Mongolian Express*	9.35pm Tue, Yaroslavsky	4 days, 5hr	R12,600
Vilnius 005	6.20pm, Belorussky	14½hr	R2890

Trans-Siberian Trains from Moscow

Destination & train no	Departure time & station	Duration	Fare
Vladimir 062	1.55pm, Kursky	2½hr	R240-320 (seat)
Yaroslavl	14 daily, Yaroslavsky	4hr	R480 (seat)
Nizhny Novgorod 062	1.55pm, Kursky	5hr	R390-470 (seat)
Kazan 002	10.08pm, Kazansky	11½hr	R2500-2860
Perm 018	6.50pm, Yaroslavsky	21hr	R4000-4300
Yekaterinburg 016	4.08pm, Kazansky	24½hr	R4770-5360
Tyumen 060	5.48pm†, Kazansky	35hr	R4900-5500
Omsk 048	7.40pm†, Kazansky	42hr	R7200-8000
Novosibirsk 026	4.20pm†, Yaroslavsky	46hr	R9200-10,000
Tomsk 038	10.40pm*, Yaroslavsky	2 days, 7hr	R9600-10,200
Krasnoyarsk 056	4.20pm, Yaroslavsky	2 day, 11hr	R11,000-11,800
Irkutsk 010 *Baikal*	11.25pm, Yaroslavsky	3 days, 15hr	R10,800-12,340
Ulan-Ude 002 *Rossiya*	9.25pm*, Yaroslavsky	3 days, 11hr	R13,000-15,000
Chita 002 *Rossiya*	9.25pm*, Yaroslavsky	3 days, 21hr	R13,800-15,100
Khabarovsk 002 *Rossiya*	9.25pm*, Yaroslavsky	5 days, 14hr	R15,600-17,400
Vladivostok 002 *Rossiya*	9.25pm*, Yaroslavsky	6 days, 2hr	R16,000-18,000

note: * odd days † even days.

Yaroslavl vokzal (Yaroslavl Station; Map p132; Komsomolskaya pl; Ⓜ Komsomolskaya) Historic 1902 art-nouveau fantasy station by Fyodor Shekhtel that caters for most trains to Siberia, the Far East, China and Mongolia.

For long-distance trains it's best to buy your tickets in advance. Tickets on some trains may be available on the day of departure, but this is less likely in summer. Always take your passport along when buying a ticket.

Tickets are sold at the train stations, but it is much easier to buy tickets from a travel agent (see p127) or *kassa zheleznoy dorogi* (railway ticket office). These are often conveniently found in hotel lobbies. Most local agencies charge a small service fee, but be careful of international travel agencies that may charge considerable mark-ups.

One agency selling airplane and train tickets with many outlets around town is **Glavagentstvo-Service** (Map pp124-5; ☎ 495-745 6548; 1-ya Tverskaya-Yamskaya ul 15; **M** Belorusskaya). Additional convenient outlets are located in Belorussky and Leningradsky vokzaly.

GETTING AROUND
To/From the Airport

All four major airports are accessible by a convenient **Aeroexpress train** (☎ 8-800 700 3377; www.aero-express.ru). If you have a lot of luggage and you wish to take a taxi, it is highly recommended to book in advance (see right) to take advantage of fixed rates offered by most companies (usually R1000 to R1500 to/from any airport).

SHEREMETYEVO

In 2008 the new express train line to Sheremetyevo opened with much fanfare, followed by much embarrassment, when the initial trains were delayed by hours. Presumably the kinks will be worked out by the time you read this, in which case the Aeroexpress train should leave Savyolovsky vokzal for Sheremetyevo airport (adult/child R250/65, 30 minutes) every hour between 5.30am and midnight. Check the schedule online in advance, as the times of departure are sort of random.

DOMODEDOVO

The Aeroexpress train leaves Paveletsky vokzal for Domodedovo airport (adult/child R150/40, 45 minutes) every hour between 6am and 11pm, every half-hour during the busiest times. This route is particularly convenient for domestic flights, as you can check into your flight at the train station.

Bus, Trolleybus & Tram

Buses, trolleybuses and trams are useful along a few radial or cross-town routes that the metro misses, and are necessary for reaching sights away from the city centre. Tickets (R25) are usually sold on the vehicle by a conductor.

Metro

The **Moscow metro** (www.mosmetro.ru) is the easiest, quickest and cheapest way of getting around Moscow. Many of the stations are marble-faced, frescoed, gilded works of art. The trains are generally reliable: you will rarely wait on the platform for more than two minutes. Nonetheless, they get packed during rush hour.

The 176 stations are marked outside by 'M' signs. Magnetic tickets (R19) are sold at ticket booths. It's useful to buy a multiple-ride ticket (10 rides for R155, 20 for R280), which saves you the hassle of queuing every time.

Taxi

Almost any car in Moscow could be a taxi if the price is right, so get on the street and stick your arm out. Expect to pay R150 to R200 for a ride around the city centre. Official taxis – which can be recognised by the chequerboard logo on the side and/or a small green light in the windscreen – charge higher rates.

Don't hesitate to wave on a car if you don't like the look of its occupants. As a general rule, it's best to avoid riding in cars that already have two or more people inside. Be particularly careful taking a taxi that is waiting outside a nightclub or bar.

To book a cab by phone, call the **Central Taxi Reservation Office** (Tsentralnoe Byuro Zakazov Taxi; ☎ 495-627 0000; www.cbz-taxi.ru).

AROUND MOSCOW

As soon as you leave Moscow, the fast-paced modern capital fades from view, while the slowed-down, old-fashioned countryside unfolds around you. The subtly changing landscape is crossed by winding rivers and dotted with peasant villages – the classic provincial Russia immortalised through the works of artists and writers over the centuries.

SERGIEV POSAD
СЕРГИЕВ ПОСАД
☎ 496 / pop 112,700 / ⏱ Moscow

According to old Russian wisdom, 'there is no settlement without a just man; there is no town without a saint'. And so the town of Sergiev Posad tributes St Sergius of Radonezh, founder of the local Trinity Monastery and patron saint of all of Russia. The monastery – today among the most important and active in Russia – exudes Orthodoxy. Bearded priests bustle about; babushkas fill bottles of holy water; crowds of believers light candles to St Sergius, Keeper of Russia. This mystical place is a window into the age-old belief system

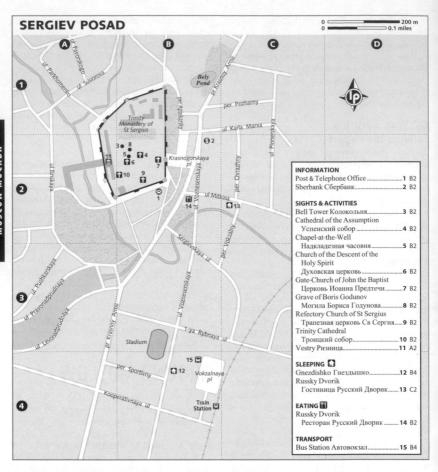

SERGIEV POSAD

INFORMATION
Post & Telephone Office 1 B2
Sberbank Сбербанк 2 B2

SIGHTS & ACTIVITIES
Bell Tower Колокольня 3 B2
Cathedral of the Assumption
Успенский собор 4 B2
Chapel-at-the-Well
Надкладезная часовня 5 B2
Church of the Descent of the
Holy Spirit
Духовская церковь 6 B2
Gate-Church of John the Baptist
Церковь Иоанна Предтечи 7 B2
Grave of Boris Godunov
Могила Бориса Годунова 8 B2
Refectory Church of St Sergius
Трапезная церковь Св Сергия 9 B2
Trinity Cathedral
Троицкий собор 10 B2
Vestry Ризница 11 A2

SLEEPING
Gnezdishko Гнездышко 12 B4
Russky Dvorik
Гостиница Русский Дворик 13 C2

EATING
Russky Dvorik
Ресторан Русский Дворик 14 B2

TRANSPORT
Bus Station Автовокзал 15 B4

that has provided Russia with centuries of spiritual sustenance.

Often called by its Soviet name of Zagorsk, Sergiev Posad is 60km from the northern edge of Moscow on the Yaroslavl road. It is an easy day trip from Moscow – a rewarding option for travellers who don't have time to venture further around the Golden Ring.

Pr Krasnoy Armii is the main street, running north to south through the town centre. The train and bus stations are on opposite corners of a wide square to the east of pr Krasnoy Armii.

Information
Post & telephone office (off pr Krasnoy Armii 127A)
Outside the southeastern wall of the monastery.

Sberbank (pr Krasnoy Armii; 9am-4pm Mon-Fri)
Exchange facilities and ATM available.

Sights
The **Trinity Monastery of St Sergius** (Troitse-Sergieva Lavra; ☎ 544 5356, 544 5350; admission free; 10am-6pm) is an active religious centre with a visible population of monks in residence; visitors should refrain from photographing them. Female visitors should wear headscarves, and men are required to remove hats in the churches.

Built in the 1420s, the squat, dark yet beautiful **Trinity Cathedral** is the heart of the monastery. The tomb of St Sergius stands in the southeastern corner, where a memorial service goes on all day, every day. The icon-festooned interior, lit by oil lamps, is largely the work of the great medieval painter Andrei Rublyov and his students.

The star-spangled **Cathedral of the Assumption** was modelled on the cathedral of the same name in the Moscow Kremlin. The cathedral dates to 1585. It is closed to the general public but included as a part of guided tours. Outside the west door is the **grave** of the tsar Boris Godunov.

Nearby, the resplendent **Chapel-at-the-Well** was built over a spring that is said to have appeared during the Polish siege. The five-tier baroque **bell tower** took 30 years to build in the 18th century, and once had 42 bells, the largest of which weighed 65 tonnes.

The **vestry** (admission R250; ⏲ 10am-5.30pm Wed-Sun), behind the Trinity Cathedral, displays the monastery's extraordinarily rich treasury, bulging with 600 years of donations by the rich and powerful – tapestries, jewel-encrusted vestments, solid-gold chalices and more.

Sleeping & Eating

All room rates include breakfast:

Russky Dvorik hotel (☎ 547 5392; www.zolotoe-koltso.ru/hoteldvorik, in Russian; ul Mitkina 14/2; s/d weekdays from R1500/1900, weekends from R1700/2100) Some of the rooms at this delightful hotel boast views of the onion domes peeking out above whitewashed walls. The place is quite modern, despite the rustic style. The fanciest room even has a Jacuzzi. The affiliated **restaurant** (☎ 45114; pr Krasnoy Armii 134; meals R500-800; ⏲ 10am-9pm) is a charming kitschy place decked out like a Russian *dacha*.

Gnezdishko (☎ 540 4214; ul Voznesenskaya 53; r R1900-2500) With only eight rooms and a small restaurant, this little inn is quaint, clean and convenient to the bus and train stations. Some rooms have views of the monastery bell tower.

Getting There & Away

The fastest transport option is the express train that departs from Moscow's Yaroslavsky vokzal (R293, one hour, twice daily) at 8.24am, returning in the afternoon. Suburban trains also run every half-hour (R110, 1½ hours); take any train bound for Sergiev Posad or Aleksandrov. To go north to Rostov-Veliky (3½ hours) or Yaroslavl (five hours), you may have to change at Aleksandrov.

Bus services to Sergiev Posad from Moscow's VDNKh metro station depart every half-hour from 8.30am to 7.30pm (R100, 70 minutes).

ROSTOV-VELIKY
РОСТОВ-ВЕЛИКИЙ
☎ 48536 / pop 33,200 / ⏲ Moscow

For a place called Rostov-Veliky, or 'Rostov the Great', this place gives the impression of a sleepy, rustic village. Perhaps for this reason, the magnificent Rostov kremlin catches visitors off guard when its silver domes and whitewashed stone walls appear amid the dusty streets. Rostov is among the prettiest of the Golden Ring towns, idyllically sited on shimmering Lake Nero. It is also one of the oldest, first chronicled in 862.

Rostov is about 220km northeast of Moscow. The train and bus stations are together in the drab modern part of Rostov, 1.5km north of the kremlin.

Sights

Rostov's main attraction is its unashamedly photogenic **kremlin** (☎ 61 717; grounds R20, exhibits each R20-35, all-inclusive R200; ⏲ 10am-5pm). Although founded in the 12th century, nearly all the buildings here date from the 1670s and 1680s, when Iona Sysoevich decided to clear away the existing buildings.

With its five magnificent domes, the **Assumption Cathedral** dominates the kremlin, although it is just outside the north wall. Beyond service hours, you can get into the cathedral through the door in the church shop on ul Karla Marksa. The cathedral was here a century before the kremlin, while the belfry was added in the 1680s. Each of 15 bells in the belfry has its own name; the largest, weighing 32 tonnes, is called Sysoi. The monks play magnificent bell concerts, which can be arranged through the excursions office, in the west gate, for R500.

The west gate (the main entrance) and the north gate are straddled by the **Gate-Church of St John the Divine** and the **Gate-Church of the Resurrection**, both of which are richly decorated with 17th-century frescoes. Enter these churches from the **monastery walls** (admission R45), which you can access from the stairs next to the north gate. Like several other buildings within the complex, these are only open from May to September. Between the gate-churches, the **Church of Hodigitria** houses an exhibition of Orthodox Church vestments and paraphernalia.

The metropolitan's private chapel, the **Church of the Saviour-over-the-Galleries**, has the most beautiful interior of all, covered in colourful frescoes. These rooms are filled with exhibits: the **White Chamber** displays religious antiquities, while the **Red Chamber** shows off *finift* (enamelware), a Rostov artistic speciality.

The town is chock full of galleries, churches and monasteries, including the sparkling **Monastery of St Jacob** on the shores of Lake Nero.

Sleeping & Eating

Rostov is a popular weekend destination, meaning that hotel prices are generally lower between Sunday and Thursday. All prices include breakfast unless otherwise indicated.

Khors (☎ 62 483; www.khors.org; per person R500; 🖳) On the grounds of the gallery, there are a handful of tiny rustic rooms with shared access to a bathroom and kitchen (which means you make your own breakfast). Tip: drag your mattress up onto the roof to awake to the sunrise over Lake Nero.

Dom na Pogrebakh (☎ 61 244; www.rostmuseum .ru; s/d/tr without bathroom R700/1000/1500, d with bathroom R2000-2500) Right inside the kremlin, and near the east gate, this place has clean, woodpanelled rooms with heavy doors and colourful tapestries. The location within the building varies, but if you can snag a room with a view of the west gate it is charming indeed.

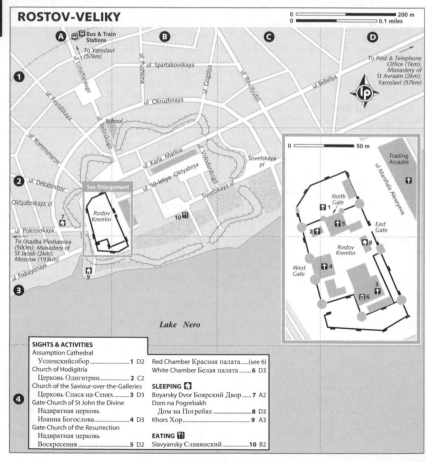

DETOUR: KUKUSHKA (КУКУШКА.РУ)

Calling all railway buffs! Midway between Sergiev Posad and Rostov-Veliky, the little town of Pereslavl-Zalessky is home to a unique railway museum known as **Kukushka.ru** (☎ 48535-49 479; www.kukushka.ru; adult/child R60/30; ⊙ 10am-6pm Wed-Sun Apr-Oct, 10am-5pm Sat & Sun Nov-Mar). The collection of locomotives occupies the tracks and depot that were used up until the middle of the 20th century. Don't miss the opportunity to ride on the hand cart (adult/child R60/30). Buses travel frequently between Moscow and Pereslavl-Zalessky (R230, 2½ hours). Not all of these stop at Sergiev Posad (one hour, three daily); others travel to Yaroslavl (R214, three hours, seven daily) via Rostov-Veliky (1½ hours).

The museum is about 16km out of town. From ul Kardovskogo (which is the main road into town from Moscow or Sergiev Posad), turn left onto Podgornaya ul and follow the road along the shoreline of Lake Pleshcheevo. At the village of Talitsy, look for the 'Muzey' sign and turn left to the museum.

Boyarsky Dvor (☎ 60 446; www.reinkap-hotel.ru; ul Kamenny most 4; standard r R1200-2000, upgraded r R1800-2200) Just outside the western Kremlin wall, this is a vast rambling place with plain but functional rooms. The downstairs cafe is a pleasant place for an evening drink.

Usadba Pleshanova (☎ 76 440; www.hotel.v-ros tove.ru; Pokrovskaya ul 34; r weekday R1700-2700, weekend R2000-3100; 🖳) This 19th-century manor house, once the residence of a merchant and philanthropic family, is now a welcoming inn with a nice restaurant, cosy library and wood sauna. Beware the 20% reservation fee.

Slavyansky (☎ 62 228; Sovetskaya pl 8; meals R400-500; ⊙ 11am-1am) About 100m east of the kremlin, this semi-swanky place gets recommendations from locals. Come here if you want traditional Russian fare in a romantic setting.

Getting There & Around
The fastest train here from Moscow is the express service from Yaroslavsky vokzal (R430, three hours, twice daily). Otherwise, some long-distance trains stop at Rostov-Veliky en route to Yaroslavl. Bus 6 runs between the train station and the town centre.

Moscow to Yekaterinburg

This leg of the Trans-Siberian journey traverses densely populated European Russia, where transport choices are abundant and travelling is fairly easy. The route itself looks like a river delta that branches into several channels, some of which rejoin far beyond the Urals. You may feel like Alice in Wonderland, unsure which bottle to open first.

The main route, taken by the Vladivostok-bound *Rossiya* and the Moscow–Běijīng train, goes through the ancient town of Vladimir, crosses the Volga at the scenic city of Nizhny Novgorod, then continues via bleak Kirov (Vyatka) to the heavily industrialised, but culturally intriguing, city of Perm, in the Urals.

Trains such as the Moscow–Yekaterinburg direct train 16, *Ural*, departing from Moscow's Kazansky vokzal (Kazan Station) follow a more southerly route via Kazan, the capital of Tatarstan. With its Unesco-listed kremlin and good connections with all cities on the main route, Kazan has become a popular detour for Trans-Siberian travellers.

Several Trans-Siberian trains, such as the 240E from Moscow to Vladivostok, ply the old northerly route, which passes through the medieval towns of Sergiev Posad and Rostov-Veliky, covered in the Moscow chapter, before merging with the main route at Kirov.

With so many fascinating places and possibilities for detours on the way, it would be simply criminal to confine yourself to the train compartment for days. Hop off and on the train, and construct your own unique Trans-Siberian route.

HIGHLIGHTS

- Unearth the roots of Russian civilisation in **Vladimir** (p158)
- Collect flowers and wake up to chiming bells and singing roosters in **Suzdal** (p160)
- Marvel at two mighty rivers converging under the walls of Nizhny Novgorod's **kremlin** (p165)
- Witness the clash of cultures and catch a Tatar at the Sabantuy fest in **Kazan** (p169)
- Chill out at the fabulous **Kungur Ice Cave** (p175)

| ROUTE DISTANCE: 1814KM | DURATION: 26 HOURS |

THE ROUTE
Moscow to Nizhny Novgorod

The beginning of this route has been immortalised by the Soviet underground writer Venedikt Yerofeyev in his novel *Moscow to the End of the Line*. The main character travels to **Petushki** (145km) on a whistle-stop *elektrichka* (suburban train) at the time of Gorbachev's liquor ban, philosophising on the virtues of alcohol and the evils of the Soviet lifestyle while toasting every station. He consumes mind-boggling cocktails, such as the 'Tear of a Young Communist League Girl', which consists of three brands of cheap Soviet eau de toilette, mouth rinse, nail polish and lemonade.

Don't try to repeat this fictional (!) experience, or you'll never reach the first stop, which happens to be **Vladimir** (191km; p158), where the train pauses for 20 minutes. As you approach the city, look out for the golden spires and domes of the Assumption Cathedral, high on the embankment to the north.

Cast your gaze northward as you pull out from Vladimir for a glimpse of the 12th-century monastery complex at **Bogolyubovo** (200km), then do a quick turn to the south-facing window to see the Church of the Intercession – the paragon of Russian church architecture, sitting in splendid isolation at the confluence of the Nerl and Klyazma Rivers.

The train then follows the valleys of the Klyazma and Oka Rivers, passing several ancient towns, such as **Kovrov** (274km), mostly known as the centre of the peculiar sport of motoball – football on motorcycles, followed by the pretty **Gorokhovets** (382km), home of the popular ski resort of **Puzhalova Gora** (www .puzhalova.ru, in Russian).

Hold your breath as you pass **Dzerzhinsk** (427km), a disastrously polluted chemical industry centre. Immediately after, there's a 12-minute stop at **Nizhny Novgorod** (441km; p163), Russia's third-most populous city, where the station is still called by its Soviet-era name of Gorky.

Nizhny Novgorod to Perm

The *Rossiya* and other services to Siberia and beyond all head northeast from Nizhny Novgorod, crossing over the mighty Volga River about 1km outside the station. You'll then chug along past the farmland and taiga of Nizhny Novgorod Oblast, passing **Semenov** (530km) – home of the Khokhloma folk-art style, towards **Kotelnich** (869km), the junction with the old Trans-Siberian route from Yaroslavl. Here, the time is Moscow time plus one hour. Kotelnich is famous as a dinosaurs' playground – numerous Permian period giant-lizard fossils have been discovered here. There is an interesting palaeontology museum in town.

Just outside Kotelnich the train crosses the Vyatka River, a meandering 1367km waterway that follows the railway route to **Kirov** (956km), which is better known by its old name – Vyatka, same as the river. There's a 15-minute stop here, but little reason to get out and explore, other than to buy some beer and clink glasses on the occasion of reaching the northernmost point of your whole Trans-Siberian journey.

Yar (1126km) is the first town you'll pass through in the Udmurt Republic, home to the Udmurts, one of Russia's four major groups of Finno-Ugric people. Around here the countryside becomes wonderfully picturesque, with plenty of pretty painted log cabins to be spotted. At **Balyezino** (1192km) there's a change of locomotive during the 19-minute halt.

After crossing the Cheptsa River at 1221km, the train enters the town of the same name. **Cheptsa** (1223km) is the junction with the line that runs between Perm and Kazan. About 40km further east, you'll cross into Perm Oblast and the foothills of the **Ural Mountains**, which stretch about 2000km from Kazakhstan to the Arctic Kara Sea. These mountains were like Aladdin's cave for the young Russia, their mineral treasures quickly filling its imperial coffers.

However the Urals rarely break 500m above sea level in Perm Oblast, so it's difficult to actually tell you're in a mountain range. As Russian academician Peter Pallas wrote in 1770, 'The middle section of the Urals range is particularly inconspicuous'. Still, with glimpses of verdant rolling landscapes and pine and birch forests, this is one of the more attractive sections of the route.

Around **Vereshchagino** (1314km), named after the late-19th-century painter Vasily Vereshchagin, who stopped here on the way to China a few months before he was killed in a naval battle with the Japanese, wind your watch forward, as local time becomes Moscow time plus two hours.

MOSCOW TO YEKATERINBURG

MOSCOW TO YEKATERINBURG

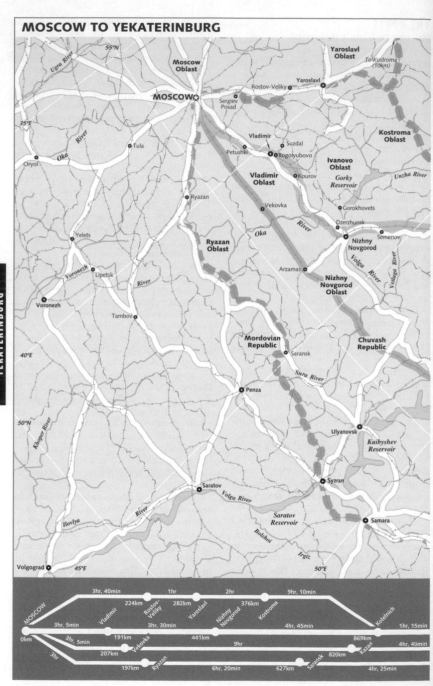

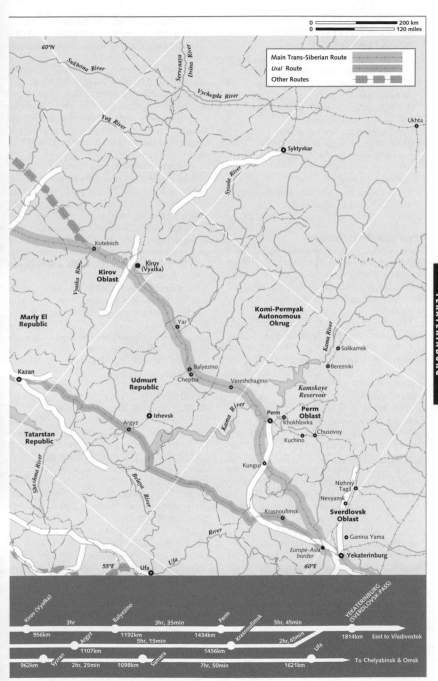

MOSCOW TO YEKATERINBURG
ROUTE PLANNER

The following is a suggested itinerary for covering the main sites of this chapter:
Day 1: Leave Moscow; 2½-hour train to Vladimir; stay Suzdal
Day 2: Tour Suzdal; return to Vladimir; train to Nizhny Novgorod
Day 3: Explore Nizhny Novgorod
Day 4: Nizhny Novgorod; boat trip to Gorodets; night train (nine hours) from Nizhny Novgorod to Kazan
Day 5: Explore Kazan
Day 6: Kazan; boat trip to Sviyazhsk; night train (15 hours) to Yekaterinburg

Perm to Yekaterinburg

The train chugs across the wide Kama River (1432km) into the industrial city of **Perm** (1434km; p172), where there's a 15-minute stop. As you pull into the station, check out the steam locomotive on the northern side of the train.

After Perm, the railway takes a sharp turn in the southeast direction towards **Kungur** (1535km), the centre of the Stroganov patrimony. This family ruled the Urals from the time of Ivan the Terrible to the reign of Peter the Great, and gave its name to beef stroganoff.

From Kungur, the railway follows the picturesque Sylva River, cutting through some hills that can almost pass for mountains – that's pretty much all you get to see of the Urals range. The crucial thing to keep an eye out for beyond here is the **Europe-Asia Border Obelisk** (1777km), a large white monument on the southern side of the train. One of several monuments marking this continental divide, it is understated, at best. For a more monumental border marker, see p186.

Approaching Yekaterinburg, the train travels along the Chusovaya River, its valley at the heart of the mining industry in the Urals. The first major station in Asian Russia – but still 260km short of the official beginning of Siberia – is **Yekaterinburg** (1814km), which merits a 15- to 30-minute stop.

Moscow to Yekaterinburg via Kazan

The first major stop east of Moscow is **Vekovka** (207km), home to a glassware factory. Along the platform, the food and drink hawkers are vastly outnumbered by factory workers flogging off sets of cut-glass tumblers, giant brandy glasses, vases, chandeliers and the like.

Arzamas-II (562km) is the junction for trains running from Nizhny Novgorod to Kazan and further south along the Volga. From here, the train traverses the Chuvash Republic. The Chuvash people are descended from the Bulgars (as are the Tatars), although most of them do not live within the territorial boundaries of this artificially drawn region.

The train stops for 16 minutes in **Kazan** (820km; p168), capital of the autonomous republic of Tatarstan. The original 19th-century train station has been handsomely restored and now houses a waiting room.

Continuing east there's a 10-minute stop at **Argyz-1** (1107km), where you may spot old steam locomotives still in use for shunting. At 1150km the *Ural* crosses the Kama River, which flows northeast to Perm.

At **Krasnoufimsk** (1456km) the local time is two hours ahead of Moscow time. This small country station is often a good place to buy berries and other forest fruits, sold by locals on the platform. From here you'll pass through the Urals' rolling mountain scenery, with lake views to the south as you near the terminus at **Yekaterinburg** (1814km; see p179).

VLADIMIR ВЛАДИМИР

☎ 4922 / pop 340,000 / ✆ Moscow
High up on Vladimir's hill, above the Klyazma River, sits the solemnly majestic Assumption Cathedral, built to announce Vladimir's claim as capital of Rus in the early 12th century. These days, Vladimir – 178km east of Moscow – feels more like a modern, industrial town than an ancient capital. Nonetheless, the grandeur of medieval Vladimir shines through the commotion.

The 'Golden Ring' is a recently coined term for this region, evoking a heroic distant past. Located northeast of Moscow, the Golden Ring is composed of some of Russia's oldest cities, where the events that shaped early Russian history occurred. Exquisite examples of Russia's most formative architecture – along with some entertaining museums – make Vladimir one of the jewels in the Golden Ring.

Orientation

Vladimir's main street is Bolshaya Moskovskaya ul (or just Moskovskaya ul), although it sometimes goes by its former name, ul III Internatsionala. The train and bus stations are 500m east on Vokzalnaya ul, at the bottom of the slope.

Information

Internet@Salon (☎ 326 471; cnr uls Gagarina & Bolshaya Moskovskaya; per hr R60; ⊙ 9am-9pm)

Post & telephone office (ul Podbelskogo; ⊙ 8am-8pm Mon-Fri)

Sberbank (Bolshaya Moskovskaya ul 27; ⊙ 9am-7pm Mon-Fri, to 5pm Sat) Exchange facilities and ATM.

Vladimir Oblast Tourist Information (☎ 447 191; www.welcome33.ru, in Russian; Bolshaya Moskovskaya ul 2; ⊙ 10am-6pm Mon-Fri, 10am-5pm Sat) Distributes some questionably useful tourist brochures.

Sights

A white-stone version of Kyiv's brick Byzantine churches, the **Assumption Cathedral** (☎ 325 201; Sobornaya pl; admission R100; ⊙ 7am-8pm Tue-Sun) was begun in 1158 – its simple but majestic form adorned with fine carving, innovative for the time. The cathedral was extended on all sides after a fire in the 1180s, when it gained the four outer domes.

Inside the working church, a few restored 12th-century murals of peacocks and prophets can be deciphered about halfway up the inner wall of the outer north aisle; this was originally an outside wall. The real treasures are the *Last Judgment* frescoes by Andrei Rublyov and Daniil Chyorny, painted in 1408 in the central nave and inner south aisle, under the choir gallery, towards the west end.

A quick stroll to the east of the Assumption Cathedral is the smaller **Cathedral of St Dmitry**

(Bolshaya Moskovskaya ul 60), built from 1193–97, when the art of stone carving in Vladimir and Suzdal reached its pinnacle. The church is permanently closed, but the attraction here is its exterior walls, covered in an amazing profusion of images. The Kyivan prince Vsevolod III, who had this church built as part of his palace, appears at the top left of the north wall, with a baby son on his knee and other sons kneeling on each side.

The grand building between the cathedrals is known as the **Palaty** (☎ 323 320; Bolshaya Moskovskaya ul 58; admission R150; ⊙ 10am-4pm Tue-Sun) and contains a children's museum, art gallery and historical exhibition. Across the small street, the **History Museum** (☎ 322 284; Bolshaya Moskovskaya ul 64; admission R50; ⊙ 10am-4pm Wed-Mon) displays many remains, and reproductions of the ornamentation from the Cathedrals of the Assumption and St Dmitry.

Vladimir's **Golden Gate** – part defensive tower, part triumphal arch – was modelled on the very similar structure in Kyiv. Originally built by Andrei Bogolyubsky to guard the main western entrance to his city, it was later restored under Catherine the Great. Now you can climb the narrow stone staircase to check out the **Military Museum** (☎ 322 559; admission R50; ⊙ 10am-4pm Fri-Wed) inside. It is a small exhibit, the centrepiece of which is a diorama of old Vladimir being ravaged by nomadic raiders in 1238 and 1293. Across the street to the south you can see a remnant of the old wall that protected the city.

The red-brick building one block west of the Golden Gate was built in 1913 to house the Old Believers' Trinity Church. Now it is a **Crystal, Lacquer Miniatures & Embroidery Exhibition**

ALTERNATIVE APPROACHES TO SIBERIA

Why not step off the beaten track and head from Moscow to Samara, on the Volga, via the ancient Russian city of Ryazan, and Saransk, capital of Mordovia – an autonomous region populated by the Mordva, a Finno-Ugric group. From Samara, continue to Ufa, the tranquil capital of the Bashkortostan Republic, sitting in the foothills of the southern Urals.

Ufa lies on the busy route that connects Siberia and the Far East with southern Russia, Ukraine and Azerbaijan. The line goes across the picturesque southern Urals to Chelyabinsk (the starting point of the historic Western Siberian line; see p47), via the access points to the Zyuratkul and Taganay national parks.

From Chelyabinsk, the line continues to Omsk in western Siberia via Petropavlovsk, across the northern tip of Kazakhstan. If you want to take this route, you'll need both a Kazakh and a multientry Russian visa. To avoid the hassle of getting the extra visas, hop on the three-hour bus from Chelyabinsk to Yekaterinburg, instead of catching the train. If someone says you've cheated, we ain't seen nothing!

(☎ 324 872; Bolshaya Moskovskaya ul 2; admission R60; ☺ 10am-4pm Wed-Mon), which features the crafts of Gus-Khrustalny and other nearby towns. The red-brick water tower atop the old ramparts houses the **Old Vladimir Exhibition** (☎ 325 451; ul Kozlov val; admission R50; ☺ 10am-4pm Tue-Sun), a nostalgic collection of old photos, advertisements and maps, including a photo of a very distinguished couple taking a ride in Vladimir's first automobile in 1896.

Sleeping

Hotel prices include breakfast.

Hotel Vladimir (☎ 324 447; www.vladimir-hotel.ru; Bolshaya Moskovskaya ul 74; s R1700, d R1850-2050, ste R2450; 🖵) This hotel near the train station used to be a state-run establishment, but it has successfully survived the transition. All the rooms have been renovated with new bathrooms and furniture, retaining a hint of old-fashioned Soviet charm in the choice of wallpaper and drapery. It is a big place with a slew of services.

U Zolotikh Vorot (At the Golden Gates; ☎ 420 823; www.golden-gate.ru, in Russian; Bolshaya Moskovskaya ul 17; s R2000-2300, d R2800-3300) The 14 rooms at this sweet little hotel are spacious and comfortable, with large windows overlooking the activity on the main street – or overlooking a central courtyard if you prefer.

Monomakh Hotel (☎ 440 444; www.monomahhotel .ru; ul Gogolya 20; s R2100-2700, d R3200, ste R4100-5100; ✕ ✕ 🖵) Off the main drag, this newish hotel has only 16 rooms, which are simply decorated but fully equipped. It offers a quiet and welcoming atmosphere.

Eating & Drinking

In addition to the places listed below, all of the hotels have restaurants on-site.

Stary Gorod (☎ 325 101; Bolshaya Moskovskaya ul 41; meals R300-400; ☺ 11am-2am) One of two side-by-side establishments on the main drag. Choose from the cosy bar, the elegant dining room or – if the weather is fine – the lovely terrace with views of the Cathedral of St Dmitry.

Traktir (☎ 324 162; Letneperevozinskaya ul 1A; meals R300-500; ☺ 11am–last guest) The liveliest place in town is this quaint wooden cottage, serving a simple menu of Russian food. In summer, the terrace opens up for cold beer and grilled shashlyk. With live music Thursday to Saturday nights (8pm to 11.30pm), it's a popular spot for young people to congregate and celebrate.

Getting There & Around

The daily express train between Moscow's Kursky vokzal (Kursk Station; R340, 2½ hours) and Nizhny Novgorod (R400, 2½ hours) stops in Vladimir, as do many slower trains. Privately run buses (R200, 3½ hours) also leave regularly from Kursky and Kazansky vokzals to Vladimir. The buses leave when they're full.

There are also scheduled buses to/from Moscow's Shchyolkovsky bus station (R190 to R225, four hours, four daily) and Nizhny Novgorod (R235 to R280, 4½ hours, seven daily). Buses go every half-hour to/from Suzdal (R40, one hour).

Trolleybus 5 from the train and bus stations runs up and along Bolshaya Moskovskaya ul, passing the main sights and hotels.

SUZDAL СУЗДАЛЬ

☎ 49231 / pop 12,000 / ☺ Moscow

The gently winding waterways, the flower-drenched meadows and dome-spotted skyline make this medieval capital the perfect fairytale setting. The town's foundation dates to 1024.

Under Muscovite rule from the late 14th century, Suzdal, 35km north of Vladimir, was once a wealthy monastic centre, with incredible development projects funded by Vasily III and Ivan the Terrible. In the late 17th and 18th centuries, wealthy merchants paid for 30 charming churches that still adorn the town. Judging by the spires and cupolas, Suzdal may almost have as many churches as people.

Suzdal was bypassed by the railroad and later protected by the Soviet government, all of which limited development in the area. So even though Suzdal is not a stop on the Trans-Siberian route, it is worth a detour to admire the abundance of ancient architectural gems and to enjoy its decidedly rural atmosphere.

Orientation & Information

The main street, ul Lenina, runs from north to south through Suzdal. The bus station is 2km east along ul Vasilievskaya.

There is an ATM that accepts international cards located at the Pushkarskaya Sloboda holiday village.

Labyrinth computer club (☎ 23 333; ul Lenina 63; per MB R4, per hr R20; ☺ 24hr) Enter from the courtyard inside the trading arcades.

Post & telephone office (Krasnaya pl; ☺ 8am-8pm) Open 24 hours for phone calls.

Sberbank (ul Lenina; ☺ 8am-4.30pm Mon-Fri) Exchange office.

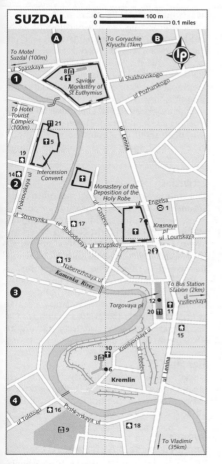

Sights

KREMLIN

The 1.4km-long earth rampart of Suzdal's kremlin, founded in the 11th century, today encloses a few streets of houses and a handful of churches, as well as the main cathedral group on Kremlyovskaya ul.

The **Nativity of the Virgin Cathedral**, its blue domes spangled with gold, was founded in the 1220s. The inside is sumptuous with 13th- and 17th-century frescoes and 13th-century gold-on-copper west and south doors.

The **Archbishop's Chambers** houses the **Suzdal History Exhibition** (☎ 21 624; admission R60; ☷ 10am-5pm Wed-Mon). The exhibition includes the original 13th-century door from the cathedral, photos of its interior and a visit to the 18th-century **Cross Hall** (Krestovaya palata), which was used for receptions. The tent-roofed 1635 **kremlin bell tower** on the east side of the yard contains additional exhibits.

TORGOVAYA PLOSHCHAD

Suzdal's Torgovaya pl (Trade Sq) is dominated by the pillared **trading arcades** (1806–11) along its western side. The arcades now house a variety of shops and cafes, as well as the excellent **Yarmarka Remesyol** (☎ 20 314; Torgovaya pl; ☷ 8am-5pm), a shop specialising in arts and crafts made in Suzdal.

There are four churches in the immediate vicinity, including the **Resurrection Church** (admission R50). Make the precarious climb to the top of the bell tower and be rewarded with wonderful views of Suzdal's gold-domed skyline.

SAVIOUR MONASTERY OF ST EUTHYMIUS

Founded in the 14th century to protect the town's northern entrance, Suzdal's biggest **monastery** (☎ 20 746; exhibits each R60-100, all-inclusive R400; ☯ 10am-6pm Tue-Sun) grew mighty in the 16th and 17th centuries after Vasily III, Ivan the Terrible and the noble Pozharsky family funded impressive new stone buildings and big land and property acquisitions. Most of the buildings on the grounds date from the 16th and 17th centuries, including the seven-domed **Cathedral of the Transfiguration of the Saviour**. Inside, restoration has uncovered some bright 1689 frescoes by the school of Gury Nikitin from Kostroma. The **tomb** of Prince Dmitry Pozharsky is by the cathedral's east wall.

The monastery buildings contain various exhibits, the most interesting of which is the old **monastery prison**, set up in 1764 for religious dissidents. It now houses a fascinating exhibit on the monastery's military history and prison life, including displays of some of the better-known prisoners who stayed there.

INTERCESSION CONVENT

This **convent** (☎ 20 889; Pokrovskaya ul; admission free; ☯ 9.30am-4.30pm Thu-Mon) was founded in 1364, originally as a place of exile for the unwanted wives of tsars. Among them was Solomonia Saburova, first wife of Vasily III, who was sent here in the 1520s because of her supposed infertility. The story goes that she finally became pregnant too late to avoid being divorced. A baby boy was born in Suzdal. Fearing he would be seen as a dangerous rival to any sons produced by Vasily's new wife, Solomonia secretly had him adopted, pretended he had died and staged a mock burial. This was probably just as well for the boy since Vasily's second wife did indeed produce a son – Ivan the Terrible.

The legend received dramatic corroboration in 1934 when researchers opened a small 16th-century tomb beside Solomonia's, in the crypt underneath the **Intercession Cathedral**. They found a silk and pearl shirt stuffed with rags – and no bones. The crypt is closed to visitors.

OTHER SUZDAL BUILDINGS

The open-air **Museum of Wooden Architecture & Peasant Life** (☎ 23 567; Pushkarskaya ul; grounds R60, exhibits each R60, all-inclusive R160; ☯ 9.30am-7pm Wed-Mon May-Oct), illustrating old peasant life in this region of Russia, is a short walk across the

river southeast of the kremlin. Besides log houses, windmills, a barn and lots of tools and handicrafts, its highlights are the 1756 **Transfiguration Church** (Preobrazhenskaya tserkov) and the simpler 1776 **Resurrection Church** (Voskresenskaya tserkov).

Almost every corner in Suzdal has its own little church with its own charm. The central dilapidated **Monastery of the Deposition of the Holy Robe**, with its landmark **bell tower** and exquisite entrance turrets, was founded in 1207, but the existing buildings date from the 16th to 19th centuries.

Activities

The rolling hills and attractive countryside around Suzdal are ideal for outdoor adventures, including horse riding and mountain biking. The **Hotel Tourist Complex** (Gostinichny Turistsky Kompleks, or GTK; ☎ 23 380; ul Korovniki 45; ☯ 10am-6pm) rents bicycles, snowmobiles and skis, as well as offering horse-riding tours.

Rural Suzdal is a great place to cleanse body and soul in the Russian *banya* (bathhouse). Beautiful, lakeside *bani* are available for rental at **Goryachie Klyuchi** (☎ 24 000; www.parilka.com, in Russian; ul Korovniki 14; ☯ 11am-1am), starting at R880 for up to four people.

Sleeping

Suzdal is experiencing a tourism boom, which means many more options for top-end travellers. All prices include breakfast unless otherwise noted.

BUDGET

Gostevoy Dom (☎ 23 264; Pokrovskaya ul 29; per person R500) If you wander around town, you are likely to see signs in private homes advertising *Gostevoy Dom* (guest house), such as this one near the Intercession Convent. This is usually an excellent option for budget travellers, who will enjoy simple, homey accommodations with shared bathrooms.

Godzillas Suzdal (www.suzdalhostel.com; Naberezhnaya ul 12; dm R600; 🖳) The popular Moscow-based Godzillas has expanded into the countryside, opening a big beautiful log-cabin facility overlooking the river. The dorm rooms each have their own bathroom and balcony. Guests can also enjoy the blooming garden and Russian *banya*, as well as the chill-out lounge and bar in the basement.

Likhoninsky Dom (☎ 21 901; ul Slobodskaya 34) Suzdal's most appealing place to stay is on a quiet street near the town centre. This 17th-century merchant's house has five charming rooms and a pretty garden. Closed for renovation at the time of research, it was scheduled to reopen in early 2009.

Motel Suzdal (☎ 21 530; www.suzdaltour.ru; ul Korovniki 45; economy s/d/tr R1670/1960/2250, modern s/d/tr R2960/3250/3540; ⊠ ▯ ⊠) One of three hotels within the GTK. This place is low on charm but high on facilities: the complex includes a fitness centre, a bowling alley, several restaurants, and a slightly more expensive hotel with upgraded rooms.

Hotel Sokol (☎ 20 088; www.hotel-sokol.ru; Torgovaya pl 2a; s R1900-2260, d R2480-2620, ste R3020-3940; ⊠) Ideally located opposite the trading arcades, this is a traditional hotel in a classical 19th-century building. Its 40 rooms are all simply decorated and fully equipped with new wooden furniture and modern bathrooms.

Pushkarskaya Sloboda (☎ 23 303; www.sloboda-gk.ru, in Russian; ul Lenina 45, enter from Pushkarskaya ul; s/d inn R2400/2700, village R3300/3600; ⊠ ⊠ ⊠) This holiday village has everything you might want from your Disney vacation – accommodation in the log-cabin 'Russian inn' or the reproduction 19th-century 'gunner's village'; three restaurants, ranging from a rustic country tavern to a formal dining room; and every service you might dream up. It's an attractive, family-friendly, good-value option, though it might be too well-manicured for some tastes.

Traktir Kuchkova (☎ 20 252; Pokrovskaya ul 35; s/d R2800/3000; ⊠) On a quiet street opposite the Intercession Convent, this guest house has a 'New Russian' ambience that does not fit in old-fashioned Suzdal, but it is not a bad option. Its 17 rooms are comfortable but overdecorated. It also has a nice *banya* and an excellent restaurant.

Kremlyovsky Hotel (☎ 23 480; www.kremlinhotel.ru, in Russian; ul Tolstogo 5; s/d from R3950/4400; ⊠ ⊠ ▯) This white-stone hotel mirrors the tall towers of the kremlin on the opposite bank of the river. The rooms are contemporary and comfortable, without a lot of fancy stuff, but they offer lovely views of the winding waterway and the rustic wooden architecture in the vicinity.

Eating & Drinking

In addition to the places listed below, all of the hotels have restaurants.

Kremlin Trapeznaya (☎ 21 763; Kremlin; meals R300-500; ☉ 11am-11pm) The attraction here is the choice location inside the Archbishop's Chambers. This place has been serving tasty, filling Russian favourites for 300 years.

Pokrovskaya Trapeznaya (☎ 20 199; Intercession Convent; meals R400-600; ☉ 10am-10pm) On the grounds of the Intercession Convent, the old refectory is now a rustic restaurant, serving hearty Russian fare in an atmospheric old wooden building.

Mead-Tasting Hall (☎ 20 803; trading arcades; tasting menu R120-150; ☉ 10am-6pm Mon-Fri, to 8pm Sat & Sun) Hidden at the rear of the trading arcades, this hall is done up like a church interior – floor-to-ceiling frescoes, arched ceilings and stained-glass windows. The menu features different varieties of *medovukha*, a mildly alcoholic honey ale that was drunk by the princes of old.

Other recommendations in the trading arcades:

Gostiny Dvor (☎ 21 778; trading arcades; meals R600-800; ☉ 11am-midnight) Enjoy the lovely vista from the outside tables, especially at sunset.

Traktir Zaryadie (☎ 24 319; trading arcades; meals R400-600) Enter from the rear of the trading arcades.

Getting There & Away

The bus station is 2km east of the centre on ul Vasilievskaya. Some long-distance buses continue on past the bus station into the centre; otherwise, a *marshrutka* will take you there.

Buses run every half-hour to/from Vladimir (R40, one hour). One bus goes directly to/from Moscow's Shchyolkovsky bus station (R250, daily, 4½ hours).

NIZHNY NOVGOROD
НИЖНИЙ НОВГОРОД

☎ 831 / pop 1.31 million / ☉ Moscow

Had something prevented this country from becoming the world's largest land empire, Nizhny (as it is usually shortened) would have been the end of your Russian rail adventure. For here Rus ends and Russia begins. No more fratricidal princes and defiant city-republics – from now on, all the stories you hear from your guides will be about tsars and their servants exploring, colonising and ruthlessly exploiting the Wild East.

Here the Trans-Siberian route crosses Russia's historical main drag – the Volga River, so you might even make a snap decision and swap the rail compartment and your chilling Siberian prospects for a cabin on a cruise ship heading down to the Caspian subtropics (you'll need our *Russia* guidebook then).

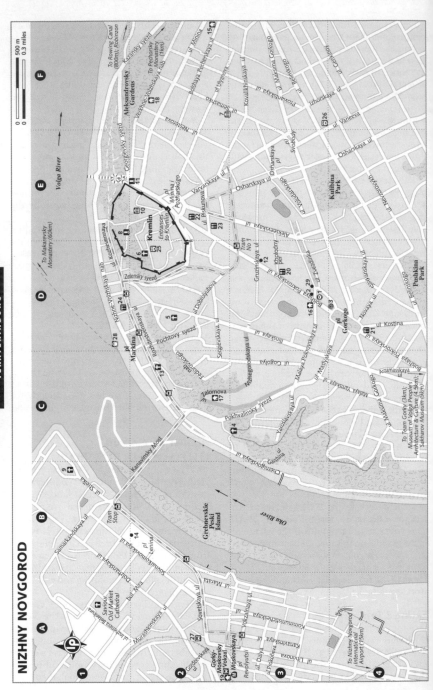

NIZHNY NOVGOROD

Like other cities downstream, Nizhny is as laid-back and scenic as you can possibly get in Russia. Its museums and old quarters with ramshackle wooden merchants' houses will fill you spiritually, while its cliffs and ravines will provide some necessary exercise before your long Siberian train confinement.

Orientation

Nizhny Novgorod, lying on the southern bank of the Volga River, is split by the Oka River. The city's kremlin sits on the high eastern bank overlooking the Volga. Outside the kremlin's southern wall, the city's main streets branch out from pl Minina i Pozharskogo. From here, the pleasant and pedestrian Bolshaya Pokrovskaya ul heads south to pl Gorkogo. The train and bus stations are side by side on the western side of the Oka.

Information

Central post office (pl Gorkogo; per hr R40; ☺ 8am-9pm) Has internet facilities.
Dirizhabl (Bolshaya Pokrovskaya ul 46; ☺ 10am-8pm) A three-storey bookshop with a good selection of maps and local guidebooks, and some books in foreign languages.
Volga Telecom (pl Gorkogo; per hr R40; ☺ 24hr) Under reconstruction at the time of research, it used to be a convenient internet facility.

Sights

Bolshaya Pokrovskaya ul, dotted with bronze figures depicting 19th-century life, ul Ilyinskaya ul, with its crumbling wooden

merchants' houses and many churches, have the greatest architectural appeal in Nizhny Novgorod. A major landmark is the **State Bank building** (Bolshaya Pokrovskaya ul 26). Built in 1913, it looks like a cross between a Russian church and a German castle.

KREMLIN

The mighty walls of the kremlin and its 11 towers date from the 16th century. Sometimes the ramparts are open for a sweeping view of the kremlin grounds and beyond; climb up through the restaurant in the Kladovaya Bashnya gate.

Inside, most of the buildings are government offices. The small, 17th-century **Cathedral of the Archangel Michael** is a functioning church. Behind it, an eternal flame burns near a striking **monument to the heroes of WWII**. At the northeast end of the grounds, the former governor's house is now the **Nizhegorodsky State Art Museum** (admission R50; ☺ 10am-5pm Wed-Mon). Exhibits range from 14th-century icons to 20th-century paintings by artists including Nikolai Rerikh and Vasily Surikov.

CHURCHES & MONASTERIES

The proliferation of onion domes and golden spires is a ubiquitous reminder of the city's rich history. The 13th-century **Annunciation Monastery** (Melnichny per, enter from Pokhvalinsky syezd; ☎ tours 430-55-78; http://www.blagovm.nn.ru/, in Russian, email -blagovestm@rambler.ru; excursions in Russian R20), above Chernigovskaya ul, is the place to see the city's oldest buildings, although an overzealous guard at the gates sometimes attempts to prevent touristy-looking people from entering. Ignore him, if possible. East of town, the 17th-century **Pechorsky Monastery**, overlooking the Volga, is much more welcoming. It houses a small **Archaeological Museum** (admission R20; ☉ 9am-7pm Wed-Sat), with a moving exhibition on Bolshevik repressions against the church on the 2nd floor. Underneath it is the **Rowing Canal**, with sandy banks that have become the city's main beach.

The stone **Assumption Church** (Ilinskaya ul), also from the 17th century, is unique in that its design was normally exclusive to wooden churches. The baroque **Stroganov Church** (Nativity Church; Rozhdestvenskaya ul) has retained its magnificent stone carvings.

On the west bank of the Oka River is the eye-catching **Nevsky Cathedral** (ul Strelka) and the handsomely restored **Yarmarka** (☎ 277 5489; www.yarmarka.ru; ul Sovnarkomovskaya 13), which used to be the location of the Nizhny Novgorod fair and now houses an exhibition hall.

MUSEUMS

Fans of Maxim Gorky can visit the **Gorky Museum** (ul Semashko 19; admission R10; ☉ 9am-5pm Tue & Wed & Fri-Sun), a wooden house where the writer lived during his 30s.

A reminder of more repressive times, the **Sakharov Museum** (☎ 466 8623; pr Gagarina 214; admission R40; ☉ 10am-5pm) is located in the flat where the dissident scientist Andrei Sakharov spent six years in exile. The Nobel laureate was held incommunicado until 1986 when a KGB officer came to install a telephone. When it rang, it was Mikhail Gorbachev at the other end, informing Sakharov of his release. The phone is a highlight of the exhibition. To get there, take *marshrutka* 4 or 104 from pl Minina i Pozharskogo.

The open-air **Museum of Volga People's Architecture & Culture** (☎ 465 1598; www.ngiamz.ru, in Russian; Gorbatovskaya ul 41; admission R30; ☉ 10am-4pm Sat-Thu) has a pleasant woodland site and a collection of traditional wooden buildings from Russian and Mordva (a Finno-Ugric people) villages. Young history enthusiasts stage colourful celebrations of five main village holidays a year. Dates vary, so check with the staff to find out if this is happening during your stay. The museum is located in the remote Shchelokovsky Khutor park, which is the final stop of bus 28 (R10, every hour) that passes ul Belinskogo in the centre.

Tours

Team Gorky (☎ 465 1999; www.teamgorky.ru; ul 40 let Oktyabrya 1a) offers canoe and bicycle tours in the Nizhny Novgorod region and beyond. Three-day adventure trips start at R5500. Dual pricing alert! Prices for some tours on their English-language site are much higher than those on the Russian one, but they swear that walk-in foreign travellers will pay the same prices.

Volga-Flot Tour (see p167) run boat tours to places such as Makaryevsky monastery.

Sleeping

Train Station Rest Rooms (Komnaty Otdykha; ☎ 244 2110; s/d without bathroom R530/710) Located in a separate building on your right as you exit the station, the rest rooms are OK to spend a night in before your next train.

Gostinitsa NGLU (☎ 436 5945; Bolshaya Pecherskaya ul 36; dm/s/d with shared bathroom R319/R678/1052) Occupying the top floors of the Linguistic University dormitory, this place is friendly to foreigners, although it does not do registrations. Rooms are in two-room apartments, and are spartan, but clean. Advance booking recommended.

Nizhegorodsky Hotel Complex (☎ 430 5387; www.hotel-nn.ru; ul Zalomova 2; s/d without river view from R2600/3100, with river view R2800/3500) A 15-minute walk from Nizhny's main drag, it is a concrete slab of a building from the outside, but rooms have been refurbished, views are fabulous and the hill slope underneath was being converted into a terraced park at the time of research.

October Hotel (Oktyabrskaya; ☎ 432 8080; www.oktyabrskaya.ru; Verkhne-Volzhskaya nab 9A; s/d incl breakfast from R3700/5550) This business hotel has a prime location overlooking the Volga. All of the rooms have been renovated and have new furniture, modern bathrooms, free wi-fi, and a hint of post-Soviet kitsch.

our pick **Jouk-Jacque** (☎ 433 0462; www.jak-hotel.ru; Bolshaya Pokrovskaya ul 57; s/d from R3750/5250) Calling something a 'mix of French and Nizhegorodian' in Russian usually means you're denouncing it for provincial vulgarism, but this cosy boutique hotel is anything but vulgar. The cheapest rooms are a bit cramped, but neat, and breakfasts are superb by Russian standards.

Eating & Drinking

The cheap and cheerful summer cafes by the city's main hangout near the Pilot Valery Chkalov monument are also a great place to mingle with locals. Other recommended places include the following.

Biblioteca (☎ 433 6934; Bolshaya Pokrovskaya ul 46; pasta R130, coffee R65; ☺ 11am-10pm) Upstairs from the Dirizhabl bookshop, this cafe's decor includes a collection of kerosene lamps hanging from the ceiling and lots of bookshelves. Food is standard Italian.

Michelle (☎ 192 914; Bolshaya Pokrovskaya ul 6; meals R150-300; ☺ 10am-11pm) This place is – first and foremost – a coffee bar, offering several varieties of aromatic brew in a simple cafe setting. The menu also features soups and sandwiches, and dishes with French nuances – innovative fare for the price.

our pick **Restoratsia Pyatkin** (☎ 430 9183; Rozhdestvenskaya ul 23; mains R200; ☺ noon-2am) This place makes one feel like a merchant feasting in his mansion after a great day's trading at the market. The menu is full of Volga specialities, such as pieces of crayfish and pike perch baked with cheese, and pike head stuffed with minced fish. It also brews an unusual apple *kvas*.

Pizza Vero (☎ 419 2438; ul Piskunova 11; pizza R300, breakfasts R150; ☺ 24hr) In a city where people tend to wake up late and go to bed early, this is one of the few places to fill your stomach after a party or an overnight train.

Merry Godmother (Vesyolaya kuma; ☎ 296 0533; ul Kostina 3; mains R350; ☺ noon-2am) In a row of 'ethnic' restaurants (Russian, German, Chinese), the godmother merrily serves hearty borsch and other Ukrainian fare.

Gorod Gorky (☎ 332 017; Bolshaya Pokrovskaya ul 30; meals R400; ☺ 11am-midnight) Irony outweighs nostalgia in this retro-Soviet place hidden in a courtyard off the main drag – look for the Музей СССР sign. Walk through the office of a waxwork Leonid Brezhnev into the dining room, littered with Soviet memorabilia and Beatles photos. The food is surprisingly good, and you can compare how much it costs today with how little it cost in 1974.

Robinzon (☎ 431 3062; nab Grebnogo kanala 108; mains R400-1100, cocktails R300) This kitschy place is from that rare breed of Russian beach restaurants. Located by the main city beach, it is unbeatable for a sunset cocktail on a hot day.

Entertainment

The **Kremlin Concert Hall** (☎ 439 1187) at the west end of the kremlin, is the home of the philharmonic, playing a full schedule of classical concerts. Shows start at 6pm. For Russian classics, the beautifully renovated **Pushkin Theatre**

of **Opera & Ballet** (☎ 218 5056; www.opera.nnov.ru, in Russian; ul Belinskogo 59) is also recommended.

Getting There & Away

The Nizhny Novgorod International Airport is 15km southwest of the city centre. S7 flies daily from Moscow (R3050, one hour). **Lufthansa** (☎ 275 9085) flies directly to/from Frankfurt four times a week (€620, 3½ hours). Airline tickets are available at agencies around the city, including the **Turbyuro** (☎ 439 3260; ul Zvezdinka 10b; ☺ 10am-7pm Mon-Sat).

The river station is on Nizhne-Volzhskaya nab, below the kremlin. The **Volga-Flot Tour** (☎ 461 8010; www.wftour.ru, in Russian; ☺ 10am-7pm Mon-Fri) office inside the station building and the cash office on the embankment sell weekend day trips to the ancient and very attractive Makaryevsky monastery (R800 to R900). Gorodets (see p168) hydrofoils (three daily, R150) leave from a dedicated pier, on the left from the station if you're facing the river.

Buses to Vladimir (R280, 4½ hours, four daily), Kostroma (R550, eight hours, daily) and Gorodets (R110, 1½ hours, every half-hour) depart from small Kanavinskaya bus station.

The Nizhny Novgorod train station still goes by its old name of Gorky-Moskovsky vokzal, so 'Gorky' appears on most timetables. It is on the western bank of the Oka River, at pl Revolyutsii. Numerous trains go to Moscow, the fastest being two daytime services to Kursk station (R500, five hours). All of these stop at Vladimir (R400, two to three hours).

Heading east, trains go along the Trans-Sib route to Perm (R3570, 15 hours, 10 trains a day) and Kazan (R320, seven hours, daily). Kazan is also served by a comfortable *elektrichka* (R320, eight hours, two daily). Tickets are available at the suburban train terminal.

The service centre at the train station is helpful for buying tickets, and also offers other services such as internet access.

Getting Around

Private buses are the main mode of transportation, and their destinations are clearly signposted. To get from the train station to the kremlin take any bus that has пл Минина и Пожарского posted on it. Slow tram 1 does the same route.

The city's metro might be extended across the river in the lifetime of this book, which will provide a useful link between pl Gorkogo and the train station.

WHATEVER FLOATS YOUR VOLGA BOAT

Before and for a few decades after the Trans-Siberian line was built, Russia's main transport artery was the Volga. Hundreds of years ago, it was already busy with boats bringing goods from as far as Baghdad and India in the south, and Scandinavian and Baltic countries in the north. Nowadays, an intricate system of channels connects the Volga to the White, Baltic and the Black Seas, enabling numerous cruise ships to take most intriguing routes, for example taking passengers from chilly, arctic Arkhangelsk to scorching hot, subtropical Astrakhan.

While on the Trans-Siberian route, you can taste the pleasures of river travel by taking a boat trip to one of several small Volga towns from either Nizhny Novgorod's or Kazan's river station.

Gorodets, a quaint town of folk artists and bakers, has been recently spruced up to appeal to day trippers from Nizhny Novgorod. Populated by Old Believers since the times of the schism, it has become famous for its gouache-on-wood folklore paintings and hard, honey-rich *pryaniki* cakes.

Two hours by boat from Kazan, the desolate egg-shaped island of **Sviyazhsk** has some of the region's most ancient architecture and a fascinating history. Its original wooden fortress, designed as a base for the Russian onslaught on Kazan during the reign of Ivan the Terrible, was built 700km upstream in the town of Myshkin, then disassembled and the logs sent floating down the river, where it was built again.

South of Kazan, the village of **Bolgar** is the descendant of Great Bulgar, the capital of a highly civilised ancient kingdom. The scattered ruins remaining from the Golden Horde era (13th to 15th centuries) are located on the outskirts of the village, on the cliffs overlooking the Volga River. You can go to Bolgar as a day trip on weekends, when excursion boats go there. Otherwise you'll have to stay overnight at **Hotel Regina** (☎ 310 44; ul Gorkogo 30; s/d R1050/R1250).

KAZAN КАЗАНЬ

☎ 843 / pop 1.1 million / ⊗ Moscow

After long stints as a Golden Horde stronghold and a provincial Russian city, Kazan has once again changed face. It now presents itself as a modern multicultural city, akin to Istanbul or Sarajevo. The most symbolic change in the cityscape is the Kul-Sharif Mosque, opened during Kazan's millennium celebrations in 2005. The mosque looks like it has always been standing in the middle of the magnificent white-walled kremlin, alongside the ancient Orthodox cathedrals, despite its predecessor being razed by Ivan the Terrible 450 years ago.

Kazan is a Tatar as much as a Russian city. Being the capital of Russia's strongest autonomy – the Republic of Tatarstan – it has what strikes some Russians as almost a foreign feel. Tatars are Turkic Muslims who are very serious about preserving their language and religion. Yet, with ethnic Russians making up almost a half of the population, Kazan seems a rather happy example of multiculturalism. Already one of the most modernised Russian cities, it will see further improvement as it prepares to host Universiade, the international student games, in 2013.

History

It is assumed that Kazan was founded as a northeastern outpost of the ancient kingdom of Volga Bulgaria, around AD 1000. After the Tatar-Mongols flattened Great Bulgar, Kazan became the capital of the region incorporated in the Golden Horde. After the Golden Horde was destroyed, the independent Kazan khanate was created in 1438. Weak from the start, it was ravaged by the troops of Ivan the Terrible and his Tatar allies from Kasimov in 1552.

Ivan the Terrible was quick to build a new (Russian) city on the ruins. Architects responsible for St Basil's Cathedral in Moscow (which honours the seizure of Kazan) were employed to plan the kremlin. Until the enlightened age of Catherine the Great, Tatars were banished from the eastern side of the Bulak canal – and the division of the city into the Russian and Tatar parts is still quite visible. The only centrally located mosque north of the canal is the new Kul-Sharif, inside the kremlin.

Kazan grew into one of Russia's economic and cultural capitals, with the country's third university opening here in 1804. Its alumni include Leo Tolstoy and Vladimir Ulyanov (Lenin), who was expelled for stirring up political trouble. In Soviet times, Kazan became the capital of the Tatar autonomous republic and a major centre of the aviation industry.

Orientation

Kazan's city centre is flanked by the Kazanka River to the north and the Volga River to the west; the train station is on the east bank of the Volga. About 500m east of the Volga shore, the Bulak canal bisects the town centre, separating the train station and surrounding former Tatar suburbs from the centre. The main pedestrian drag, ul Baumana, is just east of the canal, running from the kremlin in the northwest, down to the busy pl Tukaya.

Information

Dom Knigi (ul Baumana 58; 9am-6pm) A centrally located modern bookshop with a selection of maps and books in Tatar and foreign languages.

Kazan Tourist Information Centre (292 3010; http://gokazan.com; Kremlyovskaya ul 15/25; 9.30am-6.30pm Mon-Fri, 10am-4pm Sat) Glory to the city of Kazan for opening one of the first city tourist offices in Russia! They distribute tourist maps and promise to start issuing 'city cards' that will provide discounts in museums.

Main post & telephone office (Kremlyovskaya ul 8; 8am-7pm Mon-Fri, 9am-6pm Sat & Sun)

Tattelecom (ul Pushkina 15; per hr R32; 24hr) A large internet facility.

Sights
KREMLIN

Declared a Unesco World Heritage site in 2000, Kazan's striking kremlin is the focal point of the city's historic centre. It's home to government offices, pleasant parks and a few religious buildings that are usually open and operating. Some of the white limestone walls date from the 16th and 17th centuries.

The **Annunciation Cathedral** was built on the foundation of the razed mosque with eight minarets, and was designed by Postnik Yakovlev, who was responsible for St Basil's Cathedral in Moscow. Ironically, it is over-shadowed by the enormous **Kul Sharif Mosque**, completed in 2005, which is named after the imam who died defending the city against the troops of Ivan the Terrible in 1552.

Alongside the cathedral is the 59m-high leaning **Syuyumbike Tower** – the subject of a legend about a Tatar princess who agreed to marry Ivan the Terrible if he built the tower, and then she jumped from the tower and killed herself. A former cadet-school

building now houses the **Hermitage Centre** (admission R80; Tue-Sun 10am-5pm), which runs rotating exhibitions from the collection of St Petersburg's Hermitage (p105).

In front of the kremlin, the striking bronze figure of a man tearing barbed wire is the **Musa Dzhalil monument**, honouring a Tatar poet who was executed by the Nazis in Berlin's Moabit prison in 1944, leaving a notebook full of poems to a Belgian friend.

OTHER SIGHTS

Opposite the kremlin's main entrance, the **National Museum of the Republic of Tatarstan** (292 1484; Kremlyovskaya ul 2; admission R150; 10am-5pm Tue-Sun) is in an ornate 1770 building. The museum has a range of exhibits, from Tatar history to water and wildlife to local artists. The Gallery of Zarif is a unique exhibit by a local artist-philosopher.

Of Kazan's several Orthodox churches, the most attractive is the **SS Peter & Paul Cathedral** (ul Musy Dzhalilya 21), whose unusual architecture and heavily decorated facade defy style classifications. Built between 1723 and 1726, it commemorates Peter the Great's visit in 1722.

Another landmark is the huge red-brick **Theophany Church Belfry** (ul Baumana 78). A small chapel inside is dedicated to Russia's first musical idol – opera singer Fyodor Chaliapin, who started his career in the church's choir. The **Chaliapin Monument** stands nearby in front of the namesake hotel.

At the foot of Kremlyovskaya ul, you can't miss the overbearing classical facade of the main building of **Lenin State University**, where Vladimir Ilych himself was a student. The **university library** (cnr Astronomicheskaya & Kremlyovskaya uls) has an exquisite decorated exterior.

Many of the city's mosques are clustered in the dumpy southwest corner of town. Near the central market is the **Soltanov mosque** (ul Gabdully Tukaya 14), dating from 1867, and the **Nurullah mosque** (ul Moskovskaya 74), which has been re-built several times since 1849. The **German (St Catherine's) Lutheran church** (ul Karla Marksa 26) is on the other side of the town centre.

Events

Sabantuy is the main Tatar holiday celebrated all over Tatarstan and beyond in the middle of June. The festival features serious sporting events, such as wrestling and horse racing, as well as novelty competitions. Vladimir Putin

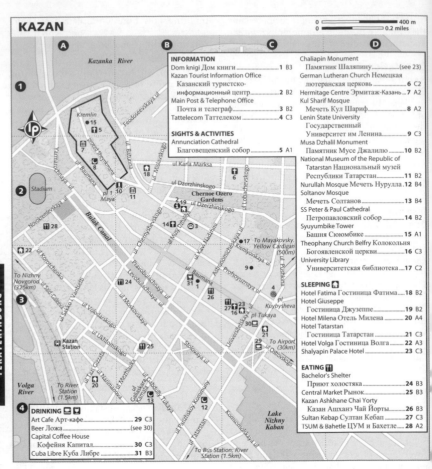

KAZAN

0 — 400 m
0 — 0.2 miles

INFORMATION
Dom knigi Дом книги 1 B3
Kazan Tourist Information Office
   Казанский туристско-
   информационный центр......................2 B2
Main Post & Telephone Office
   Почта и телеграф...............................3 B2
Tattelecom Таттелеком 4 C3

SIGHTS & ACTIVITIES
Annunciation Cathedral
   Благовещенский собор.....................5 A1

Chaliapin Monument
   Памятник Шаляпину.....................(see 23)
German Lutheran Church Немецкая
   лютеранская церковь 6 C2
Hermitage Centre Эрмитаж-Казань...7 B2
Kul Sharif Mosque
   Мечеть Кул Шариф..........................8 A2
Lenin State University
   Государственный
   Университет им Ленина...................9 B2
Musa Dzhalil Monument
   Памятник Мусе Джалилю 10 B2
National Museum of the Republic of
   Tatarstan Национальный музей
   Республики Татарстан....................11 B2
Nurullah Mosque Мечеть Нурулла.12 B4
Soltanov Mosque
   Мечеть Солтанов 13 B4
SS Peter & Paul Cathedral
   Петропавловский собор 14 B2
Syuyumbike Tower
   Башня Сююмбике 15 A1
Theophany Church Belfry Колокольня
   Богоявленской церкви..................16 C3
University Library
   Университетская библиотека 17 C3

SLEEPING
Hotel Fatima Гостиница Фатима.....18 B2
Hotel Giuseppe
   Гостиница Джузеппе......................19 B2
Hotel Milena Отель Милена 20 A4
Hotel Tatarstan
   Гостиница Татарстан 21 C3
Hotel Volga Гостиница Волга 22 A3
Shalyapin Palace Hotel 23 C3

EATING
Bachelor's Shelter
   Приют холостяка 24 B3
Central Market Рынок......................25 B3
Kazan Ashkhane Chai Yorty
   Казан Ашханэ Чай Йорты..........26 B3
Sultan Kebap Султан Кебап 27 C3
TSUM & Bahetle ЦУМ и Бахетле.... 28 A2

DRINKING
Art Cafe Арт-кафе....................................29 C3
Beer Ложа...(see 30)
Capital Coffee House
   Кофейня Капитал..............................30 C3
Cuba Libre Куба Либре..........................31 B3

Map labels:
Kazanka River
Kremlin
Stadium
Chernoe Ozero Gardens
Batak Canal
To Nizhny Novgorod (325km)
To Mayakovsky Yellow Cardigan (500m)
Kazan Station
Volga River
To River Station (1.5km)
pl Kuybysheva
pl Tukaya
To Airport (30km)
Lake Nizhny Kaban
To Bus Station; River Station (1.5km)

was once spotted at the fest wearing a green Tatar hat, and trying to catch an apple floating in a milk-filled barrel with his mouth.

Sleeping

Hotel Fatima (☎ 292 0616; ul Karla Marksa 2; r with/without bathroom from R1400/650) Spitting distance from the kremlin, this hotel is a great bargain. But without its own hot-water heater, it is subject to compulsory hot-water switch-offs in summer, which can last for weeks. The staff will warn you if this is expected.

Hotel Volga (☎ 231 6349; www.volga-hotel.ru; ul Said-Galeeva 1; s/d without bathroom R750/1200, s/d with bathroom from R1200/2200) Not far from the train station, this nicely revamped hotel has rooms for every budget (although the midrange rooms get booked early). Rooms facing the street can be noisy, but the place is clean and welcoming.

Hotel Milena (☎ 292 9992; www.milenahotel.ru; ul Tazi Gizzata 19; s/d from 1500/1700) If this hotel were a politician it would be called controversial. Some people praise it for modern comforts, proximity to the train station and free wi-fi. Others complain about the noise from the adjacent flour mill (we didn't hear anything) and indifferent staff (yes, true).

Hotel Tatarstan (☎ 238 8379; ul Pushkina 4; s/d from R1800/3600) Towering above the city centre, the namesake of the republic offers great views and generally good standards with a few Soviet oddities, such as elevators specialising in odd- or even-numbered floors and sausages with sauerkraut for breakfast.

ourpick **Hotel Giuseppe** (☎ 292 6934; www.giu seppe.ru; Kremlyovskaya ul 15/25; s/d with breakfast from R2740/3560; ⚡) Above a pizzeria of the same name, this Italian-run place has spacious, comfortable rooms. Artificially crannied walls in the corridors are meant to create the atmosphere of a Venetian villa.

Shalyapin Palace Hotel (☎ 238 2800; www.shalyapin -hotel.ru; Universitetskaya ul 7/80; s/d from R2600/4800; ⚡ 🏊) Named after Russia's greatest opera singer – whose statue greets you at the door– this large new hotel is here to compete with Hotel Giuseppe in style. Let's see who wins.

Eating

Kazan Askhane-Chai Yorty (ul Baumana 64; mains R70, pastries R20; ⏱ 9am-8pm) This cheap eatery serves hearty Tatar food, identical to what you get at the expensive House of Tatar Culinary across the street, which seems permanently closed for banquets. Go for pastry – *echpohmak* with meat, *bekken* with cabbage, *kystyby* with mashed potatoes, or *gubadiya* with sweet rice and raisins.

Sultan Kebap (☎ 238 3803; ul Baumana 74; mains R180; ⏱ 11am-11pm) A sign of special relations between Kazan and Istanbul, this is a home away from home for Turkish expats.

ourpick **Bachelor's Shelter** (Priyut kholostyaka; ☎ 292 0771; ul Chernyshevskogo 27a; mains R350) It's a relief to escape the dingy neighbourhood around the train station by sneaking in this tiny entrance, which opens into a spotlessly white oasis of style with surrealist glass paintings, and coathangers shaped like wild garlic flowers. International food, including the inevitable sushi, free wi-fi and the best latte this side of the Volga.

The colourful, sprawling **central market** (ul Mezhlauka) is good for stocking up on snacks or just for browsing. The Bahetle supermarket on the 1st floor of the **TsUM shopping mall** (ul Moskovskaya 2; ⏱ 9am-10pm) sells excellent Tatar pastries and all the supplies you'll need on the train.

Drinking & Entertainment

Capital Coffee House (☎ 292 6390; ul Pushkina 5; coffee R80, breakfast R150; ⏱ 8am-midnight Mon-Fri, noon-midnight Sat & Sun; 🖥) Apart from making good coffee and nice international food, these people promise to fix any cocktail, according to your recipe. There are three PCs with internet access (R30 per half-hour) and wi-fi (R100 per hour).

Art Cafe (☎ 236 6144; ul Ostrovskogo 38; mains R250, breakfasts R200; ⏱ 8am-6am) Another stylish

cafe, useful for breakfast or as an after-party chill-out. There is a popular pizzeria on the same premises.

BeerLozha (☎ 292 2436; ul Pushkina 5; mains R300-500; ⏱ noon-2am) Ten beers on tap and a whole range of spicy sausages feature at this Bavarian beer bar.

Mayakovsky.Yellow Cardigan (Mayakovsky.Zheltaya kofta; ☎ 264 3980; www.zheltaya-kofta.ru, in Russian; ul Mayakovskogo 24a; admission R100; ⏱ 11am-midnight Mon-Fri, 4pm-midnight Sat & Sun) It can be Tatar rap or punk bands singing covers of Soviet soundtrack faves, or something even more experimental in this club with a youthful crowd, and decor inspired by Kazimir Malevich.

Cuba Libre (☎ 253 5532; ul Baumana 58; mains R250, cuba libre R100; ⏱ noon-2am Sun-Thu, noon-5am Fri & Sat) A convivial drinking den where you can chat to friendly bartenders and other visitors while sipping Kazan's best mojito. Wild Latin dancing may erupt at any moment.

Getting There & Away

The Aviakassy booth inside Hotel Tatarstan is convenient for both air and railway tickets.

Several airlines fly daily from the **Kazan international airport** (☎ 267 8807), located 30km south of the city, to Moscow (from R2300, 1½ hours). You can also fly directly to Frankfurt (four weekly) with Lufthansa, Istanbul with Turkish Airways (two weekly) or Kaliningrad with KD-Avia (daily).

You can catch buses to Ulyanovsk (R350, four to six hours, eight daily) and Samara (R383, seven hours, two daily) at the **long-distance bus station** (www.avtovokzal-kzn.ru, in Russian; cnr uls Tatarstan & Portovaya).

Boats for Sviyazhsk and Bolgar (p168) leave from the river station at the end of ul Tatarstan. It's better to buy tickets well in advance. Buses for Bolgar (R200, 3½ hours, two daily) leave from a smallish terminal next to the river station's cash office. You can also take a boat to/from Moscow, see p146.

The beautifully restored original train station on ul Said-Galeeva now serves as a waiting room. Long-distance tickets are sold in a separate building, north of the new sleek suburban train station. Queues are smaller at ticket counters on the 2nd floor, where the service centre is also located. Frequent trains link Kazan to Moscow (R1670, 13 hours) and Yekaterinburg (R3100, 15 hours). There are one or two trains a day to Perm (R1600, 15 hours). Apart from many intercity trains,

MOSCOW TO YEKATERINBURG

Nizhny Novgorod is also served by high-speed *elektrichki* from the suburban terminal (R320, eight hours).

Getting Around

Bus 97 (every half-hour, 5am to 11pm) connects the airport with Kazan's suburbs, passing pr Pobedy station, at the end of the city's only metro line. Kremlyovskaya and pl Tukaya metro stations are located at each end of ul Baumana. Tram 7 and bus 53 link the train, bus and river stations. Tram 2 and bus 8 run from the station to pl Tukaya.

PERM ПЕРМЬ

☎ 342 / pop 1 million / ☽ Moscow + 2hr

Rising from Russia's rust belt is heavily industrialised, economically booming Perm, a confident, energetic and highly cultured city. Its museums hark back to the time of Great Perm, a mysterious Finno-Ugric medieval country. These days Perm is the home of one of Russia's best ballet schools, and opportunities for adventure and cultural tourism in the area make it worth jumping from your Trans-Siberian train and hanging around for a few days.

Orientation & Information

Perm sprawls along the south bank of the Kama River. The city centre is at the intersection of ul Lenina and Komsomolsky pr, and Perm-II station is about 2.5km southwest of here.

Main post office (ul Lenina 29; internet per hr R42; ☽ 8am-10pm Mon-Fri, 9am-6pm Sat & Sun)

Perm-36 museum office (www.perm36.ru) This was scheduled to move from the old office at ul Popova 11 to new premises, most likely at ul Gagarina 10 in the industrial Motovilikha district. Check the website. See p174 for info on the Gulag museum.

Sights

Housed in the grand Cathedral of Christ Transfiguration on the banks of the Kama, the **Perm State Art Gallery** (☎ 212 9524; www.sculpture.permonline.ru; Komsomolsky pr 4; admission R110; ☽ 10am-6pm Tue-Sat, 11am-6pm Sun) is renowned for its collection of Permian wooden sculpture. These brightly coloured figures are a product of an uneasy compromise between Christian missionaries and the native Finno-Ugric population. The latter, while agreeing to be converted to Christianity, closely identified the Christian saints these sculptures depict

with their ancient gods and treated them as such – including covering their lips with the blood of sacrificed animals.

The gallery is due to change location within the next decade, with the local authorities hoping that the new premises will have the same effect on Perm as the construction of the Guggenheim museum had on Bilbao. A recent competition for a new building design ended with two little-known Russian and Swiss architects winning. The Russian, Boris Bernaskoni, proposed that the gallery be shaped as an arch with the Trans-Siberian Railway going through it. It was unclear at the time of writing if either project would be built.

At the time of research, the **Ethnography Museum** was in the process of moving from the church building it used to occupy to the imposing **Meshkov House** (ul Ordzhonikidze 11). The museum's **Archaeological Collection** (Sibirskaya ul 15), famous for its intricate metal castings of the 'Perm animal style' used in the shamanistic practices of ancient Finno-Ugric Permians, is to open in 2009. Entry is through the courtyard.

The **Sergei Diaghilev Museum** (☎ 120 610; Sibirskaya ul 33; admission by donation; ☽ 9am-6pm Mon-Fri, closed 31 May–1 Sep) is a small, lovingly curated school museum dedicated to the impresario (1872–1929) who turned Russian ballet into a world-famous brand.

A lovely **mosque** (Osinskaya ul 5), which has served local Tatar Muslims since 1902, graces Perm's skyline; the view is particularly fine if you're standing on the other bank of the Kama. Literature buffs might also peek into **Gribushin House** (ul Lenina 13), said to be the prototype for Zhivago's 'house with figures'. **Hotel Tsentralnaya** (Sibirskaya ul 5) is the place where Grand Prince Mikhail (who formally became the tsar of Russia for a few hours between the abdication of Nicholas II and his own) spent his last night before being shot by the Bolsheviks.

Tours

Krasnov (☎ 238 3520; www.uraltourism.ru; ul Borchaninova 4; ☽ 10am-6.30pm Mon-Fri) offers a wide range of expensive excursions and adventure tours around the region, including a two-day *dacha* experience for €326 per person. Rafting and horse-riding tours advertised on the Russian-language version of the site are much cheaper and should be available for walk-in foreign

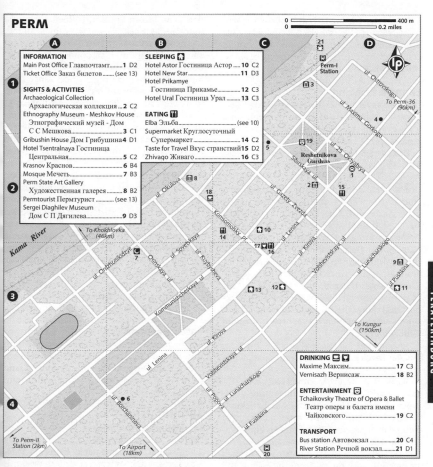

PERM

0 — 400 m
0 — 0.2 miles

INFORMATION	
Main Post Office Главпочтамт	**1** D2
Ticket Office Заказ билетов	(see 13)

SIGHTS & ACTIVITIES	
Archaeological Collection Археологическая коллекция	**2** C2
Ethnography Museum - Meshkov House Этнографический музей - Дом С С Мешкова	**3** C1
Gribushin House Дом Грибушина	**4** D1
Hotel Tsentralnaya Гостиница Центральная	**5** C2
Krasnov Краснов	**6** B4
Mosque Мечеть	**7** B3
Perm State Art Gallery Художественная галерея	**8** B2
Permtourist Пермтурист	(see 13)
Sergei Diaghilev Museum Дом С П Дягилева	**9** D3

SLEEPING	
Hotel Astor Гостиница Астор	**10** C2
Hotel New Star	**11** D3
Hotel Prikamye Гостиница Прикамье	**12** C3
Hotel Ural Гостиница Урал	**13** C3

EATING	
Elba Эльба	(see 10)
Supermarket Круглосуточный Супермаркет	**14** C2
Taste for Travel Вкус странствий	**15** D2
Zhivago Живаго	**16** C3

DRINKING	
Maxime Максим	**17** C3
Vernisazh Вернисаж	**18** B2

ENTERTAINMENT	
Tchaikovsky Theatre of Opera & Ballet Театр оперы и балета имени Чайковского	**19** C2

TRANSPORT	
Bus station Автовокзал	**20** C4
River Station Речной вокзал	**21** D1

Perm-I Station

To Perm-36 (90km)

Reshetnikova Gardens

To Khokhlovka (46km)

Kama River

To Kungur (150km)

To Perm-II Station (2km)

To Airport (18km)

tourists. Call in advance to find out about scheduled trips.

Permtourist (☎ 218 6999; www.permtourist.ru, in Russian; ul Lenina 58; ☎ 10am-6pm) arranges local excursions as well as cruises along the Kama River and further to the Volga.

Events

The annual 'ethno-futuristic' **Kamwa Festival** (www.kamwa.ru) is held in late July or early August in Perm and Khokhlovka. It brings together ancient ethno-Ugric traditions and modern art, music and fashion.

Sleeping

Hotel Ural (☎ 906 258, 906 220; ural-hotel@permtourist .ru; ul Lenina 58; s/d unrefurbished from R950/1400, refurbished R1900/2000) People who stayed here prior to the renovations will be astonished by the new high-tech lobby design, but the hotel's unrefurbished rooms are still stuck in the Soviet era.

Hotel Prikamye (☎ 219 8353; www.prikamie-hotel .ru; Komsomolsky pr 27; s/d without breakfast R1950/2600) What a revolution a tasteful colour scheme can cause in an old Soviet hospitality monster! Nicely spruced-up rooms make Prikamye a very decent option.

Hotel New Star (☎ 220 6801; www.newstar-hotel.com, in Russian; ul Gazety Zvezda 38b; s/d R2500/3400) Located in a new glassy tower with a high-tech interior that also houses a casino, this hotel has modern well-equipped rooms. The R1300 'economy-class' singles are most attractive for solo travellers, but they can be noisy.

MOSCOW TO YEKATERINBURG

Hotel Astor (☎ 212 2212; www.astorhotel.ru; Kommunisticheskaya ul 40; from s/d 2950/3600) Spotless white dominates this centrally located new hotel's colour scheme. Its reputation among business travellers is so far equally spotless.

Eating & Drinking

Taste for Travel (Sibirskaya ul 8; mains R70; ✆ 10am-10pm) This cheerful cafeteria takes you on a journey from the dumplings of Siberia to the lands of pizza and sushi.

Elba (☎ 235 1236; Kommunisticheskaya ul 40; mains R300) The cosy restaurant-bar inside Hotel Astor has an extensive menu of inventive dishes such as fig stuffed with goat cheese, spicy shrimp and tomato soup with crispy aubergines, and 'Siberian oysters' – jumbo-sized fish dumplings.

Zhivago (☎ 235 1716; ul Lenina 37; mains R400-2600; ✆ noon-11pm) The choice of name for this posh restaurant has angered Perm's literati, especially since it's a play on words – Zhivago sounds like *zhevat* – to chew. But Mr Pasternak's metal head by the entrance looks bemused rather than annoyed at people chewing the experimental dishes, such as rabbit with cuttlefish ink.

Supermarket (cnr Komsomolsky pr & ul Sovetskaya; ✆ 24hr) Stock up for your train ride at this central shop.

Maxime (☎ 212 2617; Komsomolsky pr 24; mains R170; cocktails from R90; ✆ 10am-6am) If they make all the types of coffee, tea, smoothies and cocktails listed on this convivial bar's menu, the rest of Perm will face a severe shortage of liquid.

Vernisazh (☎ 210 8037; Komsomolsky pr 10; coffee R70; ✆ 11am-10pm) Reproductions of French Impressionists hanging from the ceiling and green jalousies covering the walls rather than windows make this cafe look like a brasserie taken over by a modern artist.

Entertainment

The beautiful baroque **Tchaikovsky Theatre of Opera & Ballet** (☎ 212 3087; www.opera.permonline .ru; Kommunisticheskaya ul 25) that dominates Reshetnikova Garden is home to one of Russia's top schools of ballet.

Getting There & Away

The **ticket office** (☎ 290 6030; ✆ 9am-8pm) in the lobby of Hotel Ural is useful for airline and train tickets.

Several airlines fly to Moscow daily, including Sky Express (R3300, two hours). Lufthansa

flies to and from Frankfurt (R600, six hours) four times a week.

The **river station** (☎ 210 3609) is at the eastern end of ul Ordzhonikidze, opposite Perm-I station. Boats depart here for cruises down the Kama River to the Volga (prices range from R3000 for two-day cruises to local destinations, to R17,000 for 13-day cruises to Astrakhan).

At the **bus station** (ul Revolyutsii 68), there are numerous buses going to or via Kungur (every 30 minutes, 6am to 7pm), three buses a day to Khokhlovka (1½ hours) and two daily buses to Ufa (11½ hours).

Perm-II, the city's major train station, is on the Trans-Siberian route. Many trains travel the route from Moscow, including the *firmeny* train (a nicer, long-distance train) called the *Kama* (R3040, 20 hours). Heading east, the next major stop on the Trans-Siberian route is Yekaterinburg (R375 *platskart*, R1300 *kupe*, six hours). There are one or two trains a day for Kazan (R1600, 15 hours). Note that some trains to Kazan depart from the *gorny trakt* (mountain track) on the north side of Perm-II, as opposed to the *glavny trakt* (main track).

Getting Around

Marshrutka 1t links the bus station, the train station and the airport. Bus 42 goes between the bus station and the airport. Bus 68 and tram 4 go between the train station and Hotel Ural.

AROUND PERM

Khokhlovka Хохловка
☎ 342 / ✆ Moscow + 2hr

The **Architecture-Ethnography Museum** (☎ 212 1789; admission R35; ✆ 9am-6pm late-May–mid-Oct) is set in the rolling countryside near the village of Khokhlovka, about 45km north of Perm. Its impressive collection of wooden buildings includes two churches dating from the turn of the 18th century. Most of the structures are from the 19th or early 20th centuries, including an old firehouse, a salt-production facility and a Khanty *izba* (traditional wooden cottage). A few buses a day serve Khokhlovka from Perm (R100, one hour). At the time of research it was closed for independent tourists 'due to reconstruction'. Tours can be booked through Permtourist (p173).

Perm-36 Пермь-36

Once an ominous island in the Gulag Archipelago, **Perm-36** (☎ 8-919 492 5756; www

.perm36.ru; admission R50, ☺ by appointment) is now a fascinating museum and moving memorial to the victims of political repression.

From 1946 onwards, Perm-36 was a labour camp for dissidents. Countless artists, scientists and intellectuals spent years in the cold, damp cells, many in solitary confinement. They worked at mundane tasks such as assembling zippers, and survived on measly portions of bread and gruel.

The memorial is located in the village of Kuchino, about 25km from the town of Chusovoy, which itself is 100km from Perm. To reach it, take a bus (R210, two hours) bound for Chusovoy or Lysva, get off at Tyomnaya station, walk back to find the Kuchino turn, then walk another 2.5km to the village. The museum's Perm office (p172) can arrange a taxi for about R3000 and an interpreter for R1500 per trip. A Russian-language guided tour costs R600.

Kungur Кунгур

☎ 34271 / pop 68,000 / ☺ Moscow + 2hr

Between the architectural blandness of Perm and Yekaterinburg, Kungur is like cream between biscuits. Though the town is extremely dilapidated and has a rough working-class populace, its skyline is graced by a multitude of church cupolas, including the 18th century **Tikhvinskaya Church** in the centre and the **Transfiguration Church** on the other bank of the Sylva River, while the frozen magic of its ice cave draws a steady stream of visitors.

Founded in 1663 on the banks of the meandering Sylva River, Kungur was a copper-smelting centre during the 17th and 18th centuries. Get the full story at the **Regional Local Studies Museum** (ul Gogolya 36; admission R20; ☺ 11am-5pm Tue-Sun).

The **Kungur Ice Cave** (Ledyanaya peshchera; guided tour R300; ☺ 10am-5pm) is about 5km out of town. The extensive network of caves stretches for more than 5km, although only about 1.5km are open to explore. The grottos are adorned with unique ice formations, frozen waterfalls and underground lakes. The ancient Finno-Ugric inhabitants of the Perm region believed the cave to be the home of a fiery underground creature. You can only enter on a guided tour that take place every two hours. Tickets are available from the box office outside, and may not be available for the next tour as the number of participants is limited to 20. Take enough warm clothes to withstand negative temperatures in the first two grottos.

MOSCOW TO
YEKATERINBURG

Yekaterinburg to Krasnoyarsk

Crossing mile after mile of semi-taiga and flat level farmlands interspersed with ostensibly grim Soviet-designed cities, this stretch of the route isn't the most visually stimulating. The best way then to cover the distances between cities is in a series of overnight hops on conveniently timetabled night trains.

Once you get there however, the cities themselves have plenty to offer. Yekaterinburg, the site of events of vital importance in Russian history, is also a great base for exploring the wider Urals area. Next down the line, a day is usually enough to wander around Tyumen, where aspects of old and new Russia combine to create a pleasant, and increasingly affluent, town. The next logical stop is Tobolsk, with its picturesque old town and handsome kremlin, not to mention a thriving artistic community.

From Tobolsk another overnight train will take you to bustling Omsk, where a stroll through the city's tiny old town is almost enough to make you forget about the concrete chaos of its main streets. From Omsk another night in motion will take you to Novosibirsk, which boasts fine train museums as well as a huge amount of clubs and bars. However, much more interesting is Tomsk. Off the main Trans-Siberian route, but easily accessible on branch line trains, this atmospheric student town is famous for its wooden-lace architecture and scenic streets. A visit when snow is on the ground is both recommended and unforgettable.

HIGHLIGHTS

- Ponder Russia's often violent history at the Romanovs' execution site in **Yekaterinburg** (p179)

- Take a stroll through the student city of **Tomsk** (p199) with its picturesque wooden homes

- See firsthand the effect the oil boom has had on small Siberian towns such as **Tyumen** (p186)

- Explore the dishevelled old town of **Tobolsk** (p189), Siberia's former capital

- Discover the historic centre of **Omsk** (p192) and try to count the city's many Lenin statues

- Improve your knowledge of Trans-Siberian history at **Novosibirsk's railway museums** (p196 and p198)

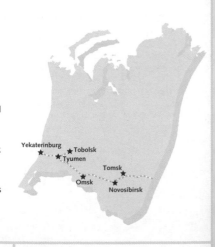

| ROUTE DISTANCE: 2287KM | DURATION: 34 HOURS |

THE ROUTE
Yekaterinburg to Omsk

Major trains halt at **Yekaterinburg** (1814km; p179) for 15 to 30 minutes. The cultural and economic capital of the Urals, the city is famous as the birthplace of Boris Yeltsin and as the place where Tsar Nicholas II and his family met their deaths at the hands of the Bolsheviks. Wander across the street for a look at the old train station, which now houses a railway museum.

Siberia officially begins at 2102km. Trains stop for 15 minutes in **Tyumen** (2138km; p186), the region's oldest Russian settlement, now a dynamic oil-rich city. There's not much to see directly outside the train station, so you'd be better off stocking up on supplies if necessary from the station shop.

From Tyumen our route detours 221km northeast off the official Trans-Siberian line to the old Siberian capital of **Tobolsk** (p189). Near the 212km marker, east-facing windows have pleasant if distant views of Tobolsk's kremlin. The town has a fine and picturesque market right on the platform, with stalls selling mainly varieties of dried and smoked fish, as well as beer and ubiquitous cheap Chinese noodles.

Back on the main Trans-Siberian route east, the next major stop is for 15 minutes at tiny **Ishim** (2428km), which is famous for its 19th-century Nikolskaya trade fairs (revived since 1991). The birthplace of the Russian fairy-tale writer Pyotr Yershov (1815–69), whose most famous work, *The Humpbacked-Horse*, was banned for many years by the tsar's censors, the town retains a striking, whitewashed 1793 cathedral. The Trans-Siberian reached this town of 65,000 in 1913 as the railway was extended from Tyumen to Omsk. At 2497km, local time becomes Moscow time plus three hours. Swampy land provides opportunities for birdwatchers, in warmer seasons at least.

Depending on what train you are on, there's a five- to 15-minute halt at agricultural-processing town **Nazyvaevskaya** (2562km). The name of the town is derived from the Russian for 'to name' and while tough to directly translate, sounds most unimaginative to Russian ears. If you're riding straight from Moscow you'll now be into day three of your journey. It's at this point that many travellers on week-long or more journeys report that disorientation sets in. If you feel like something other

than this guidebook to read, there is a steady supply of people offering papers and magazines (in Russian) on Trans-Siberian trains. Most of the salespeople are deaf, possibly due to employers in Russia getting tax breaks for taking on handicapped workers.

After the six-span Irtysh River bridge, trains pause for 25 minutes in **Omsk** (2716km; p192) where Fyodor Dostoevsky was exiled in 1849. If you are quick, you should have time to nip out and have a gaze at the fine Lenin statue right outside the station. If you are really fast, you could pop into the Pivoman shop to the left of Grandad Lenin to stock up on microbrewery beer and dried fish.

Omsk to Krasnoyarsk

If you notice an increase in passing trains after Omsk, blame it on coal from the Kuzbas Basin east of Novosibirsk going to the smelting works of the Urals. In freight terms this is the world's busiest section of railway.

Barabinsk (3035km), a 17-minute stop, was once a place of exile for Polish Jews. The surrounding Barabinsk Steppe is a boggy expanse of grassland and lakes that was formerly the homeland of the Kirghiz people. Many train engines and carriages that service the Trans-Siberian put in here for repairs at some point or other. The shop on the platform was full of drunken local teens dancing to disco music around plastic tables when we visited – check it out, they might still be there.

At around 3330km get ready for the seven-span, 870m-long bridge across the Ob, one of the world's longest rivers. During the 20-minute stop at **Novosibirsk** (3343km; p196), inspect the grand station interior, a real temple of the Trans-Siberian. Also try to have a look at the two WWII memorial statues on platform 1 depicting a family waving off soldiers to the front. The Nazis never got this far, but lots of Siberians left for the war from this station.

At 3479km, time shifts to make it Moscow time plus four hours. The 25-minute halt at **Taiga** (3565km) provides plenty of time to wish you were heading 79km north up the branch line to **Tomsk** (p199). This is not a Womble (as Brits of a certain age may expect, from the kids' TV program) but a charming old Siberian city that lost much of its regional importance when it was bypassed by the Trans-Siberian Railway. Myth says that the city fathers, fearing the dirt and pollution it

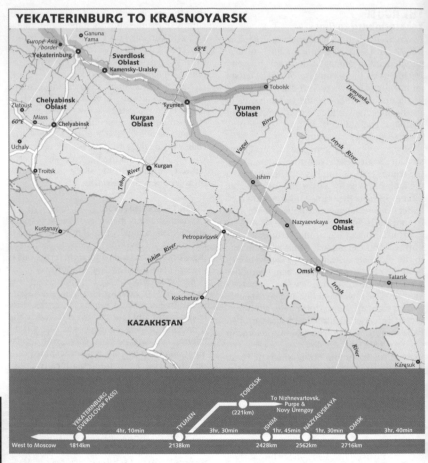

YEKATERINBURG TO KRASNOYARSK

YEKATERINBURG TO
KRASNOYARSK

would bring, declined the offer to have the town connected to the railway. However, the truth is rather more prosaic – swampland made the construction of a bridge over the River Ob problematic, and a decision was taken not to lay lines to the city.

Spot another engine-repair yard to the south as you approach the station at **Mariinsk** (3713km), a 20-minute stop. Originally named Kiysk, the town grew wealthy as the focus of a Siberian gold rush. It was renamed in 1857 to honour Tsar Alexander II's wife Maria. Many of the furniture and metal factories that operated here in Soviet times are closed now, leaving only a bakery, a meat-processing plant, and a medicinal spirit factory as the main employment options.

At 3820km the line enters Krasnoyarsky Kray, a vast territory of enormous mineral and forest wealth. It covers 2.5 million sq km, stretching all the way to the Arctic coast.

The train then makes brief stop at **Bogotol** (3846km), another example of a town being formed around the Trans-Siberian. A train station was opened here in 1893, but it was another 18 years before the subsequent settlement was awarded town status. The train then moves on to **Achinsk-1** (3914km). The small town has its origins in the founding of a fortress in the area in 1683 and, in the 19th century, soap made here was famous all over Russia. The train stops here for a few minutes before twisting through woodlands and over hills with cinematic landscapes to enjoy.

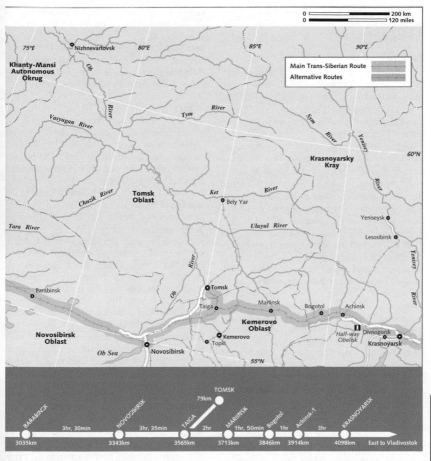

A small, easily missed white obelisk south of the train line at 3932km marks the halfway point between Moscow and Běijīng (via Ulaanbaatar).

Major services stop for 20 minutes at **Krasnoyarsk** (4098km; p206). That's just long enough to nip out and see a fine communist-era mural in red mosaics decorating a wall on the station square outside.

YEKATERINBURG
ЕКАТЕРИНБУРГ
☎ 343 / pop 1.29 million / ☽ Moscow +2hr

The capital of the 'Urals mining civilization' that flourished here in the 18th and 19th centuries (and produced myths of lizard-queens and giant ground cats guarding caves full of

lustrous treasure), is once again the locomotive of economic development in the region.

With much of its heritage bulldozed off during the Soviet times, particularly when some Boris Yeltsin was the local party boss, Yekaterinburg is a kind of a city where a few skyscrapers wouldn't do any harm. In fact, a mini-Manhattan is exactly what the local authorities are planning to erect on the banks of the city pond, in the very centre.

In the meantime, one needs to be a fan of constructivism to appreciate its architectural appeal. For others, the main attraction is the death of the Romanov family, and the original burial sites, where a cult of these new saints (officially!) is flourishing. With a couple of agencies experienced in catering to foreign travellers, Yekaterinburg is a good base for organising excursions and adventure trips around the Urals.

History

Yekaterinburg was founded as a factory-fort in 1723 as part of Peter the Great's push to exploit the Ural region's mineral riches. The city was named after two Yekaterinas: Peter's wife (later Empress Catherine I), and the Russian patron saint of mining.

Yekaterinburg is most famous as the place where the Bolsheviks murdered Tsar Nicholas II and his family in July 1918. Six years later, the town was renamed Sverdlovsk, after Yakov Sverdlov, a leading Bolshevik who was Vladimir Lenin's right-hand man until his death during the flu epidemic of 1919. The region still bears Sverdlov's name.

WWII turned Sverdlovsk into a major industrial centre, as hundreds of factories were transferred here from vulnerable areas west of the Urals. The city was closed to foreigners until 1990 because of its many defence plants.

During the late 1970s a civil engineering graduate of the local university, Boris Yeltsin, began to make his political mark, rising to become regional Communist Party boss before being promoted to Moscow in 1985.

In 1991 Yekaterinburg took back its original name. After suffering economic depression and Mafia lawlessness in the early 1990s, business has been on the upswing for the past decade.

Orientation & Information

The city centre lies between the main boulevards, pr Lenina and ul Malysheva, and runs from pl 1905 goda in the west to ul Lunacharskogo in the east. The train station is 2km north of the centre on ul Sverdlova, which becomes ul Karla Libknekhta closer to the centre.

Coffee.IN (☎ 377 6873; ul 8 Marta 8; per hr R70; ☣ 24hr) Internet cafe located on the 3rd floor of the Mytny Dvor mall.
Dom Knigi (☎ 358 1898; ul Antona Valeka 12; ☣ 10am-8pm) Best for foreign-language and local-interest books.
Main post office (pr Lenina 39; ☣ 24hr) Also offers internet and international telephone connections.

Sights

The obvious place to start your exploration of Yekaterinburg is Istorichesky skver (Historical Sq) where pr Lenina crosses a small dam forming the Gorodskoy prud (City Pond) on its north side. This area, better known as the **plotinka** (little dam), was where Yekaterinburg began back in 1723. The new **monument to the founders of the city** stands nearby, with Messrs Tatishchev and de Gennin somewhat resembling Beavis and Butthead in wigs.

East of this area, the **Yakov Sverdlov statue** is another funky-looking monument, this time from the Soviet period. Continuing north you'll reach the ostentatious **Rastorguev-Kharitonov mansion** and the restored **Ascension Church** (ul Klary Tsetkin 11).

West of here, a cluster of old wooden houses on ul Proletarskaya is known as the **Literary Quarter**. Several of the houses are museums dedicated to local writers. From there you can go back to the city pond and watch the construction activity on the other side, which the authorities are planning to transform into a mini-Manhattan.

South of metro Ploshchad 1905 goda, the **St Maximilian bell-tower** (under construction at the time of writing) is set to become one of the city's landmarks. Further down the Iset River, near metro Geologicheskaya stands the huge shell of the **TV tower** whose construction was abandoned with the fall of communism. The city's new **synagogue** (ul Kuybysheva 38A) is further along ul Kuybysheva. Inside it has a cheap **cafeteria** (☣ noon-8pm Sun-Fri) and an **internet cafe** (☣ noon-5pm Sun-Fri).

YEKATERINBURG TO KRASNOYARSK

YEKATERINBURG TO KRASNOYARSK ROUTE PLANNER

The following is a suggested itinerary for covering the main Trans-Sib stops in this chapter:

Day 1: Leave Yekaterinburg early morning; arrive in Tyumen around 9am
Day 2: Leave Tyumen for Tobolsk; arrive in Tobolsk around noon; night train to Omsk (14 hours)
Day 3 Explore Omsk; night train to Tomsk (14 to 19 hours)
Day 4: Explore Tomsk
Day 5: Take morning train to Novosibirsk; arrive early afternoon
Day 6: Take evening train from Novosibirsk to Krasnoyarsk (12 to 14 hours)

ROMANOV DEATH SITE

On the night of 16 July 1918, Tsar Nicholas II, his wife and children were murdered in the basement of a local engineer's house, known as Dom Ipatyeva (named after its owner, Nikolay Ipatyev). During the Soviet period, the building housed a local museum of atheism, but it was demolished in 1977 by then-governor Boris Yeltsin, who feared it would attract monarchist sympathisers.

Today, the site is marked by an iron cross dating from 1991, and a second marble cross from 1998 when the Romanovs' remains were sent to St Petersburg for burial in the family vault.

The massive Byzantine-style **Church of the Blood** (☎ 371 6168; ul Tolmachyova 34) dominates this site. While many believe the funds used to build this new church might have been better spent, it honours the Romanov family, now elevated to the status of saints. Rumour has it that this controversial church contains the most expensively commissioned icon in Russia.

Nearby, the pretty wooden **Chapel of the Revered Martyr Grand Princess Yelizaveta Fyodorovna** (⊙ 9am-5.30pm) honours the royal family's great-aunt and faithful friend. After her relatives' murders, this nun met an even worse end, when she was thrown down a mineshaft, poisoned with gas and buried.

MUSEUMS

Istorichesky skver is also the location of the city's major museums. Peek into the old **water tower**, one of the city's oldest structures, then head over to the old mining-equipment factory and mint buildings. These contain the **Museum of Architecture & Technology** (☎ 371 4045; ul Gorkogo 4A; admission R20; ⊙ 11am-6pm Mon & Wed-Sat), which displays mining machinery used from the 18th and 19th centuries up through WWII.

On the opposite side of the river, the star exhibit of the **Museum of Fine Arts** (☎ 371 0626; ul Voevodina 5; admission R150; ⊙ 11am-6pm Wed-Sun) is the elaborate Kasli Iron Pavilion that won prizes in the 1900 Paris Expo.

For a stunning introduction to the Urals semiprecious stones, visit Vladimir Pelepenko's private collection, also known as the **Urals Mineralogical Museum** (☎ 350 6019; ul Krasnoarmeyskaya 1A; admission R50; ⊙ 10am-7pm Mon-Fri, 10am-5pm Sat & Sun), in Bolshoy Ural Hotel. This impressive collection contains thousands of examples of minerals, stones and crystals from the region, many crafted into mosaics, jewellery and other artistic pieces.

More serious geologists will appreciate the **Ural Geology Museum** (☎ 251 4938; ul Kuybysheva 39; admission R100; ⊙ 11am-5pm Mon-Fri), which has over 500 carefully catalogued Ural region minerals and a collection of meteorites. It is inside the Urals Mining university – enter from ul Khokhryakova inside Urals State Mining University.

The **Military History Museum** (☎ 350 1742; ul Pervomayskaya 27; admission R50; ⊙ 9am-4pm Tue-Sat) is a must for military buffs.

Other unique museums:

Metenkov House Museum of Photography (☎ 371 0637; ul Karla Libknekhta 36; admission R80; ⊙ 10am-6pm daily) Features evocative photos of old Yekaterinburg.

Nevyansk Icon Museum (☎ 265 9840; ul Tolmachyova 21; admission free, ⊙ noon-8pm Wed-Sun) Icons from the 17th to the 20th century, from the local Nevyansk school (p186). The museum was created by local businessman/politician Yevgeny Royzman, famous for his controversial anti-drugs campaigns.

Railway Museum (☎ 358 4222; ul Chelyuskintsev; ⊙ noon-6pm Tue-Sat) Housed in the old train station, dating from 1881. Exhibits highlight the history of the railroad in the Urals, including a re-creation of the office of the Soviet-era railway director.

Tours

Ekaterinburg Guide Centre (☎ 359 3708; www .ekaterinburgguide.com; Eremina 10) An enthusiastic group that organises English-language tours of the city, trips into the countryside, including all destinations described in the Around Yekaterinburg section (see p185), as well as hiking and rafting expeditions. Day trips cost anything between R1900 and R5000, depending on how many persons you are. They can also help with hotel booking and long-term flat rental.

Ural Expeditions & Tours (☎ 356 5282; http:// welcome-ural.ru; ul Posadskaya 23; ⊙ 9am-7pm Mon-Fri) This group of geologists from the Sverdlovsk Mining Institute has found a unique way to market their skills and knowledge – leading trekking, rafting and horse-riding trips to all parts of the Urals, including Taganay and Zyuratkul National Parks. It has English-speaking guides. To reach the office get trolleybus 3 or 7 to the Gurzufskaya stop.

Sleeping

Resting rooms (komnaty otdykha; Sverdlovsk train station; dm 12/24hr from R440/800; ⊙ 6pm-6am) Located between floors 4 and 5 in the left wing of the

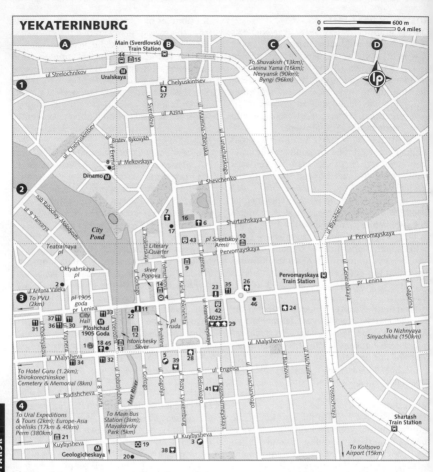

YEKATERINBURG

station, the restrooms are really only worth it if you are catching a train in the wee hours.

Bolshoy Ural Hotel (☎ 350 6896; ul Krasnoarmeyskaya 1; s/d without bathroom R885/1300, with bathroom R2240/2830) This place lives up to its name: if nothing else, it is indeed *bolshoy* (large), occupying an entire city block. The somewhat seedy atmosphere is buffered by the prime location.

Hotel Guru (☎ 228 5070; www.guruhotel.ru, in Russian; ul Repina 22; s/d R2100/2400) This is an intriguing option located inside the new building of a dance school of the same name, 10 minutes by trolleybus 3 and 7 from ul Malysheva to the Institut svyazi stop. But check if the annoying disco downstairs will be closed.

Hotel Sverdlovsk (☎ 214 3000; www.sv-hotel.ru; ul Chelyuskintsev 106; s/d from R2100/2900) The Soviet oldie located by the train station has undergone a reconstruction, but customers keep complaining about low standards.

Hotel Tsentralny (☎ 214 3000; www.hotelcentr.ru; ul Malysheva 74; s/d from R3000/4000) A historical hotel located in a grand art nouveau building has standard business-class rooms with good wi-fi signal.

Hotel Iset (☎ 350 0110; www.hoteliset.ru; pr Lenina 69/1; s/d R3200/3600) If it looks funky from the street, it is because it's shaped like a hammer and sickle when seen from the sky. Inside, curving corridors lead to nicely furnished rooms. The noise factor is high, due to its location on pr Lenina.

Park Inn (☎ 216 6000; www.ekaterinburg.parkinn
.com.ru; ul Mamina-Sibiryaka 98; s/d R5800/6600; 🖵) This
large and new hotel offers rooms with cheery
colour schemes and all the amenities you
would expect for the price.

Eating
RESTAURANTS
ourpick Mamma's Biscuit House (☎ 222 1905; pr
Lenina 26; pizza from R165; 🕑 24hr) Mamma works
nonstop to please mostly young visitors with
excellent pizzas, desserts, teas and coffees.

Light Cafe (☎ 377 6895; mains R200; 🕑 9am-mid-
night) This airy cafe serving standard European
fare and nice desserts is strategically located
and creates a good vibe.

Paul Bakery (☎ 359 8366; ul Malysheva 36; meals
R250-350) No relation to the French namesake,
this cafe, entered from ul Vaynera, is great
for a quick snack and coffee, ordered from
the counter. It is located in a compound with
several other restaurants of the Malachite empire, including the once super-popular Grand

Buffet serving Russian and European food
(mains R350).

Dacha (☎ 379 3569; pr Lenina 20a; business lunch R250,
mains R500-800) Each room in this restaurant is
decorated as a room in a Russian country
house, from the casual garden to the more
formal dining room. It's a great place to enjoy
unbeatable Russian cuisine and hospitality.

Serbian Courtyard (☎ 350 3457; pr Lenina 53; mains
R400; 🕑 noon-midnight) Patrons talk international
politics here, but whichever side in any of the
ex-Yugoslavs conflicts you might be leaning
to, they'll treat you to the best Balkan fare this
side of the Urals. A kiosk outside sells *pleck-
avicas* (burgers Balkan-style) and *chevapy*
(kebabs) to hungry students from the nearby
university for R60.

QUICK EATS & SELF-CATERING
Uspensky Food Court (☎ 371 6744; ul Vainera 10; meals
R30-100; 🕑 10am-8pm) On the top floor of the
Uspensky shopping centre, this food court
offers burgers, pizza, sandwiches, sushi and

more. Floor-to-ceiling windows provide a sweeping view of the city centre and a new perspective on the activity below.

Vilka-Lozhka (ul Vaynera 8; mains R80) A brightly coloured cheap cafeteria at the start of the main pedestrian drag.

Cafe Skver (371 2208; ul Vaynera 7b; mains R120) Barbie and Ken dance in a toy castle while you eat in this cafeteria designed as a playroom.

Uralskiye Pelmeni (☎ 350 7150; pr Lenina 69/1; lunch R200; ☽ 11am-midnight) This cafeteria-style place inside Hotel Iset building treats lunching office workers with the kind of bland food most Russians eat at home.

Drinking

Yekaterinburg has a bevy of places posing as English, Scottish or Irish pubs, although in fact they are rather expensive restaurants/ night clubs with a strict dress code. The most famous of them is the Scottish **Gordon's** (☎ 355 4535; ul Krasnoarmeyskaya ul 1; mains R400-600; ☽ noon-2am), part-owned by an Irishman. A new popular place is **Ben Hall** (☎ 251 6368; ul Narodnoy Voli 65; mains R400; ☽ noon-2am) where local rock bands play on weekends; its owner being a well-known musician himself.

Tired of this stylisation orgy? Head to the ubiquitous microbrewery **Tinkoff** (☎ 378 4008; Krasnoarmeyskaya 64; ½L beer R150; ☽ noon-2am), featuring seven home-grown brews, plus a menu of sausages, sandwiches and other tasty snacks. A more bohemian type of place, **Cafe Shepot** (☽ 371 1497; ul Rozy Lyuksemburg 16; ☽ 11am-midnight Sun-Thu, 24hr Fri & Sat) has live music most nights.

Entertainment

Philharmonic (☎ 371 4682; www.filarmonia.e-burg.ru, in Russian; ul Karla Libknekhta 38) Yekaterinburg's top venue for the classical performing arts often hosts visiting directors and soloists, as well as the regular performances of the acclaimed Urals academic orchestra.

Opera & Ballet Theatre (☎ 350 8057; www.ural opera.ru; pr Lenina 45A; tickets from R100) The level of professionalism here is not quite on par with the Philharmonic, but the ornate baroque theatre is still a lovely place to see the Russian classics.

Getting There & Away
AIR
The main airport is **Koltsovo** (☎ 224 2367), 15km southeast of the city centre. There are three

flights daily to/from Moscow (R6000, 2½ hours). Flights also leave almost daily for Irkutsk (R7500, four hours), Novosibirsk (R8860, two hours), Samara (R5800, two hours) and St Petersburg (R5700, 2½ hours). Most ex-USSR national airways have regular flights to Yekaterinburg.

Several airlines operate direct flights to Europe two or three times a week: **Lufthansa** (☎ 264 7771) flies to Frankfurt; **Malev** (☎ 264 4246) to Budapest, **Czech Airlines** (☎ 264 6213) to Prague, **Austrian Airlines** (☎ 376 6376) to Vienna and **Turkish Airlines** (☎ 264 2040) to Istanbul.

Transaero Tours Centre (☎ 365 9165; pr Lenina 50), inside the City Centre shopping mall, handles bookings for all airlines.

BUS
For Chelyabinsk (see the boxed text, p159), buses are more convenient than trains. The main **bus station** (☎ 229 9518, 229 4881; ul 8 Marta 145) is 3km south of the city centre, but most buses pass the northern bus station, conveniently located by the main train station. Here you can catch frequent buses to Chelyabinsk (R218, four hours). There is also a bus station at the Koltsovo airport serving destinations in the Sverdlovsk region and Chelyabinsk (3½ hours, R400).

TRAIN
Yekaterinburg – sometimes still 'Sverdlovsk' on timetables – is a major rail junction with connections to all stops on the Trans-Siberian route. If you are stuck at the station for a few hours, check out the excellent Railway Museum occupying the old station building (see p181) and waiting halls on the 2nd floor (admission R30) with murals depicting the history of Yekaterinburg, including US pilot Gary Powers falling from the sky after his spy plane was shot down by a Soviet missile in 1960.

Resembling an airport VIP lounge, the 'increased comfort' hall on the 1st floor (admission R100 per hour) has showers (R130) and a ticket office without queues.

Trains to/from Moscow go frequently, but the most comfortable one is the *Ural* (R4700, 26 hours, daily). All trains to Moscow stop at either Perm (*kupe/platskart* R1300/370, seven hours) or Kazan (R2760, 13 to 15 hours). Heading east, the next major stops are Omsk (R2300, 12 hours) and Novosibirsk (R1280, 21 hours). You can buy tickets at outlets

---

LAYING THE LAST TSAR TO REST

What happened to the Romanovs after their 1918 execution is a mixture of the macabre, the mysterious and the just plain messy. The bodies were dumped at Ganina Yama, an abandoned mine 16km from Yekaterinburg. When grenades failed to collapse the main shaft, it was decided to distribute the bodies among various smaller mines and pour acid on them. But the expert in charge of the acid fell off his horse and broke his leg; and the truck carrying the bodies became bogged in a swamp.

By now desperate, the disposal team opted to bury the corpses. They tried burning Alexey and Maria in preparation, but realised it would take days to burn all the bodies properly, so the others were just put in a pit and doused with acid. Even then, most of the acid soaked away into the ground – leaving the bones to be uncovered 73 years later in 1976, near Porosinkov Log, 3km from Ganina Yama. The discovery was kept secret until the remains were finally fully excavated in 1991. The bones of nine people were tentatively identified as Tsar Nicholas II, his wife Tsaritsa Alexandra, three of their four daughters, the royal doctor and three servants.

Missing were the remains of the royal couple's only son, Tsarevitch Alexey and one of their daughters, giving a new lease of life to theories that the youngest daughter, Anastasia, had somehow escaped. In 1992 bone samples were examined in the UK using DNA identification techniques. The scientists established with 'more than 98.5%' certainty that the bones were those of the royal family.

In 1994 an official Russian inquiry team managed to piece together the skulls found in the pit, badly damaged by rifle butts, hand grenades and acid. Using plaster models of the faces, DNA tests and dental records, they determined that the three daughters found were Olga, Tatyana – and Anastasia. The missing daughter was Maria, whose remains were unearthed in 2007, and formally identified along with those of her brother Alexey in 2008.

In mid-1998 the royal remains were given a proper funeral at St Petersburg's SS Peter and Paul Cathedral, to lie alongside their predecessors dating back to Peter the Great. The Orthodox Church later canonised the tsar and his family as martyrs.

---

throughout the city, including the convenient **Railway and Air Kassa** (☎ 371 0400; ul Malysheva 31D; ⏰ 7am-9pm).

Please note that some trains going from Yekaterinburg to Omsk cross through the northern tip of Kazakhstan, meaning you'll need a Kazak visa and a multiple-entry Russian visa if you choose to use them. To avoid potential problems make sure you buy a ticket for a train to Omsk via Tyumen.

Getting Around

Bus 1 links the train station and Koltsovo airport (45 minutes) from 5.30am to 11pm. *Marshrutka* 26 goes from the airport to metro Ploshchad ul 1905 goda, while *marshrutka* 39 goes to metro Geologicheskaya.

Many trolleybuses (pay on board) run along ul Sverdlova/ul Karla Libknekhta between the train station and pr Lenina. Trams 4, 13, 15 and 18 and bus 28 cover long stretches of pr Lenina, with bus 4 continuing to the main bus station.

A single metro line runs between the northeastern suburbs and the city centre, with stops at the train station (Uralskaya), Ploshchad 1905 goda and ul Kuybysheva (Geologicheskaya).

AROUND YEKATERINBURG
Ganina Yama Ганина Яма

After the Romanov family was shot in the cellar of Dom Ipatyeva, their bodies were discarded in the depths of the forests of Ganina Yama, 16km northeast of Yekaterinburg. In their honour, the Orthodox Church has built the exquisite **Monastery of the Holy Martyrs** (☎ 343-217 9146; www.g-ya.ru) at this pilgrimage site. An observation platform overlooks the mine shaft where the remains were deposited and burned. According to the Orthodox Church, this is the final resting place of the Romanov family (most of whose remains have now been reburied in St Petersburg) and is therefore sacred ground.

The nearest train station to Ganina Yama is Shuvakish, served by *elektrichka* from Yekaterinburg's central station. The monastery owns a bus that runs six times between the central station, Shuvakish station and

Ganina Yama. Ekaterinburg Guide Centre offers a three-hour tours for R1050 to R3000, depending on the number of people.

Nevyansk & Around Невьянск

This small town is in the heart of the former patrimony of the Demidovs, a family of industrialists that effectively controlled much of the Urals, blessed to develop the region by Peter I. At their decadence stage, they bought an Italian feudal title turning into counts San-Donato, to which effect there is a namesake train station in the bleak suburbs of Nizhny Tagil, birthplace of Russia's first steam locomotive (see p44). The Demidovs also aided the development of the Nevyansk icon-painting school, the most renowned in the Urals (see p181).

The main highlight here is the **Nevyansk Leaning Tower**, which sagged a bit at the time of construction and never moved again. It is an impressive structure accompanied by an equally impressive **Saviour-Transfiguration Cathedral**, which would have graced any large city. The site is controlled by the **Nevyansk History and Architecture Museum** (pl Revolyutsii 2; Nevyansk tower excursion per group R500; 9am-5pm Tue-Sun), where you buy tickets for excursion into the tower.

Seven kilometres from Nevyansk is the lovely Old Believers' village of **Byngi** where an entrepreneurial German and his Russian wife are converting an *izba* (traditional wooden cottage) into a guest house, sleeping about 15 people in the cottage, and two yurts erected in the courtyard. Rides in vintage Ural motorcycles are expected to become the main highlight. The project was not fully opera-

tional at the time of our visit. Inquire at the Ekaterinburg Guide Centre, which runs day tours to Nevyansk and the nearby old potters' village of **Tavolgi**.

There are 12 *elektrichka* (R60) to Nevyansk a day from Yekaterinburg's train station, most of them bound for Nizhny Tagil.

TYUMEN ТЮМЕНЬ

☎ 3452 / pop 507,000 / Moscow + 2hr

Founded in 1586, Tyumen was the first Russian fort in Siberia. These days the city exudes a sense of growing prosperity as the booming capital of a vast, oil-rich *oblast* (region) stretching all the way to the Arctic Circle. The city has a businesslike drive and youthful bustle, best experienced by strolling through the newly pedestrianised City Park when the weather is good. Pleasant and liveable, Tyumen has tree-lined streets and a number of attractively ramshackle pre-Soviet buildings amid all the new construction and trendy boutiques, but if you have limited time you'd be better off seeing Tobolsk instead.

Orientation & Information

The train station is located at the end of ul Pervomayskaya, 1.5km south of the main commercial artery, ul Respubliki, which runs some 5km from the fine Trinity Monastery to well beyond the bus station.

City maps are sold at **Magazin Knizhny** (Privokzalnaya ul 28A, Polyklinka Bldg; 8.30am-6pm Mon-Sat, 9am-4pm Sun), hidden away near the train station.

Main post office (ul Respubliki 56; 8am-8pm Mon-Sat, 9am-6pm Sun)

STRADDLING THE CONTINENTS

Until recently, if you wished to have one foot in Europe and one in Asia, you had to go 40km west of Yekaterinburg on the Moskovsky Trakt to the **Europe-Asia border**. Erected in 1837 at a 413m high point in the local Ural Mountains, the marker was a popular spot for wedding parties on their postnuptial video and photo jaunts.

In an attempt to make this geographic landmark more accessible to intercontinental travellers, the city has erected a new border marker, more conveniently located just 17km out of Yekaterinburg and looking a little like a mini Eiffel Tower. There are grand plans for monuments, museums, parks and gift shops, here, as well as European and Asian restaurants on their respective sides of the marker, but they are yet to be fulfilled.

Sceptics can be assured that this is more than a symbolic meeting of East and West. The site – on the watershed of the Iset and Chusovaya Rivers – was confirmed by scientists who examined geological records and studied the water flows. This clash of continents is the real deal.

Hire a taxi from Yekaterinburg or make arrangements for this excursion through Ekaterinburg Guide Centre (p181; R1050 to R2950 per person depending on the number of people).

Telephone office (ul Respubliki 51; internet per 30min R25; ☺ 24hr)

Tyumen.ru (www.tyumen.ru, in Russian) Has air and railway timetables plus information on local weather, cinema listings etc.

Web Khauz (ul Respubliki 61; internet per hr R40; ☺ 11am-8pm) Down the stairs to the left, follow the blue signs.

Sights

Behind a kremlinesque wall on the Tura riverside, the picturesque 1727 **Trinity Monastery** (Cvyato Troitsky; ul Kommunisticheskaya 10) is Tyumen's finest sight. But there are plenty more fine churches, notably the voluptuously curved baroque **Znamensky Cathedral** (ul Semakova 13) dating from 1786 and the similar **Saviour's Church** (ul Lenina).

The **Fine Arts Museum** (Muzey Izobrazitelnykh Iskusstv; ☎ 469 115; ul Ordzhonikidze 47; admission R50; ☺ 10am-5pm Tue-Sun) has an impressive and eclectic collection including an original by Vasily Kandinsky. Nearby is the large **Lenin Statue** (Tsentralnaya pl) and further southwest is the wooden **Marsharov House Museum** (☎ 461 310; ul Lenina 24; admission R40; ☺ 9.30am-12.30pm & 1.30-4.30pm Wed-Sun).

On the corner of ul Lenina and ul Pervomayskaya is the **City Park**, a great place for people watching if the weather is good. Try to find the outrageous billboard declaring (in Russian) without a hint of irony that 'Tyumen is the best city in the world'. On the way towards the train station, notice the **FD Class steam locomotive** (ul Pervomayskaya) hidden in the trees.

East of the centre, the **Geological Museum** (Muzey Geologi; Nefti i Gaza; ☎ 751 138; ul Respubliki 142; admission R40; ☺ 10am-6pm Tue-Sun) is one of the best of its type, and there's a modern **war memorial** nearby shaped like a gigantic metal candle.

Sleeping

Resting rooms (komnaty otdykha; Tyumen train station; dm/ tw R250/1000) These clean 8th-floor dorms offer panoramic views of the endless railway activity below. Exit the station via the main doorway and re-enter by a separate door on your left.

Hotel GUBD (☎ 247 434; ul Sovetskaya 124; s/tw without bathroom R400/520, with bathroom R750/950) Tyumen's best-value budget hotel has no frills yet clean rooms and is very central, if unaccustomed to foreigners. Often full, so book well ahead!

Hotel Vostok (☎ 205 350; fax 206 124; ul Respubliki 159; s/tw R850/1000) In a lively area east of the city centre, this vast Soviet monster has repainted but tired rooms with shabby private bathrooms. The cheapest options are priced at R700/800 and come without TVs. A few singles at R1350 are more comfortable and sensibly priced.

Hotel Neftyanik (☎ 461 687; fax 460 021; ul Chelyuskintsev 12; s/tw/d R1400/2000/2500) Boasting a newly built 6th floor, this concrete slab block has the best position for visiting the nicer old-town areas. Double rooms have sitting areas with comfy sofas.

Prezident Hotel (☎ /fax 494 747; ul Respubliki 33; s/d/ste R3200/4000/5500) Reached by a glass elevator through the atrium of the self-proclaimed 'World Trade Center', the good-value rooms are fully equipped but lacking in charm.

Hotel Tyumen (☎ 494 040; www.hoteltyumen.ru/en/; ul Ordzhonikidze 46; s/d R5900/7900; 🖳) Nicknamed 'Quality Hotel', it has typical international business standards, complete with a gift shop and great restaurants. The complimentary breakfast is worth writing home about.

Eating & Drinking

Stolovaya (ul Privokzalnaya 28A, Polyclinic Bldg; meals R75-150; ☺ 7.45am-3pm & 4-10pm) Fill up for less than the cost of a coffee elsewhere in this Soviet-era style cafeteria beside the station.

Pinta Taverna (☎ 250 220; ul Dzerzhinskogo 38; meals R250-400, beers R60-100; ☺ 11am-2am) Waitresses in peasant costumes and a stunted model cow star in this cosy farmyard-styled cellar restaurant found beneath the Vulkan slot-machines.

Teatralnoe Café (ul Respubliki 36/1; meals R350-550) This refined theatre-themed cafe features tasty cakes, warming soups (try the *solyanka* for R90) and a wide selection of teas and coffee. The bland pizzas are to be avoided, however.

our pick **Yermolaevo** (☎ 251 208; ul Kirova 37; meals R500-700; beer R90-140) This spacious new bar-restaurant is done up in a wooden, rustic style and serves filing traditional Russian meals. The Siberian mushroom soup (R60) is recommended. Also serves *kvas* (fermented rye-bread water) to write home about and a large selection of beers, including some home-brewed options.

Serebryany Vek (☎ 242 212; ul Turgenova 19; meals R500-700) Opposite the Archangel Mikhail Church, this squeaky clean cellar lounge cafe-restaurant offers a wide range of meals, including good fish dishes and draught beers (R90 to R150).

If you're out strolling in the City Park, pop into the great value **Snack Bar** (meals R250-400; beer

TYUMEN

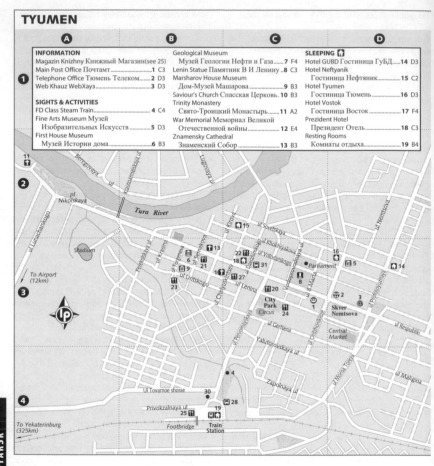

INFORMATION		Geological Museum		SLEEPING
Magazin Knizhny Книжный Магазин	(see 25)	Музей Геологии Нефти и Газа 7 F4		Hotel GUBD Гостиница ГуБД 14 D3
Main Post Office Почтамт 1 C3		Lenin Statue Памятник В И Ленину .. 8 C3		Hotel Neftyanik
Telephone Office Тюмень Телеком 2 D3		Marsharov House Museum		Гостиница Нефтяник 15 C2
Web Khauz WebХауз 3 D3		Дом-Музей Машарова 9 B3		Hotel Tyumen
		Saviour's Church Спасская Церковь .. 10 B3		Гостиница Тюмень 16 D3
SIGHTS & ACTIVITIES		Trinity Monastery		Hotel Vostok
FD Class Steam Train 4 C4		Свято-Троицкий Монастырь 11 A2		Гостиница Восток 17 F4
Fine Arts Museum Музей		War Memorial Мемориал Великой		President Hotel
Изобразительных Искусств 5 D3		Отечественной войны 12 E4		Президент Отель 18 C3
First House Museum		Znamensky Cathedral		Resting Rooms
Музей Истории дома 6 B3		Знаменский Собор 13 B3		Комнаты отдыха 19 B4

R70-100) opposite the circus for shashlyk or *pelmeni* (dumplings). Alternatively try the nearby **Kafe Sad** (ul Lenina 61; meals R 200-350, beer R60-100, snacks R50-100). Featuring a garden area when the weather is good, this cheap unpretentious bar-cafe serves the usual shashlyk, beer and vodka, as well as dried squid/fish snacks.

Kofeynya (ul Semakova 19; espresso R60; ☺ 8am-11pm) Tyumen's top coffee house has an astonishing range of special grinds, delicious cakes and maté teas served in curious, wooden bulbs shaped like opium pipes, just as they are in South America.

Getting There & Away
There are four daily flights to Moscow (R4300 to R7000, three hours) and two direct flights

a week to St Petersburg (R8021, 3½ hours, Thursday and Sunday).

Trains depart to all Trans-Siberian destinations. Useful overnight rail connections include Omsk (R1466, 8½ hours, departs 11.23pm) and Kazan (R2471, 24 hours, departs 5.36pm). Seven daily trains (4½ hours) serve Tobolsk and a *platskart* (3rd-class) ticket is around R300, depending on the train. The most convenient leaves at 7.10am. The ticket offices are just inside the entrance to the newly renovated station, on the right.

Getting Around
From the train station bus 25 serves Hotel Vostok and passes near the bus station – to get here, hop off at the Neptun/Stroitel stop then

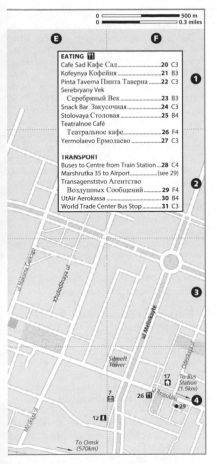

0 ____ 500 m
0 ____ 0.3 miles

EATING 🍴
Cafe Sad Кафе Сад..........................**20** C3
Kofeynya Кофейня **21** B3
Pinta Taverna Пинта Таверна **22** C3
Serebryany Vek
   Серебряный Век..........................**23** B3
Snack Bar Закусочная **24** C3
Stolovaya Столовая **25** B4
Teatralnoe Café
   Театральное кафе......................**26** F4
Yermolaevo Ермолаево **27** C3

TRANSPORT
Buses to Centre from Train Station ..**28** C4
Marshrutka 35 to Airport...............(see 29)
Transagenststvo Агентство
   Воздушных Сообщений..........**29** F4
UtAir Aerokassa **30** B4
World Trade Center Bus Stop **31** C3

Yekaterinburg and Omsk make stopping here a perfectly viable option when crossing Russia.

Tobolsk's strategic importance started to wane in the 1760s, when it was bypassed by the new Great Siberian Trakt (post road). However, until the early 20th century, it remained significant as a centre for both learning and exile. Involuntary guests included Fyodor Dostoevsky en route to exile in Omsk, and deposed Tsar Nicholas II who spent several doomed months here in 1917.

The city is also home to a thriving community of artists, many of whom are willing and pleased to make the acquaintance of visitors to the town.

Orientation & Information

The train station is 10km northeast of the modern city centre. There's an area of ugly Soviet-era concrete blocks around Hotel Slavyanskaya. Don't lose hope! Some 3km further south, the delightful kremlin overlooks the intriguing old town that lies on the Irtysh flood plain below.

Post office (Komsomolsky pr, M/R 42; ⏰ 8am-6pm) Has an attached telephone office.

Servis Tsentr (internet per hr R30; ⏰ 8am-10pm) Behind the telephone office.

Tyumen Energo Bank (White Bldg behind ul Oktyabrskaya 13; ⏰ 9am-6pm, Mon-Fri, 9am-2pm Sat) Good rates for dollars and euros.

Sights
KREMLIN

Within the tower-studded 18th-century walls of the **kremlin** (⏰ grounds 8am-8pm) are the intriguing but disused **Trading Arches** (Gostiny Dvor) and the glorious 1686 **St Sofia Cathedral**. Less eye-catching from the outside, but with splendid arched ceiling murals, is the 1746 **Intercession Cathedral** (Pokrovsky sobor). In between the two is a 1799 **bell tower**, built for the Uglich bell, which had famously signalled a revolt against Tsar Boris Godunov. The revolt failed; in a mad fury Godunov ordered the bell publicly flogged, de-tongued and banished to Tobolsk for its treacherous tolling. A tatty copy of the bell is displayed in the **Museum of the Spiritual Cultures of Western Siberia** (☎ 323 715; admission R20; ⏰ 10am-4pm Wed-Sun), an otherwise entertaining museum within the elegant **Arkhiereysky mansion**. The upper storey has a stylishly re-created 19th-century drawing room as well as plenty of stuffed animals. The middle floor has a birch-bark *chum*

walk a block east, crossing the big clover-leaf junction of uls Permyakova and Respubliki. Taxis between the bus and train stations cost R100.

Bus 13 from the train station loops around to Hotel Neftyanik; switch to frequent buses 30 or 14 in front of the Prezident Hotel for the Trinity Monastery. These follow ul Respubliki westbound but return along ul Lenina.

TOBOLSK ТОБОЛЬСК

☎ 34511 / pop 98,000 / ⏰ Moscow +2hr

Once Siberia's capital Tobolsk is one of the region's most historic towns, sporting a handsome kremlin and a charmingly decrepit old town. Tobolsk is off the Trans-Siberian mainline but direct overnight trains to both

(tepee-shaped tent made of birch bark) amid some interesting ethnographic items.

The eerie 1855 **Tyuremny Zamok** (Krasnaya pl 5; admission R20; 10am-4pm Wed-Sun) was once a holding prison. Tsarist exiles were temporarily incarcerated here awaiting a final destination for their banishment.

OUTSIDE THE KREMLIN

Built in 1887 for Tobolsk's 300th anniversary, the delightful **Fine Art Museum** (ul Oktyabrskaya 1; admission R40, video cameras R100; 10am-5pm Wed-Sun) was renovated in 2004 and soon after was visited by Vladimir Putin and later by his successor, Dmitry Medvedev. Its celebrated collection of WWI-era Russian avant-garde canvases is arguably less interesting, though, than the fine display of bone carvings. Some of these are by Minsalim Timergazeev (see p192) whose studio is attached to the nearby art shop **Minsalim Folk Trade** (240 909; raznoe72@ bk.ru; ul Oktyabrskaya 2; admission free; 9am-5pm). Here Minsalim will happily demonstrate how he turns antler fragments into a range of detailed figures as well as give visitors the low-down on Tobolsk's history and culture. His son and some members of staff speak English.

The tiny but friendly **Iska Yer** (242 400; 4-iy Mikrorayon 10; 10am-8pm) Tatar cultural centre and shop sells traditional Tatar hats, music and Tatar-Russian dictionaries for anyone planning on a trip to Kazan.

OLD TOWN

Wooden stairs lead beneath the kremlin's **Pryamskoy Vzvoz** (gatehouse) to the wonderfully dilapidated old town full of weather-beaten churches and angled wooden homes sinking between muddy lanes.

Near the 1918 **Victory Chapel**, where uls Mira and Kirova meet at a small square, is the grand **Mendeleev mansion** (ul Mira 9), which once housed the family of the famous scientist. The less-eye-catching **Tobolsk Rayon Administration Building** (ul Mira 10) was the exile-home of the last tsar, and where he was reportedly tortured, before his fateful journey to execution in Yekaterinburg. Upstairs, beyond a security check, one small room has been restored close to its 1917 appearance as the **Tsar Nicholas II Office-Museum** (Kabinet-muzey Imperatora Nikolaya II; 222 776; admission R20).

Two blocks east, the attractive **Archangel Mikhail Church** (ul Lenina 24) has a colourfully restored interior. The character of Tatiana

Larina in Pushkin's epic *Eugene Onegin* is said to have been modelled on Natalya Fonvizina, a Decembrist wife who prayed here when not cultivating pineapples in her hothouse. More photogenic is the somewhat derelict 1759 **Zachary and Elisabeth Church** (ul Bazarnaya Ploshchad) with soaring black-tipped spires. Beyond the main red-brick **mosque** (322 748; ul Pushkina 27), weave your way through the muddy lanes of attractive Tatar cottages to reach the equally splendid baroque shell of the **Krestovozdvizhenskaya Church**.

The **Siberian-Tatar Cultural Centre** (322 713; ul Yershova 30) has occasional exhibitions and Tatar musical shows.

Sleeping & Eating

Tobolsk, unsurprisingly for such a small town, does not boast many restaurants or cafes. However, the central government has begun investing large amounts of money ('More than the entire annual budget of Kazakhstan this year alone!' one local boasted) in a bid to transform it into a thriving tourist centre, and the situation may change in the near future.

Resting rooms (komnaty otdykha; 495 222; train station; dm R195) Clean and friendly, the location is utterly impractical for visiting the city but ideal if you're arriving blurry-eyed off the Omsk train or awaiting the 5.23am service to Tyumen. Showers cost R35 extra.

Hotel Novy Tobol (246 614; ul Oktyabrskaya 20; s/d/ tw R800/1250/1650) This somewhat dingy concrete slab has bathrooms in each of its old-style Soviet rooms. A few of the sad doubles have been cosmetically repapered. Music blares loud and late from the bar.

Hotel Sibir (222 390; pl Remezova 1; s R1200-1600, tw/ste R2400/2800) Across from the kremlin, this once budget hotel has recently been done up but is still good value. Rooms still have that 'just refurnished' feel about them, and the beds are comfortable. It features photos of the nearby kremlin at different times of the year. Rates include a good breakfast.

Hotel Slavyanskaya (399 101; www.slavjanskaya .ru, in Russian; 9-iy Mikro-Rayon, pr Mendeleeva; s/tw/d from R2200/4400/6000) Astonishingly well appointed for rural Siberia, the big, modern Slavyanskaya has fully Western-standard comforts. Its only disadvantage is the uninspiring new-town location. Wider beds are available for 10% extra. A few 'imperfect' rooms are significantly discounted. There's tennis, a great downstairs pub and a less appealing small nightclub.

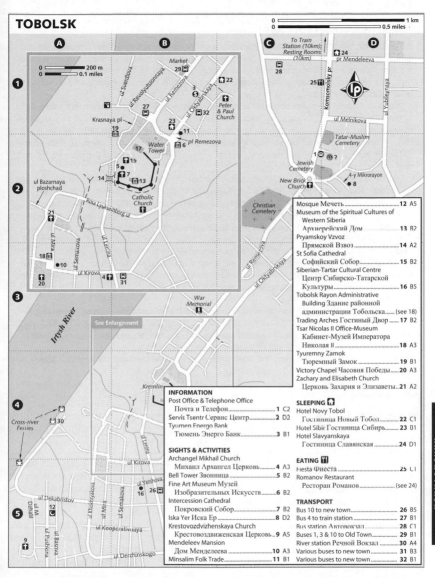

TOBOLSK

0 ——— 1 km
0 ——— 0.5 miles

INFORMATION

Post Office & Telephone Office Почта и Телефон	**1** C2
Servis Tsentr Сервис Центр	**2** D2
Tyumen Energo Bank Тюмень Энерго Банк	**3** B1

SIGHTS & ACTIVITIES

Archangel Mikhail Church Михаил Архангел Церковь	**4** A3
Bell Tower Звонница	**5** B2
Fine Art Museum Музей Изобразительных Искусств	**6** B2
Intercession Cathedral Покровский Собор	**7** B2
Iska Yer Иска Ер	**8** D2
Krestovozdvizhenskaya Church Крестовоздвиженская Церковь	**9** A5
Mendeleev Mansion Дом Менделеева	**10** A3
Minsalim Folk Trade	**11** B1
Mosque Мечеть	**12** A5
Museum of the Spiritual Cultures of Western Siberia Архиерейский Дом	**13** B2
Pryamskoy Vzvoz Прямской Взвоз	**14** A2
St Sofia Cathedral Софийский Собор	**15** B2
Siberian-Tartar Cultural Centre Центр Сибирско-Татарской Культуры	**16** B5
Tobolsk Rayon Administrative Building Здание районной администрации Тобольска	(see 18)
Trading Arches Гостиный Двор	**17** B2
Tsar Nicolas II Office-Museum Кабинет-Музей Императора Николая II	**18** A3
Tyuremny Zamok Тюремный Замок	**19** B1
Victory Chapel Часовня Победы	**20** A3
Zachary and Elisabeth Church Церковь Захария и Элизаветы	**21** A2

SLEEPING

Hotel Novy Tobol Гостиница Новый Тобол	**22** C1
Hotel Sibir Гостиница Сибирь	**23** D1
Hotel Slavyanskaya Гостиница Славянская	**24** D1

EATING

Fiesta Фиеста	**25** C1
Romanov Restaurant Ресторан Романов	(see 24)

TRANSPORT

Bus 10 to new town	**26** B5
Bus 4 to train station	**27** B1
Bus station Автовокзал	**28** C1
Buses 1, 3 & 10 to Old Town	**29** B1
River station Речной Вокзал	**30** A4
Various buses to new town	**31** B3
Various buses to new town	**32** B1

Fiesta (Komsomolsky pr 2; meals R100-250; cover R40 from 7pm Fri & Sat) This midrange cafe has a pleasant summer beer terrace, but the music can get appallingly loud in the evenings. The food is a Siberian approximation of American fast food.

Hotel Slavyanskaya houses the **Romanov Restaurant** (☎ 399 104; meals R1000-1500; ✆ noon-11pm), which features succulent 19th-century Russian dishes and is furnished with mock period furniture. The restaurant has a family portrait of Russia's last tsar and his family on the ceiling, and Dmitry Medvedev visited here shortly after winning Russia's 2008 presidential elections. Staff will happily, and proudly, show you where he sat!

MINSALIM, SIBERIAN FOLK ARTIST

Local Tobolsk folk artist Minsalim Timergazeev is an inspiringly spiritual Tatar with wild-flowing grey hair. In his art he utilises the techniques of the original Siberian peoples to carve tiny, intricate figures out of mammoth and reindeer bone dug up from the surrounding taiga. More than that, however, he is also an established part of the local artist community, and a man with deep roots in the region.

'I grew up here,' Minsalim tells me, as we stand in the building that houses his studio and gallery. 'I'm an orphan,' he goes on, 'and this was a children's home in the Soviet period. They closed it in the late '70s, when they were sure that there would be no more need for places like this under communism.' He laughs. 'We were all dreaming of our futures, dreaming of travelling to foreign lands and so on. We were all also ready to work hard, though, all prepared for labour. And so I set about learning a trade…'

His art is also a family business, and the studio offers courses in bone-carving and Siberian art for tourists from 'all over Russia and Europe. Especially Scandinavian countries, there is a real link between Siberian mythology and the myths of the peoples of the north,' explains Minsalim.

Minsalim's art is more than a way to earn a living, however. 'The whole philosophy of Siberian shamanism and mythology has formed an integral part of my life,' he tells me.

Was it, I wondered, a problem to practice Siberian folk art in the atheist Soviet era? 'Of course,' says Minsalim. 'It was extremely difficult to practice anything connected with religion.'

Minsalim is very fond of the English queen. 'Why?' I ask him. 'We don't have a monarchy,' he replies. 'You always want what you do not have,' he expounds, eyes sparkling. 'I've done a piece of work dedicated to Putin too,' he says, suddenly.

'Putin?'

'It's a fundamental part of Siberian mythology that a benevolent leadership will one day return to rule the land,' he continues, clearing away some boxes and tools to reveal a small figure. Proud and steely eyed, it is clearly Russia's second president. 'Putin has rescued Russia, like a warrior of old,' he says, almost reverently. We sit in silence and gaze at the bone talisman.

What, I wonder, does he make of Dmitry Medvedev? Minsalim waves a hand in dismissal. 'Nothing,' he answers. 'Putin will come back to power soon enough.'

As told to Marc Bennetts

Getting There & Away

From Tobolsk there are five trains a day to Yekaterinburg (R1500 to R1800, 12 hours), the most convenient leaving at 7.08pm. Two trains leave on odd-numbered days at 9.53am and 11.40pm for Omsk (R2145, 14 hours). For Tyumen, seven trains a day (R710 *platskart*, 4¾ hours) are supplemented by an equal number of daily buses (R275, five hours) via Pokrovskoe (3¼ hours), Rasputin's home village. Eight buses per day to various destinations pass Abalak.

From the **river station** (☎ 296 617) ferries run along the Irtysh to Omsk (1st/2nd/3rd class R1674/612/486, three days and seven hours) via Tara (two days and three hours). They also go north towards the Arctic.

Getting Around

Bus 4 and *marshrutka* 20 link the train station, new town and kremlin. Buses 1, 3 and 10 travel past the kremlin and loop around the old town. Bus 1 passes the mosque. Taxis from/to the station cost around R150.

OMSK ОМСК

☎ 3812 / pop 1.3 million / ❍ Moscow +3hr

Don't be put off by your first impressions of Omsk. Crossing the Irtysh River you'll see a line of giant cranes like skeletal giraffes and the usual rows of drab apartment blocks. But the old city centre, where the Om River joins the Irtysh, has parks, quirky public sculptures and a stretch of stately 19th-century buildings along ul Lenina, the main shopping drag. There's also decent-value budget accommodation and some great dining, as well as several Lenin statues – see the boxed text, p195.

History

Starting as a 1716 Cossack outpost, by 1824 Omsk had replaced Tobolsk as the seat of the governor general of Siberia. It became a major dumping ground for exiles. These included Dostoevsky, whose *Buried Alive in Siberia* describes the writer's wretched Omsk imprisonment (1849–53) during which he nearly died from a flogging. During the Civil War, Admiral Alexander Kolchak briefly made Omsk the seat of his anti-Bolshevik government until fleeing to Irkutsk where he was executed in 1919. Today Omsk is another city doing quite nicely on the proceeds of Russia's oil boom.

Orientation

From the train station, 4km south of the city centre, jump straight onto trolleybus 4 up pr Marksa, a major commercial thoroughfare with stolidly Soviet architecture. Get off at central pl Lenina, dominated by a hideous musical theatre with a roof like a giant ski jump. From near here the city's attractive old core stretches north along ul Lenina across the little Om River.

Maps are sold upstairs at the train station and also throughout the city at newspaper kiosks.

Information

Navigator Internet Kafe (ul Lenina 14/1; per hr R40, per MB R3, beers R40-80; ☺ 9am-10pm) Night shift (after 10pm) costs R90 to R120 plus R3 per MB.

Omni Travel (☎ 500 070; Hotel Mayak; ☺ 10am-5pm Mon-Fri) English-speaking travel agency offering simple city tours.

Post office (ul Gertsena 1; ☺ 8am-7pm Mon-Sat, 10am-5pm Sun)

Telephone office (ul Gagarina 34; ☺ 24hr) For calls prepay a deposit, dial the number (with ☎ 8-10 for international), then when connected press '3'.

Virt Internet Café (☎ 306 298; ul Maslinokova 7; per hr R25 plus per MB R3; ☺ 8am-1am, 24 hr weekends) Basement internet cafe popular with beer-drinking teenagers.

Sights

Several witty **statues**, including an odd Soviet 1963 'slacker' brass workman emerging from a manhole add to the elegant, century-old facades of upper ul Lenina. A **small Lenin statue** also lurks nearby.

Grandiose flourishes make the **Drama Theatre** (☎ 244 065; www.omskdrama.ru; ul Lenina; ☺ cash desk 10am-7pm) Omsk's most ornate historical building, though other fine century-old buildings can be found down ul Lenina including the pointy little 1908 **Serafimo-Alexievskaya Chapel**. The **Art Museum** (Omsky muzey iskusstv; ☎ 313 677; admission R100; ☺ 10am-6pm Tue-Sun) displays a lot of fussy decorative arts but the rectilinear 1862 building is a historical curiosity in itself. It was built as the Siberian governor's mansion and hosted passing tsars: note the original Kalmykian throne with its ebony elephant armrests and 7kg of beaten silver. In 1918–19, however, the building was home to Admiral Kolchak's counter-revolutionary government and was the heart of White Russia before the Reds eventually claimed the city.

In the gardens behind the art museum are a **war memorial** and a **Lenin statue**, with Vlad apparently preening himself in an invisible mirror. A Lenin statue used to stand outside the **former town duma** (pl Lenina), but after the town had erected a reconstruction of the green and golden domed **Assumption Cathedral** (destroyed by the atheist Soviets in the 1930s) in the square, a pious top government official apparently noticed that Lenin was pointing at the new cathedral, and ordered it removed overnight.

Activities & Tours

Fancy a **river trip**? Various pleasure boats depart regularly from just west of Yubileyny most. The scenery is nothing special but for a relaxing afternoon you could float 55km to **Achairsky Monastery** (4½ hours return). The complex has been totally rebuilt since 1992, having been used as an infamous Gulag in earlier decades. Highlights are the impressive five-storey bell tower and a holy spring that flows out beneath a cute wooden chapel in the birch woods nearby.

Sleeping

Oddly enough, there are as yet no real five star top end hotels in Omsk, although the Mayak, with its plush suites, acts as the city's 'luxury' hotel.

BUDGET

Hotel Omskgrazhdanstroy (☎ 251 247; Gospitalnaya ul 19; dm/s/tw R700/1300/1700) Remarkably good value, this little-known hotel is the wrong side of the busy ul Frunze intersection, but still walking distance from the centre. Rooms are nothing special, but are clean, large and all have private bathrooms – even the dorms.

Resting rooms (komnaty otdykha; ☎ 442 347; train station; dm R900) Rebuilt, clean and relatively inviting, they're in a separate building – exit the main station, turn left and find the door before the baggage *kassa*.

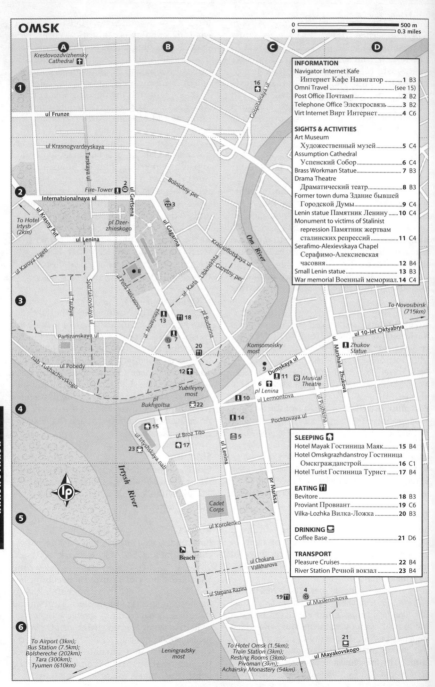

OMSK

0 — 500 m
0 — 0.3 miles

INFORMATION
Navigator Internet Kafe
   Интернет Кафе Навигатор **1** B3
Omni Travel ....(see **15**)
Post Office Почтамп...........................**2** B2
Telephone Office Электросвязь........**3** B2
Virt Internet Вирт Интернет.............**4** C6

SIGHTS & ACTIVITIES
Art Museum
   Художественный музей **5** C4
Assumption Cathedral
   Успенский Собор **6** C4
Brass Workman Statue........................**7** B3
Drama Theatre
   Драматический театр....................**8** B3
Former town duma Здание бывшей
   Городской Думы.............................**9** C4
Lenin statue Памятник Ленину **10** C4
Monument to victims of Stalinist
   repression Памятник жертвам
   сталинских репрессий **11** C4
Serafimo-Alexievskaya Chapel
   Серафимо-Алексиевская
   часовня **12** B4
Small Lenin statue **13** B3
War memorial Военный мемориал..**14** C4

SLEEPING
Hotel Mayak Гостиница Маяк...........**15** B4
Hotel Omskgrazhdanstroy Гостиница
   Омскгражданстрой.........................**16** C1
Hotel Turist Гостиница Турист **17** B4

EATING
Bevitore **18** B3
Proviant Провиант...........................**19** C6
Vilka-Lozhka Вилка-Ложка **20** B3

DRINKING
Coffee Base **21** D6

TRANSPORT
Pleasure Cruises **22** B4
River Station Речной вокзал **23** B4

YEKATERINBURG TO KRASNOYARSK

WHO IS THAT MAN?

Omsk is notable for its Lenin statues. While most Russian towns only have one or two, the rest having been torn down in the early 1990s, Omsk has at least five scattered around the city, including one right outside the main train station. This is not to say, however, that the youth of Omsk are entirely clued-up as to the identity of the balding, serious-looking fellow who haunts their town, as we discovered.

'Who's that?' asked a young boy, passing the statue near the station. 'Lenin,' his father replied. The boy thought, and then replied, 'Ah, so that's why they call it Prospect Lenina.' His father nodded. The young boy thought some more, and then posed a question that not so long ago would have been unthinkable. 'But who's Lenin?' His father was, understandably, lost for words.

Indeed, recent surveys carried out in the country's schools have shown that the nation's children know little or nothing about the leader of the 1917 Bolshevik Revolution, with answers as to the question, 'Who was Vladimir Lenin?' ranging from 'A poet,' to, bizarrely, 'The first creature to leave the sea and walk on dry land.'

Kids today, huh?

Hotel Omsk (☎ 310 721; fax 315 222; ul Irtyshskaya Naberezhnaya 30; s/tw R1400/2600) Halfway between the train station and centre, this big, drab concrete block is somewhat redeemed by its river views. Rooms are mostly unreconstructed Soviet affairs but a dozen have been fairly thoroughly rebuilt in recent years. It's often full, so book ahead. Take any bus along ul Karla Marksa to the circus then walk five minutes through Pobedy Park to the riverside.

MIDRANGE
Hotel Irtysh (☎ 232 702; www.hotel-irtysh.ru; Krasni Put' 155/1; s/d R2000/3000) About 2.5km northwest of the centre, the Irtysh is set in a forest on a bank of the river of the same name, offering the opportunity for relaxing strolls in the evening. Rooms are worn, but clean and large. There's a dark and uninviting restaurant in the basement. The breakfast included in the price is barely edible.

Hotel Turist (☎ 316 419; fax 316 414; www.tourist-omsk.ru; ul Broz Tito 2; s/tw economy R2400/2700, standard R2900/3200, 1st-class R3500/3700) A fairly central address with fine views of the river from the upper floors. Good '1st-class' rooms have recently been done up, but the 'economy' rooms are long due a similar facelift.

Hotel Mayak (☎ /fax 315 431; www.hotel-mayak.ru; ul Lermontova 2; s/tw R2860/4125; 🖵) Within the rounded end of the vaguely ship-shaped art deco river station, the Mayak has small but stylish rooms with artistic lines and good bathrooms. Popular with visiting Western businesspeople, it has friendly staff. It offers gigantic, all mod-cons luxury suites from R5300 to R7900 if you feel like splashing out.

Eating & Drinking
Vilka-Lozhka (ul Lenina 21, 2nd fl; meals R60-150) Ridiculously cheap, this self-service canteen serves honest food for honest prices. Borscht goes for R20 and pancakes for R16.

our pick **Proviant** (☎ 245 778; pr Marksa 10; meals R300-500, beer R75-120) Good jazz, beer, and a wide range of Russian/European food make this a pleasant place to spend an evening. Particularly nice cheese and potato pancakes, and live music from 7pm.

Bevitore (☎ 243 928; ul Lenina 9; meals R350-500) A hip restaurant-cafe with free wi-fi, this spacious establishment has a large range of highly recommended shashlyk dishes.

Coffee Base (☎ 30/ 5/8; ul Mayakovskogo 1/; coffees R49-100) Pleasant coffee house with sensibly priced espressos. If your palate differentiates 80% from 100% Arabica beans, consider the more expensive 'elite' blends. Food includes decent mini-bliny (pancakes), pricey cakes and steaks.

Pivoman (ul Marchenko 5; beer R60-100) Right next to the train station, to the left of Granddad Lenin, Pivoman offers over 20 types of hard-to-distinguish-from-one-another beer, plus the usual dried fish snacks (R30 to R60).

Getting There & Away
Omsk's **airport** (☎ 517 570; ul Inzhenernaya 1) is on the west bank of the Irtysh River. Destinations include Moscow (R6500, five daily) and also St Petersburg (R8500, three direct flights weekly).

Six trains a day make the 43-hour journey to Moscow, the first leaving at 9.55am, the last at 11.08pm (R2176). There are more than

YEKATERINBURG TO KRASNOYARSK

10 trains a day to Yekaterinburg, the most convenient leaving at 8.37pm and arriving at 9.40am (R2290). A train leaves at 1.30pm daily for Tobolsk (No 395, R2348, 13¾ hours), and three times a day – at 12.15am, 12.25am and at 12.44am – for Tomsk (R1350 to R1800, 14 to 19 hours). There are over 15 trains a day to Novosibirsk (R675 *platskart*, 9½ hours).

Although train tickets are sold conveniently from the **rechnoy vokzal** (river station; ☎ 398 563; pl Bukhgoltsa; ◷ 9am-7pm), the commission can be a whopping R200. Here you can also buy air tickets or catch very leisurely Rechflot ferries to Tobolsk (R1674/612 1st/3rd class, two days and 14 hours) three times monthly in summer.

Getting Around

From the train station, trolleybus 4 and *marshrutka* 335 run along pr Marksa to pl Lenina, past the main post office and on for miles up Krasny Put. Bus 60 crosses the Irtysh to the **airport** (☎ 517 570; Inzhenernaya ul 1) while trolleybus 7 or the faster *marshrutka* 366 head for the bus station further to the west. Allow over half an hour in rush-hour traffic jams.

Construction began on Omsk's metro system back in 1985, but its opening has been delayed and rescheduled for years. The current start date is 2010, with the first two stations close to the train station in the southwest of the city.

NOVOSIBIRSK НОВОСИБИРСК

☎ 383 / pop 1.5 million / ◷ Moscow +3hr

This city wouldn't exist if it wasn't for the Trans-Siberian Railway. Train enthusiasts may wish to see Siberia's biggest station, a new railway museum and a locomotive collection at nearby Seyatel. And those seeking Irish bars will be delighted by the choice. However, for atmosphere and sightseeing consider stopping in Tomsk instead.

Founded in 1893, the city grew around the Ob River bridge that was then being built for the Trans-Siberian Railway. Named Novo-Nikolayevsk until 1925 for the last tsar, it grew rapidly into Siberia's biggest metropolis, a key industrial and transport centre exploiting coalfields to the east and mineral deposits in the Urals. In the 1930s the construction of the Turkestan-Siberian (Turk-Sib) railway south from Novosibirsk to Almaty in Kazakhstan (via the Altai region) made the city a crucial transport link between Russia and Central Asia.

Orientation & Information

Despite its daunting scale, Siberia's biggest city has a relaxed and manageable centre. Vokzalnaya magistral runs 1.5km from the train station, meeting the main commercial axis, Krasny pr, at central pl Lenina.

Dom Knigi (Krasny pr 51; ◷ 10am-8pm Mon-Sat, to 7pm Sun) Has a good range of maps.

Internet Tsentr (☎ 291 8841; ul Trudovaya 1; per hr R40, per MB R2; ◷ 9am-11pm) Beneath an apartment block; take the first alley off Vokzalnaya magistral when walking from pl Lenina. Night shift (after 11pm) R150.

Main post office (ul Lenina 5; ◷ 8am-9pm Mon-Fri, to 7pm Sat & Sun)

Telephone office (ul Sovetskaya 33; ◷ 24hr)

Sights

Novosibirsk's pl Lenina is dominated by the huge, silver-domed **Opera & Ballet Theatre** (Krasny pr 36; see p199). In front, wearing a flapping coat, the dashing **Lenin statue** is flanked by waving partisans vainly trying to direct the chaotic traffic.

Close to the train station, the brand-new **West Siberian Railway Museum** (☎ 229 2033; http://zap-sib-rail.narod.ru/index-museum.htmlul, in Russian; ul Shamshurina; admission free; ◷ 8am-5pm Mon-Fri) has over 250 locomotives on display and is a must for train enthusiasts.

Platform 1 at the main train station boasts two **WWII 'family' statues** depicting a mother and her small daughter and a father and his small son waving off relatives to WWII – it was from this station that many Siberians went directly to the front.

In an elegant mansion, the **Local Studies Museum** (Kraevedchesky muzey; ☎ 218 1773; Krasny pr 23; admission R180; ◷ 10am-5.30pm Tue-Sun) has Altai shaman coats, cutaway pioneer houses and some splendid religious artefacts. The **State Art Museum** (Khudozhestvenny muzey; ☎ 223 3516; http://gallery.nsc.ru/; Krasny pr 5; adult/student R180/100; ◷ 10am-5.20pm Tue-Fri, 11am-5.20pm Sat & Sun) has an extensive collection including icons, Siberian art, works by Nikolai Gritsyuk and numerous distinctive mountainscapes by celebrated spiritual Russian painter Nikolai Rerikh.

The pretty little **Chapel of St Nicholas** (Chasovnya Svyatitelya Nikolaya; pr Krasny) was said to mark the geographical centre of Russia when built in 1915. Demolished in the 1930s, it was rebuilt in 1993 in time for Novosibirsk's centenary.

NOVOSIBIRSK

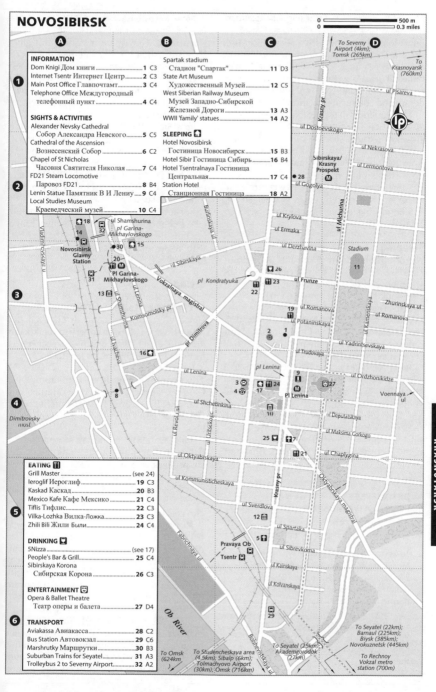

INFORMATION
Dom Knigi Дом книги **1** C3
Internet Tsentr Интернет Центр **2** C3
Main Post Office Главпочтамт **3** C4
Telephone Office Междугородный
    телефонный пункт **4** C4

SIGHTS & ACTIVITIES
Alexander Nevsky Cathedral
    Собор Александра Невского **5** C5
Cathedral of the Ascension
    Вознесенский Собор **6** C2
Chapel of St Nicholas
    Часовня Святителя Николая **7** C3
FD21 Steam Locomotive
    Паровоз FD21 .... **8** B4
Lenin Statue Памятник В И Лениу **9** C4
Local Studies Museum
    Краеведческий музей **10** C4

Spartak stadium
    Стадион "Спартак" **11** D3
State Art Museum
    Художественный Музей **12** C5
West Siberian Railway Museum
    Музей Западно-Сибирской
    Железной Дороги **13** A3
WWII 'family' statues **14** A2

SLEEPING
Hotel Novosibirsk
    Гостиница Новосибирск **15** B3
Hotel Sibir Гостиница Сибирь **16** B4
Hotel Tsentralnaya Гостиница
    Центральная **17** C4
Station Hotel
    Станционная Гостиница **18** A2

EATING
Grill Master .... (see 24)
Ieroglif Иероглиф **19** C3
Kaskad Каскад **20** B3
Mexico Kafe Кафе Мексико **21** C4
Tiflis Тифлис **22** C3
Vilka-Lozhka Вилка-Ложка **23** C3
Zhili Bili Жили Были **24** C4

DRINKING
5Nizza .... (see 17)
People's Bar & Grill **25** C4
Sibirskaya Korona
    Сибирская Корона **26** C3

ENTERTAINMENT
Opera & Ballet Theatre
    Театр оперы и балета **27** D4

TRANSPORT
Aviakassa Авиакасса **28** C2
Bus Station Автовокзал **29** C6
Marshrutky Маршрутки **30** B3
Suburban Trains for Seyatel **31** A3
Trolleybus 2 to Severny Airport **32** A2

The gold-domed 1914 **Cathedral of the Ascension** (Voznesensky sobor; ul Sovetskaya 91) has a wonderful, colourful interior with a soaring central space that's unexpected from its fairly squat exterior appearance. The 1898 **Alexander Nevsky Cathedral** (sobor Alexandra Nevskogo; Krasny pr 1a) is a red-brick Byzantine-style building with gilded domes and colourful new murals.

The local football team, Sibir, currently play at the 12,500 capacity **Spartak stadium** (☎ 2170 474; www.fc-sibir.ru, in Russian; ul Frunze 15). Games are usually played on Saturdays, and tickets cost from R100 to R500. Matches are advertised on posters around the city.

Some 30km south of the city centre near the great Ob Sea (reservoir), **Akademgorodok** is Siberia's biggest and best known science suburb.

Sleeping

Novosibirsk hotels are poor value by Siberian standards. Most will only accept foreigners when booked through a tour agency (incurring booking fees and commission).

Station Hotel (☎ 229 2376; 2nd fl, Novosibirsk Glavny train station; dm/tw/tr without bathroom R700/1500/1800, s/tw with bathroom R2800/4100) Only for those with onward rail tickets. Half-price for 12-hour stays. It's frequently full.

Hotel Tsentralnaya (☎ 222 3638; fax 227 660; ul Lenina 3; s/tw without bathroom R1000/1200, with bathroom R2500/2900) Very central, the no-frills basic rooms with shared, survivable bathrooms are Novosibirsk's best budget option. Willing to accept foreigners without advance bookings. The lifts are dodgy and floor attendants oddly protective of their toilet rolls. Breakfast not included.

DETOUR: SEYATEL – RAILWAY LOCOMOTIVE MUSEUM

СЕЯТЕЛЬ – МУЗЕЙ ЖЕЛЕЗНОДОРОЖНОЙ ТЕХНИКИ

To get to the **Seyatel – Railway Locomotive Museum** (☎ 337 9622; admission R50; ☉ 11am-5pm Sat-Thu) take *marshrutka* 1015 (R30, 30 minutes) from Novosibirsk Glavny train station to Seyatel train station. The museum has over 100 exhibits, ranging from Soviet steam engines to pre-revolution carriages. You can return to central Novosibirsk the same way or jump on an hourly *elektrichka* train (R25).

Hotel Novosibirsk (☎ 220 1120; fax 216 517; Vokzalnaya magistral 1; s/tw from R1400/2100) Opposite Novosibirsk Glavny train station, this glum 23-storey Soviet-era tower has mediocre, overpriced Soviet-era rooms. The cheapest share a toilet and washbasin between pairs of rooms and lack showers altogether. You'll pay R2900 for a private bathroom. Room rates include breakfast.

Hotel Sibir (☎ 223 1215; www.gk-sibir.sibnet.ru; ul Lenina 21; s/d from R3500/3700) The Sibir considers itself Novosibirsk's international hotel and will offer visa registrations for guests. Excellent king-bedded 'studios' (doubles R6600) have party-sized bathrooms. However, standard rooms lack style or air-con.

For a slightly cheaper option, you could take a chance with one of the women loitering outside the train station in the evenings with 'Квартира' (apartment) signs pinned to their jackets.

Eating

Choice is almost endless near pl Lenina.

our pick **Vilka-Lozhka** (ul Frunze 2; meals R100-180) Simple yet stylishly modern cafeteria decorated with primary-coloured cutlery to remarkably dramatic effect. Very cheap – pancakes cost from R12 and filling soups for R20!

Ieroglif (☎ 222 5712; Krasny pr 35; meals R350-800) This hypnotic temple of a restaurant has Chinese, Japanese and Korean offerings and a range of beers, both Russian and imported. (R80 to R150). Gets busy in the evenings, so book ahead.

Tiflis (☎ 222 8181; ul Sovetskaya 65; meals R400-800) Below the fur shop of the same name, this atmospheric tavern-cavern offers the most authentic Georgian cuisine in town. Filling and delicious *khachapuri po-adzharski* (Georgian bread with a raw egg swimming in the middle) costs R180.

Mexico Kafe (☎ 210 3420; Oktyabrskaya magistral 49; meals R400-900; ☉ 8am-1am) Dangling chillies, Aztec icons and a big charcoal grill add atmosphere while Los Gringos serenade. The great Mexican food has made it a two-times winner of the 'Best Russian Bar-B-Q' award (2006 and 2007).

Prices are relatively reasonable in the very central, Disney-esque 'Siberian village' of **Zhily-Bily** (ul Lenina 1; meals R130-450), with English menus, a salad bar and great stuffed bliny. It's upstairs above fast-food eatery **Grill Master** (burgers R50-80) through a central wooden door.

Kaskad (Vokzalnaya magistral 2; 7.30am-10pm) is a handy for the train station grocery store with a takeaway, pay-by-weight salad bar and a basic sit-down *pelmenaya*.

Drinking

There are bars galore along ul Lenina, Krasny pr and Vokzalnaya magistral. Almost all serve decent if pricey food as well as drinks.

People's Bar & Grill (Krasny pr 17; beers from R60, espresso R45; noon-2am) The preferred hangout of Novosibirsk's would-be rap stars and models. Descend the stairway opposite St Nicholas chapel.

5Nizza (ul Lenina 3; beers R80-110, snacks R50-100; noon-2am) Sharing its name with a popular Moscow reggae group, this lively bar is on the ground floor of the Tsentralnaya Hotel.

Sibirskaya Korona (ul Frunze 3; beers R70-100, snacks R50-180; noon-1am, noon-6am weekends) A noisy bar popular with local office workers on Fridays. It serves only Sibirskaya Korona beer (light, dark and nonfiltered), plus a selection of Russian/European snacks and meals.

Entertainment

Opera & Ballet Theatre (227 1537; www.opera-novosibirsk.ru; Krasny pr 36; admission R90-2000; season Oct-Jun) For classical culture don't miss an evening at this theatre. Bigger than Moscow's Bolshoi, its grand interior alone makes performances one of the city's highlights. Ticket prices depend on seats and performances. Morning shows are a lot cheaper.

Philharmonia (222 1511; www.philharmonia-nsk.ru; ul Spartaka 11; tickets R100-450) Concerts here range from classical symphonies to Dixieland jazz.

Getting There & Away

AIR

There are two airports in Novosibirsk. However, nearly all major airlines use the much bigger **Tolmachyovo** (216 9230; http://tolmachevoeng.faktura.ru), 30km west of Novosibirsk off the Omsk road. The website gives timetables. Regular international destinations include Běijīng and Seoul plus several cities in Central Asia (eg Tashkent R7600). On Friday, Saturday and Sunday there are flights to Munich (R14,609 return) and Frankfurt (R11,689 return).

There are regular domestic flights to a number of destinations, including Moscow (R7500) and St Petersburg (R9000). The central **Aviakassa** (ul Gogolya 3; 8.30am-8pm) is one of dozens of places to buy air tickets.

The much smaller **Severny** (228 3788), 6km north of the centre, handles a decreasing number of flights, including to Kyzyl in Tuva (R5900).

TRAIN

The city's huge main train station, **Novosibirsk Glavny** (ul Shamshurina 43), has numerous daily long-distance trains.

For Moscow (48 to 55 hours via Omsk, Tyumen and Yekaterinburg), comfortable train 25 (R9812, 7.20am, even days) is easy to book. However, the much cheaper 339 (R5986 10.04pm, odd days) takes one night longer, saving on hotel accommodation as well as the fare. Of a dozen possible trains to Omsk, the handiest overnighter is train 45 (R974 *platskart*, 6¾ hours, daily). For Krasnoyarsk, train 12 (R2126, 8.47pm, 12 to 14 hours, even days) is well-timed. Train no 38 leaves daily for Tomsk at 12.14am (R834, five hours).

For the Altai region, the handy 601 runs overnight to Biysk (R902, 10 hours, daily) via Barnaul (5½ hours). For Khakassia and Tuva you could go to Abakan direct (R2626, 2.48am, 23 hours, daily), or in two overnight hops via Novokuznetsk for which the best option is train 605 (R932, 9½ hours). Trains to Almaty, Kazakhstan (around R3000, 32 to 37 hours) run at 10.31am and 1.51pm daily.

Getting Around

From the train station, take trolleybus 2 to Severny airport, *marshrutka* 1122 to Tolmachyovo airport or *marshrutka* 1212 for the bus station via pl Lenina. The metro (R12) has a major north–south line running beneath Krasny pr and across the river to Studencheskaya and pl Karla Marksa. For the main train station you'll need metro stop pl Garina-Mikhaylovskogo, which is on a second three-stop line that intersects with the major line at Sibirskaya/Krasny pr.

Generally *marshrutky* are handier within the centre. A **taxi** (299 4646) to the airport costs around R500. The journey from the city centre takes about 30 to 40 minutes, depending on traffic.

TOMSK ТОМСК

3822 / pop 473,000 / Moscow +3hr

Siberia's most likable city, Tomsk is an underappreciated gem, 270km northeast of Novosibirsk. Home to some of Siberia's best traditional wooden architecture, it's also a lively university city. Although 80km off the Trans-Sib mainline, it's not really a diversion as there are handy overnight through trains from both Omsk and Krasnoyarsk.

Founded in 1604, Tomsk was an important administrative and commercial town on the Great Siberian Trakt at its Tom River crossing. When the city was bypassed by the Trans-Siberian Railway its commercial importance declined, but its renowned academic institutions and the surrounding *oblast*'s oil wealth are today bringing Tomsk a renewed economic dynamism.

Orientation & Information

The train station and next-door bus station are about 2.5km southeast of pl Lenina, which is on Tomsk's appealing main commercial street.

Accurate bus-route maps are sold at news kiosks in the stations.

Left-luggage at the train station is easy to miss; it's downstairs from within the *prigorodny kassa* (suburban train ticket office), entered by a separate door at the north end of the main station building.

Biznes Tsentr (Hotel Tomsk; internet per hr R120; 24hr) Pricey but handy when awaiting a train.

Main post office (pr Lenina 95; internet per hr R25; 9am-7.30pm Mon-Fri, 8am-5pm Sat, 9am-5pm Sun) Internet, but no postcards of Tomsk!

Netcafé (281 441; pr Lenina 32; internet per 30min R15, pay R1 per MB for faster connection; 9am-11pm) Night shift costs R160 plus traffic (11pm to 8am).

Tomskturist (528 179; pr Lenina 59; 9am-7pm Mon-Fri, 11am-4pm Sat) Can arrange individual walking tours of the city, with English-, French- and German-speaking guides. Based in a lovely wooden house opposite the university.

Sights

Tomsk is famous for 'wooden lace' architecture – carved windows and tracery on old log and timber houses. Great examples include the restored **Shushkin House** (ul Shishkova 10), the spired **Russian-German House** (1906; ul Krasnoarmeyskaya 71), the **Dragon House** (ul Krasnoarmeyskaya 68) and the fan-gabled **Peacock House** (ul Krasnoarmeyskaya 67A). Many more line **ul Tatarskaya**, which is a couple of blocks west of ul Lenina.

The site of Tomsk's original fortress on **Resurrection Hill** features the **Tomsk History Museum** (admission R20; 11am-5pm Tue-Sun) and the recently rebuilt 'Golden Gate' **wooden tower**, which is mainly interesting for the

view from its lookout turret. From the top you can see seven historic churches, but not the Dracula-gothic **Voznesenskaya Church** for which you'll need to stroll on up cobbled ul Bakunin.

Cafes, theatres and century-old architecture make for delightful strolling along pr Lenina. Start on formless pl Lenina, which mixes ugly Soviet monstrosities with the splendid 1784 **Epiphany Cathedral**, the former **trading arches** and the small but revered **Iverskaya Chapel** (Iverskaya Chasoviya; 10am-6pm). The wonderful **1000 Melochey Shop** (pl Lenina; 10am-7pm Mon-Sat, 10am-6pm Sun) features griffins and 1906 art nouveau ironwork flourishes.

Tomsk's appealing commercial district is most bustling south of per Nakhanovicha where you'll find the well-stocked if somewhat stuffy **Tomsk Art Gallery** (514 106; per Nakhanovicha 5; adult R60; 10am-5.30pm Tue-Sun). Other small museums include two rooms within the **Atashev Palace & Regional Museum** (http://museum.trecom.tomsk.ru, in Russian; pr Lenina 75; admission R30; 10am-6pm Wed-Sun), which was once a church. Across the road, the eerie prison-dungeon of the cruel NKVD (later the KGB) is now a memorable **Oppression Museum** (516 133; pr Lenina 44, rear entrance; admission R30; 2-6pm Mon-Fri). Tours are recommended, but are only available in Russian. Outside the museum there are two **monuments to victims of Stalinist repression** – the larger to local victims, the second to Poles slaughtered by Uncle Joe and his cronies.

Further south in resplendently leafy grounds, the classically colonnaded **university buildings** explain Tomsk's popular title of 'the Oxford of Siberia'. Pr Lenina ends 600m beyond at the powerful mother-and-son **WWII Memorial** in the Lagerny Gardens, behind which are views of the meandering River Tom and the taiga beyond.

Sleeping

BUDGET

Resting rooms (komnaty otdykha; Tomsk 1 train station; dm/tw R350/1050) Perfectly clean rooms with shared toilets and shower. No onward rail-ticket requirement. Curfew 1am to 5am.

TGU Hotel (534 352; 5th fl, pr Lenina 49; dm/s/tw R500/850/1300) Uniquely good-value, clean rooms have kettle, fridge and fully equipped new bathrooms (except in the dorms, which share facilities between two triples). In term-time reservations are essential (R100 booking

TOMSK

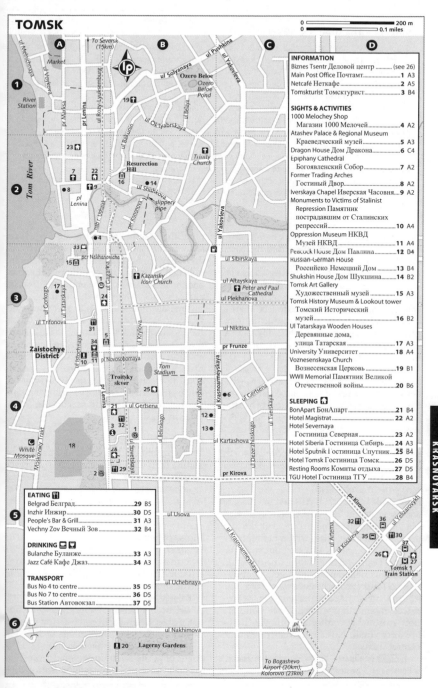

INFORMATION

Biznes Tsentr Деловой центр	(see 26)
Main Post Office Почтамт	1 A3
Netcafé Неткафе	2 A5
Tomskturist Томсктурист	3 B4

SIGHTS & ACTIVITIES

1000 Melochey Shop Магазин 1000 Мелочей	4 A2
Atashev Palace & Regional Museum Краеведческий музей	5 A3
Dragon House Дом Дракона	6 C4
Epiphany Cathedral Богоявленский Собор	7 A2
Former Trading Arches Гостиный Двор	8 A2
Iverskaya Chapel Иверская Часовня	9 A2
Monuments to Victims of Stalinist Repression Памятник пострадавшим от Сталинских репрессий	10 A4
Oppression Museum НКВД Музей НКВД	11 A4
Peacock House Дом Павлина	12 D4
Russian-German House Российско Немецкий Дом	13 B4
Shukshin House Дом Шукшина	14 B2
Tomsk Art Gallery Художественный музей	15 A3
Tomsk History Museum & Lookout tower Томский Исторический музей	16 B2
Ul Tatarskaya Wooden Houses Деревянные дома, улица Татарская	17 A3
University Университет	18 A4
Voznesenskaya Church Вознесенская Церковь	19 B1
WWII Memorial Памятник Великой Отечественной войны	20 B6

SLEEPING

BonApart БонАпарт	21 B4
Hotel Magistrat	22 A2
Hotel Severnaya Гостиница Северная	23 A2
Hotel Siberia Гостиница Сибирь	24 A3
Hotel Sputnik Гостиница Спутник	25 B4
Hotel Tomsk Гостиница Томск	26 D5
Resting Rooms Комнты отдыха	27 D5
TGU Hotel Гостиница ТГУ	28 B4

EATING

Belgrad Белград	29 B5
Inzhir Инжир	30 D5
People's Bar & Grill	31 A3
Vechny Zov Вечный Зов	32 B4

DRINKING

Bulanzhe Буланже	33 A3
Jazz Café Кафе Джаз	34 A3

TRANSPORT

Bus No 4 to centre	35 D5
Bus No 7 to centre	36 D5
Bus Station Автовокзал	37 D5

SIBERIA – THE GRAPHIC NOVEL

Graphic novels have never taken off in Russia, with even the genre's best works largely dismissed as being fit purely for children. This lack of a comic book tradition makes Nikolai Malsov's *Siberia*, released by the US-based Soft Skull Press in 2007, all the more astonishing. Drawn entirely in pencil on paper, Maslov's tale of a Soviet youth (the book's original title) spent in Siberia is bleak, bitter and beautiful.

Portraying with almost unbearable honesty the faces of the drunks and bullies he grew up with, Maslov had reportedly never actually read a graphic novel before he approached the French publisher of *Asterix* in Russia with the first pages of the book and asked him to finance the rest. The publisher agreed, allowing Maslov to quit his job as a night watchman and devote himself to his work. Maslov tells the story of his often brutal life with a complete lack of sentimentality, using matter-of-fact, almost crude frames to portray characters and everyday scenes in western Siberian villages and towns. One of the few works of art to portray everyday life in Soviet Siberia, as opposed to Solzhenitsyn-type gulag tales, Maslov's book has yet to find a publisher in his native Russia.

---

fee) but dropping in might work in midsummer. Midnight curfew. Enter from the rear; there's no lift.

Hotel Severnaya (☎ 512 324; pr Lenina 86; dm/s/d R500/1200/1500) Don't be fooled by the smart new facade. Most rooms remain ageing Soviet affairs sharing communal squat toilets. There's a sink and kettle in every room, though. Liveable, but not particularly enjoyable. A few singles (R1900) and doubles (R2400) are nicely renovated with full facilities.

Hotel Sputnik (☎ 526 660; www.sputnik.tomskturist.ru; ul Belinskogo 15; s/d/tw/tr R850/1700/1900/2400) The winner of Tomsk's first hotel competition in the 1990s, standards have slipped a touch, but the Sputnik's rooms are still good value and spotlessly clean. The cheapest singles and doubles have shared toilets. R3000 for a massive room with its own toilet and bathroom is worth considering. There's wi-fi in every room.

MIDRANGE & TOP END

Hotel Siberia (☎ /fax 527 225; pr Lenina 91; www.hotelsibir .tomsk.ru; s/d/ste R2100/2600/4000) A centrally located old hotel with clean and attractive singles and doubles and great suites with real fireplaces for R4000. Dinner costs extra, but you'd be better off eating in one of the many cafes and restaurants right outside the hotel's doors.

Hotel Tomsk (☎ 524 115; www.tomskhotel.ru; pr Kirova 65; s/tw R2460/3420) Acceptable but rather overpriced, its smartly upgraded Soviet rooms are now reasonably comfortable, though baths are very small. Not so convenient for the central sights.

our pick **BonApart** (☎ 534 650; www.bon-apart.ru; ul Gertsena 1a; s/tw/ste R2750/3400/4350) In its price range this brand-new, fully fitted private hotel is by far the best value. English is spoken, floors have key-card security and the stairs are polished light marble. It's centrally located, and the breakfast included in the price is tasty and satisfying. There's no lift, though.

Hotel Magistrat (☎ 511 111; fax 511 200; www.magistrathotel.com; pl Lenina 15; d/tw/ste R6470/7700/11,500) Behind the palatial 1802 facade, the luxurious rooms are brand new, decorated in a comfortable international style though sadly without historical idiosyncrasies. English is spoken and the restaurant is lavish. All very good, but outrageously expensive for provincial Siberia, the hotel having seen a near 200% price increase in recent years!

Eating & Drinking

There are more choices on and around pr Lenina than you can eat through in a week.

our pick **Jazz Café** (☎ 516 391; www.jazz-cafe.tomsk .ru, in Russian; pr Lenina 46; meals R200-550, beer R70-100) A hip and literally underground basement hang-out with an extensive drinks and food menu and screenings of old black-and-white films. (They were showing Chaplin's *The Great Dictator* when we popped in.) There's live music most evenings (cover charge R100 to R300). Also boasts a large book and music shop.

Belgrad (☎ 564 792; pr Lenina 51; meals R250-700) A welcoming Balkan restaurant serving fine fish dishes, Belgrad makes the perfect place to linger on cold Siberian evenings.

Inzhir (☎ 541 809; pr Kirova 66; meals R300-750) Right opposite the train station, Inzhir (Fig) serves a variety of Eastern food from Uzbek dumplings to Turkish kebabs. It's often full in the evening.

People's Bar & Grill (pr Lenina 54; meals R300-800, beers from R75; ☻ noon-2am) It's a beer and pizza hang-out in a new central location. Can get crowded at weekends. Does not take reservations over the phone. Entrance is from the rear of pr Lenina.

Vechny Zov (☎ 528 167; ul Sovetskaya 47; meals R350-900; ☻ noon-4am) Named after a popular Soviet TV serial, one of Tomsk's top dining options boasts a mock Siberian ranch outside and a cosy antique-filled home feel inside.

Bulanzhe (☎ 516 735; 2nd fl, pr Lenina 80; espresso R40; ☻ 8am-midnight) Tomsk's answer to Starbucks serves great coffee and stuffed bliny (from R40). There is another branch at ul Krasnoarmeyskaya 107.

Getting There & Away

Transport options are comprehensively listed at http://transport.sibr.ru/, in Russian.

Tomsk's **Bogashevo Airport** (☎ 270 084), about 22km southeast of town, has two flights a day to Moscow (R9000/17,000 one way/return, 7.30am and 8am). The choice is much wider from Novosibirsk's Tolmachyovo airport (p199).

From Tomsk 1 (main) train station there are daily services at 8.18am to Moscow's Yaroslavsky station (R10,351, two days and 8½ hours). For Omsk, the summer-only train 437 (R850, 15 hours, 6.02pm, even days) is convenient. For other times of the year take train 953 (R2458, 4.22am). Trains run to Barnaul on even days at 3.59pm (R960, 14¾ hours) and to Irkutsk (R3630, 34 hours) via Krasnoyarsk (R1911, 14½ hours) daily in summer, even days only in winter.

Shared taxis (R600 to 700, 3½ hours) are much faster than buses from the next-door central bus station (R300, 5½ hours, 20 daily) for Novosibirsk. Buses to Kemerovo leave five times a day (R200, two hours).

Getting Around

For the airport take the rare bus 119 from pl Lenina. Other city *marshrutky* are very frequent. Handy route 7 runs from near the train station, along pr Frunze, up pr Lenina, then east again on ul Pushkina. *Marshrutka* 11 shows you the wooden houses along ul Krasnoarmeyskaya, 29 does the same for ul Tatarskaya via pl Yuzhny, while bus 4 goes west from the train station and then runs north the length of pr Lenina.

Krasnoyarsk to Lake Baikal

At just over a thousand kilometres, this stretch of the Trans-Siberian is no more than an overnight hop, but at both ends of the route you'll discover exciting reasons to get off the rails and explore. Krasnoyarsk is one of Siberia's most forward-looking cities and also the best place to jump aboard trains bound for the BAM (Baikal-Amur Mainline; Baikalo-Amurskaya Magistral), which skirts the north of Lake Baikal and continues to places of breathtaking remoteness. Trains from here also run south to little-visited Khakassia, from where it's possible to carry on by bus to Tuva for throat singing and encounters with real-life shamans. Cruise ships are carried towards the Arctic Circle by the powerful Yenisey River, though foreigners must disembark at Igarka. The Stolby Nature Reserve, Divnogorsk dam and one of Siberia's newest ski resorts provide ample entertainment in Krasnoyarsk till it's time to move on.

If choosing one place to detrain en route from Moscow to Běijīng or Ulaanbaatar, make it Irkutsk, the de facto capital of eastern Siberia and the most engaging city in the region by far. It's also the best base from which to plot further travels around what is for most the highlight of any Trans-Siberian journey: magnificent Baikal, the world's deepest lake. Most head straight for touristy Listvyanka, 70km away, but Olkhon Island and several timeless fishing villages along the Great Baikal Trail offer tranquil retreats.

Back on the train, the Trans-Sib tracks pass right along the shore of the lake affording superb views, especially between Slyudyanka and Baikalsk. Lakeside Slyudyanka makes a feasible hop-off point as it's the terminus for the Circumbaikal Railway, as well as a hub for transport along the Tunka Valley to the Buddhist spa town of Arshan. To visit eastern Baikal, continue to Ulan-Ude.

HIGHLIGHTS

- Dance with the shamans on mysterious **Olkhon Island** (p223), steeped in myths and legends
- Branch off the Trans-Sib onto the slow but scenic **Circumbaikal Railway** (p226)
- Take a trek into the weird and wonderful rock formations at **Stolby Nature Reserve** (p207), near Krasnoyarsk
- Pull on your hiking boots and strike out along the **Great Baikal Trail** (p224)
- Cross ice-covered **Lake Baikal** (p219) on two wheels or four, on foot or by dog sled

Stolby Rock Formations
★ Lake Baikal
★ Olkhon Island
★ Circumbaikal Railway

ROUTE DISTANCE: 1088KM | DURATION: 41½ TO 44 HOURS

THE ROUTE
Krasnoyarsk to Tayshet

Heading east out of Krasnoyarsk (4098km), your fellow travellers will not have even fathomed there's a foreigner in their midst before the train crosses the 1km-long **Yenisey River bridge**, whose 1898 original won a gold medal at the 1900 Paris Expo (along with the Eiffel Tower).

The *Rossiya* makes short stops at **Zaozernaya** (4265km), from where a line runs north to the off-limits space centre of Krasnoyarsk-45, and at **Kansk-Yeniseysky** (for Kansk; 4344km). Historic Kansk, founded in 1636, boasts a scattering of century-old buildings, a freshly renovated Trinity Cathedral whose spire can be seen for miles around, an impressive bronze war memorial and an illuminated victory arch. With ample time, this is possibly the only community on this entire stretch worth getting off to see (just).

Ilanskaya (Ilansky; 4377km) has a small **museum** (10am-5pm Mon-Fri) in the 100-year-old, red-brick locomotive depot at the western end of the station, and an old locomotive and water tower behind the wooden station building. The *provodnitsa* (carriage attendant) allows passengers to roam for 20 minutes here, but will not rescue you from the police if you're arrested for taking photographs of the station (still considered espionage in Russia).

At **4474km**, the train passes into Irkutsk Oblast (region); local time becomes Moscow time plus five hours.

The *Rossiya* stops for just two minutes at **Tayshet** (4515km), but long enough for most people. This is the Trans-Siberian's westernmost junction with the BAM but most travellers change at Krasnoyarsk for through services to Severobaikalsk and Tynda. Tayshet was once an infamous transit point for Gulag prisoners.

Tayshet to Slyudyanka

If riding straight through from Moscow, you're now on day three but only halfway to the Pacific. As the railway skirts the foothills of the **Sayan Mountains**, endless taiga forests and a real sense of wilderness set in. However, at around **4560km** the line rises above the taiga and sweeps around bends for many kilometres offering good photo opportunities.

There's a 12-minute stop at mildly historical **Nizhneudinsk** (4678km), but as this comes after 10pm on the *Rossiya*, few are distracted from their vodka and bedtime instant noodles. Cossacks first built a small fortress here in 1649 and for over two centuries the town served as an important centre for gold and fur traders. The St Nicolas Church and the regional **museum** (ul Lenina 27; 8am-5pm) entice few off the rails, but an 18km hike along the Uda River to the 20m-high Ukovsky waterfalls could make for an adventurous side trip. Further east the landscape flattens out and the forests have been extensively logged. The next stop is **Tulun** (4795km), where you'll have just two minutes to contemplate the merits of the architecturally confident station building. From here a road heads 225km north to Bratsk (p261) on the BAM.

There's an overgenerous 30-minute break in proceedings at the former exile town of **Zima** (4934km), which translates ominously as 'winter'. More translation is required at **Polovina** (5087km; no stop for the *Rossiya*), whose name means roughly 'halfway' (between Moscow and Vladivostok), which it was in the early 20th century before the line was rerouted in many places. From here the train heads southeast and is joined by the Angara River around **Usole-Sibirskoe** (5118km), where a shuddering stop may jolt you from your slumber but hopefully not from your bunk altogether. The town supplies much of Russia's salt and many of its matches. By the time you reach oil-rich **Angarsk** (5145km), where there's a clock museum and a couple of good restaurants if you really want to get off, it's probably time to start collecting your belongings scattered around the compartment if you're alighting at Irkutsk.

Around the **5171km** marker, look north through the trees; 50m beyond the tracks behind two barbed wire fences are neat rows of decommissioned old tanks and rocket-launcher trucks (without rockets) rusting away thinking of their Cold War heyday. The train crosses the Irkut River 3km before **Irkutsk** (5185km; p211) station. Once nicknamed the 'Paris of Siberia', Irkutsk is the most popular Siberian stop for most transcontinental travellers, notably as a launching point to reach Lake Baikal, 70km further southeast.

Moving on from Irkutsk, the line takes a sharp right where the tracks once continued along the Angara River to Port Baikal, a

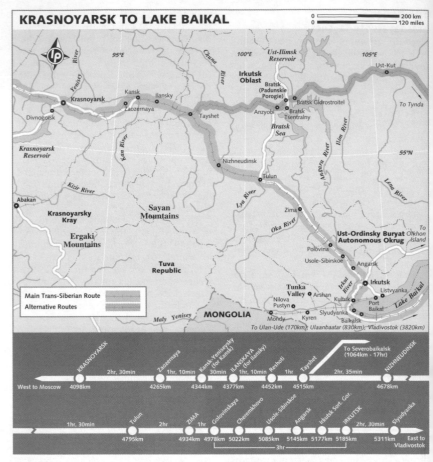

KRASNOYARSK TO LAKE BAIKAL

0 — 200 km
0 — 120 miles

Main Trans-Siberian Route
Alternative Routes

stretch flooded by the Angara Dam project. The early 1950s rerouting includes the tightest twists and the steepest descent on the entire line (providing great opportunities for photos of the train) just before **Kultuk** (5321km), where passengers get their first tantalising glimpse of **Lake Baikal**.

At **Slyudyanka** (5311km; p225), the lake is so close it's tempting to dash down for a quick dip. However, the scheduled stop here – usually no longer than three minutes – means that you could run the very real risk of being stranded in Siberia as the train chugs off without you. Our advice is to stay on the platform and snap up a snack of smoked *omul* (a fish native to Lake Baikal) from the hawkers instead.

KRASNOYARSK КРАСНОЯРСК

☎ 3912 / pop 910,000 / ⏱ Moscow +4hr

Vibrant, youthful and backed by attractive spikes of jagged forested foothills, Krasnoyarsk has a much more appealing setting than most typically flat Siberian cities. While its architecture isn't a particular strength, amid the predominantly unattractive post-WWII industrial structures are a few outstandingly well-embellished timber mansions and a sprinkling of art nouveau curves. Pleasant river trips and the nearby Stolby Nature Reserve, as well as the region's best concert halls, theatres and museums make Krasnoyarsk a most agreeable place to break a Trans-Siberian journey between Tomsk (612km west) and Lake Baikal.

Orientation

Near the Yenisey River's north bank, the city centre is a pedestrianised, ferroconcrete square where ul Uritskogo is gashed by thundering ul Veynbauma. The Stolby Reserve and ski slopes are over 10km west along the Yenisey's south bank.

Information

Internet Klub (ul Lenina 153; per hr R40; 🕑 10am–11pm) Beneath the Playboy shop.

Paradoks (☎ 239 795; pr Mira 96; per MB R4, per hr R24; 🕑 24hr) The best, most central internet access. Enter from an inner courtyard; follow the signs to the Alazani Georgian restaurant, which is opposite Paradoks.

Post office (ul Lenina 62; internet per hr R30; 🕑 8am–8pm Mon-Fri, to 7pm Sat)

ROSBank (pr Mira 7; 🕑 9am-7pm Mon-Thu, to 5.45pm Fri) Changes US dollars (pristine notes only) and travellers cheques, but service is slow.

Sberbank (ul Surikova 15; 🕑 9am-7pm Mon-Sat) Exchanges even the most dog-eared dollar notes.

Telephone office (pr Mira 102; 🕑 9am-noon & 1-6pm)

Sights

MUSEUMS & CHURCHES

The **Regional Museum** (Kraevedchesky muzey; ☎ 226 511; ul Dubrovinskogo 84; admission R70; 🕑 11am-7pm Tue-Sun) is one of Siberia's best. Its wonderfully incongruous 1912 building combines art nouveau and Egyptian temple–style features. Arranged around a Cossack explorer's ship are models, icons, historical room interiors and nature rooms where you can listen to local birdsong and animal cries. The basement hosts a splendid ethnographic section comparing the historical fashion sense of chamans from various tribal groups. The gift shop sells old coins, medals, postcards and excellent maps.

The interesting **Surikov Museum-Estate** (Muzey-usadba V I Surikova; ☎ 231 507; ul Lenina 98; admission R45; 🕑 10am-6pm Tue-Sat) preserves the house, sheds and vegetable patch of 19th-century painter Vasily Surikov (1848–1916). The heavy-gated garden forms a refreshing oasis of rural Siberia right in the city centre. More of Surikov's work is on show at the cute **Surikov Art Museum** (☎ 652 881; ul Parizhskoy Kommuny 20; admission R45; 🕑 10am-6pm Tue-Sun).

Permanently docked below the ugly brown-concrete building of the former Lenin Museum is the boat **SV Nikolai** (☎ 239 403; admission R15; 🕑 10am-8pm Tue-Sun), which transported Vladimir to exile in Shushenskoe.

For great city views climb Karaulnaya Hill to the pointy little **chasovnya** (chapel), which features on the Russian R10 banknote. At midday there's a deafening one-gun salute here. Attractive old churches abound, including the fancy 1795 **Intercession Cathedral** (Pokrovskoe sobor; ul Surikova) and the top-heavy but elegant **Resurrection Church** (Blagoveshchensky tserkov; ul 9 Yanvarya), built between 1804 and 1822, decapitated in the 1930s then retowered in 1998. Its icon-filled interior billows with incense.

STOLBY NATURE RESERVE & BOBROVY LOG SKI RESORT

Arguably Krasnoyarsk's greatest attractions are the spiky volcanic rock pillars called **stolby**. These litter the woods in the 17,000-hectare Stolby Nature Reserve (Zapovednik Stolby) south of the Yenisey River. To reach the main concentration of pillars, start by walking 7km down a track near Turbaza Yenisey (bus 50). Halfway along is a visitors centre. Alternatively, there is much easier access via a year-round **chairlift** (🕑 Tue-Sun) belonging to the new ski resort. From the top, walk for two minutes to a great lookout or around 40 minutes to reach the impressive Takmak Stolby. Tours are available, personalised in English with **SibTourGuide** (☎ 512 654; www.sibtourguide.com), priced according to itinerary, or in Russian through **KBPE** (Krasnoyarskoe Byuro Putishestvy i Ekskursy; ☎ 271 626; buro@hotelkrs.ru; 1st fl, Hotel Krasnoyarsk; per person for groups of many/3/2/1 R500/700/1000/1500; 🕑 10am-6pm Mon-Fri, to 3pm Sat), where tours last six hours. Infected ticks are dangerous between May and July and tick

---

KRASNOYARSK TO LAKE BAIKAL ROUTE PLANNER

Here's a suggested itinerary for continuing from Krasnoyarsk to Lake Baikal:

Day 1: Take overnight train from Krasnoyarsk to Irkutsk (19 hours)

Day 2: Arrive Irkutsk, then head out for a tour of the city

Day 3: Bus to Taltsy Museum of Wooden Architecture then on to lakeside Listvyanka for one night

Day 4: Return to Irkutsk, catch train for short hop to Slyudyanka for more lake views and perhaps a ride on the Circumbaikal Railway to Port Baikal

KRASNOYARSK TO LAKE BAIKAL

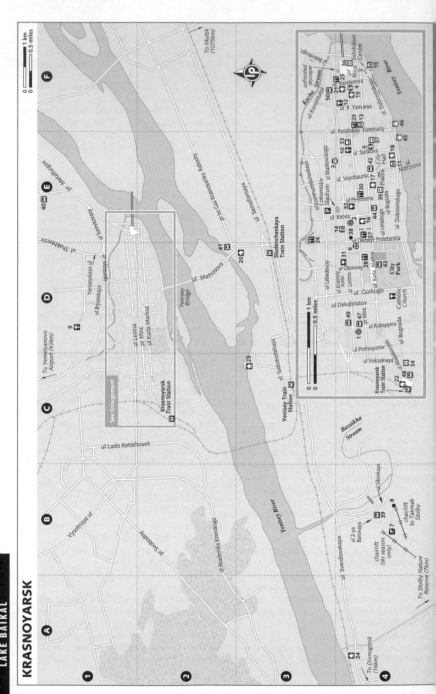

protection or predeparture encephalitis jabs are essential at this time.

Below Stolby, the slap and swish of skis and snowboards can be heard at the spanking new **Bobrovy Log ski resort** (☎ 568 686; www.bobrovylog .ru). Snow cannons keep the slopes going well into May, and in the summer months the Rodelbahn (a kind of downhill forest roller coaster), a pool and regular sports events keep the fun level high. Ask at the year-round, English-speaking **information centre** (☎ 568 686) about ski hire, lift passes and other tickets.

Tours

Experienced tour guide Anatoliy Brewhanov offers thoughtfully personalised English-speaking tour services aimed at independent travellers through **SibTourGuide** (☎ 512 654; www.sibtourguide.com). Congenial homestays and imaginative trips are on offer; check out the useful website. **KBPE** (Krasnoyarskoe Byuro Putishestvy i Ekskursy; ☎ 271 626; buro@hotelkrs.ru; 1st fl, Hotel Krasnoyarsk; ☒ 10am-6pm Mon-Fri, to 3pm Sat) is a commercial tour agency.

Sleeping

For English-speaking homestays, try Sib-TourGuide (above), which can arrange accommodation in apartments mostly in the high-rise Vyetluzhanka area, 20 minutes' drive west of the centre (but well served by city buses 91, 75 and 43).

BUDGET

Resting rooms (komnaty otdykha; ☎ 484 635; train station; dm per 12hr from R250) Clean and cheap station dorm rooms.

Turbaza Yenisey (☎ 698 110; ul Sverdlovskaya 140/7; d & tw R500-2000; P ☒) Despite the name this is a two-storey hotel. Good-value renovated rooms are simple but neat and share sparkling-clean showers. Some of the pricier doubles have private facilities. There's a glimpse of river from the communal terrace, but no cafe.

Hotel Gostiny Dvor (☎ 232 857; pr Mira 81; dm R550-700, s R700-1000, tw R1000-2200) The best cheap sleep in town enjoys a superb central position, a lovely facade and fully renovated rooms sharing brand-new toilets and showers. Kettles in some rooms; 25% booking fee.

Hotel Ogni Yeniseyya (☎ 275 262; ul Dubrovinskogo 80; s R650-1380, tw R2000) Has miserable rooms off bile-green corridors, but there are private bathrooms and visa registration is possible.

Krasnoyarskstroystrategiya (☎ 276 611; pr Mira 12; s R1100, tw R2400) Good value if utterly unpronounceable. Spruced up but now slightly overpriced ex-Soviet rooms have new furniture

KRASNOYARSK TO LAKE BAIKAL

DETOUR: YENISEY RIVER GORGE

The scenic Yenisey River gorge, with its forested hills and tiny timber villages, is popularly viewed from Krasnoyarsk to Divnogorsk hydrofoils. A 5km taxi hop beyond Divnogorsk jetty stands the impressive 1km-long **hydroelectric dam** (GES). Visiting the turbine rooms isn't allowed, but from a distance you can observe the remarkable contraption that lifts ships over the dam. **Boat rentals** are available on the reservoir beyond. **Hydrofoils** (R150, 45 minutes) buzz between Krasnoyarsk and Divnogorsk every two hours from May to late September. Pay on board.

The trip is also pleasant by road, allowing a stop in semiquaint Ovsyanka village, with its cute wooden **St Inokent Chapel** (ul Shchetinkina), an interesting **House Museum** (ul Shchetinkina 26; admission R30; ☺ 10am-6pm Tue-Sun) dedicated to famous local writer Victor Astafiev, who died in 2001, and the **Last Bow Museum** (ul Shchetinkina 35; admission R30; ☺ 10am-6pm Tue-Sun), which gives a taste of rural Siberian life.

---

and double glazing holding back the incessant traffic din. Enter from ul Karatanova.

MIDRANGE

Hotel Turist (☎ 361 470; ul Matrosova 2; s R1900-2400, tw R2200) On a busy roundabout directly across the long Yenisey Bridge from the city centre, this 16-storey Soviet monolith has variable rooms with toilet and shower. It almost always has rooms free when everything else is full.

Hotel Krasnoyarsk (☎ 749 400; www.hotelkrs.ru; ul Uritskogo 94; s/tw/ste from R2630/3780/7400; ☒) This sprawling eight-storey concrete slab dominates Krasnoyarsk's central square. It retains the Soviet-vintage *dezhurnaya* (floor-lady) system but is well kept with bright corridors, totally rebuilt full-service rooms and English-speaking receptionists. Only the suites have air-conditioning.

ourpick Siberian Safari Club (☎ 613 335; www .hotelsafari.ru; ul Sudostroitelnaya 117a; s/d R3000/4000) This intimate and well-appointed 34-room hotel occupies a pleasantly quiet spot on the riverbank and, although walls are thin, it's arguably Krasnoyarsk's best option. Attentive reception staff speak faultless English, there's a classy terrace restaurant (meals from R1000) and booking is advisable (a 25% booking fee applies to 'standard' rooms only). Bus 36 stops a 10-minute walk away.

Hotel Oktyabrskaya (☎ 273 780; www.hoteloctober .ru, in Russian; pr Mira 15; s R3800, d R5800) Comfortable and professionally run with rooms approximating chintzy Western standards, albeit without air-con. Satellite TV includes CNN and some English is spoken.

Eating

There are many eateries along pr Mira, summer cafes on the promenade near the river station,

and cheap snack stalls in the extensive **central market** (☺ 8am-6pm). On summer evenings, lively beer bars and shashlyk (kebab) grills give the concrete, fountain-filled square outside Hotel Krasnoyarsk a convivial piazza feel.

Burzhuy (☎ 661 072; 2nd fl, Metropol bldg, pr Mira 10; pelmeni R40; ☺ 10am-8pm) Cheap and very popular self-service lunch spot where office workers swap chit-chat over plates of *pelmeni* (dumplings) at formica tables. The 'ear bread' comes with countless fillings or choose from other hot dishes and salads.

ourpick Kalinka Malinka (☎ 238 824; pr Mira 91a; mains R70-200; ☺ noon-midnight) Nostalgia meets Russian MTV at this trendy, new, Soviet-theme cafe that celebrates the diverse cuisine of all the former Soviet republics minus the knick-knackery of other retro eateries. Enjoy a Eurasian feast of Ukrainian *serniki* (cottage cheese fritters), Georgian *khachapuri* (cheese bread) and Kazakh *beshparmak* (horse meat and noodles), with Moldovan wines or Russian beer. Second branch at pr Mira 85.

Krasnaya Palatka (☎ 560 686; Bobrovy Log ski resort; meals R100; ☺ 10am-10pm) Watch skiers slither down the slopes from the huge circular windows at this film-themed, self-service cafeteria. The decor is trendy but the Russian and international dishes are unexciting and perhaps appreciated more after a long day in the Stolby.

Sultan Suleyman (☎ 270 070; ul Perensona 20; meals R150-350; ☺ noon-midnight) Behind the lovely 1913 Dom Ofitserov building, midpriced Turko-Russian food is served in a semi-oriental basement. In the front is a handy fast-food joint.

Retro (☎ 277 203; pr Mira 29; meals R300; ☺ noon-midnight) Confused decor combining Marilyn Monroe, the Eiffel Tower and cobbled Central Europe, but tasty if pricey meat, seafood and salads. For dessert try 'gifts of the taiga' – ice cream with forest berries, honey and cedar nuts. English menu.

Drinking

Kinopark Pikra (ul Perensona 29a; beers R35-50) An atmospheric, great-value basement pub within a cinema-bar complex. The bar is easy to miss: follow signs to the toilets.

Traveller's Coffee (pr Mira 54; coffees R55-100; ☽ 8am-midnight) A tempting aroma of newly milled beans lures you into this Starbucks-style coffee house, which blends empire-style sofas with exposed heating pipes. Smiley service and sensibly priced milkshakes, muffins and pancakes.

Bar Chemodan (☎ 230 259; ul Lenina 116; set 3-course lunches R350, beers R280; ☽ noon-midnight) This is a wonderfully atmospheric if fiercely expensive 1920s-themed pub-restaurant stocking dozens of whiskies. The stair lift outside is for both the disabled and the inebriated.

Entertainment

Che Guevara (☎ 595 857; ul Bograda; admission after 7pm R300-500; ☽ noon-1am Sun-Wed, to 5am Thu-Sat) Has dancing or live music in a fun saloon-club with 1950s pin-ups and a commie-Cuba theme.

Rock-Jazz Kafe (☎ 523 305; ul Surikova 12; ☽ 4pm-6am Tue-Sun) Entered through a small bar beside the Dublin Irish Pub, this dark venue showcases live bands around an upturned motorcycle from 6pm most days.

Opera-Ballet Theatre (☎ 278 697; ul Perensona 2; tickets from R120) The architecturally nondescript theatre has up to five early evening shows per week from October to June.

Philharmonia (☎ 274 930; pl Mira 2b) Has three concert halls showcasing folk, pop and classical music.

Getting There & Away

AIR

From Krasnoyarsk's Yemelyanovo airport, you can fly to almost anywhere in Russia. Local airline **KrasAir** (www.krasair.ru, in Russian) has connections to Moscow (from R12,000, up to four daily), while **Katekavia** operates flights to Kyzyl (R3300, daily). **Bilet Market** (☎ 661 432; www.b-m.su, in Russian; ul Lenina 115; ☽ 8am-8pm Mon-Fri, to 7pm Sat & Sun) is a centrally located, one-stop shop for all air, bus and train tickets.

BOAT

Every few days in summer, passenger boats from Krasnoyarsk's **river station** (☎ 274 446; ☽ 8am-7pm) ply the Yenisey to Dudinka (4½ to five days, 1989km), but foreigners may not proceed beyond Igarka (which is above the Arctic Circle). After four days of going with the flow, most travellers fly back to Krasnoyarsk.

TRAIN

All major Trans-Siberian and China-bound trains stop at Krasnoyarsk. Train 055 is the best sleeper choice for Novosibirsk (R2560, 11½ hours), Yekaterinburg (R2508, 32 hours) and Moscow (R7920, two days 11 hours), while Tomsk (R565 *platskart*, 14 hours) is a 12-hour hop on train 011 (though this service leaves rather inconveniently at 3.30am). Six or more trains daily take around 19 hours to Irkutsk (R2040). Train 092 along the BAM takes 30 hours to Severobaikalsk (R2660).

A branch line currently runs south from Krasnoyarsk to Abakan, the capital of the fertile Khakassia Republic. En route this passes through Kuragino, which will in coming years become the junction for a new route as far as Kyzyl, the capital of Tuva. The first services are due to start running in 2013.

There are railway booking offices in the river and bus stations, but **Bilet Market** (☎ 661 432; www.b-m.su, in Russian; ul Lenina 115; ☽ 8am-8pm Mon-Fri, to 7pm Sat & Sun) is the most central option.

Getting Around

From assorted points near the train station, trolleybus 7 and several buses run via the city centre towards Hotel Oktyabrskaya. Some follow ul Karla Marksa, others pr Mira. Bus 50 links the city centre with attractions along the southern bank of the Yenisey (such as the Stolby Nature Reserve), while new service 37 (R10) runs from the train station direct to the ski resort. Trolleybus 2 runs along pr Mira to the bus station, from where bus 135 takes around 50 minutes to Yemelyanovo airport.

Hydrofoils to Divnogorsk depart from the river station, while regular *marshrutky* (fixed-route minibuses; R43) leave from a small bus station south of the river.

IRKUTSK ИРКУТСК

☎ 3952 / pop 591,000 / ☽ Moscow+5hr

With its fancifully rebuilt churches, grand 19th-century architecture, Anglophone tour agencies, imaginative eateries and real (if small) hostels, Irkutsk is, quite deservedly,

IRKUTSK

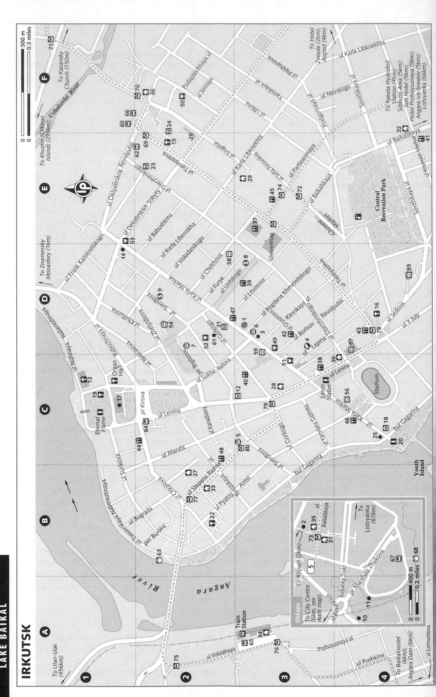

one of the most popular stops on the entire Trans-Siberian Railway. Though still 70km from its shores, it's also the nearest city to wonderful Lake Baikal and the easiest place from which to book tours and accommodation by the lake's shimmering waters. Beware that in summer even Irkutsk's largest hotels can be booked up and expensive even by Siberian standards. Book ahead.

History

Founded in 1651 as a Cossack garrison to control the indigenous Buryats, Irkutsk was the springboard for 18th-century expeditions to the far north and east, including Alaska, then known as 'Irkutsk's American district'.

As eastern Siberia's trade and administrative centre, Irkutsk dispatched Siberian furs and ivory to Mongolia, Tibet and China in exchange for silk and tea. Three-quarters of the city burnt down in a disastrous fire in 1879. However, the 1880s Lena Basin gold rush saw its grand brick mansions and public buildings restored and many still stand today.

The 'Paris of Siberia' did not welcome news of the October Revolution. The city's well-to-do merchants only succumbed to the Red tide in 1920, with the capture and execution of White Army commander Admiral Kolchak, whose controversial statue was re-erected in 2004. Soviet-era planning saw Irkutsk develop as the sprawling industrial and scientific centre that it remains today.

Orientation

The bustling train station is directly across the Angara River from the city centre. Grand ul Karla Marksa is the historic commercial centre. From the administrative centre (pl Kirova), ul Lenina parallels the river to the Raising of the Cross Church, where it becomes ul Sedova. Nearly 6km further south, this road's continuation reaches the Angara Dam (GES). Many hotels, souvenir stalls and bookshops sell city maps.

Information

BOOKSHOPS

Knigomir (ul Karla Marksa 28; ⏰ 9am-7pm Mon-Sat, 10am-5pm Sun) Sells maps of Irkutsk (R80) and many other Baikal towns, as well as Russian guides, atlases and large wall maps of Lake Baikal (R250).

INTERNET ACCESS

Epitsentr (ul Bogdana Khmelnitskogo 1; per MB R3, per hr R60; ⏰ 9am-10pm Mon-Fri, 11am-9pm Sat & Sun) Irkutsk's only surviving internet cafe located in a cellar behind a computer shop.

INTERNET RESOURCES

Baikal.ru (www.baikal.ru) Partly translated with old-postcard portraits of various Irkutsk streets.

IrkutskOut (www.irkutskout.ru, in Russian) A wealth of practical details including cafe and restaurant listings, but often goes offline.

WWW Irkutsk (www.irkutsk.org) Bags of information on every aspect of the city.

MONEY

ATMs abound.

Moy Bank (ul Gryaznova 1; ⏰ 11am-3pm & 4-6.45pm Mon-Fri) Head to counter 1 for good euro rates.

Sberbank (2nd fl, ul Uritskogo 19; ⏰ 9am-7pm Mon-Fri, 9am-5pm Sat, 10am-4pm Sun) Change even the shoddiest dollar notes at counter 8.

VTB Bank (ul Sverdlova; ⏰ 9am-6pm Mon-Fri) Only bank in town willing to accept British pounds and Chinese yuán.

POST

Post office (ul Stepana Razina 23; ⏰ 8am-9pm Mon-Fri, 9am-8pm Sat, 9am-6pm Sun) Bigger branches at per Bogdanov 8 and ul Karla Marksa 28.

TRAVEL AGENCIES

Local tour operators are useful not only for organising local excursions but also for booking hotels and train tickets. Note, though, that most have only one or two overstretched English speakers, so you may need some patience.

BaikalComplex (⏰ 461 557; www.baikalcomplex .com) Busy, well-organised operation, offering homestays

and trips tailored for Western travellers. Call to arrange a meeting.

Baikaler (⏰ 336 240; www.baikaler.com) Imaginative Jack Sheremetoff speaks very good English and is well tuned to budget-traveller needs. Original, personalised tours and a great central hostel.

Green Express (⏰ 734 400; www.greenexpress.ru; ul Dekabrskikh Sobyty 24) Big, professional outfit with a hotel in Listvyanka, yurts on Olkhon Island and many mountain biking, horse riding and other tour options.

Sights

MUSEUMS & GALLERIES

Irkutsk's pleasant if fairly standard **Regional Museum** (Kraevedchesky muzey; ⏰ 333 449; ul Karla Marksa 2; admission R100; ⏰ 10am-6pm Tue-Sun) is within a fancy 1870s brick building that formerly housed the Siberian Geographical Society, a club of Victorian-style gentlemen-explorers. The small gift shop is good for birch-bark boxes and jewellery made from purple chaorite, a unique Siberian mineral. Across the road, a newly recast **statue of Tsar Alexander III** stands bushy-bearded on the riverfront promenade, copying a 1904 original.

The grand old **Art Gallery** (ul Lenina 5; admission R100; ⏰ 10am-5.30pm Tue-Sun) has a valuable though poorly lit collection ranging from Mongolian *thangkas* (Buddhist religious paintings) to Russian-Impressionist canvases. Behind a photogenic 1909 facade, its **sub-gallery** (ul Karla Marksa 23; admission R100; ⏰ 10am-6pm Tue-Sun) is strong on Siberian landscapes and petroglyph rubbings and has some superb 17th-century icons.

A collection of Soviet tanks and missile launchers guards the **Dom Ofitserov** (ul Karla Marksa 47), which has a sporadically open museum and occasional concerts of patriotic songs.

DECEMBRIST HOUSES

After completing their terms of labour near Chita, many Decembrists settled in Irkutsk with their families, who had earlier followed them into exile (see p217). Two of the homes (those of Prince Sergei Trubetskoy and Count Sergei Volkonsky) are now touching museums with furnishings and family pictures.

The **Volkonsky House Museum** (⏰ 207 532; per Volkonskogo 10; admission R90; ⏰ 10am-6pm Tue-Sun) is a short walk behind the pretty pink **Preobrazheniya Gospodnya Church** (ul Timiryazeva). The mansion is set in a courtyard with stables, a barn and servant quarters (beware of the dog). Downstairs is an (over-)renovated piano room; upstairs is a photo exhibition including portraits of Maria and other 1820s women who romantically followed their husbands and lovers into exile. Labels are only in Russian but a R70 English-language pamphlet tells the stories. The smaller **Trubetskoy House Museum** (ul Dzerzhinskogo) was dismantled and carted off for renovation in late 2007 but should be back in 2009.

CHURCHES

The magnificent Annunciation Cathedral that once dominated pl Kirova was demolished during one of Stalin's bad moods. It was replaced by a hulking concrete **regional administrative building**, the ex-Communist Party headquarters. Tragic. Behind this ugly centrepiece, however, two notable churches still survive. The whitewashed 1706 **Saviour's Church** (Spasskaya tserkov; ☯ 8am-8pm) has remnants of murals on its facade and until a few years ago housed a museum, hence the rather colourless interior. Much more eye-catching is the fairy-tale ensemble of the **Bogoyavlensky Cathedral** (ul Nizhnaya Naberezhnaya), whose restored salmon, white and green towers add a colourful dazzle to the otherwise rather grimy riverfront.

Set in a leafy garden behind a rather noisy roundabout, the 1762 **Znamensky Monastery** is 1.5km northeast of the Bogoyavlensky Cathedral. Echoing with mellifluous plainsong, the interior has splendidly muralled vaulting, a towering iconostasis and a gold sarcophagus holding the miraculous relics of Siberian missionary St Inokent. Celebrity graves outside include the nautically themed tomb of Grigory Shelekhov, the man who claimed Alaska for Russia, and a much humbler headstone belonging to Decembrist wife, Yekaterina Trubetskaya. White-Russian commander Admiral Kolchak was executed by Bolsheviks near the spot where his **statue** was controversially erected in November 2004 at the entrance to the monastery grounds; the plinth is exaggeratedly high enough to reduce vandalism.

The 1758 baroque **Raising of the Cross Church** (Krestovozdvizhenskaya tserkov; ul Sedova 1; admission by donation) has a fine interior of gilt-edged icons and several examples of unusually intricate brickwork in a rounded style that's unique to Irkutsk and the Selenga Delta village of Posolskoe. The newest gilt spires to puncture Irkutsk's boxy skyline belong to the 18th-century **Trinity Church** (Troitsky khram; ul 5 Armii 8), where restoration work continues apace. The gigantic **Kazansky Church** (ul Barrikad) is a Disney-esque confection of salmon-pink walls and fluoro turquoise domes topped with gold baubled crosses. Get off tram 4 two stops northeast of the bus station.

OTHER HISTORIC STRUCTURES

A few charming **wooden houses** with lacy, carved decoration can still be found in Irkutsk's older quarters, especially on and around ul Dekabrskikh Sobyty east of ul Timiryazeva. The grandest brick architecture is along ul Karla Marksa, which hosts various minor museums. Opposite the Regional Museum stands the former **White House** (Bely dom; ul Karla Marksa), built in 1804 as the residence of the governors general of Eastern Siberia. It now serves as a university library.

ANGARA DAM AREA

Some 6km southeast of the centre, the 1956 **Angara Dam** extends 2km across the river. Its construction raised Lake Baikal by up to 1m, causing various human and environmental problems, but the dam itself is hardly an attraction. Moored nearby, the **Angara ice-breaker** (admission R40; ☯ 10am-6pm Tue-Sun) was originally imported in kit form from Newcastle-upon-Tyne to carry Trans-Siberian Railway passengers across Lake Baikal (the trains went on her bigger sister ship *Baikal,* which sank years ago). The steamer is now a less-than-inspiring museum reached by a permanent gangway.

Diving

It's possible to go diving in Lake Baikal. See p325 for a list of operators.

Sleeping

Travel agencies arrange homestays in Irkutsk and the villages around Lake Baikal. Prices typically can start at R500 per bed, though R800 (sometimes with full board) is more common. Check the location: the cheapest places can be 10km or more from the city centre.

BUDGET
Hostels

Irkutsk has four tiny private hostels. All have good shared toilets, shower and kitchen.

They are ideal for finding English-speaking assistance, arranging tours or meeting fellow travellers, and unlike hotels they don't charge booking fees. There are also **resting rooms** (komnaty otdykha; per hr R45, sheets R57) at the train station.

Baikalhostel (☎ 525 742; www.baikalhostels.com; apt 1, ul Lermontova 136; dm €12-14) This German-owned hostel has received rave reviews from several travellers, despite its very inconvenient and insalubrious location, several kilometres south of the train station; take *marshrutka* 12 to stop Mikrochirurgia Glaza. Excellent website.

Irkutsk Downtown Hostel (☎ 334 597; www.hostel .irkutsk.ru; apt 12, ul Stepana Razina 12; dm R500) Snug and welcoming 11-bed apartment-hostel above the Vostochny Ekspress Bank. Breakfast is included and there's internet access for R1 per minute. It may be moving to larger, more central premises, so check the website. Take tram 1 from the train station.

Admiral Hostel (☎ 742 440; apt 1, ul Cheremkhovsky 6; dm R500) The name may have been inspired by Admiral Kolchak but things are less than ship-shape here, as this newcomer is left unstaffed for long periods and lacks a true backpacker vibe. These may be just teething problems, as otherwise the spacious dorm, large kitchen and city-centre location make these decent digs.

our pick **Baikaler Hostel** (☎ 336 240; www.baikaler .com; apt 11, ul Lenina 9; dm R600; 🍽 💻) Beds are limited at this fantastic, super-central apartment hostel. Spacious dorms are cleaned every day and friendly staff will bend over backwards to help. Entrance is from the rear of the building. Free internet and wi-fi.

Hotels

Uzory (☎ 209 239; ul Oktyabrskoy Revolyutsii 17; s/tw/ tr R600/900/1350) Clean, unpretentious rooms with leopard-skin-patterned blankets but communal bathrooms and toilets. Popular with independent travellers and the best budget option when the city's hostels are all fully booked.

Hotel Profsoyuznaya (☎ 357 963; ul Baikalskaya 263; dm R649, tw R1130) Simple but well-kept Soviet-era rooms, albeit far from the centre in the distant SibExpo area. Tram 5 stops outside.

Hotel Gornyak (☎ 243 754; ul Lenina 24; s R1300-1800, tw R3000) Friendly, central and small, this hotel has reasonably presentable rooms with private

shower and toilet. However, with no breakfast or visa registration this cuts a poor deal. Enter from ul Dzerzhinskogo.

MIDRANGE & TOP END

Hotel Yevropa (☎ 291 515; www.europehotel.ru; ul Baikalskaya 69; s/d from R2500/3500; 🅿 🍽) Behind nine towering Doric columns, immaculate rooms are realistically priced at this four-star newcomer. Reception staff speak English and the Western-style buffet breakfast is reportedly the best in town.

Hotel Delta (☎ 794 090; www.grandbaikal.ru; ul Karla Libknekhta 58; s/d R3000/4400; 🅿 💻) The functional new motel-standard rooms here have little panache, but are good value for their relatively central position. Aimed primarily at business travellers.

Hotel Zvezda (☎ 540 000; www.zvezdahotel.ru; ul Yadrintseva; s/d R3500/3800, ste R5700-12,000; 🅿 🍽 💻) Within a new, Swiss chalet–style building, rooms here are modern and comfortable, service is pleasant and English is spoken. The peaceful location is 300m south of Retro 2. Its atmospheric restaurant specialises in game and exotic meats.

Sun Hotel (☎ 255 910; www.eastland.ru; ul Baikalskaya 295b; s R4000-5000, d R5000-6000; 🅿 🍽 💻) Situated in the SibExpo area near the dam, the Sun has slick rooms with impressive bathrooms, generous minibars and stylish dark-wood furnishings. Reception staff speak English but the lobby lacks facilities.

Eating

RESTAURANTS

Krendel (☎ 706 156; ul Gryaznova 1; mains R80-180, coffees R30-70, pancakes R45; 🕑 10am-2am Mon-Fri, 11am-2am Sat & Sun) The half-baked rustic theme detracts unnecessarily from tasty and sensibly priced grub at this new self-service open-all-hours cafe. The hot soups do the trick when the mercury goes south.

our pick **Kochevnik** (☎ 200 459; www.modernnomads .mn; ul Gorkogo 19; mains R150-400; 🕑 6pm-2am) Take your taste buds to the Mongolian steppe for some yurt-size portions of mutton, lamb and steak as well as filling soups and *buuzy* (steamed, palm-sized dumplings). An English menu and smiley service.

Pervach (☎ 201 288; ul Chkalova 33; meals R200-350, beers R100; 🕑 noon-1am) Pervach offers imaginative Baikal-based menus in a vaulted stone-and-brick cellar, heated by real fires in winter. Some English is spoken.

Snezhinka (☎ 344 862; opposite ul Karla Marksa 25; meals R200-350; ☯ 11am-midnight) Warm, cosy, belle époque cafe-restaurant with attentive service and consistently good food. The swirling ironwork furniture is suitably padded.

Korchma (☎ 209 102; ul Krasnykh Madyar 52; meals R250-600; ☯ noon-2am) Home-cooked traditional Russian food in a one-room cottage restaurant. It's set amid other more genuine Siberian log homes, which have so far survived intense development pressures. Meals are presented on two-tone ceramics, while an accordionist accompanies a talented, costumed folk singer (R50 to R100 cover).

CAFES & QUICK EATS

The modern but lively **Central Market** (ul Chekhova; ☯ 8am-8pm) overflows with fresh produce, while cafes and other eateries abound, especially on ul Karla Marksa.

Domino (ul Lenina 13a; bliny R40, pizza slices R70; ☯ 24hr) A popular spot because of its all-night service.

Fiesta (ul Uritskogo; snacks R50-120; ☯ noon-11pm) This is the most atmospheric and congenial of Irkutsk's numerous fast-food outlets; wi-fi is free if you eat there.

Poznaya Sytny Ryad (ul Partizanskaya 9a; meals R70-150; ☯ 10am-11pm) The most appealing of the city's cheap *pozy* joints is in a primly faux-rural timber house surrounded by the disarray of the Chinese quarter.

our pick **Russkaya Chaynaya** (☎ 201 676; ul Karla Marksa 3; mains R150-300, coffees R70-140; ☯ 10am-11pm) This wonderful place boasts a plush fin de siècle interior equipped with gleaming samovars, *matryoshka* (nesting doll) salt and pepper shakers and a collection of yesteryear tea boxes. The Astroturfed summer beer garden belongs to the Red Hall Pub below.

Na Zamorskoy (☎ 290 891; ul Timiryazeva; meals R200-400, coffees R35-200; ☯ 9am-11pm Mon-Fri, from 11am Sat & Sun) Fresh roses, rattan furniture, raffia-threaded blinds and lots of potted plants make this a soothing lunch spot. Enjoy delicious ham-and-cheese-stuffed bliny (pancakes) and an excellent latte, while watching the trams rattle past the church opposite.

Wiener Café (Venskoe Kafe; ☎ 202 116; ul Stepana Razina 19; meals R300-450, coffees R70-230; ☯ 10am-11pm) It's an alluring coffee house with marble-top tables, Parisian-bar chairs and sepia photos. Reasonably priced pastries and freshly prepared porridge make this a great breakfast retreat.

Drinking

our pick **Liverpool** (☎ 202 512; ul Sverdlova 28; imported beers R80-160; ☯ noon-3am) This Fab Four theme pub may be a bit more Wings than Beatles,

---

THE DECEMBRIST MOVEMENT

Across Siberia, notably in Irkutsk, Chita and Novoselenginsk, interesting museums commemorate the 'Decembrist' gentlemen-rebels. This group of aristocratic, liberal-leaning army officers had occupied Senate Sq in St Petersburg in an ill-conceived coup against Tsar Nicholas I. The date was 26 December 1825, hence their sobriquet.

The mutineers were poorly organised and outnumbered, but Nicholas I was loathe to mark the start of his reign with a full-blown domestic massacre. After a stand-off, which lasted most of the day, troops fired several canister shots into the square killing about 60 people. The rebellion crumbled and five leaders were executed. Another 121 organisers were sentenced to hard labour, prison and exile in Siberia where they became romantic heroes of a sort. But the real heroes were their womenfolk, many of whom abandoned their lives of comfort and sophistication to follow their husbands or lovers into exile. The first was the faithful Yekaterina Trubetskaya. The story goes that having travelled 6000km by coach to Nerchinsk, she immediately descended into the silver mines to find her husband.

Others had to wait for months in Irkutsk or Chita for permission to see their men, meanwhile setting up small social circles that encouraged 'Western civilisation' in these hitherto wild-east backwaters. Over two decades the exiled families opened schools, formed scientific societies and edited newspapers. Maria Volkonskaya, popularly known as the 'Princess of Siberia', founded a local hospital and opened a concert theatre, in addition to hosting musical and cultural soirées in her home.

The Decembrists were granted amnesty when Nicholas I died in 1855. Although many of them, including Maria Volkonskaya, returned to St Petersburg, their legacy lived on for decades.

but it's one of Irkutsk's top watering holes with an intercontinental beer menu and laid-back service. All the meals are imaginatively named after Beatles tracks, but we were assured that 'In an Octopus' Garden' contains no octopus.

U Shveyka (☎ 242 687; ul Karla Marksa 34; beers R110, meals R200-400; 🕑 noon-midnight; 🖭) This Czech-style cellar pub with staring elk heads and yin-yang condiments has a good summer beer terrace.

Cheshskaya Pivovarnaya (☎ 538 482; ul Krasnogvardeyskaya 29; beers from R110, meals R200-425) Irkutsk's unpretentious microbrewery-pub creates its own Czech Pils.

Chili (☎ 332 190; ul Karla Marksa 26; cocktails from R200, meals R250-600; 🕑 24hr) Aztec-themed night spot and all-day bar where you can join Irkutsk's moneyed youth on beige couches bathed in flamingo neon for a flashy cocktail or an outrageously overpriced meal. Very central.

Bierhaus (☎ 550 555; ul Karla Marksa; beers from R210; 🕑 noon-2am Mon-Thu, to 4am Fri & Sat, to midnight Sun) This upmarket Bavarian-style *bierstube* (beer hall with heavy wooden furniture) serves Newkie Brown and Guinness as well as German beers and sausages. English menu.

Entertainment

On summer evenings romantic couples and jolly groups of locals stroll the Angara promenade and the grassy areas behind the fine **Okhlopkov Drama Theatre** (☎ 200 477; ul Karla Marksa 14).

Circus (☎ 336 139; ul Zhelyabova; tickets R100-250) Puts on eye-boggling Cirque du Soleil–style performances. Avoid the cheapest front seats where you'll get poor views and a regular splashing.

Philharmonic Hall (☎ 241 100; ul Dzerzhinskogo 2) Historic building staging regular children's shows and musical programs from pop to classical.

Musical Theatre (☎ 277 795; ul Sedova; tickets from R500; 🕑 box office 10am-7pm Tue-Sun) Pantomimes, ballets and costumed musical-comedy shows in a big concrete auditorium.

Poznaya Disko-bar (ul Chekhova 17; admission R100; 🕑 9pm-4am) Tobacco-fogged dive, popular with student drinkers on modest budgets.

Stratosphera Night Club (☎ 243 033; www.strata-club.ru, in Russian; ul Karla Marksa 15; cover from R250; 🕑 6pm-6am Fri-Sun) Irkutsk's most central late-night hot spot, with bowling alley, two-storey disco and three-storey drink prices.

Getting There & Away

AIR

Irkutsk's antiquated little 'international' airport is handily placed near the city centre. Foreign destinations include Baku in Azerbeijan (R16,500), Tashkent (R14,500) and Dushanbe (R13,300), as well as Bangkok (R20,350), Běijīng (R17,000) and the Chinese cities of Shěnyáng (R14,000) and Dàlián (R10,000).

To Moscow's Domodedovo airport, there are direct flights with S7 Airlines (R7980 to R10,150, daily) and Aeroflot (R6650, daily). Handy regional hops include Kyzyl (R5300, Saturday) and Nizhneangarsk (R3800, three weekly). Irkutsk also enjoys direct air links to dozens of other domestic destinations, with tickets for all services sold through the convenient **Central Air Agency** (☎ 341 596; ul Gorkogo 29; 🕑 8am-8pm, to 7pm winter).

BOAT

In July and August hydrofoils buzz up Lake Baikal to Severobaikalsk and Nizhneangarsk (R2000, 11½ hours), stopping off in Port Baikal and Olkhon Island (R1500). Departures from Irkutsk are timetabled at 8.50am on Tuesday and Friday, returning the next day, but changes and cancellations are frequent. Twice daily, from June to September, hydrofoils also serve Listvyanka (R180, 1¼ hours) and Bolshie Koty (R240, 1¾ hours). All of these hydrofoils depart from the Raketa hydrofoil station beyond the Angara Dam in Solnechny Mikro-Rayon, two minutes' walk from the bus 16 stop 'Raketa'. Timetables are posted by the quay.

From a different jetty, **VSRP** (☎ 356 726) hydrofoils run to Bratsk (R1150, 12 hours) on Tuesday, Thursday and Saturday from June to late September.

BUS

From the chaotic **bus station** (☎ 209 115; 🕑 5.45am-9pm), book tickets at least a day ahead in summer for Arshan (R200, 8am and 10am), Khuzhir on Olkhon Island (R290, 9am, frequency varies seasonally) and Listvyanka (R64.50, 1¼ hours, four daily). Listvyanka services are supplemented by regular *marshrutky* (R70, 50 minutes), leaving when full. *Marshrutky* also leave several times a day for Taltsy (R70, 40 minutes).

Comfortable express coaches for Bratsk (R700, 8pm) leave from a special ticket booth and tiny left-luggage office (R50 per bag) opposite the bus station. Intercity minibuses to Ulan-Ude (R500, seven hours) depart throughout the day, but more frequently late in the evening, from the train station forecourt.

TRAIN

The elegant old train station has numbered sections. Northernmost section one sells same-day tickets; two has advance domestic ticketing. Upstairs in area three is the **Servis Tsentr** (☎ 636 501; ☺ 8am-7pm) for international tickets and the resting rooms, while downstairs is left-luggage. An unnumbered fourth area beyond sells *elektrichka* (suburban train) tickets (eg to Slyudyanka, R43.60) and is the access route to all platforms. Train tickets are also sold at the **Central Air Agency** (☎ 341 596; ul Gorkogo 29; ☺ 8am-8pm, to 7pm winter), upstairs at the airport and at the Bratsk coach ticket booth; all charge commission (around R100 for domestic journeys, R300 for international).

The best, if most expensive, train to/from Moscow is the *Baikal* (9/10; R11,570, three days and six hours), but *platskart* (open carriage) berths on slower trains such as the 43 and 339 (three days and 15 hours) only cost about R3000 via Krasnoyarsk (R900, 18 hours).

There are several alternate-day trains for Vladivostok including No 2 (R11,900, two days and 22 hours) and No 32 (R7890, three days) via Khabarovsk (two days and 12 hours). Trains for Běijīng (R10,100, two days and 22 hours) via Chita pass through Irkutsk on Tuesday at 10.31am. Those via Mongolia depart Saturday at 5.13am. Alternatively, for Ulaanbaatar (R4000), fast train No 6 (Sunday and Monday) is a full seven hours quicker than the daily No 362 (38 hours). If you're heading east, consider stopping first in Ulan-Ude (R500 *platskart*, seven to nine hours), enjoying views of Lake Baikal en route.

In July and August there are special through carriages to and from Warsaw (four days and 15 hours, weekly) and Berlin (five days, weekly).

Getting Around

Within the central area, walking is usually the best idea as one-way systems make bus routes confusing. When the new Angara bridge is completed in 2009, much of Irkutsk's public transport system will be thrown into disarray, as the current bridge linking the city centre and the train station will be closed for repairs expected to last several years.

From the train station, frequent *marshrutka* 20 runs through the city centre to the airport, trams 1 and 2 run to uls Lenina and Timiryazeva, while bus 7 crosses to pl Kirova, then loops round the centre and out past the Znamensky Monastery. *Marshrutka* 16 continues down ul Lenina, past the Raising of the Cross Church and (eventually) the Angara Dam. It then passes within 500m of the SibExpo hotels before looping back beside the Raketa hydrofoil station to the *Angara* ice-breaker. Slow tram 5 trundles from beyond the Angara Dam to the central market, where tram 4 takes over to the bus station and Kazansky Church.

WESTERN LAKE BAIKAL

Lake Baikal, the 'Pearl of Siberia', is a crystal-clear body of the bluest water. It's drinkably pure, surrounded by rocky, tree-covered cliffs and so vast that you can sail for hours without the mountain backdrops becoming appreciably closer.

Shaped like a banana, Lake Baikal – 636km from north to south, but only 60km wide – was formed by rifting tectonic plates. Though nearly 8km of the rift is filled with sediment, it is gradually getting deeper as the plates separate. It will eventually become the earth's fifth ocean, splitting the Asian continent. In the meantime it's the world's deepest lake: 1637m near the western shore. As such, it contains nearly one-fifth of the world's fresh, unfrozen water – more than North America's five Great Lakes combined.

Swimmers brave enough to face Baikal's icy waters (never warmer than about 15°C) risk vertigo, as it is possible to see down as far as 40m. In February and March you can drive right across on the 1m-thick ice, though this is safest in the north and most practical between Severobaikalsk (p265) and Ust-Barguzin (accessed from Ulan-Ude, p234).

The lake itself is a living museum of flora and fauna, 80% of which is found nowhere else on the planet, most famously the loveable black-eyed *nerpa* (freshwater seals) and salmonlike *omul* fish, which are delicious smoked. For more information on Baikal, see p93 and p99.

Taltsy Museum of Wooden Architecture
Музей Деревянного Зодчества Тальцы

About 47km southeast of Irkutsk, 23km before Listvyanka, **Taltsy** (☎ 145 249; admission R120, plus photography permit; ✆ 10am-5pm summer, to 4pm winter) is an impressive outdoor collection of old Siberian buildings set in a delightful riverside forest. Amid the renovated farmsteads are two chapels, a church, a watermill, some Evenk graves and the eye-catching 17th-century Iliminsk Ostrog watchtower. Listvyanka–Irkutsk buses and *marshrutky* stop on request at Taltsy's entrance (look out for the roadside 'Музей' sign), and the ticket booth is a minute's walk through the forest.

Listvyanka Листвянка
✆ 3952 / pop 2500 / ✆ Moscow +5hr

As the closest lakeside village to Irkutsk, this is where most independent travellers first dip their toe in Baikal's chilly waters. By far the most popular 'resort' on the lake's shores, Listvyanka offers winter dog sledding and summer boat and horse rides, and is ideal for watching the Siberian nouveau riche at play. Outside busy weekends, the village is reasonably quiet with inspiring views towards the distant snow-capped Kamar Daban Mountains.

INFORMATION
The handiest ATM is at Hotel Mayak (p222).
Post office (ul Gorkogo 49; ✆ 8am-2pm & 3-8pm Mon-Fri, to 6pm Sat) Internet costs R35 per hour.
Tourist Information Centre (✆ 496 987; hydrofoil quay; ✆ 10am-1pm & 2-6pm) Really just another commercial tour company masquerading as an information centre, though this one does endeavour to give out free maps, provide bus, ferry and hydrofoil timetables, and book accommodation. Some English spoken.

SIGHTS & ACTIVITIES
Having glimpsed Lake Baikal and eaten fresh-smoked *omul* fish at the port, many visitors are left vaguely wondering what to do next. **Fishing-boat rides** (charters per hr from R800) or gentle strolls are a common time-filler, with old log cottages to photograph up uls Gudina and Chapaeva, though ongoing gentrification is starting to impinge on their architectural integrity. About 2km west in Krestovka, the pretty if unremarkable **Svyato-Nikolskaya Church** was named for an apparition of St Nicholas, which supposedly saved its sponsor from a Baikal shipwreck. Nearby is **Retro Park** (admission R15), a garden full of wacky sculpture pieces fashioned from old Soviet-era cars and motorbikes.

Another 2km towards Irkutsk at Rogatka, tour groups are herded into the **Baikal Museum**

(✆ 250 551; ul Akademicheskaya 1; admission R150; ✆ 9am-5pm Oct-May, to 7pm Jun-Sep), where gruesomely discoloured fish samples and seal embryos in formaldehyde are now supplemented with tanks containing two frolicsome *nerpa* and various Baikal fish that you'd otherwise encounter on restaurant menus.

From December to March, the **Baikal Dog Sledding Centre** (✆ 496 829; www.baikalsled.ru, in Russian; ul Gornaya 17, Krestovka) offers thrilling dog sledding on forest tracks. The shortest run, 3km with three dogs, costs R700, but whole multiday cross-Baikal expeditions are possible with bigger dog teams. The owners' sons speak English.

On warmer winter weekends, **snowmobiles** and even **horses** can be informally hired on the ice near the Proshli Vek restaurant, while **hovercraft rides** are available from the main port area. On the beachfront, locals photograph one another in front of weirdly shaped frozen waves.

SLEEPING
There is a vast choice of accommodation. However, with minimal public transport, no taxi service and no left-luggage office, finding a room in summer without reservations can take some tiresome trekking around. Leave heavy bags in Irkutsk. Anything under R500 is likely to be very basic, with outside squat toilet, dorm-style beds or both. Virtually every Irkutsk tour agent has its own guest house or homestay in Listvyanka; value varies.

In the port area, handy but predominantly unexotic homestays abound on lakefront ul Gorkogo, ul Chapaeva (eg Nos 1, 6, 11 and 16) and ul Gudina (No 64). Slightly less convenient than the port area for public transport, Krestovka is nonetheless more of a 'real' village and offers an ever-expanding choice of accommodation.

Budget
Galina Vasilievna's Homestay (✆ 496 798; ul Kulikova 44, Krestovka; dm/tr R500/1200) Galina offers cheap, saggy dorm beds in a delightfully genuine old home with a large traditional stove-heater but minimal facilities. Ask for keys at the Dariya grocery shop in front.

Priboy (✆ 496 725; upper fl, ul Gorkogo 101; dm R500, tw R1000-2000) Within spitting distance of the lake in the port area, this glass-and-steel block of incongruity has cheap if unappealing dorms and some basic rooms with shared

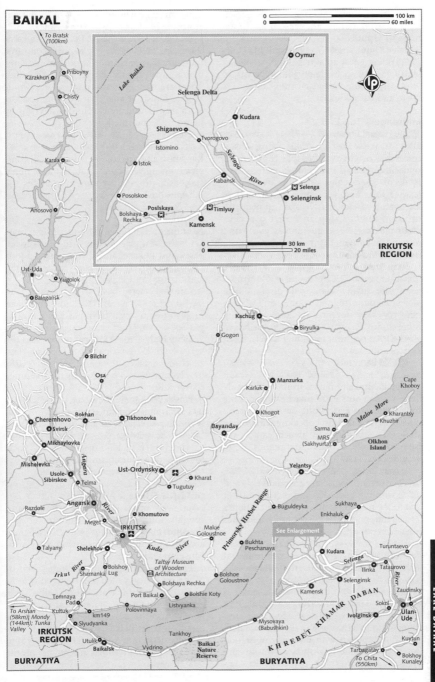

BAIKAL

toilet, shower and dubious taste in wallpaper. Downstairs is a quite fancy restaurant (open noon to 11pm).

Green House (☎ 496 707; ul Shtorkmana 3; tw R1000-2000) Timber guest house right by the market with five cosy rooms kept suitably toasty in winter by ceramic wood-burning stoves. TV room and guest kitchen.

Midrange & Top End

our pick Baikal Dream (☎ 496 758; ul Chapaeva 69; s R1000-1200, d R1300-2000) Brick-built Baikal Dream offers big bright comfortable rooms with underfloor heated bathrooms but minimalist decor. There's also a common room with leather sofas and TV, and a guest kitchen. Eager-to-please owner Nikolai will pick you up from the bus stop and cook you delicious meals. He also guarantees you won't forget his '*banya* (bathhouse) experience'. Breakfast included.

Briz (☎ 496 944; www.baikal-briz.ru; ul Gudina 71; standard tw summer R1300-1900, winter R1000-1200) A good price-quality balance with distant Baikal views, 17 pine-fragrant rooms, and a large new complex opening in 2009, meaning more choice. Firing up the guest house *banya* costs R1000 per hour including towels, birch switches and tea.

our pick Derevenka (☎ 496 737; www.village2002 .narod.ru; ul Gornaya 1; s/d R1500/2000, banya R250) On a ridge behind the Baikal front road, lovely little wooden huts with stove heaters, private toilets and hot water (but shared showers) offer Listvyanka's most appealing semibudget choice. The very friendly owners can organise snowmobile, sled and boat rentals. Rates include breakfast.

Devyaty Val (☎ 496 814; ul Chapaeva 24; d R1600-2000; ⊠) The better rooms here are relatively good value with big beds, TV and private shower and toilet in a long timber extension. There's a small indoor pool (R250 per hour) and rates include breakfast.

U Ozera (☎ 250 444; Irkutsk Hwy Km3; d winter/summer R2000/2500) New, reasonably comfortable if cramped log-built motel overlooking the lake between Krestovka and Rogatka.

Hotel Mayak (☎ 496 910; www.mayakhotel.ru; ul Gorkogo 85; s/tw summer R2200/2600, winter R1200/1800) If Baikal's planners and developers have anything to do with it, the shores of Lake Baikal will soon be lined with plasticky upmarket hotels such as the 'Lighthouse'. Rooms are Western standard but occupied by Russia's nouveau riche who lend the place an uptight atmosphere of unstylish extravagance.

Baikalskie Terema (☎ 780 120; www.gotobaikal.ru; ul Gornaya 16; d R3000-4500) For Western comforts, this fully equipped pine-furnished hotel remains Listvyanka's snazziest option so far. There are half-price room rates for 12-hour stays – handy if you arrive on the last bus from Irkutsk and are continuing next day by hydrofoil to Bolshie Koty.

Krestovaya Pad (☎ 496 863; www.baikalvip.ru; ul Gornaya 14a; summer d from R3600, winter from R2600) Big, brash and pricey, this recently built complex housing very comfortable, international standard, pine-clad rooms dominates the hillside above Krestovka.

EATING

Near the port the large fish and souvenir market is the best place to buy delicious smoked *omul* and is surrounded by greasy spoons offering relatively cheap *plov* (rice with lamb and carrots) and shashlyk.

Café Podlemore (☎ 496 472; ul Gorkogo 31; meals R80-140, coffees R30, porridge R25) This cafe has an English menu, oven-fresh pastries but nonplussed serving staff.

Shury Mury (☎ 496 858; next to information centre; meals R80-350, sandwiches R30-80; ☯ 10am-11pm) Boasting a lakeside summer terrace, this handy cafe has live music in the evenings (cover R30).

Proshli Vek (☎ 496 984; ul Lazlo 1; meals R200-500) has character and an *omul*-centric menu, while the speciality at lakeside **Pyaty Okean** (☎ 496 726; ul Gorkogo 59a; meals R200, beers R35-70; ☯ 11am-10pm) is Baikal Abyss – fish and potatoes baked in sour cream. Eat indoors or out by the gurgling Cheremshanka stream.

GETTING THERE & AWAY

Four daily buses (R64.50, 1¼ hours) and roughly hourly *marshrutky* run from outside the information centre (where bus tickets are bought) to Irkutsk, passing the Baikal Museum and Taltsy.

From mid-May to late September, hydrofoils stop at Listvyanka port between Irkutsk (R240) and Bolshie Koty (R120) daily.

Year-round a tiny, battered car-ferry lumbers across the never-frozen Angara River mouth to Port Baikal from Rogatka. It supposedly departs at 8.15am, 11.15am, 4.15pm and 6.15pm, but times are by no means guaranteed.

Various short trips by yacht, fishing boat or even hovercraft are available at the main port depending on the season. For longer cruises inquire well ahead through Irkutsk agencies.

Port Baikal Порт Байкал

☎ 3952 / pop 432 / ⊙ Moscow +5hr

From 1900 to 1904 the Trans-Siberian Railway tracks led here from Irkutsk. They continued on Lake Baikal's far eastern shore at Mysovaya (Babushkin). The rail-less gap was plugged by ice-breaking steamships, including the *Angara*, now restored in Irkutsk (p215). Later the tracks were extended south and around the lake. This Circumbaikal Railway required so many impressive tunnels and bridges that it earned the nickname 'The Tsar's Jewelled Buckle'. With the damming of the Angara River in the 1950s, the original Irkutsk to Port Baikal railway section was submerged and replaced with an Irkutsk–Kultuk short cut (today's Trans-Siberian Railway). That left poor little Port Baikal to wither away at the dead end of a rarely used branch line.

Seen from Listvyanka across the unbridged mouth of the Angara River, Port Baikal looks like a rusty semi-industrial eyesore but the view is misleading. A kilometre southwest of Stanitsa (the port area), Port Baikal's Baranchiki area is a ramshackle 'real' village, with lots of unkempt but authentic Siberian cottages and a handy selection of accommodation options. The village rises steeply, making for good short walks, with excellent Baikal lookouts easily accessible. Awkward ferry connections mean that Port Baikal remains largely uncommercialised, lacking Listvyanka's 'attractions' but also its crowds. Thus it's popular with meditative painters and hikers. Its main draw is the Circumbaikal train ride from Slyudyanka (see p226).

SLEEPING & EATING

B&B Baikal (☎ 201 489; www.baikal.tk, in Russian; ul Baikalskaya 12, Baranchiki; per person R1200, with full board R1500) Set 400m back from the lakeside in a house with a conspicuous, wood-framed picture window. Various newly decorated but unpretentious rooms share two Western-style toilets and a shower.

our pick Yakhont (☎ 250 496; www.baikalrest.ru, in Russian; ul Naberezhnaya 3, Baranchiki; tw R2600) This could be the Siberian boutique hotel you've been dreaming of. It's a traditionally designed log house decorated with eclectic good taste by well-travelled, English-speaking owners. Guests congregate in the stylish communal kitchen/dining room, above which rooms have perfect Western bathrooms. A large restaurant is under construction below the hotel. Advance bookings are essential.

If the last ferry back to Listvyanka has just left, the B&B is full and the Yakhont is too expensive, it's always possible to fall back on several basic homestays in Baranchiki. Just ask around or look out for 'сдаются комнаты' signs.

Until the Yakhont restaurant is built, Port Baikal will continue to have nowhere to eat. A couple of poorly stocked grocery kiosks are the only sources of sustenance. Both accommodation options listed here offer meals, and homestays very often have a kitchen guests can use.

GETTING THERE & AWAY

The ferry to Rogatka near Listvyanka's Baikal Museum (R23, 20 minutes) runs year-round, supposedly four times daily at 6.40am, 10.30am, 3.50pm and 5.15pm, but times can change at whim. There are direct hydrofoils to Irkutsk (50 minutes) in summer. Very infrequent trains come via the slow but scenic Circumbaikal route (p266) from Slyudyanka.

Bolshie Koty Болшие Коты

pop 350 / ⊙ Moscow +5hr

Founded by 19th-century gold miners, roadless Bolshie Koty makes an easy day trip by boat or ice-drive from Listvyanka or a picturesque hike along a section of the Great Baikal Trail (see p224). The little **museum** opposite the jetty has a few pickled crustaceans and stuffed rodents. Otherwise, the village is simply a pleasant place to stroll, snooze and watch fish dry. A few basic homestays include ul Baikalskaya 55 (lovely lakeside position) and the neater, inland ul Zarechnaya 11b. In summer great freshly smoked *omul* are sold at the port when boats arrive.

Hydrofoils originating in Irkutsk (R240) depart Listvyanka (R120, 25 minutes) at least daily in summer, staying two or three hours before returning. That's plenty for most visitors.

Olkhon Island Остров Ольхон

pop 1500 / ⊙ Moscow +5hr

Halfway up Lake Baikal's western shore and reached by a short ferry journey from

---

THE GREAT BAIKAL TRAIL

Inspired largely by the Tahoe Rim Trail (a hiking path encircling Lake Tahoe in California and Nevada), in summer 2003 a small band of enthusiasts began work on the first section of what was grandly named the Great Baikal Trail (GBT; in Russian, Bolshaya Baikalskaya Tropa, or BBT). Every summer since has seen hundreds of volunteers flock to Lake Baikal's pebbly shores to bring the GBT organisation's stated aim – the creation of a 2000km-long network of trails encircling the whole of Lake Baikal – closer to fruition. This lofty ambition may still be a far-off dream, but the GBT is nonetheless the first such trail system in all Russia.

These rudimentary bits of infrastructure, the GBT organisation hopes, will attract more low-impact tourists to the region, thus encouraging eco-friendly businesses to flourish and providing an alternative to industrial and mass tourism development. Volunteers and local activists are also involved in raising awareness of environmental issues among local people, visiting schools and fundraising. Nomination as a finalist in the 2008 *National Geographic* Geotourism Challenge is arguably the GBT's greatest achievement to date and has greatly raised its profile in the world of ecotourism.

Many Baikal explorers simply enjoy trekking the 540km of trails created thus far, but every year young and old from around the world join work crews for a few enjoyable weeks of clearing pathways, cutting steps, creating markers and cobbling together footbridges. Those eager to volunteer should visit the GBT website at www.greatbaikaltrail.ru, or contact Tanya Yurchenko, GBT's International Volunteer Coordinator (gbt.volunteers@gmail.com).

Sakhyurta (aka MRS), the serenely beautiful Olkhon Island is a wonderful place from which to view the lake and relax during a tour of Siberia. Considered one of five global poles of shamanic energy by the Buryat people, the 72km-long island's main settlement is Khuzhir, which has seen something of a tourist boom over the last few years mainly thanks to the inspiring efforts of Nikita's Guest House. For a good map of the island, go to www.baikalex.com/info/map_olkhon.html.

Although peak season is July and August, also consider visiting during the quiet winter months, when you can drive across the ice to the island until early April. Olkhon was reconnected to the electricity grid in 2005 and mobile phones now work in Khuzhir.

SIGHTS & ACTIVITIES

There are unparalleled views of Baikal from sheer cliffs that rise at the island's northern end, culminating in dramatic **Cape Khoboy**. Day-long jeep trips here (R400) including lunch can be arranged through Nikita's and Khuzhir's other guest houses.

Khuzhir's small **museum** (ul Pervomayskaya 24; admission R50; ☉ noon-7pm Mon-Fri) displays a not so much eclectic as random mix of stuffed animals, Soviet-era junk, local art and the personal possessions of its founder, Nikolai Revyakin, a teacher for five decades at the school next door.

Consider dropping by Nikita's even if you aren't staying there to admire the inventive kid's playground and general atmosphere of the place. A short walk north of Nikita's, the unmistakable **Shaman Rocks** are neither huge nor spectacular, but they make a perfect meditation focus for the ever-changing cloudscapes across the picturesque Maloe More (Little Sea). East of the rocks is a long strip of sandy beach.

The island's southern end is rolling grassland, great for off-road **mountain biking** or gentle **hiking**, and if Baikal proves too cold for a dip you can cool off in the small **Shara-Nur Lake**, where the water dyes the skin red if you wallow too long.

SLEEPING & EATING

Khuzhir has an ever-growing range of places to stay, though the vast majority of independent travellers bunk down at Nikita's. Irkutsk agencies offer a choice of basic cottage homestays in Khuzhir at around R800 with full board. If you just show up there's a fair chance of finding a similar place from around R600. Toilets are always outside the rooms and the *banya* will typically cost extra. The village is small enough that it won't take you long to find the following recommended places.

ourpick Nikita's Guest House (www.olkhon.info; ul Kirpichnaya 8, Khuzhir; full board per person R750-1000; ☉ reception 8am-11pm) Run by a former Russian table tennis champ and his wife, Siberia's premier travellers' hang-out is a fantastic place to stay and eco-friendly to boot. If it's overrun with backpackers (as it often is in the high season), the owners will find you a place to stay elsewhere in the village. The basic rooms on site are attractively decorated. Scrub up in an authentic *banya* and pig out on delicious home-cooked meals. There's a cycle hire centre and a packed schedule of excursions and activities. Staff can also register your visa (R350).

Solnechnaya (☎ 683 216; www.olkhon.com; ul Solnechnaya 14; full board R780-900) Not quite as happening a scene as Nikita's, but still a pleasant place to stay offering a good range of activities. Accommodation here is in two-storey cabins, cooler 1st-floor rooms being the more expensive.

Hotel Olkhon (☎ 708 885; www.alphatour.ru, in Russian; Baikalskaya 64; summer huts s R900 1700, d R1200-1900, hotel s R900-2700, d R1200-3500) For those who prefer toilets to flush, water to run hot and a bit less hectic backpacker scene than at Nikita's, this peaceful brick-built family hotel just off Khuzhir's main square is surrounded by an enclosure of timber Monopoly houses.

Yurt Camp Harmony (www.sokoltours.com; full board per person in 4-bed yurt R1000) Five kilometres north of Khuzhir near the tiny hamlet of Kharansty, this summer-only yurt camp has 20 large circular felt tents shaded by trees in a lakeside camping ground. It's used for the company's tours, but independent travellers can stay if there's room.

GETTING THERE & AWAY

From June to August there are at least three and usually four daily buses between Khuzhir and Irkutsk (R290, seven hours), with an additional minibus leaving from Nikita's daily at 8.30am (R600). Frequency drops off drastically outside the peak summer season. With a little warning, agencies or hostels can usually find you a ride in a private car to Irkutsk (per seat R900, whole car R3500, 5½ hours). Prices include the short ferry ride to MRS; from mid-January to March an ice road replaces that ferry. When the ice is partly formed or partly melted, the island is completely cut off from motor vehicles, though an ad hoc mini hovercraft service is sometimes operated by locals on demand.

In summer a hydrofoil service operates three times weekly from Irkutsk to Olkhon

(R1500, seven hours), dropping passengers near the ferry terminal, from where it's possible to hitch a paid lift into Khuzhir.

Maloe More Малое Море

☎ 3952 / Ⓨ Moscow +5hr

The relatively warm, shallow waters of the Maloe More (Little Sea) offer a primary do-nothing holiday attraction for Siberians. The main activities here are **swimming**, **hiking** to waterfalls and drinking. Dozens of camps, huts and resorts are scattered amid attractive multiple bays backed by alternating woodland and rolling grassland scenery. Since each widely spaced 'resort' is frequently pre-booked and hard to access without private transport, you'd be wise to first visit Irkutsk agencies and leaf through their considerable catalogues. Booking something not too far from MRS makes it easier to continue later to Olkhon Island. Arguably the most appealing bay is **Bukhta Kurkutskaya**, where the Baza Otdykha Naratey has showers and bio-toilets. Several resorts offer weekly transfers from Irkutsk for guests (around R600), including **Baikal-Dar** (☎ 266 336; www .dar.irk.ru, in Russian; d/tr incl full board R1800/2700). The further north, Olkhon-facing **Khadarta Bay**, between Sarma and Kurma, is becoming ever more popular.

From mid-June to late August *marshrutky* run daily to Kurma (R500, 5½ hours) at 9am via Sarma (R380) from in front of **Hotel Angara** (ul Sukhe-Batora 7) in Irkutsk. They return at 2pm the same afternoon. Public buses from Irkutsk serve MRS.

SLYUDYANKA СЛЮДЯНКА

☎ 39544 / pop 18,800 / Ⓨ Moscow +5hr

Lacking any architectural charm, Slyudyanka rarely tempts Westerners off the train. Yet the drab, functional town has a great lakeside setting, is backed by mountains and is the best place to start Circumbaikal train rides (see p226). It's also an ideal launching point for reaching the splendid, peak-backed Tunka Valley and its popular spa village Arshan (p227).

Slyudyanka 1, the famous all-stone **train station**, is a mere five-minutes' walk from Lake Baikal's shore. En route you pass a photogenic timber **church** in multicoloured, Scooby Doo style. Across the tracks, former locomotive workshops host an interesting though all-in-Russian **museum** (Kraevedchesky muzey; ul

Zheleznodorozhnaya 22; admission R40; 🕙 11am-5pm Wed-Sun), with archaeological finds, old railway-switching boxes and an identification guide to 47 locomotive types. Geology buffs should also consider heading to the privately run **Baikal Mineral Museum** (Muzey Samotsvety Baikala; ☎ 53 440; ul Slyudyanaya 36; admission R100; 🕙 8am-9pm), which claims to exhibit every known mineral. Take any *marshrutka* heading from the bus station up ul Slyudyanskikh Krasnogvardeytsev and ask to be dropped off at the museum. A popular picnic excursion is to **Cape Shaman**, an easy 4km stroll north towards Kultuk along Baikal's gravely shore.

With moulting lino, very basic rooms and shared showers, the friendly **Hotel Chayka** (☎ 54 073; ul Frunze 8a, M/R Perival; d R400) charges R250 for 12-hour stays. To get there from the train station, cross the long footbridge and walk two blocks further to a little **bus station** (ul Lenina); from here the hotel is 4km west by very frequent *marshrutka* 1 (last one at 11pm). A taxi costs R50. The **Mineral Museum Homestay** (☎ 53 440; ul Slyudyanaya 36; per person R500) is little more than a two-bed gar-den cottage that the museum curator rents out in the summer months. **Hostel Slyudyanka** (apt 7, ul Shcholnaya 10; dm R400) is really just an-other homestay but is very cheap and can be booked through **Hostelworld** (www.hostelworld .com). Arrange for the owners to pick you up from the station (R200) as it's tricky to find.

Located handily opposite the bus station, Slyudyanka's only eatery is **Kafe-Gril** (ul Lenina 118; meals R50-100; 🕙 10am-9pm), where inexpen-sive belly-filling stodge is served on melting plastic. At the adjacent **Bonus Supermarket** (ul Lenina 116; 🕙 9am-10pm), you can stock up on enough noodles, cheese, bread and instant porridge to keep you going all the way to Běijīng.

Trains from Irkutsk take around 3¼ hours (*elektrichka*) or 2½ hours (express). Slyudyanka 1 is the usual starting point for the Circumbaikal Railway trip. Two cheap but very scenic *elektrichki* run daily to Baikalsk, while *marshrutky* depart from outside the train station to Arshan at an ungodly 5.15am (or earlier depending on when train 125 ar-

CIRCUMBAIKAL RAILWAY

The historic Circumbaikal route (p49) from Slyudyanka to Port Baikal is one of Baikal's most popular tourist jaunts. Excruciatingly slow or a great social event? Opinions are mixed as the train chugs scenically along cliff ledges above the limpid lake waters on this lake-hugging branch line. You'll need to juggle sunglasses, a fan and a torch as the carriages are unventilated and unlit.

The most picturesque route sections are around **Polovinnaya** (approximately halfway) and the bridge area at **Km149** (one hour from Slyudyanka), where there's also a small **Rerikh museum**. Views are best if you can persuade the driver to let you ride on the front of the locomotive – possible on certain tour packages. Note that *from* Port Baikal most trains travel by night, so are useless for sightseeing.

The Circumbaikal's old stone tunnels, stolby-cliff cuttings and bridges are an attraction even if you don't ride the train: in winter it's possible to drive alongside certain route-sections on ice-roads from Kultuk. Hiking sections of the peaceful track is also popular. Walking from Port Baikal leads to some pleasant if litter-marred beaches. Or get off an Irkutsk–Slyudyanka *elektrichka* train at Temnaya Pad and hike down the stream valley for about an hour. You should emerge at Km149 on the Circumbaikal track. Continue by train to Port Baikal if you've timed things carefully.

Travelling the Circumbaikal

From a side platform at Slyudyanka 1 station, short, wooden-seated *matanya* trains currently depart at 1pm four times weekly – check timetables carefully. In summer an additional tour-ist train direct from Irkutsk departs at 7.42am on Saturday. The wonderfully detailed website http://kbzd.irk.ru/Eng has regularly updated timetables plus photographs of virtually every inch of the route.

Irkutsk agencies such as **Krugobaikalsky Ekspress** (☎ 3952-202 973; www.krugobaikalka.ru, in Russian) run organised Circumbaikal tours (R1100 including lunch), though some travellers grumble about the rather superfluous 'guides' who tag along for the entire nine-hour trip but who add little to the experience.

rives from Ulan-Ude). An additional bus to Arshan (R125, two hours) leaves around 2pm from the bus station. From here bus 103 also runs six times daily to Baikalsk.

ARSHAN АРШАН

☎ 30156 / pop 900-3800 (seasonal) / ☽ Moscow +5hr

Sawtooth Sayan peaks rise spectacularly above the cute Buddhist villages of the wide, rural Tunka Valley. This area attracts wilderness hiker-climbers, but its main draw is undoubtedly the little spa village of Arshan. It's nestled right at the foot of soaring forested mountains offering relaxing short walks to a series of rapids between sulphur-scented sips. There are plenty of longer, more challenging treks and climbs here, too. More detailed information is available at http://tunki .baikal.ru (in Russian).

From the big, six storey **Sayany Spa**, Arshan's patchily attractive main street (ul Traktovaya) fires itself 2km straight towards the mountains. Opposite the spa grounds, the **Dechen Ravzhalin Datsan** (Buddhist temple) has two sparkling new prayer wheels, a miniature stupa and a dazzlingly colourful interior. Beyond the post office, **Internet Zal** (ul Traktovaya 32; per hr R50; ☽ 11am-1pm & 2-6pm Mon-Fri, 12.30-6pm Sat & Sun) and the **bus-ticket kiosk** (ul Traktovaya 3), ul Traktovaya swerves west past the **Altan Mundarga Information Booth** (☎ 97 384; ul Traktovaya 6) and the sprawling Kurort Arshan resort.

Keep walking for 20 minutes through the forest to find the dinky little **Bodkhi Dkharma Datsan**, set in an idyllic mountain-backed glade, or walk up the stream to access the mountain footpaths.

Sleeping

Many log cottages offer basic homestays from R200 per bed. Look for 'Дом Жильё' signs.

Kurort Arshan (☎ 97 740; ul Traktovaya 1; s from R500; ☽ reception 8am-8pm summer, 9am-1pm & 4-7pm winter) Basic institutional sanatorium with various sized buildings spread through the forest, used mostly by those seeking a cure at its hot springs.

Pensionat Sagaan Dali (☎ 3952-205 315; www .sagaan.ru; ul Deputatskaya 14; d/ste R580/1160) It's inexpensive but with all the charm of a 1970s council block, rooms here are cosmetically upgraded but still have rather sad old toilets. Suites are bigger but not better. The access footpath from ul Traktovaya skirts the Sayan Sanatorium, passing a spluttering, sulphurous, spring-water faucet marked by prayer flags.

our pick **Priyut Alpinista** (☎ 97 697; www.iwf.ru; ul Bratev Domshevikh 8; tw R2000-3300) This characterful climbers' centre has the atmosphere of a Western youth hostel, but rooms have private toilets and better ones have hot showers. Rent bicycles (R120 per hour), buy climbing maps and watch videos of Arshan's attractions in the comfortable sitting room before adding comments to the 'magic tree'. It's a modest wooden building three-minutes' walk along ul Pavlova from the bus stand. The owners offer pre-erected tent places, including supplies, high in the mountains (R500 per person including food) so that hikers and mountaineers don't need to carry a rucksack.

Hotel Zamok Gornogo Korolya (☎ 92 304; ul Gagarina 18; d R2500-4000) This modern pseudo-castle has crenulations, green-tipped towers and four comfortable rooms with questionable 'artistic' taste in nude derrières.

Eating

As many visitors book full-board stays at the spas, there is only a handful of eateries for the independent traveller to choose from.

Stolovaya (ul Traktovaya 13; meals R40-70; ☽ 9am-7pm) This unrepentantly Soviet canteen is near the post office.

Zakusochnaya Khamar Daban (ul Traktovaya; meals R70; ☽ 10am-4am) Located opposite the Sayan Sanatorium, this typically austere greasy spoon serves up *pozy* and other meat-and-dough combinations for a handful of roubles.

Novy Vek (☎ 97 330; ul Traktovaya 4; mains R150; ☽ 10am-midnight) The latest addition to the Arshan dining scene, the Novy Vek has an extensive menu and a yapping FM radio.

Getting There & Away

Buses or *marshrutky* (slightly more expensive) run to Kyren (R70, 1¼ hours, 10.30am, noon and 2pm), Slyudyanka (R125, 7.30am and 2pm), Ulan-Ude (R450, 11 hours, 7.45am, four times weekly) and Irkutsk (R350, 11am and 4pm).

Lake Baikal to Vladivostok

Lake Baikal feels far from Moscow, but – before you rush south to Mongolia – there's still a lot of Russia to go. This three-day stretch covers another 4000km – that's nearly double the Moscow–Irkutsk journey – passing taiga, riverways and mountains (and three train links to the northerly BAM line) as it rolls into Russia's 'wild east', where Cossacks hunted furs (and people) and Soviet-era, Gulag-bound prisoners packed Tsar-built train carriages to Vladivostok.

This region of Russia has always lived by its own rules. Travelling this way before the Trans-Siberian was built, writer Anton Chekhov confessed he was 'in love' with it; he wrote to Moscow friends in 1890 that it 'seethes with life in a way that you can have no conception of in Europe'. And that's still apt. In this part of Russia, the Buryat Mongol group numbers nearly half a million, lending their names to towns such as Ulan-Ude and yurt camp sites in national parks, and contributing delicacies such as lamb testicles to local menus.

Out the window, the stream of Stalin-era housing blocks of passing towns may seem the same as back west, but off the tracks come surprises. Just off the Trans-Siberian line, Blagoveshchensk is a border town of tsar-era buildings, where you can cannonball into the Amur River and hear Chinese locals splash from the opposite shore. Just east you reach the Jewish Autonomous Region at Birobidzhan, Stalin's failed 'Zion' that once received thousands of migrating Jews.

The railway ends at the stunning mountains-meets-ocean setting of Vladivostok, a once-closed navy port that's no longer a dead end. It looks fully Russian, but is finally embracing its Far Eastern locale, with a flurry of new international connections – flights and boats to Korea and Japan, and train and bus connections with Hāĕrbin (Harbin), China.

HIGHLIGHTS

- Explore Lake Baikal's eastern shores from the appealing Buryat town of **Ulan-Ude** (p234), with totems and a locomotive museum

- Sleep in a Buryat yurt at **Alkhanay National Park** (p243), three hours from the Chita station

- Do a self-made cruise through Vladivostok's Golden Horn Bay by hopping on the cheap **Russky Island ferry** (p251)

- Give yourself a day off the train in **Khabarovsk** (p245), a lively and confident town with Tsar-era buildings and party cruises on the Amur River

- Listen for Chinese boat calls at the river border town of **Blagoveshchensk** (p243), with swimming spots and century-old homes

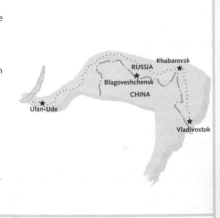

| ROUTE DISTANCE: 4104KM | DURATION: THREE DAYS |

THE ROUTE
Slyudyanka to Ulan-Ude

From **Slyudyanka** (5311km; p225) the line runs along the southern shore of Lake Baikal for 200km (5300km to 5500km), passing through a series of tunnels blasted into the cliffs along the water's edge. Many passengers press their noses to the grubby windows trying to get a view of the icy blue waters of the world's deepest lake. The best vistas come immediately after Slyudyanka, before reaching **Baikalsk** (5352km), where the air is soured by a huge, controversial pulp mill, but where, nonetheless, former President Putin enjoyed a skiing holiday in 2002.

Around 5390km, just before the village of Vydrino, the train crosses the river marking the border of Buryatiya (Buryat Republic), one of the Russian Federation's semiautonomous republics. Closely related to the Mongols, the Buryats have been undergoing something of a Buddhist revival but have largely given up their former nomadic herding lifestyles.

The town of **Tankhoi** (5420km) lies in the centre of the Baikal Nature Reserve. Further east along the shore, **Mysovaya** (5477km; for Babushkin) is the port where the Baikal and Angara used to load and disgorge their passengers and carriages before the south-bank railway was completed. The obelisk at Mysovaya zheleznodorozhny vokzal (train station) marks the spot where in 1906 tsarist forces shot revolutionary Ivan Babushkin, after whom the surrounding town is named.

Directly below the present line you can clearly make out sections of older tracks. These were half-drowned after the construction of the Angara Dam near Irkutsk raised the level of Lake Baikal.

If you are travelling west, keep a lookout for the lake from around 5507km, when the train suddenly pulls out from between the forested hillsides and reveals a glorious view of Baikal's clear blue waters and the cliffs on the other side.

Just before reaching **Selenga station** (for the town of Selenginsk; 5562km), the train line hooks up with the Selenga River, your travelling companion into Mongolia if you are Ulaanbaatar-bound. Between here and Ulan-Ude, the river valley provides ample photo opportunities, such as at 5630km, when the train rattles across the river.

Trains pull in for at least 15 minutes at **Ulan-Ude** (5640km; p234), the capital of Buryatiya. Sadly, that's not long enough to dash to the centre of this relatively exotic city to see the world's biggest Lenin head. The old steam locomotive that sits in front of the depot at the northwestern end of the platform will be the extent of your sightseeing if you're not stopping here.

Ulan-Ude to Chita

Trans-Mongolian trains (p275) say farewell to the main Trans-Sib route at **Zaudinsky** (5655km), virtually a suburb of Ulan-Ude. The mainline then follows the wide Uda Valley. At an unmarked station about half an hour out of Ulan-Ude (before Onokhoi), a marshalling yard serves as a steam loco graveyard. The scenery here is pretty as the wide, flood-prone valleys continue, their rolling meadows backed distantly by trees on the north-facing slopes. Quaint log-cabin settlements are scattered with patches of attractive woodland. You enter **Chitinskaya region** (5771km) 20km beyond Novoilyinsky. Local time becomes Moscow time plus six hours.

The *provodnitsa* (carriage attendant) unbolts the carriage door for up to 15 minutes at **Petrovsky-Zavod** (5784km), the station for the town of Petrovsk-Zabaikalsky. The station name (and the old name of the town) means 'Peter's Factory', so-called for the huge ironworks you may spot from the train. Decembrists (see p217) jailed here from 1830 to 1839 are commemorated in a large, photogenic mural at the station. There's also a good Decembrist Museum in town, though few leave the train to see it.

The tracks now head northeast following the Khilok Valley, with the **Yablonovy Mountains** (between 5800km and 6300km) forming blue shadows in the distance. At the small airbase town of **Bada** (5884km), look up from your instant noodles to admire a MiG fighter monument and a cluster of old aircraft on the runway to the north.

Around 5925km, the train slows as it leaves the valley and climbs into the mountains, affording inspiring views of the winding river and fields filled with wildflowers. It may pause briefly in **Khilok** (5934km), where there is a machine shop for repairing train engines. An old locomotive stands at the eastern end of the platform. There is another fairly lengthy stop at **Mogzon** (6054km), a good place to take

LAKE BAIKAL TO VLADIVOSTOK

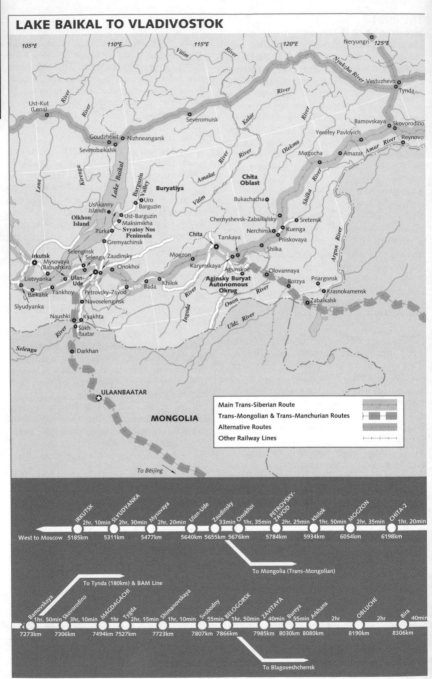

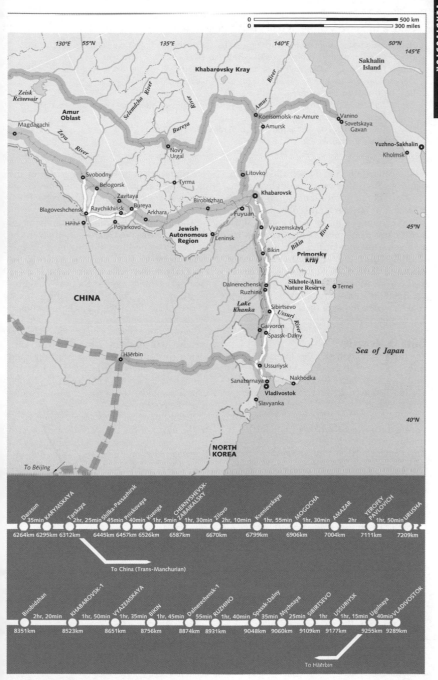

LAKE BAIKAL TO VLADIVOSTOK ROUTE PLANNER

Here's a suggested itinerary for finishing up the Trans-Siberian from Lake Baikal to Vladivostok:
Day 1: Take the train from Irkutsk to Ulan-Ude (seven hours)
Day 2: Tour Ulan-Ude. Overnight train to Chita (10 hours); take share taxi to Aginskoe for night
Day 3: Share taxi back to Chita; night train to Birobidzhan (46 hours)
Day 4: On train to Birobidzhan
Day 5: Arrive in Birobidzhan; tour synagogue. Take the bus or afternoon commuter train (three hours) to Khabarovsk
Day 6: Tour Khabarovsk; overnight train to Vladivostok (13 hours)
Day 7: Arrive in Vladivostok

on some nutrition from the babushkas on the platform. Soon afterwards the highest point (1040m) on the world's longest rail journey is reached at **Yablonovaya** (6125km).

Some trains halt for up to an hour at **Chita-2** (6198km; p239), almost long enough for a whistle-stop tour of the city's sights and certainly sufficient to explore the cathedral in the station forecourt. At the station, fans of the *Long Way Round* TV show will recognise the freight platform where Ewan McGregor et al struggled to heave their bikes aboard a Tynda-bound goods wagon.

Chita to Mogocha

For the next 250km east the Trans-Siberian route follows the Ingoda River, which is south of the train. River views open up around **Darasun** (6264km), where there's a very brief halt.

You'll have all of 18 minutes to 'admire' the platforms at **Karymskaya** (6295km), the station for the industrial town of Karymskoye. This comes shortly before **Tarskaya** (6312km), where the Trans-Manchurian peels off and heads south to the Chinese border; for details of this route, see p294.

The main Trans-Siberian route continues northeast through **Shilka-Passazhirsky** (6445km; for Shilka), where there's a five-minute halt at the remarkably modern station. Look south to see piles of train wheels on leaving the station. The hills are pretty as the route follows the Shilka River, marred by the derelict factories of Kolbon (there's no stop here).

The brakes squeal again at **Priiskovaya** (6457km), from where a 10km branch line heads north to the old silver-mining town of Nerchinsk. This is where the Treaty of Nerchinsk was signed in 1689, carving up Russian and Chinese spheres of influence in the Far East.

Around 6510km keep an eye out for the picturesque church in the Byankino Valley, as well as a few other buildings on the flood plain across the Shilka River.

Another renovated cube of a station meets the eye at **Kuenga** (6526km), after which the Trans-Sib route turns sharply north, while a 52km branch line heads to Sretensk, the eastern terminus of the Trans-Baikal Railway (see p49). Until the Amur Railway was completed in 1916, Trans-Sib passengers used to disembark from the train here to board Khabarovsk-bound steamers.

Some slower train services take a lengthy breather at **Chernyshevsk-Zabaikalsky** (6587km), giving you time to stock up from the food and drink sellers (unless it's 3am). It's named after the 19th-century exile Nikolai Chernyshevsky, whose silver-painted statue is on the platform.

Around 6660km there are sweeping views to the north of the train across the Siberian plains. The next long stop (15 minutes) is at **Mogocha** (6906km), a railway and goldmining town of 12,000 souls who endure one of the harshest climates on earth. Winter temperatures in this permafrost zone can plunge to a rail-splitting -62°C! No one gets off the train here.

Mogocha to Khabarovsk

For about 700km, starting at around the 7000km mark, the train line runs only about 50km north of the Amur River, the border with China. At one time, strategic sensitivity meant that carriages containing foreigners had their window blinds fastened down during this stretch – so please don't curse any monotony of the scenery!

At the cute red-and-green wood train station in **Amazar** (7004km), you have about a 20-minute stop; there's a nearby graveyard of steam locomotives to see. The town's nothing fancy, but may get more so – a new pulp plant in the works has drawn promises of US$500 million of Chinese investment. Around here, the terrain gets so rugged that roads stop and don't resume again until across the border at 7075km, between the Chitinskaya and Amur regions – this marks the end of Siberia and the beginning of the Russian Far East, bigger than all of non-Russian Europe.

Soon after, settled in low-lying hills, you'll stop for 21 minutes in the town of **Yerofey Pavlovich** (7111km), named for the Siberian explorer Yerofey Pavlovich Khabarov (the remainder of his name went to the big city further down the line).

You'll be well into day six of your journey from Moscow by **Skovorodino** (7306km), on the Bolshoi Never River, where there's a three-minute pause. This is where you'll need to change trains to go north along the Baikal-Amur Mainline (Baikalo-Amurskaya Magistral, or the BAM). The junction is back at **Bamovskaya** (7273km) – for more details see p259. (If you're on the *Rossiya* or any other major eastbound service, you'll have to get off at Skovorodino and catch a local train the 33km back to Bamovskaya.)

At **Magdagachi** (7494km), three hours east, there's a 15-minute stop and then a series of short stops before arriving in **Belogorsk** (7866km), another 5½ hours away. This is the place to stop off for a train or (easier) taxi van to reach the nearby border town of **Blagoveshchensk** (p243), the administrative capital of Amur Region with a ferry service to Hēihé, China. (A new bridge to China will supposedly be built near here by 2012.)

At 8184km, the border between the Amur Region and the Yevreyskaya Avtonomnaya Oblast (Jewish Autonomous Region), local time becomes Moscow time plus seven hours. **Birobidzhan** (8351km; p244) is the capital of the Jewish Autonomous Region (part of the 788,600-sq-km Khabarovsky Territory that stretches 2500km north to the Sea of Okhotsk). The stop is very short, but you can see the Hebrew letters of the station from your window. The *Rossiya* arrives at 4pm, so you could exit here, have a 90-minute look at the Jewish cultural centre and synagogue and take the 6pm commuter train to Khabarovsk.

Approaching **Khabarovsk** (8523km; p245) from the west, the train crosses a 2.6km bridge

over the 2824km-long Amur, the longest span on the whole line and the last stretch of the Trans-Siberian to be completed in 1916. The railway now runs across a new bridge, with a road along the top, completed in the 1990s. There's also a 7km tunnel under the Amur, secretly completed during WWII, and the longest such tunnel on the Trans-Sib route; it's now used only by freight trains.

If you're not overnighting in pleasant Khabarovsk, you have a 30-minute stop on the *Rossiya* – enough time to admire the Khabarov statue out front, plus the long-time renovation of the train station, which now resembles the old duma (parliament) building on central ul Muravyova-Amurskogo. You can also switch for a train to connect with the BAM at **Komsomolsk-na-Amure** (p271), from where you can reach the port at **Vanino** (p273) for a boat to Sakhalin Island.

Khabarovsk to Vladivostok

This is day seven, and your last 13 hours on the train usually pass in the night. One reason for the cover of darkness is that the line, in places, comes within 10km of the sensitive Chinese border. From Khabarovsk south to Vladivostok the route shadows the Ussuri River, the border with China. At 8597km you'll cross the Khor River.

At **Vyazemskaya** (8651km) there's a 15-minute stop; there'll be plenty of people selling bread, salmon caviar, dried fish and pickles. From here the forests are dominated by deciduous trees, such as maple and elm, which briefly blaze in a riot of autumn colours during September.

You'll probably be settling down for some sleep by the time the train reaches **Bikin** (8756km), where there's usually just a two-minute halt – the line crosses the Bikin River here and follows it south to the border between Khabarovsky and Primorsky Territories. The southern forests of the 165,900-sq-km Primorsky Territory are the world's most northerly monsoon forests and home to black and brown bears, the rare Siberian tiger and the virtually extinct Amur leopard.

There's a 15-minute stop in the dead of night at **Ruzhino** (8931km). Some 40km west of **Sibirtsevo** (9109km) – a two-minute stop – you may be able to make out Lake Khanka, a 4000-sq-km, lotus-covered lake that straddles the China–Russia border.

At **Ussuriysk** (9177km), you have 18 minutes in which to contemplate changing to the branch line west to Hāěrbīn (Harbin) in China; the train goes only twice a week and is monotonously slow. Ussuriysk, formerly named Nikolskoe in honour of the tsarevitch's 1891 visit and home to a smattering of historic buildings, was once of greater size and importance than nearby Vladivostok. There's also a line from here south to Pyongyang in North Korea, but it isn't open for passenger services.

By dawn – and after a week of travel from Moscow – you'll have your first glimpse of the Pacific to the south of the train at around 9245km. You'll now be travelling along the hilly peninsula that forms the eastern side of Amursky Gulf. At the north edge of the city, the tracks pass some forlorn, but popular, beaches around **Sanatornaya** (9269km), an enclave of big-wig summer homes and hotels.

The city rises in a series of concrete tower blocks on the hill sides; you'll pass older buildings nearer the terminus, **Vladivostok** (9289km; p250). Before leaving take a moment to admire the old locomotive on the platform beside the monument commemorating the completion of the great railroad you've just travelled along.

ULAN-UDE УЛАН-УДЭ
☎ 3012 / pop 380,000 / ☼ Moscow +5hr
Ulan means 'Red' in the local Buryat language, yet Ulan-Ude's setting is pleasantly green, cradled attractively in rolling hills. Despite an inevitable concrete suburban sprawl, it remains one of the most likeable cities in eastern Siberia. If you're coming from the west, the distinctively oriental Buryat faces make 'UU' the first strikingly Asiatic city on the Trans-Sib.

Chartered as Verkhneudinsk in 1775, Ulan-Ude was a trading post on the wealthy tea-caravan route between China and Irkutsk. Soviet industrialisation brought a large locomotive works and secretive aircraft factory. Despite the vastly expanded population, severe Stalinist pressures and the all-seeing eyes of the world's biggest Lenin head, the Buryats clung to their language and faith.

Today the city is the ideal launching point for trips to eastern Baikal, while easy quick flits to Ivolginsk allow a fascinating glimpse of the region's resurgent Buddhist tradition (see the boxed text, opposite).

Orientation & Information
The city's heart is pl Sovetov and its backbone ul Lenina, but most traffic bypasses the latter on uls Borsoeva and Baltakhinova. The commercial centre is increasingly focused on the Sagaan Morin market and shopping mall across the railway tracks on pr 50-let Oktyabrya.

Baikal Bank (pl Sovetov 1; ☼ 9am-8pm Mon-Fri, to 7pm Sat) Most centrally located place to change dollars and euros.
PhotoPlus (ul Kommunisticheskaya 16; ☼ 9am-7pm Mon-Sat, 10am-5pm Sun) Three-minute passport photos (R70) for that Mongolian visa.
Post office (ul Lenina 61; ☼ 8am-noon & 1-5pm Mon-Thu, to 4pm Fri) Multitasking office with internet room (per hour R35) and air/rail ticket windows.
Telephone office (ul Borsoeva; ☼ 9am-8pm) Internet access here is R35 per hour but there are only three PCs.

Sights
PLOSHCHAD SOVETOV
The Stalinist main square, pl Sovetov, is a Soviet marching ground but manageably proportioned and awesomely dominated by the world's largest Lenin head, which some maintain looks comically cross-eyed. The square also hides a cute little **Geological Museum** (Geologchesky muzey; ul Lenina 59; admission free; ☼ 11am-5pm Mon-Fri).

MERCHANTS' QUARTER
The town's partly pedestrianised, historical main artery is ul Lenina. Here the elegant 19th-century architecture is gradually being renovated and boutiques already occupy the smartened-up 1838 trading arcades. Viewed from the 2006 replica of an 1891 triumphal arch honouring the then imperial heir, Nicholas II, or from the adjacent 1930s Opera House (undergoing a thorough makeover at the time of research), this street is given a photogenic focus by the gold-tipped spires of the 1785 **Odigitria Cathedral** (ul Lenina 2). The building was rescued from near collapse in the late 1990s and commands an area of appealing if ramshackle old town. The carved wooden cottages extend as far as ul Kirova. The unaesthetic **Nature Museum** (Muzey Prirody Buryati; ☎ 214 149; ul Lenina 46; admission R61; ☼ 10am-6pm Wed-Sun) has big stuffed animals and a scale model of Lake Baikal showing you just how deep it is.

HISTORICAL MUSEUM
Somewhat naughtily, this **museum** (☎ 210 653; Profsoyuznaya ul 29; admission R150 or per fl R70; ☼ 10am-

THE BURYATS

Numbering over 400,000, this Mongol people is the largest indigenous group in Russia, comprising around 30% of the population of the Buryatiya Republic and 65% of the Aginsky-Buryat Autonomous District southeast of Chita.

Culturally there are two main Buryat groups. In the 19th century, forest-dwelling Western Buryats retained their shamanic animist beliefs, while Eastern Buryats from the southern steppe lands mostly converted to Tibetan-style Buddhism while maintaining a thick layer of local superstitions. Although virtually every Buryat *datsan* (Buddhist temple) was systematically wrecked during the communists' antireligious mania in the 1930s, today Buryat Buddhism is rebounding. Many (mostly small) *datsans* have been rebuilt and seminaries for training Buddhist monks now operate at Ivolginsk (p238) and Aginskoe (p242).

In the Buryat language, 'hello' is *sainbena* (or *sambaina*), 'thank you (very much)' is *(yikhe) bai yer la*. Buryatiya's trademark snack *pozy* (or *buuzy*) are dangerously juicy meatballs in ravioli-style pasta served in *poznayas* (eateries serving Central Asian food) across Eastern Siberia and beyond.

6pm Tue-Sun) charges per single-room floor. Floor 3, Buddiyskoe Iskustvo, is by far the most interesting. Its *thangka* (Buddhist iconographic paintings), Buddhas and icons were salvaged from Buryatiya's monasteries and temples before their Soviet destruction and were originally used for a museum of atheism.

ETHNOGRAPHIC MUSEUM & HIPPODROME

In a forest clearing 6km north of central Ulan-Ude, the excellent **Ethnographic Museum** (Etnografichesky muzey; ☎ 335 754; admission R70; ⌚ 9am-5pm Tue-Sun) is an open-air collection of local architecture plus some reconstructed burial mounds and the odd stone totem. It features occasional craft demonstrations and has a splendid wooden church and a whole strip of Old Believers' homesteads. *Marshrutka* (fixed-route minibus) 8 from pl Sovetov passes within 1km but on request it will detour to drop you at the door for no extra charge. En route you'll notice Ulan-Ude's attractive pair of **datsans** (Buddhist temples; Barguzinsky trakt) backed by stupas and forests fluttering with prayer flags. The nearby **hippodrome** (☎ 442 254) is the venue for major festivals, including the Surkharban (Buryativya folk festival; early June), the biggest Buryat sporting event of the year featuring archery, wrestling and exhilarating feats of horsemanship.

Tours

Sesegma (aka Svetlana), the director of **Baikal Naran Tour** (☎ 215 097; baikalnarantour@mail.ru; Room 105, Hotel Buryatiya, ul Kommunisticheskaya 47a), is infectiously passionate about Buryatiya, offering horse-riding adventures and dozens of fascinating one-off ideas.

MorinTour (☎ 443 647; www.morintour.com; Hotel Sagaan Morin, ul Gagarina 25) focuses on east Baikal, offering various ice and fishing adventures, a horse sledge trip, seal watching, rafting in the Barguzin Valley and climbing on Svyatoy Nos (Holy Nose) Peninsula.

Sleeping

Resting rooms (komnaty otdykha; ☎ 282 696; Ulan-Ude train station; r per hr R71) Well-maintained crash pad at the station.

Hotel Barguzin (☎ 215 746; Sovetskaya ul 28; s R470-960, tw R1320-2400, tr R1650-1800) Until someone opens a hostel in Ulan-Ude, the lacklustre Barguzin will continue to be the most survivable budget place to kip. Beyond the spruced-up foyer with lurking stuffed bear, rooms have en suite, TV, lino and cigarette burns. No breakfast.

Hotel Profsoyuznaya (☎ 222 373; ul Vorovskogo 25; s R1000, d R1300) Despite its scratchy towels and clumsy Soviet-era plumbing, this often overlooked former trade union hostel is a fairly decent choice, and some rooms have been upgraded. There's a 25% booking fee and no breakfast.

our pick Hotel Ayan (☎ 415 141; ul Babushkina 164; s R1300-2500, tw R1800-4000; 🖳) The inconvenient location 2km south of the city centre is more than recompensed by pristine Western-standard rooms, some with air-con. The cheapest singles are a good deal and every room has its own water heater. Floors 1 to 3 have paid wi-fi and there's also a minuscule cafe.

Hotel Sagaan Morin (White Horse; ☎ 444 019; www.morintour.com/eng/sagaan-hotel; ul Gagarina 25; s/tw/tr R1300/2400/3600) This perfectly appointed three-star tower is a popular choice among

ULAN-UDE

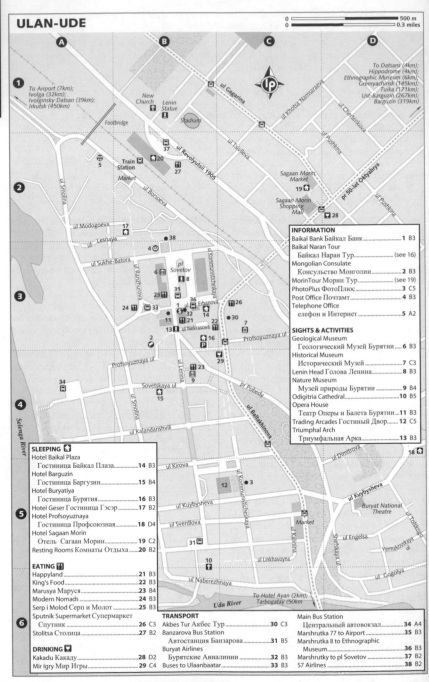

To Airport (7km);
Ivolga (32km);
Ivolginsky Datsan (39km);
Irkutsk (450km)

To Datsans (4km);
Hippodrome (4km);
Ethnographic Museum (6km);
Gremyachinsk (145km);
Tuika (171km);
Ust-Barguzin (267km);
Barguzin (319km)

INFORMATION

Baikal Bank Байкал Банк	**1** B3
Baikal Naran Tour	
Байкал Наран Тур	(see 16)
Mongolian Consulate	
Консульство Монголии	**2** B3
MorinTour Морин Тур	(see 19)
PhotoPlus ФотоПлюс	**3** C5
Post Office Почтамт	**4** B3
Telephone Office	
елефон и Интернет	**5** A2

SIGHTS & ACTIVITIES

Geological Museum	
Геологический Музей Бурятии	**6** B3
Historical Museum	
Исторический Музей	**7** C3
Lenin Head Голова Ленина	**8** B3
Nature Museum	
Музей природы Бурятии	**9** B4
Odigitria Cathedral	**10** B5
Opera House	
Театр Оперы и Балета Бурятии	**11** B3
Trading Arcades Гостиный Двор	**12** C5
Triumphal Arch	
Триумфальная Арка	**13** B3

SLEEPING

Hotel Baikal Plaza	
Гостиница Байкал Плаза	**14** B3
Hotel Barguzin	
Гостиница Баргузин	**15** B4
Hotel Buryatiya	
Гостиница Бурятия	**16** B3
Hotel Geser Гостиница Гэсэр	**17** B2
Hotel Profsoyuznaya	
Гостиница Профсоюзная	**18** D4
Hotel Sagaan Morin	
Отель Сагаан Морин	**19** C2
Resting Rooms Комнаты Отдыха	**20** B2

EATING

Happyland	**21** B3
King's Food	**22** B3
Marusya Маруся	**23** B4
Modern Nomads	**24** B3
Serp i Molod Серп и Молот	**25** B3
Sputnik Supermarket Супермаркет	
Спутник	**26** C3
Stolitsa Столица	**27** B2

DRINKING

Kakadu Какаду	**28** D2
Mir Igry Мир Игры	**29** C4

TRANSPORT

Akbes Tur Акбес Тур	**30** C3
Banzarova Bus Station	
Автостанция Банзарова	**31** B5
Buryat Airlines	
Бурятские Авиалинии	**32** B3
Buses to Ulaanbaatar	**33** B3

Main Bus Station	
Центральный автовокзал	**34** A4
Marshrutka 77 to Airport	**35** B3
Marshrutka 8 to Ethnographic	
Museum	**36** B3
Marshrutky to pl Sovetov	**37** B2
S7 Airlines	**38** B2

independent travellers and booking ahead in summer is advised. The entrance is somewhat hidden by the melee of the market outside. The owners also run a large *turbaza* (tourist camp) in the pretty Baikal village of Sukhaya, 170km north of Ulan-Ude.

Hotel Buryatiya (☎ 211 505; ul Kommunisticheskaya 47a; s R1350-1800, tw R1500-2100; 🖥) The mammoth Buryatiya, the former Intourist hotel, has 220 rooms of wildly differing sizes and standards, some like broom cupboards with Soviet plumbing, others almost palatial with sparkling European bathrooms. One advantage to staying here are the extra services (internet room, tour companies, souvenir kiosks, ATMs) on offer on the ground floor – there's even a Buddhist temple!

Hotel Baikal Plaza (☎ 210 838; www.baikalplaza.com, in Russian; ul Erbanova 12; s R2000, tw R3000, d R3500) The tired old Baikal reinvented itself in 2006, and following renovation standards have rocketed. The 68 modernised rooms are arguably UU's finest offering, and the central location overlooking the Lenin Head is unrivalled.

Hotel Geser (☎ /fax 216 151; www.geser-hotel.ru, in Russian; ul Ranzhurova 11; s/tw/ste R2500/3100/6600) For a Soviet place, this former Party hangout has relatively spacious rooms, some of which have been passably modernised. However, others retain clunky old toilets and you would expect vastly better facilities for these prices.

Eating

In summer many open-air cafes appear near the river and around the opera house, serving mostly beers and shashlyks (meat kebabs). A few fast-food vans sell burgers and snacks near the trading arches.

RESTAURANTS

Marusya (☎ 218 066; ul Lenina 46; mains R50-200; 🕑 10am-10pm) A coy 19th-century makeover with polished samovars, *matryoshki* (nesting dolls) and waitresses trussed up in pseudo folk costumes has brought the Ulger Theatre restaurant back from the dead. Enjoy inexpensive Russian meals at tightly packed tables to the sound of dreamy 1970s Russian *chansons* on CD, or flee the schmaltz for the pleasantly sunny terrace.

our pick **Modern Nomads** (ul Ranzhurova 1; mains R100-200; 🕑 11am-11pm Mon-Fri, from noon Sat & Sun) Join a group of student drinkers, snackers and diners at this clean-cut and very popular place serving Mongolian dishes with a contemporary twist.

Serp i Molod (Hammer & Sickle; ☎ 214 114; ul Erbanova 7a; mains R200; 🕑 8am-11pm) A tongue-in-cheek Soviet theme, an English menu and live music most nights make this a fun place to eat. The atmosphere improves the later it gets. Hidden just off pl Sovetov; follow the hammer-and-sickle signs.

Stolitsa (☎ 552 836; ul Revolyutsii 1905 31; meals R200-350; 🕑 11am-11pm) Perfectly situated for the train station, this surprisingly elegant upstairs restaurant has red, black and gold decor, modernist, Buddhist-influenced art and old Ulan-Ude photos. There's a menu in English and a vastly cheaper *zakusochnaya* (pub-cafe) around the side.

QUICK EATS & SELF-CATERING

Happyland (ul Lenina 52; meals R50-90; 🕑 10.30am-11pm) This everything-with-chips canteen in the cinema foyer is the cheapest source of empty calories in the city centre.

King's Food (basement, ul Kommunisticheskaya 43; meals R100; 🕑 11am-11pm) So-so food, striking pillar-box-red and jet-black decor and crass Russian MTV; on hot days use the cutlery to slice a hole in the air to breathe through.

Sputnik Supermarket (ul Kommunisticheskaya 48; 🕑 24hr) A handy but pricey central grocery.

Drinking

Kakadu (pr 50-let Oktyabrya 10; beers R35-90; snacks R20-50; 🕑 10am-11pm) Smoky basement pub with a very nominal Mexican theme. Entry is from a side alley opposite the Dauriya bar (a real dive).

Mir Igry (ul Kommunisticheskaya 52; beers R37-60, meals R90-220; 🕑 10am-11pm) This casino complex has three great bar-restaurants each with its own atmosphere. It's popular with young professionals and a great place to strike up conversations over a shot or 10 of vodka. Great beer and shashlyk garden in summer.

Getting There & Away

AIR

S7 Airlines (☎ 220 125; ul Sukhe-Batora 63; 🕑 9am-7pm Mon-Fri, to 6pm Sat & Sun) operates a direct service to Moscow Domodedovo (from R5500, daily), while planes belonging to **VIM Airlines** (www.vim -avia.com) refuel in UU twice weekly on their way between Moscow (R16,000) and Vladivostok (R9000). **Buryat Airlines** (☎ 212 248; ul Erbanova 14; 🕑 9am-7pm Mon-Fri, 9am-6pm Sat, noon-6pm Sun) has very scenic flights to Nizhneangarsk (R3450, five weekly), near Severobaikalsk, and Irkutsk (R1870, three weekly). Tickets can be bought from the Hotel Barguzin, Hotel Buryatiya, post office and **Akbes Tur** (☎ 212 212; ul Kommunisticheskaya 46; ☺ 9am-8pm Mon-Sat, 9.30am-8pm Sun).

BUS

Buses depart from various points. Use the **main bus station** (Sovetskaya ul) for Baikal's east coast, and for depart-when-full *marshrutky* to Kyakhta (R250, 4½ hours) for the Mongolian border.

Use the **Banzarova bus station** (ul Banzarova) for the Ivolginsky *datsan*: bus 104 departs early mornings, around noon and late afternoon. Alternatively, use the very frequent 130 service to Ivolga (R25), then switch to a taxi. *Marshrutky* to Arshan (R550), Irkutsk (R800) and Chita (R700) depart from the train station forecourt.

At 7.30am daily, a bus runs from a stop near the opera house roundabout to Ulaanbaatar (R950, 10 hours) via Kyakhta. Book through **Baikal Naran Tour** (☎ 215 097; baikalnarantour@mail.ru; Room 105, Hotel Buryatiya, ul Kommunisticheskaya 47a).

TRAIN

The *Rossiya* arrives from Moscow and Vladivostok every second day but there are cheaper alternatives. Běijīng-bound trains pass through Ulan-Ude on Tuesday (via Chita) and Saturday (via Mongolia). Fast trains to Ulaanbaatar (R3000, 31 hours) pass through the city on Sunday and Monday at 1.30am and waste vastly less time at the border than the 362 train (R2000, 40 hours), which departs at 7am daily. Buy international tickets from the **servis tsentr** (☎ 282 460) upstairs at the train station. For Chita, train 340 (R1500, 10 hours) is the handiest overnight option. Towards Irkutsk, day trains (from R460 *platskart*, seven to 10 hours) are popular for Baikal views.

Getting Around

Ulan-Ude has a vast, frequent but confusing public transport web. From pl Sovetov *marshrutka* 77 runs a few times hourly to the airport (R10, 20 minutes), while *marshrutka* 8 passes the *datsans,* hippodrome and Ethnographic Museum; the last buses return around 9pm. Tram 7 (R8) between ul Baltakhinova and the Hotel Odon is a relatively direct way to approach the train station, avoiding the sometimes convoluted *marshrutka* routes.

AROUND ULAN-UDE
Ivolginsky Datsan
Иволгинский Дацан

This **monastery complex** (admission free), under 40km from Ulan-Ude, was founded in 1946. While not as elaborate as Gandan Khiid in Ulaanbaatar or others around Chita, it is intriguing as the centre of Siberian Buddhism. The local Gelugpa (Yellow Hat) form of Buddhism differs slightly from that in Mongolia and Tibet, by, for example, allowing lamas to marry. When spinning prayer wheels or just walking around the temple grounds, it's polite to maintain a clockwise direction. Enter any temple building via the left door and don't use the central stairs unless you're a self-realised lama.

Viewed distantly across the grassy fields, morning sunlight glints from the gilded roof-wings of the 1972 main temple building. Up closer, however, the exterior is less impressive – slapdash paintwork, naive, tacky tiger guardian-statues and brick patterning painted onto the whitewashed walls. Some of the lovably basic prayer wheels are crafted from old tin cans. The main temple's interior (no photography please) is colourful and atmospheric despite discordantly chuntering cash registers. Nearby notice the glassed-in Bodhi Tree, convolutedly descended from the Bodh Gaya original beneath which the Buddha achieved enlightenment.

Nearing completion within the *datsan* complex is the beautiful, Korean-style wooden **Etigel Khambin Temple**, honouring the 12th Khambo Lama whose body was recently exhumed. To general astonishment his flesh had not decomposed seven decades after his death. Some 'experts' have even attested that the corpse's hair is still growing, albeit extraordinarily slowly.

The **Maitreya Festival** takes place in June and features long prayer sessions, a procession and sometimes a recorded message from the Dalai Lama. It's one of the most colourful festivals in the calendar.

The first direct bus from Ulan-Ude arrives well before the 9am *khural* (prayer service), giving ample time to wander among the prayer flags of the mosquito-infested surrounding swamp. Returning buses leave at 1.30pm, 5.30pm and 8.30pm. Alternatively, take a taxi to uninteresting Ivolga, from where *marshrutka* 130 shuttles to Ulan-Ude several times hourly (R25). Ulan-Ude tour agencies offer small group excursions to the *datsan* for around R2000 to R3000 per person.

Novoselenginsk Новоселенгинск
☎ 30145 / pop 9500 / ☺ Moscow +5hr

Worth a brief stop en route to Kyakhta (for Mongolia), stockades and wooden houses on broad dust-blown roads give this small, 19th-century town a memorable Wild West feel. Learn something of Novoselenginsk's interesting history at the **Decembrist Museum** (Muzey Dekabristov; ☎ 96 716; ul Lenina 53; admission R40; ☺ 10am-6pm Wed Sun), in a 200-year-old colonnaded house in the town's centre. Walk 2km east towards the river to see the ruins of the 18th-century Spassky Church, isolated on the grassy far bank (no bridge). That's all that remains of Staroselenginsk, the original settlement that was abandoned around 1800 due to frequent flooding. You'll also find an unremarkable obelisk commemorating Martha Cowie, the wife of a Scottish missionary who spent 22 years here translating the bible into Mongolian. Kyakhta-bound *marshrutky* all pause in Novoselenginsk from Ulan-Ude (1½ hours, six or seven daily). There's no hotel.

Eastern Lake Baikal

Sparsely scattered beach villages of old-fashioned log cottages dot the pretty East Baikal coast. A usefully practical Pribaikalsky National Park booklet is available for free to download from www.tahoebaikal.org. Further north is the dramatic Barguzin Valley, from where Chinggis (Genghis) Khaan's mother, Oilun-Ehe, is said to have originated.

Access is across a forested pass from Ulan-Ude via tiny Baturino village, with its elegantly renovated Sretenskaya Church. After about 2½ hours' drive, the road first meets Lake Baikal at pretty little Gremyachinsk, which has a wide and sandy but litter-strewn beach some 15 minutes' walk up ul Komsomolskaya.

The main road offers surprisingly few Baikal views until fishing port Turka, where there is a small museum and a newly built church but little reason to stay over. Bigger Goryachinsk, around 3km inland, is centred on a typically institutional **hot-springs kurort** (sanatorium complex; ☎ 30144-55 195; beds from R400), with cheap cottage homestays in the surrounding village. *Marshrutky* run to Ulan-Ude (R250, 3½ hours) at least three times a day.

Picturesque Baikal beaches stretch northwest of quaint little Maksimikha, a fishing hamlet with several huts and *turbazy* (holiday camps), including **Svetlaya Polyana** (tw R1200-1800; ☺ Apr-Oct). Perhaps the most dramatic views are from the low-rise town of **Ust-Barguzin**, where ul Lenina's blue-and-white carved wooden cottages culminate in a river ferry. Across the bay, the high-ridged peaks of the Svyatoy Nos Peninsula rise spectacularly sheer. Ask Baikal Naran Tour (p235) in Ulan-Ude about local homestays, visits to the new **Banya Museum** (☎ 30131-91 574; per Bolnichny 9; ☺ by appointment), tours of the peninsula and boat trips to see *nerpa* (freshwater seals) around the Ushkanny islands.

Barguzin town dates back to 1648 and has a few dilapidated historic buildings along ul Krasnoarmeyskaya and pl Lenina, where there's a basic **hotel** (ul Lenina 25; s R400-600, tw R700). However, the old town is most useful as a base for visiting the timeless Barguzin Valley, which opens out into wide horse-grazed meadows, gloriously edged by a vast Toblerone of mountain peaks. Great views across the meandering river plain from the village of Uro are easily accessible thanks to three daily buses from Barguzin (R40, 35 minutes), though taxis and private tours arranged in advance allow much better exploration. For tours, see Baikal Naran Tour (p235). The **Barguzin Nature Reserve** was set up in 1916 primarily to protect the sable antelope. Several species, including other species of antelope, the brown bear, wolf, lynx, and otters have also found refuge in the beautiful tree-covered mountainous terrain here.

To return to Ulan-Ude from Barguzin (R351, eight hours), there are buses departing 8am and 10.30am. Book ahead.

CHITA ЧИТА
☎ 3022 / pop 372,000 / ☺ Moscow +6hr

The golden domes of Chita's bombastic cathedral entice train travellers to hop off and explore this historic and patchily attractive city. Despite many architectural gems, each area is a little too diffuse to make a really memorable visual impact, but the friendly, go-ahead atmosphere makes Chita an agreeable place to linger a day or two.

Founded in 1653 Chita developed as a rough-and-tumble silver-mining town. More than 80 Decembrist gentlemen-rebels were exiled nearby, their wives setting up homes on what was known as ul Damskaya (Women's St), now lost beneath the southern end of concrete-blighted ul Stolyarova.

As a gateway to the new East Chinese Railway (p50), Chita boomed in the early 20th century and was capital of the short-lived, pro-Lenin Far Eastern Republic from 1920 till 1922 – the parliament building still stands at ul Anokhina 63. Although closed to foreigners during the Cold War and still home to a large military presence, today trade with China booms and the city is increasingly internationally minded.

Orientation & Information

The city centre is pl Lenina with a rather constipated-looking pink Vladimir Ilyich in the middle. It's three blocks northeast of the main (Chita 2) train station, one stop using any trolleybus. Wide boulevard-like ul Lenina emerges either side of the square as the city's main thoroughfare.

Internet Tsentr (ul Chaykovskogo 24; per MB R3.20, per hr R42; 🕑 9am-2pm & 3-8.30pm)

KiberPochta (ul Lenina 2; per MB R4, per hr R35; 🕑 8am-8pm Mon-Fri, to 7pm Sat, to 6pm Sun) Internet access.

Lanta (☎ 353 638; ul Leningradskaya 56; 🕑 9am-6pm Mon-Fri, 10am-6pm Sat) Local tour company.

Main post office (ul Butina 37; 🕑 8am-9pm Mon-Fri, 8am-8pm Sat, 9am-6pm Sun) Quaintly spired wooden building on pl Lenina.

VTB Bank (ul Amurskaya 41; 🕑 9am-6pm Mon-Fri) Changes US dollars, euros, Chinese yuán and even British pounds.

Sights

Ploshchad Lenina has a certain grandeur while Chita's best century-old architecture lies southeast along uls Anokhina, Amurskaya and Lenina. The original historic centre is now mostly trampled by concrete towers, but the lovely 1771 Archangel Michael log church survives and houses a small but interesting **Decembrist Museum** (Muzey Dekabristov; ☎ 310 412; ul Selenginskaya; admission R30; 🕑 10am-6pm Tue-Sun).

Beyond a gratuitous stuffed elk, the excellent **Kuznetsov Regional Museum** (Kraevedchesky muzey; ☎ 260 315; ul Babushkina 113; admission R65; 🕑 10am-6pm Tue-Sun) has engaging exhibits on the city's heritage and architectural renaissance.

The dry, Russian-language-only **Military Museum** (Muzey istori voysk ZaBVO; ☎ 343 492; ul Lenina 86; admission R30; 🕑 9am-1pm & 2-5pm) contains exhibits on Beketov's Cossacks, the Soviet invasion of Afghanistan and communist repressions. The six floors bristle with weapons, and the museum's collection of tanks

and artillery can be seen by walking up the passage between the museum and the impressive Officers' Club building next door.

Sleeping

Chita has little budget accommodation and homestays are nonexistent. Cheap digs are often jam-packed with military personnel on leave and Chinese migrants.

Hotel Taiga (☎ 262 332; 4th fl, ul Lenina 75; dm R340-510, d 880-1020) Expect plenty of teen spirit at this survivable crash pad above the Forestry College student dorms. Some rooms have TV and there's a guest kitchen. The front door is locked at midnight.

Hotel AChO (Gostinitsa Upravleniya delami Administratsi Chitinskoi Oblasti; ☎ 351 968; ul Profsoyuznaya 19; dm 625-800, s from 2000, tw R3600-4000; 🖳) Painted taupe and white, this fine brick mansion was built in 1906 for a printing magnate and used as a WWI hospital and tobacco factory before becoming a hotel. Rooms are now fully renovated with polished wooden floors, a fridge and showers with doors! Admire the wrought ironwork of the grand doorway and banisters.

Hotel Chitaavtotrans (☎ 355 011; ul Kostyushko-Grigovicha 7; dm/s/tw R900/1300/1800) Cosmetically improved but cramped rooms have TV and fridge but wobbly old shower floors. Doubles are overpriced but singles are just about spot on. Quiet yet central.

Vizit (☎ 356 945; vizit77@mail.ru; ul Lenina 93; s R2850, tw R5200; 🖳) Occupying the 5th floor of an ultramodern smoked-glass tower at the busy intersection of uls Lenina and Profsoyuznaya, this is Chita's best luxury offering with relaxing rooms with en suite, tasteful leather sofas and sparkling bathrooms. Half-price for stays of between six and 12 hours.

Hotel Dauria (☎ 262 350; ul Profsoyuznaya 17; s from R3200, tw from R3200) Renovated, very comfortable rooms with en suites have new furniture meaning this is no longer the backpacker favourite it once was. It's above the Kharbin Chinese Restaurant; 25% booking fee.

Eating & Drinking

With a couple of exceptions, Chita's dining scene amounts to an unexciting assortment of greasy spoons and crass theme restaurants with just enough choice to mean you won't go hungry. Menus are more likely to be in Chinese than English.

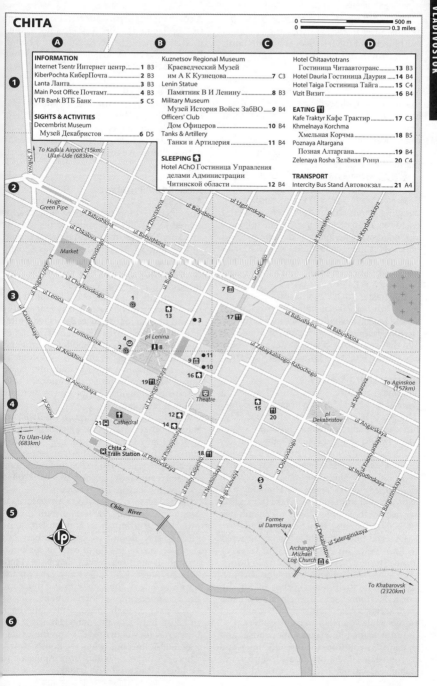

CHITA

INFORMATION
Internet Tsentr Интернет центр.......**1** B3
KiberPochta КиберПочта **2** B3
Lanta Ланта....................**3** B3
Main Post Office Почтамт...........**4** B3
VTB Bank ВТБ Банк...............**5** C5

SIGHTS & ACTIVITIES
Decembrist Museum
   Музей Декабристов **6** D5

Kuznetsov Regional Museum
   Краеведческий Музей
   им А К Кузнецова.............**7** C3
Lenin Statue
   Памятник В И Ленину **8** B3
Military Museum
   Музей История Войск ЗабВО.....**9** B4
Officers' Club
   Дом Офицеров **10** B4
Tanks & Artillery
   Танки и Артилерия **11** B4

SLEEPING
Hotel AChO Гостиница Управления
   делами Администрации
   Читинской области **12** B4

Hotel Chitaavtotrans
   Гостиница Читаавтотранс........**13** B3
Hotel Dauria Гостиница Даурия **14** B4
Hotel Taiga Гостиница Тайга **15** C4
Vizit Визит.....................**16** B4

EATING
Kafe Traktyr Кафе Трактир **17** C3
Khmelnaya Korchma
   Хмельная Корчма.............**18** B5
Poznaya Altargana
   Позная Алтаргана............**19** B4
Zelenaya Rosha Зелёная Роща **20** C4

TRANSPORT
Intercity Bus Stand Автовокзал......**21** A4

Poznaya Altargana (ul Leningradskaya 5; pozy R22; 10am-11pm) If *pozy* are your thing, this is your place, but the tasty *plov* (rice with lamb and carrots) and meatballs are an equally filling alternative.

Zelenaya Rosha (☎ 322 714; ul Lenina 65; meals R150-250, beers R50; 10am-2am) A canopy of plastic foliage covering the ceiling and a tackily dribbling water feature make this a low-lit retreat from the scorching sun outside. Down a few cheap beers or tuck into some basic Siberian comfort food. Chita's most accessible semi-public WC is in the entrance.

our pick **Khmelnaya Korchma** (☎ 352 134; ul Amurskaya 69; mains R150-300; noon-midnight Mon-Thu & Sun, noon-3am Fri & Sat;) Plastic sunflowers, dangling onion strings, folksy embroidered tea towels and a menu of borsch, *salo* (pig fat), *vareniki* (sweet ravioli-type dumplings) and *holubtsi* (cabbage rolls stuffed with rice) teleport you to rural Ukraine (almost). Nightly live music, liberal helpings and a low-priced lunch menu (R150).

Kafe Traktyr (☎ 352 229; ul Chkalova 93; mains R170-300; noon-2am) Russian home-style cooking is served at heavy wooden tables in this rebuilt wooden-lace cottage, with a quietly upmarket Siberian-retro atmosphere. The summer beer and shashlyk tent is a popular drinking spot.

Getting There & Away

The main train station is Chita 2, 6199km from Moscow and 3090km from Vladivostok. The *Rossiya* stops here on alternate days but cheaper alternatives include the 339 to Moscow and 133 and 530 to Vladivostok.

For China, the *Vostok* (020) runs to Běijīng (R5000, two days and five hours) very early Wednesday morning while trains to Mǎnzhōulǐ (R2100, 25 hours) depart on Thursday and Saturday evening. Otherwise, take the nightly service to the border town of Zabaikalsk (R1700, 11½ hours), then bus into China.

Other destinations include Blagoveshchensk (train 350; R3760, 33¾ hours, four weekly), Tynda (train 078; R1060 *platskart*, 26 hours, even days) and several Ulan-Ude services (R1470, nine to 10 hours), some overnight. For R150 commission, the helpful **service centre** (Chita 2 train station; 8am-noon & 1-7.30pm) issues tickets while you relax on comfy settees.

From near Chita 2 train station, buses and *marshrutky* run from the intercity bus stand to Aginskoe (R200, two hours, hourly) and Zabaikalsk (R700, 7.45am, noon and 2pm).

A sole minibus departs for Nerchinsk at 4pm (R350, five hours), but as there's no accommodation there, the overnight train is better. Buy bus tickets in advance from the kiosk opposite the intercity bus stand.

AROUND CHITA

South of Chita are some of Russia's greatest Buddhist sights. The most accessible is Aginskoe, which has the nation's oldest *datsan*, while Alkhanay offers a hike-through-nature alternative to Buddhist-temple-based spirituality.

Aginskoe Агинское

☎ 30289 / pop 15,000 / Moscow +6hr

For an intriguing trip from Chita, take a shared taxi (R200, two hours) to the incredibly smart Buryat town of Aginskoe, capital of the Aginsky-Buryat Autonomous Okrug. The scenery en route transforms progressively from patchily forested hills via river valleys into rolling grassy steppe land.

The highlight is a pair of old Buddhist *datsans*, 5.5km west of the centre by *marshrutky* 12 and 14. The 1816 **Aginskoe Datsan** is a white-and-gold, two-storey, Tibetan-style structure that is the hub of a Buddhist seminary. Directly to the east is the more photogenic 1883 **Tsakchen Datsan**, with a grandly impressive upper wooden frontage, partly adorned with colourful Mongolian script motifs. Getting inside is hit and miss.

On Agiskoe's central square the **Tsybikova Museum** (☎ 34 462; ul Komsomolskaya 11; admission R30; 10am-1pm & 2-5.30pm Mon-Fri) exhibits a shaman's cup made from a human skull. Opposite stands the custard-yellow 1905 St Nicholas Church, whose recent reconstruction was bankrolled by Moscow mayor, Yury Luzhkov.

Hotel Sapsam (☎ /fax 34 590; www.megalink.ru /sapsam, in Russian; tw/d R1500/1800), just off the approach road from Chita, is the town's only place to stay. Rooms are past their best, but the hotel boasts the finest eateries for miles around. Bright, self-service **Kafe Biznes Lanch** (ul Lenina 58; meals R50-100; 8.30am-2am), on the opposite side of the square to the museum, has an unpretentious Siberian menu.

It's easy enough to get a minibus back to Chita until late afternoon. Hourly minibuses run to Mogoytuy (R50) on the Chita-Zabaikalsk line, but trains are poorly timed. There's a single daily bus from Aginskoe to Duldurga (90km) for Alkhanay.

Alkhanay & Duldurga Алханай и Дулдурга

☎ 30256 / pop 7000 / ☽ Moscow +6hr

A Buryat-run national park 130km south of Chita, Alkhanay is reckoned by the local Buddhists to be the religion's fifth most important holy 'mountain'. In fact you'll see forested hills, not mountains, through which a devotional six- to seven-hour return trek takes pilgrims to a small stupa and a window rock. The latter is considered the Gate of Shambala, an entry to spiritual paradise. The beautiful flowers, pious pilgrims and bird-watching opportunities are as interesting as the scenery.

Alkhanay's entrance is 20km (R200 by taxi) from Duldurga village, where there's a helpful **Alkhanay National Park Office** (☎ 21 458; ul Gagarina 47) and two simple hotels. There's more accommodation in *turbazy* around the park entrance, including a **yurt camp** (per person R500). From July to September, the Chita-based agency **Lanta** (☎ 353 638; ul Leningradskaya 56; ☽ 9am-6pm Mon-Fri, 10am-6pm Sat) runs weekend tours, departing on Friday and including two nights' accommodation. No English is spoken.

Marshrutky from Chita to Duldurga (R230, three hours) run several times daily.

NERCHINSK НЕРЧИНСК

☎ 30242 / pop 15,300 / ☽ Moscow +6hr

Once one of Eastern Siberia's foremost towns, forgotten Nerchinsk is quietly intriguing and handily breaks up a long Chita–Blagoveshchensk journey. The venue for the immensely important 1689 border treaty with China, Nerchinsk boomed from the 1860s with discoveries of silver.

Mikhail Butin, the local silver baron, built himself an impressive crenellated palace that he furnished with what were then the world's largest mirrors, carried all the way from Paris. The mirrors form the centrepiece of the recently restored **Butin Palace Museum** (☎ 41 694; ul Sovetskaya 83; admission R50; ☽ 10am-1pm & 2-5.30pm Tue-Sat), in what remains of Butin's mansion. Nearby is the active 1825 **Voskresensky Cathedral** (ul Pogodaeva 85) and the imposing but somewhat dilapidated 1840 Trading Arches (Gostiny Dvor), slated for desperately needed renovation in the coming years.

There's nowhere to stay in Nerchinsk and most are on a bus to Priiskovaya train station before lunchtime. Criminally unwelcoming **Kafe Russkaya Dusha** (meals R50-100; ☽ 9am-3am)

sadly vacated the Trading Arches when it was gutted by fire in 2006. Relocated to a madly out-of-the-way location, 20 minutes' uphill walk from the centre, it's the only cafe so ask for directions.

From Chita, a single Nerchinsk-bound *platskart* (open carriage; R369, 10 hours) is conveniently attached to the overnight train 392 to Yerofey Pavlovich. Instead of waiting for the 7.10pm return service, take a local bus (R35) back to Priiskovaya, where connections include the 12.08pm train to Blagoveshchensk (odd-numbered days), the 9.35pm to Khabarovsk, the 2pm *elektrichka* (suburban train) back to Chita and several daily Moscow-bound services.

BLAGOVESHCHENSK БЛАГОВЕЩЕНСК

☎ 4162 / pop 210,000 / ☽ Moscow +6hr

It's sometimes easy to forget where you are out here — in deepest Asia — till you find a place like this modest border town, 110km south of the Trans-Siberian tracks and across the Amur River from China. The mix of scattered, very European-looking, tsar-era buildings and Chinese tourists walking past Lenin statues can be fascinating.

A Russian military post since 1644, the border is a happy place now, but once was tense. In 1900 Cossacks, seeking to avenge European deaths in the Chinese Boxer Rebellion, slaughtered thousands of Chinese people here. In the '60s and early '70s, Blagoveshchensk (meaning 'good news') endured round-the-clock propaganda pumped over the river.

Orientation & Information

The train station is 4km north of the river on ul 50-let Oktyabrya, which meets pl Lenina (and east–west ul Lenina) by the river.

Amur Tourist (☎ 530 035, 530 036; http://amurturist .info; ul Kuznechnaya 1; ☽ 8am-noon & 1-5pm) Helps with city tours or trips to China.

Sights

Central pl Lenina is a good starting point for a walk west down the riverside promenade. About 250m west, you'll reach the Muravyov-Amursky statue, and then the red arch by the former river port, where Anton Chekhov came through (before heading straight to a Japanese prostitute, if his lurid letters are to be believed).

A block from the river to ul Lenina then a block west is the remarkable **Amur Regional Museum** (Amursky Oblastnoi Kraevedchesky muzey; ☎ 522 414; ul Lenina 165; admission R120; 🕙 10am-6pm Tue-Sun), housed in a former tsar-era market and Soviet-era headquarters for Young Communists *(komsomol)*. Inside are plenty of interesting photos, 1960s record players, a meteor that fell in 1991 near Tynda, and an Old Blagoveshchensk map (R10) that points out the centre's many lovely tsar-era buildings.

Sleeping & Eating

Druzhba Hotel (☎ 376 140; www.hoteldruzhba.ru, in Russian; ul Kuznechnaya 1; s/d incl breakfast from R950/1600; 🍴 🖥) About 600m east of pl Lenina, this riverside Soviet survivor has a variety of rooms – the cheapest have China views but no air-con. The wi-fi access works in the lobby cafe.

Churin Hotel (☎ 441 868; churin@hotelchurin.ru; r incl breakfast from R4000; 🍴 🖥) Behind an official building, just in from ul Lenina, this business-oriented hotel is a safe bet for a bit more comfort.

At research time, construction of an overdue new hotel called **Aziya** (ul 50-let Oktyabrya) was underway; it's several blocks from the river.

The riverside's open-air food stands are busy when there's good weather. Otherwise most restaurants tend to go for Chinese fare, including **Khing An** (☎ 520 333; Shevchenko 11; mains R150-350; 🕙 11am-midnight), about 200m west of pl Lenina.

Getting There & Away

Hop off the Trans-Siberian at Belogorsk, and take a taxi van to Blagoveshchensk (R200, two hours). Buses make the return journey from Blagoveshchensk's **bus station** (☎ 442 313; ul 50-let Oktyabrya 42/2).

Several trains leave from the **Blagoveshchensk train station** (☎ 494 205), including 385/386 on odd-numbered days to/from Vladivostok (R2900, 33 hours), passing through Khabarovsk (R1690, 16 hours), and 81/82 to/from Tynda (R2540, 20 hours).

The **Passazhirskoe Port Amurasso** (☎ 595 764; ul Chaykovskogo 1), 500m east of the Druzhba Hotel, sends a dozen daily boats to Hēihé, China (one way/return R875/1150, 15 minutes). You'll need a Chinese visa and a multi-entry Russian one to return. In Hēihé, an overnight train leaves at 7.10pm daily for Hāěrbīn (Harbin; about 12 hours). The nearest Chinese consulate is in Khabarovsk.

BIROBIDZHAN БИРОБИДЖАН

☎ 42162 / pop 80,000 / 🕙 Moscow +7hr

Quiet and shady, Birobidzhan is the capital of the 36,000-sq-km Jewish Autonomous Region (Yevreyskaya Avtonomnaya Oblast) and is a couple of hours shy of Khabarovsk on the Tran-Siberian line (if you're heading east). Its concept has always been a bit more interesting than its reality (evident by the mass influx of Jews coming to 'Stalin's Zion' in the 1920s, then leaving the undeveloped swamp just as quickly). Its Jewish population never rose above about 32,000 – many saw the undeveloped swamp and left – and dipped to 17,500 by the end of the '30s when synagogues were banned here.

Since 1991 diplomatic ties between Russia and Israel have led to an outward flood of Jews. Of the estimated 22,000 who lived here then, only a few thousand remain – about 2.4% of the region's population. These days, talk revolves more around a new bridge across the Amur River to China, which may mean US$800 million of upgrades to the rail system here. It's supposed to be finished by 2010.

Orientation & Information

Parallel to the tracks to the south are the main streets ul Lenina, then ul Sholom-Aleykhema and pr 60-let SSSR, reached from the station via ul Gorkogo along Pobedy Park.

You can find internet at the **main post office** (pr 60-let SSSR 16; per hr R60; 🕙 8am-9pm Mon-Fri, 8am-8pm Sat, 9am-6pm Sun).

Sights

Halfway along Pobedy Park facing the station, head west on ul Lenina to reach Birobidzhan's two main sights in town. **Freid** (☎ 41 531, 41 529; ul Sholom-Aleykhema 14A; 🕙 10am-6pm Mon-Fri) is Birobidzhan's Jewish cultural centre.

About 100m further west, the **Regional Museum** (Kraevedchesky muzey; ☎ 68 321; ul Lenina 25; admission R100; 🕙 10am-6pm Wed, Thu, Sat & Sun, to 5pm Fri) has a smattering of exhibits on local Jewish history, plus stuffed boars and bears and a mini diorama of the Volochaevka civil war battle.

Sleeping & Eating

For a quick stop, the train station's simple **resting rooms** (komnaty otdykha; ☎ 91 605; 2-/4-bed dm R475/350, lyux R1165), with shared bathrooms and showers (R67), are probably as good as the rooms at **Hotel Vostok** (☎ 65 330; ul Sholom-

Aleykhema 1; s/d R1400/2000), by a lively market. Vostok's restaurant, though, is the best option for sit-down meals.

Getting There & Away

All Trans-Siberian trains stop here. If you're headed for Khabarovsk, hop off for half a day (storing your bag at the train station), then continue on the cheaper *elektrichka,* which leaves at 9.40am and 6pm daily to Khabarovsk (R120, three hours). *Platskartny* (3rd-class, open carriage) seats on other trains are R300.

Otherwise hourly minibuses go to Khabarovsk (R200, three hours) from beside the train station.

KHABAROVSK ХАБАРОВСК
☎ 4212 / pop 590,000 / ⏰ Moscow +7hr

One of the Trans-Siberian's most pleasant surprises – and certainly a welcome break after days of relentless taiga out the train window – Khabarovsk roars with life, optimism and plenty of pretty tsar-era buildings facing the Amur River. Unlike so many places, the city has shelled out funds to develop its riverside – a great strolling area with multicoloured tiles, parks, monuments and walkways – in the public interest. Though the terminus of the Trans-Siberian is only 14 hours southeast, it's well worth giving Khabarovsk a day (probably not more) before continuing on.

It's hot in summer, but winter temperatures give it the unglamorous title of 'world's coldest city of over half a million people'. Locals brag more about its recent victory as Russia's 'most comfortable city'.

History

Khabarovsk was founded in 1858 as a military post by Eastern Siberia's governor general, Count Nikolai Muravyov (later Muravyov-Amursky), during his campaign to take the Amur back from the Manchus. It was named after the man who got the Russians into trouble with the Manchus in the first place, the 17th-century Russian explorer Yerofey Khabarov.

The Trans-Siberian rail line arrived from Vladivostok in 1897. During the Russian Civil War, the town was occupied by Japanese troops for most of 1920. The final Bolshevik victory in the Far East was at Volochaevka, 45km west.

In 1969 Soviet and Chinese soldiers fought a bloody hand-to-hand battle over little Damansky Island in the Ussuri River. Since 1984, tensions have eased. Damansky and several other islands have been handed back to the Chinese.

Orientation

Khabarovsk's train station is about 3.5km northeast of the Amur waterfront at the head of broad Amursky bul; the airport is 9km east of the centre.

Knizhny Mir (ul Karla Marksa 37; ⏰ 9am-8pm) stocks a good range of city and regional maps for the entire Russian Far East (Khabarovsk maps are R120, an OK city guide in English and Russian is R170).

Information
INTERNET ACCESS

Internet Mir (ul Muravyova-Amurskogo 28; per hr R72; ⏰ 8am-10pm Mon-Fri, 9am-6pm Sat & Sun) Web access; next to the post office.

RedCom (ul Karla Marksa 74; per hr R72; ⏰ 9am-8pm Mon-Fri, 11am-6pm Sat)

MEDICAL SERVICES

Hotel Intourist (p248) has a doctor on its 1st floor, who can help with some cases or refer you to city specialists.

POST

Main post office (ul Muravyova-Amurskogo 28; ⏰ 8am-10pm Mon-Fri, 9am-6pm Sat & Sun)

TRAVEL AGENCIES

Either of the following can help book rail or plane tickets and assist with one-month Chinese tourist visas (about R3000 to R3500; allow seven days), as well as various city and regional tours.

Dalgeo Tours (☎ 318 829; www.dalgeotours.com; ul Turgeneva 78; ⏰ 10am-7pm Mon-Fri) English-speaking staff are helpful, though local tours get pricey.

Welcome (Velcom; ☎ 735 990; www.welcome.khv.ru; ul Dzerzhinskogo 24; ⏰ 9am-6pm Mon-Fri, 10am-2pm Sat) The name sure applies to the cheerful staff, who offer slight variants of city tours and cheaper visa fees.

Sights & Activities
MUSEUMS

One of the region's best museums, the **Regional History Museum** (Kraevedchesky muzey; ☎ 312 054; ul Shevchenko 11; admission R140, photo permits R100; ⏰ 10am-6pm Tue-Sun) has a series of well-laid-out halls in an evocative 1894 red-brick building. Highlights include a far-better-than-average

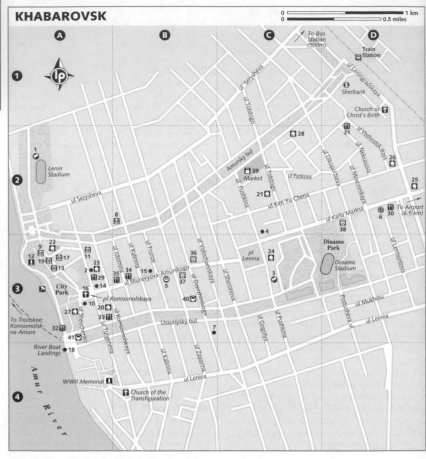

KHABAROVSK

look into native cultures and a full-on pano-rama of the snowy 1922 civil war battle at Volochaevka. There's no Gulag coverage, even though the nearby prison population was big-ger than the city's in the '30s. At research time, the museum was busy adding on a second wing called the Amur River Museum.

The nearby **Military Museum** (Voyenny muzey; ☎ 326 350; ul Shevchenko 20; admission R140; ⏰ 10am-5pm Tue-Sun) is a not uninteresting four-room frenzy of battleaxes, guns, knives and photos of moustached heroes of past conflicts, plus a back courtyard of various vehicles including a luxury officers-only rail carriage dating from 1926.

The highlights of the small **Archaeology Museum** (Muzey Arkheology; ☎ 324 177; ul Turgeneva 86; admission R180; ⏰ 10am-5.30pm Tue-Sun) are the

reproductions and diagrams of the wide-eyed figures found at the ancient Sikachi-Alyan petroglyphs (p250).

The **Far Eastern Art Museum** (Dalnevostochny Khudozhestvenny muzey; ☎ 328 338; ul Shevchenko 7; admis-sion R200; ⏰ 10am-5pm Tue-Sun) has lots of religious icons, Japanese porcelain and 19th-century Russian paintings.

The **Amur Fish Aquarium** (Muzei-akvarium Rybbi-Amura; ☎ 315 596; Amursky bul 13A; admission R130; ⏰ 11am-5pm Wed-Sun) gives props to the gilled friends from the nearby Amur.

RIVER CRUISES
Skip the overpriced river cruises offered by local agents (eg R1250 per person for two hours) and take a (at times rollicking) party

cruise; these leave regularly in summer from the riverfront. At research time, hour-long cruises (R120) left at 1.30pm, 3.30pm and 5.30pm, and 90-minute versions (R200) at 7.30pm, 9.30pm and 11.30pm.

WALKING
Khabarovsk's compact city centre is just perfect for a day's worth of looking around. Begin a stroll at pl Komsomolsk, dominated by a monument for Soviet revolutionary soldiers and the towering, reconstructed Orthodox church Khram Uspeniya Bozhey Materi. Towards the river, to your left, is the golden headquarters of the Amur Steamship Company.

Steps lead down to an impressive makeover of the riverfront, with shady parks, open-air beer and ice-cream stands, and walkways leading in both directions. Follow the bluff path to the right, where you'll pass a sassy Count Nikolai Muravyov-Amursky statue and a nearby cliff-top tower, in which a troupe of WWI Austro-Hungarian POW musicians were shot for refusing to play the Russian Imperial anthem.

Either head to the water or follow the path north then back towards the grey Hotel Intourist. You'll see the four-pillared Soviet entrance to another riverside park to your left. Go right, slightly uphill, and drop by the town's excellent Regional History Museum (p245).

Head back to pl Komsomolsk, and turn left on the city's favourite avenue, ul Muravyova-Amurskogo. The first building on the left is the striking red-and-black brick **Far Eastern State Research Library** (ul Muravyova-Amurskogo 1), built from 1900 to 1902.

A couple of blocks down, note the Mercury statue atop the mint-green **Style Moderne Tsentralny Gastronom** (ul Muravyova-Amurskogo 9), built in 1895. Another couple of blocks along is the former **House of Pioneers** (Dom Pionerov; ul Muravyova-Amurskogo 17) and parliament building, now a souvenir shop.

Continue east to pl Lenina, an elaborately renovated square filled with fountains, flowers and posing wedding couples (or ice sculptures in January); a relatively tiny Lenin looks on from the north side. Head downhill along ul Pushkina to return to the river along the green parks of bul Ussuriysky, then have a beer aboard a party cruise (opposite).

Sleeping
Dalgeo Tour's homestay service is probably only worth considering for solo travellers (US$66 per person including breakfast, but not visa registration!). All hotels listed here charge a 20% or 25% reservation fee unless otherwise noted.

BUDGET

Komnaty otdykha (☎ 383 710; 3rd fl, train station; r 12/24hr from R360/510) If you're stopping for just a night, consider the train station's quite nice resting rooms.

our pick **Hotel Tsentralnaya** (☎ 303 300, 324 759; ul Pushkina 52; s/d R1500/1700; 🌐) It's been years since the staff would let us see a room here (maybe Paul Theroux was too pissy when he stayed while researching *The Great Railway Bazaar*), but now foreigners are welcome. The 200 rooms have been spruced up considerably and half of them overlook pl Lenina.

Ekspress Vostok (☎ 384 797; ul Komsomolskaya 67; s/d R1700/2400; 🌐) Just a couple of blocks from the river and the main crawl, this fine budget hotel has tiny little rooms that manage to squeeze in an armoire, desk, balcony and wi-fi – but no breakfast.

MIDRANGE & TOP END

Versailles (Versal; ☎ 659 222; ul Amursky bul 46A; s/d incl breakfast R1900/2950; 🌐 🖥) This cheerful hotel, an easy walk from the train station, has pleasant, red-carpeted rooms with fridge and funny photos of squirrels. It's set back from the street, fronted with seal lamp posts.

Hotel Turist (☎ 439 674; www.habtour.ru, in Russian; ul Karla Marksa 67; r incl breakfast with/without air-con R2400/2100; 🌐) Its eight floors pay tribute to old-school templates, with balconies that overlook the clover-leaf web of roads outside. In all, it's not bad – rooms were redone in 2008, and, while they're still compact, there's a fresh dose of vinyl on the floors and ruby red on the curtains.

Hotel Zarya (☎ 310 101; hotel_zarya@mail.ru; ul Kim Yu Chena 81/16; r incl breakfast from R2150; 🌐 🖥) Zarya has tidy modern rooms in a plain white-brick building on a back street between the train station and centre. Its modern makeover, nice buffet breakfast, downstairs banya (bathhouse; R600 to R1000 per hour) and great staff give it a fairly boutique hotel feel.

Hotel Intourist (☎ 312 313; www.intour.khv.ru; Amursky bul 2; r from R2960; 🌐) Teeming with tour groups, this big Bolshevik still breathes as if it's 1975. Elevators are often under repair, the business centre's internet is often down and you pay an extra R500 or so for your foreign self, but views are superb on the upper floors.

Hotel Amethyst (☎ 420 760; amethyst@hotel.kht .ru; ul Lva Tolstogo 5A; s/d R3200/3400; 🌐) This cute boutique-style back-streeter has frumpy,

comfy rooms – doubles considerably larger than singles – with balconies. All come with fridge and wi-fi access. No reservation fee. Breakfast is R300.

Hotel Sapporo (☎ 226 745; sapporo1@gin.ru; Komsomolskaya 79; s/d incl breakfast R4000/4300; 🌐 🖥) Just off the main drag, the Sapporo's 20 rooms are the centre's best high-end option once you get past the banal lobby. There's a slight Japanese air in the rooms, with blonde-wood bed frames and a bit of bamboo.

Parus (☎ 327 270, 649 510; guest@parus.vic.ru; ul Shevchenko 5; s/d incl breakfast R4200/5600; 🌐 🖥) Part of a century-old brick building near the water, the Parus sure makes a grand entrance – with chandeliers, iron staircase, reading room – but rooms are rather standard, with thin carpets and cheesy art. No reservation fee.

Eating & Drinking

Many of Khabarovsk's busiest eating spots are simple cafes or open-air stands, with cheap hot dogs (R25), ice cream and beer; particularly popular are the riverside cafes.

Tsentralny Gastronom (ul Muravyova-Amurskogo 9; meals R150-300; ⏱ 11am-10pm) In a 19th-century building, this cute modern-retro, self-service cafe has a good selection of meals.

Chocolate (☎ 420 097; ul Turgeneva 74; meals R500-750; ⏱ 24hr) If you can deal with a slightly snooty air, Chocolate has slick international snacks (fajitas, burgers, brownies) and free wi-fi.

Teplan-Yaki (☎ 324 763; ul Muravyova-Amurskogo 11; teriyaki meals R600-750; sushi from R400; ⏱ noon-11pm) This popular loungey sushi spot on the main strip has a 'chill' electronica soundtrack and classy bamboo setting, with a host of sushi options.

our pick **Russky Restaurant** (☎ 306 587; Ussuriysky bul 9; meals R1000-1500; ⏱ noon-1am) Nearly all Russian restaurants get a bit kitschy, but this one goes all out – but in a way that never betrays authenticity or the sense that you're happy being there. Paintings of tsars, side-rooms in *dacha* style and traditional music kick off dinners that frequently require reservations.

If you just need groceries, the best places are **Citi HK Supermarket** (ul Karla Marksa 76; ⏱ 9am-11pm) and **Pelikan** (ul Vladivostokskaya 61; ⏱ 24hr), near the train station.

Entertainment

You may need some Russian skills to be 'entertained' in Khabarovsk.

Drama Theatre (Teatr Dramy; ☎ 303 531; ul Dzerzhinskogo 44) Lots of Chekhov.

Theatre of Musical Comedy (Teatr Muzykalnoy Komedy; ☎ 227 021; ul Karla Marksa 64; tickets R80-800) Music, jokes and the occasional heavy-metal concert (Ronnie James Dio started his 2005 tour here).

SovKino (ul Muravyova-Amurskogo 32) Screens dubbed Hollywood flicks for R100 to R150.

Shopping

Tainy Remesla (☎ 327 385; ul Muravyova-Amurskogo 17; ✲ 10am-7pm) Best souvenir shop in town, in the old House of Pioneers building.

Main market (cnr Amursky bul & ul Lva Tolstogo; ✲ 8am-7pm) Covers everything from plug adaptors to fresh produce.

Getting There & Away

If you're tired of train station ticket windows, many travel agents around town book train and air tickets. The friendliest we found in the region is **InterVizit** (☎ 316 262; ul Dzerzhinskogo 39; ✲ train tickets 10am-6pm Mon-Fri, air tickets 9am-8pm Mon-Fri, to 6pm Sat & Sun), which charges about R80 to R120 commission for train tickets.

AIR

The **airport** (☎ 263 268), about 7km east of the centre, offers domestic services to Moscow (R13,400, 8½ hours, daily), Vladivostok (from R4200, 1¾ hours, daily), Irkutsk (from R8000, three hours, daily) and other regional hubs.

Vladivostok Air (www.vladivostokavia.ru) flies twice weekly to Hāěrbīn (R6400) and Dailin (R8240) and once to Běijīng (R13,500), plus twice weekly to Niigata (R12,000), Japan. Vladivostok Air and **Asiana** (☎ 334 567; www .flyasiana.com) split almost daily flights to Seoul (R10,835). International flights usually include the R800 departure tax in the price.

Airlines have airport offices, and **Aeroflot** (☎ 783 435; ul Pushkina 50) also has an office in town.

BOAT

Between May and October, hydrofoils leave at 7am daily from the peach-coloured **river station** (☎ 468 832; Ussuriysky bul; ✲ 8am-7pm) for Komsomolsk-na-Amure (R700, six hours) on the BAM line. There is also a whirlwind of competing boats offering rides to nearby Fuyuan, China (R1600, 1½ hours), leaving around 7am and 7pm daily. These companies

include **Velkomp** (☎ 421 158) and **Tor** (☎ 468 666, 301 447).

BUS

The **bus station** (☎ 343 909; ul Voronezhskaya 19), 500m north of the train station (go by tram or autobus 6), sends hourly buses to Komsomolsk (R430, six hours).

TRAIN

Shining from a finished renovation, the lovely **train station** (☎ 382 222) has a nice, air-conditioned waiting lounge on the 3rd floor, but little in the area grocery-wise.

Heading west, *Rossiya* (1) departs on even-numbered dates for Chita (R6900, 40 hours), Irkutsk (R9500, two days 12 hours) and Moscow (R16,000, five days 10 hours), while the Novosibirsk-bound train (7) also stops in Irkutsk (R6200). Running alternate days in summer, trains 43 and 239 reach Irkutsk (R6400) or Moscow (R10,800).

Train 385 goes to Blagoveshchensk (R1690, 16 hours). See p245 for more on getting to Birobidzhan.

Heading east, Vladivostok is best reached on the daily *Okean* (6) service (R2700, 13 hours).

Train 326 departs for Tynda (R2800, 30 hours); for Komsomolsk, the best train is 67 (R1750, eight hours), while 351 continues on to Vanino (R1900, 24½ hours). These daily services all leave in the evening.

The train to Hāěrbīn (R3900) leaves at 8pm Monday and Thursday.

Getting Around

Marshrutky, trolleybuses and trams (all R12) make journeys around town. From the train station, bus 4 goes to pl Komsomolsk in the centre and trams 1 and 2 go near pl Lenina. From the airport, trolleybus 1 goes to pl Komsomolsk along ul Muravyova-Amurskogo and bus 35 goes to the train station. Bus 89 or tram 6 goes from the centre to the bus station.

A taxi to the centre from the airport is R300, and usually R200 or R250 the other way.

AROUND KHABAROVSK
Fuyuan (China) Фуюань

A shopping destination for locals, the Chinese border town of Fuyuan is reached by daily hydrofoil service from Khabarovsk from mid-May to mid-October (see left).

You'll need a Chinese visa to go, and a double-/multiple-entry Russian visa to return. Fuyuan has hotels and bus services to Hāĕrbīn.

Sikachi-Alyan Сикачи-Алян

Hard to reach by public transport, Sikachi-Alyan, 75km north of Khabarovsk, is a scrappy, mostly Nanai village with a long riverside beach and – its claim to fame – faint stone carvings of strange graphic figures, supposedly 12,000 years old.

Most visitors come to visit the tourist complex operated by Welcome (p245), which has a basic **cabin** (per person R500, incl meals R1000), traditional dwellings and a nearby beach, where you can walk to two groups of carvings, about 750m and 2.5km away. This is probably for archaeological buffs only.

All agencies in Khabarovsk offer pricey tours (Dalgeo charges R4800 per person, including lunch). You can also hire a taxi from Khabarovsk for R500 per hour and a guide (about R250 per hour) – you'd need about five or six hours.

VLADIVOSTOK ВЛАДИВОСТОК

☎ 4232 / pop 610,000 / ⏰ Moscow +7hr

At first sight, Vladivostok is something like 'Russia's San Francisco' – a real stunner, with pointed mountains springing up above a network of bays, most strikingly the crooked, dock-lined Golden Horn Bay (named for its likeness to Istanbul's). Closer up, it can be a little grey, with Soviet housing blocks squeezed between new condos and century-old mansions. But it's a great place to kick off or finish a trip – and work out those leg muscles on the hilly streets.

Big changes are coming. The city's set to host the 2012 Asia-Pacific Economic Conference, and up to US$6 billion of projects (including a bridge or two, new business hotels and roads) are in the works.

Timing-wise, June can often be grey and wet, while September and October are often the nicest, sunniest months.

History

Founded in 1860, Vladivostok (meaning 'To Rule the East') became a naval base in 1872. Tsarevitch Nicholas II turned up in 1891 to inaugurate the new Trans-Siberian rail line. By the early 20th century, Vladivostok teemed with merchants, speculators and sailors of every nation. Koreans and Chinese, many of whom had built the city, accounted for four out of every five of its citizens.

After the fall of Port Arthur in the Russo-Japanese War of 1904–05, Vladivostok took on an even more crucial strategic role. The city held out until 25 October 1922, when Soviet forces finally marched in and took control – it was the last city to fall.

In the years to follow, Stalin deported or shot most of the city's foreign population. Closed from 1958 to 1992, Vladivostok opened up with a bang – literally (mafia shoot-outs were a part of early business deals) – in the '90s, and has only started to settle down in recent years.

Orientation

The heart of central Vladivostok is where Okeansky pr intersects with ul Svetlanskaya, the city's main waterfront axis. Ul Fokina, west of Okeansky pr, is the rather scrappy 'Arbat' pedestrian shopping strip.

You can find city maps at bookshops such as **Dom Knigi** (ul Svetlanskaya 43; ⏰ 10am-7pm Mon-Sat, to 5pm Sun) and **Knigomir** (☎ 414 852; ul Aleutskaya 23; ⏰ 10am-9pm).

Information

See p331 for consulate information.

INTERNET ACCESS

Most hotels have wi-fi access; the Hotel Vladivostok lobby has free wi-fi access for all. A couple of other places to get online include **OS** (ul Fokina 4; per hr R40; ⏰ 8am-10pm) and the **post office** (ul Verkhneportovaya; per MB R2.77, per hr R3.60; ⏰ 8am-9pm Mon-Fri, 8am-10pm Sat, 9am-6pm Sun).

MEDIA

Vibirai A free Russian-language biweekly entertainment mag available at hotels and many restaurants.
Vladivostok News (www.vladivostoknews.ru) An online newspaper in English.
Vladivostok Putyevoditel Annual, free, ad-based guidebook (in Russian, with some English) available at kiosks.
Vladivostok Times (www.vladivostoktimes.ru)

MEDICAL SERVICES

MUZ Hospital No 1 (☎ 258 663; ul Sadovaya 22)

MONEY

There are currency exchange desks and ATMs all over town.

Sberbank (ul Aleutskaya 12; ☯ 8.45am-8pm Mon-Sat, 10am-5pm Sun) Accepts travellers cheques (2% commission).

POST
Post office (ul Verkhneportovaya; ☯ 8am-9pm Mon-Fri, 8am-10pm Sat, 9am-6pm Sun) Opposite the train station, with a modern business centre upstairs.

TELEPHONE
Make calls at the post office or from **Dalsvyaz** (ul Svetlanskaya 57; ☯ 9am-7pm Mon-Fri, 10am-5pm Sat).

TRAVEL AGENCIES
Most agencies can usually help get a Chinese tourist visa in three to five days for about US$100. Generally tours are quite pricey, but they can help with train and air tickets, too.
Dalintourist (☎ 410 903; www.dalintourist.ru; ul Fokina 8; ☯ 9am-7pm Mon-Fri, 9am-3pm Sat) The English-speaking manager on the 2nd floor helps with area tours and info, and can get you English speaking guides (per hour R400).
Discovery Travel Club (☎ 777 679; www.discovery club.info; Pogranichnaya 15B; ☯ 9am-noon & 1-6pm Mon-Sat) At the helm, Julia speaks excellent English and is a good source of information (if you can track her down!).

VISA REGISTRATION
OVIR (☎ 490 802; ul Posetskaya; ☯ 10am-12.30pm Tue & Thu, 2-4.30pm Wed & Fri) Registers visas for free – no English. Go to room 15 through the little red-brick entrance to the right of the police station.

Sights & Activities
On tram-lined streets around the centre you'll find plenty of tsar-era buildings. The main areas for locals to mill about are **pl Bortsov Revolyutsii** (ul Svetlanskaya & Okeansky pr) and Sportivnaya Harbour.

Much of the water facing Vladivostok is quite polluted. You'll find better swimming on Popov or Russky islands (right), or near Nakhodka (p257).

ARSENEV REGIONAL MUSEUM
At the interesting **Arsenev Regional Museum** (Kraevedchesky muzey Arseneva; ☎ 413 977; ul Svetlanskaya 20; adult/child R100/70; ☯ 10am-6pm Tue-Sun), which dates from 1890, you're likely to befriend at least a couple of grey-haired 'guards' while walking through the three floors of exhibits recounting Vladivostok's history. On the ground (1st) floor note the stuffed tiger and bear interlocked as if dancing; the 2nd floor is

filled with great 19th-century photos, including a display of the Brynner family.

FUNICULAR & AROUND
Vladivostok's favourite attraction is the well-oiled **funicular railway** (funikulyor; ul Pushkinskaya; tickets R5; ☯ 7am-8pm), which makes a fun 60-second ride up a 100m hill every few minutes. At the top, go under ul Sukhanova via the slummy underpass to a great but trashy lookout by the DVGTU (Far Eastern State Technical University) for the best views of the bay.

While you're up here, cross ul Aksakovskaya to reach the **Artetazh** (☎ 608 902; 4th fl, ul Aksakovskaya 12; admission free; ☯ 10am-6pm Tue-Fri, 11am-5pm Sat & Sun), DVGTU's humble modern-art showcase with a few intriguing piss-takes at the country's red past.

It's not a long walk from the centre. Buses 23, 31 and 49 run along nearby ul Svetlanskaya from the train station.

FORTS
Attention fort fans: Vladivostok teems with sprawling, rather unique subterranean forts (130 in all), built between the 1880s and the early 20th century. Neophytes should stick to the easily accessible **Vladivostok Fortress Museum** (Muzey Vladivostokskaya Krepost; ☎ 400 896; ul Batareynaya 4A; admission R70; ☯ 10am-6pm), overlooking Sportivnaya Harbour. Set in a fort that operated from 1882 to 1923, the museum has many models and photos (with English subtitles!), and anti-aircraft guns outside that you can point towards Japan. Reach the fort from ul Zapadnaya.

Sixteen protective forts encircle Vladivostok in a 13km arc. The best to visit is the hilltop Fort No 7, 14km north of the centre. It has 1.5km of tunnels, pretty much untouched since the last 400 soldiers stationed here left in 1923. Visiting on your own is difficult, so most go by hiring a guide and a taxi.

Many organised tours to Russky Island (below) include visits to Voroshilova fort (5km southeast of the final ferry stop).

Local adventurers run gritty tours of underground tunnels (some 3.5km long) linked with old forts. Check www.vtc.ru/~vladdig, in Russian, for details.

ISLANDS & BOATS
Just offshore, Russky Island, a fully militarised island for most of the past 150 years, only opened to foreigners this decade. It's possible

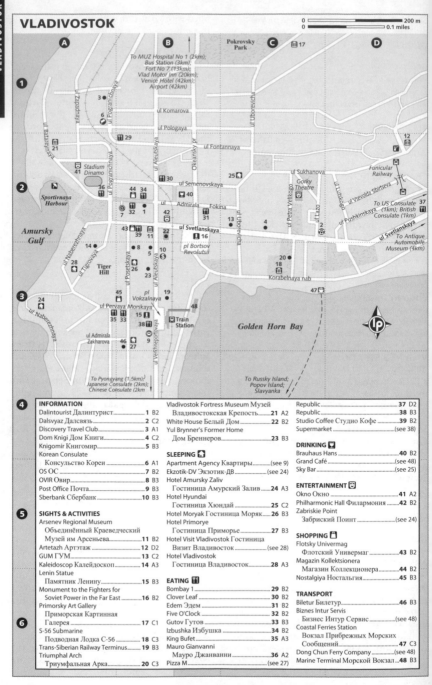

VLADIVOSTOK

to ferry out on your own and tour yourself, but it's big, and finding the forts and cannon embankments or beaches is difficult if you don't take a (costly) tour. However, it's well worth taking the ferry over and returning right away for a cheap 'bay tour'.

Ferries to Russky leave from the **coastal ferries station** (☎ 220 823), 100m east of the S-56 submarine. At research time, six daily boats were heading to a couple of points on Russky (return R50, 30 minutes) – at around 6.30am, 9.10am, noon, 2.30pm, 5.30pm and 8pm – staying for 10 minutes, then returning.

Just beyond Russky is Popov Island, better regarded for its beaches and filled with many guest houses and *dachas* (summer country houses). One or two boats go daily (return R70, 1½ hours), often requiring an overnight stay.

Travel agents offer bay cruises. Also **Kulcidoskup** (☎ 411 405, ul Tiyivuju 25/1) can arrange three hour evening cruises (from R3500).

OTHER SIGHTS

Vladivostok's bipolar art museum, the **Primorsky Art Gallery** (Primorskaya kartinnaya galereya; ☎ 427 748, 411 162; pr Partizanski 12; admission west/east R50/40; ⊙ 9am-6pm Tue-Sun), has two separate halls east of Pokrovsky Park (with separate admissions). The one to the west features 19th-century and early-20th-century oil paintings (a good one is Fechin's sassy *Golden Hairs* from 1914). The east gallery features changing exhibitions of local painters.

If you're a bit of a car (or Soviet) nerd, the newish **Antique Automobile Museum** (Muzey Avtomotostarini; ☎ 212 477; ul Sakhalinskaya 2A; admission R70; ⊙ 10am-6pm Tue-Sun), stranded under the smoke belching from a nearby factory

in east Vladivostok, is an absolute classic. A room full of Sovietmobiles (motorcycles too) from the 1930s to 1970s includes a 1948 M&M-green GAZ-20 'Pobeda' (Victory). Take bus 31 at ul Svetlanskayaand exit at the ul Borisenko's end.

WALKING

Begin from the train station, where, at the north end of the main platform a bronze marker indicates the Trans-Siberian Railway terminus (reading 9288km, the distance from Moscow).

Across the street from the station is an unusually animated Lenin statue (he points towards the nearby tram stop). Ignore him and head up ul Aleutskaya, lined with many impressive buildings from the early 1900s. A half-block down on your left is **Yul Brynner's former home** (ul Aleutskaya 15), where Yul entered his Swiss family's world in 1920. It's above the streetside concrete wall, where (ironically?) a small barber shop is now in place. Consider getting a baldie haircut, or step up to see the iffily planned plaque of a smoking Yul (he died from lung cancer in 1985).

Continue heading north, popping into the Arsenev Regional Museum (p251), before going through the underpass east along ul Svetlanskaya (previously known as ul Amerikanskaya then ul Leninskaya). Towering to the right is the forbidding White House (Bely dom), a government building that replaced green gardens with a Soviet HQ in 1983. Just beyond this place is Vladivostok's most stunning meeting point: the concrete plaza around the sombre Monument to the Fighters for Soviet Power in the Far East.

CAR CITY *Robert Reid*

It's hard to walk around the centre's traffic-jammed streets without noticing Vladivostok's gone Texas about cars. You have to have one, the bigger the better. One local with a Bentley told me he wouldn't go to a nearby cinema. He explained: 'No parking, and I don't want to walk.'

Not long ago, locals exchanged old cars in a sketchy park in eastern Vladivostok, but now they just enter one of 50 'live auction houses' across town, which broadcast 30-second internet auctions where people bid on used Japanese and Korean cars that arrive a week later. Many coming will get shipped across Russia; meanwhile, all can be seen, awaiting customs, in filled multilevel garages along Golden Horn Bay.

For fun, I stopped by an auction house at the Morskoy vokzal (sea terminal) and asked about getting a 1977 Russian Lada. 'Oh, very bad', the attendant protested. 'Locals sell those for maybe US$300. Can't we bid on a Toyota Corolla for you?'. Three-year-old Corollas go for US$12,000, plus US$500 shipping and US$3000 customs. I passed. 'Yes', he said, 'this is a very good business'.

Continue east on ul Svetlanskaya and drop by the department store **GUM** (ul Svetlanskaya 35; 🕑 10am-8pm Mon-Sat, to 7pm Sun), its exterior showing off its original Dresden-inspired architecture.

A block east, duck right through the reconstructed triumphal arch, originally built for Tsar Nicholas II in 1891 (then destroyed by Soviets and rebuilt by New Russians). Beyond to the right, you'll see the green-and-grey **S-56 submarine** (Memornalnoi Gvargeiskoi Podvodnoi Lodke S-56; ☎ 216 757; Korabelnaya nab; adult/child R50/25; 🕑 10am-8pm), where you can crawl through porthole doors to see bunk rooms and Christmas-coloured torpedoes.

Return to ul Svetlanskaya and continue east a couple of blocks, then go left on ul Pushkinskaya, which turns east to the funicular (p251) and the city's greatest view.

Sleeping

Vladivostok's pricey, at times disappointing accommodation situation will hopefully soon get a boost as Marriott and Accor are supposedly opening (overdue) new business hotels during the life of this edition.

BUDGET

Ekzotik-DV (☎ 308 063, 561 738; Hotel Amursky Zaliv, ul Naberezhnaya 9; s/d R500/1000) This scrappy, humble annexe to the Amursky Zaliv is Vladivostok's best budget deal. It's definitely not great – worn out wood-floor rooms with rust-coloured floral bedspreads and faded-tile bathrooms – but it's clean and you get a balcony overlooking the water.

Apartment agency (kvartiri; ☎ 413 415; 3rd fl, ul Verkhneportovaya 2A; from R1000; 🕑 9am-9pm) Find a homestay through this friendly, Russian-speaking agency in the post office across from the train station.

MIDRANGE & TOP END

Hotel Moryak (☎ /fax 499 499; moriak2004@mail.ru; ul Posetskaya 38; r with/without hot water R1800/1400) This grey-brick, yet cheerful place has an endearing lobby with live frogs! The colourful rooms are compact, with thin walls (and mattresses) and tiny bathrooms. Laundry is a reasonable R250 per bag.

Hotel Amursky Zaliv (☎ 412 808, 411 941; www.azimuthotels.ru; ul Naberezhnaya 9; old/new r incl breakfast R1800/2500; 🕑 Mar-Nov) This bayside hotel looms below a bizarre rooftop. The cheaper rooms

are carpeted old-school deals, and the new ones were redone in 2007 (slick bathrooms, better TVs, shockingly gold bedspreads); all have balconies.

Hotel Vladivostok (☎ 412 808; www.azimuthotels.ru; ul Naberezhnaya 10; s/d R2000/2500; 🖵) Once the only hotel alive in the centre, this 12-floor grey tower now needs a serious exterior makeover. Inside the rooms are OK – a bit dark, smoky on occasion, and with worn carpets. The lobby has free wi-fi. Also see Hotel Visit Vladivostok (below).

Venice Hotel (☎ 307 603; http://venice.far-east.ru; ul Portovaya 39; s/d R2300/3200) This small business hotel is across from the airport – perfectly fine if you have an early flight or late arrival.

our pick **Hotel Primorye** (☎ 411 422, 413 582; ul Posetskaya 20; s/d economy R2550/2750, superior R2750/3450; 🍴 🖵) Considering quality and location, this is Vladivostok's best accommodation. Economy rooms are spotless and small, but with playful details such as funny artwork. The higher-priced superiors face Golden Horn Bay. Wi-fi access throughout. There's a sauna and a cafe serving a R180 breakfast.

Hotel Visit Vladivostok (☎ 413 453; www.vizit.vl.ru; ul Naberezhnaya 10; s/d incl breakfast R3400/3800; 🍴 🖵) Welcomingly taking over the 4th floor of Hotel Vladivostok, these 36 inviting, refurbished rooms feel a world away from the grey tower they're in. There's free wi-fi and a small nautical-themed bar overlooking the water.

Vlad Motor Inn (☎ 388 888; www.vlad-inn.ru; ul Vosmaya 35, Sanatornaya; r R4600; 🍴 🖵) If you've had enough of grim Russian blocks, the 35-room Vlad is way outside the centre – 20km towards the airport – in a lovely, leafy outskirt area near an OK beach. It's seriously understyled, but rooms are very well kept. You can bus here or take the local train to Sanatornaya (R12, 40 minutes).

Hotel Hyundai (☎ 402 233, 407 250; www.hotelhyundai.ru; ul Semenovskaya 29; s/d incl breakfast from R6000/6500; 🍴 🖵) Big with Asian business travellers and groups, this 12-floor, 335-room tower has standard carpeted rooms with satellite TV, modern bathrooms and nice views. There's a sauna/pool to use, plus a nice rooftop bar (nonguests pay R450 for use of the pool).

Eating

Options coat the town, offering more class and types of food than pretty much anything between here and Moscow or Alaska.

RUSSIAN

Republic (ul Aleutskaya; meals R150-250; 9am-11pm Mon-Thu, 9am-midnight Fri, 10am-midnight Sat & Sun) Inside a glass pyramid, this perfectly respectable *stolovaya* (canteen) draws more than a couple of cheap dates with its tasty Russian-styled dishes and its own beer (R90). Its loungelike newer location (ul Svetlanskaya 83), near the funicular, is dressed up with prints of old Russian newspapers.

Izbushka (510 269; ul Fokina 9; meals R200-500; 11am-11pm) A popular little Russian eatery with two themed rooms – a taiga room and a *dacha* – and tasty food.

Gutov (414 821; ul Posetskaya 23; meals R700-1000; noon-midnight) This beer-hall place with chunky wood tables serves large Russian meals, mostly meats and fish fillets cooked up with a host of vegetable toppings.

OTHER ASIAN

Bombay 1 (Bombei 1; 432 167; ul Fontannaya 15/2, meals R250-700; noon-midnight) Vlad's only curry spot. There are R200 thali lunches from noon to 3pm and a host of North Indian–style curries served as Bollywood films play on the telly.

ourpick **Pyongyang** (Pkhenyan; 964 458; Hotel Korona, ul Verkhneportovaya 68B; meals R500-1000; noon-midnight) Staffed by newcomers from North Korea, this two-room Korean restaurant has a photo menu of excellent food (barbecue starts at R480). It's about four stops south of the train station by bus 60.

Edem (261 990; ul Fokina 22; meals R1600-2200; 11am-midnight Sun-Thu, to 2am Fri & Sat) Vladivostok's first and best sushi bar is in an attractive cellarlike space with nooks to sit in. Sushi and sashimi combos start at R1600; an eight-piece California roll is R300. 'Sushi time' is 11am to 5pm, and 6pm to 11pm only.

ITALIAN & OTHER WESTERN

ourpick **Five O'Clock** (945 531; ul Fokina 6; pastries R50; 8am-8pm Mon-Sat) Vladivostok, take note of this novel idea: coffee, brownies, cakes and quiche (R50), all made daily and sold for less than an espresso at most 'cafes'.

Studio Coffee (552 222; ul Svetlanskaya 18; meals R300-500; 24hr) Vladivostok's cool crowd comes to this indoor-outdoor cafe to enjoy a drink or remarkably well-prepared light meals – chicken sandwiches (R150), hamburgers and the like.

Pizza M (413 430; Hotel Primorye, ul Posetskaya 20; meals R350-700; 24hr) Classier than its name might suggest, the M (inside Hotel Primorye) is one of Vlad's coolest hang-outs, with two stylish rooms and good pizzas (R200 to R500).

Mauro Gianvanni (220 782; ul Fokina 16; meals R400-800; noon-midnight Sun-Thu, 24hr Fri & Sat) This slick little brick-oven pizzeria – run by an Italian guy – pumps VH1 videos in the modern interior, though most patrons sit out on the deck when the weather behaves. Crispy pizzas start at R240.

QUICK EATS & SELF CATERING

In good weather, open-air stands cook up sizzling shashlyks (R130 to R150) and *shaverma* (kebab; R70) around Sportivnaya Harbour. Some restaurants offer 'business lunches' from noon to 4pm from R200 to R300.

Clover Leaf (cnr ul Semenovskaya & Aleutskaya) mall has a 24-hour supermarket with a deli. There's another **supermarket** (ul Aleutskaya; 24hr) across from the train station. **King Bufet** (ul Pervaya Morskaya 9; meals R150-200; noon-10pm, food to 7pm) is a snazzy mezzanine cafeteria.

Drinking

Locals like grabbing a beer and sitting on the benches overlooking Sportivnaya Harbour – or any other available bench.

Sky Bar (12th fl, Hotel Hyundai, ul Semenovskaya 29; 6pm-2am) Excellent bay views.

Brauhaus Hans (406 875; ul Fokina 25A; 24hr) Hans pours a mean mug at this all-the-way German beer house, with upstairs nightly live music and all-day snacks and meals. Accessed from ul Semenovskaya.

Grand Café (302 722; 12th fl, Morskoy vokzal; noon-1am) Atop the ferry terminal, this MTV-ready club-restaurant goes for glittering parties at night and coffee-sipping snacks on its roof deck during the day. Great views.

Entertainment

Okno (555 222; 3rd fl, ul Batareynaya 3A; entry incl all drinks R3000; 10pm-3am or 4am Wed-Sat) Vlad's coolest club's entry price keeps the luxury to a high degree, not to mention gold baroque armchairs, visiting DJs and dance bands. Age limits apply (25 for guys, 21 for women).

Zabriskie Point (215 715; ul Naberezhnaya 9A; cover Mon-Thu R700-1000, Fri-Sun R500; 8pm-4am) Attached to the rear of the Hotel Amursky

Zaliv, Zabriskie is Vladivostok's main rock and jazz club. Live music at 11pm every night but Monday.

Philharmonic Hall (Filarmoniya; ☎ 264 022, 260 821; ul Svetlanskaya 15) Hosts classical music and jazz shows.

Shopping

Magazin Kollektsionera (ul Fokina 5/3; ☻ 10am-6pm) A retired navy vet has a super selection of Soviet keepsakes: cameras, watches, toy soldiers, warship clocks and so on.

Flotsky Univermag (ul Svetlanskaya 11; ☻ 10am-7pm Mon-Fri, to 6pm Sat & Sun) For unusual souvenir turf, follow the navy – those cute blue-and-white striped navy undershirts are R140.

Nostalgiya (ul Pervaya Morskaya 6/25; ☻ 10am-8pm) Nostalgiya keeps a good range of pricey handicrafts (wooden boats from R250 and way up); upstairs are many art pieces imported from around Asia and oils of Vladivostok (from R1800).

Getting There & Away

AIR

An ongoing airport renovation may allow some of Moscow's budget airlines to reach Vladivostok over the life of this book. Until then, arriving airlines include S7 Airlines (Sibir Airlines), Sakhalinskie-Aviatrassy (SAT) and Yakutia (YK).

Travel agents all over the town can sell tickets, including **Biletur** (☎ 407 700; www.airagency.ru; ul Posetskaya 17; ☻ 8am-7pm Mon-Sat, 9am-6pm Sun).

Sample one-way summer rates for direct regional flights priced a month in advance include Moscow (R12,500, eight hours, daily), Irkutsk (from R8300, four hours, four weekly) and Khabarovsk (from R4000, 1¼ hours, daily).

International links include Vladivostok Air or Korean Air flights to nearby Seoul (R12,000 to R14,000, 1½ hours, six weekly). For China, Vladivostok Air also flies to Běijīng (R8000, 2½ hours, two weekly) and also to Hāěrbin (R7800, two hours, two weekly).

For Japan, Vladivostok Air flies to Niigata (R15,000, 1¾ hours, two weekly), Osaka (R18,800, 2¼ hours, two weekly) and Toyama (R17,800, 2¾ hours, four weekly).

Also Vietnam Airlines flies to Hanoi (R12,000, six hours, one weekly).

BOAT

Boat services leaves from Morskoy vokzal, behind the train station. The **Biznes Intur Servis** (☎ 497 393; www.bisintour.com; 3rd fl, Morskoy vokzal, Okeansky pr 1; ☻ 10am-6pm Mon-Fri) sells tickets for the fairly regular ferries (supposedly every Monday) between Vladivostok and the Japanese port of Fushiki from late February to early January. The often rough trip takes 36 or more hours, costing US$440 to US$1000 one way.

Dong Chun Ferry Company (☎ 302 660; www.dongchunferry.co.kr, in Korean; Room 241, Morskoy vokzal, Okeansky pr 1; ☻ 10am-5.30pm Mon-Fri, 7am-9am Sat) sells tickets for weekly ferry services to Sokcho, Korea (one way US$232 to US$422, 24 hours), leaving 10am Saturday. In Sokcho, you can bus to Seoul (about US$15, 3½ hours) every couple of hours.

BUS

The **bus station** (☎ 323 378; ul Russkaya), 3km north of the centre, sends many buses around the Primorsky territory, such as frequent departures for Nakhodka (four hours). Some southbound destinations may be off limits to foreigners without a permit.

Ask travel agents about eight-hour bus rides to Hāěrbin, China.

TRAIN

At the time of writing, the *Rossiya* (1) was leaving the **train station** (☎ 491 005) for Moscow (R16,300, 6½ days) on odd-numbered days, passing through Khabarovsk (R2560, 12 hours), Irkutsk (R11,250, three days) and Novosibirsk (R13,780, four days four hours). A cheaper service, on even-numbered days, is the 239 – it's R10,900 for a Moscow *kupe* (compartmentalised carriage) ticket, R7500 for Irkutsk. On odd-numbered days, *Sibir* (7) to Novosibirsk (R9250, four days) is also a cheaper option for Irkutsk (R7500).

Other trains include the daily *Okean* (5) overnighter to Khabarovsk (R2600, 12 hours), and the daily train 351 to both Komsomolsk-na-Amure (R2300, 27½ hours) and Vanino (R2920, 40 hours) on the BAM line, via Khabarovsk.

Presently leaving (local time) Monday and Thursday, train 185 connects Vladivostok with Hāěrbin, China (R1500, 41 hours), from where there are daily connections to Běijīng.

If the train station windows are too busy, you can buy tickets at the **Service Centre** (☎ 248

404; ☪ 8am-noon & 1-7.45pm) at the southern end of the building, for a R185 commission.

Getting Around
TO/FROM THE AIRPORT
A rail link connecting the centre with the airport (42km north) is in the works and may be completed during the life of this book. Meanwhile, bus 107 connects the train station and airport (R55, 90 minutes) every 45 to 75 minutes from 6.40am to 5.45pm.

LOCAL TRANSPORT
Trolleybuses and trams cost R10 a ride; pay when exiting. From in front of the train station, trams 4 and 5 run north then swing east onto ul Svetlanskaya; tram 7 stays on ul Aleutskaya, running north past the market. Buses 23, 31 and 49 run from the train station along ul Svetlanskaya.

One local taxi company is **PrimTaxi** (☎ 555 555).

For local ferry information, see p251.

AROUND VLADIVOSTOK
The city's near the southern tip of the broad, mountainous Primorsky territory with tiger turf and beaches – it's a lovely region, but generally hard to access if you're not on a local agent's pricey tour. Ask about spring and summer raft tours of the 6000 rivers in the area, notably the Kema River; check www.pfst .narod.ru, in Russian, for more information.

Nakhodka Находка
☎ 42366 / pop 176,000 / ☪ Moscow +7hr
What, you want to do more? The Trans-Siberian clicks off 9288km east of Moscow at Vladivostok, but there's still four more hours of track to go.

Discovered by a desperate, storm-tossed Russian ship in 1859 – Nakhodka means 'lucky find' – Nakhodka actually served as the end of the Trans-Siberian during the Soviet years when Vladivostok was closed. A major port, expanded by the Soviets in the 1950s as Russia's only Pacific port open to foreign ships, Nakhodka's lovely bays are lined with ship-repair yards and loading docks, but there are nice beaches and rock formations nearby.

ORIENTATION & INFORMATION
The city features distinct huddled neighbourhoods connected by 15km of road, the central one being Nakhodkinski pr. The train station

('Tikhookeanski') is a walkable bus stop north of Nakhodkinski pr; the bus station is two more stops north.

The **International Marine Club Nakhodka** (☎ 56 250; marine_club@mail.ru; ul Leninskaya 22; ☪ 9am-midnight) is a seamen's hang-out, with travel info, free karaoke and email access, plus a bar that gets a bit crazy after 6pm.

There are ATMs on ul Leninskaya.

SIGHTS
Nakhodka Museum (ul Vladivostokskaya 6; admission R100; ☪ 10am-6pm Tue-Sun), at the ul Leninskaya bus stop, is a compact, but intriguing museum, with exhibits on Nakhodka's several sister cities (including Oakland, California) and a room devoted to local travellers (yes, we love this place).

From here, you can walk along the road uphill, past the train station, to reach several lookouts with views over the bay.

Area beaches are cleaner than Vladivostok's. Bus 4 heads to one OK beach area near a town called Zalatari. Better ones include Vrangel (R30, one hour) – which is also near the popular Tri Ozera (Three Lakes) – reached by bus 26 from the bus station, and Livadiya, reached via bus 22 (R38, 1½ hours).

SLEEPING & EATING
Both hotels are at the Leninskaya bus stop. Visa registration is R200.

Yuan Dun (☎ 59 995; Nakhodkinski pr 51; r from R1200) This 'Chinese hotel' is atop a hill just south of the bus stop, visible from the train tracks. Standard rooms with good bathrooms, but quite smoked in.

Piramid-Otel (☎ 52 209; pyramid-1992@yandex.ru; ul Vladivostokskaya 2, at Nakhodkinski pr; small/large r incl breakfast R2600/3200; ☒) It's housed in a grey box, but inside the super 'Pyramid' looks something like an upscale Transylvanian tavern with juicy blood-red armchairs and heavily detailed wood doors.

Anktrakt (ul Leninskaya 16; meals R200-250; ☪ 10am-10pm) This family-friendly *zakuskaya* serves simple Russian meals and omelettes.

Masis (Nakhodkinski pr 7A; meals R200-350) An excellent Armenian restaurant across from the bus station.

GETTING THERE & AROUND
Two daily trains depart from the **train station** (☎ 56 825) for Vladivostok (2nd-class R232, four hours) at around 8am and 4pm.

Frequent buses connect these cities for the same price, leaving Nakhodka's **bus station** (☎ 643 495) from 6.20am to 7.30pm daily.

Local buses cost R7. Many, including bus 2, go between the bus station, train station and ul Leninskaya. For a taxi call ☎ 690 690.

Gaivoron Гайворон

The Far East is all about its Amur (better known as Siberian) tigers, and at Gaivoron, 235km north of Vladivostok, you can see a couple at the Russian Academy of Sciences biological research reserve, run by Dr Victor Yudin. Tiger fans will cherish it, but some others might feel it's a lot of time (and money) to see a striped duo living in a 2-hectare compound.

Tours by Vladivostok agents (p251) include about 90 minutes of tiger time, lunch and a four-hour ride each way. A private tour is R2900 per person if two are going. It's not possible to go independently.

Sikhote-Alin Nature Reserve

Сихоте-Алинский Заповедник

Home to the Russian-American Siberian Tiger project, this 3440-sq-km forested reserve, headquartered in the coastal town of Terney, stretches from the Sikhote-Alin Mountains past clear salmon streams and a savannahlike oasis to the Pacific coast and rocky beaches. Chances of seeing a tiger are slim, but it's beautiful.

It's an 11- or 12-hour ride one way. Dalintourist's (p251) 'Tigerland' trip lasts six days, including a stay in its rural Arkhipovka lodge; the all-inclusive trip runs US$1900/978 if two/four people go.

Tayshet to Sovetskaya Gavan by BAM

Everyone knows the Trans-Siberian Railway, but few have heard of the 'other' Trans-Sib, its poor country cousin, the Baikal-Amur Mainline (Baikalo-Amurskaya Magistral; BAM). Stretching across almost half of Russia, the BAM begins at Tayshet as a set of points on the Trans-Siberian, curls around the top of Lake Baikal, cuts through nonstop taiga, winds around snow-splattered mountains and burrows through endless tunnels on its way east to Sovetskaya Gavan on the Tatar Strait. The majority of towns on the line were thrown up to house construction workers and sport a functionalist 1970s look. By contrast the incredibly remote and utterly wild scenery viewed from the train window is nothing short of awe-inspiring.

Costing (in today's terms) roughly US$500 million, the BAM – a 'Hero Project of the Century' – has never been recognised as the world-class engineering feat it surely is. Brutal permafrost, bridge-smashing spring floods and the odd mountain blocking the way were some of the larger obstacles engineers had to overcome, not to mention mosquitoes, bears, extreme temperatures and in some places almost daily earthquakes.

The USSR began to implode just as the first carriages began clattering along the BAM's single track, turning the route into an economic white elephant almost overnight. But many of the old-time workers you meet on trains and stations often gush with pride over their achievement and become dewy-eyed when reminiscing about the comradeship of the construction projects. Nostalgia for the USSR is strong here and many communities look and feel as though 1991-and-all-that never happened.

Other than Lake Baikal's lovely northern lip, adventures on the BAM reach some very out-of-the-way territory. Locals are likely to be surprised to see your wide-eyed face in places such as Bratsk, Tynda or Komsomolsk-na-Amure.

HIGHLIGHTS

- Step off the train at **Severobaikalsk** (p265) to explore Lake Baikal's stunningly beautiful and little-visited north

- Take a dive into the hot springs at **Dzelinda** (p269) and **Goudzhekit** (p268)

- Marvel at the 15.3km-long **Severomuysky tunnel** (p260), a victory of Soviet engineering over nature

- Tour' the BAM's nicest town, St Petersburg–styled **Komsomolsk-na-Amure** (p271), with Soviet monuments and nearby ski slopes

- Finish BAM off by taking it to its end near **Vanino** (p273); its two main-street lighthouses help break from the usual grey

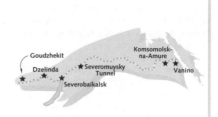

| ROUTE DISTANCE: 4308KM | DURATION: FOUR DAYS, EIGHT HOURS |

THE ROUTE
Tayshet to Severobaikalsk

The junction with the Trans-Sib at **Tayshet** (0km on the BAM and 4373km from Moscow) is the official start of the BAM, but only hardcore purists would begin in this uninspiring railway town. Most connect through on daily services from livelier Krasnoyarsk (see p206).

The first major stops along the BAM are for **Bratsk**, a sprawling city of 280,000 people on the edge of the Bratsk Sea, an artificial lake created in 1955 by the building of the Bratsk Hydroelectric Station. The railway line actually crosses the top of this gigantic 1km-long dam at the 330km mark presenting wide views on both sides. If you get off you must choose between three Bratsk stations: **Anzyobi** (293km from Tayshet) for the crushingly dreary central (Tsentralny) area, **Padunskiye Porogiye** (326km) for Energetik, or **Gidrostroitel** (339km) for the dam. Bratsk's biggest attraction is the Angara Village open-air ethnographical museum.

The taiga closes in on the line as you travel the next 600km towards the jagged mountains hemming in the northern end of Lake Baikal. At 552km, **Korshunikha-Angarskaya** is the train station for the claustrophobic 1960s iron-ore processing town of **Zheleznogorsk-Ilimsky**. A 2km walk diagonally uphill to your right as you leave the station brings you to the town's one modest attraction, the **Yangel Museum** (🕑 9am-4pm Mon-Fri), which not only celebrates a local astroscientist friend of Yury Gagarin, but also has a well-arranged exhibition on local wildlife, an art gallery and a section on ZI's twin town in Japan. The town's hotel is halfway, but visa registration could be an issue.

The only reason to leave the comfort of your bunk at **Lena** (720km; p264), the station for Ust-Kut, is to take a hydrofoil ride up the Lena River to Lensk (and eventually on to Yakutsk, the capital of the Sakha Republic). A few kilometres after Lena the line swings across the Lena River on a single-track bridge with views down on a large timber port to the north.

At **Ulkan** halt (931km), a small but eye-catching metallic Lenin relief stands against a bright red 'flag' on the east end of the platform, but you'll only have three minutes to admire it.

The scenery really improves around **Kunerma** (983km), after which the track performs a full 180-degree loop. Hurry for the camera before you disappear into the 6km-long Daban tunnel. Around half an hour before reaching Lake Baikal, some trains make a brief stop at picturesque mini-spa **Goudzhekit** (1029km; p268).

Though architecturally rather unexciting, **Severobaikalsk** (1064km; p265) makes possibly the best stop on this part of the route and the surrounding area, which takes in the northern part of Lake Baikal, is beautiful. The Thunderbirds-style station, inspired it is said by the mayor's love of ski jumping, is one of the most striking along the line, and outside there's a steam train and a statue commemorating the workers from across the USSR who toiled on the BAM.

Severobaikalsk to Tynda

This is where the BAM get serious. From Severobaikalsk to the fishing village of **Nizhneangarsk**, 30km north, the line skirts Lake Baikal, though views are often better from the road (unencumbered by tunnels). At **Nizhneangarsk 2** (1090km) station, look out for the airport (right) from where there are flights to Ulan-Ude and Irkutsk. Only local *elektrichki* stop at the Evenk village of **Kholodnaya** (1105km) by the Verkhnaya Angara River delta and the tiny hot-springs spa at **Dzelinda** (1142km; p269).

The next 1300km gives you ample time to appreciate the truly massive engineering achievement of the BAM. Many consider this the most interesting section of the line, as it climbs over densely forested, mountainous terrain along switchbacks and through several tunnels. But despite the region's remoteness, the train stops at least once an hour at communities established by BAM construction workers and their families in the 1970s and 1980s. The first major halt is the low-rise ferroconcrete station belonging to **Novy Uoyan** (1241km) though there's no reason to get off here save to stretch your legs. Trains snake across the flood plain of the Verkhnaya Angara River until the line slams into the mountains again after a minute's pause by the shack-station at **Kyukhelbekerskaya** (1241km). A few more twists and turns bring the BAM to the 15.3km-long **Severomuysky tunnel** (1400km), the longest in Russia and only completed in 2004 after years of severe technical difficulties with the permafrost. The tunnel replaced over 50km of track, which had steep gradients and was prone to avalanches.

The born-of-the-BAM town of **Taksimo** (1474km) provides the next opportunity to escape the muggy air of *platskart* and take on a few provisions at the station kiosks. Get some much needed exercise during the 30-minute stop by running to see the BAM Pioneer Monument. There are wilderness hiking possibilities in the surrounding mountains and along the River Muya, and flights operate south to Ulan-Ude from the tiny airport. Local time becomes Moscow time plus six hours shortly before **Kuanda** (1559km) where you should look out for the Golden Link Monument commemorating the uniting of the two sections of the BAM in 1984. The last lengthy stop (27 minutes) before Tynda is at **Khani** (2162km).

Tynda to Sovetskaya Gavan

After passing through the stunning Kodar and Udokan mountains, the scenery starts to smoothen out as the eastward BAM rolls across the Tynda River and into the BAM headquarters at **Tynda** (2364km; p270). Even if you don't stay, have a look at the '70s train station that looks like a science-fiction film set. Ewan McGregor went north by motorcycle from here in the TV series *Long Way Round*. But trains also go north on the still-unfinished Amuro-Yakutskaya Magistral (Amur-Yakutsk Mainline or AYaM), which stops five hours north in Neryungri; some cargo trains continue on to Tommot. Eventually the train is supposed to reach Yakutsk in the Sakha Republic; now you can arrange 24-hour taxi rides up bumpy roads from Neryungri. From Tynda, the AYaM also heads south to hook up with the Trans-Siberian, 180km south at **Bamovskaya** (7273km from Moscow).

But with two more links to the Trans-Siberian later on, it's worth continuing on the BAM. The night train out of Tynda reaches the dreary town of **Fevralsk** (3033km), on the Selemdzha River, mid-morning the next day, where you get a half hour to contemplate the permafrost below, or gold mines and pulp mills outside town.

Seven hours east, you pull into **Novy Urgal** (3315km), a coal-mining town near green hills and the white waters of the Akisma River. You can switch trains for a short cut to Khabarovsk here, or continue east. A couple hours away,

the train passes through the 2km **Dusse-Alin Tunnel** (3401km). Gulag labourers toiled (and died) over this during Stalin's watch, but it was only completed and put in use in 1982.

Most trains stop in **Postyshevo** (3633km) in the early morning; try waking up to see if locals are selling the town's famous red *ikra* (caviar) on the platform. Five hours east, the BAM pulls into its loveliest city, **Komsomolsk-na-Amure** (3837km; p271), with direct links with Khabarovsk on the Trans-Siberian, by bus or by boat.

A couple of trains leave at night to make the final dozen-hour stretch to BAM's terminus. Some train mates may joke you're on an 'international route' as the train clanks through a couple ho-hum villages passed on the way – **Kenada** (4097km) and **Toki** (4273km), they like to liken them phonetically with 'Canada' and 'Tokyo' (it's OK to fake a chuckle).

The BAM then pulls into view of a shaking Pacific bay, lined with shipyards at **Vanino** (4283km; p273). Here's the best place to exit for good, though the train does continue on to **Sovetskaya Gavan** (4309km), which is quite removed from the port town of the same name.

BRATSK БРАТСК
☎ 3953 / pop 258,000 / ◷ Moscow +5hr

A stop in Bratsk neatly breaks a Krasnoyarsk to Severobaikalsk trip into two overnight rides, but a day spent here is plenty. Bratsk's raison d'etre is a gigantic 1955 **dam** (GES), which caused the drowning of the original historic town.

New Bratsk is a confusing necklace of disconnected concrete 'subcities', whose highrise Tsentralny area is spirit-crushingly dull. It does, however, have two English-speaking tour agencies, **Taiga Tours** (☎ 416 513; www.taiga-tours.ru; 2nd fl, Hotel Taiga) and **Lovely Tour** (Lavli Tur; ☎ 439 909; baikal@lovelytour.ru; ul Sovetskaya 3, Tsentralny; ◷ 10am-7pm Mon-Fri, to 4pm Sat). Either can organise permits and guides to visit the dam's turbine rooms given two days' notice. The dam itself is 30km further north in Energetik and the BAM trains go right across it.

Between Energetik and Tsentralny, the impressive **Angara Village** (☎ 412 834; admission R100; ◷ 10am-6pm Tue-Sun, longer hr in summer) is an open-air ethnographic museum featuring a rare wooden watchtower and buildings rescued from drowned old Bratsk. A series of shaman sites and Tungus/Evenki *chum* (tepee-shaped

TAYSHET TO SOVETSKAYA GAVAN BY BAM

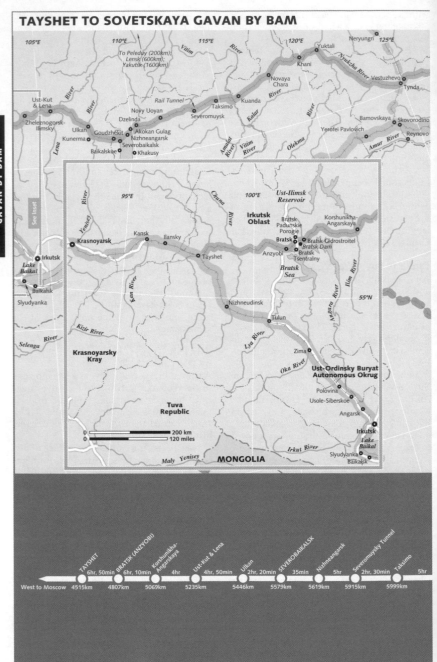

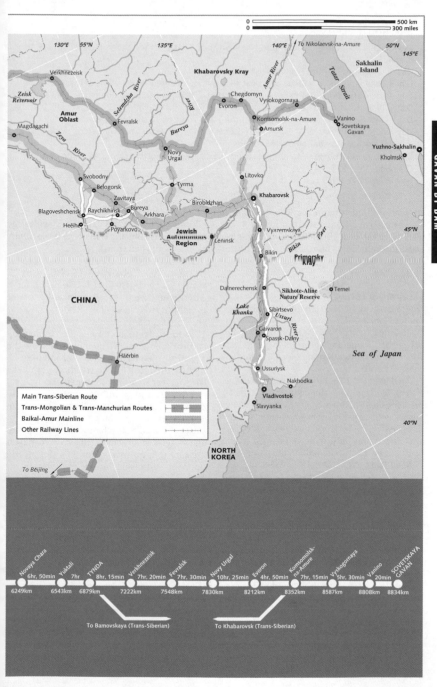

BAM ROUTE PLANNER

Day 1: Take an overnight train from Krasnoyarsk to Bratsk to see the dam holding back the Bratsk 'Sea'

Day 2: Overnight hop to Severobaikalsk

Day 3: Take a dip in Lake Baikal or a boat trip; chill out at the Baikal Trail Hostel

Day 4: Excursion from Severobaikalsk to Baikalskoe, Nizhneangarsk or one of the mini-spas at Dzelinda or Goudzhekit. Catch the night-day train to Tynda

Day 5: After spending most of the day on the train, wash off in the town's *banya*

Day 6: Explore Tynda's BAM Museum and call in on the Evenks at Zarya before catching the midnight sleeper to Komsomolsk-na-Amure

Day 7: Arrive Komsomolsk-na-Amure, spend the day exploring this surprisingly attractive city. Overnight train to Sovetskaya Gavan

Day 8: Arrive at BAM's end on the Tatar Strait

conical dwellings) lie in the woods behind. The attractive lakeside site is a lonely 3km walk from Sibirsky Traktir, an isolated highway cafe on the main *marshrutka* (fixed route minibus) routes 10 or 50. Taking a taxi makes more sense.

Sleeping & Eating

Hotel Bratsk (☎ 438 436; ul Deputatskaya 32, Tsentralny; s/tw from R500/700) Upstairs a wide variety of clean but essentially Soviet rooms all have private bathrooms and peeling paint, so unless you want a malfunctioning old TV, take the cheapest available.

Hotel Turist (☎ 378 743; ul Naymushina 28, Energetik; s/tw from R750/1500) Good-value cheaper twins (half-price for single occupancy) are clean if typically Soviet with just-functional bathrooms. The '1st-class' rooms look better but new wallpaper and carpet don't justify paying almost triple prices. It's a 15-minute walk to the dam.

Hotel Taiga (☎ 414 710; ul Mira 35, Tsentralny; s/d R1900/2400) Behind a smart new facade, wobbly Soviet-era corridors host very green bedrooms – good singles but cramped, overly intimate doubles. Some staff speak English, guest visas are registered and there's a decent hotel restaurant.

Kalipso (☎ 376 781; ul Naymushina 54, Energetik; meals R160-350; ☯ noon-7pm & 8pm-3am) The nicest pub-cafe in Energetik is at bus stop GES. It has a nautical interior, porthole windows and a beer-garden terrace that almost overlooks the lake. There are two more branches at ul Sosnova 2 and ul Kirova 27.

Getting There & Around

The three main train stations are an hour's ride apart. Padunskiye Porogiye is closest to

Energetik and Padun. Gidrostroitel is several kilometres east of the dam. For Tsentralny, get off at Anzyobi and transfer by bus or *elektrichka* (suburban train).

Eastbound there are afternoon and night trains to Severobaikalsk (R170, 14 to 17 hours) via Lena–Ust-Kut (R1150, eight hours). Afternoon trains from Severobaikalsk run west overnight to Krasnoyarsk (R1700, 13 hours) and for Irkutsk there's daily train 87 (R2050, 17 hours). Irkutsk can also be reached by comfortable coach (R700, 11 hours) from the Tsentralny **bus station** (ul Yuzhnaya) and in summer by hydrofoil (13 hours, three per week) from a river station in southeast Tsentralny.

Marshrutky 10 and 50 shuttle regularly between Hotel Turist in Energetik and the Tsentralny bus station (45 minutes). Bus 8 starts at the GES stop beside the Kalipso cafe and wiggles around Energetik's Mikro-Rayon 7 estate to a no-man's-land bus stop nearly opposite Padunskie Porogie train station.

LENA & UST-KUT
ЛЕНА И УСТЬ-КУТ

☎ 39565 / pop 70,000 / ☯ Moscow + 5hr

This 15km-long ribbon of town hugs the Lena River's north bank. Though mostly low-rise, its Soviet influences reach a concrete crescendo around Lena, the main BAM station, which stares across an overgrown square towards the river station ('Osetrovo'). Boats along the Lena River to Lensk and Yakutsk (the capital of the Sakha Republic, 2000km downstream) have been Ust-Kut's raison d'etre since it was founded in 1631.

There's not a great deal else to see, but quietly attractive old Ust-Kut, 8km west of Lena station, is worth a stroll if you're stuck here. There are some photogenic wooden cottages dotted about, and the valley has an attractive aspect despite intrusions from derelict Soviet workshops. Towards the sanatorium is the site of one of Siberia's fabled salt mines, which Yerofey Khabarov developed from 1639 to 1650. It was reactivated as a prison camp from the 1860s until WWI.

Near Lena train station, 200m east of the river station, is a **museum** (top fl, ul Rebrova-Denisova 9; ⏱ 10am-5pm Tue-Sat), with local artworks, historical artefacts and a hemp-weaving loom. Guests are so rare and staff so enthusiastic that escaping within an hour can be tough. Summer sunsets make the nearby riverside stroll pleasant, as long as you face away from the high-rises.

Sleeping & Eating

Lena Hotel (☎ 51 507; ul Kirova 88; d R1700) Across from Lena train station, this hotel has rooms with shower and toilet.

In summer there are a handful of appealingly positioned if culinary challenged beer and shashlyk (meat kebab) tents along the riverbank beside the river station. Other choices include **Kafe Ermak** (⏱ noon-3pm & 6pm-3am) at the base of the Lena Hotel, plus the minuscule **Bufet Ekspress** (⏱ 24hr) on the train station square.

Getting There & Away

Lena station (not the tiny Ust-Kut halt) is a major stop on the BAM railway with trains to Severobaikalsk (R980, 7½ hours) via Goudzhekit (seven hours) leaving odd-numbered days at 6am and even-numbered days at 2am. Three westbound trains a day stop here, including one bound for Moscow (R8500, three days and 14 hours).

From Osetrovo regular **hydrofoils** (☎ 26 394) run to Lensk, normally with one night's stop en route in Peleduy (14 hours).

SEVEROBAIKALSK
СЕВЕРОБАЙКАЛЬСК

☎ 30139 / pop 35,000 / ⏱ Moscow +5hr

Severobaikalsk, Lake Baikal's biggest shoreline town, makes a handy base from which to explore the jawdroppingly beautiful and totally unspoilt North Baikal area. It's a refreshingly uncommercial place and, although the centre is a depressingly typical maze of earthquake-proof 1970s apartment blocks, a short walk across the train tracks are some

peaceful Baikal viewpoints. Flights from Nizhneangarsk (p269) and (in February and March only) the ice-roads via Ust-Barguzin make it possible to stop at Severobaikalsk instead of Irkutsk or Ulan-Ude.

Information

INTERNET ACCESS

Internet Room (Leningradsky pr 6; per hr R38; ⏱ 10am-2pm & 3-6pm) Post office internet room.

Library (Leningradsky pr 5; ⏱ 10am-6pm Mon-Thu, 10am-2pm Fri, 10am-6pm Sat) Cheap internet. Enter through the video stall.

INTERNET RESOURCES

North Baikal Tourist Portal (www.sbaikal.ru) Comprehensive regional overview.

MONEY

Sberbank (per Proletarsky; ⏱ 9am-6.30pm Mon-Fri) Changes travellers cheques for 3% commission.

POST & COMMUNICATIONS

Post office (Leningradsky pr 6; ⏱ 10am-2pm & 3-7pm Mon-Fri, 10am-2pm & 3-5pm Sat)

Telephone office (per Proletarsky 1; ⏱ 24hr)

TOURIST INFORMATION

Baikal Hospitality Centre (☎ 8-914 875 9818; Leningradsky pr 9; ⏱ 10am-6pm, Mon-Fri, 10am-3pm Sat) Operated by the School of Environmental Education, this recently opened bona fide information centre is open year-round. Can book accommodation, sells tours and hands out advice and ideas with a smile.

Tourist Information Booth (⏱ 9am-7pm Mon-Sat Jun-Aug) Yellow kiosk on train station forecourt that's a mine of information on the North Baikal area. Can arrange permits to land on Baikal's eastern shore.

TRAVEL AGENCIES & HELPERS

The following agencies and individuals can help you arrange accommodation and Baikal boat trips, but check very carefully what is and is not included in any deal you arrange. See also agencies in Nizhneangarsk (p269).

Baikal Service (☎ /fax 23 912) This tour agency is a professional outfit with its own boat, hotel, permit arrangements and tour program, but staff don't speak English.

Maryasov family (☎ 26 491; kolonok2004@yandex .ru) English-speaking Alyona and her father Yevgeny run Severobaikalsk's hostel and information centres as well as organising adventure tours through **Tayozhik** (☎ 20 323).

Rashit Yakhin/BAM Tour (☎ /fax 21 560; www .gobaikal.com, ul Oktyabrya 16/2) This experienced

SEVEROBAIKALSK

INFORMATION
Baikal Hospitality Centre Центр
   Байкальского Гостеприимства......**1** A4
Baikal Service Байкал Сервис .... (see 15)
Internet Room **2** B4
Library Библиотека **3** A4
Post Office Почта **4** A4
Rashit Yahin (BAM Tour) **5** B2
Sberbank Сбербанк **6** B3
Telephone Office
   Междугородный Телефон **7** B3
Tourist Information Booth **8** C3

SIGHTS & ACTIVITIES
Church Церковь **9** B3
Museum Музей **10** A3
Orthodox Church **11** B3
P36 Steam Loco **12** C3
Railway Training Centre
   Учебный Центр Дорожников **13** B3

SLEEPING
Baikal Resort Дом у Байкала **14** C4
Baikal Service Bungalows
   Байкал Сервис.............................**15** D2

Baikal Trail Hostel..............................**16** D3
Podlemore Подлеморье......................**17** C3
Resting Rooms Комнаты Отдыха **18** C3
Zolotaya Rybka Золотая Рыбка **19** C4

EATING
Anyuta Анюта **20** A4
Goryache Pozi Горячее Пози.............**21** A4

Shashlyk Stand Шашлык **22** D3
Sportsbar OverTaim
   Спортсбар ОверТайм...................**23** A3
TIS ТИС **24** A4
VIST Supermarket
   Супермаркет ВИСТ **25** D3
VIST Supermarket
   Супермаркет ВИСТ **26** A4

TRANSPORT
Aviakassa Авиакасса.........................**27** A4
Buses and Marshrutky to
   Museum & Zarechny **28** A4
Buses and Marshrutky to
   Nizhneangarsk & Goudzhekit **29** C3

---

full-time travel-fixer, guide and ex-BAM worker suffered an immobilising stroke in the mid-1990s rendering his spoken English somewhat hard to follow. Nonetheless he is quick to reply to emails and is always keen to please. He rents a brilliant, central apartment (US$15, negotiable).

Sights & Activities

The friendly little **museum** (☎ 21 663; ul Mira 2; admission R50; ☽ 10am-1pm & 2-5pm Tue-Sun), 1.5km east of the town centre, has limited information on BAM history, exhibits a few Buryat artefacts and has an associated art gallery. Train buffs might prefer the colourfully painted **P36 steam loco** (pr 60 let SSSR) displayed near the Podlemore, or to peep through the railings at the outdoor signalling paraphernalia of the **Railway Training Centre** (Dorozhnogo Tsentr Uchebniya; ul Parkovaya 11A).

There are lovely lake views from a summer shashlyk stand at the eastern end of town (take *marshrutka* 3 or 103). A steep path leads down from there onto a scenic pebble beach. In winter you can walk the ice from here to the Neptuna area, where unsophisticated but photogenic *dacha*-terraces incorporate boat-garages into their lower storeys. In winter a short taxi ride across the white 'desert' of ice is a memorable experience – watch offshore fishermen freezing their hands baiting *omul* (a cousin of salmon and trout) through little ice holes.

In warmer months Severobaikalsk is a great base for relatively high-endurance hiking adventures and for very pleasant boat rides on Lake Baikal when the unpredictable weather obliges. Severobaikalsk's travel agencies can assist. If you dare brave the chilly waters, the yacht club **Bely Parus** (☎ 24 556; nordsail@mail.ru; Severobaikalsk port) rents *ails parusniye* (windsurfers), *vodnye lyzhi* (water-skis) and wetsuits.

While not historic, the town's blue-and-white plank-clad **church** (ul Truda 21) has a loveably dishevelled appearance. Services are held here at 6pm Tuesday and Saturday, and 8.30am Sunday. The more permanent-looking **Orthodox church** (Leningradsky pr) is so new it hadn't even been consecrated at the time of research, but did already sport two impressive onion domes in gleaming gold.

Sleeping

Finding a bed became a lot easier in 2008 with the opening of the Baikal Trail Hostel, bookable through Hostelworld. Homestays are organised by some of the helpers listed earlier.

Resting rooms (komnaty otdykha; train station; dm per hr R34-46) Clean, cheap dorm beds have a six-hour minimum stay. Hot shared showers are available from 5am to midnight).

Podlemore (☎ 23 179; pr 60 let SSSR 21a; s/tw/tr R452/904/975) The obvious if unmarked red-and-yellow tower beside the train station is a sanatorium that rents decent-value 7th-floor rooms with attached hot showers. Views of Baikal are across the railway marshalling yard – light sleepers might tire of the ever-disgruntled train dispatcher and her distorting loudspeaker.

ourpick Baikal Trail Hostel (☎ 23 860; www.baikal trailhostel.com; kolonok2004@yandex.ru; ul Studentcheskaya 12, apt 16; dm R500; 🖳) Initially set up to house Great Baikal Trail volunteers working in the North Baikal area, this spacious eight-bed apartment-hostel is well-equipped with kitchen, bathroom, washing machine and internet access. Breakfast is included.

Baikal Service Bungalows (☎ /fax 23 912; www .baikaltour.irk.ru; dm R700, d/tr incl breakfast R2500/3500) Hidden in a peaceful pine grove at the otherwise unpromising northeast end of town, Baikal Service has comfortable chalets with well-appointed doubles and less appealing upstairs triples with sitting rooms. Cheaper options include summer yurts, camping pitches and dorm beds in the 'student' house sharing a fridge and a good hot shower.

Baikal Resort (Dom u Baikala; ☎ 23 950; www.baikal -kruiz.narod.ru; ul Neptuna 3; tw R950-1100) Unusually comfortable for this price range, this 'resort' is really just a house and a row of cabins in a quiet area, walking distance from the lake. Rooms have a new shower and toilet, but the summer-only huts are much more cramped and have no shower.

Zolotaya Rybka (☎ 21 134; www.hotel-golden-fish .ru; ul Sibirskaya 14; tw R1200-1600) Thoroughly renovated 'cottages', each containing three rooms that share a modern shower, kitchen, tasteful sitting area and two toilets. The pleasant setting between pine trees offers glimpses of Baikal and the Neptuna area below.

Eating & Drinking

Goryache Pozi (pr Leningradsky 6; pozy R20; 🕙 9am-8pm; ✗) Basic cafe beside the market serving Central Asian food.

TIS (Railway Culture Centre, Tsentralny pl; mains R70-150; 🕙 noon-3pm & 6pm-2am) Enjoy appetising grub by day (including some veggie dishes) or a few late beers in the evening. Provides at least a bit of nightlife for Severobaikalsk's jaded youth.

Anyuta (ul Poligrafistov 3a; mains R90-180; 🕙 6pm-2am) Evening dinner spot housed in a new red-brick building amid high-rise blocks at the northern end of town.

Sportsbar OverTaim (meals R150-200, beers R50; 🕙 8pm-1am) With no sports but no cover charge either, this slightly more upmarket new pub-restaurant is popular with the youth crowd.

For cheap groceries try **VIST supermarket** Pr Leningradsky 5 (🕙 8.30am-9pm); ul Studentcheskaya (🕙 8.30am-8pm).

Getting There & Away
AIR

An **aviakassa** (☎ 22 746; Tsentralny pl; 🕙 9am-noon & 1-4pm Wed-Fri & Sun-Mon) in Dom Kultury Zhelezno dorozhnikov sells tickets for flights from Nizhneangarsk, 30km northeast, to Irkutsk and Ulan-Ude. Be aware that bad weather can seriously affect these services.

BOAT

From late June to late August a hydrofoil service runs the length of Lake Baikal between Nizhneangarsk, Severobaikalsk and Irkutsk (R2000, 12 hours) via Olkhon Island. Unfortunately, the precise timetable is only announced days before the service begins, making advance planning difficult.

Boat trips are fun and reveal the lake's vastness. Baikal's mountain backdrop looks most spectacular from about 3km offshore, so going all the way across doesn't add a lot scenically and you'll need permits to land on the almost uninhabited east coast. It's possible to negotiate cheap charters with fishermen at Severobaikalsk, Nizhneangarsk or Baikalskoe, but think carefully before taking a boat that's small, slow or seems unreliable if you're going far: storms can come from nowhere and getting help in the middle of icy-cold Baikal is virtually impossible. To rent better, long-distance boats typically costs from R1500 to R3000 per hour.

BUS

From outside Severobaikalsk's train station *marshrutky* run to Baikalskoe (two daily) and Goudzhekit (four daily). The half-hourly *marshrutky* 103 to Nizhneangarsk airport (R34, 30 minutes) passes Severobaikalsk's hydrofoil port and yacht club (2km), then follows the attractive Baikal shore.

CAR

In February and March it's possible to hitch a (paid) ride across Lake Baikal to Ust-Barguzin. Ask locals to help you locate a driver.

TRAIN

Heading towards Moscow, train 91 (even-numbered days, three days and 21 hours) starts in Severobaikalsk whereas train 75 (odd days, three days and 20 hours) comes from Tynda further along the BAM. On odd days train 71 loops round to Irkutsk (R3670, 32 hours) while on even days train 347 runs to Krasnoyarsk (R2800, 34 hours). All go via Lena (six or seven hours), Bratsk (14 to 18 hours) and Tayshet (20 to 24 hours). They also stop in Goudzhekit (R200 *platskart*, 40 minutes), though the trip is vastly cheaper and convenient by *elektrichka* (R40, one hour, twice daily).

Eastbound train 76 (R3300, 27 hours, odd days) goes to Tynda. There are also daily trains to Taksimo (eight hours) and a very slow *elektrichka* to Novy Uoyan (departs 6.30am), both via Dzelinda (two hours).

Getting Around

Marshrutka 3 connects the low-rise Zarechny suburb to Tsentralnaya pl via the museum, then continues to the train station and loops right around to the far side of the tracks, passing the Baikal Resort one way. *Marshrutka* 1 passes the access road for Baikal Service en route to the train station, Tsentralnaya pl and the museum.

AROUND SEVEROBAIKALSK
Baikalskoe Байкальское

This timeless little fishing village of log-built houses 45km south of Severobaikalsk has an incredibly picturesque lakeside location backed by wooded hills and snow-dusted peaks. Your first stop should be the small, informal **school museum** (admission R100; ☺ 10am-4pm) where hands-on exhibits tell the story of the village from the Stone Age to the seal hunts of the 20th century. The only other sight is the wooden **Church of St Inokent**, which strikes a picturesque lakeside pose.

Most come to Baikalskoe on a day trip from Severobaikalsk, but if you do want to stay the night, ask at the school where teachers are generally happy to put visitors up in their homes, or find sober hosts. There's no cafe and just a couple of shops selling basic foodstuffs.

Marshrutky leave from outside Severobaikalsk train station at 8am and 5pm on Tuesday, Friday and Sunday, returning an hour or so later. A taxi for the 45-minute drive costs from R500 each way plus waiting time; you can stop at an appealing viewpoint en route.

HIKING FROM BAIKALSKOE

A section of the Great Baikal Trail heads north from the fishing port 20 minutes up a cliffside path towards the radio mast, from which there are particularly superb **views** looking back towards the village. Beyond that Baikalskoe's shamanic **petroglyphs** hide in awkward-to-reach cliffside locations and can only be found with the help of a knowledgeable local. The well-maintained trail continues another 18 scenic kilometres through beautiful cedar and spruce forests and past photogenic **Boguchan Island** to chilly **Lake Slyudyanskoe** where there is the small **Echo turbaza** (dm R300, book through Tayozhik, p265, in Severobaikalsk). From there head along a dirt track through the forest to the Severobaikalsk–Baikalskoe road to hitch a lift, or prearrange transport back to Severobaikalsk.

Goudzhekit Гоуджекит
☎ 30139 / ☺ Moscow +5hr

Goudzhekit's lonely BAM station is beautifully situated between bald, high peaks that stay dusted with snow until early June. Five-minutes' walk to the right, the low-rise **spa** (☎ 25 852; ☺ 7am-3am) has two pools fed by thermal springs discovered accidentally in the 1970s during construction of the BAM railway. The water is a soothing 40°C and a relaxing 90-minute wallow costs just R70.

Opposite the spa there are two places to stay. **Hotel Vstrecha** (☎ 26 610; d R700) has five very comfortable rooms but no showers. Larger **Hotel Goudzhekit** (☎ 21 276; d R800) boasts a spring-water pool and a cafe. The **Pogrebok cafe** (9am-1pm) beneath the spa does a good line in salads and sandwiches.

Goudzhekit can be reached by BAM train or slower *elektrichka*, but much more convenient are *marshrutky*, which leave from in front of Severobaikalsk train station at 6.30am and 6pm, returning an hour later.

Nizhneangarsk Нижнеангарск

☎ 30130 / pop 5595 / Moscow +5hr

Although Nizhneangarsk has been around for much longer than BAM newcomer Severobaikalsk, it lacks the accommodation and places to eat to make it a decent base. That said, its 5km of typical timber houses stretching along the lakeside from the port to the airport are considerably more attractive. The centre is marked by a red, triangular monument. A small **museum** in the high school traces the town's history from the 17th century. Friendly tour agency **109 Meridian** (☎ 47 700; ul Rabochaya 143; www.109meridian .ru, in Russian; 10am-7pm Sun-Fri) based inside the airport runs reasonably priced summer bus excursions to Evenk villages and Baikalskoe, as well as multiday boat trips on Lake Baikal and up the Verkhnaya Angara. Staff can also arrange permits to land on Baikal's east shore and book accommodation in Dzelinda, Goudzhekit and Severobaikalsk. No English is spoken in the office.

SLEEPING & EATING

The appealing **Gostiny Dom** (☎ 3013-22 506; ul Rabochaya 10; tw R1600) is a wooden house-hotel. Well-appointed standard rooms have attached bathrooms. The two suites have big double beds and great views across the mudflats towards Baikal. It's a wonderfully peaceful location but there's no restaurant or any nearby cafe. Basic **Baikalsky Bereg** (ul Pobedy 53; meals R100; 8am-7pm) has an attractive lakeside location and a handwritten menu of borscht, meatballs and *pelmeni*, while the **airport snack bar** (airport) next to the 109 Meridian office stays open even when there are no flights (which is most of the time).

GETTING THERE & AWAY

Scenic low-altitude flights cross Lake Baikal to Ulan-Ude (R3450, five per week) and to Irkutsk (R3800, three per week) when the weather conditions allow.

Marshrutka 103 from Severobaikalsk runs every 30 minutes along ul Pobedy then continues along the coast road (ul Rabochaya) to the airport, returning via uls Kozlova and Lenina. The last service is at 8pm, or 6pm at weekends.

Akokan Gulag

Some 25km north of Nizhneangarsk, 3km north of the Kholodnaya turning, a forest hike leads to remnants of the small mica-mining **Akokan Gulag** (1931–33). Assuming you have a reliable guide it's about an hour's walk to reach some 'officers' huts', a collapsed watchtower and mini-railway, whose tiny bucket wagons lie beside a magical pile of mica remnants near the collapsed mine entrance. There's no public transport to Akokan. Contact helpers in Severobaikalsk (p265) or 109 Meridian in Nizhneangarsk to arrange transport or a guided tour.

Khakusy & Northeast Baikal

If you want to cross Lake Baikal, you'll need permits (available in Nizhneangarsk) before landing on lovely, shaman-haunted **Ayaya Bay** or trudging a mud-soaked 7km beyond to biologically unique **Lake Frolikha**. An easier trip is to **Khakusy** (dm/tw/tr R500/1300/1700; mid-Jun–early Sep), an idyllically isolated hot-spring *turbaza* (tour camp). Khakusy also requires permits in summer, but these are waived in February and March when it takes about an hour to drive across the ice from Severobaikalsk (around R1200 return taxi). Bathing (per person R60) is fun in the snow, and frozen steam creates curious ice patterns on the otherwise unremarkable wooden spa buildings. Occasionally the resort's summer ferry will take nonguests across.

In spring and autumn when the ice is half-melted or half-formed, all these places are totally cut off.

Dzelinda Дзелинда

Tiny timber-town Dzelinda is another hot-springs spa by the BAM railway but with a much more appealing forest location than Goudzhekit. Thermal springs keep the outdoor pools at a toasty 44°C even in winter, and when the surrounding hills are thick with snow and the temperature sinks to -35°C, a warm swim can be exhilarating. Guests stay in **timber houses** (dm R600-700), one of which has an intricately carved gable. All meals are provided. Book through 109 Meridian in Nizhneangarsk.

Elektrichka 656 leaves Severobaikalsk at 6.15pm arriving at the Dzelinda halt at 7.58pm. The spa is a short walk along a paved road through the forest.

TYNDA ТЫНДА
☎ 41656 / pop 39,000 / ⏱ Moscow + 6hr

The king of the BAM, Tynda is a nondescript BAM HQ flanked by low-lying, pine-covered hills. Many stop here, as it's a hub for trains between Severobaikalsk, Komsomolsk, and on the 'Little BAM' to Blagoveshchensk to the south, or in-progress AYaM (Amuro-Yakutskaya Magistral) to Neryungri and Tommot to the north – and overland to distant Yakutsk in the Sakha Republic.

Don't expect quaint. It's fully Soviet – nothing was here but a few shacks before BAM centralised its efforts here in 1974.

Orientation & Information
The train station – the city's most striking landmark – is across the Tynda River. A pedestrian bridge leads 1km north to the central ul Krasnaya Presnaya. There's an ATM at the train station. The **post office** (ul Krasnaya Presnaya 53; ⏱ 8am-noon & 1-7pm Mon-Fri, 8am-2pm Sat & Sun), at the street's east end, has internet.

Contact feisty adventurer **Alexey Podprugin** (☎ 8-914-552-1455; bamland@mail.ru) for kayaking, hiking and cross-country skiing trips.

Sights & Activities
The **BAM Museum** (☎ 41 690; ul Sportivnaya 22; admission R100; ⏱ by appointment 10am-6pm Wed-Sun), a couple of blocks southwest of the Orthodox cathedral (Sobor Svyatoy Troitsy), covers native Evenki culture, local art, WWII and regional wildlife, but is known for its four rooms of BAM relics and photos (no English). Two rooms cover the railway's early years – and the Gulag prisoners who built it.

Tynda's public **banya** (bathhouse; ☎ 40 030; ul Amurskaya; admission R200, lyux R540-690; ⏱ for women 1-9pm Sat, for men 1-9pm Sun) is the real McCoy when it comes to the hellishly hot steam room and chilly dunks in a pool. Freshly cut

birch branches are also available. It's in a red-brick building about 50m south of a dramatic sledgehammer-wielding **BAM worker statue** at the eastern end of ul Krasnaya Presnaya.

Zarya is a native Evenk village nearby. Bus 105 from the train station goes eight times daily (30 minutes).

Sleeping
Resting rooms (komnaty otdykha; ☎ 73 297; train station; dm per 6/12/24hr R191/325/592) Comfy and clean rooms in train station. A shower is available.

Hotel Yunost (☎ 43 534; ul Krasnaya Presnaya 49; s/d R1350/2300) This faded but fine hotel in the centre is where Dervla Murphy recuperated in her book *Through Siberia by Accident*. The reservation fee is 25%.

Getting There & Around
Trains 75/76 link Tynda with Moscow (R10,000, five days) on even-numbered days, stopping in Severobaikalsk (R2800, 26 hours). Trains 963/964 connect Tynda with Komsomolsk-na-Amure (R2850, 37 hours, daily), 81/82 with Blagoveshchensk (R2644, 16 hours, every other day), and 325/326 with Khabarovsk (R2800, 28 hours, daily). Many of these trains go on to Neryungri (R790, 5½ hours) on the AYaM line, as does the Tynda-Neryungri link (658/657).

Bus 5 outside the train station goes every 20 or 30 minutes along ul Krasnaya Presnaya.

NOVY URGAL НОВЫЙ УРГАЛ
☎ 42149 / pop 6700 / ⏱ Moscow + 7hr

This scrappy BAM crossroads town, with links south to the Trans-Siberian, satisfies those rare macabre instincts for a kept-real, fading pocket of '70s Sovietlandia – or a short cut to Khabarovsk. The town was founded in 1974 by Ukrainian railway workers.

From the station, head up the steps, where you'll see a cube-like **BAM monument**, a hospital-shaped **culture house** to your right (there's a library and club inside) and a plain main square ahead. The huge grey building on the opposite side of the square has **internet** and groceries.

The shady road going west – ul Kievskaya – leads a block to the lone attraction, a cute **BAM Museum** (☎ 7416; ul Kievskaya 7, 3rd fl; admission free; ⏱ 11am-2pm Tue-Sun), with a talkative guide.

With time, you can bus or taxi to nearby **Chegdomyn**, a mining village with a museum, North Korean monuments (and North Koreans).

TAVSHET TO SOVETSKAYA GAVAN BY BAM

WHAM BAM, IT'S THE RED ELVIS!

One of the more bizarre tours of all time rolled through Tynda in August 1979 when the 'Red Elvis' – Dean Reed, an American singer turned Marxist – did a 19-day tour on BAM, immortalised in his hilarious song *BAM* ('everybody sing along…the towns are here to stay, it's the future of our day!').

His show at Tynda's Festivalnaya Hill drew 25,000 spectators, but didn't kick off the way he wanted. But as one story recounts on the priceless website www.deanreed.de, a local refused to let an American use his horse for a dramatic cowboy entrance.

Reed's an unknown in the West these days – not surprising with songs such as *Wake Up America* and photos of him chumming around with Central American revolutionaries. That may change. In 2006 Tom Hanks bought the rights to make a film on Reed, who died under mysterious circumstances in East Germany in 1986.

Tip: Hours – and hours – of enjoyment can be had YouTubing Dean's videos.

A block south (towards the tracks) on nearby ul Donetskaya you'll find a yellow-and-white **hotel** (☎ 9786; ul Artema; r per person R400, lyux R1150), which was under renovation when we visited.

Food-wise, the best option is **Aisberg** (ul Kievskaya 5).

Train 663 goes to Khabarovsk (R1500, 15 hours), or the 963/964 stops here en route to Tynda (R2000, 23 hours) or Komsomolsk (R1350, 14 hours).

KOMSOMOLSK-NA-AMURE
КОМСОМОЛЬСК-НА-АМУРЕ
☎ 4217 / pop 280,000 / Moscow +7hr

After days of taiga and cynical grey Soviet towns, Komsomolsk-na-Amure hits the BAM adventurer like a mini St Petersburg. A convenient hub between Khabarovsk (290km south) and all points BAM, the friendly city – set up along a few grand boulevards – is worth a little time for its centre full of tsar-era style buildings in salmon, sky-blue and pink, all made under Stalin's watch. Other nearby attractions include ski slopes, Nanai villages and rafting options.

Komsomolsk began in 1932, partly by Young Communist League volunteers (*komsomol*) and mostly by Gulag labourers – to help populate the east, build a railroad, and set up an aircraft and shipbuilding factory on the Amur River. Things have slowed since the USSR days, with a dip of 30,000 in population.

Information

Gladiator (pl Lenina, Dom Kulturi Stroiteley, 2nd fl; per hr R25, plus R3 per MB; 10am-10pm) In a pillared mint-green building behind Lenin's statue, it has an internet cafe with a King Arthur theme.

Nata Tour (☎ 529 767, 8-914-189-1784; www.komso molsknata.ru, komsomolsknata@mail.ru; ul Vasyanina 12, office 110; 10am-6pm Mon-Fri) In the big grey building in back, this experienced travel service arranges homestays in town, leads 'Stalin tours' of city communist sites (incl a Gulag) for R400/300 per person for groups of two/four; also has many regional tours for fishing, rafting, skiing or homestays at Vernyaya Ekon (R2000).

Post office (pr Mira 27; 8am-7pm Mon-Fri, to 6pm Sat, to 3pm Sun)

Telephone office (pr Mira 31; 8am-11pm)

Sights

Worth it even if you can't read Russian, the well-arranged **Municipal Museum of Regional Studies** (☎ 592 640; pr Mira 8; admission R100; 9.30am-5pm Tue-Fri, 10am-5pm Sat & Sun) has several rooms filled with many old photos and knick-knacks showing how Komsomolsk rose from the tent camps of original pioneers in 1932 to an industrial Soviet city. One exhibit triumphs the Soviet *devushki* who followed the calls for 'women' to go out to this all-male city in 1937.

Just northwest of the river station, Komsomolsk's landmark sight is the impressive **WWII memorial**, which features stoic faces chipped from stone, with pillars marking the years of WWII nearby. Just east of the river station is a **beach**, well attended on nice days.

The ladies running the **Fine Art Museum** (☎ 590 822; pr Mira 16; admission R70; 10am-5.45pm Tue-Sun) will be eager to help you appreciate the two floors of changing exhibits, often modest works by regional artists. One recent exhibit we saw was of Khabarovsk-based artist Nikolai Dolbilkin, who made many of the wonderful **Soviet mosaics** around town in the '50s and '60s. In the central grey building at

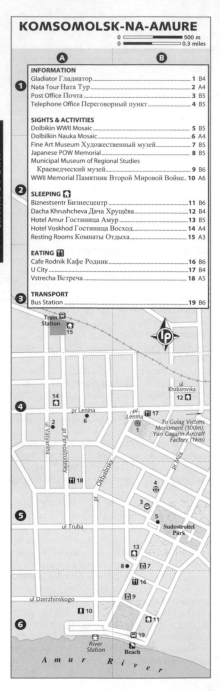

KOMSOMOLSK-NA-AMURE

0 — 500 m
0 — 0.3 miles

INFORMATION
Gladiator Гладиатор **1** B4
Nata Tour Ната Тур **2** A4
Post Office Почта **3** B5
Telephone Office Переговорный пункт **4** B5

SIGHTS & ACTIVITIES
Dolbikin WWII Mosaic **5** B5
Dolbilkin Nauka Mosaic **6** A4
Fine Art Museum Художественный музей **7** B5
Japanese POW Memorial **8** B5
Municipal Museum of Regional Studies
Краеведческий музей **9** B6
WWII Memorial Памятник Второй Мировой Войне .. **10** A6

SLEEPING
Biznestsentr Бизнесцентр **11** B6
Dacha Khrushcheva Дача Хрущёва **12** B4
Hotel Amur Гостиница Амур **13** B5
Hotel Voskhod Гостиница Восход **14** A4
Resting Rooms Комнаты Отдыха **15** A3

EATING
Cafe Rodnik Кафе Родник **16** B6
U City **17** B4
Vstrecha Встреча **18** A5

TRANSPORT
Bus Station **19** B6

Sudostroitel Park (pr Mira & ul Truba), go to the 2nd floor to see Dolbilkin's double triptych mosaic celebrating the 20th anniversary of WWII, across from Kivi Kafe; also a relief mosaic *Nauka* is at the Polytechnical Institute on pr Lenina, a block east of Hotel Voskhod.

A tiny **Gulag victims monument** – an unremarkable jagged piece of rock – is hidden in a tiny park, ominously next to the city court building on pr Lenina. There's also a simple **Japanese POW memorial**, off pr Mira.

If you have a few days to wait for permission, Nata Tour can help arrange visits of the **Yury Gagarin Aircraft Factory**, about a kilometre northeast of the centre. A tour is R700.

Sleeping

Nata Tour can arrange **homestays** (bed per person incl breakfast R1000).

Resting rooms (komnaty otdykha; ☎ 284 193; s 12/24hr R375/630, 3-bed dm R275/455) Sparkling clean, it is on the east side of the train station. Showers are R57.

Hotel Amur (☎ 590 984; ruma@kmscom.ru; pr Mira 15; s/d from R480/700) A rare budget hotel in the Far East. The Amur has 15 old-fashioned rooms (many with shared toilet and shower) in a lovely 1932 building.

our pick **Hotel Voskhod** (☎ 535 131; pr Pervostroiteley 31; r from R1600) This eight-storey grey hotel is the all-around best choice. Its renovated rooms come with wi-fi access and fans if you ask. The top-floor cafe serves good food, there's bowling next door, and it's a 10-minute walk south of the train station.

Dacha Krushcheva (☎ 540 659; ul Khabarovska 47; r R1600-2500; 🔲) Built for Nikita Khrushchev, the back-street *'dacha'* is a step back in time. The massive suites could fit a Young Pioneers troop, but only have a sofa bed and double. There's a sauna. It's for history buffs only.

Biznestsentr (☎ 521 522; bc@etc.kna.ru; ul Dzerzhinskogo 3; r R2000-4000; 🔲 🖥) A modern building behind the bus station has 17 carpeted rooms with desks and increasing elbow room per the rouble spent – a tad more comfortable than the Voskhod. There's a restaurant on site.

Eating

Cafe Rodnik (pr Mira 12; meals R150-300; 8am-11pm) This fun little eatery serves a host of Russian and Chinese dishes in a compact Chinese-style setting popular with locals. A mug of local Flora beer (a bit sweet) is R50.

U City (pr Lenina 19; meals from R150; ☾ 10am-11pm) This new one-screen cinema has a flashy ground-floor pizza-slice place (slices R50 to R60) with comfy booths and Komsomolsk's coolest kids.

Vstrecha (☎ 537 135; pr Pervostroiteley 20; meals R500-750; ☾ noon-3am) This mini banquet hall has cloud-painted ceilings and fussed-up tables wrapping around a simple disco-ball stage for live music after 9pm (when entry is R60 to R140). Food is quite good, the Russian dishes (cutlets, soups, salads) more so than the Chinese.

Getting There & Around

From Komsomolsk's pink **train station** (☎ 282 297; pr Pervostroiteley) the daily 351 service leaves for Khabarovsk (R1350, nine hours) and Vladivostok (R2300, 27 hours); train 67 also goes to Khabarovsk (R1570, nine hours).

On the BAM, train 963 heads west to Novy Urgal (R1350, 14 hours) and Tynda (R2800, 37 hours); to reach Severobaikalsk, you'll need to change in Tynda.

Local and long-distance buses leave from the simple **bus station** (☎ 591 154), near the river station. Buses bound for Khabarovsk (R430, six hours) leave every 90 minutes or so from 7am.

June through August, it's possible to travel by hydrofoil to/from Khabarovsk (R700, six hours) and north to Nikolaevsk-na-Amure (R1820, 12 hours). At research time, boats left the **river station** (☎ 591 154, 592 935) for Nikolaevsk at 7.30am, and for Khabarovsk at 1pm.

Within the city, tram 2 runs from the train station (R12), past all hotels to the river station. Bus 102 runs from the bus station every 45 minutes to the airport (R20), 25km west of town.

AROUND KOMSOMOLSK-NA-AMURE

Across the Amur River from Komsomolsk, Verkhnyaya Ekon is a Nanai village tucked in hills on the riverbanks. You can visit the **Nanai Museum**, with old shaman costumes and plenty of Nanai traditional pieces and arrange **homestays** (per person about R1500). Three daily buses come from Komsomolsk (R30, 30 minutes), but if you arrange a taxi you can visit an eerie unfinished 800m-long **BAM tunnel** at nearby Pivan village.

In winter, buses from Komsomolsk go to **Kholtimy**, a popular ski slope 60 minutes away;

the lift is R100 per ride, ski rentals are R300 per hour.

Summer is rafting time, with day-trip rides down the **Gur River**, 90 minutes south of Komsomolsk by road, finishing at the village of Voznesenskoe. Nata Tour (p271) offers day rafting trips (R2400 per person) and two-day camping trips (R3000).

VANINO & SOVETSKAYA GAVAN
ВАНИНО & СОВЕТСКАЯ ГАВАН
☎ Vanino 42137, Sov Gavan 42138 / ☾ Moscow +7hr

BAM completists or those planning on ferrying to Sakhalin Island get two grey Soviet port towns for the price of one here at the BAM's end.

Reached by train and ferry, Vanino (population 18,500) was founded during WWII. Its often foggy bay sees 20-some million tonnes of goods shipped in/out each year (including coal, lumber, gas), looked over by the two lighthouses in the middle of its grey main street.

About 36km further east, Sovetskaya Gavan (population 30,500) – originally Imperator Gavan (or Imperial Harbour), and now 'Sov Gavan' (Sov GAV-an) to most – has a bit more life (and Soviet mosaics), and heavy metal haircuts, to be honest.

Both towns have a museum, and the ride between the two revives the drama of the scenery here. Vanino's **Historical Museum** (Muzei Vystavochni Sal-Dom; ☎ 71 045; ul Matrosova; admission free; ☾ 2-7pm Tue-Fri, 10am-2pm Sat) has rooms dedicated to Russian and Japanese history in the region. It's located behind the big blue building around 300m to the east of the train station.

Sleeping & Eating

From Vanino's blue train station, take the blue pedestrian bridge, where the main road rises up to the main square at city hall. To the right, past a ticket office and bank, is the lone hotel **Vanino Hotel** (☎ 7473; r from R1500), with comfortable rooms and wi-fi access.

If it's full (and it sometimes is), there's the train station's nice **komnaty otdykha** (☎ 64 295; dm in 3-bed room for 12/24hr R255/420, shower R75) or Sov Gavan's **Hotel Sovetskaya Gavan** (☎ 46 783; s/d from R1430/2246), an old-fashioned hotel near the main square.

Both hotels have simple cafes.

Getting There & Away

A recently finished road reaches Khabarovsk in eight hours, but microbus service was already discontinued when we came by.

AIR

The airport, between the two ports, has weekday flights to/from Khabarovsk on Vladivostok Air (R4500, one hour).

BOAT

Inside the train station, during summer you can buy daily ferry tickets (if you're lucky) for Kholmsk, Sakhalin Island (four-berth/two-berth from R944/1004, 18 or many more hours, depending on weather). Delays and cancellations are common, and getting tickets is a long process. Call ☎ 42137-57 708 or 42137-73 916 for info.

TRAIN & BUS

Two trains leave Vanino nightly. The best train is 351/352, which goes to Komsomolsk-na-Amure (R1192, 11 hours), Khabarovsk (R2140, 23 hours) and Vladivostok (R2920, 41 hours).

BAM's first/last stop 'Sovetskaya Gavan-Sortirovka,' 15 minutes east, is not to be confused with the town, which is best reached from Vanino by bus 101 (R60, one hour, about five times daily) or taxi (about R500, 30 minutes).

Ulan-Ude to Běijīng via Mongolia

The Trans-Mongolian route is the most diverse leg of the cross-continental journey, cutting across three distinct cultures, landscapes and languages. It includes some of the most awe-inspiring sights of the long journey, not the least of which is the Great Wall of China, but also the Gobi Desert and the vast Mongolian steppes, still the domain of horse-bound nomads.

For centuries this same route was traversed by tea-laden camel caravans that plodded between Běijīng and Moscow in 40 days. The rail route was completed in the 1950s, cutting the journey to just a week. But Mongolia, with its frantic capital and beautiful countryside, deserves far more than a cursory glance through the train window.

This chapter only provides a taste of all that Mongolia has to offer. Many travellers hop off the train and set aside a month or more to explore this huge country. It's a rough ride from the capital down to the Gobi Desert where you can hunt for dinosaur fossils or up to the glorious Lake Khövsgöl for some rugged horse treks. In eastern Mongolia you can visit the humble homeland of Chinggis (Ghengis) Khan. Many travellers plan their visit around Mongolia's colourful Naadam Festival when wrestlers, horse racers and archers compete for glory in the 'nomad Olympics'.

Before heading for Mongolia from Russia, pause to explore Ulan-Ude (p234), where you could leave the train briefly for a minibus ride to the border, taking in the historic towns of Novoselenginsk and Kyakhta along the way. Of course, the delights of Běijīng, at the start or end of your journey, demand as much time as you can manage.

HIGHLIGHTS

- ▒ Enjoy a meal of boiled mutton, dried curds and fermented mare's milk in a herders' ger on the vast **Mongolian steppes** (p292)

- ▒ Wonder at a mystical ceremony at the country's largest and liveliest monastery, Ulaanbaatar's **Gandan Khiid** (p284)

- ▒ Browse through the weird and wonderful collection of stuffed animals, curios and artefacts at Ulaanbaatar's **Winter Palace of the Bogd Khaan** (p284)

- ▒ Catch some heated wrestling, archery and horse-racing action at the annual **Naadam Festival** (p288)

- ▒ Spot rare wild horses at **Khustain National Park** (p293) where the Przewalski horse roams free

▒ ROUTE DISTANCE: 2217KM	▒ DURATION: TWO DAYS, 6¼ HOURS

THE ROUTE

The Trans-Mongolian line branches off from the main Trans-Siberian route at Zaudinsky, about 13km east of Ulan-Ude. Mongolia and China each have their own kilometre markers. In Mongolia, the markers measure the distance to the Russian-Mongolian border, so 0km is the border town of Naushki. Once in China, the markers measure the distance to Běijīng.

For more on Mongolia, grab a copy of Lonely Planet's *Mongolia* guidebook.

Zaudinsky to Naushki

At **Zaudinsky** (5655km) the branch line turns south and continues to follow the Selenga Gol (Selenga or Selenge River), crossing at around 5701km. Here you'll see herds of cattle grazing across low green hills beside a wide, lazy river, and villages of wooden houses with brightly painted window shutters and flourishing gardens that explode with fruits and flowers in summer.

After you pass the town of **Zagustay** (5769km) the train follows the shoreline of Gusinoye Ozero (Goose Lake), surrounded by thick woods of pine and birch that are usually prevalent further north. The train crosses the Selenga again at 5885km before stopping at **Naushki** (5902km but 0km for Mongolia), a small, uneventful town that serves as the Russian border post. If you haven't gotten to the end of *War and Peace* by now you'll certainly have the chance here as the train hangs around the border for several hours for customs and passport checks.

Sükhbaatar to Ulaanbaatar

Sükhbaatar (21km) is Mongolia's chief northern border town. Set at the junction of the Selenga and Orkhon Rivers, Sükhbaatar (population 19,700), the capital of the Selenge *aimag* (province), is a quiet place founded in the 1940s and named after the revolu-

tionary hero Damdin Sükhbaatar. The train stops for over an hour, giving you time to stretch your legs, and perhaps head across the street to grab a meal in one of the small Mongolian restaurants.

Entering Mongolia brings a change of scenery; the forests thin out into the lush green pastures of the fertile Selenga Gol basin. When you cross the river at 63km you may spot cranes, heron and other waterfowl in the marshy areas on the west side of the train.

Darkhan (123km) is Mongolia's third-largest city with a population of 73,500, built only in 1961 to take pressure off a rapidly expanding Ulaanbaatar. The city is a fairly bland confection of Soviet apartment blocks but it does offer Kharaagiin Khiid, an active monastery housed in a pretty log cabin. The train stops for about 15 minutes. You can buy some *buuz* (mutton-filled dumplings) from the ladies who sell them out of plastic containers or take your chances with the *tsuivan* (steamed noodles with meat) on the train.

Should you venture off the rails, the most interesting sight in the area is Amarbayasgalant Khiid, the best-preserved Buddhist monastery in Mongolia. The three- to four- hour drive from Darkhan can be made in a taxi for around T65,000 return.

The scenery south of Darkhan is lovely, especially on the west side of the train. As the landscape becomes less verdant, gers (yurts; traditional felt tents) dot the wide grassy expanses, giving a glimpse of the grasslands to come further south. Birch and pine trees cluster on the hills in the distance. You spend 10 minutes in **Züünkharaa** (231km), where trains loaded with tree trunks and processed wood stop en route from Siberia and northern Mongolia.

North of Ulaanbaatar the rolling hills are covered with wildflowers and grazing animals, making for exquisite scenery. However, around 384km you will be able to catch views of the smokestacks and urban sprawl

---

ULAN UDE TO BĚIJĪNG ROUTE PLANNER

The following is a suggested itinerary for covering the main sites along the Trans-Mongolian route:
Day 1: Leave Ulan-Ude and take a 4½-hour train trip to Naushki, cross border, overnight on train.
Day 2: Arive in, and tour, Ulaanbaatar
Day 3: Tour Ulaanbaatar and around
Day 4: Train to Běijīng (30 hours) crossing the Chinese-Mongolian border
Day 5: Arrive in Běijīng

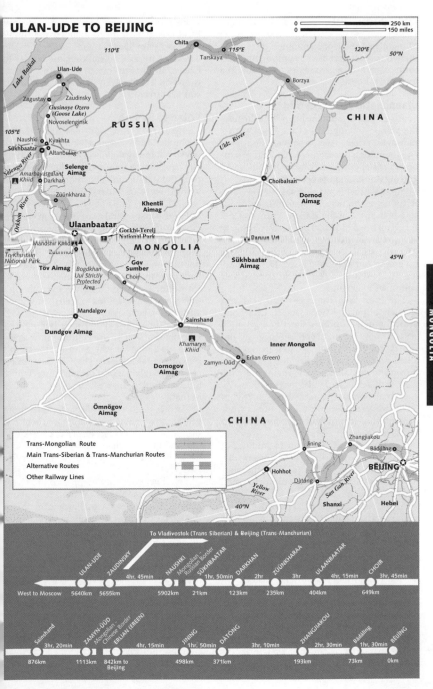

ULAN-UDE TO BEIJING

Trans-Mongolian Route
Main Trans-Siberian & Trans-Manchurian Routes
Alternative Routes
Other Railway Lines

of **Ulaanbaatar** (404km; p280) as the train descends into the valley. The train stops in the Mongolian capital for 30 minutes. If stopping off here, expect throngs of people on the platform offering tours, taxi rides or a bunk in a local guest house.

Ulaanbaatar to Zamyn-Üüd

South of Ulaanbaatar, the line winds through the gently swelling hills of the **Bogdkhan Uul** mountain range. Trees eventually disappear and the landscape becomes a 180-degree panorama of steppe, the only interruptions being grazing horses and the occasional ger.

There's a 15-minute stop at **Choir** (649km). A statue of the first Mongolian cosmonaut stands in front of the station. Prior to 1992 this grim town of 13,000 people was home to Mongolia's biggest Soviet military air base. After the Russians left, many of the buildings sat empty and were vandalised. Despite having declared itself a Free Trade Zone, Choir continues to languish.

The train then enters the flat, arid and sparsely populated Gobi Desert. In a good year, the desert sprouts short grass, which sustains a limited number of sheep, goats and camels for their ethnic Khalkh owners. In a bad year, the wells go dry, the grass turns brown and the animals die. From the train, the view of this desolate landscape is impressive. Any small bodies of water (such as at 729km on the western side of the tracks) attract wildlife, and you will probably spot horses, sheep and goats.

The train stops for around 15 minutes at **Sainshand** (876km), which means, ironically, 'Good Pond'. The *buuz* vendors on the platform sell out of their product quickly so you'll need to act fast.

As the capital of the local province, Sainshand sports a couple of museums, a modern monastery and several hotels and ger camps, should you feel the urge to jump the train and get closer to the Gobi. About one hour drive south of Sainshand is **Khamaryn Khiid**, one of the most important Buddhist monasteries in the Gobi and former home of the poet-monk Danzan Ravjaa.

In the 1920s the celebrated American explorer Roy Chapman Andrews tore through this part of the Gobi in a cavalcade of Dodge trucks in search of dinosaur skeletons. He found plenty and there are many fossils still buried in the sands.

Back on the Trans-Mongolian route, the bleak dusty landscape continues to the border town of **Zamyn-Üüd** (1113km). From here you can cross by road or rail over the border to China. If you are travelling north by local train you'll have all day in town to explore its solitary street.

Erlian to Běijīng

Compared to Zamyn Üüd, the Chinese side of the border, **Erlian** (Ereen; 842km from Běijīng), is a veritable megalopolis. The ever expanding city has a dinosaur museum, a clutch of hotels near the station and a bustling market filled with Mongolian traders. From here it takes about 13 hours to Běijīng by direct train.

For the first several hours the train continues through the Gobi, now in the so-called autonomous region of Inner Mongolia. Mongolians make up only about 15% of the population here, and since 1949 the Chinese have done their best to assimilate them, eradicating their nomadic lifestyle, even though they have been permitted to keep their written and spoken language.

It's a long journey between Běijīng and Ulaanbaatar so if you're getting a little antsy go to the dining car where most of the train's socialising takes place. The Chinese dining car is arguably the best on the entire Trans-Siberian route – but we'll let you be the judge of that.

Further south, green hills, valleys and more prosperous-looking towns appear. There is a stop at the main rail junction of **Jining** (498km) – the best place to change trains if you're not on a direct Ulaanbaatar to Běijīng service (see p291).

You'll get your first glimpse of the Great Wall as the line passes through it at about 385km. This is now Shanxi province, one of the earliest centres of Chinese civilisation. The ancient capital of this region was **Dàtóng** (371km), now an industrial metropolis of 2.7 million people. The train halts here for 10 minutes, but there are a couple of reasons for lingering longer: the awesome **Yungang Caves**, 16km west of the city, contain some 50,000 Buddhist statues carved between AD 460 and 494; and train fanatics will thrill to the Datong Locomotive Factory, the last in China to produce the 'iron rooster' steam engines until 1989. Inquire at the local **China International Travel Service** (CITS; ☎ 0352-712 4882) at the station about tours to the caves and the

RUSSIA-MONGOLIA BORDER CROSSINGS

Naushki-Sükhbaatar

Russia and Mongolia use the same rail gauge, so no bogie-changing on trains is required. However, the time saved is eaten up in drawn-out customs procedures and general hanging around – it can last some six to 11 hours!

Heading south, Naushki travellers must fill out customs forms in duplicate, and Russian border guards collect passports. Mongolian traders get the most attention from the customs officers. When you get back your passport, you can get off the train. You can change money here and there's a farmers market just outside the train station (walk to the southern end of the platform and cross the street). If you arrive in Naushki from Kyakhta it's possible to buy a ticket for the Naushki-Sükhbaatar train for R100 *kupe* (*kupeyny*; compartmentalised carriage), often just a single carriage. It departs at 1.50pm Moscow time and arrives in Sükhbaatar at 6.50pm Mongolian time. When officially 'full', a suitably tipped *provodnitsa* (female carriage attendant) may still be prepared to get you aboard for the one-hour hop across no-man's-land. The Naushki to Ulan-Ude train ride, for R320 *platskart* (*platskartny*; open carriage), is an attractive but excruciatingly slow ride (six hours). The more frequent *marshrutky* (fixed-route minibuses) from Kyakhta are faster (three hours).

The customs and immigration process is repeated by Mongolian officials in Sükhbaatar where, if you need it, there should be no problem buying a ticket for the nightly train to Ulaanbaatar that departs at 9pm. The trip takes nine hours and costs T4200 *obshchy* (4th class) or T12,800 *kupe*. *Marshrutky* (T12,000, six hours) to Ulaanbaatar depart when full from a lot outside the train station; these are a good bet in daylight hours.

Travellers on through trains from Irkutsk to Ulaanbaatar will have to wait for their carriages to be hitched to this service before they can continue on their way. There are some cafes near Sükhbaatar station, and moneychangers hang out around the station itself.

Kyakhta-Altanbulag

You can avoid the extreme tedium of the direct train crossing by taking this alternative road route into or out of Mongolia. There's a daily bus (R950, 10 hours) to Ulaanbaatar departing at 7.30am from a stop near the Opera House roundabout in Ulan-Ude. Contact Baikal Naran Tour in Ulan-Ude (see p235) for tickets. More interesting, though, is to make minibus hops to the Mongolian border from Ulan-Ude via Novoselenginsk (p239) and the once-opulent tea-route town of Kyakhta (p280). It's quite possible to briefly see both towns during the day, cross the border and still catch the nightly train to Ulaanbaatar.

The **border** (☺ 9am-noon & 2-6pm) is open to bicycles and vehicles, and some officials speak English. You can't walk across, so pedestrians need to negotiate passage with private drivers. Start as close as possible to the front of the chaotic queue: processing takes about an hour with only a handful of vehicles allowed through at any one time. The going rate is R150 per passenger across no-man's-land. The Mongolian border town, Altanbulag, is half decimated by vandals who have carted away bricks from old Soviet buildings. From here its another 26km to Sükhbaatar train station. Rides here in a shared vehicle should cost R50 or T2500.

ULAN-UDE TO BĚIJĪNG VIA MONGOLIA

factory. Note that onward tickets for trains not originating in Dàtóng can be hard to secure; you might end up only being able to get a standing-room-only ticket on an already crowded train.

From Dàtóng, the line turns east, entering Héběi province, primarily a coal-mining region, at around 300km. Héběi is characterised by its mountainous tableland where the Great Wall runs. There are good views of the wall on the eastern side of the tracks between 295km and 275km.

The train stops for about 15 minutes in the industrial city of **Zhāngjiākou** (193km). Formerly known as Khaalga, which means 'door' or 'gate' in Mongolian, this town was where the ancient tea caravans crossed the Great Wall. From here the terrain becomes increasingly mountainous and the scenery is quite dramatic. At 99km the train crosses the San Gan River. At 95km, the mountains provide a spectacular backdrop to the vibrant blue waterway. Farms and orchards surrounded by mountains make for a visually stimulating ride.

Because of the steep ascent, the train requires a banking engine; the train stops briefly at **Kanzuang** (82km) to attach/detach it (depending on which direction you are travelling). Between 80km and 50km, the train goes through a series of thrilling tunnels that cut through the mountains. Each time the train emerges into daylight there's a fabulous view of the Great Wall and the surrounding mountains. The first is at **Bādáling** (73km), immediately after a long 2km tunnel. The train then makes another, longer stop at **Qinglongqiao** (70km), where you can take photos from the platform.

At **Nankou** (53km) the rear engine is attached/detached. About an hour later, the train pulls into **Běijīng** (p304).

KYAKHTA, RUSSIA КЯХТА
☎ 30142 / pop 18,400 / ☯ Moscow +5hr
Tight against the Mongolian border, the intriguing if somewhat sad town of Kyakhta was formerly called Troitskosavsk. Kyakhta's fortunes boomed with the Chinese tea trade and by the mid-19th century up to 5000 cases of tea were arriving daily on a stream of horse or camel caravans. The caravans returned loaded with furs. This all came to an abrupt end with the completion of the Trans-Mongolian Railway, after which Kyakhta withered into a remote border garrison town.

The town's centre is around ul Lenina where you'll find the bus terminus next to the 1853 trading arches (Ryady Gostinye) and the central park. The border post is in Kyakhta's smaller Sloboda district, 4km south of the commercial centre.

The impressive shell of the 1817 Troitsky Cathedral lies at the heart of the overgrown central park. Northeast is the delightfully eccentric **museum** (☎ 92 333; ul Lenina 49; admission R100; ☯ 10am-6pm Tue-Sun), with its imaginative displays of treasures salvaged from Soviet-plundered churches and *datsani*. Running parallel to ul Lenina is ul Krupskaya, along which you'll find several attractive wooden buildings, including No 37, where the first meeting of the Mongolian Revolutionary Party was held in 1921.

In Sloboda a dwarfish Lenin glares condescendingly at the extraordinarily grand but sadly ruined **Voskresenskaya Church** (1838), with its splendid Italianate cupola. Behind Lenin is the big but rather mutilated 1842 Zdaniye Gostinogo Dvora (Historic Customs Warehouse), with an appended communist-era spire. Directly behind is the frontier post for crossing into Mongolia.

Beside the Uspensky Church, **Hotel Druzhba** (☎ 91 321; ul Krupskaya 8; dm from R280, ste R560), about 10 minutes' walk south of Kyakhta's main centre, has good-value suites with hot water, sitting room and king-sized bed.

Eating options are very limited. **Sloboda Zakusochnaya** (border post; meals from R50; ☯ 24hr) is a run-of-the-mill *pozy* joint popular with cross-border truckers. **Troika Café** (ul Lenina; ☯ 10am-midnight) serves reasonably priced Buryat and Chinese fare opposite the museum.

Ulan-Ude–Kyakhta *marshrutky* (R250, 3½ hours) take a pleasantly scenic route with a meal break in Novoselenginsk. For details of crossing to/from Mongolia, see p279.

ULAANBAATAR УЛААНБААТАР
☎ 011 / pop 1,000,000 / Moscow + 5hr
After several days of travelling across the Eurasian landmass, approaching Ulaanbaatar by train can feel otherworldly. Rolling green hills covered in pine trees harbour the occasional ger, and horsemen can be seen galloping alongside the train tracks. But any romantic expectations of a frontier outpost are rapidly quashed as the train bends into the Tuul River valley and the enormity of the Mongolian capital unfolds before your eyes.

Ulaanbaatar is a bizarre cocktail of crumbling Soviet-built apartment blocks, satanic smokestacks, the odd glass tower and derelict suburbs of gers that sprawl for 25km across an otherwise lovely valley. But don't allow the city's harsh appearance to put you off. The chaotic capital bursts with activity and will delight you with its friendly locals, quirky sights and live-for-the-moment buzz.

UB, as it's known among expats, has several excellent museums and a lively Buddhist monastery in Gandan Khiid. International cuisine is surprisingly varied and brew pubs overflow onto bright patios. If the city gets too hot you can go for a hike up Bogdkhan Uul, the forested holy peak to the south of the city. Beautiful countryside, national parks and nomadic culture can be found a short drive in any direction.

History
The first recorded capital city of the Mongolian empire, Örgöö, was established in 1639 at the Da Khuree Khiid, about 420km from Ulaanbaatar.

The monastery was the residence of the five-year-old Zanabazar, who had been proclaimed the head of Buddhism in Mongolia. In keeping with the nomadic lifestyle, the capital was moved frequently to various locations along the Orkhon, Selenga and Tuul Rivers (with a name change accompanying each move).

The capital was finally established in its present location in 1778 and grew quickly as a religious, commercial and administrative centre. Its architecture remained predominantly gers. Further name changes accompanied invasions by the Russians and the Chinese. In 1924 the city was renamed Ulaanbaatar (Red Hero) in honour of the communist triumph, and declared the official capital of an 'independent' Mongolia (independent from China, not the USSR).

From the 1930s the Soviets built the city in typical Russian style: lots of uniform apartment blocks, large brightly coloured theatres and cavernous government buildings. Tragically, the Soviets also destroyed almost all of the monasteries and temples.

A large influx of rural migrants since 2000 has put tremendous strain on the city's basic infrastructure. Housing is inadequate, roads are jammed and the city's power grid is stretched to the limit. But private investment has also poured in, causing a miniboom in glass towers, shopping malls and the like.

Orientation

The station is in the city's southwestern corner around 2km from the centre. Most of the city spreads east–west along the main road, Enkh Taivny Örgön Chóloo (Peace Ave). At the centre is Sükhbaatar Sq, named after the hero of the 1921 revolution.

The 1:10,000 *Ulaanbaatar City Map* is updated yearly. It's available at hotels, souvenir shops and the central post office. The **Map Shop** (Ikh Toiruu; ⊙ 9am-1pm & 2-6pm Mon-Fri, 10am-4pm Sat), near the Elba Electronics shop, has the best selection of maps for other parts of the country.

Information
BOOKSHOPS

Books in English (☎ 9920 3360; Peace Ave; ⊙ 11am-7pm Mon-Fri, noon-6pm Sat & Sun) Small secondhand bookshop, next to the Za Internet Cafe.

Xanadu Books & Fine Wines (☎ 319 748; Marco Polo Bldg; ⊙ 10am-7pm Mon-Sat) The selection of books is thin but they do have a few Lonely Planet titles.

EMERGENCY

It may take a few minutes to get an English-speaker on these numbers.
Emergency aid & ambulance (☎ 103)
Police emergency (☎ 102)
Robbery Unit (☎ 318 783)

INTERNET ACCESS

There are scores of internet cafes, all charging around T800 per hour; expect to pay double that for hotel business centres. Connections are generally good. You can use them to burn photos from your camera to a CD.

There is a growing number of wireless hotspots in Ulaanbaatar. Your hotel may offer free wi-fi or you can get easily get online at cafes including Café Amsterdam, Stupa Café or Michele's French Bakery (see p287).

ULAANBAATAR IN...

One Day
Catch a morning ceremony at the **Gandan Khiid** (p284). Walk back to town for lunch at **Stupa Cafe** (p287) before an afternoon exploring the **National Museum of Mongolian History** (p284) and **Museum of Natural History** (p284), both close to Sükhbaatar Sq. Take dinner at **Veranda** (see p287) and cap the night with a pint at the **Grand Khaan Irish Pub** (p288).

Two Days
On your second day, visit the **Winter Palace of the Bogd Khaan** (p284) before huffing it up to the **Zaisan Memorial** (p284). In the afternoon, visit the rather atmospheric **Monastery-Museum of Choijin-Lama** (p284), then be entertained by the **Tumen Ekh Song & Dance Ensemble** (p288).

Four Days
Get out into the countryside with a visit to **Mandshir Khiid** (p290) and **Terelj** (p292), horse riding and sleeping in a ger (traditional felt tent) camp.

Central Post Office (☎ 7010 2486; Peace Ave; per hr T700; ☺ 24hr) Also offers internet.

Internet Centre (☎ 312 512; Tserendorjiin Gudamj 65; per hr T800; ☺ 9am-2am) One of the largest internet cafes.

Za Internet cafe (☎ 320 801; Peace Ave 62; per hr T700; ☺ 24hr)

MEDIA

Pick up the English-language weekly newspapers the *Mongol Messenger* (www.mongolmessenger.mn; T400) and the *UB Post* (http://ubpost.mongolnews.mn; T600) for local news and entertainment information.

MEDICAL SERVICES

If your situation is not an emergency, consider travelling to Běijīng, where the range and quality of service is much better.

SOS Medica Mongolia Clinic (☎ 464 325; 4a Bldg, Ikh Toiruu; ☺ 9am-6pm Mon-Fri) Staffed by Western doctors on call 24 hours (☎ after hr 9911 0335). Services are pricey (examinations start from around US$195), but it's the best place to go in an emergency.

Yonsei Friendship Hospital (☎ 310 945; Peace Ave; ☺ 9am-4.30pm Mon-Fri, 10am-2pm Sat) The quality of this South Korean–sponsored clinic is not as high as SOS Medica but rates are more affordable.

MONEY

ATMs can be found in some banks, supermarkets and the lobbies of major hotels.

Golomt Bank (☎ 330 436; ☺ 24hr) Changes travellers cheques and gives a cash advance with no commission on Visa or MasterCard. There are six branches around town, including Seoul St and the corner of Juulchin Gudamj and Baga Toiruu.

State Department Store (Peace Ave 44) You can change money in the lobby.

POST

Central post office (☎ 313 421; Peace Avej; ☺ 7.30am-9pm Mon-Fri, 9am-8pm Sat & Sun)

TOURIST INFORMATION

Tourist Information Visitor Centre (☎ 311 423; www.mongoliatourism.gov.mn; ☺ 9am-8pm) The useful main office is in the central post office, on the corner of Peace Ave and Sükhbaataryn Gudamj. There are also information booths at the train station and the airport.

TRAVEL AGENCIES

Ulaanbaatar has no shortage of travel agents and tour operators (see p284) who can help organise ger visits, other excursions or obtain train tickets.

Air Market (☎ 366 060; www.air-market.net) Opposite the central post office. Good for flight tickets.

Legend Tour (☎ 315 158; www.legendtour.ru; Seoul St, Sant Asar Trading Centre, 2nd fl) Offers Russian visa support for some Western nationals. But its still best to get your Russian visa in your home country.

Dangers & Annoyances

Ulaanbaatar is a reasonably carefree and easygoing city. However, pickpockets and late-night muggings have been reported. Theft is seldom violent against foreigners, just opportunistic; it's best to carry packs on your chest. Pickpocketing is very common, especially around Naadam time; pickpockets will also attempt to get at your moneybelts or into zipped bags. Don't become paranoid; just keep vigilant and never keep any valuables in pockets. When taking a taxi from the train station into town, don't leave your bags in the trunk of the car as the taxi may be held for ransom.

STRANDED SAMMY *Michael Kohn*

As I waited for my train out of Zamyn-Üüd I got to talking with one of the local police officers. He told me that a Nigerian man was being held for having a phony passport and that the police would rather let him go but had yet to hear from his embassy, despite trying for 18 months. The wheels of Mongolian diplomacy grind slowly.

The policeman asked if I wanted to meet 'Sammy' as he was known. 'Sure', I said. 'Why not?'

So I was directed to a sandy outpost on the edge of town that served as a prison. Welcomed inside I sat down and soon Sammy appeared. He told me the story about how he'd been locked up without any access to the outside world, all because of a dodgy passport. (And you thought you had passport hassles!) When I got back to Ulaanbaatar I met with Ministry of Foreign Affairs officials and went about pestering them for two weeks. The authorities eventually caved in and bought Sammy a one-way ticket out of the country. And I never heard from him again.

ULAANBAATAR

0   300 m
0   0.2 miles

INFORMATION
Active Mongolia & Seven Summits
Camping Shop..........................**1** C5
Air Market...............................(see 1)
Books in English.........................**2** B5
Canadian Embassy......................**3** C5
Central Post Office.....................**4** C5
Centre of Cultural Heritage.......(see 70)
Chinese Embassy........................**5** D4
French Embassy..........................**6** C5
Ger to Ger...............................(see 38)
German Embassy.........................**7** C4
Golomt Bank..............................**8** B5
Golomt Bank.............................(see 45)
Internet Centre..........................**9** B5
Japanese Embassy.....................**10** C5
Karakorum Expeditions..............**11** B5
Legend Tour.............................**12** C5
Map Shop.................................**13** B5
Ministry of External Relations....**14** C5
Mobicon....................................(see 79)
Nomadic Journeys.....................(see 77)
Office of Immigration, Naturalization &
Foreign Citizens......................**15** C6
Russian Embassy.......................**16** C5
SOS Medica Mongolia Clinic.......**17** D4
Tourist Information Visitre Centre...(see 4)
Tseren Tours.............................**18** B5
UK Embassy..............................**19** D4
US Embassy..............................**20** A4
Wind of Mongolia......................**21** B5
Xanadu Books & Fine Wines.......**22** C5
Yonsei Friendship Hospital.........**23** B5
Za Internet...............................**24** B5

SIGHTS & ACTIVITIES
Gandan Khiid...........................**25** B5
Government (Parliament) House...**26** C4
Monastery-Museum of Choijin
Lama.....................................**27** C5
Mongolian Artists' Exhibition Hall...**28** C5
Mongolian National Modern Art
Gallery.................................(see 70)
Museum of Natural History........**29** C4
Naadam Stadium.......................**30** C6
National Museum of Mongolian
History..................................**31** C4

Statue of Chinggis Khaan...............**32** C4
Winter Palace of the Bogd Khaan....**33** C6
Zanabazar Museum of Fine Arts......**34** C4

SLEEPING
Bayangol Hotel..........................**35** C5
Chinggis Khaan Hotel.................**36** D4
Gana's Guesthouse.....................**37** B4
Golden Gobi..............................**38** C5
Khan Palace..............................**39** D4
Kharaa Hotel.............................**40** B5
Khongor Guesthouse..................**41** B5
LG Guesthouse..........................**42** A5
Nasan's Guest House.................**43** C5
Tiara Guesthouse......................**44** A5
UB Guesthouse (future location)...(see 80)
UB Guesthouse (old location)......**45** B5
Ulaanbaatar Hotel......................**46** C4
Voyage Hotel............................**47** B5
Zaluuchuud Hotel......................**48** C4
Zaya Backpacker Hostel.............**49** B5

EATING
Ananda Café & Meditation Centre...**50** C4
BD's Mongolian Barbeque...........**51** B5
Café Amsterdam........................**52** B5
California..................................**53** B5
Chez Bernard............................**54** C5
Dalal Eej & Merkuri Markets.......**55** B5
Khaan Buuz..............................**56** B5
Le Bistro Français......................**57** C4
Luna Blanca..............................**58** C5
Marco Polo...............................**59** B5
Michele's French Bakery.............**60** C5
Millie's Espresso......................(see 22)
Sacher's Café............................**61** C4
Silk Road Bar & Grill..................**62** C5
Stupa Café................................**63** C5
Taj Mahal...............................(see 46)
Veranda.................................(see 62)

DRINKING
Chinggis Club............................**64** C4
Dave's Place..............................**65** C5
Grand Khaan Irish Pub................**66** C5

ENTERTAINMENT
Metropolis................................**67** D4
National Academic Drama Theatre...**68** C5
Oasis.......................................**69** B5
Palace of Culture.......................**70** C4
River Sounds.............................**71** C5
State Circus...............................**72** B5
State Opera & Ballet Theatre.......**73** C5
Tengis......................................**74** B4
Tsuki House...............................**75** C5
Tumen Ekh Song & Dance Ensemble...**76** C5

SHOPPING
Egshiglen Magnai National Musical
Instrument Shop......................**77** C4
Gobi Cashmere Shop..................**78** C5
State Department Store...............**79** B5
Tsagaan Alt Wool Shop...............**80** B5

TRANSPORT
Aeroflot...................................**81** B5
AeroMongolia............................**82** A4
Air China..................................**83** D4
Bus Stop to Terelj......................**84** B5
CC Inter Tour Company.............(see 86)
EZnis.......................................**85** B5
International Railway Ticketing
Office....................................**86** A5
Korean Air...............................(see 36)
MIAT.......................................**87** C4
Taxi Stand................................**88** B5
Taxi Stand................................**89** C4

Sights

GANDAN KHIID

This **monastery** (Gandantegchinlen Khiid; ☎ 360 337; www.gandan.mn; Öndör Geegen Zanabazaryn Gudamj; admission T2500; ☺ 9am-9pm) is the largest and most important monastery in Ulaanbaatar, home to the spiritual head of Mongolia, the Khamba Lama. The name translates roughly as 'the great place of complete joy'.

The monastery was built in 1838 by the second Bogd Gegeen and even served as home to the 13th Dalai Lama for a few years after he fled Lhasa in 1904. It survived the communist purges of the 1930s and was re-opened in 1944 as a stage monastery to show to foreign dignitaries. Today there are over 800 monks in residence and in its main building, the **Migjid Janraisig Süm**, you can view the 26.5m-tall gilded statue of Buddha, a replacement for one moved to St Petersburg in 1937.

The courtyard on the right of the main entrance contains two temples, the **Ochirdary Süm** and the smaller **Golden Dedenpovaran Süm**. If you come in the morning you can witness the fascinating ceremonies that take place here.

WINTER PALACE OF THE BOGD KHAAN

Mongolia's eighth living Buddha and last king, Jebtzun Damba Hutagt VIII, lived for 20 years in this **palace** (☎ 342 195; Chingisiin Örgön Chölöö; admission T2500; ☺ 9am-5.30pm daily May-Sep, 9am-5.30pm Fri-Tue Oct-Apr). The grounds house six ornate temples; the white building on the right is the palace itself. It contains an eclectic collection of gifts received from foreign dignitaries and an extraordinary array of stuffed animals. Take bus 7 or 19 (from near the Bayangol Hotel).

MONASTERY-MUSEUM OF CHOIJIN LAMA

This **museum** (☎ 324 788; admission T2500; ☺ 9am-5pm Jun-Oct, 10am-5pm Nov-May) is also known as the Museum of Religion and hasn't operated as a monastery since 1938. There are five temples within the tranquil grounds and a concrete ger with a good selection of souvenirs and books about Buddhism and Mongolia. Sadly, a forest of glass and steel office towers are shooting up around the ancient complex, giving the place a less than pleasant backdrop.

MUSEUM OF NATURAL HISTORY

The best reason for visiting this old and rambling **museum** (☎ 321 716; cnr Sükhbaataryn Gudamj & Sambugiin Örgön Chölöö; adult/student T2500/1000; ☺ 10am-5.30pm daily May-Sep, 10am-5.30pm Wed-Sun Oct-Apr) is to see the massive dinosaur fossils and skeletons dug up from the Gobi. The museum houses two impressive complete skeletons of a *Tarbosaurus* and a *Saurolophus*, as well as petrified dinosaur eggs and fossils.

AROUND SÜKHBAATAR SQUARE

The heart of Ulaanbaatar is Sükhbaatar Square, named after the 1921 revolutionary hero who ushered in the era of communism. A statue of Damdin Sükhbaatar straddling a horse, hand aloft, stands in the centre of the square. At the northern end of the square is a marble portico housing an enormous bronze **statue of Chinggis Khaan**. His son Ögedei and grandson Kublai flank him on the west and east sides respectively.

On the east side the square, the Modernist structure is the Palace of Culture (see p289), which contains the **Mongolian National Modern Art Gallery** (☎ 331 687; admission T2000; ☺ 10am-6pm). On the northeast side of square, the cubist concrete structure is the **National Museum of Mongolian History** (☎ 325 656; cnr Juulchin Gudamj & Sükhbaataryn Gudamj; admission T2500; ☺ 10am-4.30pm Tue-Sat). This museum contains exhibits (with English captions) on ancient burial sites, folk art and culture, Buddhist ceremonial objects and the Mongol horde.

ZANABAZAR MUSEUM OF FINE ARTS

This **art museum** (☎ 326 060; Juulchin Gudamj; adult/student T2500/400; ☺ 9am-5pm May-Sep, 10am-5pm Oct-Apr) has an excellent collection of paintings, carvings and sculptures, including many by the revered sculptor and artist Zanabazar. It also contains other rare religious exhibits such as *thangka* (scroll paintings) and Buddhist statues, representing the best display of its kind in Mongolia.

ZAISAN MEMORIAL

This memorial is the tall, thin landmark on top of the hill south of the city. Built by the Russians to commemorate 'unknown soldiers and heroes' from various wars, this masterpiece of socialist realism offers sweeping views of the city and surrounding hills, as well as a workout on the climb up. Bus 7 from Bayangol Hotel will get you here.

Tours

Most guest houses offer their own range of tours. Many tour companies and travel agencies offer tours to gers.

PUREVBAT LAMA, MASTER ARTIST

Much of Mongolia's great art was destroyed in the Buddhist purges of 1937 when hundreds of temples and monasteries were burnt to the ground. G Purvebat Lama, the master artist of Gandan Khiid, is resurrecting the legacies of this Buddhist artwork. Purevbat perfected his art skills in the Himalayas, travelling for years across Nepal and India. He returned to Mongolia to re-establish the Buddhist Art School of Ulaanbaatar. We caught up with him in his studio at the monastery.

Mongolia regained its religious freedom almost 20 years ago. Has Buddhist art been resurrected in that time? Yes and no. Buddhist art created over hundreds of years was lost in the 1930s so it would be impossible to get back what was lost. But we have made small gains over the past two decades. Our collection of Buddhist art continues to grow but we probably won't ever have the number of monasteries we had before the 1930s. What is most important is to re-educate people and for this we have opened Buddhism schools so children can learn about their heritage.

What is your most recent project? This year I built a new museum in Bornur Soum, Tov aimag. It's a museum of interesting and rare cultural artefacts, including many pieces of art that were damaged during the 1930s purges. The museum also includes hundreds of skulls from lamas that were shot in 1937 – this is a way to remind people of the horror of repression.

What are some ideas you are considering for the future? We are now in the process of creating a three volume book on Buddhist art. It's an enormous project that involves the detailed study of the monasteries in Mongolia. We are also going out to the countryside to rebuild stupas that were damaged in the purges or because of neglect. Finally, I am planning to build a new museum on Tsaganii Ovoo hill, near Gandan Khiid. I have collected two million pieces of art and we need a place to display them!

What do you want your art work to achieve? I hope that by rebuilding the Buddhist culture Mongolian people will gain a better appreciation for their country. We live in a time of transition; people are travelling to different countries, being influenced by other religions and Western culture and getting distracted by the internet and mobile phones. I hope that my work will remind them what it means to be Mongolian.

As told to Michael Kohn

Active Mongolia (☎ 329 456; www.activemongolia .com; btwn Peace & Seoul Aves; ☿ 10am-6pm) In the Seven Summits camping supplies shop, it offers hiking, cycling, jeep and horse-riding trips.

Ger to Ger (☎ 313 336; www.gertoger.org; Arizona Plaza, Suite 11, Baruun Selbe Gudamj 5/3) Culturally sensitive tour group, see p292.

Karakorum Expeditions (☎ 320 182, 9911 6729; www.gomongolia.com; Gangaryn Gurav Bldg) Behind the State Circus it specialises in hiking, biking and climbing trips.

Nomadic Journeys (☎ 328 737; www.nomadicjourneys .com; Sükhbaataryn Gudamj 1) Ecoconscious tour operator that concentrates on low-impact tourism. Yak-carting and camel-trekking options with high-quality food and service.

Tseren Tours (☎ 9974 0832, 327 083; www.tserentours .com; Baruun Selbe Gudamj 14/1) Dutch/Mongolian-run outfit that does countrywide tours and biking trips.

Wind of Mongolia (☎ 9909 0593, 9973 0249; www .windofmongolia.mn; Sükhbaatar District, 5th Microdistrict, Bldg 9, Apt 57) French-run operation that does rock climbing, dog sledding (in winter) and Buddhism trips. The office is unsigned so call ahead.

Festivals & Events
Camel Polo Winter Festival Held in mid-March, this unique festival features camel polo and racing.
Naadam Mongolia's No 1 festival draws the multitudes to Ulaanbaatar on 11 and 12 July (see also p288).

Sleeping
New guest houses are opening up all the time in Ulaanbaatar. Touts meet all international trains arriving at the station – some may offer good options, but be sure to check the location before you commit. All room rates following include breakfast, although at the budget places this may just be tea, coffee and some bread and jam.

BUDGET
The private rooms at guest houses are a better deal than budget hotels. They also have the benefit of clued-up hosts who can arrange tours, and the company of fellow travellers. Many guest houses are in apartment buildings and can be difficult to find; however, most will

send someone to meet your train if you call or email ahead.

Gana's Guest House (☎ /fax 367 343; www.ganasger .mn; Gandan Khiid ger district, house No 22; dm in r/ger US$3/5, d US$15-25; 🖳) If you are looking for scruffy charm, this place has plenty. The city's oldest guest house is embedded in the ger district southwest of Gandan Khiid. You can choose between a room in the main building or the rooftop ger.

Khongor Guesthouse (☎ 316 415, 9925 2599; http:// get.to/khongor; Peace Ave 15, Apt 6; dm/s/d US$4/10/12; 🖳) Knowledgeable English-speaking Toroo offers reasonably well-appointed accommodation in three separate buildings, each convenient and central. For safe and reliable digs this is the best choice in this range. The entrance of the main guest house is around the back of the third building west of the State Department Store.

Golden Gobi (☎ 322 632, 9665 4496; www.goldengobi .com; dm/d US$5/16, d without bathroom US$14; 🖳) You'll probably hear about this funky place and its eccentric owners long before your train arrives in UB. The hosts may even take you out for a pub crawl around town! It's in the courtyard just east of the State Department Store.

UB Guesthouse (☎ 311 037, 9119 9859; www.ub guest.com; cnr Baga Toiruu & Juulchin Gudamj; dm/s/d US$5/10/16; 🖳) A popular guest house with clean rooms and a good travellers vibe. It's centrally located above Golomt Bank on Baga Toiruu west; the entrance is around the back. At the time of writing there were plans to move to a larger building opposite the State Department Store, our map indicates the new and old locations.

Nassan's Guest House (☎ 321 078, 9919 7466; www .nassantour.com; Baga Toiruu West; dm US$8, s/d/tr US$23/28/36; 🖳) Long-running guest house with a central location and a variety of room options. Not as crowded as some other guest houses, allowing a little more privacy.

Zaya Backpacker Hostel (☎ 316 696, 9918 5013; www.zayahostel.com; Peace Ave; dm US$10, s/d US$30/35, s/d without bathroom US$25/30; 🖳) The plushest guest house in the downtown area, Zaya has hardwood floors, modern bathrooms and a comfy lounge. It's on the 3rd floor of an orange apartment block behind the Peace & Friendship Building.

Handy for the train station:

LG Guesthouse (☎ 7011 8243, 9989 4672; www.lg.url .mn; Narny Gudamj; dm US$5, s/d US$12/16; 🖳) With 12 rooms this is one of the largest guest houses around. Has kitchen facilities plus a cafe.

Tiara Guesthouse (☎ 252 319, 9905 4244; www.tiara guesthouse.com; Bogd Ar Subdistrict No 5A; dm US$7; 🖳) Likable place with airy rooms and bright lounge. It's a little hard to spot: with your back to the XAAH Bank, walk through the gap to the right of the Fresco Market; after 50m turn left up the ramp.

MIDRANGE & TOP END

The three hotels following offer guaranteed privacy and, usually, your own shower.

Zaluuchuud Hotel (☎ 324 594; www.zh.mn; Baga Toiruu 43; s/d/ste incl breakfast US$35/65/90) The spiffy rooms here have been renovated to a modern, simple design and are equipped with TV, fridge and kettle.

Kharaa Hotel (☎ 313 733; Choimbolyn Gudamj 6; d/ half-lux/lux US$35/45/60; 🖳) The Kharaa is nothing spectacular but the rooms are comfortable enough, the service is friendly and it's within walking distance of the city centre. Views are better on the street side of the hotel.

Voyage Hotel (☎ 327 213; www.voyagehotel.mn; Narny Gudamj; s/d/half-lux/lux US$30/50/65/90; 🖳) Good-value midrange place with friendly service and well-maintained rooms. Convenient for the train station.

Expect 15% Value-Added Tax (VAT) to be tacked onto your bill for top-end places. A Hilton hotel is expected to open by 2009.

Ulaanbaatar Hotel (☎ 320 620; www.ubhotel.mn; Sükhbaatar Sq 14; s/d from US$60/90; 🖳) One of the very few hotels that was built and flourished during the communist era, the Ulaanbaatar harks back to that time but still has decent rooms. Excellent facilities include a sauna, billiard room, business centre, travel agency, coffee shop, two restaurants and even a practice golf range on the 6th floor.

Bayangol Hotel (☎ 312 255; www.bayangolhotel.mn; Chingisiin Örgön Chölöö 5; s/d from US$76/97; 🖳) Reliable and centrally located hotel with a couple of good restaurants and a bar. Bathrooms are small but otherwise rooms have contemporary furnishings. They also include desktop computers for work, email or internet.

Khan Palace (☎ 463 463; www.khanpalace.com; East Cross Rd; s/d from US$98/121; 🖳) This Kempinski-managed hotel is one of the best in the city. Facilities include free internet, sauna and a fitness centre. Expats rave about the breakfasts.

Eating

Ulaanbaatar's restaurants offer a surprisingly decent variety of cuisines and atmospheres.

Enjoy the choice and quality because out in the countryside it's another matter entirely!

RESTAURANTS

Luna Blanca (☎ 327 172; Juulchin Gudamj; meals T5000; ⏱ 10.30am-8.30pm; ✗ Ⓥ) Better than average vegetarian restaurant serving kebabs, soups, salads, smoothies and vegie twists on Mongolian dishes. The owners are three English-speaking sisters who learned to cook vegie food while studying in India.

our pick Veranda (☎ 330 818; Jamiyan Guunii Gudamj; mains T6000-8000; ⏱ noon-midnight) Located upstairs from Silk Road Bar & Grill, this place has seating on comfortable sofas or at tables looking over the mystical Monastery-Museum of Choijin Lama. The French-Italian cuisine is superb and the prices reasonable.

Marco Polo (☎ 318 433; Seoul St 27; pizzas T7500; ⏱ noon-midnight) This place gets our vote for the best pizza in town. Its outdoor terrace is popular in summer, while the strip show upstairs pulls in the punters year-round.

Silk Road Bar & Grill (☎ 9191 0211, 318 864; Jamiyan Guunii Gudamj; meal with drink T10,000; ⏱ 12.30-11pm) A variety of cuisines clash at this Silk Road–themed restaurant. Try a chicken shish kebab, barbecued lamb, pepper steak or choose from a good selection of soups and salads.

California (☎ 319 031; Seoul St; meal with drink T9000; ⏱ 8am-midnight Mon-Sat, 9am-midnight Sun) Popular with expats and Mongolians alike, this one is a good choice for variety and price. Notable for its American-style breakfasts, burgers, steaks, salads and lively atmosphere.

Taj Mahal (☎ 311 009; Ulaanbaatar Hotel, 6th fl; meal with drink T10,000; ⏱ noon-midnight) Excellent Indian cuisine, including a great-value *thali* (set menu) meal for T6500. Amiable owner Babu is sure to check if you're having a good time.

BD's Mongolian Barbeque (☎ 311 191; Seoul St; all-you-can-eat BBQ T10,500; ⏱ noon-midnight) This is more like an Americanised version of Mongolian barbecue, but its tasty nonetheless. Choose your ingredients and allow the chefs to grill up your meal before your eyes. It's a good place to go after a long train ride as you can eat as much as you like (within 90 minutes).

Le Bistro Français (☎ 320 022; Ikh Surguuliin Gudamj 2; meal with wine T15,000; ⏱ 9am-midnight Mon-Fri, 10am-midnight Sat & Sun) High-society folks can be found at this relaxed bistro. It serves good but pricey French-style cuisine and fine wine to the background sounds of live piano music.

CAFES & QUICK EATS

For fast Mongolian fare, cheap, tasty *buuz* are sold at small eateries around town; try Khaan Buuz, which has several outlets including one opposite the State Department Store.

Stupa Café (☎ 9911 9765; Juulchin Gudamj; Builder's Sq; snack & drink T2000; ⏱ 9am-8pm Sun-Fri; ✗) Attached to a Buddhist cultural centre, this very appealing cafe is ideal for a quiet pit stop and has some great handmade souvenirs as well as newspapers and a free English library.

Michele's French Bakery (☎ 9916 9970; off Peace Ave; snacks from T500; ⏱ 8am-8pm) Take away croissants and apple strudels or sit down with a panini or crepe. A popular haunt for expats.

Ananda Cafe & Meditation Centre (☎ 316 986; Baga Toiruu west; meals T3000; ⏱ 10am-8pm; Ⓥ) Serves herbal teas and vegie dishes made from organic produce. Profits go to supporting the Lotus orphanage. Yoga classes are available.

Café Amsterdam (☎ 8891 1832; www.amsterdam.mn; Peace Ave; lunch T5000; ⏱ 7am-10pm; ✗) A literary cafe of sorts, this place attracts journalists, writers and other creative folk. It sometimes puts on cultural events so check their noticeboard. Menu items include soups, sandwiches, teas, coffees and light European breakfasts. Some of the vegetables come from a local women's co-op.

Sacher's Café (☎ 324 734; Baga Toiruu west; breakfast T2500; ⏱ 8am-10pm) A German-run place with an excellent selection of cakes, pretzels and breads; perfect snack food for the train.

Chez Bernard (☎ 8810 0135; www.happycamel.com; Peace Ave 27; breakfast T6000; ⏱ 7am-8pm) This Belgian-owned cafe is popular with backpackers who make use of the noticeboard to swap stuff and find other travellers for countryside trips. The menu includes European-style breakfast platters, plus a selection of (over-priced) bakery items.

our pick Millie's Espresso (☎ 330 338; Marco Polo Bldg; snack & drink T6000; ⏱ 9am-4pm Mon-Sat) The preferred lunch spot for consultants, diplomats, expat businessmen and the occasional Member of Parliament. Great options include the steak sandwich, lasagne, lemon pie and fruit smoothie. Say hello to the enthusiastic hosts Millie and Daniel!

SELF-CATERING

Stock up for your train ride or a trip to the countryside by visiting the ground floor of the **State Department Store** (Peace Ave), or for a

ULAN-UDE TO BĚIJĪNG VIA MONGOLIA

THE NAADAM FESTIVAL

The high point of the Mongolian year is the Naadam Festival, held on 11 and 12 July. Part family reunion, part fair and part nomad Olympics, Naadam (meaning 'games') has its roots in the nomad assemblies and hunting extravaganzas of the Mongol armies.

Smaller Naadams are held throughout the country and are well worth attending if you want to get close to the action, witness genuine traditions, and even make up the numbers during a wrestling tournament! That said, UB's Naadam is the biggie, with parades, cheesy carnival events and souvenir salesmen outside the stadium (about 2km south of Sükhbaatar Sq). The colourful and lively opening ceremony is well worth catching even if you're not interested in the three traditional 'manly' sports of wrestling, archery and horse racing, as well as the quirky anklebone shooting.

A small ceremony occurs at around 9.30am on day one at Sükhbaatar Sq. The real action begins with the opening ceremony at the stadium, starting at 11am and lasting about two hours.

To find out what is going on during the festival, look for the events program in the two English-language newspapers; there are often sports matches and other events in the lead-up to the main two days.

Wrestling

The wrestling starts at the stadium immediately after the opening ceremony. The final rounds on day two, just before the closing ceremony, are the most exciting matches. Mongolian wrestling has no time limits; a match ends only when a wrestler falls (or any body part other than feet or hands touches the ground).

The 'eagle dance' is performed beforehand by contestants to pay respect to the judges, and again afterwards by the winner. The loser must walk under the right arm of the winner, symbolising peace between the wrestlers. Another special feature of wrestling is the uniform, complete with heavy boots, tiny tight briefs and open midriff-baring vests.

Archery

Archery is held in an open stadium next to the main stadium. Archers use a bent composite bow made of layered horn, bark and wood. Arrows are usually made from willow branches and vulture feathers.

The target is a line of up to 20 or 30 rings on the ground. Male contestants stand 75m from the target while female contestants stand 60m from it. After each shot, the judges emit a shout

---

better selection try **Dalai Eej Market** (☽ 10am-8pm) and **Merkuri Market** (☽ 10am-8pm), west of the State Circus.

Drinking

Locally brewed beers have taken off in UB. Most bars are open 11am to midnight daily and all serve food of the meat-and-potatoes variety.

Dave's Place (☎ 9979 8185; Sükhbaatar Sq) Located on the patio of the Cultural Palace, this is a great place to observe the comings and goings of central UB. Don't miss Thursday's 'Quiz Night', starting at 9.30pm (tip: read up on the local news first). In cool weather the whole operation retreats to the basement bar.

Grand Khaan Irish Pub (☎ 336 666; Seoul St) This place isn't all that Irish, but it offers a good time nonetheless. Expect big crowds, lots of smoke and free-flowing beer. The food ain't bad either.

Chinggis Club (☎ 325 820; Sükhbaataryn Gudamj 10) The beer is recommended at this German-run microbrewery, with a lively atmosphere and good German-inspired grub.

Entertainment

Check the English-language weeklies for info on coming events (see p282). The **Arts Council of Mongolia** (☎ 319 015; www.artscouncil .mn) produces a monthly cultural events calendar that covers most theatres, galleries and museums.

TRADITIONAL MUSIC & DANCE

A performance of traditional music and dance will be one of the highlights of your visit to Mongolia. **Tumen Ekh Song & Dance Ensemble** (☎ 9666 4374; State Youth & Children's

and raise their arms to indicate the quality of the shot. The winner who hits the targets the most times is declared the best *mergen* (archer).

Horse Racing

Horse racing is held about 28km west of the city at Hui Doloon Khutag. Buses and minivans travel here from the parking lot outside the stadium (T2000). Tour operators and Chez Bernard restaurant also organise vehicles or you could take a taxi (about T20,000 return). The racing, which takes place not on a track but on the open steppe, has six categories, based on the age of the horse and distance of the race (either 15km or 30km). Jockeys are children aged five to 12.

The winning horses and riders are then the subject of laudatory poems and songs performed by the crowds. The five winning riders must drink some special *airag* (fermented mare's milk), which is then sprinkled on the riders' heads and horses' backs. Spectators believe sweat from racehorses brings good luck, and will endeavour to scrape some from the horses' backsides.

Anklebone Shooting

Held in a large tent next to the archery stadium, this entails flicking a sheep's anklebone at a small target (also made from anklebones) about 3m away. Apart from providing some shade, the tent has an electric atmosphere as competitors are spurred on by the yodelling of spectators.

Tickets

Admission to the stadium (except for the opening and closing ceremonies), archery and horse racing are free, but you'll need a ticket for the opening ceremony and possibly the last round or two of the wrestling and closing ceremony. Ticket costs vary per section; the north side of the stadium (which is protected from the sun and rain by an overhang and has the best view of the opening event) is more expensive with tickets going for T30,000 (valid for both the opening and closing ceremonies). These tickets are distributed via the tour operators and hotels.

Alternatively you can get a ticket for as low as T2500 from scalpers who hang around the stadium or even from the police at the gates. The original price will be printed on the ticket; you can expect to pay twice this for the service charge. A cheap ticket will get you through a designated gate, but these sections are grossly oversold and there is no guarantee you'll get a seat. If you are a lucky seat holder you may soon find a granny or child on your lap.

Theatre, Nairamdal Park, admission T6000; 🕑 6pm) puts on a nightly cultural show in summer, complete with traditional song, dance, *khöömii* (throat singing) and contortionists. At the Tsuki House next to the State Circus, the **Moonstone Song & Dance Ensemble** (☎ 318 802; admission T7000; 🕑 2pm, 4pm, 6pm & 8pm May-Oct) puts on a similar show in cabaret fashion. One drink is included with admission and food is available. Cultural shows are also put on semiregularly at the **National Academic Drama Theatre** (☎ 324 621; cnr Seoul St & Chingisiin Örgön Chölöö; admission T7000; 🕑 6pm May-Sep) and the **Palace of Culture** (☎ 321 444) on the northeast corner of Sükhbaatar Sq.

The **State Opera & Ballet Theatre** (☎ 322 854; Sükhbaatar Sq; admission T5000-8000; 🕑 Sep-Jul) stages productions in Mongolian of many of the classics, as well as works by Mongolia's most famous poet and playwright Natsagdorj.

NIGHTCLUBS

River Sounds (☎ 320 497; Olympiin Örgön Chölöö; admission T3000-5000; 🕑 8pm-3am) Dedicated live-music venue that usually hosts jazz and occasionally rock bands.

Metropolis (☎ 9973 0569; Sky Shopping Centre; admission T5000; 🕑 8pm-4am) UB's biggest, baddest discotheque thumps all night to beats mixed by a French-Cambodian DJ.

Oasis (☎ 311 719; Seoul St; admission T4000; 🕑 6pm-late) Weird stuff usually goes down in this little club, tucked behind the 24-hour supermarket. Try it on a weekend.

CINEMA

Tengis (☎ 326 575; www.tengis.mn; Liberty Sq; regular show T2500, matinee T1500) Modern multiplex cinema that screens local movies and Hollywood blockbusters (shown in English with Mongolian subtitles).

Shopping

UB abounds with shops selling tacky tourist souvenirs as well as locally produced cashmere clothing and blankets. A few of the better places for that special Mongolian keepsake:

Egshiglen Magnai National Musical Instrument Shop (☎ 328 419; Sükhbaataryn Gudamj; ☽ 9am-6pm Mon-Sat) The place to get your *morin khuur* (horsehead fiddle).

Gobi Cashmere Shop (☎ 326 867; Peace Ave; ☽ 11am-7pm Mon-Sat) High-quality cashmere products located opposite the Russian embassy.

State Department Store (☎ 319 292; Peace Ave 44; ☽ 9am-8pm Mon-Sat, 10am-6pm Sun) Has a decent collection of souvenirs and cashmere products.

Tsagaan Alt Wool Shop (☎ 318 591; Tserendorjiin Gudamj; ☽ 10am-7pm Mon-Sat) Colourful and inventive products made from felt, including slippers and hats.

Getting There & Away

AIR

The Mongolian airline **MIAT** (☎ 322 686; www .miat.com; Baga Toiruu west) has flights to Běijīng, Berlin, Irkutsk, Moscow, Osaka, Seoul and Tokyo. **Aero Mongolia** (☎ 8808 9699, 330 373; www .aeromongolia.mn; Zaluuchuudiin Örgön Chölöö) has domestic flights and twice-weekly flights to Hohhot (China). **EZnis** (☎ 313 689; www.eznis .com; Seoul St) is another domestic carrier.

Other international carriers:

Aeroflot (☎ 320 720; Seoul St 15) To Moscow, Irkutsk and Ulan-Ude.

Air China (☎ 452 548; Ikh Toiruu, Bldg 47)

Korean Air (☎ 326 643; Tokyogiin Gudamj, Chinggis Khaan Hotel, 2nd fl) To Seoul.

BUS & JEEPS

Minivans heading for destinations in the north and west leave from the **Dragon Bus Stand** (☎ 634 902) on Peace Ave 7km west of Sükhbaatar Sq. The **Bayanzürkh Avto Vaksal** (☎ 463 386), 6km east of Sükhbaatar Sq, has buses leaving to eastern cities and Dalanzadgad. Buses depart between 7.30am and 8am. Shared vans and jeeps to all destinations also leave from the Naran Tuul Market, east of the centre.

TRAIN

For information on the international train services to and from UB, including the Trans-Mongolian, see p351.

International train tickets are available at the **International Railway Ticketing Office** (☎ 944 868; Zamchydn Gudamj) at the foreigners' booking office in Room 212 (open 8am to 8pm Monday to Friday); at weekends use the downstairs booking desk. Tickets for international trains can be booked up to one month in advance but those for the Moscow–Běijīng trains don't go on sale until the day before departure.

If you run into problems, most guest houses and hotels should be able to assist.

Getting Around

A taxi from Buyant-Ukhaa International Airport, 18km southwest of the city, should be around T10,000. Bus 11 also runs from the airport every 20 minutes to the Bayangol Hotel (T400, 25 minutes). From the train station to the city centre is about a 20-minute walk (about 2km). Alternatively, metered taxis charge a standard T400 per kilometre (check the current rate as this increases regularly); most taxi drivers are honest and will use their meters. If there is no meter, make sure they set the odometre to zero. Expect to pay around T3000 from the station to Sükhbaatar Sq. This price will be lower if you walk away from the station.

AROUND ULAANBAATAR

Mongolia's real attraction lies in the untouched beauty of the countryside, its exhilarating wide-open spaces and rich nomadic culture. Fortunately, these aspects are within reach on day trips or overnights from Ulaanbaatar. See p284 for details on tours.

Mandshir Khiid Мандшир хийд

Just over 50km south of Ulaanbaatar, Mandshir Khiid was a monastery – established in 1733 – that once contained more than 20 temples and housed 350 monks. Destroyed during the 1930s, the main temple has been restored and now functions as a museum, but the other temples remain in ruins.

The monastery itself is not as impressive as Gandan Khiid in Ulaanbaatar, but the setting is exquisite. Hidden away in the **Bogdkhan Uul Strictly Protected Area** (admission T5000), the monastery overlooks a beautiful valley of pine, birch and cedar trees, dotted with granite boulders. Behind the main temple, climb up the rocks to discover some **Buddhist rock paintings**.

You can catch a taxi straight to Mandshir Khiid from Ulaanbaatar. Alternatively, take one of the hourly minibuses to the nearby town of Zuunmod (T1000, one hour) and then walk the 5km to the monastery or take a

MONGOLIA-CHINA BORDER

This border crossing takes about five hours no matter which direction you are travelling. Some trains cross the border at night, which guarantees that you won't get much sleep. In Zamyn-Üüd, Mongolian customs officials and border guards do their thing. Officials reserve most of their energy for Chinese and Mongolian traders. This process can take up to two hours.

In Erlian, Chinese customs and passport officials repeat the process (or start it, if you are travelling west). You must fill out customs forms and departure/arrival cards. The Erlian station is usually quite lively, even at night. Once your passport is returned, catch some fresh air and explore the station and surroundings where you can change money or get something to eat. If you do get off, you will not have a chance to get back on the train for about two hours while the bogies are changed.

As in Russia, Mongolia's trains run on a 5ft (1.5m) gauge, which is slightly wider than the standard gauge used in much of the rest of the world. Before the train can continue its journey, it must make a stop at the bogie-changing shed, where the carriages are raised and the bogies are replaced with the appropriate size. The bogies are changed with the passengers still on board the train and you can see the operations happening around you. To get a better look, get off the train at the platform (after your passport has been checked) and walk back to the shed where you can watch the operations at ground level. It's a 10-minute walk from the platform to the shed.

Alternative Routes to Bĕijīng

Immediately after Naadam, with thousands of visitors heading out of Ulaanbaatar, it's practically impossible to score last-minute reservations on the direct trains and flights to Bĕijīng. If you haven't booked well in advance, all is not lost as there are alternatives.

Train tickets are often available on the twice-weekly Ulaanbaatar to Hohhot (China) service; buy a ticket as far as the main junction at Jining (T85,730 *kupe*) where you can connect with a nightly train to Bĕijīng (Y160 hard sleeper). To be sure of getting a ticket for this connection contact **CC Inter Tour Company** (☎ 245 380, 9665 8367) on the ground floor of UB's International Railway Ticketing Office (see opposite) who can make the arrangements. It charges the tögrög equivalent of Y230 for the same hard-sleeper ticket from Jining to Bĕijīng; you'll be met at Jining by its local agent, who will have your ticket.

Another option is to take the train as far as Erlian (T64,670) just across the Mongolian border. From here you can try to link up with an onward train or take a bus. From Erlian there are buses at 2pm, 3pm and 4pm to Bĕijīng (Y180, 10 hours). There is an 8am train to Jining and a train at 1.30pm on Tuesday and Saturday.

Some travellers may end up at Zamyn-Üüd by another means – possibly by local train or vehicle from UB or Sainshand. The daily Ulaanbaatar to Zamyn-Üüd train arrives in the early morning and there is a scramble to get into a jeep (T8000) to cross the border. The fare from Ulaanbaatar to Zamyn-Üüd is T18,200 and from Sainshand its T7,500. If it's Tuesday or Saturday you can take the afternoon train to Jining, on other days take the afternoon bus.

Both Zamyn-Üüd and Erlian have a reasonable selection of hotels, restaurants, moneychangers and ATMs near their respective train stations.

---

taxi. Laid-back Zuunmod (population 14,300) is also a conveniently close place to UB to catch a local Naadam festival (see p288).

Bogdkhan Uul Strictly Protected Area
Богдхан Уул

Of the Four Holy mountains that surround Ulaanbaatar, the most magnificent is Bogdkhan Uul and its highest peak, Tsetseegün Uul (2256m). The Siberian larch forest and abundance of bird and animal life make this a great place to escape the city.

The easiest way to explore Tsetseegün Uul is to hike from Mandshir Khiid (opposite). Even if you do not enter the monastery/museum, you will have to pay the T5000 admission fee for Bogdkhan Uul Strictly Protected Area. The trail is reasonably marked, but you should also use a compass. A hike from Mandshir Khiid to the Zaisan Memorial (p284) in Ulaanbaatar takes about 10 hours. With a very early start you could do it in a day, otherwise, plan on camping out on top.

GER TO GER TREKKING

Seeing Mongolia's beautiful nature from the train window will probably entice you to get off the rails. One of the best active adventure options is offered by **Ger to Ger** (☎ 313 336; www .gertoger.org; Arizona Plaza, Suite 11, Baruun Selbe Gudamj 5/3, Ulaanbaatar), a local nonprofit organisation that combines the great outdoors with a dose of traditional culture.

Trekkers travel by foot, horse and even yak cart between gers, with distances ranging from 5km to 20km. The gers act like warming huts and once you've arrived the family that maintains the ger will introduce various aspects of Mongolian culture, such as archery, cooking or horse training. Ger to Ger also provides a seminar on language and culture before you set off.

You can choose from routes in the desert, mountains or steppe, as well as levels of difficulty and duration. The closest route to Ulaanbaatar is a one-hour drive away in Gorkhi-Terelj National Park. Profits from the project go back to the local communities for small-scale development projects.

From the monastery, follow the stream east until it nearly disappears, then turn north. About three hours' walking should bring you out over a ridge into a broad boggy meadow, which you will have to cross. If you walked due north, the twin rocky outcrops of the summit should be right in front of you. When you start to see Ulaanbaatar in the distance, you are on the highest ridge and close to the two large *ovoo* (sacred pyramid-shaped collection of stones) on the summit.

From the *ovoo* you can return to Mandshir Khiid or descend to Ulaanbaatar. The quickest way is to head due north of UB's Observatory, and down to the valley where you'll cross the train tracks. The road is close by and you can catch a taxi to UB for around T3000. The longer route takes you to the Zaisan Memorial. Be careful not to drop down too soon otherwise you'll end up beside the Presidential Palace in the Ikh Tenger Valley. The guards here can be uptight about perceived 'trespassers'.

Terelj Тэрэлж

Although it's fast becoming developed, Terelj, about 80km northeast of UB and part of the **Gorkhi-Terelj National Park** (admission T3000), is still a beautiful and relaxing place to head to. At 1600m, this area is cool and the alpine scenery spectacular. There are many opportunities for hiking, rock climbing, swimming (in icy water), rafting and horseback riding (T12,000 to T20,000 per day).

One potential destination for hiking or horse riding is the appropriately named **Turtle Rock**, easily spotted along the main road through the park. From here it's less than an hour's hike up to the picturesque Buddhist meditation retreat of Aryapala from where you can look back on a stunning landscape straight out of *Lord of the Rings*.

Another place worth heading to is **Gunjiin Sün**, a Manchurian-influenced temple surrounded by forests. From the main ger camp area, Gunjiin Sün is about 30km as the crow flies, but it is easier to find if you take the longer route along the Baruun Bayan Gol. Other picturesque routes are along the Terelj and Tuul Rivers towards Khentii Nuruu.

Terelj is a great place to go camping, or guest houses can arrange accommodation in the park – sometimes staying in real gers with local families. Most of the tourist ger camps in Terelj offer similar facilities and prices – about US$30 per person, including three hearty meals, or US$15 without food. Among the better ones are **Buuveit** (☎ 322 870; www.tsolmontravel.com), which has a beautifully secluded location, and the friendly **Miraj** (☎ 325 188), 14km along the main road from the park entrance. For the slightly more adventurous, there is the **Ecotourism Ger Camp** (☎ 9973 4710; bergoo@hotmail.com; with/without meals US$16/6) run by a Dutchman named Bert. It's a 30-minute horse ride from the Terelj-Juulchin hotel, across the river. Inquire about the place at Chez Bernard (p287). Bert can organise horse trips and the area and can show you his cheese-making operation.

A bus (T1500) for Turtle Rock in Terelj leaves at 4pm from the corner of Peace Ave and Öndör Geegen Zanabazaryn Gudamj. The bus returns to Ulaanbaatar. Otherwise, hire a taxi for about T32,000 one way.

Khustain National Park
Хустайн Нуруу

Also known as Khustain Nuruu (Birch Mountain Range), this park was set up to protect the reintroduced *takhi* or Przewalski's horse. The horse (a separate species from domesticated horses) had become extinct in the wild by the late 1960s but the animals had been preserved in the zoos of Europe and Australia. A reintroduction program in the 1990s brought some back to Mongolia and they have been thriving in Khustain Nuruu. There is a sort of 'wildlife safari' feel to the place as you drive around the park looking for horses to photograph. The park is also home to wolves, steppe gazelle, boar and lynx.

You can stay at a small **ger camp** (per person without meals US$15, tent US$5) near the park entrance or at the **Moilt camp** (per person US$15) inside the park. For reservations contact the **Hustai National Park Trust** (☎ 011-245 087; www.hustai.mn).

To get to the park, travel 100km west of Ulaanbaatar and then 13km up a road off the main highway. Guest houses and tour operators offer trips here, or contact the Park Trust for transport options.

Chita to Běijīng via Hāěrbin

For connoisseurs of obscure rail routes, the Trans-Manchurian railway ranks high on the wish list. It's not on the mainline to Vladivostok, nor does it take the 'tourist route' via Mongolia; rather, the weekly *Vostok* (19/20) chugs through China's rust belt where foreign faces are few and far between.

From Chita the route cuts towards the Chinese border at Mǎnzhōulǐ, sweeps through the grasslands of Inner Mongolia and passes through Russian-influenced Hāěrbin (Harbin), one of China's more eclectic cities. Vladivostok is only a few hundred kilometres from Hāěrbin and die-hard rail fanatics could find their way onto the twice-weekly and excruciatingly slow international train connection. Most travellers, however, simply carry on towards the megalopolis that is Běijīng.

Besides its appealing obscurity, train buffs will also appreciate the Trans-Manchurian's history and its significance in East Asian affairs. The China Eastern Railway – to give it its technical name – was a geopolitical hot potato, alternately passed back and forth between the Russians, Japanese and Chinese during the tumultuous early years of the 20th century.

Another nonstandard Trans-Manchurian route is to hop across the Amur River from the Russian city of Blagoveshchensk to Hēihé, which also has regular rail connections with Hāěrbin. Whichever way you get there, Hāěrbin is a fascinating place, where elements of pre-communist Russia still poke through the surface of a thoroughly modern Chinese city. The prime time to visit is midwinter, when Hāěrbin hosts the spectacular Ice Lantern Festival.

Other possible stops en route include Hǎilāěr, where you can get a taste of Mongolian life at ger (yurt) camps near the city, and Shěnyáng, which hides some well-preserved relics of the Manchu era. In Russia you could also use Chita as a base for visiting some lesser-known Buddhist temples in the beautiful Siberian countryside.

HIGHLIGHTS

- Hang out with Russian traders in the prosperous border town of **Mǎnzhōulǐ** (p297)

- Experience the unique fusion of historic Russia and modern-day China on the cobblestone streets of Hāěrbin's **Dàolǐqū district** (p299)

- Eyeball majestic felines at the **Siberian Tiger Park** (p300), just outside Hāěrbin

- Go birdwatching in the peaceful wetlands of **Zhalong Nature Reserve** (p303)

- Brave the cold to see the spectacular ice sculptures carved at Hāěrbin's legendary **Ice Lantern Festival** (p302)

ROUTE DISTANCE: 2790KM

DURATION: TWO DAYS, EIGHT HOURS

THE ROUTE

In Russia, the kilometre markers show the distance to Moscow. Once in China, they show the distance to Hāěrbin; south of Hāěrbin, they show the distance to Běijīng.

Chita to Zabaikalsk

After **Chita** (6199km; p239), the next major stop is **Karymskaya** (6293km), from where it's 12km down the line to Tarskaya, the official start of the Trans-Manchurian route; here the train crosses the Ingoda River and heads southeast.

There is a short stop at 6444km in **Olovyannaya**, then the train crosses the Onon River, a tributary of the Ingoda. This area is said to be the birthplace of Chinggis (Genghis) Khaan (see the boxed text, p76).

The train makes another 10-minute stop at **Borzya** (6543km). There's little to see in this sparsely populated area, and even the Russian border town of **Zabaikalsk** (6666km) is a sleepy and rundown place. Zabaikalsk is where the bogies are changed before the train continues across the border into China. Passably edible meals are available at a cafe across from the station (take the bridge over the tracks and turn left).

Mǎnzhōulǐ to Hāěrbin

The Chinese border town **Mǎnzhōulǐ** (935km to Hāěrbin; p297), established in 1901 as a stop for the train, is booming thanks to cross-border trade.

Next along the line is **Hǎilāěr** (749km), the northernmost major town in Inner Mongolia, where the train stops for about 10 minutes. Should you choose to linger longer, a great option is to go to the Jinzanghan Grassland (金帐汗草原), just 40km north of Hǎilāěr, where you can eat mutton stew, sleep in a yurt (per person Y80) and ride horses (Y150 per hour). At the grasslands there is a **grasslands**

camp (☎ 133 2700 0919). A taxi here from Hǎilāěr is Y120 return.

Around 650km, the train enters the Greater Hinggan mountains. It may make stops at towns such as **Mianduhe** (634km), **Yilick Ede** (574km) and **Xinganling** (564km). From here the train descends on the eastern side of the range.

Shortly after the 15-minute halt at **Boketu** (539km), the train leaves Inner Mongolia and enters the province of Heilongjiang, meaning Black Dragon River. Known in Russian as the Amur River, Heilongjiang's namesake river marks the border with Russia in northeastern China.

The train makes another 15-minute stop at **Angangxi** (270km), then heads eastward through an area of wetlands, part of which has been designated as the Zhalong Nature Reserve (p303). The train makes a brief stop in **Daqing** (159km) at the centre of a large oilfield; look out for the rigs pumping crude oil out of the ground.

Hāěrbin (1388km from Běijīng; p299), the capital of Heilongjiang province, is...you guessed it...a 15-minute stop. If you're not stopping, the view of the skyline on the eastern side of the tracks as you leave Hāěrbin gives a sense of the city's size.

Hāěrbin to Běijīng

South of Hāěrbin, the train enters Jilin province, also part of the historic territory of the Manchus. The Japanese industrialised this region when they shaped it into the puppet state of Manchukuo (1931–45). The capital of Manchukuo, and today's provincial capital, is **Chángchūn** (1146km), where the train stops for 10 minutes. Home to China's first car-manufacturing plant (as well as 2.3 million people), it's also where the Japanese installed the last emperor Henry Puyi: his former palace is the city's attraction.

CHITA TO BĚIJĪNG VIA HĀĚRBIN

CHITA TO BĚIJĪNG ROUTE PLANNER

The following is a suggested itinerary for covering the main sights along the Trans-Manchurian route in this chapter:

Day 1: Leave Chita; overnight train to Zabaikalsk (10 hours); cross border, explore Mǎnzhōulǐ.

Day 2: Train to Hǎilāěr (2½ hours); tour the grasslands.

Day 3: Train to Hāěrbin (eight hours).

Day 4: Tour Hāěrbin and surrounding areas.

Day 5: Train to Běijīng (eight hours).

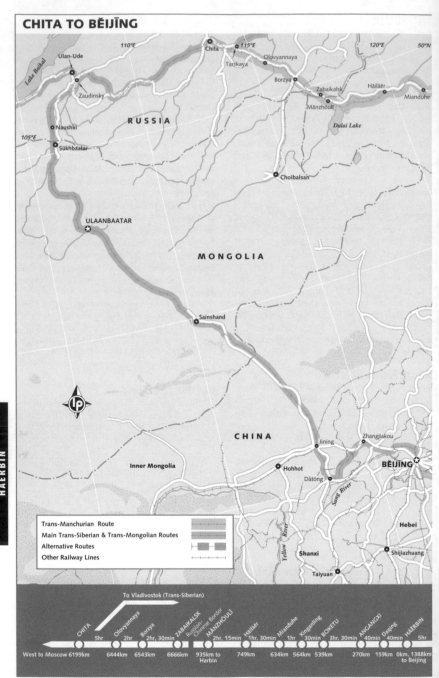

From here, the train heads southward into the head of China's sometimes blighted rust belt towards **Shěnyáng** (841km). This industrial city of 3.5 million people was a Mongol trading centre from the 11th century, becoming the capital of the Manchu empire in the 17th century. The founder of the Qing dynasty, Huang Taiji, is buried here in an impressive tomb. The train stops here for 15 minutes.

After a brief stop in Jinzhou (599km), the line roughly follows the coast. You'll get a view of the Great Wall as the train passes through the wall just north of **Shānhǎiguān** (415km). About 4km from Shānhǎiguān's centre, the Great Wall meets the sea.

The last stop before Běijīng is **Tiānjīn** (133km), a sprawling metropolis of 9.6 million people. During the 19th century this port city attracted the interest of almost every European nation with a ship to put to sea. The evidence is that Tiānjīn is a living museum of early-20th-century European architecture. You will have 10 minutes to stroll around its modern train station. If you get off in Tiānjīn, it's possible to continue to **Běijīng** (p304) on the brand-new, high-speed intercity express, which speeds to the capital in just 30 minutes (the regular train service takes 90 minutes). Traditionalists, of course, will prefer the good old mainline.

MǍNZHŌULǏ 满洲里
☎ 0470 / pop 55,400 / ⌚ Moscow +5hr
This laissez-faire border city, where the Trans-Siberian Railway crosses from China to Russia, is a pastel-painted boomtown of shops, hotels and restaurants catering to the Russian market. Unless you look Asian, expect shopkeepers to greet you in Russian.

Orientation & Information
The town centre sits between the Yǒuyì Bīnguǎn (Youyi Hotel) in the south and Beihu Park in the north. From the train station to the town centre, it's a 10- to 15-minute walk. Turn right immediately as you exit the station, then right again to cross the footbridge.

Bank of China (中国银行; Zhōngguó Yínháng; cnr Sandao Jie & Xinhua Lu; ⌚ 8am-noon & 2.30-5.30pm summer, 8am-noon & 2-5pm winter)

China International Travel Service (中国国际旅行社; CITS; Zhōngguó Guójì Lǚxíngshè; ☎ 622 8319; 35 Erdao Jie; ⌚ 8.30am-noon & 2.30-5pm Mon-Fri) On the 1st floor of Guójì Fàndiàn (International Hotel). Sells train tickets for Chinese cities.

CROSSING THE RUSSIA-CHINA BORDER

Expect to spend at least half a day crossing from Zabaikalsk to Mănzhōulĭ and vice versa, with time eaten up by thorough customs procedures on the Russian side, and the need to change the bogies on the train to match the narrower gauge used in China.

If you're not on the *Vostok* or the Mănzhōulĭ–Chita train (Friday and Saturday from Mănzhōulĭ, Thursday and Saturday from Chita), crossing this border involves taking one of the regular bus services that connect Mănzhōulĭ and Zabaikalsk.

There are daily overnight trains connecting Zabaikalsk and Chita (*kupe* R800, 12 hours); if these are full you can also take a train to Borzya and connect with a slower train to Zabaikalsk from there. Hăĕrbin and Mănzhōulĭ are also connected by a good overnight train (hard/soft sleeper Y222/338, 13 hours).

Regular buses for the border leave throughout the day from outside Zabaikalsk station (R150) or from the Mănzhōulĭ bus station (Y65), a Y10 taxi ride from the train station. Getting across by land to China is very slow as the Russians take ages to complete customs for your fellow Chinese passengers (it took us five hours). Private vehicles driven by Russians tend to get through faster, so one option is to negotiate a ride with a Russian driver either in town or at the border.

At the Chinese border post you'll have to pay Y10 departure tax: do this at the door left of the entrance and then give the receipt to the immigration officials as they stamp you out of the country. Luggage and passport inspection by Russian customs and immigration is rigorous, but you'll see that for the Chinese, who flood daily into Russia as illegal workers and traders, they're much worse. When the Chinese get through the border you can watch some of them peel off all the layers of their smuggled clothing.

There's an exchange office in the Russian customs hall where your immigration card will be registered.

Internet cafe (网吧; Wăngbā; 2nd fl, Xinhua Lu, btwn Erdao Jie & Sandao Jie; per hr Y3; ✆ 24hr)

Sights

Mănzhōulĭ is pleasantly walkable and packed with every variety of shop, restaurant and hotel; coming over from dreary Zabaikalsk it feels like another world. The town is being modernised at lightning speed but a few **Russian-built log houses** still line Yidao Jie. Train-spotters may want to visit the nearby steam-locomotive storage and repair yards at **Zalainuo'er opencast mine**, 30km east of the city. The mine has 22 steam engines in operation, most 70 to 80 years old. CITS might be able to arrange a tour that would include a ride on one of the trains.

Vast grasslands, typical of the Mongolian steppe, surround Mănzhōulĭ. CITS can arrange excursions here, including a stay in a yurt with a Mongolian family. Also consider visiting **Dalai Hu** (Dalai Lake; 达赉湖), Inner Mongolia's largest lake, 39km southeast of Mănzhōulĭ.

Sleeping & Eating

There must be a hundred hotels and guest houses in Mănzhōulĭ, all within walking distance of each other (signs are usually in Russian and Chinese). Likewise, there are plenty of restaurants, so just wander around and see what catches your fancy.

Jíxiàng Lǚguǎn (吉祥旅馆; ✆ 138 4807 7097; 11 Yidao Jie; 三道街11号; d Y100-150) Located inside a renovated Russian log cabin, this friendly budget place is easy to spot, halfway between the bus station and the Míngzhū Fàndiàn. Coming from the train station, it's on the north side of the foot bridge.

Míngzhū Fàndiàn (明珠饭店; ✆ 624 8977; fax 622 3261; 4 Xinhua Lu; 新华路4号; r incl breakfast from Y280) This hotel, at the corner of Yidao Jie, has different classes of midrange rooms. The cheaper ones can be bargained down to Y180.

Hēihăi Xī Cāntīng (黑海西餐厅; ✆ 623 7162; cnr Sandao Jie & Zhongsu Lu; dishes Y10-30; ✆ 24hr) An oceanic theme has been chosen for this friendly Chinese-Russian place. There are plenty of similar options along this street.

Getting There & Around

There are frequent trains to Hăilăĕr (Y31, three to 3½ hours) and Hăĕrbin (hard/soft sleeper Y222/338, 13 hours). Taxis charge Y10 from the station to the centre. Otherwise, most trips around town are Y7.

Buses leave all day for Hǎilaĕr (Y31, 3½ hours) from the long-distance bus station on Yidao Jie, west of Míngzhū Fàndiàn.

For details about crossing into Russia, see opposite.

HĀĚRBIN 哈尔滨

☎ 0451 / pop 3.29 million / 🕑 Moscow +5hr

Hāĕrbin feels quite unlike the cookie-cutter cities found all over China. Zhongyang Dajie, the main drag of the historic Dàolǐqū district, is pleasantly car-free and sports architecture that would not look out of place in Russian Siberia.

The European-style streets in the old town owe their influence to Hāĕrbin's days as a sort of Russian enclave in Manchuria during the construction of the Chinese Eastern Railway line (1897–1901) when thousands of Russian workers were sent here to work on the railroads.

Hāĕrbin's relaxed feel is most evident along its riverfront promenade, where locals stroll in summer or wade knee-deep into the Songhua River. Despite its quirky Russian architecture, Hāĕrbin is even more famous for its bitterly cold winters and the legendary Ice Lantern Festival. A Siberian-tiger sanctuary and the grim remains of a WWII germ-warfare base are other places of interest.

History

At the end of the 19th century, Hāĕrbin was a quiet village on the Songhua River. However, when the Russians negotiated the contract to construct the Chinese Eastern Railway line through Manchuria, Hāĕrbin's role was changed forever. Although the Japanese gained control of the new railway because of the Russian defeat in the Russo-Japanese War, Russian refugees flocked to Hāĕrbin in 1917, fleeing the Bolsheviks. The Russians continued to influence the town's development until the end of WWII, when the region was finally handed over to the Kuomintang (China's Nationalist Party).

Orientation

The main train station is in the centre of Hāĕrbin, surrounded by a cluster of hotels. The Dàolǐqū area, which also contains a few hotels and many of the city's attractions, is about 2km northwest of the train station. At the northern end of Dàolǐqū's main thoroughfare, Zhongyang Dajie, Stalin Park is on the shores of the wide Songhua River. Across the river lies Sun Island Park and the Siberian Tiger Park.

Information

Most large hotels will change US dollars. There are also many banks and ATMs along Zhongyang Dajie in the Dàolǐqū district. There's a telephone office and a convenient internet bar (Y3 per hour) on the 2nd floor of the main train station.

China International Travel Service (CITS; Zhōngguó Guójì Lǚxíngshè; ☎ 5363 3171; fax 5363 3161; 68 Hongjun Jie)

China Telecom (Guogeli Dajie)

Harbin Modern Travel Company (☎ 8488 4433; 89 Zhongyang Dajie) This office at Modern Hotel offers one-day ski trips to Yabuli from Y198.

Internet bar (Wǎngbā; 32 Xiliu Dajie; per hr Y2-4; 🕑 24hr) Off Zhongyang Dajie.

Post office (Yóujú; Tielu Jie, 🕑 8.30am-5pm) South of the train station.

Public Security Bureau (PSB; Gōng'ānjú; 26 Duan Jie; 🕑 8.40am-noon & 1.30-4.30pm Mon-Fri)

Sights

CHURCH OF ST SOPHIA 素菲亚教堂

Most of Hāĕrbin's Orthodox churches were ransacked during the Cultural Revolution and have since fallen into disrepair. But the majestic **Church of St Sophia** (Shèng Sùfēiyà Jiàotáng; cnr Zhaolin Jie & Toulong Jie; adult/student Y25/15; 🕑 9.30am-5.30pm), built by the Russians in 1907 in the Dàolǐqū district, has been beautifully restored. The church sits on a delightful open square, fronted by a fountain. It now houses the **Harbin Architecture Arts Centre**, which displays black-and-white photographs of the city from the early 1900s, as well as some icons from the Russian era. Unfortunately, there are no English captions.

DÀOLǏQŪ 道里区

Don't miss strolling the atmospheric Dàolǐqū area, along cobblestoned, pedestrianised Zhongyang Dajie and the surrounding side streets. The architecture here shows a strong imperial-Russian influence, with spires, cupolas and scalloped turrets. Thirteen preserved buildings have plaques outlining their histories, including the Modern Hotel (p302) and a former synagogue on Tongjiang Jie.

JEWISH HĀĚRBIN

In the 1920s, Hāĕrbin was home to some 20,000 Jews, the largest Jewish community

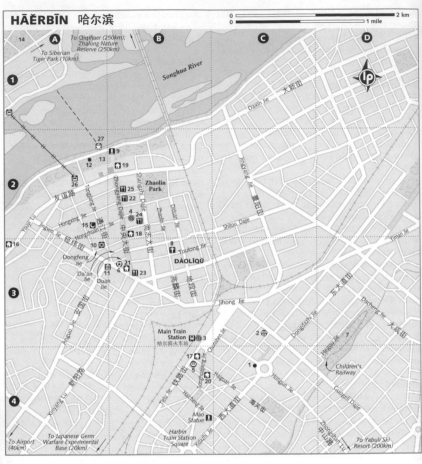

HĀĚRBĪN 哈尔滨

in the Far East at the time. The **Harbin New Synagogue** (Hāĕrbīn Yóutài Xīnhuìtáng; 162 Jingwei Jie; admission Y35; 8.30am-5pm) was built in 1921 for the community, the vast majority of which had emigrated from Russia. Restored and converted to a museum in 2004, the 1st floor is now an art gallery with pictures and photos of old Hāĕrbīn. The 2nd and 3rd floors feature photos and exhibits that tell the story of the history and cultural life of Hāĕrbīn's Jews.

A couple of blocks up Tongjiang Jie at No 82 is the **former main synagogue**. It's now been converted to host just a few shops and cafes but still has some Star of David symbols in its windows.

Further up Tongjiang Jie is the interesting **Turkish Mosque** with its distinctive minarets;

built in 1906, it's no longer operating and is closed to visitors.

In the far eastern suburbs of Hāĕrbīn is the **Huangshan Jewish Cemetery** (黄山犹太墓地), the largest in the Far East. There are over 600 graves here, all very well maintained. In 2004 the Israeli prime minister Ehud Olmert visited the cemetery – his grandfather is buried there. A taxi (Y50) takes around 45 minutes.

SIBERIAN TIGER PARK 东北虎林园
The mission of the **Siberian Tiger Park** (Dōngbĕi Hǔ Línyuán; ☎ 8808 0098; www.dongbeihu.net.cn, in Chinese; 88 Songbei Jie; adult/child Y65/30; 8am-4.30pm, last tour 4pm) is to study, breed, release and ultimately save the Manchurian (aka Siberian) tiger from extinction (see p95).

INFORMATION		
China International Travel Service	Former Main Synagogue............... **10** A3	Tiānzhù Bīnguǎn
中国国际旅行社.................................**1** C4	Harbin Architecture Arts	天竹宾馆.................................... **20** B4
China Telecom 电信局.....................**2** C3	Centre .... (see 8)	Zhōngdà Dàjiǔdiàn
Harbin Modern Travel Company	Harbin New Synagogue	中大大酒店.................................. **21** B3
哈尔滨马迭尔旅行社 .... (see 18)	哈尔滨犹太新会堂 **11** A3	
Internet Bar 网吧 **3** B3	Russian Wooden Chalet.................**12** A2	EATING
Internet Bar 网吧 **4** B2	Stalin Park 斯大林公园 **13** A2	Bì Fēng Táng 避风塘....................... **22** B2
Post Office 邮局 **5** B4	Sun Island Park	Dōngfāng Jiǎozi Wáng
Public Security Bureau 公安局....**6** B3	太阳岛公园 **14** A1	东方饺子王........................... **23** B3
Telephone Office 电信局...............(see 3)	Turkish Mosque **15** A2	Portman **24** B2
		Russia Tea House **25** B2
SIGHTS & ACTIVITIES	SLEEPING	
Children's Park 儿童公园 **7** D3	Gloria Inn ....(see 19)	TRANSPORT
Church of St Sophia	Harbin Shangri-La Hotel	Cable Car 览车................................ **26** A2
圣索菲亚教堂 **8** B3	哈尔滨香格里拉大饭店............... **16** A3	Ferries to Sun Island Park
Flood Control Monument	Kunlun Hotel 昆仑饭店................... **17** B4	太阳岛游览船........................... **27** A2
防洪胜利纪念塔 **9** B2	Modern Hotel 马迭尔宾馆 **18** B2	Harbin Railway International
	Songhuajiang Gloria Inn	Tourist Agency .... (see 17)
	松花江凯莱商务酒店 **19** B2	

The park houses some 400 of these magnificent animals, as well as a pride of African lions, a leopard, a panther and a pair of rare white tigers. While you definitely get an up-close look at the cats as you drive safarilike through the fenced-off fields, those who are not keen on zoos might want to give this supposed sanctuary a miss. The minibus drivers encourage passengers to buy chunks of meat to throw to the tigers, which makes you wonder exactly how the park is preparing these animals for the wild.

The park is located roughly 15km north of the city. From the corner of Youyi Lu and Zhongyang Dajie in Dàolǐqū, take bus 65 westbound to its terminus, then walk one block east to pick up bus 85, heading north on Hayao Lu. Bus 85 doesn't go all the way to the park. The bus stop is a 15- to 20-minute walk or a Y15 to Y20 (return) pedicab ride away from the park entrance. Alternatively, to take a taxi from the city centre, figure around Y100 (return), but expect to bargain.

You can combine the trip with a visit to Sun Island Park (right). Bus 85 stops at the western end of Sun Island Park en route from the city to the Siberian Tiger Park.

OTHER PARKS

Stalin Park (Sīdàlín Gōngyuán) is a pleasant tree-lined promenade, dotted with statues, playgrounds and a cafe in a brightly painted historic **Russian wooden chalet**, strung along the 42km embankment built to curb the unruly Songhua River. At the end of Zhongyang Dajie, the **Flood Control Monument**, built in 1958, commemorates the thousands who died in the floods up to that time.

A resort feel holds sway in summer, with ice-cream stands, photo booths and boating trips (Y30) along the river and across to **Sun Island Park** (Tàiyángdǎo Gōngyuán), which features landscaped gardens, forested areas and water parks. Buy ferry tickets for Y10 from the dock directly north of the Flood Control Monument. You can also take a **cable car** (one-way/return Y50/100) from the foot of Tongjiang Jie, one block west.

Just southeast of the centre, the **Children's Park** (Értóng Gōngyuán; cnr Guogeli Dajie & Hegou Jie; adult/child Y2/1; 4.30am-10pm May-Sep, 6.30am-8pm Oct-Apr) has the very cute Children's Railway (Y5). Its 2km of track are plied by a miniature diesel engine pulling seven cars. Engineers, ticket collectors and rail guards are all kids. Take bus 8 from the southern end of Zhongyang Dajie or bus 109 from the train station.

GERM WARFARE BASE – 731 DIVISION
侵华日军第**731**部队遗址

The extreme horrors of war are on display at the **Japanese Germ Warfare Experimental Base – 731 Division** (Qīnhuá Rìjūn Dì 731 Bùduì Yízhǐ; 8680 1556; Xinjiang Dajie; admission free; 9am-5pm, last entry 4pm), 20km south of the city.

During 1939 the Japanese army set up this top-secret research centre, where Japanese medical experts experimented on prisoners of war. More than 4000 people were infected with bubonic plague, injected with syphilis or roasted alive in furnaces. When the Soviets took Hǎěrbin in 1945, the Japanese blew the place up, but a tenacious Japanese journalist dug up the story in the 1980s. The main building of the base is now a museum, with photos and sculptures and exhibits of the equipment used by the Japanese. There are extensive English captions.

The base is a 45-minute trip on bus 343 from the train station.

Activities

The Songhua River comes alive in winter with ice skating, ice hockey, tobogganing and even ice sailing (where vessels sail on the ice surface, assisted by wind power, and reach speeds of 30km/h). Equipment for each of these sports can be hired from vendors who set up shop along the river bank. Slightly madder folk astound onlookers by swimming in gaps in the ice. To round out the winter-sports fest, head 200km southeast of Hāĕrbin to China's premier ski resort, Yabuli on Daguokui Mountain, with 20 runs and 17 lifts. **Windmill Village** (☎ 5345 5088; www.yabuliski.com; d Y380-780), the resort village, was undergoing renovations at the time of research. Weather permitting, the ski season lasts from late November until early April. CITS (p299) offers packages that include transport, ski passes, equipment hire and accommodation. One-day trips start at around Y180.

Festivals & Events

Hāĕrbin's peak tourist season is during the **Ice Lantern Festival** (Bīngdēng Jié; ☎ 8625 0068; admission to main area Y150, other prices vary; ⏰ 8am-10pm), held in Zhaolin Park and along the Songhua River, where fanciful and elaborate ice sculptures sparkle in the frigid air. Past sculptures have included a miniature Great Wall of China and a scaled-down Forbidden City. At night the sculptures are illuminated from the inside with coloured lights, turning the area into a fantasy world. Figure-skating shows, hockey tournaments and other winter events round out the calendar. Officially, the festival runs from 5 January to 15 February, although it frequently starts a week earlier and glistens into March.

Sleeping

During the Ice Lantern Festival, prices are at least 20% higher than those listed here.

BUDGET

The most convenient places to stay are along Zhongyang Dajie in Dàolǐqū or in one of the many hotels that surround the train station.

Zhōngdà Dàjiǔdiàn (☎ 8463 8888; fax 8465 2888; 32-40 Zhongyang Dajie; 中央大街32-40号; d/tr Y198/223; 🖂) With a prime location on Zhongyang Dajie, this place has received a much-needed

upgrade. The rooms are big and bright, although the bathrooms are a little cramped, and come with broadband internet access. A free Chinese breakfast is included.

Tiānzhú Bīnguǎn (☎ 8647 2109; fax 5364 3720; 6 Songhuajiang Jie; 松花江街6号; s/d Y210/238) This tower is about two blocks south of the train station; bear right as you exit. Rooms are decent and clean, if old.

MIDRANGE & TOP END

Kunlun Hotel (☎ 5361 6688; www.hljkunlun.com, in Chinese; 8 Tielu Jie; 铁路街8号; r from Y358; 🖂 💻 🖳) To the right as you exit the station, this first-class hotel is an oasis of calm with an indoor pool, sauna and six restaurants. A 15% service charge is added to all rates. Discounts of 30% available.

Modern Hotel (☎ 8488 4000; www.modern.com.cn /lshm/index1.php, in Chinese; 89 Zhongyang Dajie, 中央大街89号; s/d from Y680/980; 🖂 💻 🖳) This hotel defies its name, as it is housed in a historic Dàolǐqū building dating from 1906. Rooms are comfortable, rates include a buffet breakfast and the location is unbeatable. The entrance is around the back of the hotel. Discounts of up to 50% are often available.

Harbin Shangri-La Hotel (☎ 8485 8888; www .shangri-la.com; 555 Youyi Lu; 谊路555号; s/d US$180/200; 🖂 🖂 🖳) Not the most convenient location, but with great views of the Ice Lantern Festival. This is Hāĕrbin's most luxurious choice. Add a 15% service charge to the bill.

Half a block from Stalin Park, **Songhuajiang Gloria Inn** (☎ 8677 0000; www.gloriahotels.com; 257 Zhongyang Dajie; 中央大街257号; d from Y588; 🖂) offers plush rooms in a prime location. Next door is its poor relation, the **Gloria Inn** (☎ 8463 8855; s/tw/d/ste Y328/358/588/688), which has cheaper but still comfortable rooms.

Eating

The lanterns hanging above restaurant entrances in Hāĕrbin are actually a rating system – the more lanterns, the higher the standard and price. Red means Chinese food, while blue denotes pork-free cuisine from the Muslim Hui minority (mainly lamb dishes).

Hāĕrbin's culinary trademark is sausage, lengths of which hang in shop windows up and down Zhongyang Dajie. The street is also lined with bakeries, cafes and kiosks.

Dōngfāng Jiǎozi Wáng (Kingdom of Eastern Dumplings; ☎ 8465 3920; 39 Zhongyang Dajie; dumplings Y4-8; ⏰ 10am-10.30pm) Serves royal helpings of *jiǎozi* (dumplings) with a large choice of fill-

RARE CRANES FIND SANCTUARY

Of the world's 15 species of cranes, six can be seen at the Zhalong Nature Reserve (below). Four of the species that migrate here are on the endangered list: the red-crowned crane, the white-naped crane, the Siberian crane and the hooded crane. Both the red-crowned and white-naped cranes breed at Zhalong (as do the common and demoiselle cranes), while hooded and Siberian cranes use Zhalong as a stopover.

The red-crowned crane is a particularly fragile creature whose numbers worldwide are estimated at only about 1900. Around 220 of the birds visit Zhalong each year, although their migration was disrupted in 2005 by fires that consumed around 10% of the wetlands. The near-extinct bird is, ironically, the ancient symbol of immortality and has long been a symbol of longevity and good luck in the Chinese, Korean and Japanese cultures.

ings; try the pork with coriander or the vegie with egg. Look for the large walking dumpling out front.

Bì Fēng Táng (☎ 8469 0011; 185 Zhongyang Dajie; dishes Y9-49; 🕑 7am-2am) Bright and lively Chinese place that serves delicate, southern-style dumplings, as well as rice noodles, drunken chicken and great desserts. Good for late-night munchies.

Russia 1914 (☎ 8456 3207; 57 Xitoudao Jie; dishes Y10-80, coffees Y18-25, teas Y8-15; 🕑 9am-midnight) Housed in a historic building (from 1914), this quaint restaurant serves faux-Russian food and drink.

Portman (☎ 8468 6888; 53 Xiqi Dao Jie; mains from Y30; 🕑 11am-midnight) This restaurant has a comfortable pub atmosphere and serves tasty Western food.

Getting There & Away

If you have problems getting train tickets, contact the **Harbin Railway International Tourist Agency** (Hāěrbīn Tiědào Guójì Lǚxíngshè; ☎ 5361 6707/6718; 7th fl, Kunlun Hotel, 8 Tielu Jie) for information on travelling through to Russia. CITS may also be able to help.

The *Vostok* passes once a week, on Thursday heading to Běijīng and on Sunday to Moscow. The best connection with Běijīng is the very comfortable Z15/16 sleeper service (Y429 soft-sleeper only).

If you want to go to Vladivostok, take the train to Suífēnhé, cross the border and then take a bus – it's much faster than the train. For Blagoveshchensk, take a Hēihé-bound train.

The following table presents the costs for trains out of Hāěrbin:

Destination	Frequency (daily)	Cost hard/soft sleeper (Y)	Duration (hr)
Běijīng	3	289/420	12
Hēihé	1	153/-	12
Mǎnzhōulǐ	1	216/325	14½
Suífēnhé	2	173/215	9

Getting Around

The easiest way to get around Hāěrbin is by taxi. The minimum fare is Y8. Buses 101 and 103 (Y1) regularly travel between Stalin Park and the train station.

NORTH TO HĒIHÉ

An alternative route into Russia is to take a train to Hēihé on the banks of the Amur River across from Blagoveshchensk (p243). Along the way you could pause at Qíqíhāěr, 250km northwest of Hāěrbin and three to four hours (Y50) by train, to visit the Zhalong Nature Reserve.

Zhalong Nature Reserve 自然保护区

Twitchers will be thrilled by this **nature reserve** (Zhālóng Zìrán Bǎohùqū; admission Y50; 🕑 7am-5pm), 210,000 hectares of wetlands that are home to some 260 species of bird, including the rare red-crowned crane (see above).

Thousands of birds arrive from April to May, rear their young from June to August and depart from September to October. Even if you're not a bird fan, a trip into this peaceful countryside is bliss. During the summer, you can hire a boat to explore the freshwater marshes. Be warned: in summer giant mosquitoes are out in force – take repellent!

The reserve is 30km from Qíqíhāěr. **CITS** (☎ 0452-240 7538) offers day tours of the reserve (approximately Y100 per person, plus Y150 to Y200 for transportation), though it's easy enough to explore on your own on a half-day trip. Either take one of the erratic buses from Qíqíhāěr or a taxi (around Y150).

It's possible to stay overnight at the rather rundown **Zhālóng Bīnguǎn** (扎龙宾馆; ☎ 0452-866 9866; d Y160-298; ❄), by the parking lot. Call ahead if you're arriving in the low season to be sure the hotel is open.

Běijīng 北京

For weary Trans-Siberian Railway travellers, Běijīng will feel like the figurative pot of gold at the end of the rainbow. The long, arching ride through the Siberian wilderness and Gobi Desert comes to a halt at Běijīng's gleaming new train station and in a very short time visitors will come face to face with the city's new-found energy, pride and wealth.

The Olympics were instrumental in transforming the Chinese capital. For the first time since the Mongol invasion, Běijīng feels like an international city, brimming with overseas business, cuisine of every kind, daring modern architecture and a thriving arts scene. The billions of dollars hurled at the city in the run up to the 2008 games improved everything from the subway lines to the notorious English-language signage. Běijīngers themselves seem worldlier and more tolerant of foreign faces and attitudes.

Despite its headlong rush into the future, the best of Běijīng lies in its past. Sights such as the Forbidden City, the Temple of Heaven, the Great Wall and the Summer Palace will keep you busy for days. Duck into the fast disappearing *hutong* (narrow alleyway) neighbourhoods and discover Běijīng at its most intimate. At the end of the day you can swap your travel kit for the latest fashions and celebrate the end of your journey at a mindblowing array of nightspots.

Běijīng is the perfect bookend to the week-long rail ride but can also serve as the start of an exploration of one of the most diverse nations on Earth; grab a copy of Lonely Planet's *China* and get planning!

HIGHLIGHTS

- Romp through the seemingly endless courtyards of the **Forbidden City** (p309), once home to the Son of Heaven and all his accoutrements
- Hire a bike to skirt through the dense **hutong** (p314), Běijīng's traditional alleyways
- Ascend the dizzying heights of the **Great Wall** (p319) and look back towards Mongolia
- Celebrate the end (or beginning) of your Trans-Siberian journey at one of Běijīng's rocking **nightclubs** (p317)
- Feast on **Peking duck** (p315) and China's myriad other speciality foods

■ AREA CODE: 010	■ POPULATION: 15.6 MILLION

BĚIJĪNG

HISTORY

Běijīng (Northern Capital) – affectionately called Peking by diplomats, nostalgic journalists and wistful academics – emerged as the pre-eminent cultural and political force with the 13th-century Mongol occupation of China, when Chinggis (Genghis) Khaan descended on the city. His grandson, Kublai Khaan (c 1216–94), renamed the city Khanbalik (Khan's town). From here, Kublai ruled the largest empire in world history.

Although the capital was moved for a brief period, Emperor Yongle (of the Ming dynasty) reestablished Běijīng as the capital in the 1400s and spent millions of taels of silver to refurbish the city. Yongle is known as the architect of modern Běijīng, building the Forbidden City and the Temple of Heaven, as well as developing the bustling commercial streets outside the inner city. The Qing dynasty expanded the construction of temples, palaces and pagodas.

In January 1949, the People's Liberation Army (PLA) entered the city. On 1 October of that year Mao Zedong proclaimed a 'People's Republic' to an audience of some 500,000 citizens in Tiananmen Square.

Like the emperors before them, the communists significantly altered the face of Běijīng to suit their own image. Whole city blocks were reduced to rubble to widen major boulevards. From 1950 to 1952, the city's magnificent outer walls were levelled in the interests of traffic circulation. Before the Sino-Soviet split of the 1960s, Russian experts and technicians poured in, leaving their own Stalinesque touches.

The capitalist-style reforms of the past quarter of a century have transformed Běijīng into a modern city, with skyscrapers, slick shopping malls and freeways cutting right through the city. The 2008 Olympics thrust Běijīng into the limelight and forced it to address some of its major issues, such as the appalling air pollution and heaving traffic. While many problems persist, the city is cleaner and greener than it was before, with some world-class sporting venues to boot.

ORIENTATION

With a total area of 16,800 sq km, Běijīng is roughly the size of Belgium. Don't panic, though, as it's also a city of very orderly design, built on one giant grid, with the Forbidden City at its centre.

Beijing Train Station, one block south of Jianguomenwai Dajie, is 3km southeast of the Forbidden City, and is accessible by the metro circle line. Jianguomenwai Dajie, the most important east–west avenue, running just south of the Forbidden City, has many hotels and facilities. The east–west line of the metro follows this major road.

Five ring roads circle the city centre in concentric rings. Běijīng's Capital Airport is 27km from the city centre; see p319 for information on getting to and from the airport.

Maps

English-language maps of Běijīng can be bought at the airport, train station newspaper kiosks, and the Foreign Languages Bookstore (p308). They can also be picked up for free at most big hotels and, for Y8, branches of the Beijing Tourist Information Center (p308).

INFORMATION
Bookshops

Bookworm Café (Shūchóng; ☎ 6586 9507; www .beijingbookworm.com; Bldg 4, Nansanlitun Lu; Ⓜ Dongsishitiao) A good selection of new and used books and many good China titles, plus a great cafe with wi-fi.

WHEN TO GO

Autumn (September to early November) is the optimal season to visit Běijīng as the weather is gorgeous – clear skies and breezy days – and fewer tourists are in town. In winter, tourists are also scarce and many hotels offer substantial discounts – but it's glacial outside (dipping as low as -20°C) and the northern winds cut like a knife through bean curd. Arid spring is OK, apart from the (worsening) sand clouds that sweep in from Inner Mongolia and the static electricity that discharges everywhere. From May onwards the mercury can surge well over 30°C, reaching over 40°C at the height of summer, which also sees heavy rainstorms late in the season. Maybe surprisingly, this is also considered the peak season, when hotels typically raise their rates and the Great Wall nearly collapses under the weight of marching tourists. Note that air pollution can be very harsh in both summer and winter.

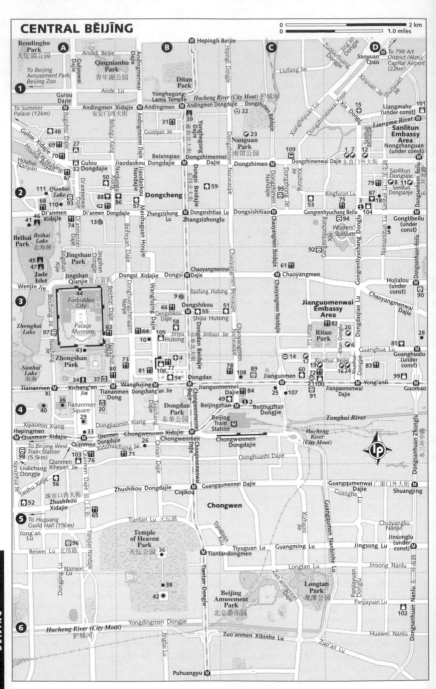

CENTRAL BĚIJĪNG

BĚIJĪNG

Foreign Languages Bookstore (Wàiwén Shūdiàn; ☎ 6512 6911; 235 Wangfujing Dajie; Ⓜ Wangfujing) Has a reasonable selection of English-language novels, as well as travel books, all on the 3rd floor.

Le Petit Gourmand (Xiǎo Měishíjiā; ☎ 6417 6095; Tongli Studio, Sanlitun Beilu; ☯ 10am-1am; Ⓜ Dongsishitiao) An excellent selection of over 10,000 books is available at this restaurant-cum-library.

Emergency
Ambulance (☎ 120)
Fire (☎ 119)
Police (☎ 110)

Internet Access
Internet cafes have become harder to find in Bĕijīng over the past few years. Many cheaper hotels and youth hostels provide internet at around Y10 per hour.

Fengyage Internet Café (Fēngyăgé Wăngbā; ☎ 6525 3712; 57 Dongsi Nandajie; per hr incl coffee upstairs/downstairs Y3/12; Ⓜ Dongsi) No English sign, but it's next to a chemist.

Hailin Star (Hăilín zhīxíng; 62 Dì'anmen Dongdajie; per hr Y3; ☯ 24hr; Ⓜ Zhangzizhonglu)

Internet Cafe (Wăngbā; per hr Y4; ☯ 24hr; Ⓜ Dongsishitiao) You'll find this cafe on the 2nd floor (up a fire escape) just east of the Bookworm Café (p305).

Internet Cafe (Wăngbā; 2nd fl, Beijing City Central Youth Hostel, 1 Beijingzhan Qianjie; per hr Y5; ☯ 24hr; Ⓜ Beijingzhan) Very new.

Media
Pick up the free monthly listings magazines the *Beijinger* (www.thebeijinger.com), *Agenda* (www.agendabeijing.com) and *City Weekend* (www.cityweekend.com.cn) from expat bars and restaurants in the Sanlitun and Qianhai Lake areas.

Medical Services
Bĕijīng has some of the best medical facilities and services in China. Note that it is much cheaper just to ask what medicines you need and then buy them at a pharmacy on the street rather than purchase them on-site at an international clinic.

Beijing Union Medical Hospital (Bĕijīng Xiéhé Yiyuàn; ☎ 6529 6114, emergencies 6529 5284; 53 Dongdan Beidajie; ☯ 24hr; Ⓜ Dongdan) Foreigners' and VIP wing in the back building.

International SOS (Bĕijīng Yàzhōu Guójì Jínjí Jiùyuán Yīliáo Zhōngxīn; ☎ clinic appointments 6462 9112, dental appointments 6462 0333, emergencies 6462 9100; www .internationalsos.com; Suite 105, Wing 1 Kunsha Building,

No 16 Xinyuanli, Chaoyang District; ☯ 9am-6pm Mon-Fri; Ⓜ Liangmahe) Expensive, high-quality clinic with English-speaking staff.

Money
Foreign currency and travellers cheques can be changed at large branches of the Bank of China (Zhōngguó Yínháng), Citic Industrial Bank, the airport and hotel money-changing counters, and at several department stores (including the Friendship Store), as long as you have your passport.

There's a Bank of China ATM in the Capital Airport arrivals hall, and several others across the city.

Bank of China Lufthansa Center Youyi Shopping City (1st fl, 50 Liangmaqiao Lu; Ⓜ Dongzhimen); Oriental Plaza (cnr Wangfujing Dajie & Dongchang'an Jie; Ⓜ Wangfujing); Sundongan Plaza (Ⓜ Wangfujing) The ATM at Sundongan Plaza is next to the main plaza entrance on Wangfujing Dajie.

Post
There are convenient post offices in the Citic building next to the Friendship Store and in the basement of the China World Trade Center. Large post offices are generally open from 9am to 5pm daily.

International Post Office (Guójì Yóudiànjú; Jianguomen Beidajie; ☯ 8am-7pm Mon-Sat; Ⓜ Jianguomen)

Tourist Information
Beijing Tourism Hotline (☎ 6513 0828; ☯ 24hr) English-speaking operators available to answer questions and hear complaints.

Beijing Tourist Information Center (Bĕijīng Lǚyóu Zīxún Fúwù Zhōngxīn; ☯ 8.30am-6pm) airport (☎ 6459 8148); Beijingzhan (☎ 6528 8448; www.bjta.gov.cn, in Chinese; 16 Beijingzhan Jie; Ⓜ Beijingzhan); Chaoyang (☎ 6417 6627; 27 Sanlitun Beilu; Ⓜ Dongsishitiao) Beijingzhan is a one-minute walk north of Beijing Train Station; Chaoyang is west of the Sanlitun Yashou Clothing Market.

Visa Extensions
The Foreign Affairs branch of the local **Public Security Bureau** (PSB; Gōng'ānjú; ☎ 8402 0101, 8401 5292; 2 Andingmen Dongdajie; ☯ 8.30am-4.30pm Mon-Sat) handles visa extensions. The visa office is on the 2nd floor on the east side of the building. First-time extensions of 30 days are generally issued on any tourist visa, but further extensions are harder to get and you might only end up with a further week. Expect to wait up to five days for your visa extension to be processed; American travellers pay Y185, Australians

Y100, Canadians Y165 and UK citizens Y160; prices can go up or down. You can also get passport photographs here (Y30 for five).

SIGHTS
Forbidden City 紫禁城

The largest and best-preserved cluster of ancient buildings in China is the **Forbidden City** (Zǐjìn Chéng; ☎ 6513 2255; admission Y60; ☼ 8.30am-4pm May-Sep, to 3.30pm Oct-Apr; Ⓜ Tiananmen Xi/Tiananmen Dong). It was home to two dynasties of emperors, the Ming and the Qing, who rarely strayed from this pleasure dome, although it was off limits to everyone else (thus, the name).

Renting the cassette for the self-guided tour (available in several languages) is worth the extra Y40; the English version is narrated by one-time 007 Roger Moore. Tickets and cassette rental are available at the Forbidden City's south gate, not to be confused with the Gate of Heavenly Peace (Tiananmen) facing onto the square of the same name. Continue through Tiananmen and go northward until you can't proceed without paying. (The booth in the centre of the first plaza sells tickets to climb Tiananmen, *not* to the Forbidden City.) A second ticket booth is located at the North Gate.

The palace is huge (800 buildings, 9000 rooms) and under constant renovation. The main **ceremonial buildings** lie along the north–south axis in the centre. Despite its vast scale, this area is frequently crowded; you may prefer to explore the **courtyards** and **pavilions** (and minimuseums within them) on either side of the main drag.

Tiananmen Square & Around 天安门广场

As the focal point for the history of communist China, **Tiananmen Square** (Ⓜ Tiananmen Xi/Tiananmen Dong/Qianmen) is sure to inspire a mix of emotions. This is where Mao's student armies waved his *Little Red Book* in surges of nationalism and where dissidents faced down tanks in the summer of 1989. Today it's largely the domain of young kite flyers and photographers snapping pictures of Chinese families in from the hinterlands. For Trans-Sib travellers having just crossed the continent, a visit here marks the end of your journey – it's fascinating to size up Tiananmen against your experience in Red Square, thousands of kilometres distant.

Although the square is the symbolic centre of the Chinese universe, what you see today is a modern reconception by Mao to project the enormity of the Communist Party. His giant portrait still hangs over the **Gate of Heavenly Peace** (Tiānānmén; ☎ 6309 9386; admission Y15, bag storage Y1-6; ☼ 8.30am-4.30pm) at the northern end of the square, flanked by the slogans 'Long Live the People's Republic of China' (left) and 'Long Live the Unity of the Peoples of the World' (right).

At the square's southern end, **Front Gate** (Qián Mén; admission Y20; ☼ 8.30am-4pm; Ⓜ Qianmen) is a remnant of the wall that guarded the ancient Inner City as early as the 15th century. It actually consists of two gates: the Arrow Tower to the south and the Main Gate to the north.

On the site of the old Outer Palace Gate, the **Monument to the People's Heroes** is a 36m obelisk

---

BĚIJĪNG IN THREE DAYS...

Start your exploration at the city centre, visiting the **Forbidden City** (above) and sights around **Tiananmen Square** (above). Grab lunch at **Quanjude Roast Duck Restaurant** (p316) or **Wangfujing Snack Street** (p316), then jump in a taxi to the **Temple of Heaven** (p312) or spend the afternoon exploring the **hutong** (narrow alleyways; p314) by bicycle, especially around mellow Qianhai Lake. After dinner hit the bars along **Nanluogu Xiang** (p317).

Rise early on day two for a journey to the **Great Wall** (p319), and spend the evening enjoying a performance of **Chinese acrobatics** (p317) before rounding off the day wining and dining in Sanlitun.

On day three take an early morning visit to the **Lama Temple** (p310) before checking out the ultramodern **National Stadium** and **Water Cube** (see the boxed text, p310) in north Běijīng, built for the 2008 Summer Olympics. Browse the bric-a-brac shops of **Liulichang** (p318) or bargain like mad at the **Sanlitun Yashou Clothing Market** (p318). In the afternoon, make an expedition to the **Summer Palace** (p312). At night, dine at the **Courtyard** (p316), snack at **Donghuamen Night Market** (p316) or spend the evening enjoying **Beijing opera** (p317) at one of the city's numerous theatres.

that bears bas-relief depictions of key revolutionary events. Just behind this monument is **Chairman Mao's Mausoleum** (Máo Zhǔxí Jìniàntáng; admission free, bag storage Y10; ◷ 8.30-11.30am & 2-4pm Mon, Wed & Fri, 8.30-11.30am Tue, Thu & Sat). Most Chinese continue to respect and revere this leader, who died in 1976, despite the atrocities carried out during his rule (Western historians say the Chairman was responsible for 40 to 70 million peacetime deaths). Expect long queues and only the briefest glimpse of the body. The official Party line is that Mao was 70% right and 30% wrong in his ruling. Appropriately, a visit to the 'Maosoleum' is about 70% solemnity and 30% absurdity, especially considering the well-stocked gift shop, which does a brisk trade in Chairman Mao thermometers and alarm clocks.

The National People's Congress, China's rubber-stamp legislature, sits on the western side of the square in the monolithic and intimidating **Great Hall of the People** (Rénmín Dàhuìtáng; admission Y30, bag storage Y2; ◷ 9am-3pm, closed when Congress is in session). Further to the west, the bulbous, titanium-and-glass **National Grand Theatre** could be mistaken for an alien mothership that has landed to refuel. Critics have questioned both its incongruous styling and the wisdom of erecting such a shimmering building in Běijīng's notoriously dust-laden air.

On the eastern side of the square, the **China National Museum** (Zhōngguó Guójiā Bówùguǎn; admission Y30; ◷ 8.30am-4.30pm) was closed for renovations at the time of research but should be worth investigating for its bronze and ceramic works.

A couple of hundred metres northeast of the square is the **Imperial City Museum** (Huáng Chéng Yìshùguǎn; ☎ 8511 5104/114; 9 Changpu Heyan; adult/student Y20/10, audio tour Y50; ◷ 9am-4.30pm; Ⓜ Tiananmen Dong), which houses a surviving section of the Imperial City wall. It's now a park decorated with a graceful marble bridge, rock features, paths, a stream and trees. Within the museum, a diorama reveals the full extent of the Imperial City and its yellow-tiled wall.

If you get up early you can watch the **flagraising ceremony** at sunrise, performed by a troop of PLA soldiers drilled to march at precisely 108 paces per minute, 75cm per pace. The same ceremony in reverse is performed at sunset.

North of the Forbidden City
LAMA TEMPLE

This exquisite **temple** (Yōnghé Gōng; ☎ 6404 4499, ext 252; 28 Yonghegong Dajie; admission Y25, English audio guide Y20; ◷ 9am-4pm; Ⓜ Yonghegong) is vast and riotously colourful. The five main halls and 10 exhibition rooms contain countless serene and smiling Buddhas, the most notable of which

---

BĚIJĪNG'S DARING NEW ARCHITECTURE

The 2008 Summer Olympics did more than bring the world's greatest athletes to Běijīng: it also lifted the curtain on some of the most daring achievements in modern architecture. First and foremost among them is the US$423 million, 91,000-seat, 'Bird's Nest' **National Stadium** (Beijing Guojia Tiyuchang; 北京国家体育场), the world's largest steel structure. Right next door is the futuristic **Water Cube** (水立方) where the swimming events were held. It is said to be the world's fastest pool; indeed 25 world records were set here during the Olympics. The stadium is now used for sporting events and concerts, while the pool is used for competitions and by the public. Both are reached by metro (Ⓜ Olympic Green station, line 8).

Another unique design in Běijīng is the new **National Grand Theatre** (www.chncpa.org; ☎ 6655 0000; 国家大剧院; Ⓜ Tiananmen Xi), also known as 'The Egg' for its instantly recognisable titanium dome shape. The 6500-seat theatre is surrounded by an artificial lake and looks impossible to enter (until you realise access is through a tunnel). It's a short walk west of Tiananmen Square.

The newest and most daring piece of modern architecture in Běijīng is the US$600 million **China Central Television (CCTV) Headquarters**. The 51-floor building consists of five continuously linked sections that defy the laws of physics. Locals have given it a variety of nicknames, including the 'big shorts', the 'twisted donut' and, ominously, 'dangerous building'. The dangerous twisted pair of shorts is located in Chaoyang District at 32 Dong San Huan Zhong Lu (中国中央电视台总部).

As if all these projects weren't enough, Běijīng had to go and build the **world's largest airport** (at the time). The incredible US$1.9 billion airport, designed by Lord Norman Foster, was opened in mid-2008.

is the 18m-high statue of the **Maitreya Buddha** sculpted from a single piece of sandalwood.

The Lama Temple was once the official residence of Count Yin Zhen, who later became emperor and moved to the Forbidden City. In 1744 the buildings were converted into a lamasery. The temple somehow miraculously survived the Cultural Revolution and was 'restocked' with novice monks from Inner Mongolia in the 1980s. Today it is the most important Tibetan Buddhist temple in China (outside of Tibet itself).

CONFUCIAN TEMPLE & IMPERIAL COLLEGE
Just a short distance down the *hutong* opposite the entrance to the Lama Temple is the **Confucian Temple & Imperial College** (Kǒng Miào & Guózǐjiān; 13 Guozijian Jie; admission Y20; ⏰ 8.30am-5pm; Ⓜ Yonghegong). The unkempt grounds and undisturbed peace are a pleasant contrast to just about every other sight in Běijīng. The **stellae** in the temple courtyard record the names of those successful in the civil-service examinations (possibly the world's first) of the imperial court. The Imperial College was where the emperor annually expounded the Confucian classics to an audience of thousands of kneeling students and professors.

BEIHAI PARK 北海公园
A relaxing place for a stroll is **Beihai Park** (Běihǎi Gōngyuán; admission Y5, Jade Islet Y10; ⏰ 6.30am-8pm, buildings open to 4pm; Ⓜ Tiananmen Xi, then bus 5), northwest of the Forbidden City. There are four gates to the park, which is formed around Beihai Lake.

The site is associated with Kublai Khaan's palace, the navel of Běijīng before the creation of the Forbidden City. Dominating **Jade Islet** on the lake, the 36m-high **White Dagoba** was originally built in 1651 for a visit by the Dalai Lama, and was rebuilt in 1741. You can reach the *dagoba* (stupa) through the **Yongan Temple**, with its halls decorated with statues of Buddhist figures and past lamas, as well as a bamboo grove. The pretty **Xitian Fanjing** (Western Paradise) temple and the **Nine Dragon Screen**, a 5m-high and 27m-long wall of coloured glazed tiles, are also worth searching out within the park.

JINGSHAN PARK 景山公园
This **park** (Jǐngshān Gōngyuán; admission Y2; ⏰ 6am-9.30pm; Ⓜ Tiananmen Xi, then bus 5) is worth visiting for its priceless views over the Forbidden

---

BĚIJĪNG MUSEUM PASS 博物馆通票

This pass (Bówùguǎn Tōngpiào) is a fantastic investment that will save you both money and queuing for tickets. For Y80 you get either complimentary access or discounted admission (typically 50%) to almost 100 museums, temples and tourist sights in and around Běijīng. Not all museums are worth visiting, but you only have to visit a small selection of museums to get your money back. The pass is effective from 1 January to 31 December in any one year and can be picked up from participating museums and sights. If you can't find one, call ☎ 6222 3793 or ☎ 8666 0651 to locate stocks. Alternatively, try the Chinese-only website www.bowuguan.bj.cn.

City immediately to its south. Its central hill, shaped from the earth excavated to create the palace moat, supposedly protects the palace from the evil spirits – or dust storms – from the north (the billowing dust clouds in the spring have to be seen to be believed). Clamber to the top of this regal pleasure garden for a magnificent panorama of the capital.

DRUM TOWER & BELL TOWER
Repeatedly destroyed and restored, the **Drum Tower** (Gǔlóu; ☎ 6401 2674; Gulou Dongdajie; admission Y20; ⏰ 9am-5pm) originally marked the centre of the old Mongol capital. Stagger up the incredibly steep steps for impressive views over Běijīng's *hutong* rooftops. Drum performances are given every half hour from 9am to 11.30am and 1.30pm to 5pm. Fronted by a Qing-dynasty stele, the **Bell Tower** (Zhōnglóu; ☎ 6401 2674; Zhonglouwan Hutong; admission Y15; ⏰ 9am-5pm) originally dates from Ming times and the current edifice dates to the 18th century. Both the Drum and Bell Towers can be reached on bus 5, 58 or 107; get off at the namesake Gulou stop.

798 ART DISTRICT 艺术新区
This disused and sprawling electronics **factory** (cnr Jiuxianqiao Lu & Jiuxianqiao Beilu; admission free) found a new lease of life several years ago as the focus of Běijīng's feisty art community. Wander the former factory workshops and peruse the artwork on view at its highlight galleries, **White Space at 798** (☎ 8456 2054; 2 Jiuxianqiao Lu; ⏰ noon-6pm Tue-Sun) and **Beijing Tokyo Art Projects**

(☎ 8457 3245; 4 Jiuxianqiao Lu; ☯ 10am-6.30pm), or admire the photographic stills at **798 Photo Gallery** (Bǎinián Yínxiàng; ☎ 6438 1784; www.798photogallery.cn; 4 Jiuxianqiao Lu).

Also worth looking into are **Long March Space** (www.longmarchspace.com; ☯ 11am-7pm Tue-Sun), where paintings, photos, installations and videos get a viewing, and the well-known **Chinese Contemporary Beijing** (☎ 8456 2421; www.chinesecontemporary.com; 4 Jiuxianqiao Lu; ☯ 11am-7pm). Ride the subway to Dongzhimen station, then jump on bus 909 (Y1, 25 minutes) and get off at Dashanzi Lukounan (大山子路口南).

Ancient Observatory 古观象台

Běijīng's ancient **observatory** (Gǔ Guānxiàngtái; ☎ 6524 2202; admission Y10; ☯ 9-11.30am & 1-4.30pm Tue-Sun; Ⓜ Jianguomen), mounted on the battlements of a watchtower lying along the line of the old Ming city wall, originally dates back to Kublai Khaan's days when it lay north of the present site.

Within the courtyard is a reproduction-looking **armillary sphere** (1439), supported by four dragons. At the rear is an attractive garden with grass, sundials and another armillary sphere. Climb the steps to the roof and an array of Jesuit-designed astronomical instruments, embellished with sculptured bronze dragons and other Chinese flourishes, making a unique combination of East and West.

During the Boxer Rebellion, the instruments disappeared into the hands of the French and Germans. Some were returned in 1902 and others were returned after WWI.

Beijing Underground City

In 1969 Mao prepared for war with the Soviet Union by ordering the construction of habitable tunnels under Běijīng that could be used in case of a nuclear attack. A section of tunnels enticingly known as the **Beijing Underground City** (Běijīng Dìxiàchéng; ☎ 6702 2657; 62 Xidamachang Jie; admission Y20; ☯ 8.30am-5.30pm; Ⓜ Chongwenmen) can be explored. English-language tours guide you along parts of this mouldering warren, past rooms designated as battlefield hospitals, a cinema, arsenals, other anonymous vaults and portraits of Mao. A detour to an underground silk factory concludes the trip – pass on the pricey duvet covers and make for the door. Emerging from the exit, head east and take a peek down the first alley on your right – **Tongle Hutong** – one of Běijīng's narrowest.

Summer Palace 颐和园

The immense park of the **Summer Palace** (Yíhé Yuán; ☎ 6288 1144; 19 Xinjian Gongmen; admission Y40-50; audio guides Y30; ☯ 8.30am-5pm) requires at least half a day of your time. Nowadays teeming with tour groups, this complex, dominated by **Kunming Lake**, was once a playground for the imperial court. Royalty came here to elude the summer heat that roasted the Forbidden City. Empress Dowager Cixi rebuilt the park in 1888 with money supposedly intended for the creation of a modern navy. (At least the empress restored the still-immobile marble boat for lakeside dining.)

The palace's main building is the **Hall of Benevolence & Longevity**, near the lake towards the eastern gate, which is where the emperor handled state affairs and received visitors. The 700m **Long Corridor** along the northern shore is decorated with mythical scenes. Visitors can also see exhibitions specific to the Empress Dowager Cixi, including her furniture and memorabilia.

Towards the North Palace Gate, **Suzhou St** is an entertaining and light-hearted diversion of riverside walkways, shops and eateries designed to mimic the famous Jiāngsū canal town. **Row boats** are available for hire.

The park is about 12km northwest of the city centre; get there by taking the metro to Xizhimen station, then a minibus or bus 375.

Temple of Heaven Park

China's finest example of Ming architecture is the **Temple of Heaven** (Tiāntán Gōngyuán; Tiantan Donglu; admission low season Y10-30, high season Y15-35, audio tour Y40; ☯ park 6am-9pm, sights 8am-6pm; Ⓜ Chongwenmen/Qianmen). This complex, set in a 267-hectare park, functioned as a stage for the solemn rites performed by the Son of Heaven, who came here to pray for good harvests, seek divine clearance and atone for the sins of the people.

The design and position of the park, as well as the shape and colour of structures within, have symbolic significance for the ancient interplay between heaven and earth. The **Round Altar**, for example, possesses an obsessive symmetry revolving around the heavenly number nine (nine rings of stone, each ring composed of multiples of nine stones etc). The altar's most mystifying feature is its ability to amplify voices emanating from the centre of the upper terrace.

Just north of the Round Altar is the **Imperial Vault of Heaven**, which is surrounded by the **Echo Wall**. Sixty-five metres in diameter, the wall allows a whisper to travel clearly from one end to the other.

The crown of the whole complex is the **Hall of Prayer for Good Harvests**. Amazingly, this temple's wooden pillars support the ceiling without nails or cement!

SLEEPING

Běijīng has a tremendous range of places to stay, from hostels to five-star luxury. The most atmospheric hotels are those built in the courtyards of the *hutong* neighbourhoods. Hotels are subject to a 10% to 15% service charge (on top of the prices quoted here), but many cheaper hotels don't bother to charge it.

Budget

Far East International Youth Hostel (Yuǎndōng Guójì Qīngnián Lüshè; ☎ 6301 8811, ext 3118; courtyard@elong .com; 113 Tieshu Xiejie; 铁树斜街113号; dm low/high season incl breakfast Y45/60; ✹ 🖳 ; **M** Qianmen) This hostel is in a pretty, old courtyard opposite the hotel of the same name. There's bike rental, a kitchen and a handy tourist desk. To get here head south on Nanxinhua Jie. About 200m after you pass Liulichang you'll see a sign (in English) on the right-hand side of the street saying 'Far East Hotel'.

Leo Hostel (Guǎngjùyuán Fàndiàn; ☎ 6303 1595; www .leohostel.com; 52 Dazhalan Xijie; 大栅栏西街52号; 12-/4-bed dm Y45/70, d with bathroom Y200-240, without bathroom Y140-160; ✹ 🖳 ; **M** Qianmen) Popular and ever busy, it's best to phone ahead to book a room at this bargain hostel tucked away down Dazhalan Xijie. It has an attractive interior courtyard decked out with plastic plants, OK dorm rooms (pricier dorms with bathroom), simple but passable doubles, a lively bar and a fine location.

Beijing Downtown Backpackers Accommodation (Dōngtáng Kèzhàn; ☎ 8400 2429; www.backpackingchina .com; 85 Nanluogu Xiang; 南锣鼓巷85号; 8-/4-/3-bed dm Y50/60/70, d fromY60; ✹ 🖳 ; **M** Andingmen) This hostel's central *hutong* location on teeming Nanluogu Xiang is hard to beat. It's close enough to the bars to crawl (or be carried) home. Free breakfast, bike rental (Y20 per day, Y300 deposit) and internet access (Y6 per hour).

Beijing City Central Youth Hostel (Běijīng Chéngshì Guójì Qīngnián Lüshè; ☎ 8511 5050; www.centralhostel .com; 1 Beijingzhan Qianjie; 北京站前街1号; 4-8 bed dm Y60, s with shower Y298-328, without shower Y120-160, tw with/without shower Y328/160; ✹ 🖳 ; **M** Beijing-zhan) For Trans-Sib travellers this is the most convenient for the Beijing Train Station. It has a handy location and clean rooms but is otherwise unspectacular. Noticeboard, info desk, kitchen and a handy internet cafe (Y5 per hour) and a bar with pool table on the 2nd floor.

OURPICK Beijing Saga International Youth Hostel (Běijīng Shíjiā Guójì Qīngnián Lüshè; ☎ 6527 2773; sagay angguang@yahoo.com; 9 Shijia Hutong; 史家胡同9号; 4-bed dm Y65, d Y218-238, tr Y258, courtyard r Y268; ✹ 🖳 ; **M** Dengshikou) Enjoying a top location on historic Shijia Hutong, this popular hostel has well-kept rooms, a spacious seating area in the main lobby, laundry and internet access (Y8 per hour). The three small courtyard rooms are at the back. Free breakfast with some rooms.

Golden Pineapple Youth Hostel (Jīn Bō Lúo Gúo Jiqīng Nían Jiǔdián; ☎ 8447 2899; www.utels.com; 18 Xinzhong Jie; 新中街18号; dm/s/d Y70/200/320; ✹ 🖳 ; **M** Dong-sishitiao) This place has the look and feel of a midrange hotel and has good-value dorms and doubles. Some of the single rooms are tiny and lack a window so you may want to look at a couple of rooms. It's on a leafy side street within walking distance of the Sanlitun bar area. It's also just a 10-minute walk from Dongzhimen airport shuttle station and subway.

Midrange

OURPICK Bamboo Garden Hotel (Zhúyuán Bīnguǎn; ☎ 6403 2229; fax 6401 2633; 24 Xiaoshiqiao Hutong; 小石桥胡同24号; s Y520, d Y760-880, ste Y990; ✹ ; **M** Gulou) This cosy, intimate and tranquil courtyard hotel is in buildings dating back to the late Qing dynasty, while the gardens belonged to a eunuch from Empress Cixi's entourage. Rooms are tastefully decorated with reproduction Ming furniture and the abundant foliage is pleasant. Reception is through the gates on your left.

Lusongyuan Hotel (Lüsōngyuán Bīnguǎn; ☎ 6404 0436; www.the-silk-road.com; 22 Banchang Hutong; 板厂胡同22号; s/d Y658/1188; ✹ 🖳 ; **M** Andingmen) Built by a Mongolian general during the Qing dynasty, this popular courtyard hotel has pocket-sized singles with pea-sized baths and just one suite. Courtyard-facing rooms are slightly dearer. The bikes (half/full day Y15/30) are pretty

BĚIJĪNG'S HUTONG

Běijīng's homely interior lies waiting to be discovered in the city's *hutong* (narrow alleyways). Criss-crossing east–west through the city, these alleyways link to create a huge, enchanting warren of one-storey, ramshackle dwellings and historic courtyard homes.

After Chinggis (Genghis) Khaan's army reduced Běijīng to rubble, the city was redesigned with *hutong*. By the Qing dynasty there were over 2000 such passageways riddling the city, leaping to around 6000 by the 1950s; now the figure has dwindled again to around 2000, home to about a quarter of Běijīng's residents. Marked with white plaques, historic homes are protected, but for many others a way of life is being ruthlessly bulldozed at a rate of over 10,000 dwellings a year.

Hutong land is a hodgepodge of the old and the new, with Qing-dynasty courtyards riddled with modern brick outhouses and socialist-era conversions, cruelly overlooked by grim apartment blocks.

Layout

Old walled *siheyuan* (courtyard homes) are the building blocks of this delightful world. More venerable courtyards are fronted by large, thick, red doors, outside of which perch either a pair of Chinese lions or *bavoguvshi* (drum stones; two circular stones resembling drums, each on a small plinth and occasionally topped by a miniature lion or a small dragon head).

Conditions in the *hutong* can be basic and many homes still lack toilets, explaining the multitude of malodorous public loos strung out along the alleyways. Other homes have been thoroughly modernised and sport varnished-wood floors, fully fitted kitchens, a Jacuzzi and air-con.

Hutong nearly all run east–west to ensure that the main gate faces south, satisfying the requirements of feng shui. This south-facing aspect guarantees a lot of sunshine and protection from more negative forces from the north. This positioning also mirrors the layout of all Chinese temples, nourishing the yang (the male and light aspect), while checking the yin (the female and dark aspect). Little connecting alleyways that run north–south link the main alleys.

Hutong Tour

The best way to see *hutong* is just to wander or cycle around the centre of Běijīng, as the alleyways riddle the town within the Second Ring Rd. Otherwise, limit yourself to historic areas, such as around the Drum Tower (p311) or the area around Nanluogu Xiang. If you want to join a tour, the **China Culture Center** (☎ 6432 9341; www.chinaculturecenter.org) operates a rewarding *hutong* and *siheyuan* tour. Any number of other pedicab tour operators infest the roads around Qianhai Lake – they will circle you like hyenas, baying '*hutong, hutong*'.

---

ancient. Taichi demonstrations are on offer, and there is internet (open 7.30am to 11pm; Y30 per hour). Rooms are typically discounted by around 40%.

Haoyuan Hotel (Hǎoyuán Bīnguǎn; ☎ 6512 5557; www.haoyuanhotel.com; 53 Shijia Hutong; 史家胡同53号; d standard/deluxe Y760/930, ste Y1080-1380; ❄ 🖳 ; Ⓜ Dongdan) This delightful Qing courtyard hotel has pleasant staff and a handful of tastefully finished rooms. Laid out with trees, the courtyard at the rear is gorgeous. There is a restaurant as well as bike rental, and rates include breakfast.

Red Capital Residence (Xīnhóngzī Kèzhàn; ☎ 6402 7150; www.redcapitalclub.com.cn; 9 Dongsi Liutiao; 东四六条9号; d from US$148; Ⓜ Dongsishitiao) An unusual guest house heady with the nostalgia of a vanished age. The five rooms are decked out

with stuff that wouldn't look out of place in a museum. For real class take a swing through town in the Red Flag limo, once the property of Mao's inner circle.

Novotel Peace Hotel (Běijīng Nuòfútè Hépíng Bīnguǎn; ☎ 6512 8833; fax 6512 6863; 3 Jinyu Hutong; 金鱼胡同3号; d west/east wing Y1494/1826; ❄ 🖳 ; Ⓜ Dengshikou) This efficient and inviting hotel has a fresh and cosmopolitan touch and a fantastic central location. The cheaper rooms – not huge but perfectly serviceable – are in the older and more scuffed west wing. Ask about promotional rates.

Top End

St Regis (Běijīng Guójì Jùlèbù Fàndiàn; ☎ 6460 6688; www.stregis.com/beijing; 21 Jianguomenwai Dajie; 建国门外大街21号; d from US$340, ste US$500-5300;

⊠ ▢ ▣ ; Ⓜ Jianguomen) Top-notch elegance complemented by professionalism and a superb location make the St Regis a marvellous choice. The splendid foyer and an enticing array of restaurants compound this hotel's undeniable allure.

Grand Hyatt Beijing (Běijīng Dōngfāng Jūnyuè Dàjiŭdiàn; ☎ 8518 1234; www.hyatt.com; 1 Dongchang'an Jie; 东长安 街1号; d US$443; ⊠ ▢ ▣ ; Ⓜ Wangfujing) Bang in the midst of the Wangfujing shopping district, this contemporary and opulent hotel offers a great location and sizable rooms.

China World Hotel (Zhōngguó Dàfàndiàn; ☎ 6505 2266; www.shangri-la.com; 1 Jianguomenwai Dajie; 建国 门外大街1号; d Y3200, ste Y5000-Y31,000; ⊠ ▢ ▣ ; Ⓜ Guomao) Acres of marble greet guests at this five-star performer, plus all your shopping and dining needs will be met at the China World Trade Center. The full tariff includes airport transfer, laundry, dry-cleaning, breakfast and local phone calls.

EATING

Some of your best memories of Běijīng are likely to be those involving eating. The best areas to look for restaurants, cafes and bars include Sanlitun and around Qianhai and Houhai Lakes. Unless stated otherwise, restaurants and cafes are open from 11am to 11pm.

For upmarket dining, Běijīng offers some exceptional restaurants that serve Chinese-influenced food with a modern twist. Reservations are necessary.

Some of the best and cheapest places to sample local cuisine are the food stalls and local markets.

Restaurants

BUDGET

Bāguó Bùyī (☎ 6400 8888; 89-3 Di'anmen Dongdajie; dishes from Y8; Ⓜ Zhangzizhonglu) Spicy Sichuān cuisine is served in a marvellous Chinese inn–style restaurant setting. There's a range of good value dishes for Y8, including Chóngqìng hot pepper chicken and chilli fish slices.

Niúgē Jiǎozi (☎ 6525 7472; 85 Dong'anmen Nanjie; meals Y15; Ⓜ Tiananmen Dong) Dumpling fans should hasten to this pocket-sized restaurant that dishes up dozens of yummy varieties – there's no English menu, though, and no English sign either, but it's opposite the building with the sign on the roof saying 'Hualong St'.

Kuān Diàn (☎ 8404 0523; 135 Jiugulou Dajie; dishes from Y20; Ⓜ Gulou) This budget dive has a charming retro-communist atmosphere with propaganda posters that look like they've been hanging there for decades. Grainy pictures of Mao stare out in the dim light, while the hipster-student clientele enjoys tasty dishes of grilled beef, barbecued chicken wings and sautéed vegetables that go great with a cold beer.

Makye Ame (Mǎjí Āmǐ; ☎ 6506 9616; 2nd fl, A11 Xiushui Nanjie; dishes from Y20; Ⓜ Jianguomen) Behind the Friendship Store, this is one of Běijīng's few Tibetan restaurants, where you can sample boiled yak with chilli and *tsampa* (roasted barley meal). There's a comfy upper room decorated with a generous crop of Tibetan ornaments.

Gongdelin Vegetarian Restaurant (Gōngdélín Sùcàiguǎn; ☎ 6511 2542; 158 Qianmen Dajie; meals Y25-40; ⏱ 10am-2.30pm & 5.30-10pm; Ⓥ; Ⓜ Qianmen) Restore your karma with dishes of mock meat that taste better than the real thing. Service is pedestrian and the decor strictly no-frills.

MIDRANGE

Green Tianshi Vegetarian Restaurant (Lüsè Tiānshí Sùcàiguǎn; ☎ 6524 2349; 57 Dengshikou Dajie; meals from Y50; Ⓜ Dengshikou) This venerable vegetarian restaurant cooks up simulated meat dishes, presented in a relaxed and attractive environment. A handy picture menu helps with the ordering.

Kaorouji (☎ 6404 2554; 14 Qianhai Dongyuan; meals Y55; Ⓜ Gulou) An old standby overlooking lovely Qianhai Lake and serving delicious coriander-laced roast mutton (Y45), as well as a good range of other Muslim Uighur dishes.

Ottos Restaurant (Rìchāng Cānguǎn; ☎ 6405 8205; Di'anmen Xidajie; meals Y60; ⏱ 11am-2am; Ⓜ Zhangzizhonglu) Loud and cavernous with a bright menu, harried staff and constant waves of diners piling in for its flavoursome Hong Kong dishes, Ottos offers no-nonsense, tasty food in decent helpings. It's east of Beihai Park's north gate.

Liqun Roast Duck Restaurant (Lìqún Kǎoyādiàn; ☎ 6702 5681; 11 Beixiangfeng Hutong; roast duck Y68; Ⓜ Qianmen) Book a table before arriving at this tiny, busy Peking-duck restaurant buried away in a maze of *hutong* in east Qianmen. No medals for service but the duck is excellent.

Steak & Eggs (☎ 6592 8088; 5 Xiushui Nanjie; meals under Y70; Ⓜ Yong'anli) If steamed buns and rice porridge aren't providing enough early morning fuel, go to this quintessential North American breakfast joint for sizeable portions of bacon, pancakes, oatmeal, fruit cups and, of course, steak and eggs. It's behind the Friendship Store.

ourpick Xiao Wang's Home Restaurant (Xiǎowáng Fǔ; ☎ 6594 3602; 2 Guanghua Dongli; meals Y70; Ⓜ Yong'anli) Treat yourself to home-style Běijīng cuisine from this excellent restaurant. Try one of the specials: fried, hot and spicy, Xīnjiāng-style chicken wings or deep-fried spare ribs with pepper salt. A very attractive branch with outdoor seating can be found in Ritan Park.

Bellagio's (☎ 8404 0523; 35 Xiaoyun Lu; dishes from Y70; Ⓜ Gulou) Why this thoroughly Taiwanese restaurant has an Italian name we know not. However, we can say the food is excellent, with a range of aromatic dishes artfully presented by spiky-haired waiters. Try one of the famed pearl teas and top off your meal with a red-bean shaved ice with fruit. Dress up for this one: Bellagio's is a late-night haunt for A-list clubbers, models, actors and wannabe actors, which makes it a fun place for people-watching.

TOP END

Quanjude Roast Duck Restaurant (Quànjùdé Kǎoyādiàn; ☎ 6525 3310; 9 Shuaifuyuan Hutong; half/whole duck Y84/168; Ⓜ Wangfujing) You've not really visited Běijīng unless you've scoffed the city's signature dish. Quanjude has an impeccable pedigree (Mao ate here) and is a fine place to sample Peking duck, as well as more specialist dishes such as duck feet with mustard sauce, salted duck's liver or deep-fried duck heart. There's also a more famous and touristy branch at Qianmen (☎ 6511 2418; 32 Qianmen Dajie; metro Qianmen).

Taj Pavilion (Tàijí Lóu Yìndù Cāntīng; ☎ 6505 5866; 1st fl, West Wing, China World Trade Center; meals from Y100; Ⓜ Guomao) Hankering for an Indian meal? The food and service here consistently get top marks.

Le Little Saigon (Xī Gòng Zài Bā Lí; ☎ 6401 8465; 141 Jiugulou Dajie; meals Y100-150; Ⓜ Gulou) This French-Vietnamese fusion restaurant has the look and feel of a Parisian brasserie and a diverse menu that spans the continents. Try the pork and spring rolls and the tasty Hanoi noodle soup. Linger a while; this is a relaxing place where you could easily spend an evening over wine.

Purple Haze (Zǐsǔtíng; ☎ 6413 0899; meals Y100-150; Ⓜ Dongsishitiao) A great neighbourhood restaurant with a loyal following, Purple Haze offers some of the best Thai cuisine in the city. The service can be downright awful but it does

have several great dishes, including red curry chicken and the signature dish, duck salad. It's along the small lane opposite the Workers' Stadium's north gate.

Courtyard (Sìhéyuàn; ☎ 6526 8883; 95 Donghuamen Dajie; meals from Y200; Ⓥ 6-10pm Mon-Sat, noon-10pm Sun; Ⓜ Tiananmen Dong) The view across to the Forbidden City is only surpassed by the cooking, which is delicious. Sunday lunch is an affordable option at Y150 per person.

Tiāndì Yījiā (☎ 8511 5556; tiandicanyin@163.com; 140 Nanchizi Dajie; meals around Y300; Ⓜ Tiananmen Dong) This refined Chinese courtyard–style restaurant is decked out with traditional furniture, water features and side rooms for snug hotpot dinners. Graze on Cantonese dim sum (served from 11am to 2pm and 5pm to 9.30pm).

Cafes & Quick Eats

Wangfujing Snack Street (Wángfǔjīng Xiǎochījiē; west off Wangfujing Dajie; kebabs from Y3, dishes from Y5; Ⓜ Wangfujing) Fronted by an ornate archway, here you'll find a good selection of small restaurants and stalls overhung with colourful banners and bursting with character and flavour. Try Xīnjiāng or Muslim Uighur cuisine such as lamb kebabs and flat bread.

Donghuamen Night Market (Dōnghuāmén Yèshì; Dong'anman Dajie; Ⓥ 3-10pm, closed Chinese New Year; Ⓜ Dengshikou) A sight in itself is this bustling night market near Wangfujing Dajie. It's for tourists, so expect to pay around Y5 for a lamb kebab (much more than you would pay for one from a *hutong* vendor).

Food Court (basement, Oriental Plaza, 1 Dongchang'an Jie; dishes from Y10; Ⓜ Wangfujing) If the outdoor stalls leave you nonplussed, try this spacious, hygienic food court offering a world of Chinese cuisine, plus other Asian dishes. You can eat very well for around Y20. Buy a prepaid card at the kiosk at the entrance; credits are deducted with each dish ordered.

Sequoia (Měizhōu Shān Kāfēiwū; ☎ 6501 5503; 44 Guanghua Lu; sandwiches Y23-35; Ⓥ 8am-8pm; Ⓜ Jianguomen) A steady stream of customers arrives at Sequoia for its satisfying coffee and deservedly popular sandwiches. The vegetarian sandwich (Y25) is wildly sought.

Kosmo (☎ 6657 0007; 5 Lotus Lane, Qianhai Xiyan; sandwiches & drinks Y30; Ⓜ Gulou) Facing Qianhai Lake, this stylish contemporary cafe, serving organic and healthy food, is a standout among the trendy offerings of Lotus Lane – and not just because it donates some of its profits to Unicef.

Self-Catering

At Běijīng's supermarkets you'll find everything you need for long train journeys. Some options:

Lufthansa Center Youyi Shopping City (Yànshā Yǒuyì Shāngchǎng; 50 Liangmaqiao Lu; ☾ 10am-8pm; Ⓜ Dongzhimen)

Super 24 (Sanlitun Lu; ☾ 24hr; Ⓜ Dongzhimen)

Yansha Supermarket (Yànshā Chāoshì; basement, Henderson Center, Jianguomennei Dajie; ☾ 10am-8pm; Ⓜ Jianguomen)

DRINKING

Sanlitun is a good place for a wild night out as it combines bars and mininightclubs. The streets around Qianhai and Houhai Lakes are atmospheric but quieter, while Nanluogu Xiang can be downright mellow. Most bars and clubs are open daily from about noon until the last customer leaves, unless otherwise specified.

Utopia (Wūtuōbāng; ☎ 136 8304 4449; 107 Nanluogu Xiang; Ⓜ Zhangzizhonglu) We went bar-hopping up and down Nanluogu Xiang and liked this pint-sized place the best. It's got a great vibe, well-worn couches and friendly waiters.

Passby Bar (Guòkè; ☎ 8403 8004; www.passbybar .com; 108 Nanluogu Xiang; ☾ 9am-2am; Ⓜ Zhangzizhonglu) One of the original bars on cafe-bar strip Nanluogu Xiang and still one of the best, with travel-oriented bar staff, a winning courtyard ambience, shelves of books and mags, and a funky feel.

Guangfuguan Greenhouse (Guǎngfúguàn de Wēnshì; ☎ 6400 3234; 36 Yandai Xijie; Ⓜ Gulou) Sink those beers in a former Taoist temple with the religious statuary still gazing on.

Tree (Yìnbì de Shù; ☎ 6415 1954; www.treebeijing.com; 43 Bei Sanlitun Nan; Ⓜ Dongsishitiao) One of the most popular drinking spots in Sanlitun, thanks to its laundry list of Belgian beers. The pizza here is downright spectacular should you get the late-night munchies.

Poachers Inn (Yǒuyì Qīngnián Jiǔdiàn; ☎ 6417 2632, ext 8506; 43 Bei Sanlitun Lu; Ⓜ Dongsishitiao) Party central on weekends, this long-running bar remains one of the most popular expat watering holes, with inflated prices and occasional live acts. It's on the same courtyard as Tree.

A couple of upmarket hotel bars with a soothing ambience and music include **Centro** (Xuànkù; ☎ 6561 8833, ext 6388; Kerry Center Hotel, 1 Guanghua Lu; ☾ 24hr; Ⓜ Guomao) and **Red Moon Bar** (Dōngfāng Liàng; ☎ 8518 1234, ext 6366; Grand Hyatt Beijing, 1 Dongchang'an Jie; Ⓜ Wangfujing).

ENTERTAINMENT

Nightclubs

Mix (Húnhè; ☎ 6530 2889; inside Workers' Stadium north gate; ☾ 8pm-late) Major hip-hop and R & B club west of Sanlitun with regular crowd-pulling foreign DJs.

Club Banana (Bānànà; ☎ 6526 3939; Scitech Hotel, 22 Jianguomenwai Dajie; cover Y20-50; ☾ 8.30pm-4am Sun-Thu, to 5am Fri & Sat) A mainstay of Běijīng's club land, Banana is loud and to the point. Select from techno, acid jazz and chill-out sections according to your energy levels or the waning of the night.

Destination (Mùdìdì; ☎ 6551 5138; www.bjdestina tion.com; 7 Gongrentiyuchang Xilu; cover Y30; ☾ 6pm-late; Ⓜ Dongsishitiao) Běijīng's premier gay dance bar is a stylish, lively place with a mixed crowd. It hosts the occasional lesbian night.

Opera

Běijīng opera (p73) is the most famous of the many forms of performance art on offer in the city. You can catch performances at the following theatres:

Chang'an Grand Theatre (Chángān Dàjùchǎng; ☎ 6510 1309; Chang'an Bldg, 7 Jianguomennei Dajie; tickets Y50-380; ☾ performances 7.15pm; Ⓜ Jianguomen)

Huguang Guild Hall (Húguǎng Huìguǎn; ☎ 6351 8284; 3 Hufang Lu; tickets Y150-180; ☾ performances 7.15-9pm; Ⓜ Hepingmen) Decorated in a similar fashion to the Zhengyici Theatre, with balconies surrounding the canopied stage, this theatre dates back to 1807.

Zhengyici Theatre (Zhèngyǐcí Jùchǎng; ☎ 6303 3104; 220 Xiheyan Dajie; tickets Y360-680; ☾ performances 7.30-9pm; Ⓜ Qianmen) Oldest wooden theatre in the country and the best place in the city to experience Běijīng opera.

Acrobatics

Chaoyang Theatre (Cháoyáng Jùchǎng; ☎ 6507 2421; 36 Dongsanhuan Beilu; tickets Y180-380; ☾ performances 7.30pm; Ⓜ Chaoyangmen) The Chaoyang Theatre is the venue for visiting acrobatic troupes, who fill the stage with plate-spinning and hoop-jumping.

Tiandi Theatre (Tiāndì Jùchǎng; ☎ 6416 0757/9893; 10 Dongzhimen Nandajie; tickets Y100-300; ☾ performances 7.15pm; Ⓜ Dongsishitiao) Around 100m north of Poly Plaza; come here to see young performers from the China Acrobatic Circus and the China National Acrobatic Troupe.

Tianqiao Acrobatics Theatre (Tiānqiáo Zájì Jùchǎng; ☎ 6303 7449; in English 139 1000 1860; Beiwei Lu, Xuanwu District; tickets Y100-200; ☾ performances 7.15-8.45pm; Ⓜ Qianmen) West of the Temple of

Heaven, this is one of Běijīng's most popular venues.

Live Music

East Shore Bar (Dōngàn; ☎ 8403 2131; 2nd fl, 2 Shishahai Nanyan; Tsingtao beers Y20; ☻ 4pm-3am; 💻) With views out over Qianhai Lake, this excellent bar hits all the right notes with its low-light, candlelit mood and live jazz sounds from 9.30pm (Thursday to Sunday). Free internet.

What Bar? (Shénme Bā; ☎ 133 4112 2757; 72 Beichang Jie; cover on live-music nights incl 1 beer Y20; ☻ 3pm- late, live music from 9pm Fri & Sat) Microsized and slightly deranged, this broom cupboard of a bar stages regular, rotating, grittily named bands to an enthusiastic audience. It's north of the Forbidden City's west gate.

SHOPPING

Whatever you want, from antiques to Versace, chances are you'll find it in Běijīng. Get lucky and some pieces might even be genuine! The best bargains include silk, cashmere and brand-name clothing (often fake). Pirated CDs and DVDs abound. While prices are fixed in the department stores, bargaining is expected – even encouraged – everywhere else. When bargaining, ask the price and counter with an offer that is 80% less, wait for the 'you crazy!' response, then work your way towards something in the middle.

Wangfujing Dajie is a lively shop-lined pedestrianised street, two blocks east of the Forbidden City. Its name, meaning 'Well of Princely Palaces', dates to the 15th century, when this area was the site of several royal palaces, long since destroyed to make way for the palaces of the people. The mammoth **Oriental Plaza** (Dōngfāng Guǎngchǎng; 1 Dongchang'an Jie; Ⓜ Wangfujing) shopping mall anchors the southern end of the street, while elsewhere along it you'll find tea emporium **Ten Fu's Tea** (Tiānfú Míngchá; ☎ 6527 4613; www.tenfu.com; 88 Wangfujing Dajie; Ⓜ Wangfujing).

Dashilar (Ⓜ Qianmen), a colourful *hutong* off Qianmen Dajie, is a jumble of silk shops, tea and herbal-medicine shops, theatres and restaurants. Also known as 'Silk St', it is a hangover from when specialised products were sold in particular areas. **Ruifuxiang** (☎ 6303 2808; 5 Dazhalan Jie) is a good place to buy silk near Dashilar.

Běijīng's premier antique street is treelined **Liulichang** (Ⓜ Hepingmen), west of Dashilar. Designed to look like an ancient Chinese vil-

lage, it's a nice place to stroll even if you don't want to buy Chinese paintings, calligraphy materials, art books or ceramics.

Pānjiāyuán ('Dirt' Market; ☻ dawn–around 3pm Sat & Sun; Ⓜ Guomao) Located off Dongsanhuan Nanlu, it's hands-down the best place to shop for arts, crafts and antiques – everything from Cultural Revolution memorabilia to Buddha heads. Come early and bargain hard. .

Sanlitun Yashou Clothing Market (Sānlǐtún Yǎxiù Fúzhuāng Shìchǎng; 58 Gongrentiyuchang Beilu; Ⓜ Dongsishitiao) Offers five floors of all the clothing you may need.

GETTING THERE & AWAY
Air

Běijīng's **Capital Airport** (☎ 6454 1100) has direct air connections to most major cities in the world and every major city in China. For more information about international flights to Běijīng, see p346.

Train

Moscow, Ulaanbaatar and Hāěrbin (Harbin) trains depart from and arrive at **Beijing Train Station** (Běijīng Huǒchēzhàn; ☎ 5101 9999; Ⓜ Beijingzhan), southeast of the Forbidden City. **Beijing West Train Station** (Běijīng Xīzhàn; ☎ 5182 6273; Ⓜ Junshibowuguan), near Lianhuachi Park, has trains for Hong Kong and Vietnam. Buses 122 and 721 connect Beijing Train Station with Beijing West Train Station.

Avoid buying tickets in the main ticket hall at Beijing Train Station, as the crowds can be overwhelming. There's a **ticketing office for foreigners** (☻ 5.30-7.30am, 8am-6.30pm & 7-11pm) in the northwestern corner of the 1st floor, accessed through the soft-seat waiting room. This is an excellent place to sit down and take a breather in the comfy armchairs provided. There's also a foreigners' ticketing office on the 2nd floor of Beijing West Train Station (open 24 hours).

The most convenient place to buy tickets to Mongolia and Russia is the **CITS International Train Ticket Center** (☎ 6512 0507; 2nd fl, Beijing International Hotel, 9 Jianguomenwai Dajie; ☻ 8.30am-noon & 1.30-5pm; Ⓜ Beijingzhan), or **BTG Travel & Tours** (☎ 6515 8010; 28 Jianguomenwai Dajie; ☻ 8am-8pm; Ⓜ Jianguomen), between the New Otani and Gloria Plaza Hotels. The latter has a desk dedicated to booking Trans-Mongolian/Trans-Manchurian trains, and can also (for a Y100 fee) book Hāěrbin to Manzhouli trains via the CITS office in Hāěrbin. The experienced travel agent **Monkey Business** (☎ 6591 6519; www.monkey

BĚIJĪNG

shrine.com; Room 201, Youyi Poachers Inn, 43 Beisanlitun Nan, Ⓜ Dongshishitiao) specialises in Trans-Siberian journeys and can provide full services, including visa support and tours in Mongolia.

GETTING AROUND
To/From the Airport

The airport is 27km from the city centre. The newly opened Airport Line light-rail link (Y25, first/last train to airport 6.30am/10.30pm, from airport 6.30am/11.05pm) runs every 15 minutes, connecting Capital Airport with Line 2 of the underground system at Dongzhimen. Express buses (Y16) also run along several routes. Line 3 (first/last bus from Capital Airport 7.30am/last flight, from Beijing Train Station 5.30am/9pm) is the most popular with travellers, running to the Beijing International Hotel and Beijing Train Station via Chaoyangmen. A taxi should cost only about Y85 from the airport to the centre (including the Y15 road toll); make sure the driver uses the meter. Join the taxi ranks and ignore approaches from drivers, as scams are common.

Bicycle

To get around the city in true Běijīng style, consider riding a bicycle, which can be rented from many hotels, especially those in the budget range. **Universal Bicycle Rental Outlet** (Shuāngrén Yizhàn; Qianhai Lake; single/tandem bike per hr Y10/20, deposit Y500; Ⓜ Gulou) has two outlets in the vicinity of Qianhai Lake.

Public Transport

Given the frequently appalling traffic, the metro (dìtiě; 地铁) is a hassle-free way to get around the centre of Běijīng. Currently nine lines are operating, with two more under construction, including Line 9, which will link Beijing West Train Station with Line 1 and Line 4. It operates from 5am to 11pm and the fare is a flat Y2. Signs are in English and easy to understand. Stations are marked by a blue sign with a capital 'D'. Beijing Train Station is a stop on the circle metro line (Beijingzhan).

Taxi

Taxis are cheap and plentiful: the standard per-kilometre charge starts from Y2, with a Y10 minimum. Make sure your driver turns on the meter, especially coming from the airport or the train station. Between 11pm and 6am there is a 20% surcharge added to the flag-fall metered fare. Drivers will rarely speak English so have a map handy to point out your destination; better still, have somebody write down your destination so you can show it to the driver.

AROUND BĚIJĪNG

GREAT WALL OF CHINA 长城

Stretching 7200km from the Bo Sea in the east to the Gobi Desert in the west, the Great Wall of China is truly a wonder, due to both its breathtaking beauty and its ancient architectural achievement. Several sections of the Great Wall, particularly at Bādálǐng, have been recently revamped for the benefit of tourists. Also renovated but less touristed are the sections at Sīmǎtái and Jīnshānlíng.

History

The 'original' construction of the Great Wall is credited to Emperor Qin Shihuang (221–207 BC), China's first sovereign emperor. He accomplished this feat by reconstructing and linking the ruins of older walls, which had been built by the vassal states under the Zhou dynasty in the 7th century BC. The result was a magnificent 4800km stretch of wall, which was meant to keep out the marauding nomads in the north. The effort required hundreds of thousands of workers, most of them prisoners. Over the course of 10 years, an estimated one million people died; legend has it that the bodies of deceased workers were used as one of the construction materials.

By the collapse of the Qin, the Great Wall had already started to crumble due to years of neglect. Emperor Han Wu-Di once again undertook the task of rebuilding the existing wall, and extending it 480km further west into the Gobi Desert. During this period, the wall served mainly as an elevated highway, along which men and equipment could be transported across mountainous terrain. Furthermore, the Hans established a system of smoke signals, by which they could warn each other of enemy attacks. Thus, the wall protected traders and explorers who were travelling the ancient caravan routes between China and Europe.

The wall that you see today is largely a product of the Ming dynasty (1368–1644). The Ming wall was taller, longer and more ornate than any earlier incarnations. It was

BĚIJĪNG

also stronger, due in part to the advanced brick technology the Ming workers used.

Bādálǐng 八达岭

Most visitors see the Great Wall at **Bādálǐng** (Bādálǐng Chángchéng; ☎ 6912 1338/1423/1520; admission Y45; ⌚ 6am-10pm summer, 7am-6pm winter), 70km northwest of Běijīng, at an elevation of 1000m. The section of masonry at Bādálǐng was first built during the Ming dynasty, and was heavily restored in the 1950s and the 1980s. Punctuated with watchtowers, the 6m-wide wall is clad in brick, typical of the stonework employed by the Ming when they restored and expanded the fortification.

The surrounding scenery is raw and impressive and this is the place to come to see the wall snaking off over the undulating hills. Also come here for guard rails, souvenir stalls, a fairground feel and the companionship of squads of tourists surging over the ramparts. Try to avoid summer weekends when the place is a crush of humanity. Come during the week instead, and if possible, during the colder months when it's covered in snow.

Cable cars exist for the weary (round-trip Y60), but don't take the slide (Y30) as it's a colossal waste of money.

The admission fee also includes a 15-minute film about the Great Wall at the **Great Wall Circle Vision Theatre** (⌚ 9am-5.45pm), a 360-degree amphitheatre, and the **China Great Wall Museum** (⌚ 9am-4pm).

GETTING THERE & AWAY

The cheapest and easiest way to get to Bādálǐng is to take bus 919 (Y12, 1½ hours) from just north of the old gate of Deshengmen, about 500m east of the Jishuitan metro stop. In summer, the first bus from Běijīng leaves at 6.30am and the last bus from Bādálǐng departs at 8.30pm (but confirm this).

CITS (☎ 6512 3075; www.cits.com.cn, in Chinese), the Beijing Tourist Information Center, big hotels and everyone else in the tourist business does a tour to Bādálǐng. Watch out for high-priced hotel tours (up to Y300 per person).

A taxi to the wall and back will cost a minimum of Y400 for an eight-hour hire with a maximum of four passengers.

Mùtiányù 慕田峪

The 2250m-long granite section of wall at **Mùtiányù** (☎ 6162 6873; admission Y45; ⌚ 6.30am-6pm), 90km northeast of Běijīng, was developed as a decoy alternative to Bādálǐng and is, on the whole, a less commercial experience. Despite some motivated hawking and tourist clutter, the stretch of wall is notable for its numerous Ming dynasty guard towers and stirring views. The wall is also equipped with a **cable car** (round-trip Y50; ⌚ 8.30am-4.30pm). October is the best month to visit, for the autumn colours of the trees that envelop the surrounding countryside.

GETTING THERE & AWAY

From **Dongzhimen long-distance bus station** (Dōngzhímén Chángtú Qìchēzhàn; ☎ 6467 4995) you can take either bus 916 (Y8, one hour) or 936 (Y5) to Huairou then change for a minibus to Mùtiányù (Y25).

Tour bus 6 (☎ 6601 8285) runs to Mùtiányù (Y50) from outside the South Cathedral at Xuanwumen, operating between 6.30am and 8.30am on Saturday, Sunday and public holidays from April to October.

Jūyōngguān 居庸关

Originally constructed in the 5th century and rebuilt by the Ming, **Jūyōngguān** (Juyong Pass; ☎ 6977 1665; admission Y40; ⌚ 6am-4pm) was considered one of the most strategically important sections of the Great Wall, only 50km northwest of Běijīng. However, this section has been thoroughly renovated to the point where you don't feel as if you're walking on a part of history. Still, if you're in a hurry, it's the closest section of the wall to the city and is usually quiet. You can do the steep and somewhat strenuous circuit in under two hours.

Jūyōngguān is on the road to Bādálǐng, so bus 919 for Bādálǐng (see left) will get you there (but tell the bus driver you want to be dropped off at Jūyōngguān Chàngchéng).

Sīmǎtái 司马台

The stirring remains at **Sīmǎtái** (☎ 6903 5025/5030; admission Y30; ⌚ 8am-5pm), 110km northeast of Běijīng, make for a more exhilarating Great Wall experience. Built during the reign of Ming-dynasty emperor Hongwu, the 19km stretch is marked by watchtowers, steep plunges and scrambling ascents.

Not for the faint-hearted, this rough section of the wall is very steep. A few slopes have a 70-degree incline and you need both hands free, so bring a day-pack to hold your camera and other essentials. The **cable car** (round-trip Y50) could be an alternative to a sprained ankle. Take strong shoes with a good grip.

Sīmǎtái has some unusual features, such as 'obstacle walls' – walls-within-walls used for defending against enemies who had already scaled the Great Wall. There's also a **toboggan ride** (Y30), and, unfazed by the dizzying terrain, hawkers make an unavoidable appearance.

GETTING THERE & AWAY

Direct minibuses depart from **Dongzhimen long-distance bus station** (☎ 6467 4995) from 6am (Y20). Otherwise take a minibus from Dongzhimen to Miyun (Y8, 1¼ hours) and change to a minibus to Sīmǎtái, or a taxi (round-trip Y120).

Weekend tour bus 12 (☎ 6601 8285) leaves from outside the South Cathedral at Xuanwumen for Sīmǎtái (Y50) between 6.30am and 8.30am Saturday, Sunday and public holidays. Backpacker hotels often run morning trips by **minibus** (not incl admission ticket Y60; ☉ 8.30am). A taxi from Běijīng for the day costs about Y400.

Jīnshānlǐng 金山岭

Though not as steep (and therefore not as impressive) as Sīmǎtái, the Great Wall at **Jīnshānlǐng** (Jīnshānlǐng Chángchéng; admission Y40), near the town of Gubeikou, has 24 watchtowers and is considerably less developed (and therefore much quieter) than any of the sites previously mentioned, despite undergoing some restoration work.

Perhaps the most interesting thing about Jīnshānlǐng is that it's the starting point for a 10km hike to Sīmǎtái. It takes nearly four hours because the trail is steep and stony. Parts of the wall along the route are in a state of ruin, but it can be traversed without too much difficulty. Upon arrival at Sīmǎtái, however, you may have to buy another ticket.

You can do the walk in the opposite direction, but getting a ride back to Běijīng from Sīmǎtái is easier than from Jīnshānlǐng. Of course, getting a ride should be no problem if you've made arrangements with your driver to pick you up (and didn't pay in advance).

To get to Jīnshānlǐng from **Dongzhimen long-distance bus station** (☎ 6467 4995), take a minibus to Miyun (Y10, 1¼ hours), then change to a minibus to Gubeikou, and get off at Bakeshiying (Y7).

Directory

CONTENTS

ACCOMMODATION

For several, if not all, nights of your Trans-Siberian journey your bed will be on the train (for train options, see p357). But at either end of your journey and most likely at points along it you'll be looking for more traditional accommodation.

Russia

Russia offers everything from cosy homestays to five-star luxury hotels. You'll occasionally come across hotels that refuse to let you stay because you're a foreigner, or that will only offer you the most expensive rooms. Otherwise you can generally stay where you like, though beware that a few of the cheapest hotels won't want to register your visa (p343).

It's a good idea to book a few nights accommodation in advance for Moscow and St Petersburg, but elsewhere it's usually not necessary. Make bookings by email or fax rather than phone, and note that many hotels charge a *bron* (booking surcharge) up to 50% of the first night's rate.

If you're looking for cheaper places to stay, head for the smaller towns or consider a homestay; many travel agencies can arrange these. Moscow, Irkutsk and St Petersburg each have backpacker hostels, most able to offer visa support. Camping in the wild is generally allowed – check with locals if you're in doubt. *Kempingi* (organised camp sites) are rare and, usually, only open from June to September. Unlike Western camp sites, small wooden cabins often take up much of the space, leaving little room for tents. Some *kempingi* are in quite attractive woodland settings but communal toilets and washrooms are often in poor condition and other facilities few.

Komnaty otdykha (resting rooms) are found at all major train stations along the Trans-Siberian route and are cheap (from R50 per hour, to R600 per day), which is why they are often booked up. Rooms are usually shared and there are shared bathrooms. At the bigger stations, such as Novosibirsk, the *komnaty otdykha* are excellent and the private luxe rooms are well worth the extra expense. At many other stations the rooms are very basic. Some will ask to see your train ticket before allowing you to stay.

In hotels *potselenye* (twin rooms) are occasionally cheaper than singles. It's often possible to pay half again when only one person is staying, especially in small towns – though in twin rooms you may end up sharing with a stranger. A *lyux* room equates to a suite with a sitting room in addition to the bedroom and bathroom. A *polu-lyux* room is somewhat less spacious. Note that size doesn't always equate to better quality.

Often each hotel floor has a *dezhurnaya* (floor lady) to keep an eye on it and to supply guests with snacks, bottled drinks or boiled water. They might even do your laundry. Check-out time is usually noon, but it's unlikely that anyone will mind if you stay an

PRACTICALITIES

All Countries

■ Electrical power in Russia, China and Mongolia is 220V, 50Hz. Sockets in Russia and Mongolia are designed to accommodate two round prongs in the European style. Chinese plugs come in at least four designs: three-pronged angled pins as used in Australia; three-pronged round pins as in Hong Kong; two-pronged flat pins as in the USA; or two narrow round pins as in Europe. For more information, check www.kropla.com.

■ Russia and Mongolia both follow the metric system. Although China also officially subscribes to the metric system, ancient Chinese weights and measures persist. Fruit and vegetables are sold by the *jin*, which is 0.5kg (1.32lb). Tea and herbal medicines are usually sold by the *liang*, which is 37.5g (1.32oz).

Russia

■ In Moscow the best source of English-language news is the daily *Moscow Times* (www.moscow times.ru) available free across the city; in St Petersburg, the *St Petersburg Times* (www.sptimes.ru) is an excellent free biweekly read. Top-end hotels in these cities usually have copies of the *International Herald-Tribune,* the *Financial Times* and occasionally some of the British broadsheets, as well as weekly magazines such as the *Economist* and *Time*. Elsewhere in Russia the pickings of English media are very slim, and most likely nonexistent. On the train you'll sometimes come across the free glossy monthly magazine *Ekspress* (in Russian). It's also common for hearing-impaired hawkers to sell newspapers, magazines and books along the carriages – a pile will be left in your compartment to leaf through.

■ Radio in Russia is broken into three bands: AM, UKV (66MHz to 77MHz) and FM (100MHz to 107MHz). A Western-made FM radio usually won't go lower than 85MHz. The BBC's World Service's short-wave (SW) frequencies in the morning, late evening and night are near 9410kHz, 12,095kHz (the best) and 15,070kHz, though the exact setting varies with locations.

Mongolia

■ In Ulaanbaatar there are two English-language weekly newspapers, the *Mongol Messenger* (www.mongolmessenger.mn) and the *UB Post* (http://ubpost.mongolnews.mn) both good for local news and entertainment information.

■ In Mongolia BBC World Service has a nonstop service at 103.1FM. Local stations worth trying include Jag (107FM), Blue Sky (100.9FM) and Radio Ulaanbaatar (102.5FM). Voice of America news is occasionally broadcast on 106.6FM.

China

■ China's main English-language newspaper is the *China Daily*. Imported English-language newspapers and magazines can be bought from five-star hotel bookshops. Look out for free expat-focused English-language listings magazines, including the *Beijinger* (www.thebeijinger.com).

■ In China listen to the **BBC World Service** (www.bbc.co.uk/cgi-bin/worldservice/psims/ScheduleSDT.cgi) or **Voice of America** (www.voanews.com)   check the websites for frequencies. **China Radio International** (CRI; www.chinabroadcast.cn) is China's overseas radio service and broadcasts in about 40 foreign languages.

---

extra hour or two. It's usually no problem storing your luggage.

Hotels with significant numbers of foreign guests also attract prostitutes; you'll usually be left alone if you make it clear you're not interested.

For a hostel dorm bed in Moscow and St Petersburg you can expect to pay around R550 to R750, while a double room with bathroom in a budget hotel in these cities will cost anything up to R3000. Elsewhere budget hotel beds can be as cheap as R500 a night with shared facilities, although R700 to R1500 is a more realistic minimum for many cities.

You'll pay R1500 to R4000 for a midrange twin (except in Moscow and St Petersburg,

---

HOMESTAY AGENCIES

The following agencies can arrange homestays mainly in Moscow and St Petersburg (as can some travel agencies; see individual city listings for details). It's worth knowing that your host family usually only gets a small fraction of the price you pay the agent.

Flatmates.ru (http://flatmates.ru/eng/) A spin off of **Way to Russia** (www.waytorussia.net)
International Homestay Agency (www.homestayagency.com/homestay/russia.html)
Host Families Association (HOFA; ☎ 901-305-8874; www.hofa.ru)
Russian Home Travel (☎ in the USA 1-800 861 9335; russiahome@aol.com)
Uncle Pasha (www.unclepasha.com)

---

where it's R3000 to R10,000). Luxury hotels in the major cities charge upwards of R10,000 for doubles. In provincial cities, expect to pay upwards of R4000, although you may get better prices through a travel agent. Top-end prices may be quoted in dollars, or sometimes euros (although you'll always pay in roubles), on top of which you'll typically pay 20% Value Added Tax (VAT) and, in Moscow and St Petersburg, 5% local tax (not included in prices quoted in this book).

China

Overall, accommodation in China is quite humdrum. The star rating at China's hotels can be very misleading. Hotels are often awarded four or five stars, when they are patently a star lower in ranking. Take time to wander around and make a quick inspection of the overall quality or stick to chain hotels with recognisable names.

Camping is not really feasible, especially within sight of a town or village. Wilderness camping is more appealing, but most areas require special permits, which are difficult to obtain. The good news, however, is that other cheap accommodation options are available. University dorms sometimes rent rooms to tourists, and there is a good range of hostels in Běijīng.

A typical hotel room is a 'twin' – two single beds in one room. A 'single room' (one bed per room) is a rarity, although they do exist. The Western concept of a 'double room' (a room with one double bed shared by two people) is also rare in China. In most cases, your choice will be between a twin room or a suite. However, two people are usually allowed to occupy a twin room for the same price as one person, so sharing is a good way to cut expenses.

A dorm bed around the centre of Běijīng goes for about Y45 to Y70. Twin hotel rooms there start at around Y240 with a shared bathroom.

Accommodation websites that may be useful:

Asia Hotel (www.asiahotels.com)
China Hotel Guide (www.china-hotelguide.com)
Ctrip (www.english.ctrip.com)
Elong (ww.elong.net)
Red Flag (www.redflag.info)
Sinohotel (www.sinohotel.com)

Mongolia

Mongolia is perhaps the world's most perfect camping destination. Excellent camp sites are everywhere, even near Ulaanbaatar in places such as Terelj. If you are travelling in the countryside, camping is an even better option, considering the lack of hotels and the expense of ger (yurt) camps. Be sure to carry enough supplies and water for the duration of your stay, as they may be hard to come by, depending on where you are.

A tourist ger camp is a 'camp ground' with traditional ger, a separate building for toilets and showers, and a restaurant-bar. The gers are furnished with two or three beds. Toilets and bathrooms, which are separate and shared, are usually clean. Most ger camps in Terelj are open from June to September. In the Gobi Desert, they are open from May to October.

Ulaanbaatar has an abundant range of guest houses targeting foreign backpackers. Most guest houses are in apartment blocks and have dorm beds as well as private rooms. Many guest houses also offer laundry services, internet connection and travel services. Some of the guest houses can also arrange for long-term guests (staying one week or more) to rent a private apartment. At US$20 to US$30 per day, an apartment is much better value than Ulaanbaatar's hotels, which are decent but overpriced. Comfortable and clean, guest house and apartment rooms usually have hot water and satellite TV, and maybe even English-speaking staff members.

Dorm beds at Ulaanbaatar guest houses start as low as US$3 (T3450), private rooms around US$10. You will be hard-pressed to find a double room at a midrange hotel for less than US$40 (T46,000).

Ger camps typically charge US$20 to US$40 per person per night, including three hearty meals, but prices are negotiable, and they may drop considerably if you bring your own food. Tour groups (p284) and travel agencies (p282) in Ulaanbaatar can arrange visits.

ACTIVITIES

The countryside traversed by the Trans-Siberian rail routes is a veritable playground for outdoor (and some indoor) activities. Some of the options, from steaming in *banya* (hot baths) to diving and ice fishing in Lake Baikal, are covered, following.

Banya

A combination of dry sauna, steam bath, massage and plunges into ice-cold water, the *banya* is a weekly event that is a regular part of Russian life (see p67). All Russian cities will have *banya*, and they're generally worth visiting.

Cycling

Poor roads and manic drivers are two of the main hazards to cyclists in Russia. Otherwise you will find rural Russians quite fascinated and friendly towards long-distance riders. Just make certain you have a bike designed for the harshest of conditions and that you carry plenty of spare parts.

Cycling is a practical means of transport, as well as an entertaining way to explore Běijīng. The neighbourhoods and *hutong* (narrow alleyways) seem to have been built with bicycles in mind, as they are the only vehicles that can fit down some of them.

In Ulaanbaatar, cycling is more enjoyable (and safer) outside the city.

Russian agencies offering organised bike tours:

Ekaterinburg Guide Center (☎ 359 3708; www .ekaterinburgguide.com; Eremina 10, Yekaterinburg) See p181 for more details.

Skatprokat (Map p110; ☎ 717 6836; www.skatprokat .ru; Goncharnaya ul 7, St Petersburg; rental per day R500; ☒ 24hr; Ⓜ Ploshchad Vosstaniya)

Team Gorky (☎ 465 1999; www.teamgorky.ru; ul 40 let Oktyabrya 1a, Nizhny Novgorod) See p166.

Diving

Fancy diving in Lake Baikal or in the seas around Russia? Such specialist trips can be arranged through the following:

Aqua-Eco (Akva-Eko; ☎ 3952-334 290; www.aquaeco .eu.org; ul K Libknekhta 12, Irkutsk)

BaikalExplorer (☎ 3952-357 199; www.baikalex.com)

Diveworldwide (☎ in the UK 0845-130 6980; www .diveworldwide.com)

RuDive (Map pp136-7; ☎ 495-005 7799; www.dive.ru /pages/page/show_lang/25.en.htm; Serpukhovsky val 6, Moscow; Ⓜ Tulskaya) Group of dive companies with the Diving Club and School of Moscow State University at its core. It offers trips in the White and Barents Seas and the Sea of Japan, including ice diving off the liveaboard boat *Kartesh* (www.barentssea.ru/index/en.htm).

SVAL (www.svaldiving.ru; ul Fridrikha Engelsa 33, Irkutsk)

Fishing

Siberia and the Russian Far East is an angler's paradise with rivers swollen with grayling and various species of salmon. Organised fishing trips, however, can be heart-stoppingly expensive. While it is possible to go it alone, most regions have severe restrictions on fishing. Travel agencies in Irkutsk (p214), Ulan-Ude (p235), Khabarovsk (p245) and Vladivostok (p251) can arrange fishing (including ice fishing) trips in their regions. When Lake Baikal is frozen you can drive across the lake from baikalsk and go ice fishing.

Hiking

The best place for trekking along the Trans-Siberian route is around Lake Baikal, with the most adventurous options being at the northern end of the lake. There's even a project to create a hiking trail around the entire lake: see p224 for details.

Many of the towns that lie along the Baikal-Amur Mainline (Baikalo-Amurskaya

---

BOOK YOUR STAY ONLINE

For more accommodation reviews and recommendations by Lonely Planet authors, check out the online booking service at www.lonelyplanet.com/hotels. You'll find the true, insider low-down on the best places to stay. Reviews are thorough and independent. Best of all, you can book online.

HIKING SAFETY

Before embarking on a hike, consider the following:

■ Be sure you're healthy and feel comfortable about hiking for a sustained period. The nearest village in Russia, China or Mongolia can be vastly further away than in other countries.

■ Get the best information you can about the physical and environmental conditions along your intended route. 'Trails' in these countries are generally nominal ideas rather than marked footpaths so employing a guide is very wise.

■ Be prepared for severe and sudden changes in the weather and terrain; always take warm and wet-weather gear.

■ Walk only in regions, and on trails, within your realm of experience.

■ Pack essential survival gear including emergency food rations and a leak-proof water bottle.

■ If you can, find a hiking companion. At the very least tell someone where you're going and refer to your compass frequently so you can find your way back.

■ Unless you're planning a camping trip, start early so you can make it home before dark.

■ Allow more time than you anticipate.

■ Consider renting, or even buying (then later reselling), a pack horse, especially in southern Siberia where this is fairly inexpensive.

Magistral, or BAM) are good bases for heading out into the wilds and further afield. Krasnoyarsk's Stolby Nature Reserve (p207) is a striking landscape in which you can easily organise a day's hike. The hills and islands around Vladivostok also provide a full range of trekking options.

Both China and Mongolia offer excellent opportunities for hiking within day trips of the capitals. The most popular (and deservedly so) locales for hikes near Běijīng are along the Great Wall (p319), with a wide variety in terms of levels of challenge and degree of remoteness.

Hiking destinations near Ulaanbaatar include Mandshir Khiid (p290), the Gorkhi-Terelj National Park (p292) and Tsetseegün Uul (p291).

Horse Riding

A visit to Mongolia is not complete without a ride on a horse. Ger camps at Terelj (p292) rent horses and can direct riders to trails with some spectacular scenery. Most travel agencies in Ulaanbaatar also organise more extensive treks.

Operators who can arrange horse riding in Russia:

Baikal Naran Tour (☎ 3012-215 097; baikalnarantour @mail.ru; room 105, Hotel Buryatiya, Ulan-Ude) See p235.
Hotel Tourist Complex (GDK; ☎ 49231-23 380; ul Korovniki 45, Suzdal) For more details, see p162.

Krasnov (☎ 3422-238 3520; www.uraltourism.ru; ul Borchaninova 4, Perm) See p172.
Ural Expeditions & Tours (☎ 343-356 5282; http://welcome-ural.ru; ul Posadskaya 23, Yekaterinburg) See p181.

River Trips & Rafting

River trips are offered across Russia from May to October, with cruises along the Volga being particularly popular. It's possible to sail between St Petersburg and Kazan, with stops at Moscow and Nizhny Novgorod en route; see p146 for details of agents in Moscow offering tickets. Shorter trips are also available from these centres.

Other river trips include excursions along the Irtysh between Omsk and Tobolsk (p192), along the Yenisey from Krasnoyarsk (p211) and on the Amur from Khabarovsk (p249). And, of course, there are also the sailings down the Angara River from Irkutsk to Lake Baikal (p218).

For those looking for a bit more adventure on the water, rafting trips can be organised out of Nizhny Novgorod, Yekaterinburg, Novosibirsk (for the Altai region of southern Siberia), and Vladivostok.

Winter Sports

With all that snow could you really pass up the chance to indulge in some winter sports while crossing Siberia? Possibilities include cross-country skiing, skating, troika rides –

even dog sledding; see p220. Lake Baikal is a particularly spectacular place to visit in winter: at Baikalsk there's a ski resort and you can go ice fishing.

BUSINESS HOURS

Usual business hours are listed inside the front cover. Exceptions to this have been noted in individual listings in this book.

Russia

Government offices open from 9am or 10am to 5pm or 6pm weekdays. In major cities 24-hour shops and kiosks selling food and drink are common. Restaurants typically open from noon to midnight except for a break between afternoon and evening meals.

Museum hours are not uniform. They close one day a week and there will be one extra 'sanitary' day per month when the facility is closed for cleaning.

China & Mongolia

Government offices and businesses operate on a five-day work week, generally from 9am to 5pm, often closing for lunch between noon and 2pm. Shops and museums are usually open on weekends, and may be closed instead for one or two days midweek. Some branches of the Bank of China may be open on the weekend.

In Ulaanbaatar, however, the banks usually open from 9am to 7pm weekdays, and there are several offering 24-hour banking. Many museums and tourist attractions have shorter hours and more days off in winter.

CHILDREN

Travelling in Russia, China or Mongolia with children can be a breeze as long as you come well prepared with the right attitudes, equipment and patience.

Practicalities

Baby-changing rooms are not common in any of the three countries and you definitely wouldn't want to use many public toilets yourself, let alone change your baby's nappy in them. Nappies, powdered milk and baby food are widely available except in rural areas.

Finding English-language kids' publications will be a challenge, although there's no shortage of toy shops.

Lonely Planet's *Travel with Children* contains useful advice on how to cope with kids

---

> **CHILDREN'S RAILWAYS**
>
> The importance of the railways to Russia is evidenced by the number of Children's Railways scattered across the country and the former states of the Soviet Union. They have actual working trains that are accurate small-scale replicas of the bigger ones. Children take part in all of the activities from ticket sales to being engineers; it's all in Russian, but it could also be interesting to watch and you could arrange for a guide to assist you with translations. The website **Children's Railways** (http://railways.id.ru/english/index.html) gives details of the parks. There's also one in Hāěrbin (Harbin; p301).

---

on the road and what to bring to make things go more smoothly.

Sights & Activities

In Moscow and St Petersburg there are the old stand-bys of the zoo, various parks and the circus, but elsewhere, diversions are more problematic. On trains, children are likely to find playmates of their own age, but as many distractions such as toys and books as you can manage would be wise. Consider using the trip as an opportunity to teach children about the region's history and geography.

Běijīng's historical and architectural masterpieces might draw yawns from the kids. That is, only until they spot the toboggans at the Great Wall at Mùtiányù (p320) and the flying saucer boats at Beihai Park (p311). Other favourite spots for children in Běijīng include **Ritan Park** (Ritan Lu; admission adult Y1; ☺ 6am-9pm; Ⓜ Chaoyangmen) and the **Beijing Zoo & Beijing Aquarium** (Zoo ☎ 6831 5131; 137 Xizhimenwai Dajie; admission winter/summer Y10/15, pandas extra Y5; automatic guide Y40; ☺ winter/summer 7.30am-5pm/7.30am-6pm; Aquarium ☎ 6217 6655; adult/child Y100/50; ☺ 9am-6pm/9am-10pm winter/summer). Hāěrbīn (Harbin) also has the Siberian Tiger Park (p300).

Unfortunately Ulaanbaatar does not cater so much to visiting children, although the dinosaur exhibit at the Museum of Natural History (p284) should certainly capture their imaginations. Mongolian food may be difficult to stomach whatever your age, but kids are sure to get a thrill from camping (at least for a couple of nights) and meeting up with local wildlife such as yaks, camels and horses.

DIRECTORY

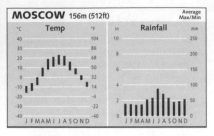

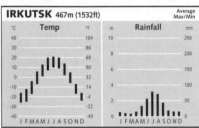

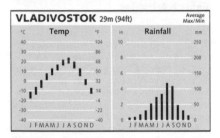

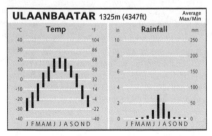

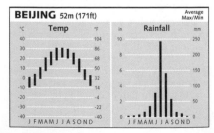

CLIMATE CHARTS

See p22 and p305 for advice on the best times to visit the regions covered by the Trans-Siberian Railway.

CUSTOMS

Russia

Customs controls in Russia are relatively relaxed these days. Searches beyond the perfunctory are quite rare. This said clearing customs, especially when you leave Russia by a land border, can be lengthy. Apart from the usual restrictions, bringing in and out large amounts of cash is limited, although the amount at which you have to go through the red channel (ie what you *have* to change to roubles) changes frequently. At the time of writing visitors are allowed to bring in and take out under US$3000 (or equivalent) in currency, and goods in value of under R65,000 and weighing less than 50kg, without making a customs declaration.

On entering Russia you might be given a customs declaration (*deklaratsia*) on which you should list any currency you are carrying as well as any items of worth. Make sure you list any mobile phones, cameras and laptops to avoid any potential problems on leaving Russia.

It's best if you can get your customs declaration stamped on entry (to do so go through the red lane at the bigger airports) and then simply show the same declaration when you exit Russia. However, sometimes customs points are totally unmanned, so this is not always possible. The system seems to be in total flux, with officials usually happy for you to fill out declarations on leaving the country, if necessary.

If you plan to export anything vaguely 'arty' – manuscripts, instruments, coins, jewellery, antiques, antiquarian books – it must be assessed by the **Committee for Culture** Moscow (Map pp136-7; ☎ 495-244 7675; ul Arbat 53; M Smolenskaya); St Petersburg (Map p110; ☎ 812-311 5196; Malaya Morskaya ul 17; M Nevsky Prospekt). The bureaucrats will issue a receipt for tax paid (usually 100% of the purchase price; bring your sales docket), to be presented to customs on your way out. If you buy something large, a photograph is usually fine for assessment purposes.

China

Chinese customs generally pay tourists little attention. There are no restrictions on foreign currency, but you should declare any cash exceeding US$5000 (or its equivalent in another currency).

Objects considered to be antiques require a certificate and red seal to clear customs. To get these, your antiques must be inspected by the **Relics Bureau** (Wénwù Jiàndìng; ☎ 010-6401 4608, no English spoken). Basically anything made before 1949 is considered an antique and needs a certificate, and if it was made before 1795 it cannot legally be taken out of the country.

Mongolia

Again, customs procedures are fairly straightforward and the main issue for the foreign traveller is the export of antiques. For any antiques you must have a receipt and customs certificate from the place you bought them; most reliable shops in Ulaanbaatar can provide this. If you don't get one of these you'll need to get one from the **Centre of Cultural Heritage** (☎ 011-312 735, 323 747) in the Palace of Culture in Ulaanbaatar. You'll need to fill in a form giving your passport number, details of where the antique was purchased and two photos of the antique itself. If you have anything that even *looks* old, it is a good idea to get a document to indicate that it is not an antique. That goes for Buddha images and statues as well.

DANGERS & ANNOYANCES

Russia, China and Mongolia are generally safe countries and crime against foreigners is rare. Pickpocketing is probably the biggest threat for the traveller, especially in crowded places such as public transport, markets and tourist attractions. The risk is greatly reduced if you keep valuables in money belts or under a layer of clothes. Hotels are generally quite safe, but leaving valuables lying around your room would be tempting providence. Always take precautions at youth hostels and guest houses, where other travellers may be trying to subsidise their journeys.

In general, Moscow's and St Petersburg's streets are about as safe, or as dangerous, as those of New York or London and, with the possible exception of Irkutsk (where some muggings have been reported), you're highly unlikely to suffer any problems in Siberia or the Russian Far East.

The key is to be neither paranoid nor carefree. Use common sense and do what you can to try to fit in with locals rather than stick out as a tourist.

On the whole the trains are reasonably safe, but it always pays to take simple precautions with your luggage. If you've got the compartment to yourself, ask the *provodnitsa* (female carriage attendant) to lock it when you leave for the restaurant car or get out at the station platforms.

Queuing is basically nonexistent in China and Mongolia and there are very specific rules for it in Russia. In most cases, neither being polite nor getting angry will help. If you have the head for it, sharpen your elbows, learn a few scowling phrases in the appropriate languages, and plough headfirst through the throng. Good luck.

Spitting is one of the banes of modern China. Campaigns to stamp it out have been partially successful in major urban centres – there is less public hawking of phlegm in Běijīng these days, but it still happens and you'll certainly see plenty of spitting in the countryside.

Mosquitoes are the great bane of summer throughout the region. Mostly, they're an annoyance, but in rural areas of Siberia they can be a grave health threat. For some precautions to take against them, see p366.

Although the situation is constantly improving, plumbing is at best erratic and at worst atrocious in all three countries.

Scams

In Russia, be very wary of officials, such as police (or people posing as police), asking to see your papers or tickets at train stations – there's a fair chance they are on the lookout for a bribe and will try to find anything wrong with your documents, or basically hold them for a ransom. The only course of action is to remain calm, polite and stand your ground. Try to enlist the help of a passer-by to translate for you (or at least witness what is going on).

Another scam involves the use of devices in ATMs that read credit card and PIN details when you withdraw money from the machines, enabling accounts to be accessed and additional funds withdrawn. In general, it is safest to use ATMs in carefully guarded public places such as major hotels and restaurants.

Always be alert when changing money, particularly in China where you should also keep an eye out for counterfeit bills.

Racism & Discrimination

Sadly, racism is a problem in Russia. It's a good idea to be vigilant on the streets around Hitler's birthday (20 April), when bands of right-wing thugs have been known to roam around spoiling for a fight with anyone who doesn't look Russian. Frightening reports of racial violence appear from time to time in the media, and it's a sure thing that if you are non-Caucasian you'll be targeted with suspicion by many (the police, in particular).

DISCOUNT CARDS

Full-time students and people aged under 26 can sometimes (but not always) get a substantial discount on admissions – flash your student card or International Student Identity Card (ISIC) before paying. If you're not a student but are under 26, ask a student agency at home for an ISIC Youth Card.

Senior citizens also *might* get a discount, but no promises: carry your pension card or passport anyway.

EMBASSIES & CONSULATES
Embassies & Consulates Abroad

Check these websites for contact details.

China www.fmprc.gov.cn/eng/and click on Missions Overseas.

Mongolia www.mongolianconsulate.com.au/mongolia/embassies.shtml

Russia www.russianembassy.net

Foreign Embassies & Consulates along the Route

Generally speaking, embassies won't be much help if you are in some kind of trouble and are the one at fault. Remember: you are bound by the local law and embassies will not be sympathetic if you end up in jail after committing a crime locally, even if such actions are legal in your own country.

In genuine emergencies you might get some assistance, but only if other channels have been exhausted. For example, if you have all your money and documents stolen, the embassy might assist with getting a new passport, but a loan for onward travel is out of the question.

If you will be travelling in these countries for a long period of time (say a month or over) and particularly if you're heading to remote locations, it's wise to register with your embassy. This can be done over the phone or by email.

RUSSIA
Irkutsk

Mongolia (☎ 3952-342 145; fax 342 143; ul Lapina 11; ⏰ 9.30am-noon, 2.30-5pm Mon, Tue, Thu & Fri) One month visa R1075, issued in two days.

Khabarovsk

China (☎ 4212-302 353, 302 432; Lenin Stadium 1) Visa applications taken from 10.30am to 1pm Monday, Wednesday and Friday. A visa can be arranged in a day for about R4200 or in a week for R2400.

Japan (☎ 4212-326 418; fax 327 212; ul Pushkina 38a)

Moscow

For a full list of embassies check http://guides.moscowtimes.ru/travel/detail.hhp?ID=13425.

Australia (Map p132; ☎ 495-956 6070; www.russia.embassy.gov.au; Podkolokolny per 10A/2; Ⓜ Kitay-Gorod)

Belarus (Map p132; ☎ 495-924 7031; www.embassybel.ru; Maroseyka ul 17/6, 101000; Ⓜ Kitay Gorod)

Canada (Map p136-7; ☎ 495-925 6000; www.dfait-maeci.gc.ca/missions/russia-russie/menu-eng.asp; Starokonyushenny per 23; Ⓜ Kropotkinskaya)

China (☎ 495-938-2006, consular 499-143 1540; www.ru.china-embassy.org; ul Druzhby 6; Ⓜ Universitet)

Finland (Map p136-7; ☎ 495-787 4174; www.finland.org.ru; Kropotkinsky per 15/17; Ⓜ Park Kultury)

France (Map p136-7; ☎ 495-937 1500; www.amba france.ru; ul Bolshaya Yakimanka 45; Ⓜ Oktyabrskaya)

Germany Embassy (☎ 495-937 9500; www.moskau.diplo.de; Mosfilmovskaya ul 56; Ⓜ Universitet, then take bus 119) Consular section (☎ 495-933 4311; Leninsky pr 95A; Ⓜ Prospekt Vernadskogo, then bus 616 or 153)

Ireland (Map p132; ☎ 495-937 5911; www.embassyof ireland.ru; Grokholsky per 5; Ⓜ Prospekt Mira)

Japan (Map p132; ☎ 495-229 2550; www.ru.emb-japan.go.jp; Grokholsky per 27; Ⓜ Arbatskaya)

Mongolia (Map pp124-5; ☎ 495-290 6792; mongolia@online.ru; Borisoglebskaya per 11; Ⓜ Arbatskaya) Consular Section (Map pp124-5; Spasopeskovsky per 7/1; Ⓜ Smolenskaya)

Netherlands (Map pp124-5; ☎ 495-797 2900; www.netherlands-embassy.ru; Kalashny per 6; Ⓜ Arbatskaya)

New Zealand (Map pp124-5; ☎ 495-956 3579; www.nzembassy.msk.ru; Povarskaya ul 44; Ⓜ Arbatskaya)

UK (Map pp124-5; ☎ 495-956 7200; www.britemb.msk.ru; Smolenskaya nab 10; Ⓜ Smolenskaya)

USA (Map pp124-5; ☎ 495-728 5000; www.moscow.us embassy.gov; Bol Devyatinsky per 8; Ⓜ Barrikadnaya)

Novosibirsk

Germany (☎ 383-223 1411; www.nowosibirsk.diplo.de; Krasny pr 28)

St Petersburg

Australia (Map p110; ☎ 812-315 1100; ul Italyanskaya 1; Ⓜ Nevsky Prospekt)

Belarus (Map pp106-7; ☎ 812-274 7212; ul Bonch-Bruevicha 3A; Ⓜ Chernyshevskaya)

China (Map pp106-7; ☎ 812-714 7670; nab kanala Griboedova 134; Ⓜ Sadovaya/Sennaya Ploshchad)

Finland (Map p110; ☎ 812-331 7600; Preobrazhenskaya pl 4; Ⓜ Chernyshevskaya)

France (Map p110; ☎ 812-332 2270; nab reki Moyki 15; Ⓜ Nevsky Prospekt)

Germany (Map pp106-7; ☎ 812-320 2400; Furshtatskaya ul 39; Ⓜ Chernyshevskaya)

Japan (Map p110; ☎ 814 1434; nab reki Moyki 29; Ⓜ Nevsky Prospekt)

UK (Map pp106-7; ☎ 812-320 3200; pl Proletarskoy Diktatury 5; Ⓜ Chernyshevskaya)

USA (Map pp106-7; ☎ 812-331 2600; ul Furshtatskaya 15; Ⓜ Chernyshevskaya)

Ulan-Ude

Mongolia (☎ 3012-211 078; ul Profsovuznaya 6; ♥ Mon, Wed & Fri)

Vladivostok

Australia (☎ 4232-427 464; ul Krasnogo Znameni 42)

China (☎ 4232-495 037; Hotel Gavan, ul Krygina 3) Visa applications are accepted 9am to 12.30pm Monday, Wednesday and Friday. A visa costs about US$125 and takes three to seven days.

Japan (☎ 4232-267 481, 267 502; ul Verkhneportovaya 46)

Korea (☎ 4232-402 222; ul Pologaya 19)

UK (☎ 4232-410 516; ul Svetlanskaya 5)

USA (☎ 4232-300 070; ul Pushkinskaya 32)

Yekaterinburg

Germany (☎ 343-359 6399; ul Kuybysheva 44)

UK (☎ 343-379 4931; www.britaininrussia.ru; ul Gogolya 15)

USA (☎ 343-379 4691; www.uscgyekat.ur.ru; ul Gogolya 15)

CHINA

Běijīng

There are two main embassy compounds in Běijīng: Jianguomenwai and Sanlitun. Embassies are open from 9am to noon and 1.30pm to 4pm Monday to Friday, but visa departments are usually only open in the morning.

The following embassies are in the Jianguomenwai area:

Ireland (☎ 010-6532 5486; fax 6532 2168; 3 Ritan Donglu)

Japan (☎ 010-6532 2361; fax 6532 2139; 7 Ritan Lu)

Mongolia (☎ 010-6532 1203; fax 6532 5045; 2 Xiushui Beijie)

New Zealand (☎ 010-6532 2731; fax 6532 4317; 1 Ritan Dong Erjie)

UK (☎ 010-5192 4000; fax 6532 1937; 11 Guanghua Lu)

USA (☎ 010-6532 3831; fax 6532 3431; 3 Xiushui Beijie)

The Sanlitun compound is home to the following:

Australia (☎ 010-5140 4111; www.austemb.org.cn; 21 Dongzhimenwai Dajie)

Canada (☎ 010-6532 3536; fax 6532 4072; 19 Dongzhimenwai Dajie)

France (☎ 010-8532 8080; fax 6532 4757; 3 Sanlitun Dong Sanjie)

Germany (☎ 010-8532 9000; fax 6532 5336; 17 Dongzhimenwai Dajie)

Netherlands (☎ 010-8532 0200; fax 6532 4689; 4 Liangmahe Nanlu)

Russia (☎ 010-6532 1381; fax 6532 4853; 4 Dongzhimen Beizhongjie) West of the Sanlitun Compound in a separate compound.

Hohhot

Mongolia (☎ 0471-492 3819; Unit 1, Bldg 5, Wulan Residential Area; ♥ 8.30am-12.30pm Mon, Tue & Thu) It's possible to get a one-month visa here in a week (Y236) or there's an express 24-hour service for Y446; you'll need a letter of invitation from a travel agency to get one.

MONGOLIA

Ulaanbaatar

Canada (☎ 328 285; fax 328 289; canada@mongolnet .mn; Bodicom Tower, 7th fl, Sükhbaataryn Gudamj)

China (☎ 320 955; fax 311 943; Zaluuchuudyn Örgön Chölöö 5) The consular section is actually on adjacent Baga Toiruu.

France (☎ 324 519; www.ambafrance-mn.org in French; Peace Ave 3)

Germany (☎ 323 325; fax 312 118; germanemb_ulan bator@mongol.net; Negdsen Undestnii Gudamj 7)

Japan (☎ 320 777, 313 332; www.mn.emb-japan.go.jp; Olympiin Gudamj 6)

Russia (☎ 327 191, 312 851; fax 327 018; www.mongolia .mid.ru; Peace Ave A6)

UK (☎ 458 133; fax 458 036; britemb@mongol.net; Peace Ave 30)

USA (☎ 329 095; http://ulaanbaatar.usembassy.gov; Ikh Toiruu 59/1)

FESTIVALS & EVENTS

For our selection of the top 10 festivals and events to attend along the Trans-Siberian routes, see p24.

January & February

Russian Orthodox Christmas (Rozhdestvo; 7 January) Begins with midnight church services.

Chinese New Year/Spring Festival This is China's biggest holiday and all transport and hotels are booked solid. To make matters worse, many hotels close down at this time and prices rise steeply. If you're in China at this time, book your room in advance and sit tight until the chaos is over. The Chinese New Year will fall on 14 February 2010, 3 February 2011 and 23 January 2012.

Lantern Festival (Yuánxiāo Jié; 元宵节) It's not a public holiday, but it is very colourful. Children make (or buy) paper lanterns and walk around the streets in the evening holding them. It falls on the 15th day of the first moon, and will be celebrated on 28 February 2010, 17 February 2011 and 6 February 2012.

March & April

Pancake Week (Maslenitsa) Folk shows and games such as sleding and snowball-throwing in Russia celebrate the end of winter, with lots of pancake-eating before Lent (pancakes were a pagan symbol of the sun). It is held late February and/or early March.

Women's Day (8 March) Celebrated in Russia like Valentines Day with women getting presents of flowers, chocolates and the like and a chance to rest up.

Camel Polo Winter Festival (mid-March) Quirky Ulaanbaatar festival.

Guanyin's Birthday The birthday of Guanyin, the Goddess of Mercy, is a fine time to visit China's Buddhist temples, many of which have halls dedicated to the divinity. It's the 19th day of the second moon and falls on 3 April 2010 and 23 March 2011.

Easter (Paskha) The main festival of the Orthodox Church year, in March or April. Easter Sunday begins with celebratory midnight services. Afterwards, people eat *kulichy* (dome-shaped cakes) and *paskha* (curd cakes), and may exchange painted wooden Easter eggs. The devout deny themselves meat, milk, alcohol and sex during Lent's 40-day pre-Easter fasting period.

May

Victory Day (9 May) A public holiday celebrating the end of WWII, or what Russians call the Great Patriotic War. Big military parades are held in Moscow and St Petersburg that are well worth attending.

Graduates Day (traditionally 25 May) A day for those finishing school in Russia, who parade about their home towns in traditional student garb.

June, July & August

Sabantuy (mid-June) Stop in Kazan to enjoy this major Tatarstan summer festival.

Maitreya Buddha Festival (June) Held at Ivolginsky *datsan* (monastery) near Ulan-Ude.

Buryatiya Folk Festival (Surkharban; June) Celebrated at the hippodrome near the ethnographic museum in Ulan-Ude; highlights include horse riding and wrestling.

Naadam (11 & 12 July) Mongolia's biggest event; see p288.

Kamwa Festival (www.kamwa.ru; late July, early August) Held in Perm and Khokhlovka this festival combines ancient ethno-Ugric traditions and modern art, music and fashion.

September & October

Birthday of Confucius The great sage has his birthday on 28 September. This is an interesting time to visit Běijīng's Confucian Temple (p311).

Mid-Autumn Festival Also known as the Moon Festival; this is the time to gaze at the moon and eat tasty *yuè bǐng* (moon cakes); it's also a traditional holiday for lovers. The festival takes place on the 15th day of the eighth moon, and will be celebrated on 3 October 2009, 22 September 2010 and 12 September 2011.

November

National Reconciliation Day (7 November) The old Great October Socialist Revolution Anniversary in Russia – still a big day for Communist Party marches. Otherwise, monarchists mourn and others drink while closing down their *dachas* for winter.

December

Russian Winter Festival (late December–January) Features tourist-oriented troika rides and folklore performances at Irkutsk and Moscow.

Sylvester and New Year (31 December & 1 January) The main winter and gift-giving festival in Russia, when gifts are put under the *yolka* (traditional fir tree). See out the old year with vodka and welcome in the new one with champagne while listening to the Kremlin chimes on TV.

FOOD

Dining options throughout Russia have improved immeasurably over recent years. It's only in small villages and remotes parts of the country where you'll struggle to find something decent to eat. In general for a budget meal you'll be looking at R300 or less, with a midrange place costing anything up to R1500 and top-end places over R1500.

There's a fantastic array of food available in China, particularly in Běijīng. Even in the capital it's still possible to dine at budget eateries for under Y30; midrange dining options will cost between Y30 and Y80, and top-end choices over Y80.

Mongolia isn't going to get many awards for its culinary offerings, although Ulaanbaatar has some surprisingly good places to eat. Expect main dishes to cost T800 to T1500 in budget joints, T2000 to T3000 in midrange places and T4000 to T8000 in most top-end restaurants.

For more on food and drink in all three countries, see p77.

GAY & LESBIAN TRAVELLERS
Russia

Young Russian urban sophisticates couldn't give a hoot who you love, but this is sadly not true for the broader population. Not everyone goes as far as Moscow's mayor Yury Luzhkov who sided with the ultraconservative protestors who broke up a gay parade in the capital in 2008, calling such events 'satanical', but in general this is a conservative country and being gay is frowned upon.

There are active gay and lesbian scenes in both Moscow and St Petersburg, and newspapers such as the *Moscow Times* and *St Petersburg Times* feature articles and listings on gay and lesbian issues, clubs, bars and events (but don't expect anything nearly as prominent as you may find in other major world centres). Away from these two major cities, the gay scene tends to be pretty much underground.

For a fine overview, visit **Gay.ru** (http://english .gay.ru) with up-to-date information, good links and a resource putting you in touch with personal guides for Moscow and St Petersburg. It's also involved in publishing the gay magazine *Kvir*. St Petersburg's **Krilija** (Wings; ☎ 812-312 3180; www.krilija.sp.ru) is Russia's oldest officially registered gay and lesbian community organisation.

China

In China, greater tolerance of homosexuality exists in the big cities than in the more conservative countryside. Still, even in urban China it's not recommended that gays and lesbians be too open about their sexual orientation in public, even though you will see Chinese same-sex friends holding hands or putting their arms around each other. The situation is slowly improving, but the police periodically crack down on gay meeting places. Check out www.utopia-asia.com/tipschin.htm for loads of tips on travelling in China, and a complete listing of gay bars nationwide.

Mongolia

Mongolia is not a gay-friendly place, nor one to test local attitudes towards homosexuality. Ulaanbaatar has a small gay community that will occasionally convene at a tolerant restaurant or bar, but it moves around every few months, so you'll need to quietly tap into the scene and ask. Insight can be found at www .globalgayz.com/g-mongolia.html and travel info at www.geocities.com/gaytomongolia/.

HOLIDAYS
Russia

New Year's Day 1 January
Russian Orthodox Christmas Day 7 January
Defender of the Fatherland Day 23 February
International Women's Day 8 March
International Labour Day/Spring Festival 1 May
Victory Day (1945) 9 May
Russian Independence Day (when the Russian republic of the USSR proclaimed its sovereignty in 1991) 12 June
Unity Day 4 November

Many businesses are closed from 1 to 7 January. Another widely celebrated holiday is Easter Monday.

China

New Year's Day 1 January
Chinese New Year (Spring Festival) Usually February
International Women's Day 8 March
International Labour Day 1 May
Youth Day 4 May
International Children's Day 1 June
Birthday of the Chinese Communist Party 1 July
Anniversary of the Founding of the People's Liberation Army 1 August
National Day 1 October

The 1 May holiday kicks off a three-day holiday, while National Day marks a week-long holiday from 1 October, and the Chinese New Year is also a week-long holiday for many. It's not a great idea to arrive in China or go travelling during these holidays as things tend to grind to a halt. Hotel prices in China rapidly shoot up during these holiday periods.

Mongolia

Shin Jil (New Year's Day) 1 January
Constitution Day 13 January; the adoption of the 1992 constitution
Tsagaan Sar (Lunar New Year) January/February; a three-day holiday celebrating the Mongolian New Year
Women's Day 8 March
Mother & Children's Day 1 June; a great time to visit parks
National Day Celebrations (Naadam Festival) 11 and 12 July
Mongolian Republic Day 26 November

DIRECTORY

However, Constitution Day, Women's Day and Mongolian Republic Day are generally normal working days.

INSURANCE

It's wise to take out travel insurance to cover theft, loss and medical problems. There are many policies available, so check the small print for things such as ambulance cover or an emergency flight home. For more details, see p363. Worldwide travel insurance is available at www.lonelyplanet.com/travel_services. You can buy, extend and claim online any time – even if you're already on the road.

INTERNET ACCESS

For some recommended websites for background information, see p33.

Most hotels in big cities along the Trans-Siberian routes have in-room broadband or wi-fi connections. Throughout this book the internet icon is used in hotel, restaurant, cafe or bar reviews to indicate terminals where you can get online.

Russia

Major cities aside, we found internet cafes have become less common. The best place to start is the main post office or telephone office, as they often have the cheapest rates (typically around R30 to R40 an hour), although they cannot be guaranteed to have a working system!

Wireless internet (wi-fi) is becoming increasingly common, particularly in Moscow and St Petersburg and other large cities, where many bars, cafes, restaurants and hotels have it. The Russian-language website www.intel.com/cd/products/services/emea/rus/247127.htm lists wi-fi hotspots in the major cities.

China

Despite massive usage, China's clumsy tango with the internet continues to raise eyebrows abroad. The number of internet cafe licences is strictly controlled, users need to show ID before going online (in the big cities) and periodic police raids keep surfers twitchy as records are kept of what was viewed by whom. Some internet cafes even digitally photograph you before you are allowed online. Rules are rigorously enforced in Běijīng, but in small towns you are rarely asked for ID.

Up to 10% of websites are traditionally inaccessible in China due to draconian censorship, but this was dramatically eased for the Olympic Games. But for checking hotmail, reading foreign newspapers online and chatting with friends, China's internet cafes are generally trouble free, even though access to some newspapers can suddenly vanish. Video-sharing sights have also come under control.

When looking for an internet cafe, look for the characters 网吧. Rates should be around Y2 to Y4 per hour for a standard, no-frills outlet, but comfier and smarter options naturally charge more (up to Y20 per hour). Deposits of Y10 are sometimes required or you may be asked for ID. Slow connections are frequent, especially on congested sites.

Internet cafes may operate a no-smoking policy, but it may not deter your neighbour from puffing away like a fiend. As most internet cafes are crowded with teenagers playing games, things can get noisy and weekends can be awesomely crowded.

Youth hostels and other backpacker accommodation options should have internet access in common areas; if not gratis, rates will be around Y5 per hour.

Mongolia

You'll find internet cafes on nearly every street in downtown Ulaanbaatar. Expect to pay between T400 to T800 per hour for online access, double or triple that for hotel business centres.

Wi-fi access is available at some spots in Ulaanbaatar. If you are staying in an apartment or otherwise have access to a phone line, you can buy a pre-paid card that gives you a dial-up connection. A 10-hour internet card costs T4000 and a 30-hour card costs T6000, but remember that you will also be charged a per-minute fee by the phone company while you are logged on, usually around T15 per minute. The cards can be bought at exchange kiosks in the State Department Store.

LAUNDRY

While self-service laundries are very rare beasts, you can get laundry done in most hotels: ask the floor attendant. In Russia it usually takes at least a day and costs around R700 a load (although we've been stung for much more so check before you hand over your washing). If you plan on doing it yourself, it's a good idea to bring along a universal sink plug as many cheap hotels don't have sinks with plugs.

There are several laundries scattered around Ulaanbaatar, where a load will cost around T4000.

LEGAL MATTERS

In Russia, and to a lesser extent in Mongolia, it's generally best to avoid contact with the police. It's not uncommon for them to bolster their puny incomes by extracting sham 'fines' from the unaware; you always have the right to insist to be taken to a police station (we don't recommend this) or that the 'fine' be paid the legal way through Sberbank. If you do need police assistance (ie you've been the victim of a robbery or an assault) go to a station with a Russian for both language and moral support. You will have to be persistent and patient, too.

If you are arrested, the police in all three countries are obliged to inform your embassy or consulate immediately and allow you to communicate with it without delay. Although you can insist on seeing an embassy or consular official straight away, you can't count on the rules being followed, so be polite and respectful towards officials and hopefully things will go far more smoothly for you. In Russian, the phrase 'I'd like to call my embassy' is *'Pozhaluysta, ya khotel by pozvonit v posolstvo moyey strany'.*

MAPS

Maps of all the major cities covered in this guide are on sale in each city, although in general you'll be best off buying regional city and area maps of Russia in Moscow or St Petersburg.

Good overseas sources for maps:

Australia
Mapland (☎ 03-9670 4383; www.mapland.com.au; 372 Little Bourke St, Melbourne, Vic)
Travel Bookshop (☎ 02-9261 8200; Shop 3, 175 Liverpool St, Sydney, NSW)

Europe
Librairie Ulysse (☎ 01 43 25 17 35; www.ulysse.fr, in French; 26 rue Saint Louis en L'Isle, 75004, Paris, France)
Stanfords Map Centre (☎ 020-7836 1321; www.stanfords.co.uk; 12-14 Long Acre, London, UK)

USA
Map Link (☎ 1800 627 7768; www.maplink.com; Unit 5, 30 S La Patera Lane, Santa Barbara, CA)

MONEY

Consult the inside front cover for a table of exchange rates. For information on costs, see p28.

The unit of Russian currency is the rouble (*ru*-bl), which is written as 'рубль' or abbreviated as 'ру' or 'р'. The rouble is made up of 100 kopecks. Kopecks come in coin denominations of one (rarely seen), five, 10 and 50. Also issued in coins, roubles come in amounts of one, two and five, with banknotes in values of 10, 50, 100, 500, 1000 and 5000 roubles.

In Russia, it is illegal to make purchases in any currency other than roubles. When you run into prices quoted in dollars (or the pseudonym 'units', often written as 'ye' – the abbreviation for *uslovnye yedenitsy,* conventional units) or euros in expensive restaurants and hotels, you will still be presented with a final bill in roubles. In this guide we list whichever currency is quoted on the ground.

The Chinese currency is the Renminbi (RMB), or 'People's Money'. Formally the basic unit of RMB is the yuán, which is divided into 10 *jiǎo*, which is again divided into 10 *fēn*. Colloquially, the yuán is referred to as *kuài* and *jiǎo* as *máo*. The *fēn* has so little value these days that it is rarely used.

The Bank of China issues RMB bills in denominations of one, two, five, 10, 20, 50 and 100 yuán. Coins come in denominations of one yuán, five *jiǎo*, one *jiǎo* and five *fēn*. Paper versions of the coins remain in circulation.

RUSSIAN STREET NAMES

We use the Russian names of all streets and squares in this book to help you when deciphering Cyrillic signs and asking locals the way. To save space the following abbreviations are used:

- bul – bulvar (бульвар) – boulevard
- nab – naberezhnaya (набережная) – embankment
- per – pereulok (переулок) – side street
- pl – ploshchad (площадь) – square
- pr – prospekt (проспект) – avenue
- ul – ulitsa (улица) – street
- sh – shosse (шоссе) – road/highway

DIRECTORY

The Mongolian unit of currency is the tö-grög (T), which comes in notes of T5, T10, T20, T50, T100, T500, T1000, T5000, T10,000 and T20,000 (T1 notes are basically souvenirs). There are also T50 and T100 coins.

ATMs

Plastic is the way to go with ATMs, linked to international networks such as Amex, Cirrus, MasterCard and Visa, common right across Russia – look for signs that say *bankomat* (БАНКОМАТ). As well as roubles, some ATMs dispense US dollars, too.

It's also pretty easy to find ATMs accepting overseas cards in Běijīng and Hāěrbīn (Harbin). In Ulaanbaatar the Trade and Development Bank's ATMs accept Visa and MasterCard.

If you are going to rely on ATMs, make certain you have a few days' supply of cash at hand in case you can't find a machine to accept your card.

Cash

There are no official facilities for exchanging money on the train itself (it's possible some of the *provodnitsas* or the restaurant staff will accept foreign cash but at very poor exchange rates – don't count on this), so you'll need to stock up at your major stops, where you should find ATMs. There are usually exchange places at border-town train stations.

You'll usually get the best exchange rates for US dollars, though euros are increasingly widely accepted and in rare cases get even better rates in bigger cities where there's a specialist bank. British pounds are sometimes accepted in big cities, but the exchange rates are not so good; other currencies incur abysmal rates if changed at all.

Any currency you bring should be in pristine condition: banks and exchange bureaus do not accept old, tatty bills with rips or tears. For US dollars make certain they are the new design, with the large offset portrait, and that they look and smell newly minted.

Credit Cards

Across Russia and China credit cards are becoming more accepted, but don't rely on them outside of the major cities. Most sizable cities have banks or exchange bureaus that will give you a cash advance on your credit card, but be prepared for paperwork in the local language.

In Mongolia, credit cards are often accepted at top-end hotels, the expensive souvenir shops, airline offices and travel agencies, but usually with an additional 3% charge. The Trade and Development Bank in Ulaanbaatar can arrange a US-dollar cash advance on your Visa, MasterCard and American Express cards. Plastic is not accepted outside the capital, though.

Moneychangers

There's no advantage to using moneychangers in either Russia or China, but in Mongolia they sometimes offer good rates for US dollars and are usually safe. However, the risks are obvious. Remember to change all your tögrög when leaving the country as it's worthless elsewhere.

Tipping

In Russia, tipping is common in upmarket restaurants – about 10% is good; elsewhere, 10% is also fine if service warrants it. Tip your guide, if you have one, a similar amount of their daily rate; a small gift is appropriate if service is especially good.

Tipping is neither required nor expected in China, except in the case of porters in upmarket hotels. In Mongolia, tipping is optional; if you round up the bill, then your server will be satisfied.

Travellers Cheques

These are worth taking if you are going to be getting off the train in large cities. The exchange rates might be more favourable than the rate for cash. However, you should always check whether there are any exchange fees incurred.

PHOTOGRAPHY

All major towns and cities will have several photographic shops to download digital snaps to CDs, buy memory cards and major brands of print film. Slide film is not widely sold so bring plenty of rolls with you. The same rare specialist shops that sell slide film will also have a smattering of camera gear by leading brands such as Nikon and Canon.

Camera batteries get sluggish in the cold, so carry your camera inside your coat and keep spare batteries warm in your pocket. For more professional tips on taking some decent photos, read Lonely Planet's *Travel Photography*, by Richard I'Anson.

Photographing People

As anywhere, use good judgement and discretion when taking photos of people. It's always better to ask first and if the person doesn't want to be photographed, respect their privacy; a lifetime living with the KGB may make older people uneasy about being photographed, although a genuine offer to send on a copy can loosen your subject up. Remember that many people will be touchy if you photograph 'embarrassments' such as drunks, run-down housing and other signs of social decay.

In Russian, 'May I take a photograph of you?' is *'Mozhno vas sfotografirovat?',* and in Mongolian it is *'Bi tany zurgiig avch bolokh uu?'.*

Restrictions

In all three countries (but especially in Russia), you should be particularly careful about taking photographs of stations, official-looking buildings and any type of military/security structure – if in doubt, don't snap! Travellers, including an author of this book, have been arrested for such innocent behaviour.

Some museums and galleries forbid flash pictures, some ban all photos and most will charge you extra to snap away. Some caretakers in historical buildings and churches charge mercilessly for the privilege of using a still or video camera.

POST

If there is a mail car attached to the train, there will be a slot in the side into which you can drop letters. However, there's no guarantee that your mail will reach its destination, so it's best to post things from cities along the way or in post boxes at the stations.

The major Russian cities, plus Běijīng and Ulaanbaatar, have international private courier firms such as **FedEx** (www.fedex.com) and **UPS** (www.up s.com).

Russia

Russia's main post offices are open 8am to 8pm or 9pm, with shorter hours on Saturday and Sunday; in big cities one office will possibly stay open 24 hours a day. Outward post is slow but fairly reliable. Airmail letters take two to three weeks from Moscow and St Petersburg to the UK, longer from other Russian cities, and three to four weeks to the USA or Australasia. To send a postcard or letter up to 20g anywhere in the world by air costs R19 or R16.10, respectively.

Incoming mail is unreliable and anything addressed to poste restante should be considered lost before it's sent. Should you decide to send mail to Russia or to receive it, note that addresses should be written in reverse order: Russia, postal code (if known), city, street address, name.

China

The Chinese postal system is efficient: airmail to Europe and North America takes about one week. It is possible to post your letters from most hotels, as well as at the post office. Packages, however, should be sent from the **International Post Office** (Guójì Yóudiànjú; Jianguomen Beidajie; ⊗ 8am-7pm Mon-Sat) in Běijīng. Officials there inspect all parcels, so don't wrap and seal them until after inspection.

Large post offices are generally open 9am to 5pm daily. Postcards to overseas destinations cost Y4.50. Airmail letters up to 20g cost Y5 to Y7 to all countries except Taiwan and Hong Kong and Macau (Y1.50). Domestic letters cost Y0.80 and postcards Y0.50.

Mongolia

The postal service is reliable but can often be *very* slow. Allow *at least* a couple of weeks for letters and postcards to arrive home from Mongolia. Foreign residents of Ulaanbaatar find it much faster to give letters (and cash to buy stamps) to other foreigners who are departing.

In most cases, you will have to post your letters from the post office. Postal rates are often relatively expensive, especially for parcels, for which there is only an 'airmail' rate – yet they often arrive months later (probably by sea). Normal-sized letters cost T700 and postcards T440 to all countries. A 1kg airmail parcel to the UK/USA will cost T14,000/18,000.

SHOPPING

See the destinations in the route chapters of this guide for suggestions on where to shop.

Apart from in tourist-orientated souvenir markets, bargaining is not the done thing in Russia. Even when it is expected, it will not be a protracted process as in parts of Asia. In China and Mongolia, in large shops and department stores where prices are clearly marked, there is usually no latitude for bargaining (but if you ask, the staff sometimes might be able to give you a small discount). Elsewhere bargaining is expected.

In all three countries the one important rule to follow is: be polite. Your goal should be to pay the local price, as opposed to the foreigners' price – if you can do that, you've done well.

Russia

The classic Russian souvenir is a *matryoshka* (set of wooden dolls stacked within dolls). Although often kitschy, they're a true folk art, and there are all manner of intricately painted designs available. A small, mass-produced set should cost just a couple of dollars, but the best examples may set you back as much as US$100. For this price you can also take along a family photo to Izmaylovsky Park in Moscow and come back the following week to collect your very own personalised *matryoshka* set.

Other items to look out for:

- *Palekh* – enamelled wooden boxes, each with an intricate scene painted in its lid
- *Khokhloma* ware – the gold, red and black wooden bowls, mugs and spoons from near Nizhny Novgorod (p163)
- *Gzhel* – blue-and-white ornamental china
- *Platok Pavlovo Posad* – the floral-designed 'Babushka scarf'
- *Yantar* – amber from the Baltic coast, though beware of fake stuff in some St Petersburg and Moscow outlets

Other ideas include paintings from the street; *plakat* (posters), both old Socialist exhortation and modern social commentary, from bookshops or specialist poster shops; and little Lenin busts at street stands and in tourist markets.

China

Although tourists are unlikely to find true antiques at bargain prices, China is still a great place to buy handmade arts and crafts and furniture. Even if the seller claims it is old, it is more likely a reproduction, but that does not mean that it is not a good buy. Most Chinese markets are chock-full of exquisite traditional furniture, iron teapots, bronze figures and Tibetan carpets, most of which are sold at prices considerably lower than in the West. Shoppers can get fantastic bargains on jewellery, especially pearls. Silk is high-quality and priced low compared to material you can buy in the West.

Mongolia

Mongolian crafts are made almost exclusively for tourist consumption, and they are expensive. Some potentially good buys are traditional Mongolian clothing and boots, landscape paintings and Mongolian games such as *khorol* (checkers) and *shagai* (dice). Cashmere sweaters are an important export item, but they are usually overpriced, especially for the limited selection. Traditional musical instruments can be a beautiful and unique memento of a trip.

TELEPHONE & FAX

City codes are listed in this book under the relevant section headings. In all three countries faxes can be sent from most post offices and upmarket hotels.

Russia

The country code for Russia is ☎ 7.

Local calls from homes and most hotels are free. To make a long-distance call from most phones first dial ☎ 8, wait for a second dial tone, then dial the city code etc. To make an international call dial ☎ 8, wait for a second dial tone, then dial 10, then the country code etc. Some phones are for local calls only and won't give you that second dial tone.

From mobile phones, just dial + followed by the country code to place an international call.

MOBILE PHONES

There are several major networks, all offering pay-as-you-go deals, including:

Beeline (www.beeline.ru/index.wbp)
Megafon (www.megafon.ru)
MTS (www.mts.ru)
Skylink (www.skylink.ru)

Reception is available right along the Trans-Siberian Railway and increasingly in rural areas. MTS probably has the widest network, but also the worst reputation for customer service. Our researchers found Beeline to be pretty reliable.

To call a mobile phone from a landline, the line must be enabled to make paid (ie nonlocal) calls. SIM and phone call-credit top-up cards, available at any mobile-phone shop and costing as little as R300, can be slot-

---

CHANGING TELEPHONE NUMBERS

Russian authorities have an annoying habit of frequently changing telephone numbers, particularly in cities. We've listed the correct phone number as at the time of research, but it's likely that some will change during the lifetime of this book, particularly in cities such as Moscow.

---

ted into your regular mobile phone handset during your stay. Call prices are very low within local networks, but charges for roaming larger regions can mount up; cost-conscious locals switch SIM cards when crossing regional boundaries.

Topping up your phone credit can be done either via pre-paid credit cards bought from kiosks or mobile-phone shops or, more commonly, via brightly coloured ATM-like machines found in all shopping centres, metro and train station and the like. Choose your network, input your phone number and the amount of credit you'd like to top up by, insert the cash and it's done, minus a small fee for the transaction. Confirmation of the top-up comes via a text message to your phone.

In this book, we have mobile-phone numbers starting with ☎ 8; be aware that, in certain circumstances, you may need to dial ☎ +7 instead.

PAY PHONES

Taksofon (pay phones, ТАКСОФОН) are located throughout most cities, and are usually in working order. Most take prepaid phonecards. There are several types of cardphones, and not all cards are interchangeable. Cardphones can be used for local and domestic or international long-distance calls.

PHONECARDS & CALL CENTRES

Local *telefonnaya karta* (phonecards), in a variety of units, are available from kiosks, shops and metro stations in Moscow and St Petersburg, and can be used to make local, national and international calls.

Sometimes better value for international calls is a call centre, where you give the clerk the number you want to call, pay a deposit and then go to the booth you are assigned to make the call. Afterwards you either pay the difference or collect your change. Such call centres

are common in Russian cities and towns – ask for *mezhdunarodny telefon*.

China

The country code for China is ☎ 86.

If calling internationally from China, drop the first zero of the area or city code after dialling the international access code, and then dial the number you wish to call. Local calls from hotel-room phones are generally cheap (and sometimes free), although international phone calls are expensive; it's best to use a phonecard.

MOBILE PHONES

China Mobile outlets can sell you a SIM card, which will cost from Y60 to Y100 depending on the phone number (Chinese avoid the number four as it sounds like the word for death) and will include Y50 of credit. When this runs out, you can top up the number by buying a credit-charging card *(chōngzhí kǎ)* for Y50 or Y100 worth of credits.

The local per-minute, nonroaming city call charge for China Mobile is 7 *jiǎo* if calling a landline and 1.50 *jiǎo* if calling another mobile phone. Receiving calls on your mobile is free from mobile phones and costs 7 *jiǎo* from landline phones. Intraprovincial calls are Y1.40 per minute. Roaming charges cost an additional 2 *jiǎo* per minute, but the call receiving charge is the same. Overseas calls can be made for Y4.80 per minute plus the local charge per minute by dialling ☎ 17951, followed by 00, the country code, then the number you want to call. Otherwise you will be charged the IDD call charge plus 7 *jiǎo* per minute.

PAY PHONES

Public telephones are plentiful, although finding one that works can be a hassle. The majority of public telephones take Integrated Circuit (IC) cards (see below) and only a few take coins. If making a domestic call, look out for public phones at newspaper stands and hole-in-the-wall shops; you make your call and then pay the owner (local calls are typically around 4 *jiǎo*). Domestic and international long-distance phone calls can also be made from main telecommunications offices.

PHONECARDS

There are two main types of prepaid phonecards: IC cards, best used for making local and long-distance calls, and internet phone (IP) cards, best for international calls. Both are sold at kiosks, shops, internet cafes and China Telecom offices and come in a variety of denominations from Y20 to Y500. Some cards can only be used in Běijīng (or locally, depending on where the card is purchased), while other cards can be used throughout China.

Purchasing the correct card can be confusing, as the instructions for use on the reverse of the card are usually only in Chinese.

With an IP card, you dial a local number, then punch in your account number, followed by a pin number and finally the number you wish to call. English-language service is usually available.

Mongolia

The country code for Mongolia is ☎ 976.

If you are calling out of Mongolia, and are using an IDD phone, just dial ☎ 00 and then your international country code. On non-IDD phones you can make direct long-distance calls by dialling the international operator (☎ 106), who may know enough English to make the right connection (but don't count on it).

The other options are making a call from a private international phone office *(Olon Ulsiin Yariin)*, which are becoming common in Ulaanbaatar but not in other cities. These charge reasonable rates to call abroad. To make the call, you need to pay a deposit in advance (a minimum equivalent of three minutes). The most expensive, but often the most hassle-free, option is to call from the business centres or reception desks at top-end hotels.

MOBILE PHONES

The three main companies are Mobicom, Skytel and Unitel. The mobile-phone network is GSM. If you bring a GSM phone you can get a new SIM card installed in Mongolia. The process is simple – just go to a mobile-phone office (a Mobicom office is conveniently located on the 3rd floor of the State Department Store, Peace Ave 44, Ulaanbaatar), sign up for basic service (around T15,000), and buy units as needed. Cards come in units of 10 (T2500), 30 (T6600), 50 (T10,250) and 100 (T19,000). It is free to receive calls, while text messaging charges are almost negligible.

If abroad, to call a mobile-phone number in Mongolia, just dial the country code (☎ 976) without the area code. Note that you drop the '0' off the area code if dialling an Ulaanbaatar number *from* a mobile phone but you retain the '0' if using other area codes.

PHONECARDS

International phonecards are sold in various outlets including the post office, the State Department Store or mobile-phone shops. The Personal Identification Number (PIN) for these cards is the last four digits of the code on the card. There are a variety of phonecards available, and you usually get what you pay for – the cheaper ones (such as Bodicom) have terrible sound quality and echo, but cost less than US$0.10 per minute.

TIME

> No one on the train knew what time it was. Some people said the train travelled on Moscow time but operated on local time, if you can figure that out. But half the people were on Běijīng time and one diplomat said he was on Tokyo time, which was the same for some reason as Ulaanbaatar time. Our Chinese porter changed his watch 15 minutes every few hours or so but this was a system of his own devising.
>
> *Mary Morris, Wall to Wall*

One of the most disorienting aspects of a Trans-Siberian trip is working out what time it is. The important thing to remember is that all long-distance trains run on Moscow time – so check carefully when you buy a ticket exactly what time *locally* you should be at the station. Once inside the station and on the train all clocks are set to Moscow time.

In the guide we list how far major cities and towns are ahead of Moscow time, eg 'Moscow + 5hr' means five hours ahead.

From the early hours of the last Sunday in September to the early hours of the last Sunday in March, Moscow and St Petersburg time is GMT/UTC plus three hours. From the last Sunday in March to the last Sunday in September, 'summer time' is in force and it's GMT/UTC plus four hours.

Most of European Russia is in the same time zone as Moscow and St Petersburg. The exception along the Trans-Siberian route is Perm, which is two hours ahead of Moscow. East of the Ural Mountains, Yekaterinburg is on Moscow time plus two hours, Irkutsk on Moscow time plus five hours and Vladivostok on Moscow time plus seven hours.

All of China is on Běijīng's clock, which is eight hours ahead of GMT. Daylight-savings time was abandoned in 1992, so the time difference with Europe and the USA is reduced by one hour during the summer months.

Mongolia is divided into two time zones. Most of the country, including Ulaanbaatar, is GMT plus eight hours, so it is the same time zone as Běijīng except during the summer when it's one hour ahead.

TOILETS

It's rare that paper will actually be available in the stalls of public toilets, so always bring a supply of toilet paper or tissue with you. Plumbing systems in all three countries often have problems digesting toilet paper. If there is a rubbish basket next to the toilet, this is where the paper should go.

Russia

Pay toilets are identified by the words платный туалет (platny tualet). In any toilet Ж (zhensky) stands for women's, while M (muzhskoy) stands for men's.

In cities, you'll now find clusters of temporary plastic toilet cubicles in popular public places, although other public toilets are rare and often dingy and uninviting. A much better option are the loos in major hotels or in modern food outlets. In all public toilets, the attendant who you pay your R10 to can provide miserly rations of toilet paper.

China & Mongolia

Public toilets in hotels, ger camps and restaurants are usually European-style, moderately clean facilities. On the other hand, public facilities in parks, stores and train stations usually require that you squat over a smelly hole. In China you'll also come across toilets without doors and separated only by a low partition, making it easy to strike up a conversation with the person squatting next to you.

Along the Route

Toilets on Russian and Mongolian trains are the Western variety, although you'll notice when you lift the seat that the bowl rim is also designed for those who would prefer to squat rather than sit. The *provodnitsas* generally do a good job of keeping the toilets clean, particularly on the more prestigious class of trains.

It is also important to remember that shortly before and after any major stops, and along any densely populated stretches of the line, the toilets will be locked; a timetable for this is usually posted on the toilet door.

On Chinese trains toilets are often of the squat variety.

HOW TO HAVE A TRANS-SIBERIAN SHOWER *Steve Noble*

Travellers often moan about not being able to shower on trains. But what is your definition of a shower? If it's high pressure hot/cold water in an elegantly tiled bathroom, you will not find this. However, if you are resourceful, adaptable and imaginative, you can shower in the toilet/washroom at the end of each *kupe* (*kupeyny*, compartmentalised carriage). Some people are happy for just an APC (armpits and crotch) wash, others prefer to splash water a little more liberally. Here are some proven methods I have tried:

- Stab lots of small holes in the bottom of a plastic (½ litre or 1L) bottle, just like your shower head at home. Fill it with water and either hold it with one hand and wash or tie some rope around the bottle neck and hook it on the back of the door. Use one bottle to wet yourself and one bottle to rinse off.
- Any size cup or bottle can be filled with water and thrown liberally over yourself.
- Use a collapsible plastic shower bag with showerhead and tap, for sale in any good camping store.
- Attach a small length of rubber hose to the tap.
- Use a sponge or quick-dry towels to have a sponge bath.

If you want hot water, get some from the samovar before you enter the toilet. Check the floor drain is unplugged before you start to shower and remember to wipe the walls down after you're done. You don't want to leave a mess and upset the *provodnitsa*!

DIRECTORY

TOURIST INFORMATION
Russia

Tourist offices like you may be used to elsewhere are few and far between in Russia. Along the Trans-Siberian routes the only places we've found them are St Petersburg (p105), Moscow (p127), Kazan (p169) and Irkutsk (p214). Elsewhere you're mainly dependent for information on the moods of hotel receptionists and administrators, service bureaus and travel firms. The latter two exist primarily to sell accommodation, excursions and transport – if you don't look like you want to book something, staff may or may not answer questions.

Russia has no overseas tourist offices and most of its consulates and embassies have little practical information. Travel agencies at home specialising in Russian travel (p351) are your best bet.

China

While Běijīng's tourist information structure is improving, on the whole tourist information facilities in China are largely rudimentary and of little use for travellers. In the absence of a national tourism board, individual provinces, cities, towns and regions promote tourism independently. The fallback position is the China International Travel Service (CITS) with branches in all major towns and cities. There is usually a member of staff who can speak English who may be able to answer questions and offer some travel advice, but the main purpose of CITS is to sell you an expensive tour.

Mongolia

Ulaanbaatar has a reasonably good tourist information centre; see p282.

TRAVELLERS WITH DISABILITIES

Russia, China and Mongolia can be difficult places for disabled travellers. Most buildings, buses and trains are not wheelchair accessible. In China and Russia, crossing busy streets often requires using underground walkways with many steps. Uneven pavements in the cities and rough roads in the countryside make for uncomfortable and potentially dangerous travel.

Travelling on Trans-Siberian trains, while not impossible for the disabled, will certainly be a challenge. People in wheelchairs will have to be carried on and off the train and into their compartments, not to mention to the utterly disabled-unfriendly toilets.

However, attitudes are becoming more enlightened and things are slowly changing. Major museums such as the Hermitage in St Petersburg offer good disabled access. The St Petersburg–based agency **Liberty** (Map pp106-7; www.libertytour.ru; Novoizmailovsky pr 24/3 – 26; Ⓜ Moskovskaya) offers wheelchair-accessible tours of the city, while in Severobaikalsk, tour guide Rashit Yakhin (p265) has plans to rent out motorised wheelchairs and buy a special vehicle to transport wheelchair users around the northern Lake Baikal region. In Běijīng tour operators offering tours for the disabled include www.tour-beijing.com and www.beijing.etours.cn.

Before setting off get in touch with your national support organisation (preferably with the travel officer, if there is one). The following organisations offer general travel advice:

Australia
Nican (☎ 02-6241 1220, 1800-806 769; www.nican.com .au; Unit 5, 48 Brookes St, Mitchell, ACT 2911)

Europe
Holiday Care Service (☎ 0845-124 9974; www.holiday care.org.uk; Tourism for All, The Hawkings Suite, Enham Pl, Enham Alamein, Andover SP11 6JS, UK)
Mare Nostrum (☎ 0711-2858 200; www.mare-nostrum .de; Am Schnarrenberg 12, Stuttgart D-70376, Germany)

USA
Accessible Journeys (☎ 800-846 4537; www.disability travel.com; 35 West Sellers Ave, Ridley Park, PA 19078) Agency specialising in travel for the disabled.
Mobility International USA (☎ 541-343 1284; www .miusa.org; 132 East Broadway, Suite 343, Eugene, Oregon, 97401)

VISAS

It's highly advisable to obtain all visas in your home country before setting out. Some tour companies can arrange your visas as part of their package. Remember if you're also travelling through Belarus, Ukraine, the Baltic countries or Central Asia, you may need visas for those countries, too.

Russia

Everyone needs a visa to visit Russia and it's likely to be your biggest single headache if you run into complications, so allow yourself at least a month before you travel to secure one. There are several types of visa, but for most Trans-Siberian travellers a tourist visa, valid for 30 days from the date of entry, will be sufficient. If you plan to stay longer, it's best to apply for a business visa. The good news is that, these days, getting a visa is usually (but not always) a straightforward process. The process has three stages – invitation, application and registration.

INVITATION

To obtain a visa, you first need an invitation. Hotels and hostels will usually issue an invitation (or 'visa support') to anyone staying with them for free or for a small fee (typically around €20 to €30). If you are not staying in a hotel or hostel, you will need to buy an invitation – costs typically range from €15 to €35 for a tourist visa depending on whether you require a single- or double-entry type and how quickly you need the invitation, and €45 to €270 for the various types of business visa. This can be done through most travel agents, via specialist agencies (see below) and online through:

Express to Russia (www.expresstorussia.com)
Russian Business Visa (www.russian-business-visa.com)
Russia Direct (www.russiadirect.co.uk)
Visa Able (www.visaable.com)
Way to Russia (http://waytorussia.net)

APPLICATION

With invitation in hand you can then apply for a visa at any Russian embassy. Costs vary – anything from US$50 to US$450 – depending on the type of visa applied for and how quickly you need it. Russian embassies are practically laws unto themselves, each with different fees and slightly different application rules; to avoid potential hassles, check well in advance what these might be. A useful website with pages for Russia, Belarus and Ukraine is **Everbrite** (www.myazcomputerguy.com /everbrite/Page2.html), which has recent posts on the application situations at various embassies and consulates.

We highly recommended applying for your visa in your home country rather than on the road – indeed the rule is that you're supposed to do this although we know from experience that some embassies and consulates can be more flexible than others. Trans-Mongolian travellers should note that unless you can prove you're a resident of China or Mongolia, attempting to get visas for Russia in both Běijīng and Ulaanbaatar can be a frustrating, costly and ultimately fruitless exercise.

REGISTRATION

On arrival in Russia, you should fill out an immigration card – a long white form issued by passport control; often these are given out in advance on your flight. You surrender one half of the form immediately to the passport control, while the other you keep for the duration of your stay and give up only on exiting Russia. Take good care of this as you'll need it for registration and could face problems while travelling in Russia – and certainly will on leaving – if you cannot produce it.

You must register your visa within three working days of arrival. If you're staying at a hotel, the receptionist should be able to do this for you for free or a small fee (typically around €20). Note that managers at the very cheapest places sometimes will not oblige. Once registered, you should receive a separate slip of paper confirming the dates you'll be staying at that particular hotel. Keep this safe – that's the document that any police who stop you will need to see.

If staying in a homestay or rental apartment, you'll either need to pay a travel

---

VISA AGENCIES

If you're really pressed for time, or especially badly affected by slow, impersonal bureaucracies, there are agencies that specialise in getting visas. In the USA, try **Zierer Visa Services** (☎ 1-866 788 1100; www.zvs.com), which has offices in Houston, New York, San Francisco and Washington DC, as well as affiliates in the UK (www.uk.cibt.com), France (www.action-visas.com/cibt), Germany (www .visum-centrale.de), Australia (https://visalink.com.au), the Netherlands (http://visumdienst.nl), Sweden and Denmark (www.cometconsular.com). Other agencies include the US-based **Russia-visa.com** (www .russia-visa.com) and the UK- and Russian-based **Real Russia** (www.realrussia.co.uk). For Chinese visas, try the US-based **China Visa Service Center** (☎ 1-800 799 6560; www.mychinavisa.com).

DIRECTORY

agency (anything from €20 to €70) to register your visa for you (most agencies will do this through a hotel) or make arrangements with the landlord or a friend to register you through the post office. See http://wayto russia.net/RussianVisa/Registration.html for how this can be done as well as a downloadable form that needs to be submitted at post offices. Note, while registering at post offices in cities and large towns is likely to be straightforward, in more remote places this procedure cannot be guaranteed.

Depending on how amenable your hotel or inviting agency is, you can request them to register you for longer than you'll actually be in one place. Otherwise every time you move city or town and stay for more than three days it's necessary to go through the registration process again. There's no need to be overly paranoid about this but the more thorough your registration record, the safer you'll be. Keep all transport tickets (especially if you spend nights sleeping on trains) to prove to any overzealous police officers exactly when you arrived in a new place.

Registration is a hassle but it's worth doing for peace of mind since it's not uncommon to encounter fine-hungry cops hoping to catch tourists too hurried or disorganised to be able to explain long gaps in their registration.

TYPES OF VISAS

Apart from the regular tourist visa, there are other types of visa that could be useful to travellers.

Business Visa

A business visa is far more flexible and desirable for the independent traveller than a tourist visa. These can be issued for three months, six months or two years, and are available as single-entry, double-entry or multiple-entry visas. They are valid for up to 90 days of travel within any six-month period.

To obtain a business visa you must have a letter of invitation from a registered Russian company or organisation, and a covering letter from your company (or you) stating the purpose of your trip. The agencies mentioned under 'Invitation', p343, can all arrange this.

Transit Visa

If you're taking a nonstop Trans-Siberian journey this visa is valid for 10 days, giving

westbound passengers a few days in Moscow; those heading east, however, are not allowed to linger in Moscow.

VISA EXTENSIONS & CHANGES

Any extensions or changes to your visa will be handled by offices of UFMS (Upravleniye Federalnoy Migratsionnoy Slyzhby), Russia's Federal Migration Service, often just shortened to FMS. It's likely you'll hear the old acronyms PVU and OVIR used for this office.

Extensions are time consuming, if not downright difficult; tourist visas can't be extended at all. Try to avoid the need for an extension by asking for a longer visa than you might need. Note that many trains out of St Petersburg and Moscow to Eastern Europe cross the border after midnight, so make sure your visa is valid up to and including this day. Don't give border guards any excuses for making trouble.

China

All foreigners need to get a visa to visit the People's Republic of China (PRC). Your passport should have at least six months' validity and one empty page. Submit your passport, a covering letter, an application, one passport photo and a money order for the appropriate fee. Processing should take four working days for a walk-in application; by mail requires more time and usually a higher fee.

Be aware that you must submit these documents to the consulate whose jurisdiction includes the state or city where you reside. Exact requirements and fees vary depending on where you apply, so be sure to check the details with your nearest Chinese consulate.

A standard visa is valid for one entry and a 30-day stay in China. A double entry is fairly straightforward. You can also get a transit visa, which is good for seven days. Requirements are more stringent for multiple entries or for longer stays in China.

At the time of writing, prices for a standard 30-day visa are US$50/30 for US/non-US citizens. For double-entry visas, it's US$75/45 and for multiple-entry visas (for six months) it's US$100/60.

Visa extensions, which are relatively easy to get, are the domain of the Public Security Bureau's (PSB) Foreign Affairs Branch; for details of the Běijīng branch see p308.

Mongolia

Most nationalities require a visa to enter Mongolia, with the following exceptions: US citizens, for stays up to 90 days; Israeli and Malaysian citizens, for up to 30 days; and Hong Kong and Singaporean citizens, for up to 14 days. To obtain a Mongolian visa, your passport must have at least six months' validity.

Standard tourist visas are valid for 30 days and cost US$30. Processing the application usually takes three to five days. For longer than 30 days, you must obtain an invitation from a travel agency or 'sponsoring organisation'.

If you are not leaving the train in Ulaanbaatar, or you are getting off only for a very short stay, you may obtain a transit visa in advance – good for 72 hours from the date of entry and costing US$15.

If you cannot get to a Mongolian consulate, you can pick up a 30-day tourist visa on arrival at the airport in Ulaanbaatar or at the land borders of Zamyn-Uüd and Sükhbaatar. You'll need US$53 and two passport photos.

For visa extensions, go to the **Ministry of External Relations** (cnr Peace Ave & Olympiin Gudamj; 9.30am-noon Mon-Fri). Enter from the back of the building. The extension is US$15 for seven days and requires a passport photo. Some guest houses will handle visa extensions for a small fee. Transit visas cannot be extended.

If you intend to stay in Mongolia for more than 30 days, you must register with the **Office of Immigration, Naturalization & Foreign Citizens** (INFC; ☎ 011-315 323; 9am-1pm & 2-5pm Mon-Fri), on the west side of Ulaanbaatar's Peace Bridge, opposite Naran Plaza.

WOMEN TRAVELLERS

Bring sanitary towels or tampons only if there is a brand you absolutely must use. Otherwise you can find locally produced products.

You need to be wary; a woman alone should certainly avoid private taxis at night. Never get in any taxi with more than one person – the driver – already in it. In Russia, any young or youngish woman alone in or near flashy bars frequented by foreigners risks being mistaken for a prostitute.

You're unlikely to experience sexual harassment on the streets in most parts of Russia, though sexual stereotyping remains strong. In more remote areas, the idea that women are somehow less capable than men may persist. In rural areas, revealing clothing will probably attract unwanted attention (whereas on hot days in Moscow women wear as little as possible).

Russian women relish the chance to talk alone with a foreign woman, and the first thing they'll tell you is how hopeless their menfolk are. When journeying by train, women might consider buying a *platskart* ticket (*platskartny;* open carriage) rather than one in a *kupe* (*kupeyny;* compartmentalised carriage), to avoid the risk of getting stuck in a closed compartment with three shady characters. If you do decide to travel *kupe* and don't like your cabin mates, tell the conductor who will more than likely find you a new place.

China is probably among the safest places in the world for foreign women to travel alone. Women are generally treated respectfully, because principles of decorum are ingrained deeply in the culture.

Mongolia doesn't present too many problems for foreign women travelling independently. The majority of Mongolian men behave in a friendly and respectful manner, without ulterior motives. However, you may come across an annoying drunk or the occasional macho idiot. The phrase for 'Go away!' is *'Sasha be!'*.

There are occasional incidents of solo female travellers reporting being harassed by their male guide. If your guide is male, it is best to keep in touch with your tour agency in Ulaanbaatar, perhaps making contingency plans with them if things go awry. Better yet, take a female guide whenever possible.

Transport

GETTING THERE & AWAY

Most travellers will start their Trans-Siberian or Trans-Mongolian trip in either Moscow or Běijīng; this section covers details for getting to or from either city. It's also possible to fly into or out of other major gateways, such as St Petersburg (see p119), Irkutsk (p218), Vladivostok (p256) or Ulaanbaatar (p290). For information on overland approaches to the railheads from Europe or Asia, see p39.

Flights, tours and rail tickets can be booked online at www.lonelyplanet.com /travel_services.

ENTERING THE COUNTRY

There are no particular difficulties for travellers entering Russia, China or Mongolia. The main requirements are a valid passport (valid for travel for six months after the expiry date of your visa) and a visa (see p342 for more details). Visas are not available at the borders.

AIR
Airports & Airlines
Moscow's **Sheremetyevo-2** (airport code SVO; ☎ 495-232 6565; www.sheremetyevo-airport.ru) and the much more congenial **Domodedovo** (airport code DME; ☎ 495-933 6666; www.domodedovo.ru)

airports host the bulk of Russia's international flights. There are also many daily international services to St Petersburg's **Pulkovo-2** (airport code LED; ☎ 812-704 3444; www.pulkovoairport.ru/eng) airport.

You don't necessarily have to fly into either Moscow or St Petersburg – other cities along the Trans-Siberian route with direct international connections are Irkutsk, Kazan, Khabarovsk, Nizhny Novgorod, Novosibirsk, Perm, Vladivostok and Yekaterinburg.

Běijīng's **Capital Airport** (airport code PEK; ☎ 010-6454 1100; http://en.bcia.com.cn/) is served by both international and domestic connections, as is Ulaanbaatar's **Chinggis Khaan Airport** (airport code ULN; ☎ 198, 011-983 005).

Airlines flying internationally to/from Mongolia are Aeroflot, Aero Mongolia, Air China, Korean Air and MIAT; see p290 for details. Airlines flying into Russia and China include the following. Phone numbers are for Moscow, unless otherwise stated.

Aeroflot Russian International Airlines (airline code SU; ☎ 495-223 5555; www.aeroflot.ru/eng)

Air Baltic (airline code BT; ☎ in Latvia 9000 6006; www.airbaltic.com)

Air Berlin (airline code AB; ☎ in Germany 01805-737 800; www.airberlin.com)

Air China (airline code CA; ☎ 495-292 3387; www.china -airlines.com/en/index.htm)

Air France (airline code AF; ☎ 495-937 3839; www .airfrance.com)

Alitalia (airline code AZ; ☎ 495-967 0110; www.alitalia .com)

Austrian Airlines (airline code OS; ☎ 495-995 0995; www.aua.com)

THINGS CHANGE...

The information in this chapter is particularly vulnerable to change. Check directly with the airline or a travel agent to make sure you understand how a fare (and ticket you may buy) works and be aware of the security requirements for international travel. Shop carefully. The details given in this chapter should be regarded as pointers and are not a substitute for your own careful, up-to-date research.

CLIMATE CHANGE & TRAVEL

Climate change is a serious threat to the ecosystems that humans rely upon, and air travel is the fastest-growing contributor to the problem. Lonely Planet regards travel, overall, as a global benefit, but believes we all have a responsibility to limit our personal impact on global warming.

Flying & Climate Change

Pretty much every form of motorised travel generates CO_2 (the main cause of human-induced climate change) but planes are far and away the worst offenders, not just because of the sheer distances they allow us to travel, but because they release greenhouse gases high into the atmosphere. The statistics are frightening: two people taking a return flight between Europe and the USA will contribute as much to climate change as an average household's gas and electricity consumption over a whole year. See p39 for details on how to minimise using flights to get to the railheads.

Carbon Offset Schemes

Climatecare.org and other websites use 'carbon calculators' that allow travellers to offset the level of greenhouse gases they are responsible for with financial contributions to sustainable travel schemes that reduce global warming, including projects in India, Honduras, Kazakhstan and Uganda.

Lonely Planet, together with Rough Guides and other concerned partners in the travel industry, supports the carbon offset scheme run by climatecare.org. Lonely Planet offsets all of its staff and author travel. For more information, check out our website: www.lonelyplanet.com.

bmi (airline code BD; ☎ in UK 0870-6070 555; www.flybmi.com)
British Airways (airline code BA; ☎ 495-363 2525; www.britishairways.com)
China Southern Airlines (airline code CZ; ☎ in Běijīng 010-950 333; www.cs-air.com)
Click Air (airline code IB; ☎ 902 790 790; www.clickair.com)
ČSA (Czech Airlines; airline code OK; ☎ 495-973 1847, 978 1745; www.csa.cz/en/)
Delta Air Lines (airline code DL; ☎ 800-700 0990; www.delta.com)
Dragonair (airline code KA; ☎ in Běijīng 010-6518 2533; www.dragonair.com)
El Al Israel Airlines (airline code LY; ☎ 495-232 1017; www.elal.co.il)
Estonian Air (airline code OV; ☎ in Tallinn 372-640 1160; www.estonian-air.ee)
Finnair (airline code AY; ☎ 495-933 0056; www.finnair.com)
German Wings (airline code 4U; ☎ in Germany 0870-252 1250; www.germanwings.com)
Japan Airlines (airline code JL; ☎ 495-730 3070; www.jal.co.jp/en)
KD Avia (airline code KD; ☎ 495-641 1074; www.kdavia.eu)
KLM (airline code KL; ☎ 495-258 3600; www.klm.com)
Korean Air (airline code KE; ☎ 495-725 2727; www.koreanair.com)
Lithuanian Airlines (airline code TE; ☎ 370-5-252 5555; www.flylal.com)

LOT Polish Airlines (airline code LO; ☎ 800-5082 5082; www.lot.com)
Lufthansa (airline code LH; ☎ 495-980 9999; www.lufthansa.com)
MIAT Mongolian Airlines (airline code OM; ☎ 495-241 0754; www.miat.com)
Niki (airline code HG; ☎ in Austria 0820-737 800, in Russia 800-5550737; www.flyniki.com)
Qantas (airline code QF; ☎ in Běijīng 010-6567 9006; www.qantas.com.au)
Rossiya (airline code FV; ☎ 495-995 2025; http://eng.pulkovo.ru/en/)
SAS (airline code SK; ☎ 495-775 4747; www.flysas.com)
S7 Airlines (airline code S7; ☎ in Moscow 495-777 9999, in Novosibirsk 383-298 9090; www.s7.ru)
Singapore Airlines (airline code SQ; ☎ 495-775 3087; www.singaporeair.com)
Swiss International Airlines (airline code LX; ☎ 495-937 7767; www.swiss.com)
Thai Airways International (airline code TG; ☎ 495-647 1082; www.thaiair.com)
Transaero Airlines (airline code UN; ☎ 495-788 8080; www.transaero.com)
Turkish Airlines (airline code TK; ☎ 495-980 5202; www.thy.com)
Ural Airlines (airline code U6; ☎ in Yekaterinburg 343-345 3645; www.uralairlines.ru)
Utair (airline code UTA; ☎ in Tyumen 3452-492 462; www.utair.ru)

Vim Airlines (airline code NN; ☎ 8-800-700 0757, 495-783 0088; www.vim-avia.com)

Vladivostok Air (airline code XF; ☎ in Vladivostok 495-626 8888, 4232-307 000; www.vladivostokavia.ru)

Windjet (airline code IV; ☎ in Italy 89-2020; w3.vola windjet.it)

Tickets

Good deals on air tickets can be found both online and through discount travel agencies. Fares quoted in this book are based on the rates advertised by travel agencies and online at the time of research (May to September 2008). The quoted airfares do not necessarily constitute a recommendation for the carrier.

There are many websites specifically aimed at selling flights. Many large travel agencies also have websites, but not all of them allow you to look up fares and schedules. See p351 for a list of agencies that specialise in tours along the Trans-Siberian routes; some of these will offer discount fares, too.

Websites worth checking include the following:

www.cheapflights.com Really does post some of the cheapest flights but get in early to get the bargains.

www.dialaflight.com Offers worldwide flights out of Europe including the UK.

www.expedia.com A good site for checking worldwide flight prices.

www.kayak.com Great search engine for flight deals with links through to its selections.

www.lastminute.com This site deals mainly in European flights, but does have worldwide flights, mostly package returns.

www.statravel.com STA Travel's US website. There are also UK and Australian sites (www.statravel.co.uk and www.statravel.com.au).

www.tch-fly.de/en German agency Transport Clearing House can pull up flights with Air Berlin and Niki, with connection onwards with Russian airlines Transaero, Ural, Siberian Airlines, Krasair, Domodevskie Avia, Vladivostok Air, Samara Air, Sky Express, Polet, UT Air and Azal.

www.travel.com.au A good site for Australians to find cheap flights. A New Zealand version also exists (www .travel.co.nz).

To bid for last-minute tickets online try **Skyauction** (www.skyauction.com). **Priceline** (www .priceline.com) aims to match the ticket price to your budget. Another cheap option is an air courier ticket but it does carry restrictions: for more information check out organisations such as **Courier Association** (www.aircourier.org) or the **International Association of Air Travel Couriers** (IAATC; www.courier.org).

Australia & New Zealand

Two well-known agencies for cheap fares, with offices throughout Australia, are **Flight Centre** (☎ 133 133; www.flightcentre.com.au) and **STA Travel** (☎ 134 782; www.statravel.com.au).

The cheapest flight you're going to get to Russia would be something like Sydney to Seoul and then Seoul to Moscow: a Korean Air deal starts at A$1500 return. Seoul is also the most convenient transfer point for flights on to Vladivostok or Khabarovsk.

To Běijīng the low-season return fares from Sydney start at around A$1100.

The *New Zealand Herald* has a travel section in which travel agencies advertise fares. **Flight Centre** (☎ 0800-243 544; www.flightcentre .co.nz) and **STA Travel** (☎ 0800-474 400; www.statravel .co.nz) have branches in Auckland and elsewhere in the country; check the websites for complete listings.

Air fares from New Zealand to Russia and China are similar to those from Australia.

Canada

Canadian discount agencies, also known as consolidators, advertise their flight specials in major newspapers such as the *Toronto Star* and the *Vancouver Sun*. The national student travel agency is **Travel CUTS** (☎ 1866-246 9762; www.travelcuts.com).

In general, fares from Canada to Russia cost 10% more than from the USA. From Vancouver to Moscow return flights start from C$1400 (with two changes of plane); from Montreal C$1200 (with one change of plane). From Vancouver to Běijīng you'll pay from around C$700.

China

There are multiple options for getting to and from China. Moscow, naturally, has the best connections with daily flights offered by Air China and Aeroflot to Běijīng (from Y6000 return). There are five flights a week between Shànghǎi and Moscow (Y6830 return). Transaero flies weekly from Moscow Domodedovo to Hong Kong and Sānyà. There are also direct flights from Běijīng to Irkutsk, Khabarovsk, Novosibirsk and Vladivostok; Dailin to Irkutsk and Khabarovsk; Hā'ěrbīn (Harbin) to Khabarovsk and Vladivostok, and Shěnyáng to Irkutsk.

Three carriers fly the Běijīng–Hong Kong route: Air China, China Southern Airlines and Dragonair. Tickets between Běijīng and Hong Kong start at about Y2530 one way.

Continental Europe

There are several budget airlines, as well as all the major airlines. Travel agencies may also offer some sort of deal, so shop around. Standard return fares to Moscow from major Western European cities start at around €250, or €900 to Běijīng.

FRANCE

Nouvelles Frontières (☎ 08 25 00 07 47; www.nouvelles -frontieres.fr, in French) has many branches in Paris and throughout France. Also try **Anyway** (☎ 08 92 89 38 92; www.anyway.fr, in French) and **Lastminute** (☎ 08 92 70 50 00; www.fr.lastminute .com, in French).

GERMANY

Germany is an excellent jumping-off point for Russia, with not only plenty of connections to a range of Russian cities with Lufthansa but also connections through budget airlines such as German Wings. Many Russian airlines also fly direct between Germany and Russia including **Don Aeroflot** (www.aeroflot-don .ru, in Russian) and **KMV Avia** (www.kmvavia.ru, in Russian) and **S7** (www.s7.ru).

Recommended agencies in Germany include **Just Travel** (☎ 089-747 3330; www.justtravel .de), **STA Travel** (☎ 069-7430 3292; www.statravel.de) and **Travel Overland** (☎ 01805-276370; www.travel -overland.de in German).

ITALY, NETHERLANDS & SPAIN

Italian company **CTS Viaggi** (☎ 199-501 150; www .cts.it, in Italian) specialises in student and youth travel fares.

Recommended agencies in the Netherlands are **Airfair** (☎ 0900-77 17 717; www.airfair.nl, in Dutch) and **NBBS Riesen** (☎ 0900-10 20 300; www.nbbs.nl, in Dutch).

Try **Barcelo Viajes** (☎ 902 116 226; www.barcelo viajes.com, in Spanish) in Spain.

Japan

Reliable discount agencies in Japan include **No 1 Travel** (☎ 03-3205 6073; www.no1-travel.com), **Across Travellers Bureau** (☎ 03-3340 6745; www.across -travel.com), and **STA Travel** (☎ 03-5391 2922; www .statravel.co.jp) with branches in both Tokyo and Osaka.

Return flights from Tokyo to Moscow are around ¥170,000, although at certain times of the year 60-day excursion fares on Aeroflot can go as low as ¥60,000 return. Air China and Japan Airlines have several flights per week from Tokyo and Osaka to Běijīng. Return fares start from ¥30,000.

Other useful connections are from Niigata to Khabarovsk and Vladivostok, and from Osaka and Toyama to Vladivostok.

Korea

Seoul in South Korea is a possible international travel hub for Siberia and the Russian Far East, with almost daily flights to Khabarovsk and Vladivostok and weekly ones to Novosibirsk and Yuzhno-Sakhalinsk (for getting to Sovetskaya Gavan). There are also flights connecting Pusan and Vladivostok. Air China, Asiana Airlines and Korean Air have daily flights between Běijīng and Seoul.

Mongolia & Central Asia

Ulaanbaatar is connected with Moscow (one way/return from US$361/580) and Irkutsk (US$117/210). There are also flights to/ from Běijīng with **MIAT** (www.miat.com) and Air China.

There are dozens of connections to Central Asia. From Moscow there are many direct flights. Also from Novosibirsk you can reach Almaty in Kazakhstan; Andizhan and Tashkent in Uzbekistan; Dushanbe and Khudzhand in Tajikistan; and Bishkek in Kyrgyzstan.

Singapore, Thailand & Vietnam

In Singapore, **STA Travel** (☎ 6737 7188; www.sta travel.com.sg) offers competitive discount fares for Asian destinations and beyond, including Běijīng. Singapore, like Bangkok, has hundreds of travel agents, so you can compare prices on flights.

Khao San Rd in Bangkok is the budget travellers' headquarters. Bangkok has a number of excellent travel agencies but keep in mind that there are also some suspect ones; seek the advice of other travellers before handing over your cash to anyone. **STA Travel** (☎ 02-236 0262; www.statravel.co.th; Rm 1406, 14th fl, Wall St Tower, 33/70 Surawong Rd) is a reliable place to start. Aeroflot has direct flights to Moscow from Bangkok. S7 flies to Novosibirsk, and several other Russian airlines offer seasonal charters.

There's also a weekly Vietnam Airlines flight between Hanoi and Vladivostok.

UK & Ireland

Newspapers and magazines such as *Time Out* and *TNT Magazine* in London regularly advertise low fares to Moscow. Start your research with the major student or backpacker-oriented travel agencies such as STA and Trailfinders. Through these reliable agents you can get an idea of what's available and how much you're going to pay – however, a bit of ringing around the smaller agencies afterwards will often turn up cheaper fares.

Reputable agencies in London:

ebookers (☎ 0871-223 5000; www.ebookers.com)

Flight Centre (☎ 0870-499 0040; www.flightcentre .co.uk)

STA Travel (☎ 0871-230 0040; www.statravel.co.uk)

Trailfinders (☎ 0845-058 5858; www.trailfinders.com)

Travelbag (☎ 0800-804 8911; www.travelbag.co.uk)

Shop around and you might get a low-season one-way/return fare to Moscow for UK£150/200. Flights to St Petersburg cost around UK£200/250. Aeroflot and bmi generally offer the cheapest deals. Also check out deals with KD Avia that fly out of Gatwick to Kaliningrad and beyond. Return fares from London to Běijīng start at UK£350.

USA

Discount travel agencies in the USA are known as consolidators (although you won't see a sign on the door saying Consolidator), and they can be found in the *Yellow Pages* or the travel sections of major daily newspapers such as the *New York Times*, the *Los Angeles Times* and the *San Francisco Examiner*. You'll generally come across good deals at agencies in San Francisco, Los Angeles, New York and other big cities.

STA Travel (☎ 1-800 781 4040; www.statravel.com) has a wide network of offices.

Economy-class air fares from New York to Moscow or Běijīng can go as low as US$750 return. From Los Angeles you're looking at return fares to Moscow of around US$925, and US$650 to Běijīng.

LAND

Both Russia and China share borders with 14 countries, so if you're planning on travelling overland to join or leave the Trans-Siberian

route there is no shortage of options. See p39 for some ideas.

More often than not it will be by train that you cross into or leave this region, but there are also several useful bus services; we list some here. You should also check well in advance whether or not you will need a visa for any of the countries you will be passing through en route to Russia or China.

Border Crossings

See p279 for details of the border crossing between Russia and Mongolia, (p291) for the Mongolia and China crossing, and p298 for the Russia-China crossing. For other overland routes into China, see Lonely Planet's *China* guidebook for details.

Belarus & Poland

Minsk is well connected by train with Moscow (R2830, 11 hours, 20 daily) and St Petersburg (R3000, 15 hours, daily). Changing the wheels to/from Russia's wider gauge adds three hours to the journey. There's at least two buses a week from Minsk to Moscow and one a week to St Petersburg.

Warsaw is connected with Moscow (R4500, 18 to 21 hours, two daily) and St Petersburg (R3000, 29 hours, daily). The Moscow trains enter Belarus near Brest. The St Petersburg trains leave Poland at Kuznica, which is near Hrodna (Grodno in Russian) in Belarus. You'll need a Belarus visa or transit visa.

Estonia

The nearest border crossing from Tallinn is at Narva. There are daily trains between Tallinn and Moscow (R3300, 15 hours) and St Petersburg (R1485, 9½ hours). Tallinn is also connected with St Petersburg by seven express buses daily (R900, 7½ hours).

Finland

There are currently three daily trains between St Petersburg and Helsinki with plans to add four high-speed rail services from late 2009: see p119 for details. There's also the daily 31/34 *Leo Tolstoy* service between Moscow and Helsinki (R5320, 13½ hours). There are many daily buses between Helsinki and St Petersburg. For more details, see p119.

Kazakhstan

There are trains every two days between Moscow and Almaty (R6260, three days and six hours) in addition to a variety of services from Siberia, eg Novosibirsk. Beware that some domestic Russian trains cut through Kazakhstan en route, including Chelyabinsk–Omsk, Chelyabinsk–Magnitogorsk and those Yekaterinburg–Omsk services routed via Kurgan. Visa checks are not always made leaving Russia, but coming back in you may find yourself in serious trouble if you don't have a Kazakhstan visa and a double-/multiple-entry Russian visa, too.

Latvia & Lithuania

From Latvia, handy overnight trains run daily between Rīga and Moscow (R4020, 16 hours) and St Petersburg (R3280, 13 hours). There are two daily buses from Riga to St Petersburg (R700 to R1050, 11 hours); see p119. There are also two to three buses daily to Moscow (R800, 14 hours) including one that is operated by **Ecolines** (www.ecolines.ru; R1425).

Services link Vilnius in Lithuania, with Moscow (R2890, 15 hours, three daily) and St Petersburg (one way/return R2230/2735, 15¼ hours, every other day). The St Petersburg trains cross Latvia, and the Moscow ones cross Belarus for which you'll need a Belarus visa or transit visa.

Mongolia

Kupe prices for a berth between Ulaanbaatar and Běijīng cost the equivalent of R6635. Apart from the Trans-Mongolian train connecting Moscow and Běijīng, there's a direct train twice a week from Ulaanbaatar to Moscow (R15,000, four days and five hours) as well as a daily service to and from Irkutsk (R4000, 25 to 35 hours). There's also a bus service connecting Ulan-Ude and Ulaanbaatar (p238).

UK & Western Europe

Travelling overland by train from the UK or Western Europe takes a minimum of two days and nights. It is, however, a great way of easing yourself into the rhythm of the Trans-Siberian Railway – see p39 for more details.

Ukraine

Most major Ukrainian cities have daily services to Moscow, with two border crossings: one used by trains heading to Kyiv, the other by trains passing through Kharkiv.

Trains from Kyiv to Moscow (R2000 to R2400, 9½ hours, 18 daily) go via Bryansk (Russia) and Konotop (Ukraine), crossing

at the Ukrainian border town of Seredyna-Buda. The best trains to take (numbers are southbound/northbound) between Moscow and Kyiv are the 1/2 and 3/4. The best train between Moscow and Lviv is 73/74 (R2200, 23 hours, daily via Kyiv). Between Moscow and Odessa (R2200 to R2600, 23 hours, daily via Kyiv) there's the 23/24, the *Odesa*. There are also daily trains to/from St Petersburg to Lviv (31 hours via Vilnius) and Kyiv (24 hours).

Trains between Kharkiv and Moscow (R1800 to R2200, 13 hours, about 14 daily via Kursk) cross the border just 40km north of Kharkiv. The best train is the night train, the 19/20 *Kharkiv*. Between Moscow and Simferopol (26 hours, daily via Kharkiv), the best train is 67/68, the *Simferopol*. Trains between Moscow and Donetsk (22 hours, three daily), Dnipropetrovsk (20 hours, twice daily), Zaporizhzhya (19 hours, twice daily) and Sevastopol (29½ hours, daily) all go through Kharkiv.

There are also daily international trains passing through Ukraine to/from Moscow's Kievsky vokzal. These include the 15/16 Kyiv–Lviv–Chop–Budapest–Belgrade, with a carriage to Zagreb three times a week.

There is a handful of weekly buses travelling from Kharkiv across the border into Russia on the E95 (M2) road. The official frontier crossing is 40km north of Kharkiv, and is near the Russian border town of Zhuravlevka.

RIVER & SEA

The Amur River, which forms part of the border between Russia and China, can be crossed by ferries from Khabarovsk to Fuyuan (p249) and from Blagoveshchensk to Hēihé (p244).

There are ferries between St Petersburg and the Kaliningrad Region from which Germany, Poland or Lithuania are a short hop; see p119. For details of ferries from Vladivostok to Japan and South Korea, see p256.

Běijīng's nearest seaport is Tiānjīn's port district of Tanggu. Ships travel between Tiānjīn and Kobe, Japan, once a week.

TOURS

If you have time, and a certain degree of determination, organising your own trip to Russia is easily done. But for many travellers, opting for the assistance of an agency in drawing up an itinerary, booking train tickets and accommodation, not to mention helping with the visa paperwork, will be preferable. See p22 to choose which suits you best.

The following agencies and tour companies provide a range of travel services. Numerous more locally based agencies can provide tours once you're in Russia; see the destination chapters for details. Many local companies work in conjunction with overseas agencies so if you go to them directly you'll usually pay less.

Australia
Eastern Europe/Russian Travel Centre (☎ 02-9262 1144; www.eetbtravel.com)
Passport Travel (☎ 03-9500 0444; www.travelcentre .com.au)
Russian Gateway Tours (☎ 02-9745 3333; www .russian-gateway.com.au)
Sundowners (☎ 03-9672 5300; www.sundownersover land.com) Specialises in Trans-Siberian and Trans-Mongolian packages and tours.
Travel Directors (☎ 08-9242 4200; www.traveldirectors .com.au) Upmarket Trans-Siberian tour operator.

Canada
Trek Escapes (☎ 1866-338 8735; www.trekescapes.com) Canada's top adventure-tour agency offers Trans-Siberian packages run by Sundowners and Imaginative Traveller. Has branches in Calgary, Edmonton, Toronto and Vancouver.

China
Monkey Business (☎ 8610-6591 6519; www.monkey shrine.com) Tours on the Trans-Siberian, Trans-Manchurian and Trans-Mongolian trains, with stopover options.
Moonsky Star Ltd (☎ 852-2723 1376) Monkey Business' Hong Kong partner.

Germany
Lernidee Reisen (☎ 030-786 0000; www.lernidee -reisen.de, in German)

Japan
MO Tourist CIS Russian Centre (☎ 03-5296 5783; www.mo-tourist.co.jp) Has tours and can help arrange ferries and flights to Russia.

UK
Beetroot Experience (www.beetroot.org) Offers budget trips geared towards backpackers.
Go Russia (☎ 020-3355 7717; www.justgorussia.co.uk) Cultural and adventure holiday specialist.
GW Travel Ltd (☎ 0161-928 9410; www.gwtravel .co.uk) Offers luxury Trans-Siberian tours on the *Golden Eagle* (see p360), a private train made up of Pullman-style carriages where all the sleeping compartments have attached showers.

Imaginative Traveller (☎ 0845-077 8802; www .imaginative-traveller.com)
Intourist Travel (☎ 020-7792 5240; http://intouristuk .com/index.php)
Regent Holidays (☎ 0845-277 3317; www.regent -holidays.co.uk)
Russia Experience (☎ 020-8566 8846; www.trans -siberian.co.uk) Very experienced and reliable operator.
The Russia House (☎ 020-7403 9922; www.therussia house.co.uk) Agency experienced with dealing with corporate and business travel needs.
Russian Gateway (☎ 08704-46 1812; www.russian gateway.co.uk) Small specialist agency that offers mainly city-break packages and river cruises via its sister company **Russiana River Cruises** (www.russiana.co.uk).
Russian National Tourist Office (☎ 020-7495 7570; http://visitrussia.org.uk) Offers tours across the country.
Scott's Tours (☎ 020-7383 5353; www.scottstours.co.uk /index.php)
Steppes East (☎ 01285-880 980; www.steppeseast .co.uk) Specialises in catering to offbeat requirements.
Voyages Jules Verne (☎ 020-7616 1000; www.vjv .co.uk) Offers a variety of upmarket tours in Russia.

USA
Cruise Marketing International (☎ 800-578 7742; www.cruiserussia.com) Books tours on cruises along Russian waterways such as the Volga River.
Exeter International (☎ 813-251 5355; www.russia tours.com) Specialises in luxury tours to Moscow and St Petersburg.
Far East Development (☎ 206-282 0824; www .traveleastrussia.com) Eco-adventure tour company specialising in Far East Russia and Siberia.
Go To Russia Travel (☎ 404-827 0099; www.goto russia.com) Has offices in Atlanta, San Francisco and Moscow; offers tours and a full range of travel services.
Mir Corporation (☎ 206-624 7289; www.mircorp.com) Award-winning operation with many different tours.
Red Star Travel (☎ 206-522 5995; www.travel2russia .com)
Sokol Tours (☎ /fax 724-935 5373; www.sokoltours .com) Tour options include train trips, Tuva and Kamchatka.
VisitRussia.com (☎ 1800-755 3080; www.visitrussia .com) Has offices in New York, Moscow and St Petersburg and can arrange package and customised tours.

GETTING AROUND

For most, if not all, of your Trans-Siberian journey you're going to be getting around on the train, but sometimes you might need or want to take an internal flight, a boat or a bus. The following apply mainly for getting around Russia, with significant differences mentioned for China and Mongolia. There's also some information for those thinking of driving or cycling through Russia (see p355).

AIR
Russia

It's no problem buying a ticket either on-line (see below) or with *avia kassy* (ticket offices) all over most large towns and cities. Generally speaking, you'll do better booking internal flights once you arrive in Russia. Fares are generally 30% cheaper (60% on major Moscow routings) for advance bookings or evening departures.

Tickets can also be purchased at the airport desks right up to the departure of the flight and sometimes even if the city-centre office insist that the plane is full. Return fares are usually double the cost of one-way fares.

Make sure you reconfirm your flight at least 24 hours before take-off: Russian airlines have a nasty habit of cancelling unconfirmed tickets. Airlines may also bump you if you don't check in at least 90 minutes before departure. Unlike the train, the idea of schedules being kept remains in the realms of fantasy: delays and cancellations are common.

The mechanical safety of the planes is an issue, as are the safety procedures (or lack of) for protection against terrorist attacks. Both **Aeroflot Russian Airlines** (www.aeroflot.com) and **Transaero** (www.transaero.ru/english) have consistent safety records.

To minimise the danger of loss or theft, try not to check-in any baggage: many planes have special stowage areas for large carry-on pieces. Russian airlines can be very strict about charging for bags that are overweight, which generally means anything over 20kg.

China

The Civil Aviation Administration of China (CAAC; Zhōngguó Mínháng) is the civil aviation authority for numerous airlines, including **Air China** (www.airchina.com.cn), **China Eastern Airlines** (www.ce-air.com) and **China Southern Airlines** (www.cs-air.com).

CAAC publishes timetables in both English and Chinese in April and November each year, and these are available at airport desks and CAAC offices in China. Tickets are easy to purchase from branches of CAAC nationwide, other airline offices and travel agents or from the travel desk of your hotel. At most times there is an oversupply of airline seats (except during major festivals and holidays). Ask around for discounts. Return tickets cost twice the single fare.

On domestic and international flights the free-baggage allowance for an adult passenger is 20kg in economy class and 30kg in 1st class. You are also allowed 5kg of hand luggage, though this is rarely weighed.

Mongolia

Although Mongolia has 44 functioning airports only 12 of these have paved airstrips. Almost all of the destinations are served directly from Ulaanbaatar. The state-owned airline **MIAT** (www.miat.com) flies only to a handful of cities in very old planes; their pilots are very experienced, however, and they've not had a fatal crash since 1998. Possible alternatives are **Aero Mongolia** (☎ 011-283 029; www.aeromongolia.mn) and **Blue Sky Aviation** (☎ 011-312 085; www.bsamongolia.com), which has a nine-seat Cessna that can be chartered for any part of the country.

AIR TICKETS VIA THE WEB

You may prefer to use the web to purchase air tickets. Online agencies specialising in Russian air tickets with English interfaces include **Avantix** (☎ 495-787 7272; www.avantix.ru) and **Pososhok.ru** (☎ 495-234 8000; http://avia.waytorussia.net).

Using modern 737s, **Sky Express** (☎ 495-580 9360; www.skyexpress.ru/en//) is a Russian low-cost carrier with services between Moscow and Kaliningrad, Kazan, Murmansk, Perm, Rostov-on-Don, Sochi, St Petersburg, Tyumen and Yekaterinburg.

Primorskoye Aeroagentsvo (☎ 4232-407 707; www.airagency.ru), a Vladivostok-based agency with branches in Moscow and St Petersburg, as well as across the Russian Far East, can also quote fares and have English-speaking agents.

TRANSPORT

TRANSPORT

THE GAI

Not to put too fine a point on it, many officers of the State Automobile Inspectorate, GAI (*gah-yee*, short for Gosudarstvennaya Avtomobilnaya Inspektsia), are nothing short of highway bandits. GAI officers are authorised to stop you (they do this by pointing their striped, sometimes lighted, stick at you and waving you towards the side of the road), issue on-the-spot fines and can shoot at you if you don't pull over.

Watch for speed traps on major roads into Moscow and St Petersburg. There are permanent GAI checkpoints at the boundary of many Russian cities and towns, while in cities the GAI is everywhere, stopping cars often for no reason and collecting 'fines'. For serious infractions, the GAI can confiscate your licence, which you'll have to retrieve from the main station.

Get the shield number of the 'arresting' officer. By law, GAI officers are not allowed to take any money at all – fines should be paid via Sberbank. However, in reality Russian drivers normally offer to pay the GAI officer approximately half the official fine, thus saving money and the time eaten up by Russian bureaucracy, both at the police station and the bank.

BOAT
Russia

In summer it's possible to travel long distances across Russia on passenger boats. You can do this either by taking a cruise, which you can book through agencies in the West or in Russia, or by using scheduled river passenger services. The season runs from late May through to mid-October, but is shorter on some routes.

There are numerous boats plying the routes between Moscow and St Petersburg, many stopping at some of the Golden Ring cities on the way; and along the Volga River from Moscow to other Trans-Siberian cities such as Nizhny Novgorod and Kazan. In Siberia and the Russian Far East there are services along the Ob and Irtysh Rivers (between Omsk and Tobolsk), the Yenisey from Krasnoyarsk, the Lena from Ust-Kut via Lensk to Yakutsk, the Amur from Khabarovsk to Komsomolsk, as well as across Lake Baikal from Irkutsk to Nizhneangarsk.

Beware that boat schedules can change radically from year to year (especially on Lake Baikal) and are only published infuriatingly close to the first sailing of each season.

BUS

Long-distance buses complement rather than compete with the rail network. They generally serve areas with no railway or routes on which trains are slow, infrequent or overloaded.

Russia

Most cities have a main intercity *avtovokzal* (автовокзал; bus station). Like long-distance bus stations everywhere they are often scoun-drel magnets, and are rarely pleasant places to visit after dark. Tickets are sold at the station or on the bus. Fares are normally listed on the timetable and posted on a wall. As often as not you'll get a ticket with a seat assignment, scribbled almost illegibly on a till receipt. Prices are comparable to 2nd-class train fares; journey times depend on road conditions. A sometimes hefty fee is charged for larger bags.

Marshrutky (just a diminutive form of *marshrutnoye taksi,* meaning a fixed-route taxi) are minibuses that are quicker than the rusty old buses and rarely cost much more. Where roads are good and villages frequent, *marshrutky* can be twice as fast as buses, and well worth the double fare.

China

Chángtú gōnggōngqìchē (long-distance buses) are one of the best means of getting around China. Services are extensive, main roads are improving and with the increasing number of intercity highways, bus journeys are getting quicker (often quicker than train travel). It's also easier to secure bus tickets than train tickets and they are often cheaper. Buses also stop in small towns and villages, so you get to see parts of the countryside you wouldn't see if you travelled by train, although breakdowns can be a problem.

On the downside, some rural roads and provincial routes are in shocking condition, dangerously traversed by nerve-shattering hulks. Long-distance bus journeys can be cramped and noisy, with Hong Kong films on overhead TVs and three-dimensional sound. Drivers lean on the horn at the slightest detection of a vehicle in front.

Routes between large cities sport larger, cleaner and more comfortable fleets of private buses, such as comfy Volvos; shorter and more far-flung routes still rely on rattling minibuses into which the driver crams as many fares as possible.

On popular long-haul routes, *wòpù qìchē* (sleeper buses) may cost around double the price of a normal bus service, but many travellers swear by them. Some have comfortable reclining seats, while others have two-tier bunks. Watch out for your belongings on them, however.

CAR & MOTORCYCLE
Russia
Russian main roads are a really mixed bag – sometimes they are smooth, straight dual carriageways, sometimes rough, narrow, winding and choked with the diesel fumes of the slow, heavy vehicles that make up a high proportion of Russian traffic. Driving much more than 300km in the course of a day is pretty tiring.

Russian drivers use indicators far less than they should, and like to overtake everything on the road – even on the inside. Priority rules at roundabouts seem to vary from area to area: all you can do is follow local practice. Russian drivers rarely switch on anything more than sidelights – and often not even those – until it's pitch black at night. Some say this is to avoid dazzling others, as for some reason dipping headlights is not a common practice.

A useful general site for motorcyclists, with some information on Russian road conditions, is www.horizonsunlimited.com.

FUEL
Western-style petrol stations are common. Petrol comes in four main grades: 76, 93, 95 and 98 octane. Prices range from R22.5 to R30 per litre. Unleaded petrol is available in major cities; BP petrol stations usually sell it. *Dizel* (diesel) is also available (around R24 a litre). In the countryside, petrol stations are usually not more than 100km apart, but you shouldn't rely on this.

ROAD RULES
Russians drive on the right-hand side of the road and traffic coming from the right has the right of way. Speed limits are generally 60km/h in towns and between 80km/h and 110km/h on highways. There may be a 90km/h zone, enforced by speed traps, as you leave a city. Children under 12 may not travel in the front seat, and safety-belt use is mandatory. Motorcycle riders (and passengers) must wear crash helmets.

The maximum legal blood-alcohol content is 0.03%. This is a rule that is strictly enforced. The normal way of establishing alcohol in the blood is by a blood test, but apparently you can be deemed under the influence even without any test.

Traffic lights that flicker green are about to change to yellow, then red.

DRIVING ACROSS RUSSIA

For intrepid car travellers the challenge of driving across the vast expanse of Russia is irresistible. Most famously, *Corriere della Sera* journalist Luigi Barzini documented the road trip he made from Běijīng to Paris in 1907, led by Prince Scipione Borghese. The journey took them two months, during which time they frequently resorted to driving along the railway rather than the mud tracks that constituted Siberian roads.

More recently, Ewan McGregor and Charley Boorman wrote about their Russian adventures in *Long Way Round* (www.longwayround.com/lwr.htm); their round-the-world route took them from Volgograd all the way to Yakutsk and Magadan via Kazakhstan and Mongolia. The celebrity bikers had a camera crew and support team following them. For a more accurate view of the trials suffered by ordinary mortals read *The Linger Longer*, by brothers Chris and Simon Raven who somehow coaxed a rusty Ford Sierra from the UK to Vladivostok.

Should you be planning to drive the 11,000km from St Petersburg to Vladivostok along the unofficial Trans-Siberian highway it's worth knowing that the rockiest section remains the 2100km Amur Hwy, opened in 2004, between Chita and Khabarovsk. About 800km of this road remains gravel-topped, meandering and pock-marked. Full completion of the asphalt road is slated for 2009 or 2010. For some information in Russian on this section of road see http://amur-trassa.ru.

You'll need to be 18 years old and have an International Driving Permit with a Russian translation of your licence, or a certified Russian translation of your full licence (you can certify translations at a Russian embassy or consulate).

Don't forget your vehicle's registration papers, proof of insurance (be sure it covers you in Russia) and a customs declaration promising that you will take your vehicle with you when you leave. To get the exact details on all this it's best to contact your automobile association (eg the AA or RAC in the UK) at least three months before your trip.

China

The authorities remain anxious about foreigners driving at whim around China, so don't plan on hiring a car and driving wherever you want. Road conditions in China should abolish any remaining desire to get behind the wheel. Bilingual road signs are making a slow appearance along some highways, but much remains to confuse would-be drivers from abroad.

If you want to use a car, it's easy enough to book a car with a driver. Basically, this is just a standard long-distance taxi. Travel agencies such as CITS or even hotel booking desks can make the arrangements. They generally ask excessive fees, so be prepared to negotiate. If you can communicate in Chinese or find someone to translate, it's not particularly difficult to find a private taxi driver to take you wherever you like for less than half the CITS rates.

Mongolia

Travelling around Mongolia with your own car or motorcycle – without a driver – is not recommended. What look like main roads on the map are often little more than tyre tracks in the dirt, sand or mud. All maps are inadequate, and there is hardly a signpost in the whole country. The roads here are used by nomads who, by their nature, keep moving so even the roads are seminomadic, shifting like restless rivers. Remote tracks quickly turn into eight-lane dirt highways devoid of any traffic making navigation tricky – some drivers follow telephone lines when there are any, or else ask for directions at gers (felt tents) along the way. Towns with food and water are few and far between, and very few people in the countryside will speak anything but Mongolian

or, if you are lucky, Russian. If all this hasn't put you off, keep in mind that foreigners have been jailed for being involved in traffic accidents, even if they were not at fault.

Ulaanbaatar has a couple of car-rental agencies but they require that you be driven by one of their drivers, which is a good idea.

HITCHING

Hitching is never entirely safe in any country in the world, and Lonely Planet doesn't recommend it. Travellers who hitch should understand that they are taking a small but potentially serious risk.

Russia

Hitching in Russia is a very common method of getting around. In cities, hitching rides is called hailing a taxi, no matter what type of vehicle stops (see opposite for more information). In the countryside, especially in remote areas not well served by public transport, hitching is a major mode of transport, though you'll need to pay for a ride.

China

Passengers are expected to offer at least a tip when hitching in China. Some drivers might even ask for an unreasonable amount of money, so try to establish a figure early to avoid problems later. Even when a price is agreed upon, don't be surprised if the driver raises it when you arrive at your destination and creates a big scene (with a big crowd) if you don't cough up the extra cash. Indeed, they may even pull this scam halfway through the trip, and if you don't pay up you get kicked out in the middle of nowhere.

In other words, don't think of hitching as a means to save money – it will rarely be any cheaper than the bus. The main reason to do it is to get to isolated outposts where public transport is poor. There is, of course, some joy in meeting the locals this way, but communicating is certain to be a problem if you don't speak Chinese.

Mongolia

Because the country is so vast, public transport so limited and the people so poor, hitching (usually on trucks) is a recognised – and, often, the only – form of transport in the countryside. Hitching is seldom free and often no different from just waiting for public transport to turn up. It is *always* slow – after stopping at gers to drink, fixing flat tyres, breaking down, running out of petrol and getting stuck in mud and rivers, a truck can take 48 hours to cover 200km.

Hitching is not generally dangerous personally, but it is still hazardous and often extremely uncomfortable. Don't expect much traffic in remote rural areas; you might see one or two vehicles a day on many roads, and sometimes nobody at all for several days. The best place to wait is the petrol station on the outskirts of town, where most vehicles stop before any journey.

LOCAL TRANSPORT

For details of local trains see below. Also see the Getting Around sections of the various destinations for details of local bus, metro, tram and boat services.

Taxi

RUSSIA

There are two main types of taxis in Russia: the official ones, metered taxis you order by phone or the rarer four-door sedans with a chequerboard strip down the side and a green light in the front window that cruise the streets of Moscow; and 'private' taxis (any other vehicle on the road).

Hail rides by standing at the side of the road and flagging passing vehicles with a low, up-and-down wave (not an extended thumb). State your destination and negotiate the fare before getting in. You are expected to pitch in for petrol; paying what would be the normal bus fare for a long-haul ride is considered appropriate. If the driver's game, they'll ask you to *sadites* (get in), but always act on the cautious side before doing this. Check with locals to determine the average taxi fare in that city at the time; taxi prices around the country vary widely. The better your Russian, generally the lower the fare. If possible, let a Russian negotiate for you: they'll do better than you will.

As a precaution have the taxi stop at the corner nearest your destination, not the exact address, if you're staying at a private residence. Trust your instincts. If a driver looks creepy, take the next car, and don't get in a car with more than one person inside.

TRAIN

For more detailed information about train travel in Mongolia and China, see Lonely Planet's *Mongolia* and *China* guides.

Russia

Russian Railways (RZD or Rossiyskie Zheleznye Dorogi; www.eng.rzd.ru/wps/portal/rzdeng/fp) runs one of the largest networks in the world. It has a remarkable record for punctuality, with trains almost invariably departing each station to the minute allotted on the timetable. However, there are underlying reasons for this punctuality: managers have a large portion of their pay determined by the timeliness of their trains. This not only inspires promptness, but it results in the creation of generous schedules. You'll sometimes find your train stationary for hours in the middle of nowhere only to start up and still roll into the next station on time.

Timetables are posted in stations and are revised twice a year. The Russian rail network mostly runs on Moscow time, so timetables and station clocks from St Petersburg to Vladivostok will be written in and set to Moscow time. The only exception is suburban services, which are listed in local time.

Most stations have an information window; expect the attendant to speak only Russian and to give a bare minimum of information. Sometimes you may have to pay a small fee (around R10) for information. See p358 for ways to crack the timetable code on your own.

CLASSES

The regular long-distance service is a *skory poezd* (fast train), which rarely gets up enough speed to merit being called 'fast', but is indeed much quicker than the frequently stopping *passazhirsky poezd* (passenger trains) found mainly on routes of 1000km or less. A *prigorodny poezd* (suburban train), nicknamed an *elektrichka,* is a local service linking a city and its suburbs or nearby towns, or groups of adjacent towns.

The premium trains are *firmennye poezdy* and often have proper names (eg *Rossiya*). These generally have cleaner and more upper-class carriages, polite attendants, more convenient arrival and departure times and a reasonable (or at least functioning) restaurant car. Sometimes the ticket prices will also include your linen and breakfast.

Russians make themselves very much at home on trains. This often means they'll be travelling with plenty of luggage. It also means some juggling of the available space will become inevitable.

In all but local trains there's a luggage bin underneath each of the lower berths that will hold a medium-sized backpack or small suitcase. There's also enough space beside the bin to squeeze in another medium-sized bag. Above the doorway (in 1st and 2nd class) or over the upper bunks (in 3rd class) there's room for a couple more rucksacks.

In all classes of carriage with sleeping accommodation, if you've not already paid for a pack of bedding linen and face towels (called *pastil*) in your ticket price, the *provodnitsa* (the female carriage attendant; see p361) will offer it to you for a small charge, typically around R60. In 1st class the bed is usually made up already.

All compartments are air-conditioned in summer and heated in winter – that's why the windows are locked shut (though sometimes you'll be able to open them). There is a speaker above the window through which the *provodnitsa* can inflict her music on you – you can switch this off with the knob.

Note that no account is taken of sex when allocating a cabin, so a single woman might find herself sharing with three men. If you don't feel comfortable, ask the *provodnitsa* if you can swap – it's often possible.

If you want true luxury, you'll need to shell out for the trips offered by **GW Travel Ltd** (see p352) or associated companies, which use the *Golden Eagle* private rail cars that are complete with plush compartments and showers; see p360 for more details.

Deluxe 1st class

These are only available on the 3/4 Trans-Mongolian train. These two-berth compartments are roomy, have wood-panelling, are carpeted and have a sofa. A shower cubicle is shared with the adjacent compartment.

1st Class/SV

Most often called SV (which is short for *spalny vagon*, or sleeping wagon), 1st-class compartments are also called *myagky* (soft class) or

---

READING A TRAIN TIMETABLE

Russian train timetables vary from place to place but generally list a destination; train number; category of train; frequency of service; and time of departure and arrival, in Moscow time unless otherwise noted (see following).

Trains in smaller city stations generally begin somewhere else, so you'll see a starting point and a destination on the timetable. For example, when catching a train from Yekaterinburg to Irkutsk, the timetable may list Moscow as the point or origin and Irkutsk as the destination. The following are a few key points to look out for.

Number

Номер *(nomer)*. The higher the number of a train, the slower it is; anything over 900 is likely to be a mail train.

Category

Скорый *(Skory)*, Пассажирский *(Passazhirsky)*, Почтово-багажный *(Pochtovo-bagazhny)*, Пригородный *(Prigorodny)* – and various abbreviations thereof. These are train categories and refer, respectively, to fast, passenger, post-cargo and suburban trains. There may also be the name of the train, usually in Russian quotation marks, eg 'Россия' *(Rossiya)*.

Frequency

Ежедневно *(yezhednevno, daily)*; чётные *(chyotnye, even-numbered dates)*; нечётные *(nechyotnye, odd-numbered dates)*; отменён *(otmenyon, cancelled)*. All of these, as well, can appear in various abbreviations, notably еж, ч, не, and отмен. Days of the week are listed usually as numbers (where 1 is Monday and 7 Sunday) or as abbreviations of the name of the day (Пон, Вт, Ср, Чт, Пт, С and Вск are, respectively, Monday to Sunday). Remember that time-zone differences can affect these days. So in Chita (Moscow + 6hr) a train timetabled at 23.20 on Tuesday actually leaves 5.20am on Wednesday. In months with an odd number of days, two odd days follow one another (eg 31 May, 1 June). This throws out trains working on an alternate-day cycle so if travelling near month's end pay special attention to the hard-to-decipher footnotes on a timetable. For example, '27/V – 3/VI Ч' means that from 27 May to 3 June the train runs on even dates. On some trains, frequency

lyux. They are the same size as in 2nd class but have only two berths, so there's more room and more privacy for double the cost. Some 1st-class compartments also have TVs on which it's possible to watch videos or DVDs supplied by the *provodnitsa* for a small fee (there's nothing to stop you from bringing your own, although they'll need to work on a Russian DVD player, compatible with region 5). You could also unplug the TV and plug in your computer or other electrical equipment.

These carriages also have the edge in that there are only half as many people queuing to use the toilet every morning. A couple of special services between Moscow and St Petersburg, and Moscow and Kazan offer luxury SV compartments each with their own shower and toilet.

2nd Class/Kupe

The compartments in a *kupeyny* (2nd class, also called 'compartmentalised') carriage (often shortened to *kupe*) are the standard accommodation on long-distance trains. These carriages are divided into nine compartments, each with four reasonably comfortable berths, a fold-down table and enough room between bunks to turn around.

In every carriage there's also one half-sized compartment with just two berths. This is usually occupied by the *provodnitsa*, or reserved for railway employees, but there is a slim chance that you may end up in it, particularly if you do a deal directly with a *provodnitsa* for a train ticket.

3rd Class/Platskartny

A reserved-place *platskartny* carriage, sometimes also called *zhyostky* ('hard class', or 3rd class) and usually abbreviated to *platskart*, is essentially a dorm carriage sleeping 54. The bunks are uncompartmentalised and are arranged in blocks of four down one side of the corridor and in twos on the other, with the lower bunk on this side converting to a table and chairs during the day.

---

depends on the time of year, in which case details are usually given in similar abbreviated small print: eg '27/VI – 31/VIII Ч; 1/IX – 25/VI 2, 5' means that from 27 June to 31 August the train runs on even dates, while from 1 September to 25 June it runs on Tuesday and Friday.

Arrival & Departure Times

Corresponding trains running in opposite directions on the same route may appear on the same line of the timetable. In this case you may find route entries such as время отправления с конечного пункта *(vremya otpravlenia s konechnogo punkta)*, or the time the return train leaves its station of origin. Most train times are given in a 24-hour time format, and almost always in Moscow time (Московское время, *Moskovskoye vremya*). But suburban trains are usually marked in local time (местное время, *mestnoe vremya*). From here on it gets tricky (as though the rest wasn't), so don't confuse the following:

- время отправления *(vremya otpravleniya)* Time of departure.

- время отправления с начального пункта *(vremya otpravleniya s nachalnogo punkta)* Time of departure from the train's starting point.

- время прибытия *(vremya pribytiya)* Time of arrival at the station you're in.

- время прибытия на конечный пункт *(vremya pribytiya v konechny punkt)* Time of arrival at the destination.

- время в пути *(vremya v puti)* Duration of the journey.

Distance

You may sometimes see the расстояние *(rastoyaniye)* – distance in kilometres from the point of departure – on the timetable as well. These are rarely accurate and usually refer to the kilometre distance used to calculate the fare. Note that if you want to calculate where you are while on a journey, keep a close look out for the small black-and-white kilometre posts generally on the southern side of the track. These mark the distance to and from Moscow. In between each kilometre marker are smaller posts counting down roughly every 100m. The distances on train timetables don't always correspond to these marker posts.

TRANSPORT

RIDING THE GOLDEN EAGLE *Simon Richmond*

In 2005 GW Travel stumped up US$22 million for 12 custom-built carriages featuring en-suite sleeping cabins with top notch amenities. Two years later, the *Golden Eagle's* maiden journey from Moscow to Vladivostok was attended by HRH Prince Michael of Kent. Not since the era of the British royal's distant cousin Tsar Nicholas II had such a luxurious train service traversed Siberia.

The private train's 15-day itinerary between Moscow and Vladivostok tweaks the traditional Trans-Siberian route to go via the Tatarstan capital of Kazan and detours into Mongolia to pause for a day in Ulaanbaatar. Other stops include Novosibirsk for a trip to the Railway Locomotive Museum at Seyatel; a picnic beside Lake Baikal; and a visit to an Old Believers' village near Ulan-Ude. A couple of times a year, depending on demand, GW Travel also runs the luxury train on a 14-day journey along the BAM route via Severobaikalsk, Tynda and Komsomolsk-na-Amure.

Starting at US$16,600 for single occupancy of a 5.5-sq-m Silver Class cabin and US$20,000 for a 7-sq-m Gold Glass cabin, these tours are the rail equivalent of a voyage on the QEII, and so attract a similar well-heeled and older-age clientele. Modern, comfortable but not overly lavish cabins sport a sofa that converts into a bed with another pull down bed above that. The air-con can be set to the desired temperature and there's a flat-screen TV connected to a DVD/CD player. En-suite bathrooms have decent showers and, in Gold Glass, heated ceramic floor tiles. Unlike on regular Russian trains, the toilets can be used any time – even while in stations – since they don't drop their waste directly on the track.

Just as in a decent hotel there's a laundry service aboard the train, a hair dresser is available, beds are made up during dinner then packed away during breakfast at the same time that linens and towels are exchanged. All meals and copious amounts of alcohol while on the tour are included as are excursions by bus at each of the train halts, and other diversions such as Russian-language and cooking lessons on the train.

Hearty four-course meals with wine are taken in an ornate dining car that certainly evokes the glory days of the Trans-Siberian. If the train is busy, as it can be with possibly more than 100 passengers per journey, the adjoining lounge-bar, complete with piano and pianist, can also be used to house the overflow.

During my two-day taster of the *Golden Eagle* from Moscow to Yekaterinburg, I was highly impressed with the professionalism, organisation and friendliness of the staff, the quality of the train's facilities and the food provided. If creature comforts are something you require during an extended journey across the largest country on earth, then this luxury train is the way to go. On the downside, I missed the interaction with locals that you get on regular Russian services and was frustrated by the regimented bus tours at the various stops (as were several other passengers).

A passenger, Charles Cuddington, comments:

'The train did not disappoint. The cabin was comfortable, the car attendants attentive, the food exceeded expectations both in quality and quantity and the on-board management/entertainment was efficient and entertaining.

I was surprised at the mix of fellow travellers. I had not expected the number of different nationalities – American, Australian, Swiss, French, Belgium as well as Brits. The characters themselves could have been created by Agatha Christie herself for a *Murder on the Trans-Siberian Express* story, but fortunately everyone got on well enough that there was no body at the end of the journey!'

If you don't mind the lack of privacy, we recommend *platskart*. They're ideal for one-night journeys. In summer the lack of compartment walls means they're not usually as stuffy as a *kupe* can be. Many travellers (women in particular) find *platskart* a better option than being cooped up with three (possibly drunken) Russian men. It's also a great way to meet ordinary Russians. What

is likely to clinch the deal is that *platskart* tickets cost half to two-thirds the price of a 2nd-class berth.

However, on multiday journeys some *platskart* carriages can begin to resemble a refugee camp, with clothing strung between bunks, a great swapping of bread, fish and jars of tea, and babies sitting on potties while their snot-nosed siblings tear up and down the corridor. Only the hardy would want to do Moscow to Vladivostok or similar nonstop journeys this way.

If you do travel *platskart*, it's worth requesting specific numbered seats when booking your ticket. The ones to avoid are 1 to 4, 33 to 38, 53 and 54, found at each end of the carriage, close to the samovar and toilets, where there is lots of activity. Note 39 to 52 are the doubles with the bunk that converts to a table – you may want to avoid these ones too, especially if you're tall.

4th Class/Obshchy
Also called 4th class, *obshchy* (general) is unreserved. On long-distance trains the *obshchy* carriage looks the same as a *platskart* one, but when full, eight people are squeezed into each unenclosed compartment so there's no room to lie down. Suburban trains normally have only *obshchy* class, which in this case means bench-type seating. On a few daytime-only intercity trains there are higher-grade *obshchy* carriages with more comfortable, reserved chairs.

LEFT LUGGAGE
Many train stations have either a secure камера хранения (*kamera khraneniya*, left-luggage room) or автоматические камеры хранения (*avtomaticheskiye kamery khraneniya*, left-luggage lockers). Make sure you note down the room's opening and closing hours and, if in doubt, establish how long you can leave your stuff for. Typical costs are around R100 per bag per day (according to size) or R100 per locker.

Here is how to work the left-luggage lockers (they're generally the same everywhere). Be suspicious of people who offer to help you

work them, above all when it comes to selecting your combination.

- Buy two *zhetony* (tokens) from the attendant.
- Put your stuff in an empty locker.
- Decide on a combination of one Russian letter and three numbers and write it down.
- Set the combination on the inside of the locker door.
- Put one token in the slot.
- Close the locker.

To open the locker, set your combination on the outside of your locker door. Even though it seems as if the knobs on the outside of the door should correspond directly with those on the inside, the letter is always the left-hand-side knob, followed by three numbers, on both the inside and the outside. After you've set your combination, put a token in the slot, wait a second for the electrical humming sound and then pull it open.

RESERVATIONS
For details of buying train tickets, both before you leave home and once you're in Russia, see p27.

STOPS
Every carriage has a timetable (in Cyrillic) posted in the corridor, which notes how long the train will stop at each station. These timetables, however, are not set in stone, so always ask the *provodnitsa* how long you're going to be at a station. Usually, stops last from two to five minutes, but at least twice a day the train stops for 15 or 20 minutes, allowing time to get off, stretch your legs and stock up on food from sellers on the platform.

TRANSPORT

SHE WHO MUST BE OBEYED
On any long-distance Russian train journey you'll soon learn who's in charge: the *provodnitsa*. Though sometimes male *(provodniki)*, these carriage attendants are usually women. Some of them sport the most distinctive hairdos you'll come across this side of a drag-queen convention.

Apart from checking your ticket before boarding the train, doling out linen, and shaking you awake in the middle of the night when your train arrives, the *provodnitsa*'s job is to keep her carriage spick-and-span (most are very diligent about this) and to make sure the samovar is always fired up with hot water. They will have cups, plates and cutlery to borrow, if you need them, and can provide drinks and snacks for a small price; some have even been known to cook up meals and offer them around.

On long journeys the *provodnitsa* works in a team of two; one will be working while the other is resting. Butter them up the right way and your journey will be all the more pleasant.

China

China has some 52,000km of domestic train lines. Although carriages can be crowded, trains are the best way to get around the country in reasonable speed and comfort.

There are a variety of classes of travel. Hard seat (*yìngzuò*; 硬座) is actually generally padded, but this class can still be hard on one's sanity – it can be dirty, noisy and smoky. You may or may not have a seat reservation.

On short express journeys (such as Běijīng to Tiānjīn) some trains have soft-seat (*ruǎnzuò*; 软座) carriages, where overcrowding and smoking are not permitted.

Hard-sleeper (*yìngwò*; 硬卧) carriages are made up of doorless compartments with half a dozen bunks in three tiers, and sheets, pillows and blankets are provided. It does very nicely as an overnight hotel.

Soft-sleeper (*ruǎnwò*; 软卧) carriages have four comfortable bunks in a closed compartment; on Z-class trains (the best) you'll also have your own TV. Z-class trains also have luxury two-berth compartments with their own shower and toilet facilities.

Once you are on the train, the conductor may be able to upgrade your ticket if space is available in other carriages. The cost of the upgraded ticket is pro-rated to the distance travelled in the higher class.

For more info on China's railways and trains, consult the following sites:

Duncan Peattie's Chinese Railways Home Page (www.chinatt.org/) English-language timetable information for trains in China.

The Man in Seat 61 (www.seat61.com/china.htm)

Railways of China (www.railwaysofchina.com)

Mongolia

Mongolia's rail network is primarily made up of the Trans-Mongolian Railway, with both the domestic and international trains using this same line. It was built during the Soviet era so there are lots of similarities between the Mongolian and Russian train systems. Note that you can't use the Trans-Mongolian Railway for domestic transport.

If you're travelling from Ulaanbaatar, it is important to book a soft seat well in advance – this can be done up to 10 days before departure. There may be a small booking fee. In general, booking ahead is a good idea for any class, though there will always be hard-seat tickets available.

Health

CONTENTS

Although on the whole Russians are far from a healthy people, the dangers to visitors are quite minimal. The same goes for China. As for Mongolia, its cold, dry climate and sparse human habitation mean there are few of the infectious diseases that plague tropical Asian countries. However, there are a few health issues to be aware of. This chapter offers very basic advice; for more details check the internet resources provided and pick up Lonely Planet's *Asia & India: Healthy Travel*.

BEFORE YOU GO

Prevention is the key to staying healthy while away. A little planning before departure, particularly for pre-existing illnesses, will save trouble later. See your dentist before a long trip, carry a spare pair of contact lenses and glasses, and take your optical prescription with you. Bring medications in their original, clearly labelled containers. A signed and dated letter from your physician describing your medical conditions and medications, including generic names, is also a good idea. If carrying syringes or needles, be sure to have a physician's letter documenting their medical necessity.

INSURANCE

Good emergency medical treatment is not cheap in this region, so seriously consider taking out a policy that covers you for the worst possible scenario, such as an accident requiring an emergency flight home. Find out in advance if your insurance plan will make payments directly to providers (the preferable option) or reimburse you later for overseas health expenditures. Note: some policies specifically exclude 'dangerous activities', which can apply to scuba diving, motorcycling and trekking. Some policies ask you to phone back (reverse charge) to a call centre in your home country, where an immediate assessment of your problem is made.

RECOMMENDED VACCINATIONS
Diphtheria & Tetanus
Recommended for everyone, vaccinations for these two diseases are usually combined.

Hepatitis A
Vaccines including Avaxim, Havrix 1440 and VAQTA provide long-term immunity after an initial injection, then a booster at six to 12 months. Alternatively, an injection of gamma globulin can provide short-term immediate protection; it's reasonably effective, unlike the vaccine, but because it is a blood product, there are current concerns about its long-term safety. Hepatitis A vaccine is also available as Twinrix, combined with hepatitis B vaccine. Three injections over a six-month period are required, the first two providing substantial protection against hepatitis A.

> **TRAVEL ADVISORIES & SARS**
>
> The Severe Acute Respiratory Syndrome (SARS) health crisis that plagued China and Russia is no longer a problem. For the latest travel advisories, check the following websites (which are also good for general travel advice):
> **Australia** (www.smartraveller.gov.au)
> **Canada** (www.voyage.gc.ca)
> **New Zealand** (www.mft.govt.nz)
> **UK** (www.fco.gov.uk/travel)
> **USA** (www.travel.state.gov/travel/warnings.html)

Hepatitis B

This vaccination, which involves having three injections with a booster at 12 months, is recommended for Russia. Rapid courses are available.

Japanese B Encephalitis

Consider vaccination if spending a month or longer in parts of the Russian Far East and Siberia, or if making repeated trips to at-risk areas. It involves three injections over 30 days.

Polio

You should keep up to date with this vaccination, normally given in childhood – a booster every 10 years ensures immunity.

Rabies

Consider having vaccination if you're spending a month or longer travelling, especially if cycling, handling animals, caving or travelling to remote areas; children should also have it. Pretravel vaccination involves having three injections over 21 to 28 days. If someone who has been vaccinated is bitten or scratched by an animal, they'll need two booster injections; those not vaccinated require more.

Tuberculosis

If you'll be living among local people in high-risk areas for three months or more, consider being vaccinated for TB.

Typhoid

Available as an injection or oral capsules. A combined hepatitis A/typhoid vaccine is available; check with your doctor.

INTERNET RESOURCES

The World Health Organization's (WHO) publication *International Travel and Health* is revised annually and is available online at www.who.int/ith/. Other useful websites include the following:

- www.ageconcern.org.uk – advice on travel for the elderly
- www.fitfortravel.scot.nhs.uk – general travel advice for the layperson
- www.mariestopes.org.uk – information on women's health and contraception
- www.mdtravelhealth.com – travel health recommendations for every country; updated daily

IN RUSSIA, CHINA & MONGOLIA

AVAILABILITY & COST OF HEALTH CARE

Medical care is readily available across Russia but the quality can vary enormously. The biggest cities and towns have the widest choice of places, with both Moscow and St Petersburg well served by sparkling international-style clinics that charge handsomely for their admittedly generally excellent and professional service; except to pay around US$50 for an initial consultation.

Some foreigners (eg British) are theoretically entitled to free treatment in state-run noncommercial clinics, according to bilateral agreements from Soviet times. In practice this means that in Moscow they might be treated for free in cases of major injury. In remote areas doctors won't usually charge you either, but it's recommended to give them gifts – such as a bottle of Armenian cognac, chocolate or money.

In some cases, medical supplies required in hospital may need to be bought from a pharmacy and nursing care may be limited. Note that there can be an increased risk of hepatitis B and HIV transmission via poorly sterilised equipment.

Běijīng and Hāěrbīn (Harbin) and other metropolitan areas of China have good medical facilities well up to international standards. Mongolia, however, suffers from a serious lack of medical facilities. In short, an ill person is better off in Ulaanbaatar than in the countryside, and better off in Beijing than in Ulaanbaatar. If you must obtain medical assistance in Mongolia, seek out a hospital or private clinic that caters to foreigners and be sure to bring a translator. In China and Mongolia expect to pay anything up to US$100 for an initial consultation at a private clinic.

Apart from the chief *provodnitsa* (carriage attendant) probably having a first-aid box, there is no medical assistance available on the train itself.

INFECTIOUS DISEASES

Influenza

This will be your main health concern across Russia and China, particularly in winter. Symptoms include muscle ache, high fever,

---

DRINKING WATER

- Never drink tap water.
- Check the seal on bottled water is intact on purchase.
- Avoid ice and fresh juices if you suspect they have been watered down.
- Boiling water is the most efficient method of purifying it. Trains have a *samovar* (hot-water heater) in every carriage.
- The best chemical purifier is iodine. It should not be used by pregnant women or those with thyroid problems.
- Water filters should also filter out viruses. Ensure your filter has a chemical barrier such as Iodine and a small pore size, eg less than four microns.

---

runny nose, cough and sore throat. Vaccination is particularly recommended for those aged 65 and over.

Rabies
Spread through bites or licks on broken skin from an infected animal. It is always fatal unless treated promptly. Animal handlers should be vaccinated, as should those travelling to remote areas where a reliable source of post-bite vaccine is not available within 24 hours; see opposite.

Tick-borne Encephalitis
Spread by tick bites, this is a serious infection of the brain and vaccination is advised for those in risk areas who are unable to avoid tick bites (such as campers, forestry workers and walkers). Two doses of vaccine will give a year's protection, three doses up to three years'. For more information, see www.masta-travel-health.com/travel-health-library.aspx?page_group=14#p.

Typhoid & Hepatitis A
Spread through contaminated food (particularly shellfish) and water, typhoid can cause septicaemia (blood poisoning); hepatitis A causes liver inflammation and jaundice. Neither is usually fatal but recovery can be prolonged; see opposite and p363.

TRAVELLER'S DIARRHOEA
To prevent diarrhoea, avoid tap water unless it has been boiled, filtered or chemically disinfected (with iodine tablets) and steer clear of ice. Only eat fresh fruits or vegetables if cooked or peeled; be wary of dairy products that might contain unpasteurised milk. Eat food that is hot through and avoid buffet-style meals. If a restaurant is full of locals the food is probably safe.

If you develop diarrhoea, be sure to drink plenty of fluids, preferably an oral rehydration solution (eg Dioralyte). A few loose stools don't require treatment, but if you start having more than four or five stools a day, you should start taking an antibiotic (usually a quinolone drug) and an antidiarrhoeal agent (such as Loperamide). If diarrhoea is bloody, persists for more than 72 hours or is accompanied by fever, shaking, chills or severe abdominal pain you should seek medical attention.

ENVIRONMENTAL HAZARDS
The temperatures on the trains are generally kept at a comfortable level, but once out in the wide open spaces of Russia, Mongolia and China the main environmental hazards to be careful of are heat exhaustion in summer and frostbite in winter.

Heat Exhaustion & Heatstroke
Best avoided by drinking water on a constant basis, heat exhaustion occurs following excessive fluid loss with inadequate replacement of fluids and salt. Symptoms include headache, dizziness and tiredness. Dehydration is already happening by the time you feel thirsty. To treat heat exhaustion, replace lost fluids by drinking water and/or fruit juice, and cool the body with cold water and fans. Treat salt loss with salty fluids such as soup or Bovril, or add a little more table salt to foods than usual.

Heat stroke is much more serious, resulting in irrational and hyperactive behaviour and eventually loss of consciousness and death. Rapid cooling by spraying the body with water

---

AVIAN INFLUENZA *Dr Trish Batchelor*

Avian influenza, or 'bird flu', presents only a very remote risk to travellers at this time. In 2004 and 2005 the avian H5N1 virus caused illness in domestic birds around the world. This virus is passed from healthy migratory birds to domestic birds such as chickens and ducks, which then may sicken and die. Transmission has occurred from domestic birds to humans, however, it is rare, and requires close contact with an infected bird or its droppings. By September 2008, the World Health Organization had reported a total of 387 cases out of which 245 people had died. The majority of these cases occurred in Indonesia, Vietnam, Egypt, China and Thailand.

The WHO recommends the following precautions for travellers to affected countries: avoid live poultry markets; avoid eating raw or undercooked poultry or eggs; wash hands frequently; and seek medical attention if you develop a fever and respiratory symptoms (cough, shortness of breath etc).

You can keep up to date on the current situation by visiting the website of the **World Health Organization** (www.who.int/en).

---

and fanning is ideal. Emergency fluid and electrolyte replacement by intravenous drip is recommended.

Hypothermia & Frostbite

Proper preparation will reduce the risks of getting hypothermia. Even on a hot day in the mountains the weather can change rapidly; carry waterproof garments and warm layers, and inform others of your route.

Acute hypothermia follows a sudden drop of temperature over a short time. Chronic hypothermia is caused by a gradual loss of temperature over hours.

Hypothermia starts with shivering, loss of judgment and clumsiness. Unless rewarming occurs, the sufferer deteriorates into apathy, confusion and coma. Prevent further heat loss by seeking shelter, warm dry clothing, hot sweet drinks and shared bodily warmth.

Frostbite is caused by freezing and subsequent damage to bodily extremities. As it develops the skin blisters and then becomes black. Adequate clothing, staying dry, keeping well hydrated and ensuring adequate calorie intake best prevent frostbite. Treatment involves rapid rewarming. Avoid refreezing and rubbing the affected areas.

Insect Bites & Stings

LEECHES

You'll often find leeches in damp forest conditions; they attach themselves to your skin to suck your blood. Trekkers often get them on their legs or in their boots. Salt or a lighted cigarette end will make them fall off. Do not pull them off, as the bite is then more likely to become infected. Clean and apply pressure if the point of attachment is bleeding. An insect repellent may keep them away.

LYME DISEASE

This is a tick-transmitted infection that may be acquired throughout the region. The illness usually begins with a spreading rash at the site of the tick bite, accompanied by fever, headache, extreme fatigue, aching joints and muscles, and mild neck stiffness. If untreated, these symptoms usually resolve over several weeks, but over subsequent months disorders of the nervous system, heart and joints may develop. There is no vaccination against the disease. Treatment by antibiotics should be sought as soon as possible for best results.

MOSQUITOES

A problem in summer all across Russia, mosquitoes here may not carry malaria but can cause irritation and infected bites. Use some form of insect repellent and keep covered up.

From May to September in the rural areas bordering Mongolia, China and North Korea, take extra special care as mosquito bites can cause Japanese encephalitis. If visiting rural areas you should consider the immunisation.

TICKS

From May to July, tick-borne encephalitis (p365) is a risk anywhere in rural Russia. Always check all over your body if you have been walking through a potentially tick-infested area as ticks can cause skin infections and other more serious diseases. If you find a tick attached, press down around its head with tweezers, grab the head and gently pull upwards. Avoid pulling the rear of the body as this may squeeze the tick's gut contents through the attached mouth parts into the skin, increasing the risk of infection. Smearing chemicals on the tick will not make it let go and is not recommended.

Snake Bites

Avoid getting bitten – do not walk barefoot or stick your hand into holes or cracks. Half of those bitten by venomous snakes are not actually injected with poison (envenomed). If bitten by a snake, do not panic. Immobilise the bitten limb with a splint (eg a stick) and apply a bandage over the site firmly, similar to a bandage over a sprain. Do not apply a tourniquet, or cut or suck the bite. Get the victim medical help as soon as possible so that antivenene can be given if necessary.

TRAVELLING WITH CHILDREN

All travellers with children should know how to treat minor ailments and when to seek medical treatment. Make sure the children are up to date with routine vaccinations, and discuss possible travel vaccines well before departure as some vaccines are not suitable for children under a year.

If your child is vomiting or has diarrhoea, lost fluid and salts must be replaced. It may be helpful to take rehydration powders for reconstituting with boiled water.

Children should be encouraged to avoid and mistrust any dogs or other mammals because of the risk of rabies and other diseases. Any bite, scratch or lick from a warm-blooded, furry animal should immediately be thoroughly cleaned. If there is any possibility that the animal is infected with rabies, immediate medical assistance should be sought.

WOMEN'S HEALTH

Emotional stress, exhaustion and travelling through different time zones can all contribute to an upset in the menstrual cycle. If using oral contraceptives, remember some antibiotics, diarrhoea and vomiting can stop the pill from working and lead to the risk of pregnancy – remember to take condoms with you just in case. Time zones, gastrointestinal upsets and antibiotics do not affect injectable contraception.

Travelling during pregnancy is usually possible but always consult your doctor before planning your trip. The most risky times for travel are during the first 12 weeks of pregnancy and after 30 weeks.

SEXUAL HEALTH

Condoms are available across Russia, China and in Ulaanbaatar from pharmacies and certainly should be used. The **International Planned Parent Federation** (www.ippf.org) can advise about the availability of contraception in different countries.

When buying condoms in the region, look for a European CE mark, which means they have been rigorously tested, and then keep them in a cool dry place or they may crack and perish.

HIV & AIDS

Infection with human immunodeficiency virus (HIV) may lead to acquired immune deficiency syndrome (AIDS), which is a fatal disease. Russia is experiencing one of the fastest rises of reported HIV and AIDS cases in the world. China is also experiencing a rapid increase in HIV rates.

Any exposure to blood, blood products or body fluids may put the individual at risk. The disease is often transmitted through sexual contact or dirty needles – vaccinations, acupuncture, tattooing and body piercing can be potentially as dangerous as intravenous drug use. HIV/AIDS can also be spread through infected blood transfusions. If you do need an injection, ask to see the syringe unwrapped in front of you, or take a needle and syringe pack with you.

Sexually Transmitted Diseases

HIV/AIDS (above) and hepatitis B (p364) can be transmitted through sexual contact; see the relevant sections for more details. Other STDs include gonorrhoea, herpes and syphilis; sores, blisters or rashes around the genitals and discharges or pain when urinating are common symptoms. In some STDs, such as wart virus or chlamydia, symptoms may be less marked or not observed at all, especially in women. Chlamydia infection can cause infertility in men and women before any symptoms have been noticed. Syphilis symptoms eventually disappear completely but the disease continues and can cause severe problems in later years.

While abstinence from sexual contact is the only 100% effective prevention from STDs, using condoms is also effective. The treatment of gonorrhoea and syphilis is with antibiotics. Different STDs each require specific antibiotics.

HEALTH

Language

CONTENTS

CHINESE

The Chinese spoken in Manchuria is the dialect spoken in Běijīng. It is the official language of the People's Republic of China (PRC) and is usually referred to in the west as 'Mandarin' – the Chinese call it *pǔtōnghuà* (common speech).

For a more detailed guide to the language, get a copy of Lonely Planet's *Mandarin Phrasebook*.

PRONUNCIATION

Chinese is a tone language. This means that variations in pitch within syllables are used to determine word meaning. For example, in Mandarin the word *ma* can have several different meanings, depending on which tone is used:

High tone: *mā*, 'mother'.
Rising tone: *má*, 'hemp' or 'numb'.
Falling-rising tone: *mǎ*, 'horse'.
Falling tone: *mà*, 'scold' or 'swear'.

In pinyin, apostrophes are sometimes used to separate syllables, eg *ping'an* prevents the word being pronounced as *pin'gan*. The English 'v' sound doesn't occur in Chinese. For beginners, the trickiest sounds are **c**, **q** and **x** because their pronunciation isn't remotely similar to English.

c	as the 'ts' in 'bits'
ch	as in 'church', but with the tongue curled back
h	guttural, a bit like the 'ch' of 'loch'
q	as the 'ch' in 'chicken'
r	as the 's' in 'pleasure'
sh	as in 'ship', but with the tongue curled back
x	as the 'sh' in 'ship'
z	as the 'ds' in 'suds'
zh	as the 'j' in 'judge' but with the tongue curled back

USEFUL WORDS & PHRASES

Hello.
你好   *Nǐ hǎo.*
Goodbye.
再见   *Zàijiàn.*
Thank you.
谢谢   *Xièxie.*
You're welcome.
不客气   *Búkèqi.*
I'm sorry.
对不起   *Duìbùqǐ.*
May I ask your name?
您贵姓?   *Nín guìxìng?*
My (sur)name is ...
我姓 ...   *Wǒ xìng ...*
Where are you from?
你是从 ...   *Nǐ shì cōng ...*
哪儿来的?   *nǎr láide?*
I'm from ...
我是从 ... 来的   *Wǒ shì cōng ... láide.*
No. (don't have)
没有   *Méi yǒu.*
No. (not so)
不是   *Búshì.*
No, I don't want it.
不要   *Búyào.*
I don't understand.
我听不懂   *Wǒ tīngbudǒng.*
Could you speak more slowly, please?
请你说慢一点，   *Qǐng nǐ shuō màn yìdiǎn,*
好吗?   *hǎo ma?*

IN TOWN

How much is it?
多少钱?   *Duōshǎo qián?*
That's too expensive.
太贵了   *Tài guìle.*
Bank of China
中国银行   *Zhōngguó Yínháng*
change money
换钱   *huàn qián*
telephone
电话   *diànhuà*
Where is the ...?
... 在哪里?   *... zài nǎli?*

EMERGENCIES – CHINESE

I'm sick.
我生病   *Wǒ shēng bìng.*
Help!
救命啊   *Jiùmìng a!*
Thief!
小偷   *Xiǎo tōu!*
emergency
紧急情况   *jǐnjí qíngkuàng*
hospital
医院   *yīyuàn*
police
警察   *jǐngchá*
foreign affairs police
外事警察   *wàishì jǐngchá*

hotel
旅馆   *lǚguǎn*
tourist hotel
宾馆/饭店/   *bīnguǎn/fàndiàn/*
酒店   *jiǔdiàn*
Is there a room vacant?
有没有空房间？   *Yǒu méiyǒu kōng fángjiān?*
Yes, there is/No, there isn't.
有/没有   *Yǒu/Méiyǒu.*
single room
单人房   *dānrénfáng*
twin room
双人房   *shuāngrénfáng*
toilet (restroom)
厕所   *cèsuǒ*
men/women
男/女   *nan/nün*
toilet paper
卫生纸   *wèishēng zhǐ*
bathroom (washroom)
洗手间   *xǐshǒu jiān*

TRAIN TALK

train station
火车站   *huǒchē zhàn*
ticket office
售票处   *shòupiào chù*
I want to go to ...
我要去 ...   *Wǒ yào qù ...*
buy a ticket
买票   *mǎi piào*
one ticket
一张票   *yìzhāng piào*
two tickets
两张票   *liǎngzhāng piào*
hard-seat
硬席/硬座   *yìngxí/yìngzuò*

soft-seat
软席/软座   *ruǎnxí/ruǎnzuò*
hard-sleeper
硬卧   *yìngwò*
soft-sleeper
软卧   *ruǎnwò*

NUMBERS

0	零	*líng*
1	一/幺	*yī/yāoo*
2	二/两	*èr/liǎng*
3	三	*sān*
4	四	*sì*
5	五	*wǔ*
6	六	*liù*
7	七	*qī*
8	八	*bā*
9	九	*jiǔ*
10	十	*shí*
11	十一	*shíyī*
12	十二	*shíèr*
20	二十	*èrshí*
21	二十一	*èrshíyī*
100	一百	*yìbǎi*
200	两百	*liǎngbǎi*
1000	一千	*yìqiān*

MONGOLIAN

The official national language of Mongolia is Mongolian. Since 1944, the Russian Cyrillic alphabet has been used to write Mongolian (see p371). The only difference between Mongolian and Russian Cyrillic is that the Mongolian version has two additional characters (ө and ү), for a total of 35. Double vowels indicate that the vowel is stressed.

For a more detailed look at the language, pick up a copy of Lonely Planet's *Mongolian Phrasebook*.

USEFUL WORDS & PHRASES

Hello.
Сайн байна уу?   sain bai·na *uu*
(literally: How are you?)
Fine. How are you?
Сайн. Та сайн байна уу? sain ta sain bai·na *uu*
What's new?
Сонин сайхан   *so*·nin *sai*·khan
юу байна?   yu bai·na
Nothing really.
Тайван сайхан.   *tai*·van *sai*·khan
(literally: It's peaceful.)

EMERGENCIES – MONGOLIAN

Help!
Туслаарай! — tus-*laa*-rai
Call a doctor!
Эмч дуудаарай! — emch duu-*daa*-rai!
I'm ill.
Миний бие өвдөж байна. — mi-*nii* bi-ye öv-döj bai-na

Goodbye.
Баяртай. — ba-yar-*tai*
What's your name?
Таны нэрийг хэн — ta-*ny* ne-riig khen
гэдэг вэ? — ge-deg *ve*
My name is ...
Миний нэрийг ... гэдэг. — mi-*nii* ne-riig ... ge-deg
Yes.
Тийм. — tiim
No.
Үгүй. — ü-*güi*
Thanks.
Баярлалаа. — ba-yar-la-*laa*
Excuse me.
Уучлаарай. — uuch-*laa*-rai
What country are you from?
Та аль улсаас ирсэн бэ? — ta a-li ul-*saas* ir-sen *be*
I'm from ...
Би ... улсаас ирсэн. — bi ... ul-*saas* ir-sen
Do you speak English?
Та англиар ярьдаг уу? — ta an-*gliar* yair-dag uu
I don't understand.
Би ойлгохгүй байна. — bi *oil*-gokh-güi bai-na

Do you have a (town) map?
Танайд (хотын) зураг байна уу? — ta-*naid* (kho-*tyn*) zu-rag bai-na uu
Where's the train station?
Галт тэрэгний буудал хаана байдаг вэ? — galt te-re-ge-*nii* buud-al *khaa*-na bai-dag *ve*
hotel
зочид буудал — zo-chid *buu*-dal
Do you have any rooms available?
Танайд сул өрөө байна уу? — ta-*naid* sul ö-*röö* bai-na uu
I'd like a single room.
Би нэг хүний өрөө авмаар байна. — bi neg khü-*nii* ö-*röö* av-*maar* bai-na
I'd like a double room.
Би хоёр хүний өрөө авмаар байна. — bi kho-yor khü-*nii* ö-*röö* av-*maar* bai-na
What's the price per night/week?
Энэ өрөө хоногт/долоо хоногт ямар үнэтэй вэ? — ene ö-*röö* kho-nogt/do-loo kho-nogt *ya*-mar ün-*tei* ve

RUSSIAN

Russian is written in a variant of the Cyrillic alphabet (see p371). It's easy to find English speakers in the big cities but not so easy in the smaller towns (sometimes not even in tourist hotels).

For a more detailed guide to the language, get a copy of Lonely Planet's *Russian Phrasebook*.

PRONUNCIATION

The 'voiced' consonants (ie when the vocal cords vibrate) **б**, **в**, **г**, **д**, **ж**, and **з** are not voiced at the end of words (eg хлеб, 'bread', is pronounced *khlyep*) or before voiceless consonants.

Two letters have no sound but are used to modify the pronunciation of other letters. A consonant followed by the 'soft sign' **ь** is spoken with the tongue flat against the palate, as if followed by a faint 'y'. The 'hard sign' **ъ** is rarely seen; it occurs after consonants and indicates a slight pause before the next vowel.

USEFUL WORDS & PHRASES

Two words you're sure to use are the universal 'hello', здравствуйте (*zdrast*-vuy-te), and пожалуйста (pa-*zhal*-sta), the word for 'please' (commonly included in all polite requests), 'you're welcome', 'pardon me', 'after you' and more.

Hello.
Здравствуйте. — *zdrast*-vuy-te
Hi.
Привет. — pri-*vyet*
Good morning.
Доброе утро. — *do*-bra-e *u*-tra
Good afternoon.
Добрый день. — *do*-bri dyen'
Good evening.
Добрый вечер. — *dob*-ri *vye*-cher
Goodbye.
До свидания. — da svi-*da*-ni-ya
Bye.
Пока. — pa-*ka*
How are you?
Как дела? — kak de-*la*
What's your name?
Как вас зовут? — kak vas za-*vut*
My name is ...
Меня зовут ... — me-*nya* za-vut ...

THE RUSSIAN CYRILLIC ALPHABET

Cyrillic	Roman	Pronunciation
А, а	a	as the 'a' in 'father' (in stressed syllable); as the 'a' in 'ago' (in unstressed syllable)
Б, б	b	as the 'b' in 'but'
В, в	v	as the 'v' in 'van'
Г, г	g	as the 'g' in 'god'
Д, д	d	as the 'd' in 'dog'
Е, е	ye/e	as the 'ye' in 'yet' (in stressed syllable and at the beginning of a word); as the 'e' in 'ten' (in unstressed syllable)
Ё, ё *	yo	as the 'yo' in 'yore'
Ж, ж	zh	as the 's' in 'measure'
З, з	z	as the 'z' in 'zoo'
И, и	i	as the 'ee' in 'meet'
Й, й	y	as the 'y' in 'boy' (not transliterated after ы or и)
К, к	k	as the 'k' in 'kind'
Л, л	l	as the 'l' in 'lamp'
М, м	m	as the 'm' in 'mad'
Н, н	n	as the 'n' in 'not'
О, о	o/a	as the 'o' in 'more' (in stressed syllable); as the 'a' in 'hard' (in unstressed syllable)
П, п	p	as the 'p' in 'pig'
Р, р	r	as the 'r' in 'rub' (rolled)
С, с	s	as the 's' in 'sing'
Т, т	t	as the 't' in 'ten'
У, у	u	as the 'oo' in 'fool'
Ф, ф	f	as the 'f' in 'fan'
Х, х	kh	as the 'ch' in 'Bach'
Ц, ц	ts	as the 'ts' in 'hits'
Ч, ч	ch	as the 'ch' in 'chin'
Ш, ш	sh	as the 'sh' in 'shop'
Щ, щ	shch	as 'sh-ch' in 'fresh chips'
Ъ, ъ	-	'hard sign' (see opposite)
Ы, ы	i	as the 'i' in 'ill'
Ь, ь	'	'soft sign' (see opposite)
Э, э	e	as the 'e' in 'end'
Ю, ю	yu	as the 'u' in 'use'
Я, я	ya/ye	as the 'ya' in 'yard' (in stressed syllable); as the 'ye' in 'yearn' (in unstressed syllable)

* Ё, ё are often printed without dots

Where are you from?
Откуда вы?   at·ku·da vi
I'm from ...
Я из ...   ya iz ...
Yes.
Да.   da

No.
Нет.   nyet
Please.
Пожалуйста.   pa·zhal·sta
Thank you (very much).
(Большое) спасибо. (bal'·sho·e) spa·si·ba
Excuse me.
Простите.   pras·ti·te
I'm sorry.
Извините.   iz·vi·ni·te
No problem/Never mind.
Ничего.   ni·che·vo

Do you speak English?
Вы говорите по-английски?
vi ga·va·ri·te pa an·gli·ski
I don't understand.
Я не понимаю.
ya nye pa·ni·ma·yu
Could you write it down, please?
Запишите, пожалуйста?
za·pi·shi·te pa·zhal·sta
Can you help me, please?
Помогите, пожалуйста.
pa·ma·gi·te pa·zhal·sta

EMERGENCIES – RUSSIAN

I'm ill.
Я болен.   ya bo·len (m)
Я больна.   ya bal'·na (f)
I need a doctor.
Мне нужно врач.   mnye nuzh·na vra·ch
hospital
больница   bal'·ni·tsa
the police
милицию   mi·li·tsi·yu
Help!
Помогите!   pa·ma·gi·te
Thief!
Вор!   vor

IN TOWN

I need ...
Мне нужно ...   mnye nuzh·na ...
Do you have ...?
У вас есть ...?   u vas yest' ...
How much is it?
Сколько стоит?   skol'·ka sto·it
Where is ...?
Где ...?   gdye ...
hotel
гостиница   gas·ti·ni·tsa

LANGUAGE

room
номер · *no·*mer
telephone
телефон · te·le·*fon*
Toilet
Туалет · tu·a·*let*
Men
Мужской (М) · muzh·*skoy*
Women
Женский (Ж) · zhen·*ski*

Do you have a ... room?
У вас есть ...?
u vas yest' ...
   single
   одноместный номер
   ad·na·*myest*·ni *no·*mer
   double
   номер с двуспальней кроватью
   *no·*mer z dvu·*spal'*·ney kra·*va·*t'yu

Where is the toilet?
Где здесь туалет? · gdye zdyes' tu·al·*yet*
How much is a room?
Сколько стоит номер? · *skol'*·ka *sto*·it *no·*mer
Do you have a cheaper room?
У вас есть дешевле · u vas yest' de·*shyev*·le
   номер? · *no·*mer

TRAIN TALK
I want to go to ...
Я хочу ехать в ...
ya kha·*chu* ye·khat' v ...
When is the next train?
Когда следующий поезд?
kag·*da* slye·du·yu·shi *po*·ist
When does it leave?
Когда отправляется?
kag·*da* at·prav·*lya*·it·sa
Are there SV/kupe/platskartny tickets on train number ... to ...?
Есть билеты для СВ/для купе/в плацкарте на поезд
   номер ... до ...?
yest' bil·*ye*·tih dlya es ve/dlya ku·*pe*/f plats·*kar*·tye na *po*·ist
   *no·*mir ... na ...
I'd like to buy an SV/kupe/platstkartny ticket for train number ... to ...
Я хотел/хотела бы купить билет для СВ/
   для купе/в плацкарте на поезд номер ... до ...
ya kha·*tyel* (m)/kha·*tye*·la (f) bih ku·*pit'* bil·*yet* dlya es ve/
   dlya ku·*pe*/f plats·*kar*·tye na *po*·ist *no·*mir ... na ...
Which platform does the train leave from?
С какой платформы отходит поезд?
s ka·*koy* plat·*for*·mih at·*kho*·dit *po*·ist

Please tell me why I can't buy a ticket.
Скажите, пожалуйста, почему я не могу купить
   билета!
ska·*zhih*·tye pa·*zhal*·sta pa·chi·*mu* ya nye ma·*gu* ku·*pit'*
   bil·*ye*·ta
There's no train today.
Сегодня не будет поезда.
si·*vod*·nya nye *bu*·dit pa·iz·*da*
The train is full.
Все билеты на этот поезд проданы. (literally: all
   tickets are sold)
fsye bil·*ye*·tih na et·at po·ist *pro*·da·nih
There are no SV/kupe/platskartny tickets left for the train.
Билеты для СВ/для купе/в плацкарте уже все
   распродались.
bil·*lye*·tih dlya es ve/dlya ku·*pe*/f plats·*kar*·tye u·*zhye* vsye
   ras·pra·*da*·lis'
Tickets for that service aren't on sale until ...
Билеты на этот город будут на продаже с ...
bil·*ye*·tih na e·tat *go*·rat *bu*·dut na pra·*da*·zhye s ...
You're at the wrong ticket window. Please go to window ...
Вы стоите не в том месте. Обращайтесь к окошку ...!
vi sta·*i*·tye nye f tom *myes*·tye a·bra·*shai*·tyes k a·*kosh*·ku ...

map
карта · *kar*·ta
platform
платформа · plat·*for*·ma
train station
железнодорожный · zhi·lyez·na·da·*rozh*·nih
   (ж. д.) вокзал · vag·*zal*
ticket, tickets
билет, билеты · bil·*yet*, bil·*ye*·tih
ticket office
билетная касса · bil·*yet*·na·ya *ka*·sa
timetable
расписание · ras·pi·*sa*·ni·ye
one-way
в один конец · v a·*din* kan·*yets*
return, round trip
туда и обратно · tu·*da* i a·*brat*·na
baggage
багаж · ba·*gash*
arrival
прибытие · pri·*bih*·ti·ye
departure
отправление · at·prav·*lye*·ni·ye

TIME, DAYS & NUMBERS
When?
Когда? · kag·*da*
At what time?
В котором часу? · f ka·*to*·ram cha·*su*

LANGUAGE

today

сегодня   se·*vod*·nya

tomorrow

завтра   *zaft*·ra

day after tomorrow

послезавтра   pos·le·*zaf*·tra

yesterday

вчера   vche·*ra*

Dates are given day-month-year, with the month usually in Roman numerals. Days of the week are often represented by numbers in timetables (Monday is 1).

Monday	понедельник	pa·ne·*dyel'*·nik
Tuesday	вторник	*ftor*·nik
Wednesday	среда	sre·*da*
Thursday	четверг	chet·*vyerk*
Friday	пятница	*pyat*·ni·tsa
Saturday	суббота	su·*ho*·ta
Sunday	воскресенье	vas·kre·*syen'*·e

January	январь	yan·*var'*
February	февраль	fev·*ral'*
March	март	mart
April	апрель	ap·*ryel'*
May	май	may
June	июнь	i·*yun'*
July	июль	i·*yul'*
August	август	*av*·gust
September	сентябрь	sen·*tyabr'*
October	октябрь	ok·*tyabr'*
November	ноябрь	na·*yabr'*
December	декабрь	de·*kabr'*

How much/many?

Сколько?   *skol'*·ka

1	один	a·*din*
2	два	dva
3	три	tri
4	четыре	che·*ti*·re
5	пять	pyat'
6	шесть	shyest'
7	семь	syem'
8	восемь	*vo*·sem'
9	девять	*dye*·vyat'
10	десять	*dye*·syat'
11	одиннадцать	a·*di*·na·tsat'
12	двенадцать	dve·*na*·tsat'
13	тринадцать	tri·*na*·tsat'
14	четырнадцать	che·*tir*·na·tsat'
15	пятнадцать	pyat·*na*·tsat'
16	шестнадцать	shest·*na*·tsat'
17	семнадцать	sem·*na*·tsat'
18	восемнадцать	va·sem·*na*·tsat'
19	девятнадцать	de·vyat·*na*·tsat'
20	двадцать	*dva*·tsat'
21	двадцать один	*dva*·tsat' a·*din*
22	двадцать два	*dva*·tsat' dva
30	тридцать	*tri*·tsat'
40	сорок	*so*·rak
50	пятьдесят	pyat'·des·*yat*
60	шестдесят	shes·des·*yat*
70	семьдесят	*syem'*·des·yat
80	восемьдесят	*vo*·sem'·de·syat
90	девяносто	de·vya·*no*·sta
100	сто	sto
1000	тысяча	*ti*·sya·cha
1,000,000	(один) миллион	(a·*din*) mi·li·*on*

Glossary

This glossary is a list of Russian (R), Chinese (C) and Mongolian (M) terms you may come across during your Trans-Siberian journey. See p85 for words that will help you while dining. Also see the Language chapter, p368, for some other useful words and phrases.

aimag (M) – province or state within Mongolia
airag (M) – fermented mare's milk
apteka (R) – pharmacy
arkhi (M) – the common word to describe homemade vodka
aviakassa (R) – air-ticket office
avtomat (R) – automatic ticket machine
avtostantsiya (R) – bus stop
avtovokzal (R) – bus terminal

babushka (R) – grandmother
BAM (R) – Baikalo-Amurskaya Magistral (Baikal-Amur Mainline)
bankomat (R) – ATM
banya (R) – bathhouse
bashnya (R) – tower
bei (C) – north
benzin (R) – petrol
biblioteka (R) – library
bilet (R) – ticket
binguan (C) – tourist hotel
biznesmen/biznesmenka (R) – literally, businessman/woman, but often used to mean a small-time operator on the fringe of the law
Bogd Gegen (M) – hereditary line of reincarnated Buddhist leaders of Mongolia, the third highest in the Buddhist hierarchy, which started with Zanabazar
Bogd Khaan (M) – Holy King; title given to the eighth Bogd Gegen (1869–1924)
bolnitsa (R) – hospital
bulvar (R) – boulevard

CAAC (C) – Civil Aviation Administration of China, which controls most of China's domestic and foreign airlines
CCP (C) – Chinese Communist Party
Chángtú gōnggōngqìchē (C) – long-distance buses
CIS (R) – Commonwealth of Independent States; an alliance of independent states comprising the former USSR republics, with the exception of the three Baltic countries
CITS (C) – China International Travel Service
CTS (C) – China Travel Service

dacha (R) – country cottage, summer house
dajie (C) – avenue
datsan (R) – Buddhist monastery
detsky (R) – child's, children's
dezhurnaya (R) – woman looking after a particular floor of a hotel
dom (R) – house
dong (C) – east
duma (R) – parliament
dvorets (R) – palace

elektrichka (R) – also *prigorodny poezd*; suburban train
elitny (R) – elite, typically used an adjective to describe an exclusive place
etazh (R) – floor (storey)

fen (C) – one-tenth of a *jiao*, in Chinese currency (which makes it miniscule)
firmeny poezda (R) – trains with names (eg *Rossiya*); these are generally nicer trains
FSB (R) – Federalnaya Sluzhba Bezopasnosti, the Federal Security Service, the successor to the KGB

GAI (R) – Gosudarstvennaya Avtomobilnaya Inspektsia; State Automobile Inspectorate (traffic police)
gavan (R) – harbour
gazeta (R) – newspaper
ger (M) – traditional, circular felt yurt
glavpochtamt (R) – main post office
gol (M) – river
gorod (R) – city, town
gostinitsa (R) – hotel
gostiny dvor (R) – trading arcade
granitsa (R) – border
gudamj (M) – street
Gulag (R) – Glavnoe Upravlenie Lagerey (Main Administration for Camps); the Soviet network of concentration camps
GUM (R) – Gosudarstvenny Univermag; State Department Store

hu (C) – lake
hutong (C) – narrow alleyway

Inner Mongolia (M) – a separate province within China
inostranets (R) – foreigner
Intourist (R) – the old Soviet State Committee for Tourism, now hived off, split up and in competition with hundreds of other travel agencies
izba (R & M) – traditional single-storey wooden house

Jebtzun Damba (M) – also known as Bogd Gegen; a hereditary line of reincarnated spiritual leaders of Mongolia
jiao (C) – one-tenth of a yuàn, in Chinese currency
jie (C) – street

kamera khraneniya (R) – left-luggage room
karta (R) – map, or multiride metro pass cards
kassa (R) – ticket office, cashier's desk
Kazakh (M) – Turkic ethnic group from Central Asia, also found in the west of Mongolia; people from Kazakhstan
KGB (R) – Komitet Gosydarstvennoy Bezopasnosti; Committee of State Security; now the FSB
khaan (M) – a king or chief
Khalkh (M) – the major ethnic group living in Mongolia
khiid (M) – Buddhist monastery
khorol (M) – traditional Mongolian game similar to checkers
khram (R) – church
kino (R) – cinema
kladbishche (R) – cemetery
kniga/knigi (R) – book/books
komnaty otdykha (R) – literally 'resting rooms'; cheap lodgings in Siberian train stations
Komsomol (R) – Communist Youth League
kopek (R) – kopeck; the smallest, worthless unit of Russian currency
kray (R) – territory
kreml (R) – kremlin, a town's fortified stronghold
Kuomintang (C) – Chiang Kaishek's Nationalist Party, the dominant political force after the fall of the Qing dynasty; now Taiwan's major political party
kupeyny (R) – *kupe*; compartmentalised carriage

lama (M) – Tibetan Buddhist monk or priest
lavra (R) – senior monastery
Living Buddha (M) – common term for reincarnations of Buddhas; Buddhist spiritual leader in Mongolia
lu (C) – road
lyux (R) – a lyux room in a hotel is a kind of suite, with a sitting room in addition to the bedroom and bathroom

Mafia (R) – anyone who has anything to do with crime, from genuine gangsters to petty criminals
magazin (R) – shop
Manchus (C) – non-Chinese ethnic group from Manchuria (present-day northeast China) that took over China and established the Qing dynasty
manezh (R) – riding school
marshrutky (R) – minibus that runs along a fixed route
matryoshka (R) – set of painted wooden dolls stacked within dolls
mestnoe vremya (R) – local time
militsia (R) – police
more (R) – sea
morin khuur (M) – horsehead fiddle
most (R) – bridge

MPRP (M) – Mongolian People's Revolutionary Party
muzey (R) – museum; also some palaces, art galleries and nonworking churches
muzhskoy (R) – men's (toilet)

Naadam (M) – game; the Naadam Festival (see p288)
naberezhnaya (R) – embankment
nan (C) – south
novy (R) – new
nuruu (M) – mountain range

oblast (R) – region
obshchy (R) – 4th-class train compartment
okrug (R) – district
örgön chölöö (M) – avenue
OVIR (Otdel Viz I Registratsii) – old Department of Visas and Registration; now known under the acronym UFMS, although outside Moscow OVIR or PVU is still likely to be in use
ovoo (M) – shamanistic collection of stones, wood or other offerings to the gods, usually placed in high places
ozero (R) – lake

Paskha (R) – Easter
pereryv (R) – break (when shops, ticket offices, restaurants etc close for an hour or two during the day)
pereulok (R) – lane or side street
peshchera (R) – cave
Pinyin (C) – the system of writing the Chinese language in the Roman alphabet, adopted by the Communist Party in 1958
PLA (C) – People's Liberation Army
platskartny (R) – *platskart*, also *zhyosky*; 3rd class (or hard seat) in an open carriage of a train
ploshchad (R) – square
poezd (R) – train
posolstvo (R) – embassy
PRC (C) – People's Republic of China
prichal (R) – landing, pier
prigorodny poezd (R) – also *elektrichka*; suburban train
prospekt (R) – avenue
provodnik/provodnitsa (R) – male/female carriage attendant on a train
PSB (C) – Public Security Bureau; the arm of the police force that deals with foreigners
PVU (Passportno-Vizovoye Upravleniye) – old passport and visa department, formerly OVIR, but now known as UFMS

rayon (R) – district
rechnoy vokzal (R) – river terminal
remont, na remont (R) – closed for repairs
Renminbi (C) – literally 'people's money', the formal name for the currency of China; shortened to RMB
Rozhdestvo (R) – Christmas
ruǎn wò (C) – soft-seat sleeper

ruǎn zuò (C) – soft-seat carriage
rubl (R) – rouble*ruǎn zuò*

sad (R) – garden
samovar (R) – urn with an inner tube filled with hot charcoal used for heating water for tea
selo (R) – village
sever (R) – north
shosse (R) – highway
siheyuan (C) – traditional house with courtyard
selo (R) – village
skory (R) – fast
Sodruzhestvo Nezavisimykh Gosudarstv (R) – SNG; Commonwealth of Independent States (CIS)
selo (R) – village
sotovye telefony (R) – mobile phone
spalny vagon (R) – also SV; sleeping wagon
stupa (M) – Buddhist religious monument composed of a solid hemisphere topped by a spire, containing relics of the Buddha; also known as a pagoda, or suburgan in Mongolian
süm (M) – Buddhist temple

taiga (R) – northern pine, fir, spruce and larch forest
teatr (R) – theatre
tögrög (M) – unit of currency in Mongolia
traktir (R) – tavern
troika (R) – vehicle drawn by three horses
Tsagaan Sar (M) – 'White Moon' or 'White Month'; a festival to celebrate the start of the lunar year
tserkov (R) – church
tualet (R) – toilet

UFMS (R) – Upravleniye Federalnoy Migratsionnoy Slyzhby (Federal Migration Service) often shortened to UFMS or FMS. It's likely you'll hear the old acronyms PVU and OVIR used for this office.
ulitsa (R) – street
univermag, universalnyy magazin (R) – department store
urtyn-duu (M) – traditional singing style
uul (M) – mountain

valyuta (R) – foreign currency
vokzal (R) – station
vostok (R) – east

xi (C) – west

yezhednevno (R) – daily
yìng wò (C) – hard-seat sleeper
yìng zuò (C) – hard seat, though often padded
yuàn (C) – the Chinese unit of currency, also referred to as RMB
yug (R) – south
yurt (R) – nomad's portable, round tent-house made of felt or skins stretched over a collapsible frame of wood slats

zal (R) – hall, room
zamok (R) – castle, fortress
zapad (R) – west
zapovednik (R) – nature reserve
zhenskiy (R) – women's (toilet)
zheton (R) – token (for metro etc)

The Authors

SIMON RICHMOND
Coordinating Author, St Petersburg

After studying Russian history and politics at university, Simon's first visit to the country was in 1994 when he wandered goggle eyed around St Petersburg, and peeked at Lenin's mummified corpse in Red Square. He's since traversed the country on the Trans-Siberian, Trans-Mongolian and Trans-Manchurian lines as well as parts of the BAM and Turk-Sib lines. An award-winning writer and photographer, Simon has written about Russia for several publications including the Russian edition of *Newsweek*. He's the co-author of both past editions of Lonely Planet's *Trans-Siberian Railway* as well as the last three editions of *Russia*. Catch him online at www.simonrichmond.com.

MARC BENNETTS
Yekaterinburg to Krasnoyarsk

Initially enticed to St Petersburg by the works of Gogol and Dostoevsky, Marc later moved to Moscow, where he has lived since 1998. During that time he has followed the fortunes of Russian football, and in 2008 his book *Football Dynamo – Modern Russia and the People's Game* – was released. He has also written about Russia for a number of guides and magazines. Marc currently works for a Russian news agency and is researching his second book – to be either a vampire novel set in Siberia or a look at modern Russian–British relations.

MARC DI DUCA   Krasnoyarsk to Lake Baikal, Lake Baikal to Vladivostok, Tayshet to Sovetskaya Gavan via BAM

Born a mile from the Stockton-to-Darlington Railway (the first in the world), Marc has a natural affinity with ribbons of steel. He's been riding the ex-USSR's rails since the late-1990s when a trip from Kiev to Crimea took him through the endless sunflower fields of Ukraine. Thousands of miles later, Marc still loves the ceremony of Russian Railways – buying food for the trip, the *provodnitsa* – and keeps returning for more. Marc has worked on several Ukraine and Russia-related titles, most recently Lonely Planet's *Russia*. He can usually be found in Sandwich, Kent, where he lives with his Kievite wife, Tanya.

LONELY PLANET AUTHORS

Why is our travel information the best in the world? It's simple: our authors are passionate, dedicated travellers. They don't take freebies in exchange for positive coverage so you can be sure the advice you're given is impartial. They travel widely to all the popular spots, and off the beaten track. They don't research using just the internet or phone. They discover new places not included in any other guidebook. They personally visit thousands of hotels, restaurants, palaces, trails, galleries, temples and more. They speak with dozens of locals every day to make sure you get the kind of insider knowledge only a local could tell you. They take pride in getting all the details right, and in telling it how it is. Think you can do it? Find out how at **lonelyplanet.com**.

MICHAEL KOHN

**Ulan-Ude to Běijīng via Mongolia,
Chita to Běijīng via Hāěrbin, Běijīng**

Michael first experienced the Trans-Sib in 1997 when he took the train from
Běijīng to Ulaanbaatar in the dead of winter where he had a three-year stint
as the editor of the *Mongol Messenger*. Over the years since, he has travelled
to every corner of the country and even made the very random train journey
from Choibalsan to the Russian border. Michael has also worked for a variety
of news outlets in Mongolia, including the BBC, Associated Press and the *New
York Times*. He has worked on a dozen other Lonely Planet titles, including
China, *Mongolia* and *Russia*. Michael is online at www.michaelkohn.us.

LEONID RAGOZIN

**Moscow to Yekaterinburg,
Yekaterinburg to Krasnoyarsk**

Leonid devoted himself to beach dynamics when he studied geology at
Moscow State University. For want of nice beaches in Russia, he helped gold
prospectors in Siberia and sold InterRail tickets and Lonely Planet books to
Russians before embarking on a journalist career. After eight years with the
BBC, he was poached by Russian *Newsweek*. He has coerced his superiors
into sending him to far-flung destinations. If you see a Russian boarding a
Bolivian Air Force 1 plane, searching for Circassians in Kosovo or celebrating
St Patrick's Day in Belfast with ex-militants, it's probably him.

ROBERT REID

**Lake Baikal to Vladivostok,
Tayshet to Sovetskaya Gavan via BAM**

Raised in Oklahoma, Robert (www.reidontravel.com) eventually turned from
Richie Rich comics to Dostoevsky and his subsequent Russian studies got him
to spend the 'first summer of Russia' (1992) in Moscow and St Petersburg.
His favourite parts of Russia tend to be further east, though – the little
forgotten towns found on the BAM and way east of Lake Baikal. He lives
in Brooklyn, New York.

MARA VORHEES

Moscow, Moscow to Yekaterinburg

Mara has been travelling to Russia since the days of the Cold War. She spent
the first half of the 1990s learning Russian before working on a foreign-aid
project in the Urals. She has ridden the Trans-Siberian, cruised the Volga
River, circled the Golden Ring and mastered the Moscow metro. Her stories
about Moscow have appeared in *National Geographic Traveler,* among others.
She is the author of Lonely Planet's *Moscow* and *St Petersburg* city guides.
When not in Russia, she lives in in Somerville, Massachusetts with her husband and cat. Check out her adventures on www.maravorhees.com.

Behind the Scenes

THIS BOOK

This 3rd edition of *Trans-Siberian Railway* was co-ordinated by Simon Richmond with contributions by Marc Bennetts, Marc Di Duca, Michael Kohn, Leonid Ragozin, Robert Reid and Mara Vorhees.

This guidebook was commissioned in Lonely Planet's London office, and produced by the following:

Commissioning Editors Amanda Canning, Will Gourlay, Korina Miller, Jo Potts, Sally Schafer
Coordinating Editor Evan Jones
Coordinating Cartographer Valentina Kremenchutskaya
Coordinating Layout Designer Jim Hsu
Managing Editors Brigitte Ellemor, Geoff Howard
Managing Cartographer Mark Griffiths
Managing Layout Designers Celia Wood, Sally Darmody
Assisting Editors Michelle Bennett, Jessica Crouch, Helen Koehne, Helen Yeates, Nigel Chin
Assisting Cartographers Alissa Baker, Anita Banh, Bonnie Wintle, Diana Duggan, Marion Byass, Brendan Streager, Alex Leung, Tony Fankhauser, Amanda Sierp
Cover Designer Pepi Bluck
Project Managers Eoin Dunlevy
Language Content Coordinator Quentin Frayne

Thanks to Lucy Birchley, Clara Monitto, John Mazzocchi, Daniel Corbett, Mark Germanchis, Adam Bextream, James Hardy, Wayne Murphy, Imogen Bannister, Ali Lemer

THANKS
SIMON RICHMOND

Amanda Canning put in the yards as this book's initial commissioning editor and was a pleasure to work with, as were the dream team of authors – *bolshoi spasibo* all round but especially to Leonid Ragozin, who worked overtime (literally!) to make sure we captured Russia in all its messy, fascinating glory. It's always a pleasure returning to St Petersburg and catching up with old friends such as Peter, Sasha and Andrey who greeted me with delicious ginger-infused vodka and melt-in-the-mouth *pirogi* and, as always, provided many fun-filled nights and insights into their beloved city. Cheers to my drinking buddy Matt Brown, for being on the ball about all things Piter. Thanks also to Herve Le Bail, Jennifer Fell, Ilya Gurevich, Dr Dimitri Ozerkov, Andrei Dmitriev, Vyacheslav Bochkov, Valery Katsuba, Sergei Politovsky, marathon train traveller Ed Greig, Chris Hamilton and Paul and Veronica at Express to Russia for assistance with my visa. It was a treat being able to spend a few days on the *Golden Eagle*, in particular in the company of fellow passengers Charles Cuddington, Richard Lewis and Richard and Carol Gray. I'm also grateful to Yulia Fadeeva on the return journey to St Petersburg on the Demidovsky Express. For his support while I'm on the road and at home, thanks to the adorable Twanda.

THE LONELY PLANET STORY

Fresh from an epic journey across Europe, Asia and Australia in 1972, Tony and Maureen Wheeler sat at their kitchen table stapling together notes. The first Lonely Planet guidebook, *Across Asia on the Cheap,* was born.

Travellers snapped up the guides. Inspired by their success, the Wheelers began publishing books to Southeast Asia, India and beyond. Demand was prodigious, and the Wheelers expanded the business rapidly to keep up. Over the years, Lonely Planet extended its coverage to every country and into the virtual world via lonelyplanet.com and the Thorn Tree message board.

As Lonely Planet became a globally loved brand, Tony and Maureen received several offers for the company. But it wasn't until 2007 that they found a partner whom they trusted to remain true to the company's principles of travelling widely, treading lightly and giving sustainably. In October of that year, BBC Worldwide acquired a 75% share in the company, pledging to uphold Lonely Planet's commitment to independent travel, trustworthy advice and editorial independence.

Today, Lonely Planet has offices in Melbourne, London and Oakland, with over 500 staff members and 300 authors. Tony and Maureen are still actively involved with Lonely Planet. They're travelling more often than ever, and they're devoting their spare time to charitable projects. And the company is still driven by the philosophy of *Across Asia on the Cheap*: 'All you've got to do is decide to go and the hardest part is over. So go!'

BEHIND THE SCENES

MARC BENNETTS

Thanks to – Minsalim, Margarita, Golnur and Rafik in Tobolsk; Ludmila Ivanovo and Albina in Novokuznetsk; Larisa and Yelena in Kemerovo; Sayat and Kayrat in Kosh Agash. And all my fellow authors for their useful comments.

MARC DI DUCA

Many thanks to Amanda Canning for entrusting me with eastern Siberia, and to Simon Richmond for his expert guidance and support as coordinating author. I am also indebted to my fellow authors for their advice and wisdom in all matters Russian. Many, many thanks go to Jack and the gang in Irkutsk, Svetlana and Tatiana in Ulan-Ude, Leonid and family in Moscow, Sean and Aylana in Kyzyl, Anatoly in Krasnoyarsk, Boyir and family in Chita, Alex in Ust-Barguzin, and Alyona in Severobaikalsk. Finally a huge *spasibo* to my wife Tanya for all the days we spend apart.

MICHAEL KOHN

In Mongolia, thanks to my wife Baigalmaa and friends Guido and Toroo (of the Khongor Guesthouse). In China, thanks to Maryanne for putting me up and to Athena for translation help. In Ulan-Ude thanks to Svetlana for getting me around town. Cheers to my fellow train passengers for camaraderie. Special thanks to coordinating author Simon, the editors and my fellow authors for virtual support along the way.

LEONID RAGOZIN

Most of all, I'd like to thank Simon Richmond for all his patience, help and advice throughout the project and Masha Makeeva for enduring my long absences and maps flying around our bedroom. I am also very grateful to Yaroslav Blanter whose online guide to Russia inspired me to visit Bolgar and Sviyazhsk, Denis and Svetlana Kamenshchikov for taking care of me in Yekaterinburg, Konstantin and Olga Brylyakov for many years of help to all LP authors and for a ride to Nevyansk, and Dmitry Mouzychenko and his friend Juliana for an unexpected party in Nizhny and a tip on Gorodets.

ROBERT REID

Thanks to Will Gourlay and Amanda Canning at LP for the job, and Simon Richmond and my fellow authors for letting me bounce off wild ideas in our all-author chat group. Many locals made my life easier, particularly the hilarious woman working the ticket counter at the Blagoveshchensk river port who chased me down outside to hand me a (jokingly requested) photo of the ship captain. 'Young man! A souvenir for you!'

MARA VORHEES

No place to stay in Moscow is so comfy cosy as flat No 24 on the Sadovaya-Triumfalnaya. Grazie, Mirjana, for feeding me fruit and always offering opinions! Tim, I owe you so many beers by now. Not to mention all your people, especially Max and Yulia – спасибо! Lyonya, thank you for making me raki, among other things (many other things). I am grateful to my co-authors, especially our fearless leader Simon and Muscovites Marc B and Leo R. And, Jerz, thank you for the garden, the wine rack, the bike rides, the coffee, the music, the love.

OUR READERS

Many thanks to the travellers who used the last edition and wrote to us with helpful hints, useful advice and interesting anecdotes:

Carlos Arroyo, Mark Barr, Jane Boyd, Haydn Brooks, Sue Buparai, William Burke, Kay Burnham, Richard Chapman, Rob Croft,

---

SEND US YOUR FEEDBACK

We love to hear from travellers – your comments keep us on our toes and help make our books better. Our well-travelled team reads every word on what you loved or loathed about this book. Although we cannot reply individually to postal submissions, we always guarantee that your feedback goes straight to the appropriate authors, in time for the next edition. Each person who sends us information is thanked in the next edition – and the most useful submissions are rewarded with a free book.

To send us your updates – and find out about Lonely Planet events, newsletters and travel news – visit our award-winning website: **lonelyplanet.com/contact**.

Note: we may edit, reproduce and incorporate your comments in Lonely Planet products such as guidebooks, websites and digital products, so let us know if you don't want your comments reproduced or your name acknowledged. For a copy of our privacy policy visit lonelyplanet.com/privacy.

Christopher Culver, Anna Cumming, Fabiana Cymrot, Eduardo De Aysa, Margriet De Jong, Marco De Oliveira, Jennifer Difilippo, Francois Dube, Geraldine Dunbar, Tali Emdin, Kate Evans, Stephan Ferreira, Sally Fowler, Kate Franks, Montserrat Garcia Calvo, Alex Gelfand, Phil Gillette, Chris Gleed-Owen, Edward Greve, Keith Hack, Martin Hajek, Alex Humberg, Christine Hüttinger, Mark Janson, Adam Jones, Evgeny Karachakov, David Kennedy, Fiona King, Antti Koskinen, Linda Lablans, Tim Lewis, Reto Locher, Lissy Lovett, Carrie Macmillan, Christopher And Emily Mcgill, Andrew Moncrieff, Roy Oltmans, Marieke Prommenschenckel, Tim Passey, Shanna Pedersen, Matt Pepe, Ann Persson, Gillian Peskett, Mary Power, Frank Pridding, Roger Ratcliff, Stephen Rich, Jelmer Samplonius, Marianne Schmid, Andrew Schraff, Sam Sinnayah, Ludmila Souckova, Helen Sutton, Dan Taylor, Anne Laure Thevoz, Eric Van Der Sneppen, Saskia Van Vugt, Martina Vondrova, Kristin Westdal, Sebastian Zahn, Andreas Zeman

ACKNOWLEDGMENTS
Many thanks to the following for the use of their content:

Globe on title page ©Mountain High Maps 1993 Digital Wisdom, Inc.

Index

INDEX

INDEX

INDEX

INDEX

MAP LEGEND

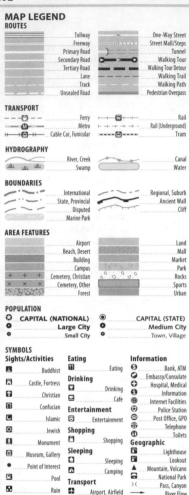

ROUTES
- Tollway
- Freeway
- Primary Road
- Secondary Road
- Tertiary Road
- Lane
- Track
- Unsealed Road
- One-Way Street
- Street Mall/Steps
- Tunnel
- Walking Tour
- Walking Tour Detour
- Walking Trail
- Walking Path
- Pedestrian Overpass

TRANSPORT
- Ferry
- Metro
- Cable Car, Funicular
- Rail
- Rail (Underground)
- Tram

HYDROGRAPHY
- River, Creek
- Swamp
- Canal
- Water

BOUNDARIES
- International
- State, Provincial
- Disputed
- Marine Park
- Regional, Suburb
- Ancient Wall
- Cliff

AREA FEATURES
- Airport
- Beach, Desert
- Building
- Campus
- Cemetery, Christian
- Cemetery, Other
- Forest
- Land
- Mall
- Market
- Park
- Rocks
- Sports
- Urban

POPULATION
- ◉ CAPITAL (NATIONAL)
- ● Large City
- ● Small City
- ◎ CAPITAL (STATE)
- ● Medium City
- ○ Town, Village

SYMBOLS

Sights/Activities
- Buddhist
- Castle, Fortress
- Christian
- Confucian
- Islamic
- Jewish
- Monument
- Museum, Gallery
- Point of Interest
- Pool
- Ruin
- Zoo, Bird Sanctuary

Eating
- Eating

Drinking
- Drinking
- Cafe

Entertainment
- Entertainment

Shopping
- Shopping

Sleeping
- Sleeping
- Camping

Transport
- Airport, Airfield
- Bus Station

Information
- Bank, ATM
- Embassy/Consulate
- Hospital, Medical
- Information
- Internet Facilities
- Police Station
- Post Office, GPO
- Telephone
- Toilets

Geographic
- Lighthouse
- Lookout
- Mountain, Volcano
- National Park
- Pass, Canyon
- River Flow
- Waterfall

LONELY PLANET OFFICES

Australia
Head Office
Locked Bag 1, Footscray, Victoria 3011
☎ 03-8379 8000, fax 03-8379 8111
talk2us@lonelyplanet.com.au

USA
150 Linden St, Oakland, CA 94607
☎ 510 250 6400, toll free 800 275 8555
fax 510 893 8572
info@lonelyplanet.com

UK
2nd fl, 186 City Rd,
London EC1V 2NT
☎ 020-7106 2100, fax 020-7106 2101
go@lonelyplanet.co.uk

Published by Lonely Planet Publications Pty Ltd
ABN 36 005 607 983

© Lonely Planet Publications Pty Ltd 2009

© photographers as indicated 2009

Cover photograph: A *prodvodnista* (carriage attendant) standing in front of No 9/10 *Baikal* train, Simon Richmond/Lonely Planet Images. Many of the images in this guide are available for licensing from Lonely Planet Images: www.lonelyplanetimages.com.

Printed by Hang Tai Printing Company.
Printed in China.

Mixed Sources
Product group from well-managed
forests and other controlled sources
www.fsc.org Cert no. SGS-COC-005002
© 1996 Forest Stewardship Council
FSC

Although the authors and Lonely Planet have taken all reasonable care in preparing this book, we make no warranty about the accuracy or completeness of its content and, to the maximum extent permitted, disclaim all liability arising from its use.